THE HANDBOOK OF DUAL LANGUAGE BILINGUAL EDUCATION

This handbook presents a state-of-the-art overview of dual language bilingual education (DLBE) research, programs, pedagogy, and practice. Organized around four sections—theoretical foundations; key issues and trends; school-based practices; and teacher and administrator preparation—the volume comprehensively addresses major and emerging topics in the field. With contributions from expert scholars, the handbook highlights programs that honor the assets of language-minoritized and marginalized students and provides empirically grounded guidance for asset-based instruction. Chapters cover historical and policy considerations, leadership, family relations, professional development, community partnerships, race, class, gender, and more. Synthesizing major issues, discussing central themes, and advancing policy and practice, this handbook is a seminal volume and definitive reference text in bilingual/second language education.

Juan A. Freire is Associate Professor in the Department of Teacher Education at Brigham Young University, USA.

Cristina Alfaro is the Associate Vice-President of International and Transborder Affairs and Professor of Multilingual and Global Education at San Diego State University, USA.

Ester J. de Jong is Professor and program leader in the Culturally and Linguistically Diverse Education program at the University of Colorado Denver, USA.

THE HANDBOOK OF DUAL LANGUAGE BILINGUAL EDUCATION

Edited by
Juan A. Freire
Cristina Alfaro
Ester J. de Jong

NEW YORK AND LONDON

Designed cover image: getty images

First published 2024
by Routledge
605 Third Avenue, New York, NY 10158

and by Routledge
4 Park Square, Milton Park, Abingdon, Oxon, OX14 4RN

Routledge is an imprint of the Taylor & Francis Group, an informa business

Library of Congress Cataloging-in-Publication Data
Names: Freire, Juan A., editor. | Alfaro, Cristina, editor. | De Jong, Ester J., editor.
Title: The handbook of dual language bilingual education / edited by Juan A. Freire, Cristina Alfaro, Ester J. de Jong.
Description: First edition. | New York : Routledge, 2024. | Includes bibliographical references and index.
Identifiers: LCCN 2023018144 (print) | LCCN 2023018145 (ebook) | ISBN 9781032215877 (hbk) | ISBN 9781032205427 (pbk) | ISBN 9781003269076 (ebk)
Subjects: LCSH: Education, Bilingual--Handbooks, manuals, etc. | Second language acquisition--Handbooks, manuals, etc. | Linguistic minorities--Education. | Educational equalization. | Multicultural education.
Classification: LCC LC3719 .H26 2024 (print) | LCC LC3719 (ebook) | DDC 370.117/5--dc23/eng/20230503
LC record available at https://lccn.loc.gov/2023018144
LC ebook record available at https://lccn.loc.gov/2023018145

ISBN: 9781032215877 (hbk)
ISBN: 9781032205427 (pbk)
ISBN: 9781003269076 (ebk)

DOI: 10.4324/9781003269076

Typeset in Sabon
by KnowledgeWorks Global Ltd.

Visit the support material at: www.routledge.com/9781032205427

CONTENTS

ACKNOWLEDGMENTS

We would like to acknowledge that we have had the pleasure to stand on the shoulders of many giants. On a personal note, we would like to first thank our ancestors for the linguistic, cultural, wisdom, and spiritual legacy we inherited from them. We are immensely grateful to our students and colleagues whose words and actions give life to this volume. We also thank our families for their invaluable support while working on this volume. This handbook is the result of a large number of people, starting with the mentors we have had in the academic field.

Juan would like to thank Verónica E. Valdez, who served as his academic madre during his doctoral program, and the different colleagues with whom he's engaged in scholarly work. Juan is also especially grateful for Cristina's and Ester's collaboration and for having graciously and enthusiastically accepted to work with him on this handbook.

Cristina would like to acknowledge her mentors—Antonia Darder, Patricia Gándara, and Alberto Ochoa—whose support and solidarity have challenged her to become an ideologically clear and critically conscious scholar, transborder/international leader, and Professor of Multilingual and Global Education. Cristina is especially grateful to her family, students, and colleagues for providing her with the richest spaces and moments of learning and teaching upon which to ground her theory, practice, leadership, and activism.

Ester is grateful for the teachers and administrators she has had the honor of working with, and for the scholars who have continuously fought to forge pathways into bilingual education that center students as bi/multilingual students—María Estela Brisk, Rebecca Field Freeman, Susan McGilvray-Rivet.

They have shown her that it is not sufficient to challenge the status quo, it is equally important to engage in action for change.

And, of course, we would like to thank the extraordinary contributing authors who accepted to write these powerful and cutting-edge chapters for this handbook. All of whom responded with enthusiasm and authentic commitment to this work—(y con cariño). We are also grateful for the support provided by everyone at Routledge.

BIOGRAPHY

Juan A. Freire, Ph.D., is an associate professor in the Department of Teacher Education at Brigham Young University. His research centers on equity in dual language bilingual education. He is the co-editor of the book *Overcoming the Gentrification of Dual Language, Bilingual, and Immersion Education: Solutions-Oriented Research and Stakeholder Resources for Real Integration* (2023).

Cristina Alfaro, Ph.D., is the Associate Vice-President of International and Transborder Affairs at San Diego State University where she also served as Provost Chair of Diversity, Equity, and Inclusion. Dr. Alfaro is a Multilingual and Global Education Professor and Past Chair of the Dual Language and English Learner Education Department in the College of Education where she championed and led the largest bilingual teacher education program in the state of California. As a researcher, she has examined and published on the role of educator critical ideological consciousness and pedagogical practices that situate access and equity at the core of dual language bilingual education.

Ester J. de Jong, Ed.D.,is a professor in the Culturally and Linguistically Diverse Education program at the University of Colorado Denver. Her book *Foundations of Multilingualism in Education* lays out a principles-based approach to educational equity for bilingual learners.

LIST OF CONTRIBUTORS

Cristina Alfaro, Ph.D., is the Associate Vice-President of International and Transborder Affairs at San Diego State University where she also served as Provost Chair of Diversity, Equity, and Inclusion. Dr. Alfaro is a Multilingual and Global Education Professor and Past Chair of the Dual Language and English Learner Education Department in the College of Education where she championed and led the largest bilingual teacher education program in the state of California. As a researcher, she has examined and published on the role of educator critical ideological consciousness and pedagogical practices that situate access and equity at the core of Dual Language-Bilingual Education.

Xochitl Archey, Ph.D., is an assistant professor in the School of Education's (SOE) Multilingual and Multicultural unit at California State University, San Marcos (CSUSM). Her work is situated in the intersections of bilingual education and (dis)ability studies and captures the educational experiences of Emergent Bilinguals with (dis)abilities. Frameworks of educational equity and social justice are central to her scholarship.

Elvira G. Armas, Ed.D., is Director of the Center for Equity for English Learners and Affiliated Faculty in the School of Education at Loyola Marymount University. Throughout her career, Dr. Armas is an active collaborator with pre-12th-grade educators in the areas of leadership, curriculum, integrated standards-based instruction, assessment, and family/community engagement in culturally and linguistically diverse settings. For over 3 decades, she has served as a bilingual classroom teacher, mentor, district advisor, staff developer, grant writer, project director, and curriculum materials developer. She has co-authored articles, policy briefs, and chapters about issues related to teaching, learning, family/community engagement, assessment and accountability. She has taught second language and literacy methods as well as foundational courses at several universities.

Ale Babino is an associate professor of Literacy and Learning at Texas Woman's University, where she teaches and researches at the intersection of bilingual and literacy education. Based on her experiences as a dual language teacher, her work explores how power, systems, and language affect the educational outcomes for Latinx, bilingual students. Specifically, she explores how (emergent) bilinguals become biliterate and bicultural to varying degrees across contexts, with an emphasis on DLBE and teacher preparation programs.

Sjana Baker is a citizen of the Little Traverse Bay Bands of Odawa Indians and resides in her homelands of Northern Michigan. She is a lifelong learner of her language, Anishinaabemowin, and focuses her research on Anishinaabemowin education and community engagement. She graduated from the University of California, Los Angeles in 2022 with her Master of Arts degree in American Indian Studies, where her thesis concentrated on the benefits and uses of various learning technologies in Anishinaabemowin community classes.

Reka Barton is a postdoctoral faculty fellow at the University of San Diego. Her research uses multimodal methodology to explore educational experiences of Black girls at the intersections of race, language, and equity.

Eurydice Bouchereau Bauer is the John E. Swearingen Chair of Education in the Department of Instruction and Teacher Education at the University of South Carolina. Her research focuses on the literacy development, instruction, and assessment of students (preschool-grade 5) from diverse linguistic, economic, and cultural backgrounds, with a specific focus on bilingual literacy. She is the Director of the Center of Bilingualism Matters @UofSC, which focuses on serving the language needs of South Carolina and the greater region. She currently serves as the Lead Editor for *Journal of Literacy Research*. Dr. Bauer's research has been published in the *Journal of Literacy Research*, *Reading Research Quarterly*, *Research in the Teaching of English*, *International Journal of Bilingualism*, and *The Reading Teacher*, among others.

Katie A. Bernstein is an associate professor of early childhood/emergent bilingual education in Mary Lou Fulton Teachers College at Arizona State University. As an applied linguist, a former early childhood teacher, and an early childhood education researcher, she studies young multilingual children and the contexts that shape their learning—from peer interactions to teacher beliefs to state language policies. She is author of the 2020 book, *(Re)defining Success in Language Learning: Positioning, Participation and Young Emergent Bilinguals at School.*

Rebecca Blum Martinez is Emerita Professor of Bilingual Education at the University of New Mexico. Her research includes the study of language development in bilinguals and second language development across varied learning contexts. Her recent publications include a co-authored chapter entitled, *A watershed moment in the education of American Indian students: A judicial strategy to mandate the State of New Mexico to meet the unique cultural and linguistic needs of American Indian students in New Mexico public schools*; and a co-edited volume, *The Shoulders We Stand On: A History of Bilingual Education in New Mexico*. She is a NABE board member, and national advisor to the non-profit EL Education organization

Allison Briceño is an associate professor at San José State University where she coordinates the Multilingual and Multicultural Literacy Education master's program. She co-authored the book, *Conscious Classrooms: Using Diverse Texts for Inclusion, Equity, and Justice* (2022, Benchmark).

Amanda Cataneo is a Ph.D. candidate in the department of Teaching and Learning Policy and Leadership at the University of Maryland, College Park. Her research interests include teacher education and teacher identity in dual language bilingual education programs.

Claudia Cervantes-Soon, Ph.D., is an associate professor at Arizona State University and a former K-12 bilingual educator. Her research draws on ethnographic approaches, decolonial theory, critical pedagogies, and Chicana/Latina feminisms to examine sociocultural, pedagogical, and policy factors affecting the education of historically marginalized youth in bilingual and borderlands communities. She is coeditor of the book *Critical Consciousness in Dual Language Bilingual Education: Case Studies on Policy and Practice.*

Laura C. Chávez-Moreno, Ph.D., is an assistant professor at UCLA's César E. Chávez Department of Chicana/o & Central American Studies. Dr. Chávez-Moreno is an award-winning scholar, recently recognized with a 2022 National Academy of Education/Spencer Foundation Postdoctoral Fellowship. Her work appears, among other publications, in *Educational Researcher* (2022), *American Educational Research Journal* (2021), *Journal of Teacher Education* (2021), *Handbook of Latinos & Education* (2nd ed., 2021), *Journal of Latinos & Education* (2022), *Handbook of Research on Teachers of Color and Indigenous Teachers* (2022), and *Research in the Teaching of English* (2022).

Woongsik Choi is an assistant professor of ESL/Bilingual Education at Illinois State University. As a multilingual teacher-researcher, his research interests include inclusive and equitable pedagogy and teacher preparation in TESOL/bilingual education.

Zach A. Coulter is a Ph.D. student in Curriculum and Instruction with a specialization in ESOL/Bilingual Education at the University of Florida, Gainesville, Florida. His research focuses on teacher collaboration in two-way dual language bilingual education programs.

CSUDH Colectivo Plurilingüe, the CSUDH Colectivo Plurilingüe is a collective of professors, lecturers, K-12 teachers and administrators, and current and former graduate students invested in critical approaches to Dual Language Learning in Los Angeles. This chapter was written collaboratively and communally represents the ideas, research, and voices of the following contributors: Nallely Arteaga, Cynthia Lozano, Carmen Lopez, Miguel Casar, Anna Arredondo-Kim, Yesenia Fernández, Natalie Nuñez, Beth Mossman, Maria Morales-Thomas, and Jen Stacy.

Kristin J. Davin, Ph.D., is an associate professor and Program Director of World Language Education at the University of North Carolina at Charlotte. Her most recent book is *Promoting Multilingualism in Schools: A Framework for Implementing the Seal of Biliteracy* (ACTFL, 2022).

Sarah De La Garza, Ph.D., is the Assistant Director of Dual Language Partnerships at The University of Texas at San Antonio. Her research interests focus on emergent bilingual student success and educator preparation, especially for dual language bilingual education. She is also the recipient of the Texas Association of Bilingual Education's 2022 Dissertation of the Year Award.

M. Garrett Delavan is an assistant professor in Georgia State University's Department of Middle and Secondary Education. He taught language in public schools for 18 years and now researches equity in language education policy and curriculum. He is co-editor of the book *Overcoming the Gentrification of Dual Language, Bilingual, and Immersion Education: Solutions-Oriented Research and Stakeholder Resources for Real Integration.*

Hoan Do, Ph.D., is currently affiliated with Clinical Outcomes Solutions, LLC. She served as Research Associate at the Center for Equity for English

Learners at Loyola Marymount University at the time of the writing of this chapter. Previously, Hoan taught English as a Foreign Language and Study Skills courses at Vietnam National University and participated in the Common European Framework of Reference for Languages. She received a doctoral degree in Educational Research and Evaluation in 2021 from Ohio University. Her research interests include teaching English to Speakers of Other Languages (TESOL), critical theories, statistical methods, and psychometrics.

Christina L. Dobbs is an assistant professor in English Education for Equity and Justice at Boston University. Her research focuses on adolescent writing development, supporting culturally and linguistically diverse secondary students, disciplinary literacy, and teacher beliefs and professional learning. Additionally, she does research about the experiences of women of color in the academy. Her recent books include *Investigating Disciplinary Literacy* (2017) and *Disciplinary Literacy Inquiry & Instruction* (2019). She is a former high school teacher in Houston, Texas, as well as a literacy coach and reading specialist.

Lisa M. Dorner, Ph.D., is an associate professor in Educational Leadership and Policy Analysis and the Director of the Cambio Center at the University of Missouri-Columbia. She is not only a teacher and researcher but also a life-long learner who loves language, intercultural connection, and the idea of educación. Read more at lisamdorner.com

Mallory Earl graduated from Brigham Young University in 2022 with a bachelor's degree in Elementary Education with a double minor in Teaching English as a Second Language and Dual Language Immersion.

Joe Elliott is a former elementary dual-language bilingual teacher and is currently an assistant professor of education at Elmhurst University near Chicago, Illinois. He is passionate about supporting pre-service and in-service teachers in culturally and linguistically diverse settings, as well as advocating for emergent bilinguals across all language program models. Joe's dissertation is titled: *Understanding Dual Language Teachers' Language Ideologies Using Translanguaging Theory and Pedagogy: A Mixed Methods Approach.*

Kathy Escamilla is a professor emerita of Education in the Division of Equity, Bilingualism and Biliteracy at the University of Colorado, Boulder. Her research focuses on issues related to the development of bilingualism and biliteracy for Spanish-speaking emerging bilingual children in the U.S. schools. She has authored three books and over 50 research articles on topics related to (bi)literacy. She served two terms as the President of the National Association for Bilingual Education, and one term as the Chair of the Bilingual

Special interest group at AERA. Her best professional memories, however, are from being a bilingual teacher in Colorado and California.

Christian Faltis is a professor of Bilingual Education and Chair of the Department of Education at Texas A&M International University and Professor Emeritus at UC Davis where he held the Dolly and David Fiddyment Endowed Chair in Teacher Education. An AERA Fellow and AERA Distinguished Scholar, Christian is also an accomplished artist. He was the recipient of the Bilingual Research SIG Lifetime Achievement Award in 2018 from AERA.

Erika Feinauer is an associate professor of Teacher at Brigham Young University. She researches bilingualism, biliteracy, and social identity processes among minoritized students. She also prepares pre-service teachers to teach in culturally competent and inclusive ways.

Lily Wong Fillmore, Jerome Hutto Professor of Education, Emerita, University of California at Berkeley. She is a linguist and an educator; her research and writing have focused on language and cultural issues related to the education of Latino, Asian, American Indian, and Alaskan Native children. Since her retirement from the Berkeley faculty in 2004, she has worked with educators in urban school districts (Denver, Boston, NYC, San Francisco, Albuquerque, and Fresno) and with the Council of Great City Schools to improve academic language and literacy instruction for English learners and other language minority students.

Juan A. Freire, Ph.D., is an associate professor in the Department of Teacher Education at Brigham Young University. His research centers on equity in dual language bilingual education. He is co-editor of the book *Overcoming the Gentrification of Dual Language, Bilingual, and Immersion Education: Solutions-Oriented Research and Stakeholder Resources for Real Integration.*

Eugene García is Professor Emeritus at Arizona State University. He served as Professor and Vice President for Education Partnerships at ASU from 2006 to 2011 and as Dean of the Mary Lou Fulton College of Education from 2002 to 2006. He joined ASU from the University of California, Berkeley, where he was Professor and Dean of the Graduate School of Education (1995–2001). He has served as an elected member of a local school board and a Senior Officer in the U.S. Department of Education. He has published extensively in areas of early learning, bilingual development, and equal educational opportunity. He has authored or co-authored 16 books and over 200 articles and book chapters.

Ofelia García is Professor Emerita in the Ph.D. programs in Urban Education & Latin American, Iberian and Latino Cultures at The Graduate Center, City University of New York. She has published extensively and has received many distinguished awards. See www.ofeliagarcia.org

Suzanne García-Mateus is an assistant professor of Bilingual Education and the Director of the Monterey Institute for English Learners at California State University, Monterey Bay. Her research critically examines the intersection of language, race, and class in the dual language bilingual education classroom. She is co-editor (2023) of the book *Gentrification & Bilingual Education: A Texas TWBE School across Seven Years.*

Armando Garza Ayala is an assistant professor of Language, Literacy, and Sociocultural Studies at the University of New Mexico. Using sociocultural and critical frameworks, Dr. Garza Ayala's research and teaching interests focus on the use of linguistic and cultural tools in K-12 mathematics/science education with bilingual and emergent bilingual Latina/o/x marginalized students, and language and literacy justice of minoritized student populations and communities.

Verónica González, Ph.D., is an assistant professor of Bilingual Education in the division of Curriculum and Instruction at California State University, Los Angeles. Her research focuses on dual language educators' ideologies and practices surrounding the implementation of sociocultural competence.

Patrick J. Graham is the Department Chair and Associate Professor in the Master of Science in Secondary Education for the Deaf of Hard of Hearing program at the National Technical Institute for the Deaf at the Rochester Institute of Technology. Dr. Graham's research focuses on Body Habitus in Deaf Education, Culturally Responsive Pedagogy, Special Education, and Language Deprivation.

Dan Heiman is an assistant professor of Bilingual/Biliteracy Education at the University of Texas at El Paso and a former elementary bilingual teacher in the borderlands. He is co-editor of the book *Critical Consciousness in Dual Language Bilingual Education: Case Studies on Policy and Practice.*

Amy J. Heineke is a professor of Education at Loyola University Chicago (USA). Her recent publications include *Inclusive Texts in Elementary Classrooms: Developing Literacies, Identities, and Understandings* (2022) and *Promoting Multilingualism in Schools: A Framework for Implementing the Seal of Biliteracy* (ACTFL, 2022).

Kathryn I. Henderson is an associate professor in the Department of Bicultural-Bilingual Studies, College of Education and Human Development at The University of Texas at San Antonio. She taught elementary school in Guadalajara, Mexico before working in teacher preparation. She is the current Graduate Advisor of Record for the Culture, Literacy, and Language Ph.D. program. Her education interests include language ideologies, language policy, and dual language bilingual education. She has presented regularly in local, regional, and international conferences and published in journals such as the *Modern Language Journal*, *Language Policy, TESOL Quarterly,* and *Journal of Language, Identity and Education.*

Ana M. Hernández, Ed.D., is a professor of Multilingual and Multicultural Education in the School of Education at CA State University San Marcos. Her research examines dual language pedagogy, teacher preparation, cross-cultural equity, and educational leadership. She provides professional development for educators of culturally and lingually diverse students. Her field experience stems from 32 years as a bilingual teacher in grades K-8.

Sera J. Hernández, Ph.D., is an associate professor and Chair of the Dual Language and English Learner Education Department at San Diego State University. Her research bridges the fields of educational linguistics and the anthropology of education to examine the sociocultural, linguistic, and political contexts surrounding educational language policies, bilingual teacher preparation, and bilingualism and biliteracy practices. Her scholarship has been featured in journals such as the *Review of Research in Education*, *Language Policy,* and the *Journal of Latinos and Education.*

Susan Hopewell is an associate professor and Chair of the Equity, Bilingualism, and Biliteracy program area in the School of Education at the University of Colorado Boulder. Her research centers on holistic biliteracy development in Spanish/English bilingual programs. She is co-author of *Biliteracy from the Start: Literacy Squared in Action* (2014, Caslon/Brookings).

Elizabeth R. Howard is an associate professor of bilingual education in the Neag School of Education at the University of Connecticut, where she conducts research on dual language education, biliteracy development, and the preparation of teachers to work with multilingual learners. Her most recent book is *Dual Language Tandem Teaching: Coordinating Instruction across Languages through Cross-Linguistic Pedagogies* (2023).

Elena Izquierdo is a professor in the Department of Teacher Education at The University of Texas at El Paso in Bilingualism/Biliteracy and Dual

Language Bilingual Education. She is a linguist by training, Applied Linguistics and Bilingual Education, Georgetown University, and an educator in practice with 13 years as an administrator in Washington, D.C. serving as the principal of one of the first National Dual Language models in the country. Her expertise, research, and experiences are in the areas of Equity and Leadership in DLBE and Biliteracy. Her most current book publication is *Dual Language Education: Teaching and Leading Through Two Languages*, Springer, 2019.

Oscar Jimenez-Castellanos is the Director of P-12 Research at The Education Trust in D.C. His research focuses on education policy and finance with a particular emphasis on multilingual learners. He previously served as Murchison Endowed Professor and Chair at Trinity University, Associate Professor and Director at Santa Clara University, and Associate/Assistant Professor in Mary Lou Fulton Teachers College at Arizona State University.

Ester J. de Jong, Ed.D., is Professor in the Culturally and Linguistically Diverse Education program at the University of Colorado Denver. Her research focuses dual language bilingual education, integrated approaches to the schooling of bilingual learners, and teacher preparation. Her book *Foundations of Multilingualism in Education* lays out a principles based approach to educational equity for bilingual learners.

Jongyeon Joy Ee, Ph.D., is an associate professor in the School of Education at Loyola Marymount University. Her research agenda centers around educational equity and equal access to quality education in different contexts. She has explored education for immigrant students, dual language bilingual education, school segregation, and racial disparities.

Noah Katznelson is a Ph.D. candidate in the Language, Literacy, and Culture program at U.C. Berkeley School of Education. Through her research, she critically examines the relationship between neoliberalism and language education policy.

Chris Kurz, Ph.D., is a professor and Director of the Mathematics and Science Language and Learning Lab at Rochester Institute of Technology, USA. His research areas include STEM language and literacy, Deaf math and science experience, and international deaf literacy. He directs international projects using the World Around You (WAY) crowdsourcing platform that has an online library of free signed storybooks and resources for Deaf young children in multiple sign languages and provides training in signed storybook development and translation.

Magaly Lavadenz, Ph.D., is Leavey Presidential Endowed Chair in Ethics and Moral Leadership and founding Executive Director, Center for Equity for English Learners in the School of Education at Loyola Marymount University. Her research addresses the intersections of policies and practices for English/ Multilingual learners, their teachers, and school leaders. Her work is published in numerous articles, chapters, monographs, and books, including *Latino Civil Rights in Education: La Lucha Sigue*, co-edited with Anaida Colón Muñiz. As a community-engaged scholar-activist, she has held leadership positions as President of Californians Together, California Association for Bilingual Education (CABE), the California Association for Bilingual Teacher Education, and the California Council on Teacher Education.

Saúl I. Maldonado is an associate professor of Dual Language and English Learner Education at San Diego State University and co-editor of the volume, *Assessment and Evaluation in Bilingual Education* (2022). Maldonado investigates mathematics and science achievement in K-12 schools, bilingual teacher education, and culturally responsive evaluation and assessment.

Melinda Martin-Beltran is an associate professor of Applied Linguistics and Language Education in the Department of Teaching & Learning, Policy & Leadership at the University of Maryland. Using sociocultural and critical frameworks, she studies how multilingual students and teachers use discourse to interact, learn, build relationships and expand linguistic repertoire. Informed by her experiences as a bilingual teacher in the United States and Latin America, she focuses on transformational and humanizing teaching/learning practices that build upon culturally and linguistically diverse students' funds of knowledge.

Teresa L. McCarty lives and works in the unceded homelands of the Gabrielino-Tongva and pays respect to their sovereignty in this place. At the University of California, Los Angeles, she is Distinguished Professor and G.F. Kneller Chair in Education and Anthropology, and Faculty in American Indian Studies. Her research focuses on Indigenous education, language education planning and policy, Indigenous language reclamation, and the critical ethnography of education. She is a member of the National Academy of Education and a Fellow of the American Educational Research Association and the International Centre for Language Revitalisation.

Sarah C. K. Moore is Clinical Assistant Professor of Applied Linguistics and Language Education in the Department of Teaching and Learning, Policy and Leadership, College of Education, University of Maryland College Park. Her research relates to language policy, language rights, and educational linguistics. She is author (2021) of *A History of Bilingual Education in the U.S.: Examining the Politics of Language Policymaking.*

Trish Morita-Mullaney is an associate professor at Purdue University. Her research focuses on the intersections between language learning, gender, and race and how these intersecting identities shape individual and structural policy-making for emergent bilinguals. Her recent work is published in *American Educational Research Journal* (2016), *Current Issues in Language Planning* (2022), *International Journal of Bilingual Education and Bilingualism* (2022), *TESOL Quarterly* (2020; 2023), *and Theory into Practice* (2020).

Eduardo R. Muñoz-Muñoz, Ph.D., is an associate professor in the Teacher Education Department at San José State University where he coordinates the Critical Bilingual Authorization Program Bilingüismo y Justicia. His current scholarly activity focuses on language ideologies, critical policy analysis, and heteroglossic teacher preparation.

Melissa A. Navarro Martell, Ph.D., is an assistant professor in the Department of Dual Language and English Learner Education at San Diego State University. Her research and teaching center the need to prepare critically conscious multilingual educators on the sociopolitical, ideological, cultural, and linguistic aspects of teacher preparation in general, and K-8 equitable STEM and dual-language education specifically.

Idalia Nuñez is an assistant professor of Language and Literacy at the University of Illinois at Urbana-Champaign. Her research interests are on bilingual education, bilingualism, biliteracy, and the translanguaging practices and knowledge of Chicanx/Latinx students, families, and communities. Dr. Nuñez's research, teaching, and advocacy efforts are on supporting the educational needs of students from culturally and linguistically diverse backgrounds. Her research has been published in *Research in the Teaching of English, Literacy Research: Theory, Method, and Practice, Equity and Excellence in Education*, etc.

Alberto Ochoa is Professor Emeritus of Education, a former PI for the Southern Area International Language Network, and was Chair of the Department of Policy Studies (now Dual Language Education) at SDSU. Directed one of nine National Origin Desegregation Centers in the nation from 1975 to 1987. He has published in the areas of action research, cross-cultural and intercultural education, teacher education bilingual/biliteracy, parent advocacy and leadership, language policy, and cultural Integration. Co-founder of the Parent Institute for Quality Education that celebrated its 35th anniversary.

Irina Okhremtchouk is a professor of Educational Administration and Leadership in the Department of Equity, Leadership Studies, and Instructional Technologies at San Francisco State University (SFSU). She also coordinates SFSU's Educational Administration and Leadership certification and MA programs. Okhremtchouk is charged with preparing well-rounded and well-informed equity-driven school leaders and administrators who are ready to build inclusive school communities, and work persistently to eliminate racism, inequalities, and injustices. Okhremtchouk's research and expertise are in school organization, policy, and finance. Specifically, her scholarly work stems from a deep interest in translating research into better-informed public policy and practice.

Edward M. Olivos is a professor of Education Studies at the University of Oregon. His research focuses on the relationship between bicultural parents and schools as well as the development of bilingual educators. He is the author of *The Power of Parents: A Critical Perspective of Bicultural Parent Involvement in Public Schools* (2006, Peter Lang Publishers, Inc.) and co-editor of *Bicultural Parent Engagement: Advocacy and Empowerment* (2011, Teachers College Press).

Deborah Palmer is a professor of Equity, Bilingualism and Biliteracy at the University of Colorado Boulder. A former DL bilingual teacher, she conducts critical ethnography and discourse analysis with bilingual teachers. She is co-editor of the forthcoming book *Critical Consciousness in Dual Language Bilingual Education: Case Studies on Policy and Practice* (2022).

Angela Palmieri, Ed.D., was born in Caracas, Venezuela, and was raised in Los Angeles, CA. She is a bilingual education specialist, an adjunct professor of education, and an educational consultant. Her doctoral research focused on exploring teacher perceptions of sociocultural competence in dual language education.

Maite T. Sánchez, Ph.D., is an assistant professor of Bilingual Education at Hunter College, CUNY. Her research focuses on language education policy and practice in support of racialized bilinguals, translanguaging pedagogy, and bilingual teacher preparation. She is co-editor (2022) of the book *Transformative Translanguaging Espacios: Latinx Students and their Teachers Rompiendo Fronteras sin Miedo*.

Jody Slavick, Ph.D., is a research associate and the Director for Professional Development for the Literacy Squared® Project at the University of Colorado Boulder. Her research interests include the design and implementation of bilingual programs, strategies to facilitate biliteracy, and working with teachers to promote the bilingual/bicultural development of their emerging bilingual students.

Sonia Soltero is a professor and Chair of the Department of Leadership, Language and Curriculum at DePaul University and former Director of its Bilingual-Bicultural Education Graduate Program. Soltero has numerous publications on bilingual and Latino education including three books, the latest entitled *Dual Language Education: Program Design and Implementation*. She co-chairs the English Learners Advocacy Council in Higher Education (ELACHE), is a member of the Executive Board of the National Association of Bilingual Education, and co-editor of Global Perspectives. Soltero has been involved in bilingual education for more than 30 years as a university professor, researcher, former dual language public school teacher, professional developer, and education advocate.

Michelle Soto-Peña, Ph.D., is an assistant professor in the Department of Bilingual and Elementary Education at California State University, Fullerton. Her interests focus on policies and practices that promote educational access and equity for historically minoritized students in dual immersion educational settings, and ethnic studies in bilingual elementary education. She has also served as an advocate to several California state organizations related to educational equity for emerging bilinguals, including the English Learner Leadership & Legacy Initiative (ELLLI), the California Association of Bilingual Teacher Educators (CABTE), and the California Commission on Teacher Credentialing (CCTC) Bilingual Authorization Program Standards update.

Luis Urrieta, Jr. is an Indigenous (P'urhépecha)/Latino interdisciplinary and transdisciplinary researcher, born in East Los Angeles, but with family origins in San Miguel Nocutzepo and Tócuaro, Michoacán, Mexico. He is a Professor of Cultural Studies and Education at the University of Texas at Austin and holds the *Charles H. Spence, Sr. Centennial Professorship in Education*.

Kaila Willardson graduated from Brigham Young University with a bachelor's degree in elementary education and a minor in dual language immersion in 2022. She is at the beginning of her career in teaching and research. This is her first published work.

Wayne E. Wright is the Associate Dean for Research, Graduate Programs, and Faculty Development, and is Professor and the Barbara I. Cook Chair of Literacy and Language Education in the College of Education at Purdue University. He is author of *Foundations for Teaching English Language Learners: Research, Theory, Policy, and Practice* (3rd ed., 2019), and co-author of *Foundations of Bilingual Education and Bilingualism* (7th ed., 2021).

William Zahner is an associate professor and the director of the Center for Research in Mathematics and Science Education at San Diego State University. His research focuses on creating equitable mathematics classrooms for multilingual learners, and his work has been published in *ZDM Mathematics Education*, *Review of Educational Research*, and the *Journal of Adolescent and Adult Literacy*.

Manqian Zhao is a postdoctoral faculty fellow at George Mason University. Her research explores Mandarin-English biliteracy development among multilingual learners in Mandarin dual language programs.

SETTING THE STAGE

An Introduction to *The Handbook of Dual Language Bilingual Education*

Ester J. de Jong, Juan A. Freire, Cristina Alfaro

What Is Dual Language Bilingual Education?

Dual language bilingual education (DLBE) can be defined as a content-based program that lasts at least five years and aims for academic achievement, bilingualism and biliteracy, and sociocultural competence (Howard et al., 2018). More recently, critical/ideological/sociopolitical consciousness has been added as an additional key goal for DLBE to reach its vision for equity and social justice (Alfaro, 2019; Freire, 2020; Hernández et al., 2022; see Chapters 3 and 11 in this volume). DLBE programs are also known as dual language education, dual language immersion, dual immersion, and immersion. In this volume, we purposefully selected the use of the term "dual language bilingual education" to honor the long struggle and tradition of bilingual education in the United States, while recognizing the importance of distinguishing asset-based/developmental programs from deficit orientated/temporary approaches. Sánchez et al. (2017) contend that what transforms dual language education into DLBE is when these programs consider the sociolinguistic realities and the bilingual continuum of all students, especially for language-minoritized students, in their bilingual learning. García et al. (2018) add that the term DLBE reconnects the program with its original civil rights roots as modern-day programs were "beginning to lose the original intent of providing bilingual communities with a meaningful and equal educational opportunity for their children" (p. 44).

DLBE programs have increasingly gained popularity across the United States as policy makers, educators, families, and communities recognize the value and benefits of multilingualism and experience the positive impact of DLBE on student learning and school success (Alfaro, 2018, 2019).

DOI: 10.4324/9781003269076-1

A growing number of states and school districts are paying particular attention to the establishment and growth of DLBE programs (Cervantes-Soon et al., 2021; Delavan et al., 2022; Wall et al., 2019), often in conjunction with other efforts that value the development of language proficiency in more than one language, such as the Seal of Biliteracy (see Chapter 20 in this volume). These efforts, in turn, have great implications for teacher and leadership preparation (see Chapters 34 and 37 in this volume).

DLBE programs can be divided by the target population for which the program is designed. Four program models can be distinguished: (1) heritage programs for language revitalization in (usually indigenous) communities; (2) one-way developmental/maintenance bilingual education programs for English-learner-designated students; (3) two-way programs that seek to balance English-learner-designated students and English speakers; and (4) one-way foreign/world language immersion programs for English speakers. This handbook is specifically concerned with the first three models that focus on providing access to DLBE for minoritized language speakers. The reader is referred to Coffey and Wingate's (2018) *New Directions for Research in Foreign Language Education* (Routledge) for more on foreign/world language programs.

Bilingual Education and DLBE in the United States

Bilingual education has a long tradition of resisting the assimilationist tendencies that have characterized educational policies in the United States. Although bilingual schooling was integral to many immigrant communities in the 1800s–1900s (Kloss, 1977/1998), modern bilingual education finds its roots in the Civil Rights Movement. Historically, counter-hegemonic movements for educational social justice, access, and equity have fought exclusionary forces that relegate linguistically and culturally diverse students to inferior educational conditions and spaces. Different groups, such as Chicano activists in the Southwest and the Young Lords, from New York, advocated for bilingual education while fighting against white hegemony (Flores, 2016). Collective efforts among those working for community-based organizations, schools, as well as colleges and universities led to advocacy for bilingual education. For example, the complex history of bilingual education in New Mexico, covering Dine, and Pueblo languages, shows critical actions, initiatives, and activists that have impacted bilingual education (Blum Martinez & López, 2020). Similarly, Olsen (2022) documents California as a central stage for these critical movements, especially with regard to the impact on im/migrant bi/multilingual students and their families.

Over time, different bilingual education programs have been designed and implemented. Some of these programs were truly community-based and emancipatory in nature (Torrez-Guzmán & de Jong, 2015; Flores & García, 2017), valued the linguistic and cultural resources that students and families brought to school to support teaching and learning, and denounced the oppressive conditions in the education of students and their families (Colón-Muñiz & Lavadenz, 2016). In the fall of 1964, for example, Cuban refugees opened the first dual language bilingual program at the Coral Way elementary school in Florida. Although it was open to Cuban children and English-speaking children, the original intention was to maintain Cubans' Spanish (Coady, 2019).

Despite the sustained efforts of bilingual education activists and advocates, more commonly, schools reverted to an approach that used students' home languages but only temporarily as a bridge to English language proficiency. Be it more gradual than English-only programs, these so-called transitional bilingual education programs ultimately aimed for monolingualism in English and students' assimilation into the mainstream (Baker & Wright, 2021). Moreover, the English-only movement gave place to anti-bilingual education campaigns and legislation. Combined with other federal educational legislation, many states saw a significant loss of bilingual education programs. Over the last two decades, however, efforts to reclaim bilingual education emerged under the new umbrella term "dual language education." These efforts re-positioned bilingual programs as an asset-based approach and explicitly identified bilingualism and biliteracy as desired outcomes. At the same time, a focus on economic and cognitive arguments of the benefits of bilingualism and the increased inclusion of white, monolingual English speakers from advantaged economic backgrounds has led to a distancing of DLBE from its civil rights origins and its centering of minoritized communities.

Focus, Aims, and Audience of the Handbook

This volume aims to reclaim bilingual education as it could be envisioned for minoritized language speakers through an authentic bi/multilingual lens. Despite three decades of policy and practice in the United States, a comprehensive synthesis of the research specifically focused on DLBE does not yet exist. Much of the discourse about bilingual education has been framed in defense against monolingual, assimilationist discourses that stress standardization, efficiencies, and the importance of English proficiency to become a productive member of U.S. society (similar arguments are heard in other nation-states and the treatment of minoritized languages in schools; Márquez Román & Castellanos Villalobos, 2020; Trillos Amaya, 2020). Within this frame, research on bilingual education still prioritized English outcomes to prove that the program was effective, considered rapid exit from programs as a valid indicator of success, and rarely considered a range of other variables besides English proficiency as integral to the effectiveness of the schooling for minoritized language speakers (Flores & García, 2017). Much of the work failed to decenter the hegemonic forces and legacies of whiteness, colonization, racism, and other forms of oppression (Chávez-Moreno, 2021; Flores, 2013; Freire et al., 2022). Rather than constructing a research-based counternarrative to monolingual English-only approaches, this research ultimately reinforced the assimilationist, monolingual dominant discourses. It left out and marginalized important voices and perspectives that questioned the focus on language as the sole mediator for school success (Hornberger & Link, 2012).

With this handbook, then, we aimed to frame DLBE in its own right from a bilingual, pluralistic stance in an effort to construct a research-based alternative discourse and set future directions for critically and pluralistically grounded research (Freeman, 1996). We intended to center equity and social justice at the center for language-minoritized and other minoritized students, their families, and communities. Castek et al. (2007) state that "a Multilingual Perspective views multilingualism as a powerful national asset and multilingual students as global citizens who have the potential to create global connections that will transform the future in dynamic ways" (p. 113). Multilingual learners are thus not only recognized for the linguistic and cultural assets they bring; they are positioned as leaders who can transform practices for a more just world.

Taking a multilingual perspective redefines how research, policy, and practice approach superdiversity in educational settings as it discursively shifts the focus away from approaching diversity as a problem to constructing diversity, including multilingualism, as a resource for social justice. This shift leads to different renewed problem-posing, analysis, and consideration of new research questions. We would like to argue that a research agenda in DLBE contexts grounded in equity and justice must address the following five themes.

Theme 1. Equity, Status, and Power

A strong thread throughout the research is the increased need for criticality as dual language bilingual programs experience mission creep, are implemented in gentrifying neighborhoods, and try to resist the dominant narrative. More research is needed on how to analyze such power dynamics and their impact on student experiences and learning. We need more research-based examples on how educators, at all levels, are engaged in developing and implementing critical approaches and processes of decolonizing, and disrupting raciolinguistic ideologies in DLBE; often under challenging socio-political and ideological constraints, including heritage bilingual and one-way developmental/maintenance programs.

Theme 2. Partnerships and Community Engagement

Equity work cannot be accomplished by single individuals or entities. The chapters point to a great need to understand authentic partnership building to support DLBE. Such partnerships are needed not only between schools and families, but also between schools and communities/community-based organizations, and schools/school districts and institutes of higher education.

Theme 3. Educator Preparation

A quality DLBE program stands and falls with the quality of its leadership and personnel involved in working with bi/multilingual learners. Despite some existing frameworks and professional development standards, it is surprising to see how little research has focused on how to best prepare professionals to specifically work in DLBE contexts, including principals, teachers, and paraprofessionals but also school counselors and school psychologists. How can teacher and administrator preparation prepare their graduates to resist the monolingual ideologies and English hegemony?

Theme 4. Diversity, Identity, and Intersectionalities

A major advancement in the field is the increased recognition of students' complex, dynamic, and multiple identities and to go beyond single or static linguistic or cultural identities in DLBE research. Critical consciousness of the role of culture, language, and identities as they intersect with gender, class, religion, and other identities is a central issue for research moving forward. With the recognition of intersectionality comes the task of understanding how educators can construct learning environments that are affirmative of these identities, even within contexts where multiple perspectives are not included.

Theme 5. Critical Language Policies

Tollefson (2006, p. 42), posits that "critical" in critical language policy research has three interrelated meanings: (1) it refers to work that is critical of traditional mainstream approaches to language policy research; (2) it includes research that is aimed at social change; and (3) it refers to research that is influenced by critical theory. More research is needed that is grounded in the sociopolitical, socio-ideological, and socio-historical dimensions inherent in language policy, planning, implementation, management, and accountability measures in different states and locations.

We chose to focus this handbook of research on strength-based DLBE programs, that is programs where educators affirm minoritized students' languages and cultural experiences and identities, have a commitment to and proactively construct counternarratives to the dominant monolingual discourse, and support the development of bilingualism and biliteracy for their students. Building on the depth and breadth of prior research done by exceptional DLBE scholars in the past, we purposefully selected emerging and experienced scholars for their expertise on a range of enduring and emerging topics and key issues in DLBE. We asked them to synthesize extant empirical research as it specifically relates to DLBE as defined in this volume and to provide directions for future research.

This handbook of research on DLBE will support upper-level undergraduate and graduate students, researchers, academics, professionals, and policy makers in the fields of DLBE, bilingualism studies, education, language education, and ethnic studies.

Organization of the Handbook

The Handbook of Dual Language Bilingual Education is organized in a comprehensive manner that captures a broad range of relevant topics. This volume is organized around four sections, with some sections including longer and other shorter chapters.

Section 1: Theoretical Foundations and Outcomes (Chapters 1–11)

The chapters in this section are organized into three categories: (1) theoretical foundations; (2) history, programs, and policy; and (3) DLBE outcomes. This section will discuss foundational issues around the creation, interpretation, and appropriation of DLBE, such as theoretical frameworks that have guided DLBE, history, types of DLBE programs and their development over time, and research on programmatic outcomes related to the three main universal goals of DLBE and the fourth or foundational proposed goal of critical consciousness. This section will synthesize both classic and contemporary research and cross-sectional, as well as longitudinal work.

Section 2: Key Issues and Trends (Chapters 12–22)

This section is divided into three categories: (1) social justice issues, (2) programmatic issues, and (3) racial/ethnic groups. The key issues and trends include hot topics and areas of debate pertinent to minoritized students in DLBE as indicated in each one of the categories. This section will cover key trends and contemporary issues as they have shaped the field of DLBE and continue to be debated by scholars, teacher educators, and other stakeholders.

Section 3: School-Based Practices (Chapters 23–33)

This section includes four categories: (1) student relationships; (2) pedagogical issues; (3) discourses, power, and school research; and (4) family and community. This section will engage the reader in findings from school-based research on language and literacy development, content-development, language use, identity, equitable learning opportunities, and family and community activism in DLBE programs.

Section 4: Teacher and Administrator Preparation (Chapters 34–38)

This section will include chapters addressing two categories: (1) teacher education and professional development, and (2) leadership and partnership. This section will address literature and directions for teacher and administrator preparation programs, professional development, and collaboration with universities and districts.

Organization of the Chapters

Each chapter in this volume synthesizes major issues and discusses central themes and research trends in its given topic and addresses implications to advance DLBE through research, policy, and practice. The chapters address the following three areas:

1. **Overview of issue** – An introduction that provides the reader with the main idea about the topic, a research agenda with questions that organize the content, and a discussion of the pressing issues surrounding the chapter topic.
2. **Main findings from research** – Similar to a literature review, although organized by headings such as "central themes," or a similar heading that points to a review of current research. The reviewed research can vary from qualitative, quantitative, and mixed-methods research. Some of the literature review has also included non-empirical work, such as theoretical literature, that has contributed to DLBE debates and the field.
3. **Implications and future directions for DLBE** – Brief implications for research, policy, and practice based on the chapter topic, including future research, research questions, and research directions.

With *The Handbook of Dual Language Bilingual Education*, we hope that the readers will maintain and renew their commitment to language-minoritized and other minoritized groups in DLBE. Our work is far from over, we need more scholars and practitioners to engage in a renewed vision and mission in agency, advocacy, equity, and social justice work both locally and globally. We must extend our capacity to begin anew, to reconstruct, to refuse the bureaucratic mindset, to understand life as a process, and live to become (Freire, 1998, 2000).

References

Alfaro, C. (2018). The sociopolitical struggle and promise of bilingual teacher education: Past, present, and future. *Bilingual Research Journal*, *41*(4), 413–427.

Alfaro, C. (2019). Preparing critically conscious dual-language teachers: Recognizing and interrupting dominant ideologies. *Theory Into Practice*, *58*(2), 194–203.

Baker, C., & Wright, W. E. (2021). *Foundations of bilingual education and bilingualism* (8th ed.). Multilingual Matters.

Blum Martinez, R., & López, M. J. H. (Eds.). (2020). *The shoulders we stand on: A history of bilingual education in New Mexico*. University of New Mexico Press.

Castek, J., Leu, D. J., Coiro, J., Gort, M., Henry, L. A., & Lima, C. (2007). Developing new literacies among multilingual learners in the elementary grades. In L. L. Parker (Ed.), *Technology-mediated learning environments for young English learners: Connections in and out of school* (pp. 111–153). Lawrence Erlbaum.

Cervantes-Soon, C., Gambrell, J., Kasun, G. S., Sun, W., Freire, J. A., & Dorner, L. M. (2021). "Everybody wants a choice" in dual language education of El Nuevo Sur: Whiteness as the gloss for everybody in media discourses of multilingual education. *Journal of Language, Identity & Education*, *20*(6), 394–410.

Chávez-Moreno, L. C. (2021). The problem with Latinx as a racial construct vis-à-vis language and bilingualism: Toward recognizing multiple colonialisms in the racialization of Latinidad. In E. G. Murillo, Jr., D. Delgado Bernal, S. Morales, L. Urrieta, Jr., E. R. Bybee, J. Sánchez Muñoz, V. B. Saenz, D. Villanueva, M. Machado-Casas, & K. Espinoza (Eds.), *Handbook of Latinos and education* (pp. 164–180). Routledge.

Coady, M. R. (2019). *The Coral Way bilingual program*. Multilingual Matters.

Coffey, S., & Wingate, U. (2018). *New directions for research in foreign language education*. Routledge.

Colón-Muñiz, A., & Lavadenz, M. (2016). *Latinos civil rights in education: La lucha sigue*. Routledge.

Delavan, M. G., Freire, J. A., & Morita-Mullaney, T. (2022). Conscripted into thinking of scarce, selective, privatized, and precarious seats in dual language bilingual education: The choice discourse of mercenary exclusivity. *Current issues in language planning*. Advance online publication. https://doi.org/10.1080/14664208.2022.2077032

Flores, N. (2013). Silencing the subaltern: Nation-state/colonial governmentality and bilingual education in the United States. *Critical Inquiry in Language Studies*, *10*(4), 263–287.

Flores, N. (2016). A tale of two visions: Hegemonic whiteness and bilingual education. *Educational Policy*, *30*, 13–38.

Flores, N., & García, O. (2017). A critical review of bilingual education in the United States: From basements and pride to boutiques and profit. *Annual Review of Applied Linguistics*, *37*, 14–29.

Freeman, R. D. (1996). Dual-language planning at oyster bilingual school: "It's much more than a language". *TESOL Quarterly*, *30*(3), 557–582.

Freire, P. (1998). *Teachers as cultural workers: Letters to those who dare teach*. Westview Press.

Freire, P. (2000). *Pedagogy of the oppressed.* Continuum.
Freire, J. A. (2020). Promoting sociopolitical consciousness and bicultural goals of dual language education: The transformational dual language education framework. *Journal of Language, Identity & Education*, *19*(1), 56–71.
Freire, J. A., Gambrell, J. A., Kasun, S. G., Dorner, L., & Cervantes-Soon, C. (2022). The expropriation of dual language bilingual education: Deconstructing neoliberalism, whitestreaming, and English hegemony. *International Multilingual Research Journal*, *16*(1), 27–46.
García, O., Menken, K., Velasco, P., & Vogel, S. (2018). Dual language bilingual education in NYC: A potential unfulfilled. In M. B. Arias & M. Fee (Eds.), *Profiles of dual language education in the 21st century* (pp. 38–55). Center for Applied Linguistics.
Hernández, S. J., Alfaro, C., & Martell, M. A. N. (2022). Bilingual teacher educators as language policy agents: A critical language policy perspective of the Castañeda v. Pickard case and the bilingual teacher shortage. *Language Policy*, *21*, 1–23.
Hornberger, N. H., & Link, H. (2012). Translanguaging and transnational literacies in multilingual classrooms: A biliteracy lens. *International Journal of Bilingual Education and Bilingualism*, *15*(3), 261–278.
Howard, E. R., Lindholm-Leary, K. J., Rogers, D., Olague, N., Medina, J., Kennedy, D., Sugarman, J., & Christian, D. (2018). *Guiding principles for dual language education* (3rd ed.). Center for Applied Linguistics. http://www.cal.org/twi/guidingprinciples.htm
Kloss (1977/1998). *The American bilingual tradition.* Center for Applied Linguistics and Delta Systems.
Márquez Román, A., & Castellanos Villalobos, M. L. (2020). La exclusion del derecho a la educación bilingüe indígena en México. In I. U. López Bonilla, & M. L. Castellanos Villalobos (Eds.), *Prolegómenos de intervención jurídica: Planteamientos clínicos en homenaje al Dr. Rafael Sánchez Vázquez* (pp. 55–69). Dykinson.
Olsen, L. (2022). *A legacy of courage and activism: Stories from the movement for educational access and equity for English learners in California.* Californians Together.
Sánchez, M. T., García, O., & Solorza, C. (2017). Reframing language allocation policy in dual language bilingual education. *Bilingual Research Journal*, *41*(1), 35–51.
Tollefson, J. W. (2006). Critical theory in language policy. In T. Ricento (Ed.), *An introduction to language policy: Theory and method* (pp. 42–59). Blackwell Publishing.
Torres-Guzmán, M. E., & de Jong, E. J. (2015). Looking back, sideways, and forward: Language and education in multilingual settings. In M. Bigelow & J. E. Kananen (Eds.), *The Routledge handbook of educational linguistics* (pp. 428–445). Routledge.
Trillos Amaya, M. (2020). Los derechos lingüísticos en Colombia: Avances y desafíos. *Lingüística y Literatura*, *77*, 173–202. http://www.scielo.org.co/scielo.php?script=sci_arttext&pid=S0120-55872020000100173
Wall, D. J., Greer, E., & Palmer, D. K. (2019). Exploring institutional processes in a district-wide dual language program: Who is it for? Who is left out? *Journal of Latinos and Education*, *21*(1), 87–102. https://doi.org/10.1080/15348431.2019.1613996

SECTION I

Theoretical Foundations and Outcomes

Theoretical Foundations

1

THEORETICAL FOUNDATIONS OF DUAL LANGUAGE BILINGUAL EDUCATION

Ofelia García, Cristina Alfaro, Juan A. Freire

Introduction

At the end of the 20th century, many bilingual education programs in the United States were transformed into dual language programs (also called dual language immersion and two-way immersion) (Lindholm-Leary, 2001). The different naming for these programs signaled an ideological shift that reflected a distancing from the struggles of primarily Chicanx, Puerto Rican, and Native American communities during the Civil Rights movement to develop educational programs for their children that reflected their own knowledge systems, histories, and cultural and linguistic practices. The word "bilingual" became the "B-word" (Crawford, 2000) and was eliminated from every piece of legislation and from federal and state departments of education following the No Child Left Behind Act of 2002 (García, 2009). In the erasure of the word "bilingual," U.S. language-minoritized communities were dispossessed of their educational programs (Freire et al., 2021), now substituted by programs that were to teach two languages and *two groups* of children, that is, were to be "two-way," rather than focusing on *educating language-minoritized children bilingually*.

True, since the 1980s, the developmental maintenance bilingual education programs that had been the vision of the Chicanx, Puerto Rican, and Native American communities to improve the socioeconomic conditions of their communities had been slowly substituted by transitional bilingual education programs and in some cases by English as a second language (ESL) programs. Dual language programs held the promise of giving back the possibility of bilingual and biliterate development. But as these programs grew, a process akin to what David Harvey (2004) called "accumulation by

DOI: 10.4324/9781003269076-4

dispossession" occurred. Harvey used this term to refer to neoliberal capitalist policies that resulted in the centralization of wealth and power in the hands of a few by dispossessing others of their own resources. Similarly, Freire et al. (2021) used the term "expropriation" to illustrate how many dual language programs are engaged in "the act of co-opting or dispossessing language resources, opportunities, and rights of language-minoritized individuals ... to benefit majoritarian communities" (p. 28). As transitional bilingual education programs throughout the country were shut down, dual language programs, more palatable to the language majority, sprung up. These programs were also of benefit to the dominant English-speaking white communities who, keeping up with global neoliberal interests, became interested in their children's bilingual and biliteracy development. The surge of dual language programs can then be seen as following the logic of neoliberalism to both serve the interests of the dominant class and pacify resistance by marginalized groups (Delavan et al., 2017). In addition, these programs also had a political purpose of bringing those who had previously been excluded into "global capitalism's all-consuming framework and structure" (Mignolo & Walsh, 2018, p. 57).

The implementation of two-way dual language programs reduced program capacity for language-minoritized children by half and expropriated them of the right to be educated bilingually as a group. Half the seats were now reserved for those who were learners of the language other than English, most frequently Spanish, but also Mandarin, Cantonese, French, Arabic, and others. In so doing, the language other than English was curricularized (Valdés, 2018) to the same extent as English, slowly distancing it from the minoritized community and its language practices (Alfaro, 2019; Alfaro & Bartolomé, 2017; Freire & Feinauer, 2022), and in the process, making it acceptable to the dominant group. Spanish, for example, started to be taught as if it was a "language elsewhere" (Mena & García, 2020), and not used as the language of a U.S. Latinx community with a long history. As a result, dual language programs have led to the gentrification of communities and the takeover of bilingual education spaces by privileged populations (Valdez et al., 2016; Chapter 13 in this volume).

Dual language programs became a strategy of what Silvia Rivera Cusicanqui (2012), the Bolivian feminist decolonial scholar, calls "crossdressing," which she describes as new forms of colonization that reproduce a conditional inclusion, "a mitigated and second-class citizenship that molds subaltern imaginaries and identities into the role of ornaments through which the anonymous masses play out the theatricality of their own identity" (p. 99). Language-minoritized children in some dual language programs became nothing more than enhancements for the benefit of language majorities eager to become bilingual (Valdez et al., 2016). The identities of language-minoritized children were not authentically performed but were dressed up for a world stage. Crossdressing relates to the idea of gatopardismo, a term based on the 1954 novel of the Italian author Giuseppe di Lampedusa, which refers to a political strategy of advocating for change, but in practice only superficially modifying existing power structures (see also Freire et al., 2021; Martínez, 2017). Many dual language programs exert a form of crossdressing and gatopardismo under the dominance of majoritarian populations.

As two-way dual language programs spread, the growing language-minoritized communities started to perceive how these programs could also be beneficial for their own bilingual children. For example, in many communities across the United States where Latinx make up the overwhelming numerical majority, Latinx educational authorities and educators started advocating for dual language programs. These programs were a good alternative to the ESL programs or the very few Transitional Bilingual Education programs that were available for students classified as "English Language Learners." These dual language programs also offered the opportunity to bilingually educate Latinx children who were fluent in English. Language-minoritized and racialized children whose bilingualism falls along all points of the bilingual continuum are educated in these dual language programs.

But regardless of the student composition of dual language programs, they traditionally were, for the most part, theoretically grounded in colonial theories of language that perceived *language as an object to be "had,"* and traditional sociolinguistic theories of *bilingualism as additive and of language separation.* In this chapter, we consider alternative theories of language and bilingualism that dual language-*bilingual* programs must take up to provide a socially and cognitively just education that is inclusive and equitable for all. We ask: How can we engage in a project of *dual language bilingual education* (DLBE) theoretically grounded from the ground up, from those who have been pushed to the margins, in ways that does not respond to colonial language constructions of dominance and power? How can we loosen restrictive worldviews in order to transform subjectivities and consciousness, and open up opportunities for change? In doing so, we take inspiration from the many examples of work already being done by committed and critical bilingual educators.

In this chapter, we first look at the past to move forward, as we make a call to commit to the origins of bilingual education for a transformed DLBE in the future. Then, we ground our theoretical framework on *decolonial theory and nepantlera theory,* as well as *raciolinguistic ideologies* (see Chapter 14 of this volume for literature review on raciolinguistics in DLBE). These theoretical perspectives broaden the ways in which language, bilingualism and biliteracy are theorized within dual language education, and we describe how this is so. We show how through taking up these lenses, *language, bilingualism* and *biliteracy* can be reconceptualized in ways that reconstitute

DLBE. This then leads us to propose the adoption of a critical flexible dual language bilingual allocation policy at the program level and critical pedagogical practices at the classroom level.

"Past-future" at a Time of Change and Theories "Otherwise"

Indigenous Aymara and Quechua groups appeal to the concept of *Pachakutik* to refer to a "change in the sun," a moment that signals a new cycle and desire for substantive change in the political environment (Cusicanqui in Cacopardo, 2018). For us, the pandemic caused by COVID-19, and the movements associated with Black Lives Matter and #Me Too, have been Pachakutiks in our lives, enabling us to clearly see what Cusicanqui calls "past-future" that engages us in walking forward looking back because, as she says, looking at the past can orient us in the present world (Cusicanqui in Cacopardo, 2018) toward an "otherwise," meaning "a transformation conceived and impelled from the margins, from the ground up, and for society at large" (Mignolo & Walsh, 2018, p. 59).

We find Cusicanqui's notion of past-future necessary for dual language bilingual programs. As DLBE scholars we must look to the past and the commitment of the brave Latinx and Native American educators during the Civil Rights movement to educate their children bilingually, sustained by their own histories, knowledge-systems, cultural and linguistic practices, stories, songs, poetry, and desires for socioeconomic improvement (for more, see Blum Martínez & Habermann López, 2020; García & Sung, 2018; San Miguel & Valencia, 1998). It is instructive to listen to the words of a leading Mexican American educational anthropologist of the time, Henry T. Trueba. Bilingual-bicultural education, he says, "ultimately will *open the door to full Chicano participation in the socioeconomic opportunities*" (our italics, 1973, p. 2). And he defined a Chicano as someone who "perceives his *culture as unique*, that is, *different from the Mexican and the Anglo cultures*, and who *actively works to defend* his *cultural heritage* and his *social and civil rights* in order to improve his economic, political, social and religious life" (our italics, 1973, p. 2). Clearly bilingual-bicultural education was part of Chicanx activism, a way to defend their civil rights and open doors to socioeconomic opportunities, to maintain Spanish, but also to assert unique cultural and linguistic practices, ones that didn't quite fit either the Mexican or the Anglo cultures.

The theoretical foundations of traditional dual language programs of colonial language, additive bilingualism, and language separation were of benefit to the mostly white English-speaking majority that wanted to accumulate languages. Dual language *bilingual* programs must refocus their theoretical foundations about knowledge, language, and bilingualism to meet the social desires of the language-minoritized community first. The bilingualism of the community and their lives in borderlands (Anzaldúa, 2012) must be repositioned as central (Alfaro & Gándara, 2021; Freire, 2016).

We will enter Pachakutik as we commence a new cycle in DLBE supported by theories "otherwise," namely, theories that capture "an other thinking" (Mignolo, 2000, p. 69), those that are refocused on language-minoritized communities. The theories "otherwise" that are the focus of this chapter are decolonial theory, nepantlera theory, and raciolinguistic ideologies.

Decolonial Theory

We draw from Latin American *decolonial theory* (Dussel, 1995; Espinosa-Miñoso, 2014; Grosfoguel, 2002; Lugones, 2008; Mignolo, 2000; Quijano, 2000; among others) to query mainstream epistemologies about standard named languages and additive double bilingualism and duality. Decolonial scholars have provided a roadmap of how to situate our epistemological perspective on what Boaventura de Sousa Santos (2007) has called "the other side of the line," instead of always seeing with a "hegemonic eye" that renders otherwise thinking as nonexistent, incomprehensible, or magical, and that hides histories of domination. "The other side of the line" refers to the epistemologies and practices of colonized people that have been invalidated and are deemed as inferior or nonexistent. In order to make visible and recover colonized epistemologies and practices from the "the other side of the line," de Sousa Santos (2007) makes a call for a "post-abyssal thinking" (Santos, 2007). Post-abyssal thinking requires acknowledging an *ecology of knowledges*, a concept that recognizes the heterogeneity and diversity of experiences as equal, as well as the proliferation of alternatives (Santos, 2007). Even though this *interknowledge* is important, "[p]reference must be given to the form of knowledge that guarantees the greatest level of participation to the social groups involved in its design, execution, and control, and in the benefits of the intervention" (Santos, 2007, p. 73). For DLBE programs to benefit marginalized bilingual communities, they must be aligned with theoretical perspectives that respond to the ideologies, the epistemologies, the practices, and the desires, of the minoritized group (Alfaro, 2019; García et al., 2021).

Dual language bilingual programs must delink from the abyssal and epistemic assumptions about language and bilingualism, as well as racist and heteropatriarchal oppression. That is, the theoretical grounding of these programs must engage instead with the subjective reconstitution of those seen as minoritized bilinguals. To *delink from this epistemological matrix of power*, one would need to take up a *different locus of enunciation* (Mignolo, 2000) other than that of the nation-state, its schools, and the dominant monolingual class. The loci of enunciation can be described as "border gnosis," which refers to "the subaltern reason striving to bring to the foreground the force and creativity of knowledges subalternized during a long process of colonization of the planet" (Mignolo, 2000, p. 13). Theoretically, we must move toward *another logic*, by drawing on the locus of enunciation of the marginalized group, thus changing the terms, not just the content, of the conversation that we have been having about bilingualism and schools (Mignolo, 2000). We align DLBE theoretically to the actual language and cultural experiences of diverse communities, rectifying histories of sociopolitical, linguistic, cultural and knowledge exclusions, while extending complex understandings of language and bilingualism.

Nepantleras Theories: Beyond Borders

In 1987, the Chicana scholar Gloria Anzaldúa published *Borderlands/La Frontera*. The concept of borderlands referred to a geopolitical and psychic space, the "lifeblood of two worlds merging to form a third country, a border culture" (Anzaldúa, 2012, p. 25). This space was defined by the border itself, and yet it enabled becoming a "crossroads." In later work, Anzaldúa moved beyond borderlands by appealing to the Nahuatl word, nepantla. Nepantla refers to "el lugar entre medio." It transcends duality and recognizes the in-between spaces in which minoritized communities dwell and where possibilities and transformations can occur. In this nepantla, one can tap into what Anzaldúa calls "el cenote," "an inner underground river of information" (2002, p. 6), "a subterranean reservoir of personal and collective knowledge" (p. 66). This cenote pushes against linguistic, cultural, national, and any other boundaries, "[r]igid borders [that] hinder communication and prevent us from extending beyond ourselves" (p. 66).

Anzaldúa calls for nepantleras who function disruptively. Anzaldúa adds: "Like tender green roots growing out of the cracks, they eventually overturn foundations, making conventional definitions of otherness hard to sustain" (2002, p. 84). Educators and scholars studying dual language bilingual programs must become nepantleras, overturning the foundations of privilege upon which these programs were built, ensuring that everyone is included. To do so, Anzaldúa recommends activism, a notion that she describes as "putting our hands in the dough and not merely thinking or talking about making tortillas. It means creating spaces and times for healing to happen, espacios y tiempos to nourish the soul" (p. 89). What are the spaces and times that we can create in dual language bilingual programs to ensure that the soul of language-minoritized children is nourished? How do we put our hands in the theoretical dough that has shaped them in ways that minoritize them, not simply to make tortillas, but to transform reality?

To transform dual language bilingual programs we must take up a perspective from the cracks/rajaduras "[that] enable us to reconfigure ourselves as subjects outside the us/them binary ... to construct alternative roads, create new topographies and geographies ... Look at the world with new eyes, use competing and global systems of knowledge, and rewrite identities. Navigating the cracks is the process of reconstructing life anew" (Anzaldúa, 2002, p. 79). Dual language bilingual programs must reconfigure themselves to be free from linguistic and cultural artificial borders. Dual language bilingual programs need to be inclusive and go beyond the binary of us/them, opening up interstices that reflect that in-between space capable of connecting language-minoritized people with our cenote—the source of water and freshness in an unjust world.

Raciolinguistic Ideologies

The study of how race and racism in the United States has impacted the lives of racialized people developed throughout the 20th century and culminated with the work of legal scholars around the systemic structural racism that was built into the legal foundations of the country to exclude and deprive racialized people of societal and educational opportunities (Bell, 1980; Crenshaw, 1988). The study of language ideologies has focused on the processes through which language has been constructed in ways that serve the interests of the dominant class, limiting access to minoritized communities that are rendered without human agency (Alfaro & Bartolomé, 2017; Irvine & Gal, 2000). Even though language-minoritized groups have been also racialized, the study of the two categories of exclusion—race and language—had never been addressed jointly. Traditionally, issues of educating racialized bilinguals were simply considered issues of language. This changed with the work on raciolinguistic ideologies by Nelson Flores and Jonathan Rosa (Flores & Rosa, 2015; Rosa & Flores, 2017; see Chapter 14 in this handbook). Dual language bilingual scholars and educators need to pay attention to how raciolinguistic ideologies inform how language operates in DLBE classrooms.

Raciolinguistic ideologies hold that it is not language itself, but the social categories (white/non-white, monolingual/bilingual, native-non-native, or immigrant) that produce the *perception* of signs that are in turn negatively evaluated by those Rosa and Flores call "white listening subject," listeners with institutionalized power. As Flores and Rosa (2015) say: "No language variety is objectively distinctive or nondistinctive, but rather comes to be enregistered as such in particular historical, political and economic circumstances" (p. 632). By separating languages strictly, traditional dual language programs deem the language practices of minoritized bilinguals as inferior and non-academic (Alfaro & Bartolomé, 2017; Freire & Feinauer, 2022). The work on raciolinguistic ideologies makes it obvious that these perceptions are product of a subjectivity based on claimed racial superiority. Rather than protect separations that tend to reify superiority of language practices of those deemed racially superior, DLBE programs must make students conscious of the raciolinguistic ideologies that operate and work against them by normalizing minoritized knowledge systems and cultural and linguistic practices.

DLBE Taking Notice of Decolonial/Nepantlera Theories and Raciolinguistic Ideologies

We have proposed decolonial theory, nepantlera theory, and raciolinguistic ideologies to reframe the theoretical foundations of DLBE. Now, the reader might be wondering, how do scholars and educators engaged in DLBE take up position as nepantleras? Where are the rajaduras in the traditional theoretical foundations of dual language bilingual programs? What do we need to crack in order to see through the realities of children, and especially minoritized bilingual children, in dual language bilingual programs?

We need to crack the notion of *language,* unbind it as an object of study, and situate it in the sociocultural complexity that surrounds speakers' real language use, in its heteroglossia (Bakhtin, 1981). In the field of bilingual education, heteroglossia can be understood as the acknowledgment of the languaging practices of bi/multilingual communities as fluid, interacting, and dynamic, without strict boundaries (García, 2009). Hence, as we crack the notion of *language*, we also need to crack the concept of *bilingualism* as double monolingualism/additive bilingualism. We need to drive away from colonial and raciolinguistic approaches in DLBE and perceive the dynamic *translanguaging* of bilingual speakers (García & Li, 2014; Otheguy et al., 2015; Li, 2018; Chapter 26 in this volume), understanding students' positionality in nepantla spaces (Freire, 2016) and referring to bilingual speakers' and learners' agentive use of their entire linguistic/semiotic repertoire to communicate and learn. Through this translanguaging perspective, *biliteracy* is theorized as the agency exerted by bilinguals to make meaning around print and texts by bringing forth their entire life experience, including all their linguistic/semiotic resources (García & Kleifgen, 2019). Taking up a decolonial/nepantlera theoretical perspective and a raciolinguistic lens that shifts our perspective to the actual practices of minoritized bilinguals from the ground up, we consider next the theoretical foundations to understand language, bilingualism, and biliteracy "otherwise."

Language and Languaging

As Makoni and Pennycook (2007) have shown, language has been an ideological invention that has operated as an instrument of colonialism and nation-building to produce and naturalize forms of social inequality. As explained by the Peruvian sociologist Aníbal Quijano (1991, 2000) and the Brazilian Lynn Mario Menezes de Souza (2007), language, as normalized today, was a product of colonialization. At the point of the Encounter in the Americas, language, as well as race, gender, religion, and culture were created as categories that justified the superiority and dominance of the white Europeans. The biologization of race then created a category of "non-humans" who did not have a valid language and were unable to enter into legitimate dialogue (Flores & Rosa, 2022). In coining the concept of "coloniality," Quijano points out that the exploitation and domination of racialized groups continues after the colonizers left, and is now carried out not solely through labor, but through the structuring of knowledge-systems, language, race, and gender into superior and inferior. Language is a product of a particular colonial epistemology, yet it appears to be, and is accepted as, a natural object, required to be educated.

The construction of a named language, that is, what we have learned to call English, Spanish, Chinese, Vietnamese, etc., has little to do with the languag*ing* of people. The Chilean biologists Maturana and Varela (1984) coined the term "lenguajear" [languaging] to refer to what differentiates human beings from other organisms. Human beings do more than simply communicate and interact, they language (as a verb) to also observe, reflect, and describe their interactions. This languaging process of human beings engages the histories, the social, the cognitive, the emotional, the affective, and the lived ethnographies of all interlocutors, involving the subjectivities of speakers. This languaging is, of course, very different from the ways in which language has been constructed as an object by the writing of grammars supported by empires and nation-states for domination (Mignolo, 2000). Mignolo adds that this constructed language then "becomes the point of reference to measure and rank languaging practices that do not comply with the regulatory force of language" (Mignolo, cited in Delgado & Romero, 2000, p 17). Critical approaches in sociolinguistics have shown how named languages were, and continue to be, constructs of nation-state building and colonial expansion to support an ideology of racial, class, and gender superiority in multilingual societies.

Dual language bilingual programs must then center the languaging of its students, rather than simply the named language which has been increasingly narrowly conceived as "academic." Increasingly, educators appeal to the concept of academic language as the reason for the failure of racialized students. Many scholars have worked to identify the features of academic language, without questioning the nature of what they are describing (García & Solorza, 2020). Their descriptions reflect the features found in texts and ways of speaking produced by dominant white monolingual people, making it "academic" simply because of the power held by that group (Alfaro & Bartolomé, 2017; Poza, 2016). This dominant group monopolizes how language is used in schools, branding as "deficient" all other ways of languaging by bi/multilingual communities, speakers of African American English, and other language-minoritized communities. These language practices are portrayed from a raciolinguistic approach as non-academic, inferior, conceptually deficient. Languaging goes beyond the borders of language drawn by the dominant group that emphasizes linguistic practices that have been normalized as the only standard and, instead, includes all the language practices of people, as they live, communicate, and desire differently. It pays attention to the heteroglossic nature of language (Bakhtin, 1981) and to the right of all speakers/languagers to *do* language in ways that fit their different ecologies of knowledge and lives.

Bilingualism and Translanguaging

The sociolinguistic study of bilingualism in the second half of the 20th century focused on the difference between the ways in which bilingual speakers and monolingual speakers used language. The study of "language contact" was pioneered by Uriel Weinreich (1953/1979), focusing on the linguistic phenomena that were said to characterize bilingual ways of using language—the presence of loans and calques, and the use of code-switching. In comparison to monolingual ways of using language, bilingual language was full of what were seen as interferences.

To control what were said to be interferences from the point of view of dominant monolingual speakers, strict boundaries had to be drawn between named standard languages. The education of bilinguals developed around the idea that true bilingualism was *additive*, with one separate "second language" being added to the bilingual speakers' "first language" (Lambert, 1974). This ranking of languages relates to the sociolinguistic concept of *diglossia*, that is, the idea that for societal bilingualism to be stable, the two named languages need to be compartmentalized and kept strictly separate (Fishman, 1967). One language had to be used for what were seen as "high" functions in "formal" domains, and the other for "low" functions in "informal" domains. These diglossic descriptions of bilingual use never considered the power differentials that were responsible for enforcing a strict linguistic hierarchy.

The ways of knowing and languaging of bilingual-minoritized speakers in the United States is, as Trueba said a long time ago, unique, and is not limited by the national borders that they have gone across—physically, spiritually, or emotionally. Their languaging cannot be compared to those who are monolingual, dominant, and white, neither in the United States nor in the countries from which they or their ancestors originate. The reality of multilingual practices is more complex than that described from the point of view of white scholars who are still holding up the model of a monolingual. Many multilingual speakers have grown up with different language practices that make it difficult to categorically name a language as first, second, or third. There is nothing diglossic about their language use, which reflects their own dynamic language practices. As Ndhlovu and Makalela (2021) have said, the mainstream understanding of multilingualism was pre-eminently colonial and needs to be decolonized.

In the 21st century, language education policies and practices in the Global North were suddenly impacted by the complexity of identities and language practices that were present in classrooms. The negative raciolinguistic reaction to this greater heterogeneity in schools was violent, with policies and practices controlling even more the boundaries that had been drawn around named languages. Traditional dual language programs are a case in point. The dynamic language practices of bilingual students were severely policed, so that their language did not contain "interferences." But in doing so, not only were language-minoritized communities expropriated of the academic value of their dynamic language practices to learn but they also became the possessors of the achievement gap, of the word gap, of the lack of academic language, of the inability to meet language standards that were evaluated with monolingual assessments.

Bilingual-minoritized speakers engage in *translanguaging*, a term that has been coined by sociolinguists to refer to the languaging of bilingual people that transcends, goes beyond, the concept of two named languages (García & Li, 2014; Li, 2018; see also Chapter 16 of this volume). Otheguy et al. (2015) have defined translanguaging as "the deployment of a speaker's full linguistic repertoire without regard for watchful adherence to the socially and politically defined boundaries of named (and usually national and state) languages" (p. 283). Bilinguals do not "have" two languages; they "do" language with a *unitary language/semiotic repertoire*, a network of features and meanings from which they select those that are more fitting to their situations (Otheguy et al., 2019). Translanguaging points to this *emergent unitary network* of linguistic/semiotic features. The language performances of bilinguals are never dual and separate; instead, they do the opposite—they *assemble* (Pennycook, 2017) and bring together all of their languaging with all multimodalities, their emotions, their lives, their experiences, their funds of knowledge, their bodies, and relevant objects, including technology, as they engage in meaning-making. In supporting this unitary repertoire, translanguaging is a political act (Flores, 2014), disrupting the linearity with which second language acquisition and bilingual studies have proceeded, and going beyond the coloniality of language that nation-states and their schools have defended. Translanguaging theory has enormous repercussions for DLBE programs, and many scholars have called for its inclusion (see, for example, Freire & Feinauer, 2022; García-Mateus & Palmer, 2017; Hamman, 2018; Martínez, 2017; Palmer et al., 2014; Sánchez & García, 2022; Tian & Link, 2019).

It is true that named languages have had real and material effects in our lives. It is also true that named languages are important for the identity purposes of many. Language and bilingualism are important concepts, but they have *social* reality, not a *psycholinguistic* one. That is, there is no dual correspondence in the minds of bilinguals of one language and the other, although one learns the social mores of when to use features that are externally and socially defined as belonging to one language or another. Translanguaging takes the *internal* perspective of what bilinguals *do* with language, instead of the *external* perspective of named languages associated with nation-states that speakers are said to "have."

There is no such thing as learning an additional language or acquiring a second language. Bilingual children acquire new linguistic features that they then integrate into a unitary repertoire, as all children do. The repertoire of bilingual children has more features than that of monolinguals, that is, it is more extensive. Yet, in schools, even in most dual language programs, bilingual students are allowed to use only less than half of the features of their repertoire in class and in assessments. This creates the illusion that bilingual children can be two monolinguals in one. And beyond the illusion is the reality that insisting that bilingual children act like monolinguals only produces failure—failure that they cannot meet the standards that systems have artificially set up, and that then produce subjectivities of inferiority that keep them in subordinate positions.

Translanguaging focuses on redressing the asymmetry of languages and denouncing the coloniality of power and knowledge (Mignolo, 2000, p. 231). The South African scholar Leketi Makalela (2017) appeals to the concept of ubuntu, "I am because you are. You are because I am," to describe what he calls *ubuntu translanguaging*. Multilingual South African speakers use an interwoven network of language because no language is complete without the other, and all depend on each other for the total sum of meaning (Ndhlovu & Makalela, 2021). Édouard Glissant, the Martiniquais philosopher once said: "To understand [opacities] one must focus on the texture of the weave and not on the nature of its components" (1990, p. 190). Translanguaging theory keeps the epistemological eye on the ways in which bilingual people weave their languaging, and not on the separate components of what are seen as languages. The weave is where DLBE needs to focus. Bilingualism as two named languages is of value. But to educate for social and cognitive justice, *the focus has to be on the weave*, how learners interlace their linguistic/semiotic features to learn, to make meaning, to create, to produce, to imagine, to have ideas, and to be creative.

Translanguaging in dual language bilingual programs has much to do with what W.E. du Bois (1903) has called "lifting the veil" (1903). The borders around named languages are abolished as we lift the veil to truly see and center minoritized bilingual students in DLBE. Racialized bilingual students must learn to see and hear themselves without any reference to monolingual students. Students in dual language bilingual programs must understand that what is natural in bilingualism is translanguaging, suppressed by the monolingual ideology of modernity and nationalism, as well as the enduring coloniality of dominance. And yet, they must also see language and bilingualism as important social realities that need to be extended to include their languaging and translanguaging.

Biliteracy and Translanguaging

One of the most important functions of school has been the development of literacy. But as scholars of what is known as New Literacy Studies have consistently shown, literacy is a practice that is socially constructed and locally negotiated (Street, 1984). Similarly, biliteracy needs to be locally negotiated to meet the needs and desires of language-minoritized communities. Nancy Hornberger (1990) has defined *biliteracy* as "any and all instance in which communication occurs in two or more languages in or around writing" (p. 213), which theoretically can be inclusive of the language practices of bilingual students. However, traditional biliteracy approaches in the education of bilingual students have adhered to the "one-named-language as input and the same-named-language as output" principle (García, 2009). In traditional dual language classrooms, bilingual students are asked to make meaning only with the authorized language of the written text, preventing them from bringing to bear their whole meaning-making repertoire. These borders of literacy disadvantage language-minoritized students, expropriate their linguistic resources, and raciolinguistically position them as inferior. Nancy Hornberger's continua of biliteracy has posited that biliteracy is better obtained when learners can draw on all their practices and not just those that are privileged in schools (Hornberger & Skilton-Sylvester, 2000). When literacy performances of bilingual students are viewed through translanguaging, the literacy act is no longer located in, and limited by, the printed page, but in the relations formed across signs, texts, images, languages, objects, bodies, thoughts, and emotions.

A translanguaging approach to biliteracy would not only pair the literacy in the two languages closer together as in the approach known as biliteracy squared (Escamilla et al., 2013, see Chapter 29 in this volume), it would also leverage the students' translanguaging to make meaning in all their encounters with written texts. Rather than keeping the spoken/written/signed/linguistic modes separate from other meaning-making modes, it would bring down these barriers. It is important for DLBE programs to have spaces for students to hear, speak, read, and write in one language or the other. But even more important is to encourage students to always leverage their translanguaging so that they can liberate themselves from artificial borders and the policing of those who impose named languages and bilingualism as colonial apparatus. As dual language bilingual students enter this process, biliteracy efforts need to extend "reading the world" (Freire & Macedo, 1987), to a nepantla world. This sociopolitical act can help bilingual students become socially and politically repositioned as they encounter raciolinguistic discourses and fight colonization.

Decolonizing, Nepantlerizing, and Disrupting Raciolinguistic Bilingual Allocation Policies and Pedagogical Practices

The decolonial/nepantlera/raciolinguistics theoretical foundations of language, bilingualism, and biliteracy that we have been considering have repercussions for theorizing language allocation policies and pedagogical practices in DLBE. This section considers how these theoretical foundations can transform the rigid language allocation policies of traditional dual language programs, as well as traditional pedagogical practices.

Critical Flexible Dual Language Bilingual Allocation Policy

Programmatic planning for dual language bilingual programs often includes a language allocation policy in which a designated time is given to each one of the named languages. The typical types are 90:10 and 50:50. Decolonizing, nepantlerizing, and disrupting raciolinguistic ideologies unsettle these traditional language allocation policies (Freire & Delavan, 2021). *Critical flexible dual language bilingual allocation policies* then emerge (Freire & Delavan, 2021; Sánchez et al., 2018), since strictly binary categorization principles do not hold. A critical flexible dual language bilingual allocation policy positions children not as learners of one named language or another, but as *emergent bilinguals*, positioned along different points of a bilingual/multilingual continuum, all engaging with translanguaging practices. Although spaces for the two languages of instruction may be observed, these do *not follow diglossic principles* of strict separation or blindly fit a quantifiable "model" prescribed by external authorities. Instead, the allocation of languages in instructional spaces is *localized* and responds to the different characteristics of local students, as well as the community/family wishes for the bilingual education of their own children. A language policy that is attentive to the power differentials in the coloniality of language and schooling, and the raciolinguistic ideologies that have created subjectivities of inferiority, needs to create cracks in rigid language allocation policies and strict language separation policies.

In order to combat language separation policies, dual language bilingual programs need to provide translanguaging spaces (García et al., 2017; Li, 2011), which function as ways for students to breathe, to act on their agency to assemble all their meaning-making resources, to learn generatively. To do so, teachers must offer flexibility within instructional spaces allocated to one language or the other so that students can use all their repertoire during the *process* of learning and languaging. With consciousness and care, teachers can, of course, encourage students to generate *products* in one named language or another, but always drawing from their entire linguistic/semiotic repertoire. These translanguaging spaces encourage *collaboration, co-learning, and co-laboring* among students and teachers. *Critical engagement across difference* is possible in these translanguaging spaces, encouraging bilingual children and teachers with different histories of settlement and immigration, diverse raciolinguistic and sociopolitical/socioeconomic experiences, and various complex language and cultural practices to not only understand each other's subjectivities, but to potentially transform their own subjectivities and those of bilingual communities.

Critical Pedagogical Practices in Dual Language Bilingual Programs

Critical/sociopolitical *consciousness* is necessary to transform pedagogical practices in DLBE (Alfaro, 2018, 2019; Freire, 2016, 2021; Palmer et al., 2019, see Chapters 3 and 12 in this volume) in ways that emanate from decolonial, nepantlera, and raciolinguistic theories. Freire (2016) proposed that as dual language bilingual educators understand how language-minoritized students operate in nepantla spaces, these teachers need to contest restrictive language policies in tandem with supporting students' critical/sociopolitical consciousness as one of the goals of DLBE. Dual language programs have proliferated, and many times have served as instruments of gentrification that have kept educators and communities ignorant of histories and theories that hurt. As Anzaldúa (2002) says, "conocimiento hurts, but not as much as desconocimiento" (p. 557). Critical pedagogical practices in DLBE must be grounded in language-minoritized people's histories, struggles, and subjectivities and focus on regenerating the "broken weave" that language separation has produced.

Freire and Feinauer (2022) suggested that leveraging bilingual-minoritized students' full repertoire, their translanguaging, can promote the goal of critical consciousness in DLBE. García et al. (2017) have argued that teachers need to develop a juntos/together translanguaging stance with students' practices and understandings at the center, before they can develop equitable pedagogical practices. Sánchez et al. (2018) have identified three ways in which teachers' pedagogical practices can incorporate translanguaging: (1) translanguaging documentation, which refers to leveraging the students' translanguaging to assess and document what students know and are able to do; (2) translanguaging rings, which uses translanguaging to scaffold instruction for students whose language performances fall at different points of the bilingual continuum; (3) translanguaging transformation, which provides transformative spaces to shift students' subjectivities about themselves and their language practices as valuable. These translanguaging pedagogical practices legitimize minoritized bilingual students' full linguistic repertoires as academic.

Conclusion

The theoretical perspectives laid out in this chapter draw from decolonial theory, nepantlera theory, and raciolinguistic ideologies. These perspectives help explain how language, languaging, translanguaging, bilingualism, and biliteracy work for bilingual-minoritized students. This theoretical grounding also contributes to transforming policies and pedagogical practices in ways that support the struggles of bilingual education activists of the past (Alfaro, 2019; Blum Martínez & Habermann López, 2020; Delavan et al., 2017; Rosa & Flores, 2017).

As Gloria Anzaldúa (2002) has said: "Our task is to light up the darkness" (p. 8), a darkness that has been produced by conceptualizing language solely as a colonial apparatus, what Mignolo (2000) calls "the darker side of modernity." For dual language bilingual programs to fulfill their promise, we must return to Anzaldúa's calls to the activism of nepantleras that have the potential to normalize our language practices. Dual language bilingual programs cannot just make tortillas, especially if they're going to be consumed by the dominant group. Dual language bilingual teachers have to crack the shell, break the eggs, and cook up new subjectivities for their minoritized bilingual students in ways that will move the programs toward social equity (Alfaro & Hernández, 2016; Sánchez & García, 2022). Educators must put their hand in the dough to mix, to juntar, to shape differently for diverse children, to heal and nourish each of them, to create translanguaging spaces where other knowledges, other languaging, other literacies can be valued. Only then, will these transformed DLBE programs, become all that they could and should be.

References

Alfaro, C. (2018). The sociopolitical struggle and promise of bilingual teacher education: Past, present, and future. *Bilingual Research Journal*, *41*(4), 413–427.

Alfaro, C. (2019). Preparing critically conscious dual language teachers: Recognizing and interrupting dominant ideologies. Reimaging dual language education in the U.S. *Theory into Practice Journal*, *58*(2), 194–203.

Alfaro, C., & Bartolomé, L. (2017). Preparing ideologically clear bilingual teachers: Honoring working-class non-standard language use in the bilingual education classroom. *Issues in Teacher Education*, *26*(2), 11–34.

Alfaro, C., & Gándara, P. (2021). Binational teacher preparation: Constructing pedagogical bridges for the students we share. In P. Gándara, & B. Jensen (Eds.), *The students we share: Preparing US and Mexican educators for our transnational future* (pp. 45–69). SUNY Press.
Alfaro, C., & Hernández A. M. (2016). Ideology, pedagogy, access and equity (IPAE): A critical examination for dual language educators. *The Multilingual Educator*, 8–11.
Anzaldúa, G. (2002). (Un)natural bridges, (un)safe spaces. In G. Anzaldúa, & A. L. Keating (Eds.), *This bridge we call home: Radical visions for transformation* (pp. 1–5). Routledge.
Anzaldúa, G. (2012). *Borderlands/La frontera. The new mestiza* (2nd ed.). Aunt Lute Books.
Bakhtin, M. M. (1981). *The dialogic imagination: Four essays* (M. Holquist, Ed.; C. Emerson & M. Holquist, Trans.). University of Texas Press.
Bell, S. (1980). Brown v. Board of Education: The interest-convergence dilemma. *Harvard Law Review*, *93*(3), 518–533.
Blum Martínez, R., & Habermann López, M. J. (2020). *The shoulders we stand on: A history of bilingual education in New Mexico*. University of New Mexico Press.
du Bois, W. E. (1903). *The souls of Black folk*. A.C. McClurg & Co.
Cacopardo, A. (2018). "Nada sería posible si la gente no deseara lo imposible." Entrevista a Silvia Rivera Cusicanqui. *Andamios*, *15*(37), 179–193.
Crawford, J. (2000). *At war with diversity. U.S. language policy in an age of anxiety*. Multilingual Matters.
Crenshaw, K. (1988). Race, reform and retrenchment: Transformation and legitimation in anti-discrimination law. *Harvard Law Review*, *101*(7), 1331–1387. https://doi.org/10.2307/1341398
Cusicanqui, S. R. (2012). Ch'ixinakax utxiwa: A reflection on the practices and discourses of decolonization. *The South Atlantic Quarterly*, *111*(1), 95–109. https://doi.org/10.1215/00382876-1472612
Delavan, M. G., Valdez, V. E., & Freire, J. A. (2017). Language as whose resource?: When global economics usurp the local equity potentials of dual language education. *International Multilingual Research Journal*, *11*(2), 86–100. https://doi.org/10.1080/19313152.2016.1204890
Delgado, E., & Romero, R. (2000). Local histories and global designs: An interview with Walter Mignolo. *Discourse*, 22(3), 7–33.
Dussel, E. (1995). *The invention of the Americas: Eclipse of "the other" and the myth of modernity*. Continuum.
Escamilla, K., Hopewell, S., & Butvilofsky, S. (2013). *Biliteracy from the start: Literacy squared in action*. Caslon.
Espinosa-Miñoso, Y. (2014). Una crítica descolonial a la epistemología feminista crítica. *El Cotidiano*, *184*, 7–12.
Fishman, J. A. (1967). Bilingualism with and without diglossia: Diglossia with and without bilingualism. *Journal of Social Issues*, *23*(2), 29–38.
Flores, N. (2014). Let's not forget that translanguaging is a political act. [Online] *Educational Linguist*. https://educationallinguist.wordpress.com/2014/07/19/lets-not-forget-that-translanguaging-is-a-political-act/
Flores, N., & Rosa, J. (2015). Undoing appropriateness: Raciolinguistic ideologies and language diversity in education. *Harvard Education Review*, *85*(2), 149–171. https://doi.org/10.17763/0017-8055.85.2.149

Flores, N., & Rosa, J. (2022). Undoing competence: Coloniality, homogeneity, and the overrepresentation of whiteness in applied linguistics. *Language Learning*. Advance online publication. https://doi.org/10.1111/lang.12528

Freire, J. A. (2016). Nepantleras/os and their teachers in dual language education: Developing sociopolitical consciousness to contest language education policies. *Association of Mexican American Educators Journal*, *10*(1), 36–52.

Freire, J. A. (2021). Conscientization calls: A white dual language educator's development of sociopolitical consciousness and commitment to social justice. *Education and Urban Society*, *53*(2), 231–248.

Freire, J. A., & Delavan, M. G. (2021). The fiftyfication of dual language education: One-size-fits-all language allocation's "equality" and "practicality" eclipsing a history of equity. *Language Policy*, *20*(3), 351–381.

Freire, J. A., & Feinauer, E. (2022). Vernacular Spanish as a promoter of critical consciousness in dual language bilingual education classrooms. *International Journal of Bilingual Education and Bilingualism*, *25*(4), 1516–1529.

Freire, J. A., Gambrell, J., Kasun, G. S., & Dorner, L. M. (2021). The expropriation of dual language bilingual education: Deconstructing neoliberalism, whitestreaming, and English-hegemony. *International Multilingual Research Journal*, *16*(1), 27–46.

Freire, P., & Macedo, D. (1987). *Reading the word and the world*. Bergin & Garvey.

García, O. (2009). *Bilingual education in the 21st century: A global perspective*. Wiley.

García, O., Flores, N., Seltzer, K., Wei, L., Otheguy, R., & Rosa, J. (2021). Rejecting abyssal thinking in the language and education of racialized bilinguals: A manifesto. *Critical Inquiry in Language Studies*, *18*(3), 203–228.

García, O., Johnson, S., & Seltzer, K. (2017). *The translanguaging classroom: Leveraging student bilingualism for learning*. Caslon.

García, O., & Kleifgen, J. A. (2019). Translanguaging and literacies. *Reading Research Quarterly*, *55*(4). https://doi.org/10.1002/rrq.286

García, O., & Li, W. (2014). *Translanguaging: Language, bilingualism and education*. Palgrave Macmillan Pivot.

García, O., & Solorza, C. (2020). Academic language and the minoritization of U.S. bilingual Latinx students. *Language and Education*, *35*(6), 505–521. https://doi.org/10.1080/09500782.2020.1825476

García, O., & Sung, K. K. (2018). Critically assessing the 1968 bilingual education act at 50 years: Taming tongues and Latinx communities. *The Bilingual Research Journal*, *4*(4), 318–333. https://doi.org/10.1080/15235882.2018.1529642

García-Mateus, S., & Palmer, D. (2017). Translanguaging pedagogies for positive identities in two-way bilingual education. *Journal of Language, Identity, and Education*, *16*(4), 245–255. https://doi.org/10.1080/15348458.2017.1329016

Glissant, E. (1990). *Poetics of relation*. University of Michigan Press.

Grosfoguel, R. (2002). Colonial difference, geopolitics of knowledge and global coloniality in the modern/colonial capitalist world-system. *Review*, *25*(3), 203–224.

Hamman, L. (2018). Translanguaging and positioning in two-way dual language classrooms: A case for criticality. *Language and Education*, *32*(1), 21–42. https://doi.org/10.1080/09500782.2017.1384006

Harvey, D. (2004). The "New" imperialism: Accumulation by dispossession. *Socialist Register*, *40*, 63–87.

Hornberger, N. (1990). Creating successful learning contexts for bilingual literacy. *Teachers College Record*, *92*(2), 212–229.

Hornberger, N., & Skilton-Sylvester, E. (2000). Revisiting the continua of biliteracy: International and critical perspectives. *Language and Education*, *14*(2), 96–122.

Irvine, J. T., & Gal, S. (2000). Language ideology and linguistic differentiation. In P. V. Kroskrity (Ed.), *Regimes of language: Ideologies, polities*, and identities (pp. 35–84). School of American Research Press.

Lambert, W. E. (1974). Culture and language as factors in learning and education. In F. E. Aboud & R. D. Meade (Eds.), *Cultural factors in learning and education* (pp. 91–122). Western Washington University.

Li, W. (2011). Moment analysis and translanguaging space: Discursive construction of identities by multilingual Chinese youth in Britain. *Journal of Pragmatics*, *43*(5), 1222–1235. https://doi.org/10.1016/j.pragma.2010.07.035

Li, W. (2018). Translanguaging as a practical theory of language. *Applied Linguistics*, *39*(1), 9–30. https://doi.org/10.1093/applin/amx039

Lindholm-Leary, K. J. (2001). *Dual language education*. Multilingual Matters.

Lugones, M. (2008). Colonialidad y género. *Tabula Rasa*, *9*, 73–10.

Makalela, L. (2017). Bilingualism in South Africa: Reconnecting with ubuntu translanguaging. In O. García, A. Lin, & S. May (Eds.), *Bilingual and multilingual education* (pp. 297–310). Springer.

Makoni, S., & Pennycook, A. (2007). *Disinventing and reconstituting languages*. Multilingual Matters.

Martínez, R. A. (2017). Dual language education and the erasure of Chicanx, Latinx, and indigenous Mexican children: A call to re-imagine (and imagine beyond) bilingualism. *Texas Education Review*, *5*(1), 81–92.

Maturana, H., & Varela, F. (1984). *El árbol del conocimiento: Las bases biológicas del entendimiento humano*. Lumen/Editorial Universitaria.

Mena, M., & García, O. (2020). 'Converse racialization' and 'un-marking' language: The making of a bilingual university in a neoliberal world. *Language in Society*, *50*(3), 343–364. https://doi.org/10.1017=S0047404520000330

Menezes de Souza, L. M. T. (2007). Entering a culture quietly: Writing and cultural survival in indigenous education in Brazil. In S. Makoni & A. Pennycook (Eds.), *Disinventing and reconstituting languages* (pp. 135–169). Multilingual Matters.

Mignolo, W. (2000). *Local histories/global designs: Essays on the coloniality of power, subaltern knowledges and border thinking*. Princeton University Press.

Mignolo, W., & Walsh, C. (2018). *On decoloniality: Concepts, analytics, praxis*. Duke University Press.

Ndhlovu, F., & Makalela, L. (2021). *Decolonising multilingualism in Africa*. Multilingual Matters.

Otheguy, R., García, O., & Reid, W. (2015). Clarifying translanguaging and deconstructing named languages: A perspective from linguistics. *Applied Linguistics Review*, *6*(3), 281–307. https://doi.org/10.1515/applirev-2015-0014

Otheguy, R., García, O., & Reid, W. (2019). A translanguaging view of the linguistic system of bilinguals. *Applied Linguistics Review*, *10*(4), 625–651. https://doi.org/10.1515/applirev-2018-0020

Palmer, D. K., Cervantes-Soon, C. G., Dorner, L., & Heiman, D. (2019). Bilingualism, biliteracy, biculturalism, and critical consciousness for all: Proposing a fourth fundamental goal for two-way dual language education. *Theory into Practice*, *58*(2), 121–133.

Palmer, D. K., Martínez, R. A., Mateus, S. G., & Henderson, K. (2014). Reframing the debate on language separation: Toward a vision for translanguaging pedagogies in the dual language classroom. *The Modern Language Journal*, *98*(3), 757–772. https://doi.org.10.1111/modl.12121

Pennycook, A. (2017). Translanguaging and semiotic assemblages. *International Journal of Multilingualism*, *14*(3), 269–282. https://doi.org/10.1080/14790718.2017.1315810

Poza, L. (2016). *Barreras:* Language ideologies, academic language, and the marginalization of Latin@ English language learners. *Whittier Law Review*, *37*(3), 401–421.

Quijano, A. (1991). Colonialidad y modernidad/racionalidad. *Perú Indígena*, *29*, 11–21.

Quijano, A. (2000). Coloniality of power, ethnocentrism, and Latin America. *Nepantla*, *1*(3), 533–580.

Rosa, J., & Flores, N. (2017). Unsettling race and language: Toward a raciolinguistic perspective. *Language in Society*, *46*(5), 621–647. https://doi.org/10.1017/S0047404517000562

San Miguel, G. Jr, & Valencia, R. (1998). From the Treaty of Guadalupe Hidalgo to Hopwood: The educational plight and struggle of Mexican Americans in the Southwest. *Harvard Educational Review*, *68*(3), 353–412.

Sánchez, M. T., & García, O. (Eds.) (2022). *Transformative translanguaging Espacios: Latinx students and teachers rompiendo fronteras sin miedo*. Multilingual Matters.

Sánchez, M. T., García, O., & Solorza, C. (2018). Reframing language allocation in dual language bilingual education. *Bilingual Research Journal*, *41*(1), 37–51. https://doi.org/10.1080/15235882.2017.1405098

Santos, B. de S. (2007). Beyond abyssal thinking: From global lines to ecologies of knowledges. *Review (Fernand Braudel Center)*, *30*(1), 45–89.

Street, B. V. (1984). *Literacy in theory and practice*. Cambridge University Press.

Tian, Z., & Link, H. (Eds.). (2019). Positive synergies. Translanguaging and critical theories in education. *Translation and Translanguaging in Multilingual Contexts*, *5*(1), entire issue.

Trueba, H. T. (1973). Bilingual bicultural education for Chicanos in the Southwest. ED 084 073.

Valdés, G. (2018). Analyzing the curricularization of language in two-way immersion education: Restating two cautionary notes. *Bilingual Research Journal*, *41*(4), 388–412. https://doi.org/10.1080/15235882.2018.1539886

Valdez, V., Freire, J. A., & Delavan, M. G. (2016). The gentrification of dual language education. *The Urban Review*, 48: 601–627. https://doi.org/10.1007/s11256-016-0370-0

Weinreich, U. (1953/1979) *Languages in contact: Findings and problems*. Mouton.

2

THEORETICAL FOUNDATIONS

Conceptualizing Sociocultural Competence for Transformation in Dual Language and Bilingual Education (DLBE)

Verónica González, Michelle Soto-Peña, Reka Barton, Angela Palmieri

Despite the cultural, linguistic, and racial diversity present in the United States, cultural hegemony has served as a nation-building tool to assimilate racially and linguistically minoritized communities into whiteness. This has resulted in the colonization and commodification of indigenous peoples, in the enslavement of Black people and anti-blackness, and in restrictive immigration policies against Latinxs and Asians (Spring, 2016). Similarly, nation-building projects, which have positioned English as the sole language of this country, have led to policies that have stripped, or have attempted to strip, the aforementioned groups from their tongues. Resultantly, schools have worked as a microcosm of these efforts and oftentimes work to reproduce asymmetrical power relations. As the growing research on the inequities that permeate dual language bilingual education (DLBE) programs evidences, DLBE is not panacea and can also work to reproduce the status quo despite countering the hegemony of English by teaching in another language. This is evident in the growing gentrification and cooptation of DLBE which privileges whiteness and world language frameworks over heritage frameworks meant to center equity for minoritized students and families (Delavan et al., 2021; Flores & García, 2017; Freire et al., 2022). The reported anti-blackness in DLBE programming further supports the aforementioned claim (Frieson, 2022a; Palmer, 2010). Despite the contradictions that exist within DLBE, there are opportunities to center the needs of minoritized communities within the problematization,

DOI: 10.4324/9781003269076-5

conceptualization, and operationalization of sociocultural competence—one of the stated goals of DLBE.

Sociocultural competence in DLBE, however, is an abstract, ever-evolving, and multilayered phenomenon (Palmieri, 2021) whose implementation is influenced by educators' ideologies (Freire, 2020; González, 2020). The ambiguity behind its implementation results in sociocultural competence being overshadowed and undermined, as well as implemented in superficial ways divorced from analysis of power dynamics (Freire, 2020; González, 2020). As Freire (2020) claims, "Typically in DL education, the bicultural goal is addressed superficially or reduced to merely becoming acquainted and getting along with the 'other'" (p. 13). Reported challenges to the implementation of sociocultural competence include a lack of time, lack of culturally relevant materials, inadequate knowledge, deficit beliefs about social justice being inappropriate for younger students, parent pushback and disapproval, and misalignment with administrators (Freire, 2020; Freire & Valdez, 2017; González, 2020; Palmieri, 2021). Insights on barriers to sociocultural competence implementation are critical since they can inform the development of more socially just forms of DLBE.

This chapter explores how sociocultural competence is interpreted and how these theoretical interpretations are operationalized in DLBE settings. We first problematize the concept of culture in the context of sociocultural competence by reviewing the work of prominent scholars in the field, both past and present. Next, through an analysis of peer review and conceptual texts, we provide interpretations of sociocultural competence as well as examples of its operationalization in relation to ideologies and practices. Google Scholar and ERIC were used as search engines and search terms included: sociocultural competence, dual language bilingual education, as well as synonyms and precursors, such as cross-cultural competence, global competence, culturally relevant pedagogies, and identity development. Considering that the authors in this chapter conducted dissertation studies related to sociocultural competence, those findings are included as well. The following questions, grounded through the theoretical framework of culturally sustaining pedagogies (CSP) (Paris & Alim, 2017), guide this chapter:

1 How has culture been interpreted in relation to language learning and schooling?
2 How has sociocultural competence been conceptualized in DLBE?
3 What are the ideologies and practices that relate to the operationalization of sociocultural competence for transformation in DLBE?

Theoretical Framework

CSP is a framework developed by Paris and Alim (2017) in response to schooling in the United States being assimilationist and driven by a white imperial project that denies the diversity of minoritized students. CSP advocates for sustaining cultural pluralism in schools and for the positive transformation of education by "demand[ing] a critical, emancipatory vision of schooling that reframes the object of critique from our children to oppressive systems" (p. 3). CSP builds on the work of Gloria Ladson-Billings (1995), who asserts classroom teachers should work toward incorporating meaningful instructional strategies and curricula that make significant connections between students' home and school lives. This pedagogical approach is built on the belief that racially and linguistically minoritized students possess deeply rooted funds of knowledge that when effectively activated can add depth to the content and curricula presented in the classroom (González et al., 2006). Paris and Alim further Ladson-Billings' work and problematize the concept of culture by embracing it as dynamic and always changing. Through CSP, they argue that educators must move away from solely promoting heritage practices and the perpetuation of stereotypes. CSP challenges static perceptions of culture by centering intersectionality (i.e., gender, sexual orientation, language, race, and ethnicity) and challenging oppressive structures (i.e., heteronormativity, patriarchy, and white supremacy) that are embedded within diverse cultural practices. Thus, by positioning CSP as both theory and practice, Paris and Alim (2017) illuminate the need to interpret culture as participation in experiences that cannot be generalized based on ethnic or racial group affiliation, but rather sustaining students' ways of being in relation to systems of oppression. CSP advocates for educators to work alongside students to problematize culture, concurrently fostering critical consciousness. Similarly, the conceptualization of sociocultural competence in this chapter advocates for dynamic conceptualizations of culture that go beyond solely celebrating students' "heritage" practices and toward fostering "racial justice and positive social transformation" (p.13) by preparing students to "fight back." The following literature review discusses the evolution, tensions, and practices that exist within conceptualizations of sociocultural competence.

Problematizations of *Culture* in the Context of Socio*cultural* Competence

The Merriam-Webster dictionary defines sociocultural as "of, relating to, or involving a combination of social and cultural factors" (Merriam-Webster, 2022a) and competence as "the quality or state of having sufficient knowledge, judgment, skill, or strength" (Merriam-Webster, 2022b). By combining these two definitions, one may infer the meaning of sociocultural competence as having an in-depth understanding of the interconnectedness between society and culture. However, the aforementioned definition of sociocultural competence is ambiguous in the varied ways society and culture are interpreted and defined. This is evident in the tension that exists in the conceptualization and operationalization of sociocultural competence in DLBE; thus, a problematization of culture in relation to society is of foremost importance.

Sociocultural theorists draw on the connections between language and culture by arguing that language is an integral element in sociocultural development because it serves as a means to communicate with one another, build relationships, and create a sense of community (Schulz, 2007). As posited, language is positioned as intrinsic to the expression of culture because it is a means of communicating values, beliefs/customs, and it is an important social function that fosters feelings of group identity and solidarity. For example, Vygotsky (1978) asserts that with the guidance of knowledgeable individuals, children learn the language and norms of a culture, and therefore, language and culture serve as vital frameworks through which humans experience, communicate, and understand reality. Sociocultural theory formed from his seminal work where scholars and practitioners began to reframe culture away from an individual construct that resides in a person's mind, to one that is also influenced by the external or outer factors that shape human cognition (Cole, 1996). While Vygotsky's theories assert the process of meaning making is strongly correlated to the social interactions of one's community, his understanding of culture is limited to the learner's immediate surroundings and not critical to the power dynamics embedded within society or the learning of additional languages.

As scholars theorized the interconnection between language and culture, world language scholars reinforced the notion that language instruction cannot be divorced from culture (Peck, 1998). They assert language is both a symbol and product of culture. This is evident in the frameworks, standards, and lessons articulated within the field of world languages. For example, contemporary World Language Standards (WLS), adopted in 2019 by the California Department of Education, categorizes language learning into three facets—language standards, culture standards, and interconnections between the two. When examining the standards for culture, students are expected to learn various elements of the target culture under study (i.e., communication norms, cultural materialism [products], and cultural practices and perspectives). However, while world language teachers have recognized the need to incorporate more activities aligned with promoting students' cultural and intercultural understanding to "help combat the ethnocentrism that often dominates the thinking of our young people" (National Standards in Foreign Language Education Project, 1999, p. 47), the question lingers as to how such cultural teaching should and could most effectively occur at the classroom level (Dema & Moeller, 2012) and beyond the heritage culture/s of the non-English language being studied.

The problematization of culture, especially in relation to teaching and learning, is not a new endeavor. The civil rights movements of the 1960s, which included the Third World Liberation Front as well as the Chicano Movement, were a call to action to decenter white-centric curriculum and center the cultural experiences of racially and linguistically minoritized students within schooling. This is evident in the East Los Angeles walkout demands which called for "Bilingual-Bi-cultural education [to] be compulsory for Mexican-Americans" (Chicano Student News, 1968). These demands paved the way for fields such as ethnic studies and critical multicultural education that, when implemented with fidelity, foster counter-hegemonic spaces in schools. Such spaces strive to foster students' self-empowerment through an intentional focus on their academic and social identities, awareness of social justice issues, and the criticality of social action (Banks, 2009; Dee & Penner, 2017; Sleeter & Zavala, 2020; Verhoeven et al., 2019). However, despite these efforts for more culturally and linguistically relevant and sustaining spaces, the incorporation of culture in schools takes on various forms.

Nieto (1994) explains the variations and contradictions of the implementation of culture in schools by describing how multicultural education must go beyond teaching tolerance. She outlines the following four common approaches to the incorporation of multicultural education in schools: (1) tolerance, (2) acceptance, (3) respect, and (4) affirmation, solidarity, and critique. The first—tolerance—includes educators' "tolerating" differences without an understanding of how social differences intersect with power dynamics; consequently, failing to decenter whiteness. Meanwhile, through the affirmation, solidarity, and critique approach, students' differences are leveraged and they become part of classroom pedagogy by critiquing fixed notions of culture and working toward transforming schools. Comparatively, according to Banks (2009), the incorporation of multicultural curriculum in schools can be analyzed through a continuum that involves the following approaches: (1) contributions, (2) additive, (3) transformation, and (4) social action. The contributions level focuses on superficial notions of culture such as heroes and holidays, while the social action level includes students identifying problems in their communities and taking action toward ameliorating them. In intersecting ways, the aforementioned problematizations of culture in relation to schools underscore the importance of decentering mainstream curriculum that privileges whiteness as well as challenging superficial and stagnant notions of culture. Nieto (1994) and Banks (2009) also illustrate how differing ideologies surrounding culture can result in varied implementations, thus highlighting the importance of educators' ideologies in relation to sociocultural competence, especially in the fostering of spaces that work toward transformation.

Conceptualizations of Sociocultural Competence in DLBE

The cultural component in DLBE, currently termed sociocultural competence, has been coined in distinct ways. Sociocultural competence has emerged in DLBE research as cross-cultural competence and high self-esteem (Lindholm, 1990), positive cross-cultural attitudes and behaviors (Christian, 1996; Howard et al., 2003), cross-cultural awareness/understanding (Genesee &

Gandara, 1999; Gort, 2008), biculturalism (Bearse & de Jong, 2008; Gort, 2008), identity development (Feinauer & Howard, 2014; Hamman-Ortiz & Palmer, 2023; Howard et al., 2018; Reyes & Vallone, 2007), and culturally relevant practices (Freire & Valdez, 2017). An analysis of the research on sociocultural competence demonstrates that its conceptualization has evolved from a focus on cross-cultural competence/awareness/understanding that includes a focus on the attitudes between students from different ethnic, racial, and linguistic groups to a focus on biculturalism and identity development. This latter conceptualization has been coupled with critical perspectives that advocate for fostering critical/sociopolitical consciousness (Cervantes-Soon et al., 2017; Freire, 2020) to work toward the transformation of schools and society. Thus, positioning sociocultural competence to embrace heritage frameworks that advocate for minoritized communities while, simultaneously, challenging world language frameworks that threaten to commodify DLBE.

Regardless of the many names and conceptualizations for sociocultural competence, the recognition of the importance of centering culture within DLBE is echoed throughout. Feinauer and Howard (2014) define sociocultural competence as an understanding of how students come to understand and view themselves within the socially and culturally diverse classrooms that DLBE programs often provide. Cervantes-Soon et al. (2017) describe sociocultural competence as students understanding their identities and those of others "within particular histories of power, colonization, imperialism and difference" (p. 419). According to the Guiding Principles for Dual Language Education (GPDLE), a tool that has been used by DLBE programs across the United States, through sociocultural competence DLBE programs should strive toward valuing students' culture and language through curriculum and pedagogy that encompasses identity development, cross-cultural competence, and multicultural appreciation for all students (Howard et al., 2018, p. 3). Similarly, these perceptions of sociocultural competence are student-centered and focus on student identity in relation to self, and society; however, there is a lack of recognition between sociocultural competence and its relationship with educators and families. Greater clarity is needed on how to operationalize sociocultural competence through theoretical antecedents that are culturally sustaining and that include the various members who participate in DLBE.

Operationalizing Sociocultural Competence in DLBE

In an attempt to highlight the possibilities for transformation within DLBE, this section looks toward scholars who operationalize sociocultural competence through critical theoretical antecedents. This first includes an analysis of ideological constructs that challenge the status quo through understandings of the interconnections between culture, race, language, and power. Next, practices influenced by the aforementioned ideologies, or the lack thereof, are described. This supports the analysis that the ideologies held by key DLBE program contributors play a fundamental role in how sociocultural competence is conceptualized and operationalized.

Ideologies Foundational to Sociocultural Competence

In an effort to center minoritized students in the conceptualization of sociocultural competence, contemporary scholars extend the work of Freire (1970) and argue that in order to employ learning experiences that interrogate and dismantle systems of oppression, educators must first undergo an interrogation of their own biases to develop critical consciousness and, consequently, ideological clarity (Alfaro, 2019; Alfaro & Bartolomé, 2017). Through ideological clarity, teachers "perceive potentially negative ideologies more lucidly and intervene more proactively to thwart the potential discriminatory manifestation of such ideologies" (Alfaro, 2019, p. 196). Alfaro (2019) and Alfaro and Bartolomé (2017) argue that DLBE teachers need to be equipped with the ideological clarity necessary to recognize and denounce hegemonic forces within their practices, especially as they relate to challenging deficit notions of language that position the language practices of students from a lower socioeconomic status as deficient.

Cervantes-Soon et al. (2017) also underscore the importance of centering critical consciousness within DLBE efforts. They argue that to combat the growing inequities in the implementation of two-way DLBE programs critical consciousness must be added as a fourth goal. As the authors argue "teaching for critical consciousness and human connection requires that the whitestream curriculum is decentered for all students" (p. 421). Palmer et al. (2019) further promote the importance of critical consciousness by stating that It should be placed at the forefront and used to radicalize the other goals of DLBE, including sociocultural competence. By proposing sociopolitical consciousness as an additional goal of DLBE, Freire (2016, 2020) argues that teachers can become advocates for their students' language interests, while students can become empowered to join their teachers in these advocacy efforts. Freire positions the goal of sociopolitical consciousness as students "fight[ing] against inequities and discrimination through social justice activism in order to transform their educational lives" (p. 46). In other words, if critical consciousness is infused in the ecosystem of DLBE programs (curriculum, pedagogy, policies, and leadership), then key educational members (students, teachers, parents, and administrators) will better maintain a focus on equity and fulfill their potential to support a more integrated and socially just society.

Building on the goal of critical consciousness, Chávez-Moreno (2021) proposes that DLBE educators and students become grounded in critical-racial consciousness (CRC), an ideological lens that centers race and racial ideologies to address the normalization of race-evasiveness in the United States. Through CRC, Chávez-Moreno argues that teachers must examine their raciolinguistic ideologies and include CRC as part of DLBE equity efforts. The author posits the argument for CRC through an examination of a middle school two-way 50/50 DLBE (Spanish-English) program where teachers blamed Latinx students' underperformance on racist explanations rather than examining the lack of cultural relevance prevalent in their practices. Chávez-Moreno notes that if DLBE "teachers narrowly define their teaching and their Latinx youths' needs as about language/literacy, the language of instruction will be of little significance given that ideologies of deficit and pathology will contribute to reproducing inequities" (p. 22). Thus, the author highlights the need to intentionally center students' lived experiences in ways that go beyond the depositing of information in two languages while, simultaneously, acknowledging the racialized experiences of Latinx students in the United States.

At the core, these assertions call for more equitable DLBE spaces, where teachers are guided by their North Star (Love, 2019), a political act of love (Darder, 2011), and the conscious effort to dismantle systems of power and oppression to build a just and transformative world. In DLBE settings, sociocultural competence—aligned with critical consciousness and critical-racial consciousness—can serve as a vehicle to achieve these goals, so long as the educators driving this vision are ideologically clear and centered on justice.

Educators

An example of how educators can begin the process of developing sociopolitical/critical consciousness is demonstrated in a study conducted by Freire (2020) where he facilitated a one-year collaborative professional development with an intentional focus on biculturalism and sociopolitical consciousness. Through this experience, eight kindergarten through sixth grade two-way DLBE (Spanish-English) teachers, all new to culturally relevant pedagogy (CRP), had the opportunity to examine and critique their beliefs and practices as they designed lessons. The aim was for the teachers to operationalize the transformational DLBE framework introduced by Freire which merges CRP and the goals of DLBE: (1) academic achievement, (2) bilingualism/biliteracy, (3) biculturalism, and (4) sociopolitical consciousness. Although the teachers worked collectively to align their curriculum to the goals of biculturalism and sociopolitical consciousness, Freire notes that teachers' practices still varied throughout the school year and that most of their practices lacked bicultural and sociopolitical characteristics. Instead, using Banks (2009) levels of multicultural content, Freire explicates how the majority of the lessons were characterized at the "additive level" which includes "content-based cultural connections" (p. 6) added to the mainstream curriculum. This study is advantageous because it serves as a reminder of the difficulty yet importance of creating collaborative professional development opportunities where teachers' ideologies are addressed in relation to curriculum development.

Further examples of the operationalization of sociocultural competence are noted in a qualitative single case study conducted by González (2020) at a transitional kindergarten (TK) through eighth-grade one-way/developmental 90/10 DLBE (Spanish-English) program in Southern California which serves predominantly Latinx students. Findings demonstrate that educators understand sociocultural competence as multilayered and as including the development of students' identity, an awareness of diversity, discussions related to justice, and taking action. González observed how the second-grade team worked to sustain students' identities through classroom pedagogies that centered their *funds of knowledge*. For instance, rather than having students solely describe a food that is part of their culture, students were engaged in a thorough investigation of a family recipe which consisted of interviewing an elder and preparing the dish alongside them. One teacher shared how one student interviewed her abuelita (grandmother) and learned that her strawberry tamal recipe was influenced by her experience working in the strawberry fields. Meanwhile, the eighth-grade team engaged students in problematizing injustices in their community through service projects where students had the opportunity to work alongside a local nonprofit organization. For example, one student volunteered with a local organization that supports migrants crossing the US-Mexico border by leaving water supply and nonperishable food across the border. Besides volunteering, students had to conduct a thorough investigation of the social problem their selected nonprofit worked to ameliorate. During the presentation, the aforementioned student engaged in a discussion on the over militarization of the border and its relationship to increases in migrant deaths. Although some transformative practices were observed and educators expressed commitment to the implementation of sociocultural competence, there were also "gaps in knowledge" that led to the implementation of practices that reproduce the status quo. For instance, a finding suggests that teachers (mis)conceptions of race work to undermine racism within attempts to foster sociocultural competence. This was evident in a lesson described by a first-grade teacher where students were going to sort images of people from diverse racial backgrounds by the continent where they were presumably from. Besides perpetuating stereotypes, such a lesson also undermines the heterogeneity that exists across continents. Similarly to Freire (2020), this study demonstrates the complexities in implementing sociocultural competence as well as the lack of consistency in sustaining critical practices.

González (2020) posits that an additional barrier to the implementation of sustainable sociocultural competence in the studied DL program consists of disconnects between teachers and administrators. For instance, the tenets of justice and action were echoed more strongly among administrators, while teachers elevated the tenets of identity and diversity awareness a lot more. Also, although the administration team claimed that sociocultural competence was of utmost importance, several teachers hesitated when asked to describe how administrators supported its implementation. One teacher stated that he had not heard of sociocultural competence since he graduated from his teacher preparation program nearly a decade before. Other teachers shared concerns about implementing community circles, which they viewed as key to the implementation of sociocultural competence, out of fear that the administration team would do an impromptu classroom visit and signal them as being off task. Meanwhile, the administrator team minimally described the practices the teachers employed in relation to the implementation of sociocultural competence. This juxtaposition between administrators and teachers signals the need for professional development in relation to sociocultural competence as well as a lack of a school-wide consensus regarding its conceptualization and implementation. Consequently, affirming the need for DLBE programming to have a school-wide consensus on the conceptualization of sociocultural competence rooted in critical ideologies that propel educators to collectively work toward transformation.

Similarly, Palmieri (2021) conducted an exploratory qualitative study where she interviewed 21 kindergarten through eighth-grade DLBE teachers and asked them to explain their perceptions of sociocultural competence. Teachers represented various language groups (i.e., Spanish, Mandarin, Japanese, and Italian) and program models (i.e., 90/10, 50/50 and one-way, two-way) across several schools in California. Palmieri identified six patterns that describe how the DLBE teachers perceive sociocultural competence, which include: (1) critical consciousness, (2) CRP, (3) teacher identity development, (4) student identity development, (5) empathy development and cultural awareness, and (6) target or partner culture/s development. In relation to the pattern of critical consciousness, a middle school two-way 90/10 DLBE (Spanish-English) teacher explained that sociocultural competence means taking action when it comes to identifying and addressing societal inequities. In a similar way, a first-grade one-way 50/50 DLBE (Mandarin-English) teacher shared that she addresses sociocultural competence by teaching children about justice and how to be conscious of the problems that exist in society, such as racism and discrimination. These participants' responses suggest the development of critical consciousness within their understanding of sociocultural competence since they perceive building an awareness of inequalities, including racism, as the focus of instruction. However, despite the presence of the aforementioned critical conceptualizations of sociocultural competence, Palmieri underscores that the majority of participants stressed the use of heritage cultural practices to immerse or teach students about the perceived culture of the partner language. One of the participants, a first-grade one-way 50/50 DLBE (Japanese-English) teacher, explained that she incorporates Japanese culture as often as possible, mostly in the form of song, dance, and art. Another participant, a sixth-grade one-way 90/10 DLBE (Italian-English) teacher, stated that she creates a "cultural bubble" in her classroom where she exposes students to Italian culture. These latter examples highlight the notion of culture being perceived as monolithic and static, which does not allow for an accurate understanding of the dynamic nature of the cultural practices that exist within communities that speak the partner language as well as within a DLBE classroom. The work of McCarty and Lee (2014) offers some guidance to the DLBE field by stressing the importance of Tribal Sovereignty—"Indigenous rights to self-governance and to autochthonous lands and lifeways" (International Labour Organisation, 1989 as cited in McCarty & Lee, 2014, p. 102). Through Tribal Sovereignty, indigenous peoples create their own educational systems and practices that protect and sustain indigenous language and knowledge. The Native American Community Academy (NACA) employ several pedagogical practices that honor and sustain indigenous cultural traditions. McCarty & Lee (2014) describe two examples of pedagogical practices employed–weekly morning community circles and assessment practices. Weekly morning community circles are described as a school created tradition reflective of various indigenous practices where students gather with music and song. Teachers were mindful that as they engaged in this practice, they would not reproduce generalized perceptions that indigenous people are a monolithic group. Assessment practices is another approach toward sustaining indigenous practices and beliefs. Rather than assessing students solely on content knowledge, educators also assessed students on their development of care, empathy, and quality relationships they build with their peers (McCarty & Lee, 2014). Each practice exemplifies decolonized pedagogical practices where connecting and community are centered in the curriculum employed.

Although the scope of this chapter focuses on how sociocultural competence is operationalized within DLBE settings, it is important to note alternative approaches toward language revitalization and preservation. According to McCarty & Lee (2014), the NACA employ a Native-language immersion program that is inherently connected to the setting, environment, and practices. Through experiential learning, students engage in various cultural revitalization practices where they use Native languages in context. Situational Navajo is cited as one teaching method employed where educators create "everyday situations (i.e., cooking, cleaning) to foster conversations in the language that require verb use and physical responses" (McCarty & Lee, 2014, p.110). In this example, one can note how language revitalization and development is inherently interconnected with NACA efforts in reclaiming and sustaining indigenous and cultural practices sovereign from standardization of education adopted by colonial power.

Students

As educators grapple with making sense of sociocultural competence within DLBE classrooms, student identity development has emerged as a salient theme when examining classroom practices. One example is noted in the work of López (2011) who examined the language ideologies of two first-grade students of different linguistic and racial experiences in a two-way 90/10 DLBE (Spanish-English) classroom. In order to understand children's linguistic ideologies, López (2011) read a children's book that described the bilingual experiences of a young girl. After engaging in the exercise, she describes how Johanna, a Latina native Spanish speaker, saw bilingualism as important because she is a language broker for her family. Meanwhile, Cody, a white native English speaker, saw no benefit to learning Spanish because, besides not using it at home, he struggled with the language. López's study evidences that young children form ideological stances about language and language use at a very young age; thus, teachers need to intentionally address students' perceptions of their bilingualism to recognize, affirm, and empower their bilingual identities at an early age.

Chaparro (2019) highlights the unintended consequences of the racialization of children by examining the linguistic development and racial/ethnic identities of three young children in a two-way 90/10 DLBE (Spanish-English) program. Each child was a part of the same DLBE classroom but represented a different cultural and ethnic background—Santiago, a biracial Costa Rican and white middle-class student; Zoe, a white middle-class student; and Larissa, a Mexican American working-class student. Utilizing an ethnographic approach to inquiry, Chaparro (2019) found that student self-perceptions and linguistic development varied based on their racial background. Santiago internalized society's negative perceptions of the Latinx community and rejected the Spanish language and the identity of being a "Spanish boy." In turn, his bilingual and biliterate development suffered. Meanwhile, Zoe, who was identified as white, quickly acquired Spanish and was consistently positioned as the "teacher" to her peers. In sharp contrast, Larissa, even though a native Spanish speaker, was consistently positioned as the struggling student across all subjects because her literacy skills did not match those of the dominant school environment. Chaparro concludes that students' bilingual and biliterate identity construction is largely influenced by racial and economic hierarchies which impact perceptions of linguistic ability through the process of *raciolinguistic socialization*. Consequently, despite the presence of Spanish and Spanish-speaking cultures in two-way DLBE programs, Latinx students' funds of knowledge may still be undermined if systems of oppression are not directly and intentionally interrogated within the curriculum developed and employed.

In an effort to dismantle the oppression experienced by students from minoritized backgrounds as demonstrated above, Heiman and Yanes (2018) utilize a critical autoethnographic approach as a space of resistance to the rapid expansion of white interest within a gentrifying two-way DLBE (Spanish-English) program. Through a critically conscious lens, Ms. Yanes, a fifth-grade Latina DLBE teacher, centered and elevated the perspectives and experiences of minoritized students and families by employing a language-as-empowerment framework. For instance, Ms. Yanes fostered her students' identities by allowing them to discuss critical issues such as their evolving thoughts and fears surrounding Trump's presidency in relation to immigration and deportation. By creating a space where students could analyze how inequities intersect with their lived realities in Spanish, Ms. Yanes tapped into students' full selves while building their critical consciousness. Additionally, Ms. Yanes facilitated her students' sense of advocacy by encouraging them to defend their DLBE program model through bilingual public comment at a school board meeting. Designing such transformative opportunities for students, besides positioning language as a tool for empowerment, also served to elevate student voice and to, again, build their critical consciousness. Concurrently, the spaces for student identity development fostered by Ms. Yanes, allowed for resistance of white supremacy in DLBE by framing the language as a tool for empowerment.

Similar to the created spaces for student identity development that Heiman and Yanes (2018) call attention to, through a close discourse analysis, García-Mateus and Palmer (2017) explore the co-construction of the identities of emergent bilingual students in a first-grade two-way DLBE (Spanish-English) program whose teachers embraced dynamic bilingualism. Findings revealed that translanguaging offered equitable, empowering educational, and language learning opportunities to minoritized students. More specifically, a translanguaging pedagogy resulted in greater metalinguistic awareness, while developing students' bilingual identities. Part of the co-construction of bilingual identities that García-Mateus and Palmer (2017) allude to is also evident in Hamman-Ortiz's (2023) ethnographic case study of a second-grade two-way 90/10 DLBE (Spanish-English) classroom which investigated how students make sense of becoming bilingual. This study offered an in-depth, and under researched lens into the sense-making that young students are engaged in as they negotiate their emerging bilingual identities within their DLBE settings. The study explored young emerging bilinguals with the following questions guiding the inquiry: (1) How do students in a second-grade two-way classroom make sense of becoming bilingual? (2) What shapes their investment in this process? And (3) What are similarities and differences in how Latinx and non-Latinx students experience their emerging bilingualism? The findings offered contrasting views of Latinx and non-Latinx students around their feelings concerning the uniqueness of being bilingual. While Non-Latinx students perceived their bilingualism as something special, Latinx students saw their bilingualism as something normal. Again, highlighting the need for educators to intentionally create spaces where minoritized students explore their evolving bilingual identities.

The necessity to create spaces for students to examine the construction of their bilingual identities does not end at the elementary level. de Jong et al. (2023) carried out an exploratory study which examined the experiences of middle school students in an urban two-way DLBE program. Through the lens of students' sense of belonging, the study examined how middle school students described their experiences being enrolled in a DLBE program at the primary and secondary level. Using quantitative and qualitative data, the study found that students experienced a sense of belonging through a culture of care, peer relationships, and community-building activities. Additionally, translanguaging practices supported students' identities as bilinguals and were a way to include students whose language proficiency was still in the emerging stages. de Jong et al. (2023) conclude that two-way DLBE programs are uniquely situated to engage in practices that support students' sense of belonging and, through these practices, create, open up, and sustain identity options for bilingual learners in middle school.

Both Frieson (2022b) and Barton (2022) have conducted studies responding to Valdés' (2018) cautionary note urging not to overlook the presence of Black students in DLBE programming. In Frieson's (2022b) study, she examined the biliteracy practices of Black Language (BL) speakers in a kindergarten through first-grade two-way 90/10 DLBE (Spanish-English) program. The author's work highlights the "brilliance" of the biliteracy practices that these speakers used in biliteracy centers, including the communicative contexts in which BL speakers drew upon BL as a valuable resource. By drawing on a raciolinguistic framework, which analyzes the connections between race and language, Frieson (2022b) deconstructs the roles that BL harnesses in disrupting raciolinguistic ideologies in bilingual spaces. Her work reinforces that to truly serve the unique, linguistic needs of Black students who speak BL in DLBE programs, our attention to the linguistic features of BL is necessary. The work of Frieson aligns with Barton's (2022) study which highlights the narratives of seven first through fifth-grade Black elementary school girls in a two-way 90/10 DLBE (Spanish-English) program and the magic they possess as Black Girl Multilinguals. Using a critical visual methodology, findings suggest that Black Girl Multilinguals are both free and languageful, and they transverse their social and academic spaces while embodying their full linguistic repertoire, and demonstrating their #blackgirlmultilingualmagic. The visual and interview transcriptions together provided evidence that the Black Girl Multilinguals practiced a freedom in and across their linguistic repertoires that ignored limitations and boundaries of language allocation and fixed language settings, thus, offering spaces of self-expression.

As Frieson's (2022b) and Barton's (2022) studies evidence, Black students are also negotiating their identities with regard to language, race, and culture within DLBE; consequently, these perspectives also warrant attention in the critical understandings and practical implementations of sociocultural competence in DLBE. It is this centering of race and racial experiences that is necessary to truly operationalize sociocultural competence in DLBE classrooms with a deliberate attention to creating equity-centered spaces for Black students as well. Black students are often left out of conversations regarding DLBE (Valdés, 2018), are not given equitable access to DLBE programs (Palmer,

2010), and/or are deemed inferior linguistically (Flores, 2020). Without bringing Black students and families into conversations regarding DLBE, there is no true fidelity to implementing sociocultural competence for transformation.

Conclusion

The importance of fostering sociocultural competence in DLBE, through critical theoretical frameworks and counter-hegemonic epistemologies, cannot be understated, as it is the precursor to creating programs that embrace social justice and center equity, especially for minoritized students. Considering tensions between world language versus heritage frameworks present in DLBE programs (Valdés, 2018), transformational implementations of sociocultural competence must take precedence in DLBE efforts. In reviewing the literature, this chapter offered an exploration of the questions: (1) How has culture been interpreted in relation to language learning and schooling? (2) How has sociocultural competence been conceptualized in DLBE? And (3) What are the ideologies and practices that relate to the operationalization of sociocultural competence for transformation in DLBE?

The findings of this literature review suggest that there is a disconnect in the conceptualization and operationalization of sociocultural competence in DLBE. Despite the need to center critical ideologies that problematize the interconnections between race, language, culture, and power, the educator section demonstrates that there is limited knowledge and consensus around the implementation of sociocultural competence. Additionally, there are limited intentional opportunities for educators to develop the ideological clarity necessary to design spaces and lessons that go beyond surface-level approaches to implementing sociocultural competence. As a result, when examining the implications of sociocultural competence in relationship to students, it is evident that although teachers try to work toward students' identity development, systems of power such as race and class still interrupt the successful and positive associations of minoritized students in these programs. Resultantly, students internalize negative connotations about their racialized identities. It is important to note that the majority of literature focusing on students examines their identity in relation to languaging. Although this is critical, it is as equally important to begin to study how students make sense of other aspects of their identities (i.e., race, ethnicity, gender, and sexual orientation). Additionally, more research is needed that addresses how opportunities for self-empowerment and advocacy are created for students within DLBE. It is also critical to explore how decolonial approaches to language revitalization and knowledge sustainment within Indigenous peoples may help guide the field of DLBE toward transformational conceptualizations of sociocultural competence.

Finally, race, language, and power and its effects on the competing values and desires of DLBE programming must be acknowledged and encountered to allow for the sustainable implementation of sociocultural competence. While there is still much more to do in realizing equitable and transformative sociocultural competent classrooms for all DLBE students, understanding the historical and current interpretations, conceptualizations, and operationalizations of sociocultural competence fosters an opportunity to understand the nuanced perspectives existing within DLBE and, thus, move the work forward with intentional praxis and criticality.

References

Alfaro, C. (2019). Preparing critically conscious dual-language teachers: Recognizing and interrupting dominant ideologies. *Theory into Practice*, *58*, 194–203.

Alfaro, C., & Bartolomé, L. (2017). Preparing ideologically clear bilingual teachers: Honoring working-class non-standard language use in the bilingual education classroom. *Issues in Teacher Education*, *26*(2), 11–34.

Banks, J. A. (2009). *Teaching strategies for ethnic studies*. Pearson.

Barton, R. (2022) *Picture this: Black girl multilingual magic* [Doctoral dissertation, The Claremont Graduate University]. ProQuest Dissertations Publishing.

Bearse, C., & de Jong, E. J. (2008). Cultural and linguistic investment: Adolescents in a secondary two-way immersion program. *Equity & Excellence in Education*, *41*(3), 325–340.

Cervantes-Soon, C. G., Dorner, L., Palmer, D., Heiman, D., Schwerdtfeger, R., & Choi, J. (2017). Combating inequalities in two-way language immersion programs: Toward critical consciousness in bilingual education spaces. *Review of Research in Education*, *41*, 403–427.

Chaparro, S. E. (2019). But mom! I'm not a Spanish boy: Raciolinguistic socialization in a two-way immersion bilingual program. *Linguistics and Education*, *50*, 1–12.

Chávez-Moreno, L. C. (2021). Racist and raciolinguistic teacher ideologies: When bilingual education is "Inherently Culturally Relevant" for Latinxs. *The Urban Review*, *54*(4), 1–22.

Chicano Students. (1968). Student demands. *Chicano Student News: Mano a Mano*, *1*, 3. https://achieve.lausd.net/cms/lib/CA01000043/Centricity/Domain/922/Chicano%20Student%20Movement%20Newspaper.vol1.march68.pdf

Christian, D. (1996). Two-way immersion education: Students learning through two languages. *The Modern Language Journal*, *80*(1), 66–76.

Cole, M. (1996). *Cultural psychology: A once and future discipline*. Harvard University Press.

Darder, A. (2011). Chapter 9: Teaching as an act of love: Reflections on Paulo Freire and his contributions to our lives and our work. *Counterpoints*, *418*, 179–194.

de Jong, E. J., Coulter, Z., & Tsai, M. C. (2023). Two-way bilingual education programs and sense of belonging: Perspectives from middle school students. *International Journal of Bilingual Education and Bilingualism*, *26*(1), 84–96.

Dee, T. S., & Penner, E. K. (2017). The causal effects of cultural relevance: Evidence from an ethnic studies curriculum. *American Educational Research Journal*, *54*(1), 127–166.

Delavan, G. M., Freire, J. A., & Menken, K. (2021). Editorial introduction: A historical overview of the expanding critique(s) of the gentrification of dual language bilingual education. *Language Policy*, *20*(3), 299–321.

Dema, O., & Moeller, A. K. (2012). *Teaching culture in the 21st century language classroom*. Faculty Publications: Department of Teaching, Learning and Teacher Education, 181. http://digitalcommons.unl.edu/teachlearnfacpub/181

Feinauer, E., & Howard, E. (2014). Attending to the third goal: Cross-cultural competence and identity development in two-way immersion programs. *Language Immersion Education, 2*(2), 257–272.

Flores, N. (2020). Anti-Blackness is a dual language issue. *Bilingual Education Research SIG Newsletter*, Fall 2020.

Flores, N., & García, O. (2017). A critical review of bilingual education in the United States: From basements and pride to boutiques and profit. *Annual Review of Applied Linguistics, 37*, 14–29.

Freire, J. A. (2016). Nepantleras/os and their teachers in dual language education: Developing sociopolitical consciousness to contest language education policies. *Association of Mexican American Educators Journal, 10*(1), 36–52.

Freire, J. A. (2020). Promoting sociopolitical consciousness and bicultural goals of dual language education: The transformational dual language educational framework. *Journal of Language, Identity & Education, 19*(1), 56–71.

Freire, J. A., Gambrell, J., Kasun, G. S., Dorner, L. M., & Cervantes-Soon, C. (2022). The expropriation of dual language bilingual education: Deconstructing neoliberalism, whitestreaming, and English-hegemony. *International Multilingual Research Journal, 16*(1), 27–46.

Freire, J. A., & Valdez, V. E. (2017). Dual language teachers' stated barriers to implementation of culturally relevant pedagogy. *Bilingual Research Journal, 40*(1), 55–69.

Freire, P. (1970). *Pedagogy of the oppressed.* Bloomsbury Publishing USA.

Frieson, B. L. (2022a). "It's like they don't see us at all": A critical race theory critique of dual language bilingual education for Black children. *Annual Review of Applied Linguistics, 42*, 47–54.

Frieson, B. L. (2022b). Remixin' and flowin' in centros: Exploring the biliteracy practices of Black language speakers in an elementary two-way immersion bilingual program. *Race Ethnicity and Education, 25*(4), 585–605.

García-Mateus, S., & Palmer, D. (2017). Translanguaging pedagogies for positive identities in two-way dual language bilingual education. *Journal of Language, Identity & Education, 16*(4), 245–255.

Genesee, F., & Gandara, P. (1999). Bilingual education programs: A cross-national perspective. *Journal of Social Issues, 55*, 665–685.

González, N., Moll, L. C., & Amanti, C. (Eds.). (2006). *Funds of knowledge: Theorizing practices in households, communities, and classrooms.* Routledge.

González, V. (2020). *Beyond language: Critical and sustainable sociocultural competence in dual language program (publication No. 28412152)* [Doctoral dissertation, The Claremont Graduate University]. ProQuest Dissertations Publishing.

Gort, M. (2008). "You Give Me Idea!": Collaborative strides toward bilingualism, biliteracy and cross-cultural understanding in a two-way partial immersion program. *Multicultural Perspectives, 10*(4), 192–200.

Hamman-Ortiz, L. (2023). Becoming bilingual in two-way immersion: Patterns of investment in a second-grade classroom. *International Journal of Bilingual Education and Bilingualism, 26*(1), 69–83.

Hamman-Ortiz, L., & Palmer, D. (2023). Identity and two-way bilingual education: Considering student perspectives: Introduction to the special issue. *International Journal of Bilingual Education and Bilingualism, 26*(1), 1–6.

Heiman, D., & Yanes, M. (2018). Centering the fourth pillar in times of TWBE gentrification: "Spanish, love, content, not in that order". *International Multilingual Research Journal, 12*(3), 173–187.

Howard, E. R., Lindholm-Leary, K. J., Rogers, D., Olague, N., Medina, J., Kennedy, B., Sugarman, J., & Christian, D. (2018). *Guiding principles for dual language education* (3rd ed.). Center for Applied Linguistics.

Howard, E. R., Sugarman, J., & Christian, D. (2003). *Trends in two-way immersion education: A review of the research*. Center for Applied Linguistics.

Ladson-Billings, G. (1995). But that's just good teaching! The case for culturally relevant pedagogy. *Theory Into Practice*, *34*(3), 159–165.

Lindholm, K. (1990). Bilingual immersion education: Criteria for program development. In A. Padilla, H. Fairchild, & C. Valadez (Eds.), *Bilingual education: Issues and strategies* (pp. 91–105). Sage.

López, M. M. (2011). Children's language ideologies in a first-grade dual-language class. *Journal of Early Childhood Literacy*, *12*(2), 176–201.

Love, B. L. (2019). *We want to do more than survive: Abolitionist teaching and the pursuit of educational freedom*. Beacon Press.

McCarty, T. L., & Lee, T. (2014). Critical culturally sustaining/revitalizing pedagogy and Indigenous education sovereignty. *Harvard Educational Review, 84*(1), 101–124.

Merriam-Webster. (2022a). *Competence*. Merriam-Webster. Retrieved May 31, 2022, from https://www.merriam-webster.com/dictionary/competence

Merriam-Webster. (2022b). *Sociocultural*. Merriam-Webster. Retrieved May 31, 2022, from https://www.merriam-webster.com/dictionary/sociocultural

National Standards in Foreign Language Education Project. (1999). *Standards for foreign language learning in the 21st century*. Author.

Nieto, S. (1994). *Affirmation, solidarity, and critique: Moving beyond tolerance in multicultural education*. Multicultural Education.

Palmer, D. (2010). Race, power, and equity in a multiethnic urban elementary school with a dual-language "strand" program. *Anthropology & Education Quarterly*, *41*(1), 94–114.

Palmer, D. K., Cervantes-Soon, C., Dorner, L., & Heiman, D. (2019). Bilingualism, biliteracy, biculturalism, and critical consciousness for all: Proposing a fourth fundamental goal for two-way dual language education. *Theory into Practice*, *58*(2), 121–133.

Palmieri, A. (2021). *Teacher perceptions of sociocultural competence in dual language education (publication no. 28776683)* [Doctoral dissertation, University of California, Los Angeles]. ProQuest Dissertations Publishing.

Paris, D., & Alim, S. (2017). *Culturally sustaining pedagogies*. Teachers College Press.

Peck, D. (1998). *Teaching culture: Beyond language*. New Haven Teachers Institute.

Reyes, S. A., & Vallone, T. L. (2007). Toward an expanded understanding of two-way bilingual immersion education: Constructing identity through a critical, additive bilingual/bicultural pedagogy. *Multicultural Perspectives*, *9*(3), 3–11.

Schulz, R. A. (2007). The challenge of assessing cultural understanding in the context of foreign language instruction. *Foreign Language Annals*, *40*, 9–26.

Sleeter, C. E., & Zavala, M. (2020). *Transformative ethnic studies in schools: Curriculum, pedagogy, and research*. Teachers College Press.

Spring, J. (2016). *Deculturalization and the struggle for equality: A brief history of the education of dominated cultures in the United States*. Routledge.

Valdés, G. (2018). Analyzing the curricularization of language in two-way immersion education: Restating two cautionary notes. *Bilingual Research Journal*, *41*(4), 388–412.

Verhoeven, M., Poorthuis, A. M., & Volman, M. (2019). The role of school in adolescents' identity development. A literature review. *Educational Psychology Review*, *31*(1), 35–63.

Vygotsky, L. S. (1978). *Mind in society. The development of higher psychological processes*. Harvard University Press.

3

ESTABLISHING A TRANSFORMATIVE FOUNDATION FOR DUAL LANGUAGE BILINGUAL EDUCATION

Critical Consciousness at the Core

Daniel Heiman, Claudia Cervantes-Soon, Deborah K. Palmer, Lisa M. Dorner

Overview of the Issue

This chapter explains critical consciousness as the necessary foundation to guide dual language bilingual education (DLBE). In previous work, we demonstrated that despite its good intentions and innovative and additive approaches, DLBE in the United States is highly susceptible to reproduce and exacerbate inequities and marginalization for language-minoritized and historically underserved students (Cervantes-Soon et al., 2017), and we issued an urgent call to center critical consciousness in DLBE as a way to combat inequities at the policy, practice, and knowledge levels (Palmer et al., 2019). Building on this and other critical work in the field of bilingual education, we define our evolving notion of critical consciousness as an essential foundation and goal for DLBE and discuss its significance.

While we initially conceived critical consciousness as an additional pillar to the three existing ones promoted by DLBE programs, namely high academic achievement, bilingualism and biliteracy, and cross-cultural competence, as work continues in this area we are compelled to revise our proposal. Here we argue that critical consciousness should not be viewed as simply one more pillar, but rather should be the foundation that propels

DOI: 10.4324/9781003269076-6

all work in DLBE, be it academic, linguistic, or sociocultural. In doing so, critical consciousness can transform the purposes, interactions, policies, and practices of DLBE toward a more holistic, decolonizing, and humanizing education for all children involved, but especially for historically marginalized students and their communities. Because critical consciousness is never static nor final, there is always space for growth. Therefore, critical consciousness as a foundation generates a cyclical process of conscientization resulting in more critical consciousness. In this way, critical consciousness is both a driving force and an end goal. With this in mind, this chapter addresses the following questions:

What is critical consciousness and why is it important in DLBE?

1 In what ways can critical consciousness be enacted in DLBE?
2 How has recent research in DLBE conceived and drawn upon critical consciousness?
3 What are the implications for future research, policy, and practice when placing critical consciousness as the foundation of DLBE?

What Is Critical Consciousness and Why Is It Important in DLBE?

Notions of critical consciousness have been key in many scholarly, educational, and activist communities, including those working within indigenous, critical race theory, feminist, Marxist, anticolonial, and post-structuralist frameworks, among others. We draw from educator and philosopher Paulo Freire's (1970) conceptualization of critical consciousness, whose work teaching literacy to adult workers in Brazil helped him realize that injustice is maintained when the oppressed are unable to discern the structures of power that shape their realities. To P. Freire, critical consciousness, or "reading the world," is an ongoing sociopolitical process of questioning the roots of one's historical, material, and social conditions, and breaking the "culture of silence" that reproduces the status quo through the internalization of myths bred and promoted by the oppressor. Critical consciousness is the heart of emancipatory education, and it requires engaging in praxis, a process that involves: (1) critical reflection and analysis generated by questioning myths and recognizing the systems that structure inequities; (2) recognizing our agency, including our own role in perpetuating systems of oppression and our potential to disrupt them; and (3) critical action for social transformation, both individual and collective. As opposed to "banking education," which emphasizes the transmission of predetermined knowledge, the process of conscientization involves continuous dialogue with others to identify conflicting perspectives and contradictions in experience and to collectively reflect and act upon the world.

The argument to infuse critical consciousness in DLBE can be historicized from the race radical roots of bilingual education that aimed to empower Latinx communities and enact social change (Darder, 2012; Flores, 2016; Pacheco & Chávez-Moreno, 2022). Drawing on this history, Bartolomé (2004) emphasized the urgency for bilingual educators to develop political clarity (understanding of how macro-level forces impact micro-level processes) and ideological clarity (mapping of individuals to mainstream ideologies). She argued that both are key interrogation processes in the development of critical consciousness in bilingual education (Alfaro, 2019; Freire, 2016).

However, as DLBE programs began to proliferate across the nation, a disconnect from these critical roots became evident, especially in regions without a longstanding presence of bilingual education. Thus, scholars began to emphasize the need to attend to critical consciousness. For example, J. Freire's (2014, 2020) *transformational dual language education framework* proposed a fourth goal of *sociopolitical* consciousness to interact in fluid ways with the other three goals. At around the same time, Cervantes-Soon (2014), witnessing the marginalization of Latinx families in a DLBE program in the southeast United States, proposed *critical* consciousness "as an essential goal" (p. 78).

Meanwhile, in the area of teacher preparation, Alfaro and Bartolomé (2017) and Alfaro (2019) proposed a framework for the development of critical consciousness for teachers in DLBE that echoed J. Freire's and Cervantes-Soon's call for critical/sociopolitical consciousness. Soon after, Cervantes-Soon et al. (2017) carried out a thorough review of the literature documenting inequalities in DLBE and concluded with a more elaborated articulation of this proposed fourth goal of critical consciousness. The same team proposed a framework involving four *actions* toward critical consciousness (Palmer et al., 2019) that were intended to guide practice.

With this genealogy in mind, we now offer a review of research that has taken up this notion since, and in light of the review we put forth this adjustment to our original proposal: critical consciousness, we will argue here, must be a *foundational* goal that reorients both the field and DLBE programs on the ground. Our field's collective conceptualization of critical consciousness continues to evolve; however, infusing critical consciousness as a foundational goal has the potential to radicalize educators' conceptions of the three most commonly adopted goals in DLBE, bilingualism/biliteracy, high academic achievement, and cross-cultural competence. In other words, critical consciousness can help us interrogate these goals to discern their purposes and processes, with the end goal of a humanizing and liberatory education.

P. Freire (1970) describes radicalization, not as sectarian fanaticism, but as a creative critical spirit and commitment to engage in deeper more meaningful ways with others "in an effort to transform concrete, objective reality" (p. 37). P. Freire (1970) explained:

> the more radical the person is, the more fully he or she enters into reality so that, knowing it better, he or she can transform it. This person is not afraid to confront, to listen, to see the world unveiled. This person is not afraid to meet the people or to enter into dialogue with them. This person does not consider himself or herself the proprietor of history or of all people, or the liberator of the oppressed; but he or she does commit himself or herself, within history, to fight at their side. (p. 39)

P. Freire's radicalization calls for "confront[ing]" one's world/objective reality, entering into dialogue "within [the] history" of this same world/reality that challenges us to critically listen to, "fight" with, and acompañar "the people" (p. 39). The following discussion aims to advance understanding of the ways practice must shift to place critical consciousness as a foundational goal of DLBE.

Key Actions for Critical Consciousness in DLBE

As part of the cycle of praxis that characterizes P. Freire's notion of conscientization, we previously identified four *actions*[1] that are particularly central to developing critical consciousness in DLBE (Palmer et al., 2019). These are: (1) continuously interrogating power, i.e., calling out oppression, pushing those in power to take note of injustice and to transform systems; (2) historicizing schools, i.e., deconstructing mainstream explanations (and/or erasures) of the past and foregrounding individuals' and communities' local histories; (3) critical listening, i.e., engaging students, educators, and families with others for meaningful and transformative connection and thereby embodying a relation of curiosity and attention, sharing, caring, reciprocity, and responsivity; and (4) engaging with discomfort, i.e., experiencing and learning from the inevitable unsettledness in recognizing, reflecting on, and acting against the ways in which our own privilege, sense of entitlement, or silence reify and reproduce social injustice. All these actions are connected to one another and often overlap. We proposed that P. Freire's (1970, 2005) praxis cycle – the idea of engaging in reflection, dialogue, and action to humanize our connections to one another – can involve these four actions in the teaching and learning process for stakeholders across DLBE: teachers, children, parents, leaders, and policymakers. We also argued that through these practices, we both build critical consciousness and do critically conscious work. That is, as individuals engage in these actions through the praxis cycle, they both work directly toward justice and foster their own and others' growth in critical consciousness, which in turn results in a greater and deeper enactment of humanizing pedagogies.

In what follows, we review recent research that has explored and presented aspects of critical consciousness in DLBE, both studies that directly applied frameworks of critical/sociopolitical consciousness and broader research that has critically interrogated practices in DLBE. This review provides concrete examples of the four actions we originally recommended and describes emerging themes across this literature that shed light onto how critical consciousness can transform the three traditional goals of DLBE.

How Has Recent Research in DLBE Conceived of and Drawn upon Critical Consciousness?

We reviewed research from 2015 to the present that focused on critical/sociopolitical consciousness, i.e., grappling with how to work toward equity and justice in DLBE. While this does not provide a complete review of all work on critical consciousness in DLBE, it offers a snapshot of the most recent scholarship. In total, we reviewed 47 articles/books. For our analysis, we asked two key questions for each action of critical consciousness we had previously recommended: (1) What are stakeholders taking action about (e.g., what are people historicizing)? And (2) Who is taking the action (e.g., who is doing the historicizing)? We also coded each article for any other actions taken to build critical consciousness in DLBE.

Interrogating Power

An important part of developing and acting upon critical consciousness is recognizing who has power, how that power is activated, and how it is institutionalized. Through this interrogation, educators can take action against injustices and oppressive structures, especially those that deny access and opportunity for minoritized students and families. Of all the actions for critical consciousness documented in the DLBE research we reviewed, interrogating power was the most common (across nearly half of the research). Interrogating power has happened at both the larger state level and within schools and classrooms, usually with teachers and administrators as the primary actors. Fewer studies have documented how parents and students question unjust or inequitable practices in DLBE, although they have done so, sometimes in collaboration with educators. Researchers also have potential to partner and interrogate power in DLBE (Flores et al., 2020; Frieson, 2021; Martinez Negrette, 2021).

We found four instances of interrogating power at state and district levels. Freire et al. (2022) highlighted school leaders who, with support from teachers and their greater Latinx communities, at two public charter schools in

Utah, continually resisted state-level policies that resulted in fewer resources and lack of access to professional development, funding, and marketing for their 90:10 programs. As the only two DLBE programs in the state not following a 50:50 model at the time and serving a far greater proportion of Spanish-speaking, designated English Learners than their 50:50 counterparts, they worked to understand state-level policies and to seize opportunities – such as attending state legislative committee hearings – to press for change within the state board's policies on DLBE; ultimately, their advocacy led to a new definition and acceptance of 90:10 models at the state level (Freire et al., 2022). Meanwhile, Indiana district-level leaders, who were bilingual and had extensive histories in teaching EL and/or bilingual education, have interrogated power and fought for better principal leadership of dual language programming for emerging bilinguals. Despite their commitment, they experienced little success until state grant funding pushed for new DLBE initiatives (Morita-Mullaney, 2019). In Arizona, advocates, educators, and legislators came together to interrogate how restrictive language policies that imposed a 4-hour block of structured English immersion for designated English learners led to pervasive segregation and incurred damages on these students and their teachers, including exclusion from DLBE. Their ongoing and strategic interrogation of power, based on their knowledge of the state's history and dominant values, led to the passing of a bill that removed barriers for designated English learners to access 50-50 dual language bilingual programs (Kaveh et al., 2021). Also in Arizona, principals questioned a state policy requiring students seeking access to DLBE to first demonstrate English proficiency; the principals adjusted their approach and modified their communication with transnational/immigrant parents, and they ultimately allowed these students into their dual language program anyway (Bernstein et al., 2020).

While these studies examined pushes for policy change in state and district contexts, other research has interrogated power at the school level. In the following studies, school leaders and teachers worked to adapt a variety of policies and practices especially around (1) parent involvement; (2) language allocation/separation; and (3) recruitment/enrollment. For instance, Burns (2017) documented how one Western school's Latina parent liaison witnessed and then confronted white parents who were dominating the parent-teacher organization and its activities. Research has also documented educators interrogating power around language use/separation and the monoglossic mindsets of programs (e.g., Flores et al., 2020; Freire & Feinauer, 2022; Varghese & Snyder, 2018). In Babino and Stewart's (2018) study, for example, regardless of language allocation policies, teachers used multiple languages and translanguaging to "covertly remodel their programs to meet students' holistic needs" (p. 272). Studies also illustrate the interrogation of power related to issues of enrollment, recruitment, and gentrification in DLBE (e.g., Dorner & Lee, 2020; Heiman & Murakami, 2019). For instance, a district leader in the Midwest and parent leaders in Texas interrogated power as they posed questions to their colleagues around how to reshape enrollment to ensure access to minoritized, Spanish-speaking children when gentrification in the DLBE programs resulted in decreased numbers of designated English Learners (Dorner et al., 2021).

A few studies have documented DLBE teachers and students interrogating power at the classroom level. This work at questioning power can happen with students as young as kindergarten and first grade (Frieson, 2021; García-Mateus & Palmer, 2017), third grade (Salas et al., 2021), and fifth grade (Heiman, 2021). Frieson (2021), for example, shared the rich translanguaging practices of young Black children in a DLBE kindergarten/first-grade program as they agentically moved across Black Language, Spanish, and standardized English in direct violation of the classroom's strict standard language enforcement policies. Relatedly, many studies in teacher education have documented or made a call to develop teachers' critical consciousness; it is clear that preservice and in-service teacher education programs are important contexts for interrogating power in DLBE (e.g., Caldas, 2021; Freire, 2021; Heiman et al., 2021; Oliveira et al., 2020; Palmer, 2018).

Finally, research itself has the potential to interrogate power in DLBE. We agree with Flores et al.'s (2020) call for more research to step up to this responsibility; yet some research already has. For example, Martinez Negrette (2021) documents very young children discerning and navigating socially constructed racial ideas and tracks teacher and students' co-construction of a deeply problematic marginalized identity for one Black student in a DLBE kindergarten classroom, posing the question: "How is research in DLI contexts speaking against anti-blackness in DLI programs?" All of us in the field of DLBE need to lean into this question moving forward, as Frieson (2021) reminds us that "Black lives *still* (emphasis in original) do not matter, even in contexts where bilingualism claims to be 'celebrated'" (p.3).

Historicizing Bilingual Education and Its Communities

When we historicize, we focus on the stories and narratives that often remain underexplored in mainstream spaces. Developing critical consciousness requires engaging in the praxis cycle around personal, community, and school histories, with continued reflection and action to center and humanize marginalized histories. How have we each – teachers, students, leaders, families, researchers, and policymakers – come to be part of DLBE communities, and what are the histories that should be shared of our communities both inside and outside schools?

Historicizing often manifests as teachers or schools explicitly including often-marginalized histories or narratives as they make choices for curriculum or pedagogy (e.g., Freire & Feinauer, 2022; Heiman, 2021; La Serna, 2020; Lopez et al., 2021). The teacher described in Lopez et al. (2021), for example, intent upon ensuring critical culturally sustaining family engagement in her classroom, collected stories from her students' families and integrated these into her language arts curriculum, asserting that "when teachers act as brokers between school, home, and community, they demonstrate the potential to transform systems through honoring the CCW [community cultural wealth] of their students" (p. 2). Similarly, the teacher in Heiman's (2021) study developed a unit of study exploring the history of gentrification in her community because of the disparate impact this phenomenon was having upon different families in her classroom community. La Serna's (2020) analysis offers a counter-example regarding the problems with a failure to historicize. In this study, a team of DLBE teachers working to integrate culturally responsive pedagogies in their elementary school included some examples of rich, culturally sustaining literature in their curriculum and used it to teach the language arts standards. However, they made no move to leverage the stories or perspectives these books offered to historicize. Their efforts, in this way, failed to move their school toward critical consciousness.

Significant efforts to engage in historicizing appear to be happening in bilingual/dual language teacher preparation and professional development, to engage preservice and in-service bilingual/dual language teachers in examining their own histories (Cervantes-Soon, 2018; Palmer, 2018; Stacy et al., 2020; Varghese & Snyder, 2018) or the histories/contexts of the communities they serve (Bernstein et al., 2020; Espinoza et al., 2021; Heiman et al., 2021). For example, Varghese and Snyder (2018) describe four bilingual preservice teachers' (co)construction of a figured world of DL teaching during their year of preparation within a mainstream elementary teacher preparation program; for all four of their participants, "their desire to teach Latinx students and bring Spanish to the classroom emerged from their own histories of loss and struggle" (p. 152). For the preservice bilingual teachers in Espinoza et al.'s (2021) analysis, exploring their students' family and community histories and building this into their lessons further nourished their development of critical consciousness.

Finally, the field of bilingual education research is itself working to historicize. Education researchers and policymakers are reframing our history to ensure inclusion of narratives of struggle and resistance, e.g., in New York City (García et al., 2018) or nationally (Flores, 2016; Pacheco & Chávez-Moreno, 2022). For example, Pacheco and Chávez-Moreno (2022) examine documents from the Chicana/o/x Civil Rights movement in the 1960s, locating and highlighting the same arguments that are being made today, grounded in developing critical consciousness in support of what they term "Bilingual Education for Self determination against Oppression," especially young people's roles in this process (p. 522). J. A. Freire and Feinauer (2022) historicize the vernacular language practices of US Spanish speakers in making their argument that teachers must embrace and draw from students' bilingualism or risk perpetuating damaging deficit ideologies that will undermine their students' academic and biliterate achievement.

Critical Listening

Critical listening feeds reflection and is meant to move us to action; it requires – and engenders – empathy and caring and can lead to deepened trust and stronger relationships. It involves deliberately making space to center the voices and narratives of those who have been historically marginalized and silenced in the larger society and within the school community, allowing them to express in their own terms, and taking seriously the messages being conveyed. It also involves listening to silences and erasures, and considering how those are tied to power relations and structures of inequity (Schultz, 2010). For example, one might consider whose language practices do not have a place in the curriculum; whose identities are invisible; whose narratives are distorted or given no attention; who dominates classroom discourse; how students are being talked about; whose bodies are contained, surveilled, and controlled; and whose parents' opinions and ideas become priorities. In this way, critical listening is an extension of interrogating power as one first has to recognize whose voices are the most prominent and powerful. It also inevitably leads to discomfort, as some are compelled to speak for the first time, making themselves vulnerable, while others are decentered or recognize the need to step aside. Critical listening cannot simply be an empty platform for new voices that give the illusion that inequities are vanishing, nor an increased practice of polite interactions and superficial friendships. Instead, critical listening is a messy and unsettling process and should be backed up by action and transformation that affect all social relations and that directly address the concerns, contradictions, and complexities that are brought to light.

Critical listening needs to happen at all levels of educational systems, from classroom interactions to system-wide and policy decision-making. Research has documented critical listening in DLBE classrooms/among students (Caldas, 2018; García-Mateus, 2021; Heiman, 2021; Salerno et al., 2020), with families (Chaparro, 2020; Freire, 2021; Heiman & Nuñez-Janes, 2021), in administrative leadership (Burns, 2017), and in teacher preparation (Heiman et al., 2021; Palmer, 2018) – with varying impact and connection to action.

García-Mateus (2021) and Heiman (2021) both documented the intentional work of critically conscious teachers to develop lessons that engage their diverse young students – particularly their privileged English-speaking and/or white students in two-way DLBE – in activities that required critical listening. Cervantes-Soon et al. (2020) also shed light on the ways in which a teacher in a DLBE program serving primarily African American and Latinx students engaged in critical listening by remaining open to students' expressions of interest and opportunities for spontaneous learning, as well as by thoughtfully listening to students' feelings and fostering dialogue, empathy, and community. This critical listening is notable given the larger school context characterized by implicit anti-Blackness and continuous surveillance that severely restricted student agency. In all these cases, researchers noticed these teachers as isolated cases at their school, asserting that more systematic inclusion of such experiences across grade levels and years would have more potential to shift power dynamics.

Arts-based projects have also proven a generative space for research that engages students in critical listening practices. García-Mateus (2021) and Caldas (2018) have explored the possibilities of drama pedagogies to support first- and second-grade children's critical reflection about marginalized and intersectional identities. Salerno et al. (2020) documented high-school students interacting with one another across differences during an after-school DLBE club, negotiating intersectional identities and roles as they coauthored a children's story. While the students certainly challenged and listened to one another in productive ways, the researchers commented on possible opportunities the researchers who organized the context may have missed, especially the need to push students to more critically engage with one another, and to move to action.

Finally, research has documented and developed opportunities for critically listening to families in DLBE. Chaparro's (2020) antropoesía, or poetic rendering of transcriptions of the words of Latinx mothers, explicitly calls upon the reader to listen critically in order to better understand the experiences of immigrant parents in DLBE schools. Meanwhile, Freire (2021) offers an example of a white teacher who, having experienced a series of "conscientization calls" throughout her life, was able to critically listen to parents of color in her school, to further develop critical consciousness, and act in solidarity with those families against injustice.

Engaging with Discomfort

Educators, students, and researchers will inevitably experience discomfort as we learn about, address, and fight inequities and oppression. Being uncomfortable is essential to expand the parameters of one's thinking. Discomfort emerges most in the research as felt by adults, particularly teachers and administrators, while a few studies highlight student or parent engagement with discomfort.

In a number of studies, as teachers and administrators interrogated power, historicized bilingual education and communities, or listened critically, they were taking "covert" action against the local or state-level policies.

For example, teachers in Babino and Stewart (2018) used translanguaging and multiple languages in classrooms that were supposed to be separated as "English" or "Spanish" only. Similarly, the principals in Bernstein et al. (2020) went against state-level policies to covertly support EL-identified children's access to DLBE. In both instances, educators managed their own feelings of discomfort as they chose to follow their hearts, rather than oppressive policies.

Other studies portrayed moments where students or parents faced moments of discomfort. For instance, when the Latinx parent liaison Ana had to confront white parents about their dominating perspectives and activities in the PTO organization in Burns' study (2017), both Ana and her parents exhibited discomfort. Heiman (2021) documented students' critical listening to one Latina mom emotionally describing her personal experience with gentrification (i.e., displacement from the neighborhood surrounding the school, stress, longer commutes, and distance from community). Listening to her narrative resulted in youths' discomfort, especially for white students, as they witnessed the distress of their peer's mother. Similarly, the teacher in Garcia-Mateus (2021) used process drama and Gloria Anzaldúa's (1993) children's book *Friends from the Other Side* to purposefully push white students to consider their own biases and preconceived notions of Mexico. The teacher then encouraged Mexican-origin students to speak back to their classmates' biases and share their authentic transnational experiences. García-Mateus and Palmer (2017), drawn from the same study, illustrated the potentially positive identity construction that marginalized students may experience when encouraged to lean into discomfort in (critically conscious) adult-supported, drama-based peer interaction around children's literature, this time a poem titled *Teacher* (Medina, 1999). Meanwhile, Pacheco and Hamilton (2020) documented children bearing witness to each other's discomfort in DLBE, and taking action to support their peers when they experienced marginalization, in a process they called "bilanguaging love."

Emerging Themes: Acompañamiento, Translanguaging, and Affirming Identities

Research has surfaced several emerging themes that shed light on the ways that engaging in the actions for critical consciousness can transform the three original goals of DLBE. First, Heiman and Nuñez-Janes (2021) propose *acompañamiento,* emerging from border pedagogies (Dyrness & Sepúlveda, 2020), as a necessary tool, particularly in two-way DLBE contexts in which Latinx children and families' interests must be centered. Teachers and leaders – and fellow students – can accompany marginalized students and their families, to support and uplift their experiences. Similarly, Pacheco and Hamilton (2020) described the acompañamiento work of second-grade immigrant Latinx students as *bilanguaging love.*

Second, Pacheco and Hamilton (2020) and others have drawn a connection between the actions required to move toward critical consciousness, and the work bilingual people do when *translanguaging* in a monoglossic society (Frieson, 2021; Freire & Feinauer, 2022; García-Mateus & Palmer, 2017; Mortimer & Dolsa, 2020; Sánchez & García, 2021). Heiman et al. (2022) noted that translanguaging in DLBE embodies a critique of colonial and contemporary language policies. If given the space, translanguaging can be a tool for making the coloniality of power visible and for naming the world in the oppressed's own terms as it disrupts curricular and linguistic impositions. Research has shown how translanguaging is central for both teachers and students. Venegas-Weber (2018) has described "bilingual pedagogical noticing" as "bilingual teachers' conscious leveraging of their linguistic and cultural resources as pedagogical tools to assert their more holistic bilingual identities and to develop a critical and *mestiza* consciousness within the spaces they are trying to create for themselves and for their students in DLI programs" (p. 169, emphasis in original). Calling it "critical metalinguistic and social consciousness," García-Mateus and Palmer (2017) showed that supporting students' bilingual identities required accepting and engaging their bilingual language practices in classroom experiences – and that students' translanguaging practices are one way they assert these identities, thereby interrogating power. Mortimer and Dolsa (2020) analyzed the bilingual languaging of border-dwelling high school students who – counter to policymakers and school leaders in their district – explicitly included newcomers into their DLBE program through discourse moves, demonstrating the possibilities of translanguaging to engage in radical inclusion. Finally, Frieson (2021) provided a vivid example of young Black children engaging in "language architecture" (Flores, 2020) by mapping the connection between their agentic work to express their multilingual selves, and the work we all must do to radically transform DLBE programs to be welcoming of intersectional identities and the wide-ranging vernacular language practices that accompany/construct them.

Third, affirming identities has been proposed as a potential fourth core goal in DLBE (de Jong, 2016; Palmieri, 2021; Reyes & Vallone, 2007). Recent literature has continued to assert that the bilingual and intersectional identities of marginalized students and families must be centered in DLBE programs (García-Mateus & Palmer, 2017; Mortimer & Dolsa, 2023; Salerno et al., 2020; Varghese & Snyder, 2018). This idea cuts across all the elements of critical consciousness that we have described. Therefore, we posit that by engaging actions of critical consciousness, DLBE programs are better equipped to truly affirm their historically marginalized students' identities in ways that do not rely on cultural stereotypes or assumed identities.

Summary and Future Research

The articles reviewed above all touch on particular actions of critical consciousness, straddling multiple actions, and speaking to the interactions between them (Palmer et al., forthcoming). Crucially, many of the articles explicitly address parts but not all of the praxis cycles. Some focus more on reflexivity, while others focus on action. In general, there is a need for research that documents DLBE schools and communities working toward critical consciousness and engaging the full cycle.

Implications for Practice and Research

Having unpacked the role and significance of critical consciousness we now identify some of the imperatives for future work in DLBE. We first focus on implications for practice with attention to the inevitable challenges inherent in this work. We then discuss implications for research, both in terms of process and focus to inform critical praxis in DLBE.

Radicalizing the DLBE Vision

It is important to consider that the ways in which our field has tried to achieve the three goals of DLBE – bilingualism/biliteracy, high academic achievement, and cross-cultural competence – which appear to have furthered DLBE's vulnerability to gentrification, appropriation, and linguistic co-optation, and exacerbated the erasure of students from historically marginalized communities, in exchange for acceptance from the dominant group. This is evident in the anti-Blackness (Cervantes-Soon et al., 2020; Frieson, 2021; Martinez Negrette, 2021) and anti-indigeneity (Martínez et al., 2017) that continue to go unchallenged in DLBE programs, in teachers' constant pressures to abide by an imposed curriculum to which students are unable to relate, and in the many ways in which students' genius and authentic learning are missed and repressed by the standardized testing that DLBE continues to hold as its seal of quality (Palmer et al., 2015). Moreover, the three pillars as currently conceived limit the transformative potential of DLBE contexts by dictating what we should value (Freire, 2020; Freire & Feinauer, 2022): academic achievement as measured by standardized tests of whitestream curriculum over meaningful learning situated in the lives of students; a bilingualism that still delegitimizes the authentic and creative languaging of students of color; and a sociocultural competence rooted in elite cosmopolitanism and voyeuristic othering, which fails to recognize Blackness, queerness, undocumentedness, and the many other intersectional identities of students, as well as the ways in which power relations continue to silence certain groups (Flores et al., 2020).

Establishing critical consciousness as the foundation of DLBE, and establishing practices of regularly historicizing, interrogating power, critically listening, and leaning into discomfort can help us interrogate these three pillars and any other goals by asking what these goals mean, who benefits, in what ways, and on whose terms. The emerging themes documented in the literature, that is acompañamiento, translanguaging, and affirming identities, offer additional insight into how bilingualism, teaching, learning, and social relations are radically transformed when critical consciousness is centered. Centering critical consciousness liberates us to recognize and pursue what really matters to our communities. What does it mean to be bilingual and biliterate outside of the white gaze and how do we conceive and cultivate that? To transform the goal of bilingualism/biliteracy is to embrace translanguaging and elevate our students' authentic language practices in the DLBE classroom. Is learning truly encapsulated by achievement on a standardized test? Should we even endeavor to measure learning, and if so why – and how? To affirm our students' identities is to acknowledge – and teach, and learn from – ways of knowing that emerge from subaltern communities, rather than continuously elevating the dominant whitestream curriculum reflected in standardized assessment. What does it look like when members of the dominant group actually engage with a critical, sociocultural consciousness? Might they learn what it means to *acompañar* marginalized communities? At the same time, do DLBE classrooms always need to include members of the dominant group in order to develop cross-cultural, humanizing connections?

Situating critical consciousness as a foundation – and recognizing it as a continuous, messy, and potentially transformative process – can help us reimagine what DLBE could be and can help us work toward transforming the three established goals and "radicalizing" bilingual education to uplift and serve racially and linguistically marginalized students and families.

The Bumpy Long Road of Conscientization

While the transformative potential of critical consciousness is undeniable, it is important to recognize that the work of conscientization is not easy nor immediate. In our review of the literature and in our own research, we have witnessed instances when authentic work toward critical consciousness did not yield desired results. García-Mateus et al. (2021), for example, follow one white student through her six years of schooling at a DLBE elementary school, unfortunately showing that despite concerted efforts on the part of at least some of her teachers, the child displays little evidence of critical consciousness. Cervantes-Soon et al. (2020) document a teacher's heroic (but not overall successful) efforts to humanize the educational experiences of his young African American and Latinx students in a DLBE program at a highly surveilled public school. This work reinforces Flores et al.'s (2020) warning that critical consciousness-raising may have limited impact within a white supremacist society. Therefore, any work of conscientization cannot follow a formula, nor can it be done in isolation. Hegemonic and neoconservative efforts are always at work and manifest in various ways. For example, we are writing this in a particular moment in which state legislatures throughout the country are passing laws restricting or in some cases forbidding teachers from historicizing (i.e., anti-Critical Race Theory laws). Teachers are under attack for *talking about* and therefore interrogating and critically listening to structural inequities/racism. The process of conscientization is an embodied and collective one, as well as one that is never complete. Therefore, we must consider who should be at the table, and how to create spaces – from the classroom to the district office – to explicitly and continually engage in praxis.

Implications for Humanizing Research

Just as DLBE must have critical consciousness as a foundation, so should our research, and humanizing approaches are essential for bringing such praxis into our studies (Cervantes-Soon et al., 2017). Research is not a neutral endeavor as academic disciplines remain part of a larger colonial project and therefore often shape researchers' inquiry and analytical processes, reinforcing extractive approaches and colonial power relations of the researcher as "the knower" or "helper" and the researched as objects or providers of unprocessed data. Much of the research that is used to market DLBE programs draw upon normative measures of language and academic learning that appeal to the interests and disembodied goals of the dominant group (e.g., Cloud et al., 2000; Collier & Thomas, 2004; Lindholm-Leary, 2004). As we continue to make efforts to counter colonial ideologies and gentrification within our own research, it is important to consider how to engage in research in more humanizing ways, developing mutually productive collaborations with DLBE stakeholders wishing to center critical consciousness in which they can help shape the research process and talk back. While this type of research has already been taking place with educators, engaging children and families from historically marginalized communities, not as informants, but as co-intellectuals and collaborators is not common practice. In other words, we need to recognize who is included at the table, who is excluded, and what their roles are or could be in the research process. Doing so may help transform the research into a more ethical, moral, and political enterprise that does not simply seek to extract knowledge (Bejarano et al., 2019; Palmer & Caldas, 2015; San Pedro, 2021).

Future research should also move beyond assessments of whether DLBE is reaching its goals, toward interrogating those very goals, and the assumptions, tools, and constructions of language and learning that are the basis for analysis. There are particular areas of concern that need urgent attention, such as the pervasiveness of anti-Blackness, and the colonial frameworks that define curriculum and instruction. Future research should also begin to document the centrality of discomfort in the process of conscientization and praxis, as transformative action often comes with risk. The risk in DLBE often involves upsetting members of the dominant group and losing their support, which has been an important feature that differentiates DLBE from other bilingual models. In particular, it is essential to examine the process of critical reflexivity among speakers of standardized English and members of the dominant group and the role privilege plays in creating or reproducing inequities. We must examine the conditions to facilitate such reflexivity, how discomfort manifests, and whether it actually results in further action and transformation in DLBE. Finally, it is crucial that future research examines processes that foment critical consciousness in the preparation of future DLBE teachers and with administrators, as they are the ones who will be and are working on the ground alongside DLBE communities.

Conclusion

The work of conscientization is difficult and ongoing, and those working alone can quickly get overwhelmed and discouraged. Remember that the entire process of praxis happens collectively among multiple stakeholders over time; together we must explore how to support each other in this work and truly create change. Only by working together and continuously can we forge a vision of healing and joy and develop collective strategies beyond linguistic and academic boundaries with the end goal of social transformation and decolonization.

Note

1 Our terminology has shifted from "elements" to "actions" to more accurately represent that these are dynamic; they are things we *do*.

References

Alfaro, C. (2019). Preparing critically conscious dual-language teachers: Recognizing and interrupting dominant ideologies. *Theory Into Practice*, *58*(2), 194–203. https://doi.org/10.1080/00405841.2019.1569400

Alfaro, C., & Bartolomé, L. (2017). Preparing ideologically clear bilingual teachers. *Issues in Teacher Education*, *26*(2), 11–34.

Anzaldúa, G. (1993). *Friends from the other side/Amigos del otro lado*. Children's Book Press.

Babino, A., & Stewart, M. A. (2018). Remodeling dual language programs: Teachers enact agency as critically conscious language policy makers. *Bilingual Research Journal*, *41*(3), 272–297. https://doi.org/10.1080/15235882.2018.1489313

Bartolomé, L. I. (2004). Critical pedagogy and teacher education: Radicalizing prospective teachers. *Teacher Education Quarterly*, *31*(1), 97–122.

Bejarano, C. A., Juárez, L. L., García, M. A. M., & Goldstein, D. M. (2019). *Decolonizing ethnography*. Duke University Press.

Bernstein, K. A., Katznelson, N., Amezcua, A., Mohamed, S., & Alvarado, S. (2020). Equity/social justice, instrumentalism/neoliberalism: Dueling discourses of dual language in principals' talk about their programs. *TESOL Quarterly*, *54*(3), 652–684. https://doi.org/10.1002/tesq.582

Burns, M. (2017). "Compromises that we make:" Whiteness In the dual language context. *Bilingual Research Journal*, *40*(4), 339–352. https://doi.org/10.1080/15235882.2017.1388303

Caldas, B. (2018). Juxtaposing William and Graciela: Exploring gender nonconformity through drama-based pedagogy in a dual-language classroom. *TESOL Journal*, *9*(4), e00420. https://doi.org/10.1002/tesj.420

Caldas, B. (2021). Hablando Pa'tras: Developing critical conscious bilingual teacher education programs in Mexican-American/Latinophobic times. *Journal of Language, Identity & Education*, *20*(1), 1–3. https://doi.org/10.1080/15348458.2021.1864202

Cervantes-Soon, C. G. (2014). A critical look at dual language immersion in the new Latin@ diaspora. *Bilingual Research Journal*, *37*(1), 64–82. https://doi.org/10.1080/15235882.2014.893267

Cervantes-Soon, C. G. (2018). Using a Xicana feminist framework in bilingual teacher preparation: Toward an anticolonial path. *The Urban Review* 50, 857–888. https://doi.org/10.1007/s11256-018-0478-5

Cervantes-Soon, C. G., Degollado, E. D., & Nunez, I. (2020). The black and brown search for agency: African American and latinx children's plight to bilingualism in a two-way language program. In N. Flores, A. Tseng, & N. Subtirelu (Eds.), *Bilingualism for all? Raciolinguistic perspectives on dual language education in the United States* (pp. 199–219). Multilingual Matters.

Cervantes-Soon, C. G., Dorner, L., Palmer, D., Heiman, D., Schwerdtfeger, R., & Choi, J. (2017). Combating inequalities in two-way language immersion programs: Toward critical consciousness in bilingual education spaces. *Review of Research in Education*, *41*(1), 403–427. https://doi.org/10.3102/0091732X17690120

Chaparro, S. E. (2020). Pero Aquí se Habla Inglés: Latina Immigrant Mothers' experiences of discrimination, resistance, and pride through Antropoesía. *TESOL Quarterly*, *54*(3), 599–628. https://doi.org/10.1002/tesq.593

Cloud, N., Genesee, F., & Hamayan, E. (2000). *Dual language instruction: A handbook for enriched education*. Heinle & Heinle.

Collier, V. P., & Thomas, W. P. (2004). The astounding effectiveness of dual language education for all. *NABE Journal of Research and Practice*, *2*(1), 1–20.

Darder, A. (2012). Culture and power in the classroom: *Educational foundations for the schooling of bicultural students*. Routledge.

de Jong, E. J. (2016). Two-way immersion for the next generation: Models, policies, and principles. *International Multilingual Research Journal*, *10*(1), 6–16. https://doi.org/10.1080/19313152.2016.1118667

Dorner, L., Cervantes-Soon, C., Heiman, D., & Palmer, D. (2021). "Now it's all upper-class parents who are checking out schools:" Gentrification facing two-way bilingual policy enactment across scales, contexts, and stakeholders. *Language Policy*, *20*, 1–27. https://doi.org/10.1007/s10993-021-09580-6

Dorner, L. M., & Lee, S. W. (2020). Una Búsqueda de la Equidad y la Justicia: District leaders attempt to expand dual language bilingual education for equity. *Journal of Cases in Educational Leadership*, *23*(3), 3–15. https://doi.org/10.1177/1555458920916910

Dyrness, A., & Sepúlveda, E. III (2020). *Border thinking: Latinx youth decolonizing citizenship*. University of Minnesota Press.

Espinoza, K., Nuñez, I., & Degollado, E. D. (2021). "This is what my kids see every day": Bilingual pre-service teachers embracing funds of knowledge through border thinking pedagogy. *Journal of Language, Identity & Education*, *20*(1), 4–17. https://doi.org/10.1080/15348458.2021.1864204

Flores, N. (2016). A tale of two visions: Hegemonic Whiteness and bilingual education. *Educational Policy*, *30*(1), 13–38. https://doi.org/10.1177/0895904815616482

Flores, N. (2020). From academic language to language architecture: Challenging raciolinguistic ideologies in research and practice. *Theory into Practice*, *59*(1), 22–31. https://doi.org/10.1080/00405841.2019.1665411

Flores, N., Phoung, J., & Venegas, K. (2020). "Technically an EL": The production of raciolinguistic categories in a dual language school. *TESOL Quarterly*, *54*(3), 629–651.

Flores, N., Tseng, A., & Subtirelu, N. (2020). *Bilingualism for all? Raciolinguistic perspectives on dual language education in the United States*. Multilingual Matters.

Freire, J. A. (2016). Nepantleras/os and their teachers in dual language education: Developing sociopolitical consciousness to contest language education policies. *Association of Mexican American Educators (AMAE)*, *10*(1), 36–52.

Freire, J. A. (2020). Promoting sociopolitical consciousness and bicultural goals of dual language education: The transformational dual language educational framework. *Journal of Language, Identity & Education*, *19*(1), 56–71. https://doi.org/10.1080/15348458.2019.1672174

Freire, J. A. (2021). Conscientization calls: A white dual language Educator's development of sociopolitical consciousness and commitment to social justice. *Education and Urban Society*, *53*(2), 231–248. https://doi.org/10.1177/0013124520928608

Freire, P. (1970). *Pedagogy of the oppressed*. Continuum.

Freire, P. (2005). *Education for critical consciousness*. Continuum.

Freire, J. A., Delavan, G., & Valdez, V. (2022). Grassroots resistance and activism to one-size-fits-and separate-but-equal policies by 90:10 dual language schools en comunidades latinas. *International Journal of Bilingual Education and Bilingualism*, *25*(6), 2124–2141. https://doi.org/10.1080/13670050.2021.1874868

Freire, J. A., & Feinauer, E. (2022). Vernacular Spanish as a promoter of critical consciousness in dual language bilingual education classrooms. *International Journal of Bilingual Education and Bilingualism*, *25*(4), 1516–1529. https://doi.org/10.1080/13670050.2020.1775778

Freire, J. A. (2014). *Spanish-English dual language teacher beliefs and practices on culturally relevant pedagogy in a collaborative action research process* (Publication No. AAI3672850) [Doctoral dissertation, University of Utah]. ProQuest Dissertations Publishing.

Frieson, B. L. (2021). Remixin' and flowin' in centros: Exploring the biliteracy practices of Black language speakers in an elementary two-way immersion bilingual program. *Race Ethnicity and Education*, *0*(0), 1–21. https://doi.org/10.1080/13613324.2021.1890568

García, O., Menken, K., Velasco, P., & Vogel, S. (2018). Dual language bilingual education in NYC: A potential unfulfilled? In B. Arias, & M. Fee (Eds.), *Profiles of dual language education in the 21st century* (pp. 38–55). Multilingual Matters.

García-Mateus, S., Strong, K. A., Palmer, D. K., & Heiman, D. (2021). One white student's journey through six years of elementary schooling: Uncovering whiteness and privilege in two-way bilingual education. In N. Flores, A. Tseng, & N. Subtirelu (Eds.), *Bilingualism for all? Raciolinguistic perspectives on dual language education in the United States*. Multilingual Matters.

García-Mateus, S. (2021). "Yeah, things are rough in Mexico. Remember we talked about hard times?" Process drama and a teachers role in critically engaging students to dialogue about social inequities in a dual language classroom. *The Urban Review*, *53*(1), 107–126. https://doi.org/10.1007/s11256-020-00555-1

García-Mateus, S., & Palmer, D. (2017). Translanguaging pedagogies for positive identities in two-way dual language bilingual education. *Journal of Language, Identity & Education*, *16*(4), 245–255. 10.1080/15348458.2017.1329016

Heiman, D. (2021). 'So is gentrification good or bad?': One teacher's implementation of the goal in her TWBE classroom. *Anthropology & Education Quarterly*, *52*(1), 63–81. 10.1111/aeq.12362

Heiman, D., Bybee, E. R., Rodríguez, H. M., & Urrieta, L. (2021). "Era como si esas casas no encajaban con la comunidad": Caminatas with futurxs maestrxs bilingües in a gentrifying Latinx community. *Journal of Language, Identity & Education*, *20*(1), 30–44. https://doi.org/10.1080/15348458.2021.1864207

Heiman, D., Cervantes-Soon, C., & Hurie, A. (2022). Well good para quién?': Disrupting two-way bilingual education gentrification and reclaiming space through a critical pranslanguaging pedagogy. In M. Sánchez, & O. García (Eds.), *Transformative translanguaging espacios: Latinx students and their teachers rompiendo fronteras sin miedo* (pp. 47–70). Multilingual Matters.

Heiman, D., & Murakami, E. (2019). "It was like a magnet to bring people in": School administrators' responses to the gentrification of a two-way bilingual education (TWBE) program in central Texas. *Journal of School Leadership*, *29*(6), 454–472. https://doi.org/10.1177/1052684619864702

Heiman, D., & Nuñez-Janes, M. (2021). "Research shows that I am here for them": Acompañamiento as language policy activism in times of TWBE gentrification. *Language Policy*, *20*(3), 491–515. https://doi.org/10.1007/s10993-020-09577-7

Kaveh, Y. M., Bernstein, K. A., Cervantes-Soon, C., Rodriguez-Martinez, S., & Mohamed, S. (2021). Moving away from the 4-hour block: Arizona's distinctive path to reversing its restrictive language policies. *International Multilingual Research Journal*, 1–23. https://doi.org/10.1080/19313152.2021.1973261

La Serna, J. J. (2020). Culturally relevant pedagogy in two-way immersion classrooms. *Bilingual Research Journal*, *43*(4), 400–416. https://doi.org/10.1080/15235882.2020.1861126

Lindholm-Leary, K. J. (2004). The rich promise of two-way immersion. *Educational Leadership*, *62*(4), 56–59.

Lopez, M., Butvilofsky, S. A., Le, K., & Gumina, D. (2021). Project recuerdo: Honoring latinx Families' knowledge within the school. *The Reading Teacher*. https://doi.org/10.1002/trtr.2062

Martinez Negrette, G. (2021). 'He looks like a monster': Kindergarten children, racial perceptions, and systems of socialization in dual language education. *Race Ethnicity and Education*, *0*(0), 1–19. https://doi.org/10.1080/13613324.2021.1924138

Martínez, R. A., Durán, L., & Hikida, M. (2017). Becoming "Spanish learners": Identity and interaction among multilingual children in a Spanish-English dual language classroom. *International Multilingual Research Journal*, *11*(3), 167–183. https://doi.org/10.1080/19313152.2017.1330065

Medina, J. (1999). *My name is Jorge on both sides of the river*. Wordsong/Boyds Mills Press.

Morita-Mullaney, T. (2019). At the intersection of bilingual specialty and leadership: A collective case study of district leadership for emergent bilinguals. *Bilingual Research Journal*. https://doi.org/10.1080/15235882.2018.1563005

Mortimer, K., & Dolsa, G. (2023). Ongoing emergence: Borderland high school DLBE students' self-identifcations as lingual people. *International Journal of Bilingual Education and Bilingualism*, *26*(1), 7–19. https://doi.org/10.1080/13670050.2020.1783636

Oliveira, G., Chang-Bacon, C. K., Cho, E., & Baez-Cruz, M. (2020). Parent and teacher perceptions of a Brazilian Portuguese two-way immersion program. *Bilingual Research Journal*, *43*(2), 212–231. https://doi.org/10.1080/15235882.2020.1773961

Pacheco, M., & Chávez-Moreno, L. (2022). Bilingual education for self-determination: Re-centering Chicana/o/x and Latina/o/x student voices. *Bilingual Research Journal*, *44*(4), 522–538. https://doi.org/10.1080/15235882.2022.2052203

Pacheco, M., & Hamilton, C. (2020). Bilanguaging love: Latina/o/x bilingual Students' subjectivities and sensitivities in dual language immersion contexts. *TESOL Quarterly*, *54*(3), 548–571. https://doi.org/10.1002/tesq.585

Palmer, D. (2018). *Teacher leadership for social change in bilingual and bicultural education*. Multilingual Matters.

Palmer, D., & Caldas, B. (2015). Critical ethnography. In K. King, Y.J. Lai, & S. May (Eds.), *Research methods in language and education*. (pp. 1–12). Springer. https://doi.org/10.1007/978-3-319-02329-8_28-1

Palmer, D. K., Cervantes-Soon, C., Dorner, L., & Heiman, D. (2019). Bilingualism, biliteracy, biculturalism, and critical consciousness for all: Proposing a fourth fundamental goal for two-way dual language education. *Theory into Practice*, *58*(2), 121–133. https://doi.org/10.1080/00405841.2019.1569376

Palmer, D. K., Henderson, K., Wall, D., Zúñiga, C. E., & Berthelsen, S. (2015). Team teaching among mixed messages: Implementing two-way dual language bilingual education at third grade in Texas. *Language Policy*, 1–21. https://doi.org/10.1007/s10993-015-9361-3

Palmieri, A. (2021). *Teacher perceptions of sociocultural competence in dual language education*. Unpublished dissertation. University of California at Los Angeles.

Reyes, S. A., & Vallone, T. L. (2007). Toward an expanded understanding of two-way bilingual immersion education: Constructing identity through a critical, additive bilingual/bicultural pedagogy. *Multicultural Perspectives*, *9*(3), 3–11.

Salas, S., Acosta, J., & La Serna, J. (2021). Teacher disequilibrium, programmatic doublespeak, and "a day without immigrants. *Journal of Curriculum and Pedagogy*, *0*(0), 1–19. https://doi.org/10.1080/15505170.2021.1928570

Salerno, A. S., Kibler, A. K., & Hardigree, C. N. (2020). 'I'll be the hero': How adolescents negotiate intersectional identities within a high school dual-language program. *International Journal of Bilingual Education and Bilingualism*, *0*(0), 1–14. https://doi.org/10.1080/13670050.2020.1784086

San Pedro, T. (2021). *Protecting the promise: Indigenous education between mothers and their children*. Teachers College Press.

Sánchez, M., & García, O. (2021). *Transformative translanguaging espacios: Latinx students and their teachers rompiendo fronteras sin miedo*. Multilingual Matters.

Schultz, K. (2010). After the blackbird whistles: Listening to silence in classrooms. *Teachers College Record*, *112*(11), 2833–2849. https://doi.org/10.1177/016146811011201101

Stacy, J., Fernández, Y., & McGovern, E. R. (2020). El Instituto: Centering language, culture, and power in bilingual teacher professional development. *Journal of Culture and Values in Education*, *3*(2), 120–137. https://doi.org/10.46303/jcve.2020.16

Varghese, M. M., & Snyder, R. (2018). Critically examining the agency and professional identity development of novice dual language teachers through figured worlds. *International Multilingual Research Journal*, *12*(3), 145–159. https://doi.org/10.1080/19313152.2018.1474060

Venegas-Weber, P. (2018). Teaching and knowing in nepantla: "I wanted them to realize that, that is being bilingual. *International Multilingual Research Journal*, *12*(3), 160–172. https://doi.org/10.1080/19313152.2018.1474622

History, Programs, and Policy

4 THE HISTORICAL ROOTS OF ACTIVISM FOR DUAL LANGUAGE BILINGUAL EDUCATION

Sarah CK Moore

This chapter explores the historical roots of activism that led to Dual Language Bilingual Education (DLBE) programs in the United States. Antecedent to contemporary DLBE were Spanish-medium schools in post-colonial communities; activists for their language preservation promoted bilingual education. The true "roots" of activism for today's DLBE are tied to efforts against legal, school-based segregation on the basis of racial/ethnic conceptions, language background, and national origin. As such, the chapter first revisits the genesis and outcome of the 1945/1947 *Mendez v. Westminster* case. Later descriptions of activism highlight contributions by figures who cultivated the potential for DLBE for Multilingual Learners (MLLs). A concluding section describes a series of assemblies prompted by Mexican-American civil rights activists in the 1960s, whose recommendations included focus on DLBE as remedy for societal ills. Ultimately, various examples at the roots of activism convey shared commitments to agency, *compromiso*, and pursuit of a more just society.

Early Bilingual Education

Although the Coral Way bilingual school, developed in Miami for middle-class Cuban refugees during the early 1960s, is often referenced as the first DLBE program in the United States, other examples of early multilingual education are often overlooked. Californios, for example, were descendants of Spanish and Mexican recipients of land grants "tolerated" by Yankees in the late 19th century. Despite English-only school requirements in California, "the schools in Santa Barbara—then a predominantly Californio town—managed to ignore the order" (Weinberg, 1995, p. 145). Parochial schools

DOI: 10.4324/9781003269076-8

administered by the Catholic Church, which conducted Spanish-medium instruction, were also well established in New Mexico during the 19th century. "The schools of Bishop Jean Baptiste Lamy guided heir students according to the educational norms of the Vatican in the Spanish language, with English learning included" (Gonzales, 2020, p. 78, [citing Bullis, 2012; McKevitt, 1992; Milk, 1980; Read, 1911; Steele, 2000; Wiley, 1965]). The overwhelming influence and hegemony of English as preferable to Spanish in schools during periods prior to statehood is historically established. A departure from rural areas, where Spanish monolingualism among Nuevomexicanos and its express use as medium of instruction was customary, state leaders often advocated for use of Spanish in schools only as a mechanism for transitioning to attaining English proficiency. An 1891 measure required teachers' proficiency in both Spanish and English.

However, Gonzales (2020) notes, between 1891 and 1904, the first four superintendents of the State Department of Education (SDE) "sought to safeguard Spanish language learning in rural schools" (p. 82). The first of whom, Amado Chaves "pointed to the 'paramount importance' of the language in the whole of the America's, command of Spanish by Nuevomexicanos as being 'of far greater practical value to our children than the rest of modern or dead languages'". Chaves declared:

> It is a crime against nature and humanity to try and rob the children of New Mexico of this, their natural advantage, of the language which is theirs by birth-right, to deprive them unjustly of the advantages, great and numerous, which those have who command speech in two languages.
>
> *(Gonzales, 2020, p. 82, [citing Lozano, 2018, p. 83])*

Although House Bill 155, which passed the New Mexico legislature in 1919, required rural teachers be proficient in both English and Spanish, its impact may have been negligible. Gonzales (2020) notes, "In the actuality of the classroom, instruction tended to be in Spanish with English studied incidentally, 'if at all'" (p. 86). During this period, xenophobia raged in, but importantly outside the state, flagrantly from President Theodore Roosevelt, who staunchly claimed non-English speakers were un-American. Despite these claims, formidable advocates for bilingual education in the state were also outspoken. A prominent University of New Mexico professor of Spanish, D. B. Morrill, and the state's Governor from 1919 to 1920, Octaviano Larrazolo, "who was an immigrant from Mexico, had a greater vision: a truly bilingual state". Both criticized the imposition of Roosevelt's English for Americanization rhetoric on educational language policymaking in the state.

Larrazolo (who in 1928 later became the first Latino Senator), and others argued that Nuevomexicanos were part of the broader culture of Latin America and as such, could help the United States become more economically competitive by leveraging themselves and communities as Spanish-speaking resources. During his tenure as Governor, around 1920, he proposed Spanish language requirements in secondary and higher educational settings, including "compulsory use of bilingual textbooks" (Gonzales, 2020, p. 87). Although Larrazolo's full vision was not realized, he remained committed to bilingual education in New Mexico and the SDE did ultimately implement bilingual laws. Although due to limited guidance at the state level, models for bilingual programs and instruction were weak, "One researcher says it represented 'a means of treating Hispano children with dignity, thus enhancing the learning process'" (Gonzales, 2020, p. 89 [citing Getz, 1997, p. 38, 32]). These initiatives were, unfortunately overturned by the New Mexico State Board of Education in 1923, replaced by restrictivist English-only policies, and it was not until a new program was created in the early 1960s in Pecos that bilingual education again emerged. For exhaustive and in-depth documentation on the history of bilingual education in New Mexico, see Blum Martínez and Haberman López (2020).

School Segregation: Separate and Not Equal

Perhaps among the most prohibitive policies aimed at MLL students prior to the 1960s were pervasive systems of school segregation based on language, race, ethnic background, and/or national origin. As noted by Weinberg (1995), "By 1920, a pattern had emerged for Texas as a whole: Separate schooling in greatly inferior facilities for Mexican-American students; deliberate refusal to make educational use of the child's cultural heritage, especially the Spanish language; and a shorter school year" (p. 145). In California, the Méndez family sought to combat the established order of separate, and not equal, schooling.

Mendez v. Westminster School District

After Gonzalo and Felícitas Méndez[1] moved to Orange County, California, in 1943, his sister brought their three children, along with her two, to register at the Seventeenth Street School in Westminster. They had taken over the lease of a farm from the Munemitsu family, who were forcibly moved to an Arizona Japanese internment camp. Although Gonzalo's sister's children were accepted for enrollment (their surname was French and skin tones lighter than the Méndez children's), she was told the other three should instead enroll at the nearby "Mexican school". Robbie (2016) described:

> Aunt Sally had married a Mexican who was part French and so her children, Alice and Virginia, had light skin and light hair as well as a French last name. The Méndez children, Sylvia, Gonzalo Jr. and

> Jerome, had dark skin, jet black hair and a Mexican last name ... though all the children were born in America and they all spoke English, the Westminster school officials refused to admit them (p. 60).

Mr. Méndez again attempted to enroll his children the next day but was turned away and told his children must attend the "Mexican" school. Although all children rode the same bus to school, those of Mexican origin "turned to walk another half mile to their school in the barrio" where "flies, the stench of manure, and an electric cattle fence surrounded their playground" (p. 60). Using newly garnered income generated from taking over the farm, they hired a civil rights attorney who had recently won a segregation case in Los Angeles, David Marcus, who suggested the case be filed as a class action. Gonzalo spent considerable time meeting with other Mexican origin families and ultimately convinced four others to join the lawsuit, filed March 2, 1945, on behalf of 5,000 students in Orange County (Robbie, 2016, p. 61).

In addition to their segregated status, "Mexican" schools were vastly inferior to those for Anglo students. Those in "'Mexican"' schools

> were taught a curriculum quite different from the one offered in other schools. The boys studied gardening, boot making, blacksmithing, and carpentry, to prepare them for the low-paying trades that the schools assumed would be the only ones such boys could or should enter. The girls studied sewing and homemaking.
>
> *(Strum, 2014, p. 309)*

The Méndez family, as well as William Guzmán, Frank Palomo, Thomas Estrada, and Lorenzo Ramírez, filed suit against several school districts. Plaintiffs claimed that under the Equal Protection Clause of the Fourteenth Amendment "school districts denied them equal protection of the laws, as a class, by forcing them to attend schools solely for children whose ancestry was Mexican" (Green, 2008, p. 549). As Robbie (2016) noted, "what really motivated Mr. Méndez to fight the segregation was the fact that he did not want his children to grow up with hate in their hearts for the children who went to the beautiful school" (p. 61). Appealed by the school district defendants, the *Mendez* case was tried twice.

> [In the initial trial] Marcus presented testimony from students, parents and school officials to show the pattern of discrimination in which children of Mexican descent were routinely sent to Mexican schools under the guise of teaching those students English and Americanizing them, when in fact the children were never tested and many were already fluent English-speakers. Marcus submitted as evidence a master's thesis

written by one of the school superintendents that essentially stated that Mexican children were inferior intellectually, physically, and hygienically, and that they could never compete with Anglo children.

(Robbie, 2016, p. 61)

In *Mendez,* Judge McCormick initially found in 1946 racial segregation to be illegal and the "pedagogical excuses for segregation were found unjustified" (Blanton, 2004, p. 113). Notably, "this was also the first time English-only pedagogy failed a legal test as a justification for segregation" (Blanton, 2004, p. 113).

The *Mendez v. Westminster* School District "represented the first major and successful challenge to segregated schooling in California" (Moll, 2010, p. 451). It was among the earliest cases in which social science research was used as "testimony to the harms of segregation" (p. 451). A portion of the research utilized in *Mendez* were findings in George Sánchez's (1940) publication, *Forgotten People: A Study of New Mexicans.*

As part of the second *Mendez* trial, Attorney Robert L. Carter, under direction from Thurgood Marshall, working for the National Association for the Advancement of Colored People (NAACP), wrote an Amicus Brief. NAACP leaders believed judicial precedent could be set to challenge other school segregation cases. Carter would go on to write the argument in *Brown v. Board of Education,* which was modeled on his earlier penned *Mendez* brief. The Ninth Circuit court decision "was so monumental and far-reaching that it would lead to the end of *de jure* segregation of California's schools 16 months later" and "that the language segregation policy was a pretense for blanket discrimination against the students of Mexican ancestry" thus, illegal (Valencia, 2005, p. 405).

Two months after the court's 1947 Ninth Circuit ruling, then-Governor of California Earl Warren signed the Anderson Bill, "repealing the statutes that had allowed for the segregation of Asian American and Native Americans, and children with disabilities, making California the first state to end public school segregation" (Robbie, 2016, p. 62). Just six years later in 1954, Warren would be Supreme Court Chief Justice who led the 9-0 *Brown v. Board of Education* decision. Sylvia, the Méndez' daughter, finally allowed into the white school in 1948, remains an outspoken activist in promoting the role of the *Westminster* case as the predecessor of the landmark *Brown* decision, a historical artifact largely obscured in today's recognition of the long-standing activists' fights for more equitable education for MLLs. She was awarded a Presidential Medal of Freedom by Barack Obama in 2011. Sylvia Mendez Elementary School, a Spanish/English DLBE program in the Berkeley Unified School District, was renamed in 2018 to honor the Méndez family's activism, advocacy, and leadership. Two full decades before the Invisible Minority, *Pero No Vencibles* (1966), the Méndez family emerged as among earliest advocates for equal education access, regardless of language background.

Activism

The following sections are glimpses of similar lesser known activists, followed by accounts of key meetings that led to broad expansion of DLBE in the United States, in part through forming the early basis for the 1968 Bilingual Education Act.

George I. Sánchez

One biographer described George I. Sánchez as arguably "the single most important Mexican American intellectual between the Great Depression and Great Society" (Blanton, p. x). Sánchez authored the publication used by lawyers in the *Mendez* case, *Forgotten People: A Study of New Mexicans* (1940), which "offered as an interpretative study of the social and economic conditions faced by that sector of the population of New Mexico that is of Spanish extraction" (Sánchez, 1940. p. vii). It specifically addressed the Spanish-speaking and Native peoples in Taos County and the disparities between their lived experiences and structures, policies, and language use in schools. The 1940 publication became the basis for subsequent litigation regarding implications of segregated schooling for language learners—as previously discussed, for the *Mendez v. Westminster School District*. Sánchez strategized with Thurgood Marshall around possibilities for other future trials challenging school-based segregation.

Joshua Fishman, sociolinguist of the University of Pennsylvania, now widely regarded as instrumental in the early promotion of DLBE programs, inquired regarding Sánchez's opinion on mother tongue maintenance among Mexican-Americans. He requested Sánchez contribute an essay on related topics for the project Fishman was directing, Survey of Language Resources of American Ethnic Groups, funded by the Office of Education. As described by Blanton (2014, p. 230), Sánchez's manuscript was ultimately rejected "as not being interpretively in step with the rest of the essays". Fishman's resulting publication was *Language Loyalty in the United States,* a seminal study substantively leveraged as a tool in the fight for bilingual education—it constituted findings from the earlier research project. Sánchez went on to present two versions of the rejected paper in Los Angeles at Occidental College in 1963 and again in 1965; it was later published in an edited volume by his protégé, Dr. Julian Samora[2] (1966) entitled, *La Raza: Forgotten Americans.* Sánchez's chapter is the first and framed as the text's pillar—"History, Culture, and Education".

Sánchez's involvement in bilingual education, as opposed to through scholarship, had more to do with politics—he "shaped Yarborough's opinions on Mexican American education over the years" and "helped Senator

Yarborough with his bilingual education bill" (Blanton, 2014, p. 231). As Blanton (2014) recounted in a Sánchez biography:

> During the legislative process Sánchez wrote for Yarborough's staff a three-page, single-spaced memo full of speech lines and arguments favoring bilingual education. He added influential Canadian studies on cognition and bilingualism, the national self-interest involved in language resources, hemispheric relations, and how this bill demonstrated the Great Society's first real interest in Mexican Americans. (p. 231)

A prepared statement made by Sánchez for the Senate Subcommittee Hearings on Bilingual Education concluded:

> Whether my proposed legislation passes or not, I urge you to insist to your local authorities to do everything within their power to provide a bilingual education for your children, whether their home language is Spanish, French, German, or Chinese. Bilingualism, *per se,* is the gift of the educated man. Let us be educated Americans. Let us be bilingual.

Sánchez is one example of countless professors, regional leaders, state legislators, and other localized trailblazers whose shared activism led to initial, early developments in DLBE and on a national scale, the BEA. The involvement of many others was also instrumental. The three profiles that follow are only samples of the numerous other distinguished influencers whose activism was comparably powerful.

María Urquides

Maria Luisa Legarra Urquides was born, the youngest of eight, on December 8, 1908, in Tucson, Arizona. She attended "Mexican-only" schools. A third-generation Mexican-American, she attended Tempe State Teachers College and graduated valedictorian of her class in 1928 with a teaching certificate. Urquides first taught at Davis Elementary School and transitioned in the 1950s to study secondary school curriculum at the University of California, Berkeley. "As an educator, she became a leader in spearheading a bilingual-bicultural approach to teaching language among her students. In time, she became known as 'the mother of bilingual education' for her work in a new and emerging field of study at the national as well as local level" (Arizona Women's Hall of Fame, 2002, n.p.).

As noted by Combs (2008), "She was particularly troubled that Mexican students fluent in Spanish were nonetheless unable to read and write it ... she began to work closely with Adalberto Guerrero, who was attempting to create a Spanish Honors class for Spanish-speaking students" (p. 870). Begun in 1959, the class' popularity and students' success were so notable that in 1965, Pueblo High School received the Peacemaker School Award from the National Education Association (NEA). "In a very real sense, this was an early program of bilingual instruction although it did not bear that designation at the time" (Combs, 2008, p. 870). When Pueblo received the award, "she lobbied the NEA concerning the need to address other difficulties faced by Latino students" (Combs, 2008, p. 870).

In his role as the NEA's Western representative, Monroe Sweetland committed $2,000 from NEA's Department of Rural Education to conduct a study of the teaching of Spanish-speaking students in the Southwest. "The teachers who were surveyed saw Spanish and Mexican culture as assets rather than deficits. They believed that the Spanish language could facilitate the acquisition of English and that there were many benefits to becoming bilingual and bicultural" (Combs, 2008, p. 870). The resulting report, The Invisible Minority, became impetus for a 1966 NEA conference held in Tuscon, The Spanish-Speaking Child in the Schools of the Southwest: *Las Voces Nuevas del Sudoeste* (see later discussion). Adalberto Guerrero described the Tucson survey:

> Monroe Sweetland ... had confided in Maria Urquides that there was pending legislation which provided funding for successful innovative educational programs for minority students. Maria informed him about the special Spanish program, and they agreed to form the NEA-Tucson Survey Team to determine if there were other similar programs in the Southwest which might be emulated.
>
> *(Robbins, 2015, p. 198)*

Urquides has been recipient of numerous awards, including the NABE Pioneer Award retired from the Tuscon Unified School District in 1978. A 1986 dissertation devoted to documenting her life (Gonzalez, p. 1) described Urquides' contributions:

> she legitimately carried with her the title as the "Mother of Bilingual Education." Besides spearheading the National Education Association's efforts regarding bilingualism, she served on presidential commissions from the time of Eisenhower to Nixon to further the cause of education for the Spanish speaking Hispanic student. In the border states of the Southwest and in Washington, Dr. Urquides spoke, lobbied, and implored both supporters and opponents to understand the problems encountered by that particular minority in the Anglicized public school system. Her efforts to incorporate bilingual education into the schools

had as its intention to provide the Spanish speaking student the opportunity to learn and excel in a multi-cultural environment.

Urquides found in Beto Guerrero a staunch advocate. He recalled "including materials and visual aids that Mexican Americans could identify with. Many people thought we were crazy for doing this" (Gonzalez, 1986, p. 63). Describing her nickname as "the mother of bilingual education", Guerrero recounted:

> *Y quien nos llevaba de la manita a las juntas con estos hombres de Washington? Fue Maria. Y quien impulso el symposium aqui en Tucson? Maria fue. Asi es que a ella le hemos dado ese sobre nombre por 10 tanto que tuvo que moverse para que al acto de la educacion bilingue se hiciera una realidad en los Estados Unidos.*
>
> *(Gonzalez, 1986, p. 68)*

Adalberto Guerrero

Adalberto "Beto" Guerrero was born in 1929 in Bisbee, Arizona, one of seven children to parents Ramón Quiñones Guerrero and Guadalupe Méndez Guerrero. Ramón became heavily involved in union activities stemming from "persistent inequities and racial discrimination" and Guadalupe "instilled in their seven children a love of reading through her graphic narrations of stories and novels, fairy and folk tales, historical anecdotes, riddles, and games" (Combs, 2008, p. 332). Beto was particularly proud of his father's contributions to the union. In 1944 (and again in 1945 after a brief return), Guerrero dropped out of high school to follow "the only life for a real man" (Combs, 2008, p. 333). After service in the Army, he applied to the University of Arizona, earned his Bachelor's degree in 1957, and began teaching at Pueblo High School. There he encountered the disastrous results of students' systemic misplacement by the school. Guerrero created a four-year program of Spanish for Spanish speakers. "He believed that if he could instill in the students pride about their linguistic and cultural origins, they would visualize themselves as succeeding in other subjects as well" (Combs, 2008, p. 233).

Based on the success of the Spanish for Spanish Speakers class at Pueblo, he was recruited to teach a methods course for advanced Spanish language teachers in Guadalajara at the University of Arizona's National Defense Education Act program. Guerrero maintained connections with both Pueblo and the program and continued contributing to development of its curriculum. After it received the national Peacemaker Award from the NEA, Guerrero was one of six Tucson educators who conducted surveys and visited programs for Spanish-speaking children across the Southwest as part of the

NEA's Survey on the Teaching of Spanish to the Spanish-speaking students in the Southwest. After its final report was written in 1966, *The Invisible Minority*, its project director, María Urquides, was invited to present at a press conference event by Monroe Sweetland of the NEA; she declined and invited Guerrero to attend in her absence. At the two-hour event, "Guerrero recalled that most of the reporters seemed unaware that Native Americans were not the only minority group in the western United States" (Combs, 2008, p. 334).

As a Sweetland biographer recalled, "Guerrero, who would become a valued Sweetland ally, provided practical, on-the ground confirmation for bilingual approaches in teaching English to Spanish-speaking students. Sweetland was the facilitator, arranging major regional conferences and eventually congressional hearings on bilingual education" (Robbins, 2015, pp. 196–197). Guerrero's testimony during hearings prior to floor debates on the BEA, May 19, 1967, were groundbreaking:

> He introduced himself as a teacher at Pueblo High School and at the University of Arizona. Then he switched to Spanish for several moments; pausing, he switched back to English, observing that most of his audience was lost, because they were unfamiliar with Spanish. "This is precisely what happens to many of our students when they enter school," leaving them with the notion they are not as smart as their peers who understand English. Bilingual programs would improve student self-esteem and give them pride in their language and culture. They should be aware that they "have a very rich cultural background." He thanked Senator Yarborough for sponsoring a bill that had the potential to "provide more equitable educational opportunities" for students in the Southwest who had been "an invisible minority."
>
> *(Robbins, 2015, p. 201)*

Still living in Arizona in 2011, Guerrero told the *Arizona Daily Star* of the English-only movement and Proposition 203

> that history was repeating itself, with opponents of bilingual education promoting the same failed pedagogies of the past. Their objectives were always to deny teaching Mexican American children their language, history, and culture. The eighty-one-year-old Guerrero told his interviewer: "We have the right to instruct our children in a manner that reflects us".
>
> *(Robbins, 2015, p. 206)*

In addition to educators like Urquides and Guerrero, negotiations, navigation, and facilitation by mid-level, regional actors played important roles impacting policymaking for early activism targeting promotion of DLBE.

Monroe Sweetland

Monroe Mark Sweetland was born on January 20, 1910, in Salem, Oregon to Dr. G. J. Sweetland, who was a doctor and athletic director at Willamette University and Ethel Mildred Sweetland. As early as age 11, he began politically organizing with a friend to elect a candidate for city caucus. He was politically active, early on as a socialist and later within the Democratic Party. Sweetland ran several times for elected office, but a core period of his career were years working as a Western delegate of the NEA, as a key proponent for bilingual education and the BEA. At his memorial service in 2006, "his daughter Barbara Sweetland Smith remarked that her father always considered his background work leading to passage of the Bilingual Education Act the most significant accomplishment of his life" (Robbins, 2015, p. 196).

Sweetland worked closely with Urquides and Guerrero on early developments that radically enhanced the trajectory of bilingual education and development of the BEA by bringing national attention to not only the educational inequities faced by Mexican-American students but more practically speaking, the programs most beneficial for teaching Spanish-speaking students. "Reynaldo Martinez,[3] who often traveled with Sweetland during these years, characterized the trips as 'painful,' because they 'stayed in the cheapest motels and ate Spartan meals'" (Robbins, 2015, p. 196).

Speaking of Sweetland and the BEA, "That law", Senate Majority Leader Harry Reid said on the occasion of Sweetland's 94th birthday, "opened the doors of education and opportunity to young people in the West and other parts of the country who are native speakers of Spanish. Oregon and our entire country are a better place because of this good man". Publication of *The Invisible Minority,* which substantively influenced policy discussions around the need for improved educational opportunities for native Spanish-speaking students, relied heavily on collaboration among Urquides, Guerrero, and Sweetland.

The Invisible Minority, Pero No Vencibles

As a result of Urquides' and Sweetland's lobbying NEA leadership concerning the challenges faced by Spanish-speaking students, it "agreed to fund a study on constructive approaches to educating Mexican students". Urquides was named as a Chair of the project (Combs, 2008, p. 870). Other committee members included Guerrero and Paul Allen of the University of Arizona; and Martina Garia, Rosita Cota, Henry Oyama, and Paul R. Streiff, all of Tucson Public Schools. Sweetland, of the NEA, was NEA Consultant for the project and later publication.

The study, the NEA Tucson Survey on the Teaching of Spanish to the Spanish Speaking, reported on findings from a survey of schools across the southwest and documented "successful bilingual and Spanish language educational programs in … Laredo and El Paso, Texas; Albuquerque and Pecos, New Mexico; Merced, California; Pueblo, Colorado; and Tucson, Arizona. Troubling statistics were also a fundamental highlight—although 72% and 75% of the overall male and female populations had spent one or more years in secondary settings, comparatively, only a striking 48.5% and 52% of Latinx males and females had done so" (Moore, 2021, p. 44 citing the NEA, 1966). The resulting report, *The Invisible Minority,* was published in the summer of 1966; authors declared:

> To meet the problem fully, however, further legislation and substantially increased appropriations are needed. An extended series of needs could be listed …. But the urgent need is for ACTION and innovation in local school districts almost everywhere.
>
> *(NEA, 1966, p. 1)*

The NEA-Tucson Survey Committee shared nine recommendations for the improvement of education for native speakers of Spanish. Five of the nine applicable to bilingual education are listed below (NEA, 1966, pp. 17–18):

1 Instruction in pre-school and throughout the early grades should be in both Spanish and English.
2 English should be taught as a second language.
4 A well-articulated program of instruction in the mother tongue should be continued from pre-school through the high school years.
5 All possible measures should be taken to help Mexican-American children gain a pride in their ancestral culture and language.
6 State laws which specify English as the language of instruction and thus, by implication at least, outlaw the speaking of Spanish except in Spanish classes should be repealed.

As was noted by Vega (1983), these points are "particularly important because they appear in one form or another" (p. 30) in the BEA and in Texas state legislative documents in 1969 and 1973.

Lupe Anguiano

Although the influences of Urquides, Guerrero, and Sweetland are relatively evident, based on analyses of historical archives and other biographical documentation, the roles of other activists, whose contributions may have been equally, but differently pivotal, in early expansion of DLBE are lesser known—if at all. Lupe Anguiano's experiences are a single example of the countless civil servants whose devotion to realizing expansion of DLBE, especially through the BEA, are rarely highlighted. Anguiano, whose mother was Spanish and father Huichol (or Wixárika, Indigenous people of Mexico and the United States), was born in La Junta, Colorado, on March 12, 1929. She was an outspoken rights activist who volunteered for farm workers' rights led by César Chávez and fought for women's rights representing Raza Unidas with Gloria Steinam, Shirley Chisolm, and Betty Friedan, among others (See Rivers, 2020). One of the myriad hidden figures who played a focal role in early development of the BEA, when interviewed in 2020, despite having spent the majority of her life in other rights activist roles, Anguiano spoke almost entirely about her experience in developing the BEA and the importance of bilingual education.

Based on her work with teens recruited from gangs in Los Angeles through Teen Post "to give the youth the experience of learning to communicate and learning to take action" (Wright, 2016, p. 67), California Congressman George Brown selected Anguiano to attend a White House meeting regarding Mexican-American issues. In a meeting with Vice President, Hubert Humphrey:

> Lupe spoke about her experiences in dealing with teenagers, working with those in poverty, her efforts in the education field as a teaching nun, and the issues of gang violence that plagued East Los Angeles. She also made a pitch for much-needed bilingual education, providing support for the efforts of Senator Ralph Yarborough from Texas who had introduced the bilingual bill.
>
> *(Wright, 2016, pp. 71–72)*

The following day, an aide to the Vice President invited Anguiano to move to Washington, DC, to help with development of the BEA as an appointee of the President. As recounted, she "was called to President Lyndon Johnson's White House to a meeting aimed at studying the needs of Mexican Americans in the South" (Rivers, 2020, n.p.). She was later appointed to the Office of Education where "she worked with both [Texas Senator] Yarborough and [Secretary of Health, Education Welfare, John] Gardner who at the time had developed a language education model for the children of ambassadors". Anguiano also studied the case of Coral Way and bilingual programs serving Cuban refugee children in Miami, Florida, and "became a driving force to get the BEA passed in 1968" (Rivers, 2020, n.p.).

Equity in schooling and promoting language rights were among many other demands being made by Chicanx, Latinx, and others on behalf of seeking social justice for "Spanish-speaking" communities. These often culminated with, or were predicated by, large-scale assemblies.

Delineating Demands: Activism through Assembly

A series of meetings "helped to create the kinds of support which brought the common problems of Chicanos to national prominence" (Vega, 1983, p. 28). These included the Tucson event that coincided with the NEA's *The Invisible Minority Report*, as well as convenings in Albuquerque (1966), El Paso (1967), and two events in San Antonio (1967). Unlike the individuals' contributions described thus far, these are meaningful because they were collective activist movements for Latinx human and civil rights for which bilingual-bicultural education was viewed as one among many antidotes to the societal ills upon which these communities were imposed.

Albuquerque

Historically perhaps the most remarkable event among early activism for Chicanx rights were the actions taken by 50–60 (the number varies depending on sources) Chicanx protestors who attended a meeting on March 28, 1966, of the Equal Opportunity Commission (EEOC) "to investigate the Chicano's employment problems" (Acuña, 2000, p. 332). Protestors there "angrily stormed out of the official meeting" (Vega, 1983, p. 28) and stated (San Miguel, 1987) "We, the delegates representing Mexican American organizations from throughout the six Pacific and Southwestern states, realize that further participation in this conference ... will be valueless". And further "Through its actions both here and in Washington, DC, the Commission has shown its total lack of interest and understanding of the problems facing our nation's six million Mexican Americans" (p. 166). Although the commission was designed to promote equal employment, "it did not have one Mexican on its staff" (Acuña, 2000, p. 332).

President Johnson later appointed Vicente T. Ximenes as the EEOC's first Mexican-American Commissioner, created the Inter-Agency Committee for Mexican-American Affairs, and "agreed to convene a conference where Mexican-American leaders would be invited to publicly present testimony on the social, economic and political problems which afflicted ... the progress of the Mexican-American citizen" (Vega, 1983, p. 29).

Tucson

Several months after publication of *The Invisible Minority*, between October 30 and 31, a symposium was hosted by the NEA in Tucson, Arizona, and attended by 450 educators and political leaders. The Spanish-Speaking Child in the Schools of the Southwest: *Las Voces Nuevas del Sudoeste*, it marked the "first national convening aimed at addressing the specialized educational needs of language minority students, families and communities ... and the first major step in the development of the BEA" (Moore, 2021, p. 46).

Prompted in part by study results, it convened a diverse range of stakeholders, including not only educators and community organizers, but also future BEA sponsor, Senator Ralph Yarborough, who claimed the meeting contributed to its inspiration. The Tucson meeting constituted the third NEA Commission on Professional Rights and Responsibilities (PR&R). It succeeded two earlier conferences focused on issues of civil rights, integration, and equitable access to schooling for African-American students. Two goals of the conference were "to increase local and state support for bilingual instruction in public schools for the Mexican-American student ... [and] an increase in ESEA appropriations as well as the enactment of specific legislation on bilingual education" (Vega, 1983, p. 29).

Dr. Monroe Sweetland of the NEA invited Senator Ralph Yarborough to the meeting under the guise of speaking about how to pass the BEA. Upon arrival, the Senator was surprised by his true intentions, which rather were "to educate him on the need for bilingual education" (Vega, 1983, p. 30, citing Yarborough, R., Personal Communication, March 27, 1979). A 1973 dissertation investigating genesis of the BEA, Sanchez highlighted the importance of the meeting for realizing bilingual education on a national scale:

> The Tucson Conference was viewed by all the major participants for this study as the turning point in the efforts by many Mexican-American educators to see that the regional problem of equal educational opportunity for Mexican-Americans was escalated to a national level. (p. 155)

At the end of the symposium, state teachers' representatives urged the NEA to give its highest priority to developing 'bilingual-bicultural curricula' for schools with large numbers of "Mexican American children" (Robbins, 2015, p. 204).

El Paso

The conference event promised by Johnson when he met with Albuquerque protestors never materialized. Instead, a second conference on the problems of Mexican-Americans was held in in El Paso on October 26, 1967. However, these excluded César Chávez, Corky Gonzalez, and Reies Tijerina—the equivalent of holding meetings to address Civil Rights for African Americans at the exclusion of Martin Luther King, Jr., for example. At the meetings, Mexican-Americans decided to walk out and to hold an alternative conference—'la verdadera conferencia' as they termed it—in the barrios of El Paso. "They called their group La Raza Unida ... both the hearings and Raza Unida conference provided the first national forums for articulating the problems of Mexican Americans" (San Miguel, 1987, p. 168). San Miguel

(1987) cited a statement drafted by La Raza, declaring "the time of subjugation, exploitation, and abuse of human rights of La Raza in the United States is hereby ended forever" it "affirms the magnificence of La Raza, the greatness of our heritage, our history, our language, our traditions, our contributions to humanity and our culture" (p. 168).

Vega (1983) noted that "to many Chicanos the conference was nothing more than a scheme by the Democratic leadership to attract the support of the Mexican-American vote for the 1966 presidential elections" (p. 31). Carlos F. Truan, who would direct efforts for later Texas-based legislation promoting bilingual education, testified that:

> In the past, the Indian, the Negro, the Filipino, the Puerto Rican, and all the other peoples in a situation similar to that of the Mexican-American have been the object of moral responsibility. Not so the Mexican-American. He has been, and continues to be, the most neglected, the least sponsored, the most orphaned major minority group in the United States. (p. 32)

Most presentations at the conference continued descriptions of the same "social ills" already discussed in previous meetings and were again the subjects of future meetings. The request from Mexican-American advocacy groups by this time was drawing increasingly clear—the need for a "federal program which specifically addressed itself to their unique educational needs" (Vega, 1983, p. 32).

San Antonio I

From April 13 to 15, 1967, 700 conference attendees met at the Texas Conference for the Mexican-American: Improving Educational Opportunities in San Antonio, to discuss improved educational opportunities for Mexican-Americans. Twenty-five resolutions were adopted during the meetings, the first of which (put forth by Governor Connally) was to develop Texas as a bilingual state. The second, introduced by the state's Commission of Education, Dr. J. W. Edgar, was to "equip all Mexican-American children with the ability to read, write, and speak Spanish and English" (Vega, 1983, p. 33). One resolution recommended that intelligence and academic tests be conducted in both Spanish and English to better ensure reliable results (this was enacted into Texas law in 1973).

San Antonio II

The U.S. Commission on Civil Rights held hearings in San Antonio on December 9–14, 1967, regarding the state of education for Mexican-American children in the Southwest. Among the speakers was Dr. Jack Forbes, of both Native Powhatan-Renapé and Delaware-Lenápe, as well as Swiss and Celtic heritage, who spoke of the historical nature of schooling in the Southwest since the 1870s, where schools

> have not been neutral, culturally speaking. Those schools have been controlled by the Anglo-American population and the curricula throughout have been Anglo in character. ... this kind of school quite obviously has not been good, for Mexican-American children. The same kind of school has not been good for American Indian children. It has not been good for other non-Anglo children. It tends to lead to a great deal of alienation, a great deal of hostility ... to a great deal of confusion, where the child comes out of that school really not knowing who he is, not knowing what he should be proud of, not knowing what language he should speak other than English, being in doubt as to whether he should completely accept what Anglo people have been telling him and forget his Mexican identity, or whether he should listen to what his parents and perhaps other people have said and be proud of his Mexican identity.
>
> *(Southwest Intergroup Relations Council, 1970)*

His statement was documented by Mario Obledo (1970),[4] of the Southwest Intergroup Relations Council, who reported "a depressing stream of testimony concerning the devastating effect of common educational practices upon Mexican-American children in the Southwest region" (p. 1). Professor Sánchez testified that it is "normal practice to retain Spanish-speaking children in the first grade for two or even three years, because of deficiency in English while instruction goes on entirely in English. He added that this policy is psychologically ruinous and without pedagogical reason" (p. 2). Obledo indicated that "By the end of the second day of such testimony people in the audience were limp with a weariness both physical and emotional" (p. 2).

The final testimony came from Harold C. Brantley, administrator of the United Consolidated School District of Webb County, who described amalgamation of local schools by the "joining of three common school districts which made up almost all of Webb County other than the City of Laredo" (Obledo, 1970, p. 3). Brantley portrayed the population of the district as including 987 pupils, 47% of whom were Mexican-American and roughly half Anglo, "with a handful of black children enrolled". The program began in Fall 1964, after Brantley visited Miami, Florida, to observe the Coral Way bilingual program there, developed to serve the needs of Cuban refugees in the area. Brantley reported he had traveled the country speaking about the bilingual program he directed and his most important point of advice was to get started with programs right away without delay due to a lack of personnel, funding, materials, or conditions—"Don't wait until you get all of the coons up one tree to start, just get with it and start!" (Obledo, 1970, p. 5).

Although bilingual education was not the central focus of these assemblies, they represent a shifted approach to framing the roots of activism for DLBE because the movements associated with these meetings directed attention toward the benefits of bilingual education as a remedy to compromised educational equity. As was noted in Brantley's concluding testimony, hasty establishment of new bilingual programs reflected their promise for reconciling previously disparate, unequal and segregated systems of schooling.

Learning from the Past for Future Directions

Historical activism promoting language rights through provision of DLBE emerged in several forms. It is critical not to exclude antecedents to contemporary bilingual education—those programs that emerged from monolingual Spanish-speaking communities in post-colonial regions like New Mexico and California. Beyond those, later DLBE would not be possible without trailblazing families, communities, and students like the Méndez's and their counterparts who fought in *Mendez v. Westminster* and Sylvia Méndez, whose life is committed to expanding familiarity on the role of their case as fundamental to the subsequent *Brown v. Board of Education* litigation that ended legal school segregation. Still other figures created collective agency by joining forces, as did Urquides, Guerrero, and Sweetwater. Contemporaneously, both more obscure figures like Anguiano and public leaders in Washington wrestled to promote DLBE through establishment and implementation of the BEA. Still others practiced activism through the Mexican-American civil rights movement, parts of which were crowned by assemblies demanding equal rights.

These profiles and examples of activism share common characteristics. They were united in *compromiso* for equitable schooling, language preservation, and civil rights. They recognized and exercised their own *agency* in pursuit of safeguarding multilingualism and expanding DLBE in the United States. Returning to Sánchez's (1966) analyses of schooling, "The lessons of history, the experience of other countries, the dictates of ordinary judgment suggest various ways for the school to approach the education of children with a mother tongue other than that which is the language of the school" (p. 19). His recommendations from nearly sixty years ago are appropriate for future activism and advocacy for DLBE in the United States.

First, "the talent potential for large numbers of bilingual teachers is here, and it would require no great effort to recruit Spanish-speaking high school graduates to enter teacher education programs if there were reasonable assurance of employment" (Sánchez, 1966, p. 20). A notion similar to the trajectory of Beto Guerrero, who as a teenager dropped out of high school, but was later accepted into a teacher education program and went on to lead a vibrant professional career in scholarship on language educator preparation as a professor at the University of Arizona.

Second, "schools, even without bilingual teachers, could give status to the vernacular of the Spanish-speaking child and employ teachers who would give him a sense of satisfaction and belonging in his accomplishment in the Spanish language and culture it represents" (Sánchez, 1966, p. 21). A proposition analogous to the curriculum developed by Guerrero and Urquides, who "was particularly troubled that Mexican students fluent in Spanish were nonetheless unable to read and write it". They counteracted the school's language suppression by instead creating a robust and prosperous Honors level Spanish for Spanish Speakers course first offered in 1959 at Pueblo High School, in Tucson, Arizona.

Third, (Sánchez,1966) "the Spanish-speaking child of the Southwest is socially and economically disadvantaged. In health, wealth, and welfare he is at or near the bottom of the scale when compared with his fellow Americans" (p. 21). Scholars (de Jong & Howard, 2009; Flores & McAuliffe, 2022; Palmer, 2010) have investigated the extent to which DLBE programs may, in fact, amplify, rather than ameliorate school segregation. Seventy-five years since *Mendez v. Westminster* and seventy years since *Brown v. Board of Education*, schools are more racially segregated today than at the time of these landmark decisions. If the future of DLBE programs remains in pursuit of equitable schooling, the need for advocates and, indeed, *activism* for truly realizing social justice for educational access remains as critical now as in past generations.

Notes

1 Early in the *Mendez v. Westminster* case, court transcripts incorrectly documented it as *Mendez*, despite the plaintiff's surname spelling, Méndez (see Strum, 2014). It is now typically referred to as *Mendez*, although in some cases *Méndez* is retained.

2 Julian Samora is known as the first Mexican-American to earn a doctorate in sociology and anthropology, led pioneering efforts that contributed to the development of Latinx Studies programs, and was instrumental in the founding of National Council of La Raza. As was noted in his 1996 *New York Times* obituary, "Dr. Samora found it especially grating as a child to walk through his hometown of Pagosa Springs and find a sign at the entrance to the public park reading: 'No Mexicans, Indians or Dogs.'" Dr. Samora was committed to advancing rights for Mexican-Americans.

3 Reynaldo Martínez was in his own right a trailblazer and pioneer in both pursuits for bilingual education and Democratic politics. He was recruited to pitch for the Washington Senators out of college and later served as high school classmate, Representative Harry Ried's, Chief of Staff for a period during the 1980s; for twelve years, he was the only Latino Chief of Staff on the Hill.

4 In his *New York Times*, Obituary, Mario G. Obledo (Martin, 2010) is referred to as "Godfather of the Latino Movement". He was awarded the Presidential Medal of Freedom by Bill Clinton in 1998, who said he had "created a powerful chorus for justice and equality". With Pete Tijerina, he founded the Mexican-American Legal Defense Fund in 1968 and later the Hispanic National Bar Association, the Southwest Voter Registration Education Project, and the National Coalition of Hispanic Organizations. *The Washington Post* described Obledo as "outspoken on issues including immigration reform and bilingual education, and he refused to accept what he considered the scant attention mainstream political candidates gave Latinos" (Brown, 2010).

References

Acuña, R. (2000). *Occupied America: A history of Chicanos* (4th ed.). Longman.

Arizona Women's Hall of Fame. (n.d.). Maria Urquides (1908-1994). Retrieved 15 May, 2023 from https://www.azwhf.org/copy-2-of-mae-sue-talley.

Blanton, C. K. (2004). *The strange career of bilingual education in Texas, 1836-1981*. Texas A & M Press.

Blanton, C. K. (2014). *George I. Sánchez: The long fight for Mexican American integration*. Yale University Press.

Blum Martínez, R., & Habermann López, M. J. (2020). *The shoulders we stand on: A history of bilingual education in New Mexico*. University of New Mexico Press.

Brown, E. (2010, August 23). Mario G. Obledo, 78, Latino civil rights pioneer, dies. *The Washington Post*. Retrieved October 20, 2021 from https://www.washingtonpost.com/wp-dyn/content/article/2010/08/22/AR2010082202747.html

Combs, M. C. (2008). Urquides, María (1908-1994). In J. M. González (Ed.), *Encyclopedia of bilingual education* (Vol. II, pp. 869–870). Sage.

de Jong, E., & Howard, E. (2009). Integration in two-way immersion education: Equalising linguistic benefits for all students. *International Journal of Bilingual Education and Bilingualism*, *12*(1), 81–99.

Flores, N., & McAuliffe, L. (2022). 'In other schools you can plan it that way': A raciolinguistic perspective on dual language education. *International Journal of Bilingual Education and Bilingualism*, *25*(4), 1349–1362.

Gonzales, P. B. (2020). Promise and frustration: The history of Spanish-language bilingual education in New Mexico, 1848-1970. In R. Blum Martínez & M. J. Haberman López (Eds.), *The shoulders we stand on: A history of bilingual education in New Mexico*. University of New Mexico Press.

Gonzalez, E. Q. (1986). *The education and public career of Maria L. Urquides: a case study of a Mexican American community leader*. Doctoral Dissertation, The University of Arizona.

Green, P. E. (2008). Méndez v. Westminster. In J. M. González (Ed.), *Encyclopedia of bilingual education* (Vol. II, pp. 549–551). Sage.

Martin, D. (2010, August 20). Mario Obledo, Hispanic Rights Leader, Dies at 78. *The New York Times*.

Moll, L. C. (2010). Mobilizing culture, language, and educational practices: Fulfilling the promises of Mendez and Brown. *Educational Researcher*, *39*(6), 451–460.

Moore, S. C. K. (2021). *A history of bilingual education in the U.S.: Examining the politics of language policymaking*. Multilingual Matters.

National Education Association. (1966). The invisible minority. *Report of the NEA-Tucson survey on the teaching of Spanish to the Spanish-speaking*. http:/ww. eric. ed.gov/ERlCWebPortal/search/detailmini. Jsp

Obledo, M. (1970). A bilingual approach: Education for understanding the story of the bilingual program of education in the United Consolidated School District Webb County, Texas. Southwest Intergroup Relations Council. Retrieved on May 23, 2023 from https://files.eric.ed.gov/fulltext/ED075106.pdf

Palmer, D. (2010). Race, power, and equity in a multiethnic urban elementary school with a dual-language "strand" program. *Anthropology & Education Quarterly*, *41*(1), 94–114.

Rivers, K. (2020, March 12). "Let your light shine". Lupe Anguiano: Lifelong activist. *Ventura County Reporter*. Oxnard, Ventura County, CA. Retrieved October 20, 2021 from https://vcreporter.com/2020/03/let-your-light-shine-lupe-anguiano-lifelong-activist/

Robbie. S. (2016). The meaning of Méndez. In A. Colón-Muñiz & M. Lavadenz (eds.), *Latino Civil Rights in education: La lucha sigue*. Routledge.

Robbins, W. (2015). *A man for all seasons: Monroe Sweetland and the liberal paradox*. Oregon State University Press.

San Miguel Jr., G. (1987). *Let them all take heed: Mexican Americans and the campaign for educational equity in Texas, 1910–1981*. University of Texas Press.

San Miguel Jr., G. (2004). *Contested policy: The rise and fall of federal bilingual education policy in the United States 1960–2001*. University of North Texas Press.

Sanchez, G. (1973). *An analysis of the Bilingual Education Aact, 1967-68*. University of Massachusetts Amherst.

Sánchez, G. I. (1940). Forgotten people: A study of New Mexicans. *Albuquerque, N. M.: The University of New Mexico press.* Peabody Journal of Education, 92(3), 302–321.

Sánchez, G. I. (1966). History, culture, and education. In J. Samora (Ed.), *La Raza: Forgotten Americans* (pp. 1–26). University of Notre Dame Press.

Strum, P. (2014). "We always tell our children they are Americans": *Mendez v. Westminster* and the beginning of the end of school segregation. *Journal of Supreme Court History*, *39*, 307–328.

Valencia, R. R. (2005). The Mexican American Struggle for Equal Educational Opportunity in *Mendez v. Westminster*: Helping to Pave the Way for *Brown v. Board of Education. Teachers College Record*, *107*(3), 389–423.

Vega, J. E. (1983). *Education, politics, and bilingualism in Texas*. University Press of America.

Weinberg, M. (1995). *A chance to learn: A history of race and education in the United States*. Cambridge University Press.

Wright, D. (2016). *Uncompromised: The Lupe Anguiano story*. Opportunity Development Enterprises, LLC.

5

DLBE PROGRAM TYPES FOR DIFFERENT TARGET POPULATIONS

Wayne E. Wright, Woongsik Choi

Overview

Dual language bilingual education (DLBE) is a broad label for a wide variety of program models and configurations that target various student populations, separately or in combination, for purposes of developing proficiency in two (or more) languages. According to Howard et al. (2018), DLBE "refers to any program that provides literacy and content instruction to all students through two languages and that promotes bilingualism and biliteracy, and grade-level academic achievement, and sociocultural competence for all students" (p. 3).

There are many different types of education programs for emergent bilingual students in the United States. They can be largely divided into monolingual programs and bilingual programs (Wright, 2019). However, as shown in Figure 5.1, some English-medium programs may not be entirely monolingual. As Wright (2019) asserts, all programs for students designated as English language learners (ELLs) should include the use of bilingual or translanguaging strategies to increase comprehension and support students' positive identity development as bilinguals. Thus, no classroom in any type of program serving ELL-designated students and other multilingual students should strictly be English-only.

However, a distinction needs to be made between the bilingual *support* provided in English-medium instruction programs (e.g., Sheltered English Immersion) and bilingual *instruction* provided in bilingual education programs where one or more content areas are taught in the ELL-designated students' home language (Wright, 2019). Bilingual *support* in English-medium classrooms typically takes the form of quick explanations from a teacher,

 DOI: 10.4324/9781003269076-9

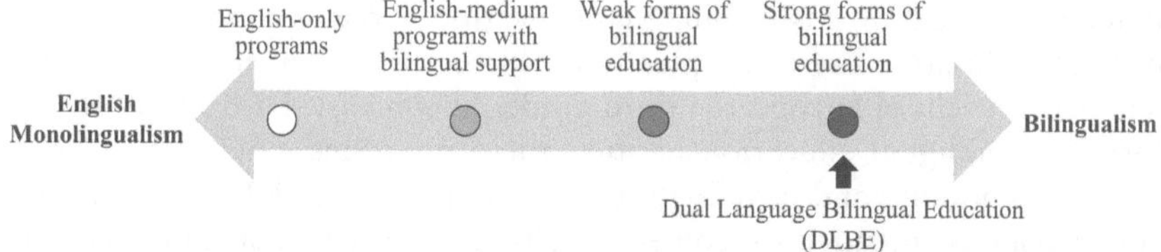

Figure 5.1 U.S. Education Programs for Language-Minoritized Students

paraprofessional, or peer; allowances for students to use their home languages or to engage in translanguaging; or providing other short/temporary oral or written supports in the home languages. Such bilingual and translanguaging supports are feasible even in classrooms where teachers do not speak the home language(s) of their students. While such supports can be effective and even empowering when they allow bilingual students to draw upon all of their linguistic resources for classroom learning purposes, there is no sustained programmatic effort to further develop the home languages (García et al., 2016).

In contrast, home language *instruction* is the distinguishing feature of bilingual education program models. It entails sustained teaching of entire lessons and specific content areas in the home language of the ELL-designated students. In most bilingual programs, this includes literacy instruction designed to help ELL-designated students attain grade-level reading and writing proficiency in their home languages. Home language literacy may be developed before, or simultaneously with, English literacy. Providing such instruction requires, at a minimum, (a) qualified and trained teachers who are proficient bilinguals in English and the target language with good reading and writing skills in both languages; (b) sufficient availability and use of teaching materials in English and the target language; and (c) appropriate formative and summative bilingual assessments. These distinctions are important given that many programs for bilingual students are mislabeled and thus are what Hinton (2015) calls "bilingual-in-name-only" (BINO). Such BINO programs may include classrooms originally designated as DLBE, but due to political issues (e.g., pressure to prepare students for high-stakes English-only tests), poor planning (e.g., lack of clear goals; lack of bilingual curricular materials), or other problems (e.g., insufficient qualified bilingual teachers), there is a shift to English-medium instruction with minimal bilingual supports (Hinton, 2015; Palmer & Lynch, 2008).

Baker and Wright (2021) provide a typology that makes a distinction between "weak" and "strong" forms of bilingual education (see Figure 5.1). Weak forms of bilingual education include transitional programs for ELL-designated students which aim for quick transition to English mainstream instruction after only a few years of home language instruction. A common outcome of weak forms of bilingual education is relative monolingualism in English because there is typically no further development of the home language in school beyond the third grade. In contrast, DLBE is a "strong form" of bilingual education because these programs extend for several years of schooling and have high levels of bilingualism, biliteracy, and biculturalism as intended outcomes. Additional goals of academic achievement, sociocultural and global competences (Howard et al., 2018), and the development of critical consciousness (Cervantes-Soon et al., 2017) further make DLBE not only a strong form of bilingual education but a strong form of education overall. Figure 5.1 shows where DLBE is positioned on a continuum of the aforementioned types of programs for emergent bilingual students.

The predominance of weak forms of bilingual education has led many political leaders and educators to view bilingual education as a remedial program for students with "limited English proficiency," thus taking a language-as-problem orientation (Ruiz, 1984, 2010) and a deficit view of bilingual students. This deficit view also has origins in the original Bilingual Education Act of 1968 which included poverty criteria to identify targeted students (Wright, 2005), thus clearly marking bilingual education as a "remedial or compensatory program" (Lyons, 1995). Such weak forms were predominant as they were bilingual programs most supported by federal and state policies and funding (Moore, 2021). Strong forms, including DLBE, have helped move bilingual education into the realm of enrichment education with an orientation that views language as a valuable resource (Ruiz, 2010). Alternative names such as *two-way* (or *one-way*) *immersion*, *dual immersion*, *dual language immersion* or simply *dual language* seem to avoid the use of the word "bilingual" in order to distance these enrichment programs from association with remedial forms of bilingual education. Following García (2009), we prefer to use the term "Dual Language Bilingual Education (DLBE)" which emphasizes the fact that dual language is indeed a form of bilingual education. DLBE programs have been growing in popularity and receiving increasing state policy and funding support, particularly for forms inclusive of non-ELL-designated students.

This chapter will first provide an overview of the various types of DLBE program models and structures and their targeted populations as documented in academic research. Next, the chapter will cover key issues in the provision of DLBE for different student populations, including the inclusion of speakers of non-standard varieties of English and/or the target language, the inclusion of students who speak home or heritage languages other than the target languages, and the need for DLBE educators to address issues of power and equity in their DLBE programs. Finally, the chapter will briefly discuss implications and future directions for DLBE research and programs.

DLBE Program Types for Different Target Populations

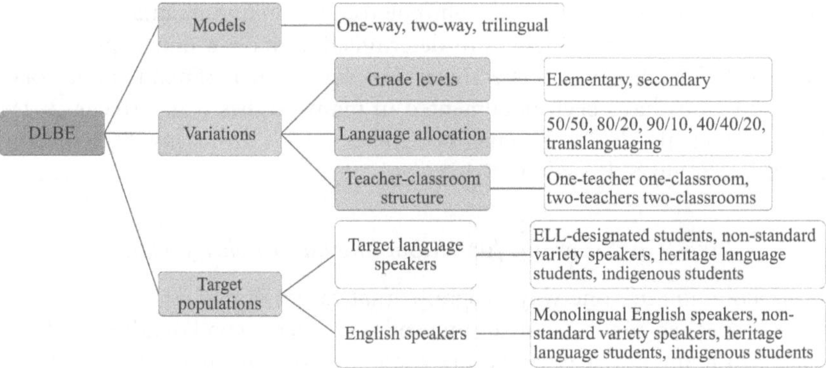

Figure 5.2 DLBE Program Types and Target Populations

Main Findings from Current Empirical Research

Empirical research conducted in schools with DLBE programs reveals that these programs vary in terms of model types, grade levels, language allocations, structures, teachers, and student demographics (Figure 5.2). One important distinction is made between *one-way*, *two-way*, and *trilingual* programs.

One-Way Models

One-way (immersion) models generally target students who are dominant speakers of the same language, with the goal of bilingualism and biliteracy in a target language and English. However, there is variation in terms of who these target students are.

One-Way Programs for ELL-designated Students

In some one-way programs, the targeted students are ELL-designated students who speak the same home language. These programs "aim to help the students develop both English and their home language, so they become fully bilingual and biliterate, achieving academically through both languages and developing positive sense of their cultural heritage and ethnolinguistic identities" (Wright, 2019, p. 104). These one-way DLBE programs for ELL-designated students are more accurately called *developmental* or *maintenance bilingual education programs* (also sometimes called *"late-exit" bilingual programs*). They typically extend throughout elementary school (e.g., grades K-5 or K-6). In contrast to the weaker forms of bilingual education that focus on transitioning to English-only instruction after just a few years, these one-way programs continue to develop and maintain the home language, even after students are determined to have attained proficiency in English. The design and effectiveness of developmental/maintenance one-way programs have been documented in many studies (e.g., Alvear, 2019; Escamilla et al., 2013; Thomas & Collier, 2012; Umansky & Reardon, 2014; Valentino & Reardon, 2015).

One-Way Programs for "Monolingual" English Speakers

More common are one-way programs that target dominant and proficient English speakers who wish to attain proficiency in a second or additional language. In many one-way programs, these are language-majority students—so-called native English speakers—who begin the program as monolingual speakers of English, but who wish (or more likely with parents who wish for them) to learn a "foreign" or world language such as Spanish, French, Mandarin Chinese, or Japanese (Sung & Tsai, 2019). A "total" or "full" immersion approach typically occurs throughout the elementary school grades with instruction beginning primarily in the target non-English language. The amount of English instruction slowly increases each year until about fourth grade. Then, equal time is given to instruction in both languages until the end of elementary school (e.g., grade 5 or 6). Some programs will extend throughout the secondary school years. Traditionally such programs were referred to as *bilingual immersion programs* or *foreign/world language immersion programs*. Alternatively, they were simply called *immersion programs* by the name of the target language (e.g., *Spanish immersion*, *Chinese immersion*, *French Immersion*) (de Courcy, 2002). These programs generally operate out of foreign/world language education departments designed to serve majority English speakers and thus are disconnected from bilingual education departments and the traditions, histories, and paradigms of bilingual education for language-minority students (Freire et al., 2017).

One-Way Programs for Heritage Language Students

In other one-way programs, the proficient and dominant English speakers are heritage speakers of the target language. For example, many 1.5, 2nd, or 3rd generation students from immigrant families are dominant English speakers with varying levels of oral proficiency and literacy skills in their heritage language. Typically, students have some ability to understand and speak the language due to exposure or use of the language at home. For these students, a one-way program may be better described as a form of a *heritage language education program*. It may follow the same structure as the *foreign/world language immersion program* but should be designed to recognize the students as bilinguals and further develop their knowledge and skills of their heritage language (see, e.g., Grivet et al., 2021, on French DLBE programs in Louisiana).

At the secondary school level, these programs may have names such as *Heritage Spanish*, *Khmer-for-Khmer speakers*, or *Vietnamese for heritage speakers* (see, e.g., Chik & Wright, 2017). However, in states such as Tennessee, where heritage language learner policies and programs are nearly absent, heritage language is often taught to a mixed group of students in world language classes (e.g., high school Spanish), imposing responsibilities on the world language teachers to address the differing strengths and needs of heritage speakers (Soler & Fuentes, 2021).

One-Way Programs for Indigenous Students

In other cases, the dominant English speakers in a one-way program are heritage speakers of endangered indigenous languages such as Navajo, Hawaiian, or Yupik. These heritage language programs are not just about helping students attain proficiency in their indigenous languages but are a key part of larger language revitalization efforts to prevent further loss of endangered indigenous languages, or even to resurrect a previously "dead" (or "dormant") indigenous language (Baker & Wright, 2021).

The Native American Languages Act of 1990/1992 established the federal government's role in supporting the preservation of Native American languages. This act "emerged from the grass-roots efforts of bilingual educators and Native language revitalization activists" (Warhol, 2011, p. 293). Following the 2007 Esther Martinez Native American Languages Preservation Act, funding from the U.S. Department of Education was provided to indigenous language programs. For example, the Puente de Hózhó Elementary School in Arizona offers a Diné (Navajo)-English DLBE program along with Spanish-English DLBE (McCarty, 2018). This program provides K-5 education in Diné and English to Native American students.

Two-Way Models

Dual language education traditionally referred to *two-way immersion (TWI)* programs serving roughly the same number of English proficient students and ELL-designated students who speak the same target language (e.g., Spanish). The two-way model is designed to benefit all students in becoming bilingual, biliterate, and bicultural. For the ELL-designated students, a well-designed two-way program enables them to develop literacy skills and learn academic content in the language they know the best, while also helping them to learn English (Crawford, 2004). The English-proficient students—typically monolingual English speakers—benefit from the opportunity to learn a new language, while still receiving literacy instruction and support in their home language of English. In principle, the two-way program creates equal ground; English-dominant students must rely on ELL-designated students as they learn their target home language, and ELL-designated students must rely in turn on English-dominant students as they learn English (Wright, 2019). Both student groups benefit from the cross-cultural learning experiences, which help them understand and appreciate their own and each other's cultures (Lindholm-Leary, 1994). The Coral Way Elementary School established the first modern two-way program in Dade County, Florida, in 1963, serving both Spanish-speaking students (from the Cuban community) and English-speaking students (from predominantly middle-class families). The rich history of the Coral Way program, including its experimental design and strong advocacy from the Cuban community to develop the program, is well documented by Coady (2020). Freeman (1998) provides a detailed ethnographic account of the James F. Oyster Bilingual Elementary School, established in 1971 (now called the Oyster-Adams Bilingual School). Freeman described the development of the two-way dual language program as an initiative of local parents and politicians to cross language, cultural, ethnic, and social class lines. At the time of Freeman's study, the school served a diverse group of students with "60% Hispanic, 20% White, 15% Black, and 5% Asian and other language minorities"; "two in every 5 children came from low-income families" (Baker & Wright, 2021, p. 235).

Trilingual Models

Many communities of contemporary society are indeed multilingual, and more than two named languages are used and taught. Thus, some DLBE programs introduce instruction in a third language at the beginning or later in the program (Wright & Chan, 2019). Such programs are called *trilingual education* or sometimes "*three-way immersion*" (Malakoff & Hakuta, 1990, p. 39). Although trilingual programs are less common in the United States, such multilingual education programs are found in many multilingual societies across the globe (e.g., Hong Kong, India, Kenya, Spain) (Aldekoa et al., 2020; Phakeng et al., 2018; Wang & Kirkpatrick, 2019). For instance, Aldekoa et al. (2020) report on a Basque-Spanish-English trilingual model in the Basque Autonomous Community of Spain.

In the U.S. context, trilingual models tend to be an extension of a two-way model. Some trilingual programs add a third language minimally or in later grades. Henn-Reinke (2012), in her book *Considering Trilingual Education*, researched Riverview Elementary School's International Academy in San Diego, California. The school has both Spanish and Chinese (Mandarin) DLBE programs. Students in the Spanish program receive about 30 minutes of Chinese language instruction, and vice-versa for the students in the Chinese DLBE programs. Similarly, Wright and Chan (2019) note that students in the Spanish-English two-way DLBE program at the private International School of Indiana start studying in a third language in the secondary grades (e.g., Mandarin).

In other trilingual models, the third language is taught simultaneously with two focal languages. Wright and Chan (2019) describe the private Oasis Trilingual Community School in the greater Los Angeles area where students simultaneously study Mandarin Chinese, English, and Spanish. Weeks (2021) investigated students' reading achievement in a public charter district in Texas, where students received instruction in English, Spanish, and Chinese at the elementary level. However, as the students proceed to secondary grades, they learn Spanish and Chinese through daily language development instruction.

Trilingual programs may primarily benefit and be more successful for language-majority students who do not face the pressure of losing their home language. Consider, for example, Canadian immersion programs where English-French programs add a third minority language group (e.g., Hebrew) (Genesee & Lambert, 1983; Malakoff & Hakuta, 1990). However, when targeted for language-minority students, trilingual models can raise their sociocultural competence to address social justice issues altogether. For example, the inclusion of Korean language in Los Angeles Unified's DLBE program helped heal and bond the community together as African American, Hispanic, and Korean-speaking children learned each other's languages after the community was "torn apart by racial riots" in 1994 (Kimura-Gorecki, 1996, p. 41).

Variations in Grade Levels

Most DLBE programs begin in kindergarten and extend throughout the elementary school grades (e.g., grade 5 or 6). Some DLBE programs are in K-8 schools and thus can serve students through the middle school grades. Some school districts provide pathways for graduates from elementary school DLBE programs to continue the program through middle school and high school, with at least one class period continuing to develop grade-level literacy skills in the target non-English language, and/or content classes taught in a non-English language. Morita-Mullaney et al. (2020) describe a Spanish-English K-12 DLBE program in an Indiana school district where three courses continue to be taught in Spanish in middle and high schools: Spanish language arts, science, and social studies.

While the assumption is that the students will begin the program in kindergarten, the reality is that newcomer ELL-designated students arrive in U.S. schools at all grade levels. Such late arrival may be used as an excuse for exclusion from DLBE programs, even though placement in ongoing DLBE programs may provide the most support for the newly arrived students, with accommodations as needed to help the student catch up with their grade-level peers. In some cases, DLBE programs begin in later grades, even in secondary schools, to accommodate newcomer students.

Variations in Language Allocations

DLBE programs have traditionally relied on strict separations of when each language could be used for instruction and/or spoken by the students (Howard et al., 2018). Designations were typically indicated by the percentage of instructional time allocated for each language. Historically most two-way programs followed a 50/50 model—50% of instruction in English and 50% of instruction in the target language (e.g., Spanish) (Figure 5.3). How this division of time is structured can vary. In some programs, one language is used in the first half of the day, and the other in the second half of the day. In other programs, the language may alternate by day—for example, Monday-English, Tuesday-Spanish, Wednesday-English, etc. There is some critique that in a 50/50 model there is more focus on equality and pragmatic values than on equity (Freire & Delavan, 2021).

In a model of DLBE that was initially designed for use in schools along the southern Texas border where the majority of students are Latinx, the Gomez and Gomez Dual Language Enrichment Model (www.gomezandgomez.com) follows a unique 50/50 model that divides language of instruction by content area as well as by time (Gómez et al., 2005). However, such division by content may result in less than 50% of instruction time in Spanish during the first years of the program and thus does not meet the minimum threshold for inclusion in the Center for Applied Linguistics Directory of two-way programs (Palmer et al., 2015).

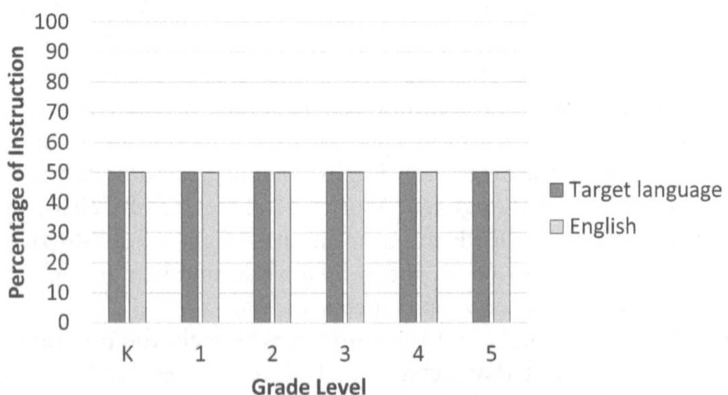

Figure 5.3 50/50 Model

Adapted from Wright (2019, p. 107).

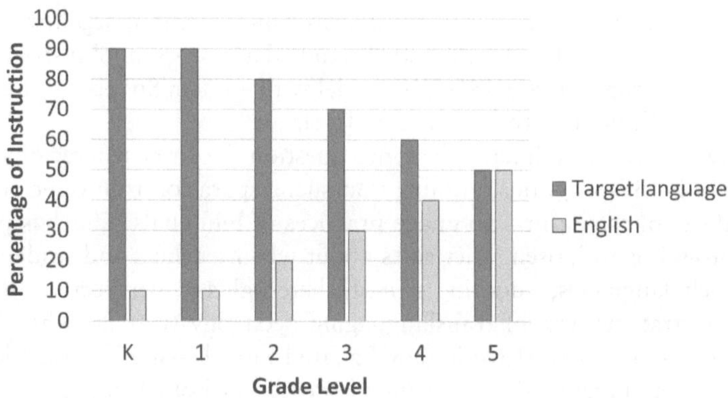

Figure 5.4 90/10 Model
Adapted from Wright (2019, p. 107).

Some two-way and many one-way programs begin with much more time dedicated to the non-English target language, particularly during the first year or two of the program. For example, in a 90/10 model that begins in kindergarten, 90% of instruction time is in the target language, and only 10% in English. As students move up in grade level, the balance between the languages shifts to 80/20, 70/30, 60/40, and eventually to 50/50 by grade 5 (Figure 5.4). Some programs, such as the Navajo-English DLBE at Puente de Hózhó Elementary School in Arizona (https://www.fusd1.org/domain/2229), start with an 80/20 or 70/30 balance to allow more time at the beginning of the program for English instruction.

As an illustration of a trilingual education program, at the Oasis Trilingual Community School, students study three languages simultaneously in a 40/40/20 model (Figure 5.5)—40% in Mandarin, 40% in English, and 20%

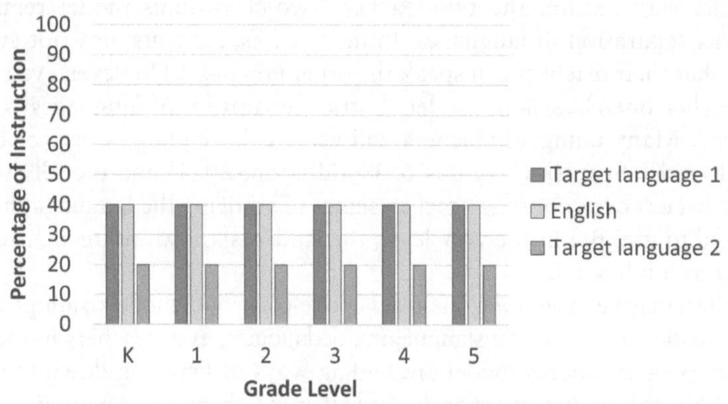

Figure 5.5 40/40/20 Model

in Spanish—from grades K-6 (https://oasistrilingualschool.org/curriculum/) (Wright & Chan, 2019). Weeks (2021) studied a Texas school district trilingual program that offers a 45/45/10 model with 45% in Spanish and English and 10% in Chinese at the elementary level.

More recent research has called into question the strict separation of languages in DLBE programs, arguing that such separation is in opposition to the realities of the natural language practices of bilinguals. This has pushed some programs to loosen strict rules about when teachers and students can use which languages, adopting a more heteroglossic perspective that encourages strategic uses of translanguaging pedagogy (García et al., 2016). In Escamilla et al.'s (2013) Literacy Squared model, paired literacy lessons facilitate simultaneous development of literacy in both languages, explicit lessons are taught to develop cross-language connections, assessments account for biliteracy development, and teachers use languages strategically and flexibility to enhance student learning and to respond to students' language alterations.

Variations in Teacher-Classroom Structures

50/50 two-way models can vary in terms of the number of teachers and classrooms. In some models, a single bilingual teacher teaches both English and the target language in the same classroom. In other models, there are two teachers—one who teaches only in English, and one who teaches only in the target language. The teachers work in pairs, and students physically move from the English classroom to the non-English classroom (and vice-versa) in the middle of the school day. The target language teacher is bilingual, though typically will only speak to the students in the target language. The English teacher is typically a monolingual English speaker or has a beginning level of proficiency in the target language.

By its very nature, the two-teachers two-classrooms model reinforces the strict separation of languages. In many cases, students may not even be aware that their teachers can speak the other language. However, even in the one-teacher one-classroom model, a strict separation of languages is often enforced. Many bilingual teachers will use a color-coding system of blue = English, red = Spanish (Przymus & Huddleston, 2021) and literally wear a color card or corresponding scarf to signal to students the language they are expected to use. But at the very least, the students know and recognize their teacher as a bilingual.

While it may be easier for a one-teacher one-classroom model to adopt a more heteroglossic view with translanguaging pedagogies, even teachers in the two-teachers two-classrooms model are finding ways of breaking down the walls which keep the languages separate. For example, through co-planning, teachers can coordinate their lessons to complement each other in a paired-literacy fashion and share in the planning of explicit cross-language lessons and use of bilingual materials across both classrooms. Teachers can also combine their classes on occasion to co-teach lessons utilizing translanguaging pedagogies.

Linguistic Diversity of the "English" and "Target" Language Speakers

When considering students in DLBE programs, it is necessary to go beyond the traditional distinction between "English-only" students and "English-learner" students. Such dualism often results in underrepresenting, if not excluding, certain minoritized languages or non-standard varieties. In a two-way model, in particular, the assumption is (approximately) half of the students are "native" speakers of standard American English, and the other half are "native" speakers of the standard variety of the target language, and that students in both groups begin as monolingual learners of a "new" language.

In reality, there is often great ethnic and linguistic diversity in terms of who these "native" speakers are (de Courcy et al., 2002). Consider, for example, this description from Starr (2017), who researched sociolinguistic variation and acquisition in a Mandarin-English two-way program at Meizhang School, a private school on the West Coast of the United States:

> Approximately two-thirds of the first- and second-grade parents are ethnically Chinese. The largest group of ethnically Chinese parents are 1st, 1.5, and 2nd generation Taiwanese Americans, with varying degrees of proficiency in Mandarin. The next largest group is from the Southern Chinese dialect areas of China including Sichuan, Shanghai and Hong Kong, or from Southern Chinese dialect speaking groups in Southeast Asian countries such as Malaysia, Indonesia, and Singapore. A handful of parents are from other areas of Mainland China. Of the non-Chinese parents, around half are American-born native English speakers of European, East Asian and South Asian ancestry. The other half are native speakers of various other East Asian, Asian Pacific, Middle Eastern, and European languages. The majority of non-Chinese parents do not speak any Mandarin, although there are some with various levels of Mandarin proficiency. (p. 9)

Starr also notes that many of the students are of "mixed ethnicity, with parents who each belong to different categories described above" (p. 9). Some students have one European and one Chinese parent, and others are adoptees who, in some cases, have a different ethnic background than their adopted parents. These variations observed by Starr challenge the oversimplistic notions of English speakers and target language speakers in DLBE programs.

Beginning with the "English speakers" in a two-way program, among this group, there may be students who are already bilingual or multilingual, speaking one or more languages other than the target language of the program, at varying levels of proficiency. In Starr's example above, the English speakers included children from families who also spoke East Asian, Asian Pacific, Middle Eastern, and European languages. Among the English speakers in a Spanish-English two-way program, there may be heritage speakers of Mandarin, Korean, Arabic, Karen, Hmong, or Swahili, just to name a few.

Likewise, in terms of the "target language speakers," among this group may be multilingual students who speak it as an additional language to the languages or varieties they may speak at home. For example, some Spanish-English bilingual programs serve indigenous students from Mexico who speak languages such as Nahuatl, Mixteco, or Zapoteco (Morales et al., 2019); or indigenous students from Guatemala who speak K'iche', Mam, or Chuj (Bernstein et al., 2020). In many French DLBE programs, the "native" and "heritage" French speakers are often immigrant students from countries where French is a colonial language and used as the medium of instruction in school such as Haiti, the Democratic Republic of the Congo, and Cameroon (Jaumont, 2017). These students may speak one or more national or local languages in addition to French (e.g., Haitian Creole, Lingala, Swahili, Fulani).

Even when students do speak English as their "native" or predominant home language, the variety may differ from the standard variety assumed and/or taught by the DLBE program. For example, many DLBE programs are inclusive of African American students who speak a variety of African American Vernacular English at home and thus are learning Standard American English at the same time they are learning the target language (e.g., Spanish) (Bauer et al., 2020; Frieson & Scalise, 2021). In cases where Latinx students are counted among the "English" speakers (i.e., not ELL-designated) (Block, 2011), some may speak a variety of Chicano-English that is used in their homes or the local community, although such bilingual Chicanx children are often subject to "erasure" in DLBE programs that believe in linguistic purism (Martínez, 2017).

Likewise, there is dialect variation among target language "native" speakers. The "native" and "heritage" French speakers from Haiti and African nations speak varieties of French much different from the standard variety spoken in Paris. There are also wide varieties of Spanish depending not only on what country the student or their family is from (e.g., Mexico, Guatemala, Peru, Spain), but also on variations within countries (e.g., different regions of Mexico). Many Puerto Rican students struggle with the variations in vocabulary and pronunciation when served in programs that assume students speak the standard variety of Spanish spoken in Mexico City, as do students from more rural areas of Mexico, and those born and raised in the

United States speaking the variety of Spanish of their home and community. DLBE teachers also face challenges when their variety of Spanish is different from either the variety assumed by the program, and/or different from the variety spoken by the majority of their students. Consider, for example, the challenges for bilingual teachers recruited from Spain, Puerto Rico, or even Mexico who teach mostly U.S.-born Mexican American students. Without proper training and sociolinguistic understandings, such teachers are often shocked at what they consider to be the "improper" Spanish spoken by the students and their families.

In Starr's example above of the Mandarin-English two-way program, the "Mandarin speakers" came from a variety of homes with parents at varying levels of Mandarin coming from diverse regions of Greater China, including Taiwan, Hong Kong, Southern Mainland China, and from the Chinese diaspora in Southeast Asia nations like Malaysia, Indonesia, and Singapore. Each spoke variations of Mandarin, as well as regional varieties and dialects of Chinese. Starr also noted the complexity of Mandarin as the "target language" of the program:

> Chinese American communities must negotiate between the Taiwanese standard, *Guoyu,* and the Mainland Chinese standard, *Putonghua,* which are quite similar in their spoken form. In their written form however, there are significant differences that come to the fore in an educational context. First, in Taiwan Chinese is written with traditional characters and in Mainland China it is written with simplified characters. In addition, schoolchildren in Taiwan learn a specialized phonetic alphabet called *Zhuyin fuhao*, which uses unique symbols, while in Mainland China children learn *pinyin*, standardized Mandarin romanization. (pp. 9–10)

Given the predominance of Taiwanese American families, the "standard" version selected for use in the program was the Taiwanese standard, and students learned traditional characters and Zhuyin fuhao. One can imagine the disadvantage this decision places on teachers, students, and parents who speak a different standard or non-standard form of Chinese language, and who use the pinyin system of romanization. Similar issues may arise, for example, in a Hmong bilingual program given variations between White Hmong and Blue/Green Hmong, and continuing debates over standardized Hmong spellings.

Another assumption is that "English" speakers and "target language" speakers begin the program as monolingual speakers of these languages and thus will become "sequential" bilinguals as a result of the DLBE program. In reality, many of the target language speakers are already emergent or simultaneous bilinguals, including U.S.-born students who have been exposed to two or more languages growing up in their homes and their communities (Baker & Wright, 2021). In many immigrant families, one or both parents may have varying levels of English proficiency. Also, older siblings (if any) are likely to be English speakers and use it at home if they have also attended school in the United States.

As noted above, many of the English-proficient students in DLBE programs are former ELL-designated students or other heritage speakers of the target language and thus are already bilingual with varying levels of proficiency in that language. For example, Lee et al. (2021), in their study of a Korean-English 50/50 two-way model in an urban area of Southern California, found the following composition among the 26 students in the first-grade classroom (p. 181):

- 25% Korean-dominant
- 30% English-dominant
- 45% more balanced bilingual students (as described by the teachers)
- 20 Korean ethnicity
    - 8 born in Korea
    - 12 born in the United States
- 6 of non-Korean ethnicity
    - 1 African American, 1 Filipino, 2 White, and 2 mixed-heritage (Japanese/White, Chinese/White)

Henderson and Palmer (2020) note that a particular critique of the Gomez and Gomez Dual Language Enrichment Model, designed to serve predominantly Latinx students, is the requirement to identify each student's "dominant" or "primary" language in order to assign them to either the English- or Spanish-dominant groups. As Henderson and Palmer observe: "for many [students], especially in South Texas, students' primary language really is *both* Spanish and English." The decision of which language to assign to children can be challenging for educators, and a harrowing one for parents, all of which seem a bit counterproductive if the program's purpose is to encourage all students to be—and become—bilingual, biliterate, and bicultural.

Implications and Future Directions for DLBE Research and Programs

As shown above, DLBE programs differ in terms of the number of languages, grade levels, language allocation, and teacher-classroom structure. However, terms to describe different types of DLBE programs are used inconsistently. DLBE researchers need to clearly identify the types of DLBE models and variations when describing the research context. One concern is that the description may become too lengthy. It may be helpful to use codification such as *DLBE-2 50/50 2T2C* (two-way DLBE using a 50/50 two-teachers two-classrooms model) to enhance consistency, brevity, and discoverability (Keefer & Haj-Broussard, 2020).

More empirical research studies are needed on trilingual models and secondary-level programs. Given trilingual programs are less common in the United States, research is still emerging and specificity is lacking (Phakeng et al., 2018). It is yet unclear how effectively these programs develop high levels of proficiency across all program languages and academic achievement of students in all language groups, while addressing complex power dynamics among the three languages. Also, secondary-level DLBE programs are less studied because they are a comparatively new phenomenon in the United States. This is more so in DLBE programs for non-Spanish languages such as Korean and Mandarin (Lee & Wang, 2021).

Lastly, the examples above, and many more which are documented in the research literature, reveal the linguistic reality on the ground of the student target populations is often much more complex than the oversimplified notion of monolingual "native speakers" of two different languages in a two-way program learning each other's languages. These same linguistic complexities are also present in one-way and trilingual programs. Thus, it is important for DLBE researchers and teachers to have some sociolinguistic training and understanding so as to recognize and value all of the linguistic varieties among the students in their classrooms. Such a shift is needed, particularly when researchers and educators may have internalized ideologies of linguistic purism. In the concluding remarks of her study, Starr (2017) acknowledged the shift in her own attitude and beliefs:

> When I first began my fieldwork at the Meizhang school, I must confess that I was rather scandalized by the amount of non-standard Mandarin used by some of the teachers. "They never would be hired to teach at the university level," I scoffed to myself. ... Looking back over my fieldwork data, I now realize that the students were not only learning standard Mandarin, but also how to interpret the dialect differences that were prevalent in the local Mandarin-speaking community. Students who had completed both the first and second grades would be familiar with two different Mandarin dialects from both North and South, preparing them to travel across China and handle the range of Mandarin they would encounter. In English, students were gaining experience with British, Canadian and other regional dialects that they would never encounter in a conventional American school. In hindsight, the diversity at Meizhang wasn't a drawback at all: it was a benefit to the students. (pp. 158–159)

Developing such sociolinguistic understandings and shifts in ideologies is just a first step. Looking to the future, there may be a need to rethink our current oversimplified models with programs that can better account for the linguistic realities of the target populations being served.

There is already growing critique and some promising changes in practice regarding the strict separation of the two target languages during instruction. As Henderson and Palmer (2020) note, "such strict separation is artificial" (p. 12). They argue, "since bilinguals have the ability to draw on language features across their repertoire, more linguistical flexibility—thoughtful linguistically responsive pedagogy—should be encouraged in order to best develop bilingualism and support rich academic learning and deep thinking" (p. 12). Recent efforts towards translanguaging pedagogies are beginning to shift practices in some DLBE programs (García & Kleyn, 2016; García & Li, 2014; García et al., 2016; Sánchez et al., 2017; Sayer, 2013). These shifts include efforts to deliberately plan instruction time for bilingual language use, to teach bridging lessons, and to develop metalanguage and cross-language understandings (Beeman & Urow, 2012; Escamilla et al., 2013).

How can DLBE programs that are premised on valuing bilingualism and biculturalism better embrace the languages, non-standard dialects, and cultures of students whose home language and heritage language varieties are not targets for development in the program? We expect mainstream and ELL teachers in linguistically and culturally diverse English-medium classrooms to embrace and value the diversity of the students in their classrooms, engage in culturally sustaining pedagogies (Paris & Alim, 2017), and adopt a heteroglossic approach that includes ways to enable all students to draw on their entire linguistic repertoire when learning a new language and academic content through that language (de Jong, 2011; Wright, 2019). Nothing less should be expected of our bilingual teachers in DLBE programs, thus the need to go beyond the two target standard language varieties and their associated (perceived) cultures.

References

Aldekoa, A., Manterola, I., & Idiazabal, I. (2020). A trilingual teaching sequence for oral presentation skills in Basque, Spanish and English. *The Language Learning Journal*, *48*(3), 259–271. https://doi.org/10.1080/09571736.2020.1741666

Alvear, S. A. (2019). The additive advantage and bilingual programs in a large urban school district. *American Educational Research Journal*, *56*(2), 477–513. https://doi.org/10.3102/0002831218800986

Baker, C., & Wright, W. E. (2021). *Foundations of bilingual education and bilingualism* (7th ed.). Multilingual Matters.

Bauer, E. B., Colomer, S. E., & Wiemelt, J. (2020). Biliteracy of African American and Latinx kindergarten students in a dual-language program: Understanding students' translanguaging practices across informal assessments. *Urban Education*, *55*(3), 331–361. https://doi.org/10.1177/0042085918789743

Beeman, K., & Urow, C. (2012). *Teaching for biliteracy: Strengthening bridges between languages*. Caslon Publishing.

Bernstein, K. A., Katznelson, N., Amezcua, A., Mohamed, S., & Alvarado, S. L. (2020). Equity/social justice, instrumentalism/neoliberalism: Dueling discourses of dual language in principals' talk about their programs. *TESOL Quarterly*, *54*(3), 652–684. https://doi.org/10.1002/tesq.582

Block, N. (2011). The impact of two-way dual-immersion programs on initially English-dominant Latino students' attitudes. *Bilingual Research Journal*, *34*(2), 125–141. doi.org/10.1080/15235882.2011.598059

Cervantes-Soon, C., Dorner, L., Palmer, D., Heiman, D., Schwerdtfeger, R., & Choi, J. (2017). Combating inequalities in two-way language immersion programs: Toward critical consciousness in bilingual education spaces. *Review of Research in Education*, *41*, 403–427.

Chik, C., & Wright, W. E. (2017). Overcoming the obstacles: Vietnamese and Khmer heritage language programs in California. In O. Kagan, M. Carreira, & C. Chik (Eds.), *A handbook on heritage language education: From innovation to program building* (pp. 222–236). Routledge.

Coady, M. (2020). *The coral way bilingual program*. Multilingual Matters.

Crawford, J. (2004). *Educating English learners: Language diversity in the classroom* (5th ed.). Bilingual Education Services, Inc.

de Courcy, M. (2002). *Learners' experiences of immersion education: Case studies of French and Chinese* (Vol. 32). Multilingual Matters.

de Courcy, M., Warren, J., & Burston, M. (2002). Children from diverse backgrounds in an immersion programme. *Language and Education*, *16*(2), 112–127.

de Jong, E. J. (2011). *Foundations for multilingualism in education: From principles to practice*. Caslon Publishing.

Escamilla, K., Hopewell, S., Butvilofsky, S., Sparrow, W., Soltero-González, L., Ruiz-Figueroa, & Escamilla, M. (2013). *Biliteracy from the start: Literacy squared in action*. Caslon.

Freeman, R. D. (1998). *Bilingual education and social change*. Multilingual Matters.

Freire, J. A., & Delavan, M. G. (2021). The fiftyfication of dual language education: One-size-fits-all language allocation's "equality" and "practicality" eclipsing a history of equity. *Language Policy*, *20*(3), 351–381. https://doi.org/10.1007/s10993-021-09579-z

Freire, J. A., Valdez, V. E., & Delvan, M. G. (2017). The (dis)inclusion of Latina/o interests from Utah's dual language education boom. *Journal of Latinos and Education*, *16*(4), 276–289.

Frieson, B. L., & Scalise, M. (2021). Linguistic artistry and flexibility in dual-language bilingual classrooms: Young Black children's language and literacy practices. *Bilingual Research Journal*, *44*(2), 213–230. doi.org/10.1080/15235882.2021.1942323

García, O. (2009). *Bilingual education in the 21st Century: A global perspective*. Wiley-Blackwell.

García, O., Johnson, S. I., & Seltzer, K. (2016). *Translanguaging classrooms: Leveraging student bilingualism for learning*. Caslon Publishing.

García, O., & Kleyn, T. (2016). *Translanguaging with multilingual students: Learning from classroom moments*. Routledge.

García, O., & Li, W. (2014). *Translanguaging: Language, bilingualism, and education*. Palgrave Macmillan.

Genesee, F., & Lambert, W. E. (1983). Trilingual education for majority-language children. *Child Development*, *54*(1), 105–114.

Gómez, L., Freeman, D. E., & Freeman, Y. S. (2005). Dual language education: A promising 50–50 model. *Bilingual Research Journal*, *29*(1), 145–164.

Grivet, C. S., Haj-Broussard, M., & Broomé, R. (2021). School administrators' perspectives of French immersion programs. *Foreign Language Annals*, *54*(1), 114–138. https://doi.org/10.1111/flan.12512

Henderson, K. I., & Palmer, D. K. (2020). *Dual language bilingual education: Teacher cases and perspectives on large-scale implementation*. Multilingual Matters.

Henn-Reinke, K. (2012). *Considering trilingual education*. Routledge.

Hinton, K. A. (2015). "We only teach in English": An examination of bilingual-in-name-only classrooms. *Research on Preparing Inservice Teachers to Work Effectively with Emergent Bilinguals*, 24, 265–289. https://doi.org/10.1108/S1479-368720150000024012

Howard, E., Lindholm-Leary, K., Rogers, D., Olague, N., Medina, J., Kennedy, B., ... & Christian, D. (2018). *Guiding principles for dual language education* (3rd ed.). Center for Applied Linguistics.

Jaumont, F. (2017). *The bilingual revolution: The future of education is in two languages*. TBR Books.

Keefer, N., & Haj-Broussard, M. (2020). Language in educational contexts. *Journal of Culture and Values in Education*, *3*(2), 1–12. https://doi.org/10.46303/jcve.2020.9

Kimura-Gorecki, K. L. (1996). Bilingual policies are affected by alternative programs and public opinion: A study of alternative bilingual programs and public opinion in California from 1994-1996. *Theses Digitization Project*. 1153. https://scholarworks.lib.csusb.edu/etd-project/1153

Lee, J. S., Lee, W., & Sun, H. (2021). Raciolinguistic positioning of language models in a Korean-English dual language immersion classroom. In N. Flores, A. Tseng, & N. C. Subtirelu (Eds.), *Bilingualism for all? Raciolinguistic perspectives on dual language education in the United States* (pp. 177–198). Multilingual Matters.

Lee, J. S., & Wang, T. (2021). A review of Korean/English and Mandarin/English dual language programs in the United States. *Language Teaching for Young Learners*, *3*(1), 28–65. https://doi.org/10.1075/ltyl.19020.lee

Lindholm-Leary, K. J. (1994). Promoting positive cross-cultural attitudes and perceived competence in culturally and linguistically diverse classrooms. In R. A. DeVillar, C. J. Faltis, & J. P. Cummins (Eds.), *Cultural diversity in schools: From rhetoric to practice* (pp. 189–206). State University of New York Press.

Lyons, J. (1995). The past and future directions of federal bilingual education policy. In O. Garcia & C. Baker (Eds.), *Policy and practice in bilingual education: Extending the foundations* (pp. 1–15). Multilingual Matters.

Malakoff, M., & Hakuta, K. (1990). History of language minority education in the United States. In A. M. Padilla, H. H. Fairchild, & C. M. Valadez (Eds.), *Bilingual education: Issues and strategies* (pp. 27–45). SAGE Publications.

Martínez, R. A. (2017). Dual language education and the erasure of Chicanx, Latinx, and indigenous Mexican children. *Texas Education Review*, *5*(1), 81–92. https://journals.tdl.org/txedrev/index.php/txedrev/article/download/31/25

McCarty, T. L. (2018). So that any child may succeed: Indigenous pathways toward justice and the promise of Brown. *Educational Researcher*, *47*(5), 271–283. https://doi.org/10.3102/0013189X18768549

Moore, S. C. K. (2021). *A history of bilingual education in the US: Examining the politics of language policymaking*. Multilingual Matters.

Morales, P. Z., Saravia, L. A., & Pérez-Iribe, M. F. (2019). Multilingual Mexican-origin students' perspectives on their indigenous heritage language. *Association of Mexican American Educators Journal, 13*(2). https://doi.org/10.24974/amae.13.2.430

Morita-Mullaney, T., Renn, J., & Chiu, M. M. (2020). Obscuring equity in dual language bilingual education: A longitudinal study of emergent bilingual achievement, course placements, and grades. *TESOL Quarterly, 54*(3), 685–718. https://doi.org/10.1002/tesq.592

Palmer, D. K., & Lynch, A. W. (2008). A bilingual education for a monolingual test? The pressure to prepare for TAKS and its influence on choices for language of instruction in Texas elementary bilingual classrooms. *Language Policy, 7*(3), 217–235. https://doi.org/10.1007/s10993-008-9100-0

Palmer, D. K., Zuñiga, C. E., & Henderson, K. I. (2015). A dual language revolution in the United States? On the bumpy road from compensatory to enrichment education for bilingual children in the United States. In W. E. Wright, S. Boun, & O. Garcia (Eds.), *Handbook of bilingual and multilingual education* (pp. 449–460). Wiley-Blackwell.

Paris, D., & Alim, H. S. (Eds.). (2017). *Culturally sustaining pedagogies: Teaching and learning for justice in a changing world.* Teachers College Press.

Phakeng, M. S., Planas, N., Bose, A., & Njurai, E. (2018). Teaching and learning mathematics in trilingual classrooms. In R. Hunter (Ed.), *Mathematical discourse that breaks barriers and creates space for marginalized learners* (pp. 277–293). BRILL. https://doi.org/10.1163/9789004378735_014

Przymus, S. D., & Huddleston, G. (2021). The hidden curriculum of monolingualism: Understanding metonymy to interrogate problematic representations of raciolinguistic identities in schoolscapes. *International Journal of Multicultural Education, 23*(1), 67–86. https://doi.org/10.18251/ijme.v23i1.2435

Ruiz, R. (1984). Orientations in language planning. *NABE Journal, 8*(2), 15–34.

Ruiz, R. (2010). Reorienting language-as-resource. In J. E. Petrovic (Ed.), *International perspectives on bilingual education: Policy, practice, and controversy* (pp. 155–172). Information Age Publishing.

Sánchez, M. T., García, O., & Solorza, C. (2017). Reframing language allocation policy in dual language bilingual education. *Bilingual Research Journal, 41*(1), 37–51. https://doi.org/10.1080/15235882.2017.1405098

Sayer, P. (2013). Translanguaging, TexMex, and bilingual pedagogy: Emergent bilinguals learning through the vernacular. *TESOL Quarterly, 47*(1), 63–88.

Soler, G. I., & Fuentes, R. (2021). Navigating a policy vacuum in the new Latino diaspora: Teaching Spanish as a heritage language in Tennessee high schools. *Foreign Language Annals, 54*(1), 91–113. doi.org/10.1111/flan.12505

Starr, R. L. (2017). *Sociolinguistic variation and acquisition in two-way language immersion: Negotiating the standard.* Multilingual Matters.

Sung, K., & Tsai, H.-M. (2019). *Mandarin Chinese dual language immersion programs.* Multilingual Matters.

Thomas, W. P., & Collier, V. (2012). *Dual language education for a transformed world.* Dual Langauge Education of New Mexico – Fuente Press.

Umansky, I. M., & Reardon, S. F. (2014). Reclassification patterns among Latino English learner students in bilingual, dual immersion, and English immersion classrooms. *American Educational Research Journal, 51*(5), 879–912. https://doi.org/10.3102/0002831214545110

Valentino, R. A., & Reardon, S. F. (2015). Effectiveness of four instructional programs designed to serve English learners: Variation by ethnicity and initial English proficiency. *Educational Evaluation and Policy Analysis, 37*(4), 612–637. https://doi.org/10.3102/0162373715573310

Wang, L., & Kirkpatrick, A. (2019). *Trilingual education in Hong Kong primary schools*. Springer.

Warhol, L. (2011). Native American language education as policy-in-practice: An interpretative policy analysis of the native American languages act of 1990/1992. *International Journal of Bilingual Education and Bilingualism*, *14*(3), 279–299. https://doi.org/10.1080/13670050.2010.486849

Weeks, K. K. (2021). *Tri means three: A comparative study of bilingual and trilingual methods in third grade reading achievement scores in Texas school districts* (Order No. 28416143). Available from ProQuest Dissertations & Theses Global. (2540466388). https://www.proquest.com/dissertations-theses/tri-means-three-comparative-study-bilingual/docview/2540466388/se-2?accountid=13360

Wright, W. E. (2005). *Evolution of federal policy and implications of No Child Left Behind for language minority students* (EPSL-0501-101-LPRU). Tempe, AZ. http://nepc.colorado.edu/publication/evolution-federal-policy-and-implications-no-child-left-behind-for-language-minority-stu

Wright, W. E. (2019). *Foundations for teaching English language learners: Research, theory, policy and practice* (3rd ed.). Caslon.

Wright, W. E., & Chan, V. (2019). Multilingualism in North America. In S. Montanari & S. Quay (Eds.), *Multidisciplinary perspectives on multilingualism: The fundamentals* (pp. 77–100). De Gruyter Mouton.

6

A FRAMEWORK FOR SUCCESS

Dual Language Education Building Blocks

Sonia W. Soltero

Introduction

For the past two decades, interest in dual language education (DLE) has grown exponentially across the United States as evidenced by increased statewide initiatives (e.g., Utah, Delaware, Washington, Indiana) and districtwide implementation (e.g., NYC Department of Education, Portland Public Schools, Dallas ISD, Elgin School District U-46). While the desire to expand access to DLE to more students is laudable, districts and schools cannot ensure program quality and sustainability without comprehensive program planning and ongoing self-evaluation. Building a shared understanding of what constitutes effective DLE is essential for creating programs of high academic quality, which are sustainable over time and generate the highest academic, bilingual/biliterate, and cross-cultural student outcomes.

The elements in the *Dual Language Building Blocks* discussed in this chapter are grounded in current and seminal research in the fields of bilingual education, bilingualism/biliteracy, second language acquisition, and sociocultural education. While much of the research in the field tends to focus on classroom practice, an increasing body of literature is helping to inform the development and implementation of effective bilingual education programs. The research points to decision-making processes both at the school and system levels that best enhance learning experiences and outcomes for multilingual learners (Arias & Fee, 2018; de Jong, 2014; Scanlan & López, 2012; Scanlan et al., 2019; Soltero, 2016, 2018; Tedick & Björklund, 2014). The *Building Blocks* provide a macro-level road map to guide districts and schools in designing, planning, implementation, and improvement of DLE

DOI: 10.4324/9781003269076-10

programs. They can also be leveraged as an advocacy tool for promoting access, equity, and integration for developing bilinguals who are acquiring English as a second language.

The *Dual Language Building Blocks* are contextualized around the *why*, *what*, *who*, *how*, and *when* of program design and implementation. The *why* lays out the rationale for effective DLE and how it can elevate developing bilinguals (English learners) and their communities in leveraging the linguistic and culturally diverse demographics of the United States. Behind the *why* are the cognitive, academic, economic, and sociocultural advantages of developing bi-multilingualism and bi-multiliteracy in school, juxtaposed with the increasing demands for a multiliterate workforce. The *what* describes the goals, models, and characteristics of effective culturally responsive DLE. The *how* represents the essence of the *Building Blocks* that explain key aspects necessary for creating sustainable high-quality programs. Embedded in the building blocks are the *who* and the *when* that need to be considered by districts and schools in gaging staff and leadership capacity to carry out implementation and sustainability efforts.

The Why: Demographic Context and the Benefits of Multilingualism

Demographics and Linguistic Capital

Multilingualism is widespread around the world in large part because of the rise in global digital communication, growth in international travel and commerce, and increased migration. Grosjean (2021) reports that an estimated half of the world's population is at least bilingual, with many being multilingual. The boost in multilingualism and multiliteracy is also a result of more people around the world choosing to educate their children in a second language (L2), particularly in the most populous languages: English, Spanish, Chinese, and Arabic.

The number of speakers of languages other than English (LOTE) in the United States has tripled since 1980 with 67.3 million in 2018. Seven home languages have more than a million speakers each: Spanish (41.5 million), Chinese (3.5 million), Tagalog (1.8 million), Vietnamese (1.5 million), Arabic (1.3 million), French (1.2 million), and Korean (1.1 million) (Zeigler & Camarota, 2019). The largest increases are in states that have not historically had large populations of bilinguals. Spanish remains the most spoken home language other than English in the United States with more Spanish speakers than in any country in Latin America except for Mexico, Colombia, and Argentina.

The plurilingual tapestry of the United States is made up of a rich variety of languages: First Nations languages like Navajo, Yupik, Cree, Ojibwe;

indigenous languages from other parts of the world, such as Nahuatl, Quichua, Mam; creole languages like Haitian Kreyòl, Jamaican Patois, Cape Verdean Creole; low incidence languages like Karen, Swahili, Samoan; populous languages, such as Chinese, Spanish, Hindi, Arabic; as well as American Sign Language and American English dialects. These linguistic diversities present exciting opportunities for expanding DLE in more languages and as pipelines for increasing the bilingual education and world language teacher and leadership workforce in those languages. While the United States is without a doubt rich in linguistic diversity, the recent decline in new immigration coupled with an accelerated shift to English has created an urgent need for systemic opportunities for students to develop high levels of bi-multilingualism and bi-multiliteracy in PK-12 schools and higher education.

Benefits of a Multiliterate Society

de Jong et al. (2019) broaden Ruiz's (1984) influential language planning orientations that view language either as a problem, as a right, or as a resource, by proposing a fourth paradigm. They posit that "The bi/multilingualism-as-a-resource orientation extends Ruiz's notion of language as a resource to explicitly address a bi/multilingual perspective that highlights the benefits of bi/multilingualism for the individual, the community, and for society" (p. 115). Research points to significant economic and career advantages for bi-multiliterate individuals, including increased employment opportunities, career advancement, and higher wages (Callahan & Gándara, 2014). Bilingual workers typically earn more than monolingual counterparts, especially in areas where demand for bilinguals is high. Bilinguals were found to earn higher wages even when they did not use their bilingual skills for work purposes. In these cases, employers perceived them as having additional desirable skills just for being bilingual (Christofides & Swidinsky, 2010). Market analysts in the United States indicate increasing demands for bilingual, biliterate, and bicultural professionals, especially in high density Latino and Asian areas.

The growing recognition that proficiency in more than one language benefits both individuals and society is backed by extensive research in education, neuroscience, sociolinguistics economics, and political science (Bialystok, 2011; Callahan & Gándara, 2014; Krizman et al., 2012). Increasing the number of high school students who graduate with multilingual and multiliterate proficiency and skills enhances their economic competitiveness, advances intercultural competences and intergroup relations, and strengthens political stability and national security. Bi-multiliteracy, the ability to read and write in two or more languages, increases these advantages exponentially (Soltero, 2016).

The Seal of Biliteracy is another compelling argument for implementing DLE across the PK-12 grade span. The Seal is an official recognition awarded by a state's Department of Education to students who demonstrate biliterate competencies in a LOTE and in English on a normed-reference language test in their senior year of high school. Students who earn this distinction have the Seal officially recorded in their diplomas and high school transcripts. California was the first state that legislated the Seal of Biliteracy in 2011, and by 2022, all but one state has made it a state law. Many districts also confer Seal of Biliteracy Pathway Awards in elementary and middle schools that recognize and celebrate students' progress toward acquiring biliteracy. Care must be taken to ensure students who are developing English as their L2 have ample opportunities to earn the Seal and not prioritize English-dominant students in world language programs (Heineke & Davin, 2020).

Cognitive and Academic Benefits of Being Bilingual and Biliterate

Research findings confirm the many cognitive benefits of bilingualism. The most compelling conclusions are that bilinguals, when compared to monolinguals, have better executive functioning in cognitive processing, higher attention control, and can better cope with neurological diseases (Bialystok, 2011). Neuroscientists and psycholinguists' research point to a "bilingual advantage" and the positive effects of acquiring two languages as well as the wide-ranging capacity of the human brain to learn multiple languages. Evidence suggests that the use of two languages by bilinguals helps them "fine-tune" their auditory nervous system and to juggle language in ways that improve attention and working memory (Krizman et al., 2012).

Bialystok et al. (2012) research on the effects of bilingualism on cognitive functions found that bilinguals, compared to monolinguals, perceive differences and hold attention longer because they have a more efficient and developed executive control. Their findings suggest that bilinguals perform better on cognitive tasks using different brain networks that lead to improved working memory, more effective multitasking, and increased inhibition of irrelevant information. They conclude that "lifelong experience in managing attention in two languages reorganizes specific brain networks, creating a more effective basis for executive control and sustaining better cognitive performance throughout the lifespan" (p. 241).

Research conducted during the past two decades consistently found that students who participate in well-designed and well-implemented DLE programs for an extended time show significant biliterate and academic gains (de Jong, 2014; de Jong & Bearse, 2014; Howard & Sugarman, 2007; Lindholm-Leary, 2016; Lindholm-Leary & Block, 2010; Lindholm-Leary & Borsato, 2005, 2006; Lindholm-Leary & Hernández, 2011; Soltero, 2016, 2018; Steele et al., 2017; Thomas & Collier, 2015). DLE students perform at or above grade level on standardized reading and math tests in English;

score on par with their statewide peers by fifth-to-seventh grades, if not sooner; achieve at or above grade level in reading and math tests measured in the L2; and close the achievement gap by about fifth grade in comparison to students in English-only programs. Studies focusing on middle and high schools concluded that, compared to their counterparts in general education programs, DLE students are as or more likely to be enrolled in higher level math courses; as or more likely to pass high school exit exams; less likely to drop out of school; and more likely to close the achievement gap by the end of high school (Lindholm-Leary, 2012). The significant increase of DLE programs across the United States is "due in large part to the strong research base that has consistently demonstrated the benefits of immersion education" (Tedick et al., 2011, p. 5). These research findings offer critical foundations for challenging uninformed ideologies and misguided practices.

The What: Dual Language Education

DLE, sometimes referred to as bilingual immersion, is an additive language model within the broader umbrella of bilingual education with a subset of model types characterized by:

- differences in scope of program implementation (a school strand or whole school)
- student language population served (one-way or two-way)
- language allocation (50-50, 80-20, or 90-10)
- language of initial literacy instruction (sequential or simultaneous)
- classroom organization (self-contained or team-teaching).

Regardless of model type, three universal goals guide DLE: (1) bi/multilingual and bi/multiliterate proficiencies; (2) academic achievement; (3) cross-cultural competencies. These goals serve as the compass for all decision-making and guide how programs are structured within the specific needs, demographics, and circumstances of each school (Soltero, 2016; Tedick & Lyster, 2020). Maintaining the highest levels of program quality and effectiveness requires that districts and schools ensure certain foundational programmatic elements remain in place, including qualified and committed teachers; knowledgeable school leaders; district policies that align with dual language principles; linguistic and culturally responsive curriculum, instruction, materials, and assessments; and family and community engagement and support.

Integrity of DLE: Prioritizing English Learners

As with other "innovative" education trends that either by design or happenstance become selective programs privileging higher income English-speaking students, two-way DLE, when unchecked, may favor the linguistic needs and desires of the dominant group over the academic and linguistic needs of students who are developing English as their new language (Cortina et al., 2015; Freire & Alemán, 2021; Hernández, 2017; Valdez et al., 2016). Guadalupe Valdés (1997) brought to light these very risks over two decades ago, cautioning that two-way programs must ensure English learners' language and culture do not become a commodity for the benefit of the dominant English-speaking group. Similarly, Valdez et al. (2016) argue that the "gentrification" of DLE poses a dangerous trend that dilutes the equity effects of DLE. They contend that if we are not careful, it "may soon constitute the next wave of inequitably distributed enrichment education in the U.S. by following a broader pattern of enrichment tracking practices, such as in gifted and talented programs and STEM programs that have tended to further privilege already privileged students" (p. 604).

To avoid potentially damaging consequences for English learners in two-way programs, school leaders and educators must address these power differentials in concrete ways. Cortina et al. (2015) advise schools "to address the power imbalance ... so that such programs do not become merely foreign language programs for the more affluent students" (p. 11). When these power differentials are minimized, two-way dual language programs can serve as the conduit for authentic cultural and social class integration. Palmer and Martínez (2013) add that professional development includes "a more critically contextualized understanding of the power dynamics that operate in bilingual classroom contexts" (p. 269).

The How, Who, and When: Dual Language Building Blocks

Increasing number of states have undertaken districtwide expansion of DLE programs but not always with the necessary planning and development of infrastructure that ensures quality and sustainability. In a large-scale study of DLE in Portland Oregon, Steele et al. (2017) conclude that en masse DLE program expansion is likely to diminish their quality if districts are not careful about program planning and implementation. They add that "efforts to scale beyond the level adopted by Portland would entail many logistical and staffing challenges, and the promise of immersion may be squandered if efforts are not put in place to ensure program quality" (p. 303).

Program development involves a full year of planning; comprehensive needs-assessments and ongoing program evaluation; DLE school and district long-term strategic plan; modifying existing English-centric instructional materials, curriculum, and assessments; adequate district personnel to support new and continuing DLE programs; emphasis on the needs of English learners; systems of support; and extensive family engagement (Alfaro & Hernández, 2018; Lindholm-Leary, 2012; Soltero, 2016, 2021).

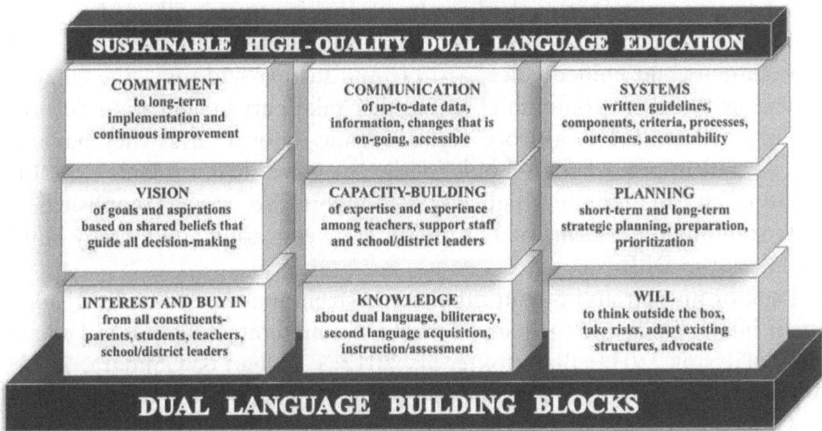

Figure 6.1 Dual Language Building Blocks

Determining whether a school has the necessary conditions to start a program is revealed through a needs-assessment of existing infrastructures, resources, and availability of licensed/endorsed bilingual teachers. A significant factor in achieving the highest academic, linguistic, and cultural outcomes for students depends on well-designed, adequately resourced, and carefully implemented programs (Alanís & Rodriguez, 2019). The *Dual Language Building Blocks* (Figure 6.1) provide a framework for school and district leaders, teachers, and other educators to establish long-term program effectiveness and maintain high quality standards. Starting from the bottom and moving up, each block is examined from left to right in more detail in the section below.

Interest and Buy-In

Buy-in is defined as the acceptance of and willingness to actively support and participate in support a new or existing undertaking, while stakeholders are typically characterized as groups that affect or are affected by that undertaking. Stakeholders who have buy-in around DLE become essential allies and collaborators, while those that lack buy-in can pose serious roadblocks to effective long-term implementation.

Because DLE programs do not work well in isolation, buy-in must come both from within the school (micro level) as well as external to the local setting (macro level). Cortina et al. (2015) refer to "community as a network of actors" made up of school/district leaders, teachers, parents, education groups, community education agencies, and other affiliated organizations. The authors maintain that this network of actors must work together "to evidence a commitment to the long haul, dual language will need to move with these alliances and population shifts and continue to strengthen with their support and unified voice" (p. 11) and further add that "the empowerment networks of community actors that take part in education decision making ... have led to a process of academic innovation as they have reshaped and improved the schools' design to serve their students" (p. 14). Creating and maintaining high levels of buy-in are best accomplished by understanding the benefits of a bi-multiliterate education and thereby building interest in DLE.

Lack of interest and buy-in often comes from inadequate understanding about bilingualism and the many benefits of a biliterate/multicultural education (Bialystok, 2011; Bialystok et al., 2012; Callahan & Gándara, 2014). Additionally, resistance or opposition to bilingual education tends to focus on concerns around funding, students' academic progress in English, staffing, and a desire to maintain the English-centric status quo (Mehisto & Genesee, 2015; Zamudio et al., 2011). Therefore, a starting point in program planning is determining levels of interest from the school community, including families, teachers, support staff, school leaders as well as central office administrators. This can be accomplished through surveys, town halls, and focus groups. The preliminary interest-baseline that results from this analysis helps to identify those areas that require additional efforts in building buy-in. It is important to note that initial enthusiasm for DLE may diminish over time due to changes in school and district staff, leadership, demographics, and state/district mandates (Boyle et al., 2015). A reboot in buy-in and interest is sometimes needed for long-established programs to ensure continued commitment and consistency in the face of changes that may undermine its effectiveness and longevity.

Knowledge

Interest and buy-in are predicated on the level of knowledge that the school community has about the theoretical and research underpinnings of DLE, multilingualism, bi-multiliteracy, and culturally responsive education (Block, 2011; Feinauer & Howard, 2014). Misconceptions abound about the predominance of English above all else, and the English-centric belief that students must assimilate linguistically and culturally to be academically successful (Bunch, 2013; García, 2009; Hernández, 2017). Many incorrect assumptions continue to persist about bilingualism and bilingual education including that bilingualism causes confusion in children; an L2 is acquired quickly; native language instruction is detrimental to or delays developing academic English; and English learners require heavy doses of discreet skills in English (Escamilla et al., 2022; Soltero, 2011). Misinformation about the acquisition process of an L2 and the development of bilingualism has serious implications for pedagogical decisions and policy at both the micro and macro levels (Genesee, 2018). When teachers and school leaders have extensive knowledge of culturally and linguistically responsive instruction and assessment practices, the school community and district leadership are better positioned to function from a shared understanding that informs sound decision-making (Goulah & Soltero, 2015).

A solid knowledge base prepares educators and leaders to fully understand the complexities involved in creating quality sustainable DLE programs and positions them to effectively advocate for DLE. Advocacy efforts include networking, participating in policymaking, creating advocacy plans, and building knowledge at all levels. Strategies to do the latter can be achieved by ensuring that those with DLE expertise are at the district "decision-making table".

Alfaro and Bartolomé's (2017) notion of "ideological clarity" is important in knowledge-building and advocacy efforts. Ideological clarity refers to a continual process in which teachers analyze their own understandings of the status quo and how it compares to institutionalized inequities and prejudices. This in turn helps them to develop self-awareness about their own beliefs and biases that may perpetuate injustices for marginalized groups and uphold privileges for the dominant group. Teachers and school leaders are uniquely positioned to apply their own ideological clarity to create democratic and safe environments for their students. Alfaro and Hernández (2018) add that "Equity gives DLE teachers a lens to filter how they can apply their ideological clarity to create safe and democratic environments, examine group member participation, and balance the status of language with instruction. It is not easy for a bilingual teacher to maintain social equity within the classroom since the English language is the language that represents power in the United States" [translation, p. 491].

Research highlights the critical role of ongoing professional development that engages educators in the co-construction of knowledge (Boyle et al., 2015; de Jong, 2014; Feinauer & Howard, 2012; Lindholm-Leary, 2012; Palmer & Martínez, 2013; Palmer et al., 2019; Soltero, 2011). Yaden (2019) asserts that a cycle of continuous learning is an effective approach to promoting "collective inquiry that leads to practical application of the learning" (p. 79). She argues that coordinated professional learning through structured networks of DLE schools with similar educational mission creates shared learning experiences and facilitates a more "focused, relevant, and participant-centered" professional development approach. Creating a multiyear professional development plan that includes ongoing opportunities for professional inquiry and learning, partnering with universities, peer observations, and visiting established DLE schools, helps to expand the knowledge base and build capacity.

Will

School leaders, district administrators, and classroom teachers frequently face pressures from shifting mandates and policy demands, particularly around high-stakes assessments and adoptions of curricular programs that often contradict foundational principles of DLE (Menken, 2017; Menken & Solorza, 2015; Roque et al., 2016; Soltero, 2016; Tedick & Lyster, 2020). For DLE programs to be successful, educators and educational leaders must think outside and beyond the English-centric box and shift to a multilingual, biliterate/multiliterate, and culturally responsive educational paradigm. This necessitates what Souto-Manning et al. (2016) call "courageous leadership" in which school/district leaders take an active role in contradicting negative assumptions by demonstrating positive outcomes of well-planned and well-supported DLE programs. Menken (2017) adds that "for school leaders to successfully implement and sustain dual language bilingual education programs, they must be able to negotiate and resist top-down policies and external pressures promoting English-only instruction" (p. 3).

Even though DLE has become an increasingly desirable alternative to English-only or transitional bilingual education schooling, the fact remains that we live in a racially divisive time that fuels anti-immigrant sentiments and assimilationist policies (Callahan & Gándara, 2014; Christian, 2018; Genesee, 2018). Advocacy is particularly pertinent at this inflection point as we contend with persistent English-centric narrow views of education, literacy, and assessment, the dangers of DLE "gentrification", and an ever-increasing rate of bilingual teacher burn-out (Amanti, 2019; Freire & Alemán, 2021). Engagement in advocacy efforts guards against incompatible district and state policies that weaken DLE goals and outcomes (Christian, 2018; Soltero, 2016).

According to Boyle et al. (2015), "The development, implementation, and sustainability of dual language programs depend heavily on the policy environment in which they function. The range of allowable program types, support mechanisms, and funding are generally dictated by state level rules" (p. xvii). The report points to inconsistencies in policies across states around funding formulas, teacher licensure requirements, restrictive vs additive language programs, reporting and definitions of bilingual and DLE models, as well as standardized assessments and other metrics.

The will to "lead with courage" in the face of these challenges requires district/school leaders to adjust existing policies and expectations in ways that align with the foundational premises of DLE. Key areas include reducing the amount of testing; utilizing assessments in LOTEs; removing the high-stakes nature of standardized assessments; extending the time to demonstrate academic results on standardized tests to align with the length of time it takes to develop academic L2; adopting authentic LOTE curricular programs and instructional materials; and using curriculum and materials that are specially designed for L2 development.

Vision

Tedick and Lyster (2020) assert that well-informed and knowledgeable leadership are uniquely positioned to "develop and communicate a school-wide shared vision for the program and for the promotion of bilingualism and biliteracy and ensure that there is a plan to bring that vision to fruition" (p. 43). Facilitating the formulation of both district and school vision statements is most effectively done in collaboration with a representative cross-section of the district/school community that includes school/district leaders, teachers, support staff, students, parents/families, and members of the community. Scanlan and López (2015) add that school communities should also engage in "regenerating" their vision and mission statements. They posit that unlike revising or updating the vision, regenerating implies a more comprehensive renewal or restoration of the school's beliefs, values, and aspirations that align with linguistically and culturally responsive education.

Research on organizational effectiveness point to the critical role that collaboratively generated vision statements play on their long-term sustainability (Bennis & Nanus, 1985; Stemler et al., 2011). Generally, vision and mission statements are developed to (1) facilitate coherence within an organization by providing direction and purpose; (2) serve as a checks-and-balances mechanism; (3) guide organizational decision-making; and (4) give meaning to work that inspires and motivates members of an organization (Braun et al., 2012). A vision statement describes a "long-term, future-oriented, and comprehensive view" that focuses on the big picture and is intended to be both aspirational and inspirational, while the mission delineates specific objectives and tasks to accomplish the vision.

Vision and mission statements are based on a set of shared beliefs that represent the school/district goals and desires, guide decision-making, and provide a sense of purpose and direction for the entire school and district community (Hunt, 2011; Scanlan & López, 2015; Soltero, 2011). These statements should highlight language and cultural diversity as valuable assets and resources that strengthen students' views about themselves and others while developing their bi-multiliterate, sociocultural, and academic competencies. The degree to which DLE is reflected in the school/district vision shows the extent of the commitment to the program.

Capacity-Building

Decades of research have emphasized the critical role that well-prepared and committed teachers and school leaders play in program quality and effectiveness (Genesee, 2018; Goulah & Soltero, 2015; Menken, 2017; Soltero, 2018; Tedick & Lyster, 2020). The most effective and successful DLE programs are guided by dedicated teachers, visionary district leaders, and long-term districtwide commitment (Alanís & Rodríguez, 2008; DeMatthews & Izquierdo, 2018; Menken, 2017; Soltero, 2016; Tedick & Lyster, 2020). While district leaders have defining roles in decisions around budget allocation, personnel, curriculum, adoption of instructional materials, assessment, family outreach, and so much more, teachers are the fundamental backbone of DLE. District leadership must therefore provide them with the right conditions, resources, and ongoing supports needed to be successful (Bunch, 2013; Menken & Solorza, 2015; Palmer & Martínez, 2013). DLE programs are not easy to implement, not only because they require long-term implementation but also entail additional preparation and curricular content beyond that required of general education classroom teachers. This calls for significant investment of time, energy, and funding to increase the knowledge and expertise of teachers, support staff, and school leaders.

It is vital for districts to create a deliberate teacher and school leader recruitment, hiring, and retention plan. In terms of retention, school leaders should be cognizant of teacher burnout in DLE programs and create organizational systems that minimize teacher fatigue. Amanti (2019) cautions that the heavy lift DLE teachers undertake results in prolonged, overextended, and uncompensated work. She posits that "the unique, often invisible, aspects of the working conditions of DLBE [dual language bilingual education] teachers, whose intersectional identities lend to additional linguistic labor as they navigate the structure, context, and realties of teaching in DLBE programs" (p. 458). It is common for bilingual teachers to spend significant time creating their own materials in the LOTE, translating English-only mandated district curriculum, and supplementing text adoptions with linguistic and culturally authentic materials. In addition, bilingual teachers are often tapped outside of their classrooms to translate school documents and/or serve as interpreters for families. These conditions are particularly acute in newly launched programs.

In their national report on DLE, Boyle et al. (2015) concluded that "Hiring qualified and skilled teachers with appropriate levels of language proficiency is essential to the effectiveness of any dual language program. However, the rising number of programs around the country and a scarcity of teachers with the necessary language skills has led to a shortage of qualified dual language teachers" (p. 78). Given these shortages and the challenges in recruiting qualified bilingual teachers, it becomes imperative that districts and schools create deliberate structures to retain them. Key components that ameliorate the additional work that bilingual DLE teachers undertake include weekly structured planning time; remuneration for creating and translating materials; reducing unnecessary work; multiyear targeted and differentiated professional development plan; native language and specialized L2 instructional support from DLE coordinators and bilingual coaches; and public recognition for their additional work.

Planning

DeMatthews and Izquierdo (2016) correctly characterize the planning of DLE as a "messy process" and add that "Rather than rush to implementation by individually drafting a plan or adopting a 'canned or pre-packaged program,' principals must understand that DLE cannot be forced onto families and teachers but must be developed through dialogue and an exploration of school community context and needs" (p. 63). School leaders must navigate numerous challenges to ensure program quality and longevity, including forming a broad range of inclusive support services, ensuring equitable access to all educational opportunities, and understanding funding and policy mechanisms that impact their schools (Genesee, 2018; Menken, 2017). Strategic planning is a systematic and comprehensive process focused on long-term success that entails gathering information, engaging families and communities, conducting school visits, participating in professional development, and creating a plan of action (Alanís & Rodríguez, 2008; Soltero, 2011, 2016).

Schools and districts that engage in comprehensive program planning and design are more apt to show long-term success and consistent gains in students' biliterate academic achievement and increased sociocultural competencies (García, 2009 Howard & Sugarman, 2007; Lindholm-Leary 2012, 2014; Lindholm-Leary & Borsato, 2005, 2006; Lindholm-Leary & Hernández, 2011). Research shows that carefully planned dual language programs are more likely to:

1 Offer high quality cohesive and well-coordinated curriculum and instruction.
2 Attract and retain committed and highly qualified teachers.
3 Generate greater parent/family satisfaction with their children's education.
4 Mitigate economic, societal, and educational inequities through access to and inclusion in rich and engaging additive bilingual education.

Deliberate long-term planning ensures that interdependent organizational aspects of effective and sustainable programs are in alignment. Soltero's (2016) *5Cs* ground planning and implementation around programmatic cohesion, consistency, coordination, compatibility, and commitment. Research indicates that these features characterize sustainable high quality DLE (Arias & Fee, 2018; Collier & Thomas, 2017; de Jong, 2014; Genesee, 2018;

Lindholm-Leary, 2001, 2012; Soltero, 2018; Steele et al., 2018; Tedick & Lyster, 2019).

- *Cohesion:* all curricular areas—LOTE, English, and bilingual language arts, culture, content, learning standards, and assessments—are connected, integrated, and aligned.
- *Consistency:* instructional and curricular elements are evident throughout the program, including compatible instructional approaches, language-appropriate materials, and assessments.
- *Coordination:* across and within grade levels in areas like language allocation, culture curriculum, instructional materials, and family involvement efforts.
- *Compatibility:* all programs within the school complement/enhance each other and have compatible pedagogical philosophy and approaches.
- *Commitment:* further elaborated below as one of the key building blocks.

Effective and sustainable programs engage in at least one full year of planning before implementation. Because decisions about program models are determined by local contexts and demographics, as well as district/state mandates, the planning year is critical in designing a program model that best fits those characteristics. In addition, short-term planning must be accompanied by a long-term strategic plan that looks beyond the first years of implementation.

Commitment

DLE requires long-term commitment because development of bi-multiliteracy, multicultural competencies, and academic achievement can only happen over extended time and across the grade spans. Genesee (2018) highlights that "we know from many years of research that the benefits of dual language take time to materialize ... language is the most complex skill humans acquire and it takes time to become fully proficient in a new language" (p. 137). He adds that "for students to achieve high levels of dual language proficiency in school, educators must create developmentally sound learning environments that are integrated across grade levels" (p. 137). This necessitates macro-level long-term commitment that can withstand conditions such as turnover in district/school leadership, ideological English-centric forces, high-stakes accountability, and misguided pedagogical pressures that hinder program sustainability. Commitment is exemplified by leaders who have the know-how and the will to adapt to changes in school demographics and education policies while adhering to the program's foundational principles.

The inescapable challenge around long-term commitment is how to contend with leadership and policy changes at the school/district level, as well as the constantly evolving broader educational landscape. Cortina et al. (2015) offer Pastor's (2013) ten elements of social movements as a useful tool to conceptualize DLE, focusing on the three most relevant features: (1) a vision and frame; (2) an authentic base in key constituencies; and (3) a commitment to the long haul. The authors suggest that to demonstrate a commitment to this long haul "dual language will need to move with these alliances and population shifts and continue to strengthen with their support and unified voice" (p. 11).

The most effective and sustainable programs have teachers and principals who believe in the value of additive bilingual education; embrace students' and families' languages and cultures; adopt a long-term vision for the program; advocate on its behalf within and outside the school; and are fully committed to its continuous improvement (Alanís & Rodríguez, 2008, 2019; DeMatthews & Izquierdo, 2018; de Jong, 2014; Mehisto & Genesee, 2015; Palmer et al., 2019; Roque et al., 2016; Soltero, 2016). Commitment must be established at all levels of implementation and by all the "network of actors" in the local learning community (families, teachers, support staff, school leaders, and the student themselves) and at the district level. The extent to which the needs of DLE are prioritized in areas like teacher support and mentoring, inclusion of authentic native language material and assessments, equity in allocation of funds, and attention to students' academic and biliterate progress, indicate the level of commitment and long-term investment.

Systems

Successful organizational DLE systems provide implementation parameters and criteria, communicate clarity about expectations and outcomes, set direction for short- and long-term courses of action, ensure alignment across the various elements of DLE, and offer the necessary structures for program continuity and sustainability (Soltero, 2011, 2016). These systems are most effective when created collaboratively with key stakeholders and, in doing so, establish shared understanding and increased buy-in and commitment (DeMatthews & Izquierdo, 2016; Lindholm-Leary, 2012; Scanlan and López, 2015). Written procedures, guidelines, and policies should be disseminated to DLE educators, support staff, and administrators involved in decision-making that affect the program.

These written documents help ensure consistency and cohesion by providing a centralized repository of information that include program description and criteria; program vision/mission; language allocation policies; instructional practices and materials; authentic assessment tools; bilingual homework guidelines; district/state requirements; resources. A "DLE Handbook" is an effective way of housing this information that is easily accessible to teachers, support staff, and school leaders. Because changes in staff are common, having this type of written document is useful in maintaining continuity and abiding by the program's stated criteria and goals.

Communication

Districts and schools are complex organizations with many moving pieces not always well calibrated or aligned. District and school organizational structures tend to be siloed and not set up for effective cross-departmental or cross-program communication (Scanlan et al., 2019; Soltero, 2016). For DLE to be successful, systematic and frequent communication must happen through cross-departmental district collaboration, between district and program leadership, as well as across school programs, grade levels, and content area teachers. Lack of communication often leads to decisions that go against the premises of DLE, unwittingly setting program ups for failure.

Decisions based on the needs of general education programs that pertain to teacher recruitment and hiring, curricular development and planning, districtwide adoption of instructional and intervention programs, assessment tools and mandates, to name a few, frequently do not consider the specialized needs of DLE and result in negative implications for their effectiveness (Lindholm-Leary, 2012; Valero & Makishima, 2019). Districts/schools benefit greatly from systematic ways of sharing up-to-date data, information, and changes in policies/mandates that relate to and impact DLE programming.

Premised on educational organizational research and distributed leadership theory (Spillane, 2012), the *Districtwide Dual Language Decision-Making Framework* (Figure 6.2) outlines a conceptual mapping of areas that have direct impact on program sustainability and quality. At the center of

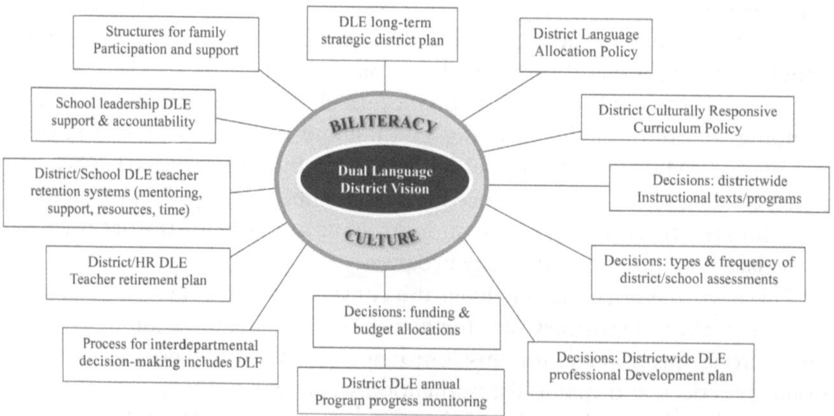

Figure 6.2 Districtwide Dual Language Decision-Making Framework

this decision-making framework is the district's vision for DLE based on the two major aspects that distinguish DLE from other district programs: students' development of bilingualism/biliteracy, and cultural competencies. Areas of consideration include development of a DLE district strategic plan; funding and resource allocation; program progress monitoring, accountability, and supports; teacher and school leader recruitment and retention plan; language allocation policies; culturally responsive curriculum and assessments; district texts adoption and instructional materials; DLE professional development; and interdepartmental decision-making that considers DLE.

Conclusion

DLE has proven to be a promising path toward making the United States a more multiliterate society and to bridge the language and academic inequities that many linguistically diverse communities have historically experienced. Cultivating a multilingual and multiliterate workforce positions us to better respond to the educational, economic, and social needs of our sizable linguistic and culturally diverse population. This calls for districts and schools to offer expanded PK-12 multilingual academic opportunities for all students, but especially for those whose heritage or first language is not English.

The long-term effectiveness of DLE depends on comprehensive program planning, design, implementation, and sustainability. The *Dual Language Building Blocks* described in this chapter, preceded by a summary of the many compelling advantages for students to develop bi-multiliteracy and cultural competencies, provide a framework for creating programs that increase their viability, longevity, and effectiveness. More importantly, well-designed programs can help mitigate the economic, societal, and educational inequities for linguistically diverse students through access to and inclusion in rich and engaging additive bi-multiliterate programs.

Decisions to implement DLE involve comprehensive understandings of the philosophical views and values of a school community regarding diversity, bilingualism, and multiculturalism (Soltero, 2021). Applying Alfaro and Bartolomé's "ideological clarity" to both teachers and educational leaders, we should not lose sight that the critical premise of DLE is access, equity, and inclusion for those students who are most at the margins. When the goals of DLE are perceived to be highly desirable and worth the long-term investment of resources and commitment by schools, communities, and districts, they are more likely to endure and succeed.

References

Alanís, I., & Rodríguez, M. A. (2019). Sustaining a dual language immersion program: Features of success. *Journal of Latinos and Education*, 7(4), 305–319.

Alfaro, C., & Bartolomé, L. (2017). Preparing ideologically clear bilingual teachers honoring working-class non-standard language use in the bilingual education classroom. *Issues in Teacher Education*, *26*(2), 11–34.

Alfaro, C., & Hernández, A. (2018). Un autoanálisis crítico para docentes de la enseñanza bilingüe: Ideología, pedagogía, acceso y equidad (IPAE). A critical self-examination for dual language educators: Ideology, pedagogy, access, and equity (IPAE). *Revista de Sociología de la Educación*, *11*(3), 487–496.

Amanti, C. (2019). The (invisible) work of dual language bilingual education teachers. *Bilingual Research Journal*, *42*(4), 455–470.

Arias, M. B., & Fee, M. (2018). *Profiles of dual language education in the 21st century*. Multilingual Matters.

Bennis, W., & Nanus, B. (1985). *Leaders: The strategies for taking charge*. Harper & Row.

Bialystok, E. (2011). Reshaping the mind: The benefits of bilingualism. *Canadian Journal of Experimental Psychology*, *65*(4), 220–235.

Bialystok, E., Craik, F., & Luk, G. (2012). Bilingualism: Consequences for mind and brain. *Trends in Cognitive Sciences*, *16*(4), 240–250.

Block, N. (2011). The impact of two-way dual-immersion programs on initially English-dominant Latino students' attitudes. *Bilingual Research Journal*, *34*(2), 125–141.

Boyle, A., August, D., Tabaku, L., Cole, S., & Simpson-Baird, A. (2015). *Dual language education programs: Current state policies and practices*. Office of English Language Acquisition, U.S. Department of Education.

Braun, S., Wesche, J. S., Fey, D., Weisweiler, S., & Peus, C. (2012). Effectiveness of mission statements in organizations. A review. *Journal of Management & Organization*, *8*(4), 430–444.

Bunch, G. C. (2013). Pedagogical language knowledge: Preparing mainstream teachers for English learners in the new standards era. *Review of Research in Education*, *37*(1), 298–341.

Callahan, R., & Gándara, P. (2014). *The bilingual advantage: Language, literacy and the US labor market*. Multilingual Matters.

Christian, D. (2018). Making space for dual language education: The role of policy. In M. B. Arias & M. Fee (Eds.), *Profiles of dual language education in the 21st century* (pp. 115–132). Multilingual Matters.

Christofides, L. N., & Swidinsky, R. (2010). The economic returns to the knowledge and use of a second official language: English in Quebec and French in the rest-of-Canada. *Canadian Public Policy/Analyse de Politiques*, *36*(2), 137–158.

Collier, V. P., & Thomas, W. P. (2017). Validating the power of bilingual schooling: Thirty-two years of large-scale, longitudinal research. *Annual Review of Applied Linguistics*, *37*, 203–217.

Cortina, R., Makar, C., & Mount-Cors, M. F. (2015). Dual language as a social movement: Putting languages on a level playing field. *Current Issues in Comparative Education*, *17*(1), 5–16.

de Jong, E. J. (2014). Program design and two-way immersion programs. *Journal of Immersion and Content-Based Language Education*, 2(2), 241–256.

de Jong, E. J., & Bearse, C. I. (2014). Dual language programs as a strand within a secondary school: Dilemmas of school organization and the TWI mission. *International Journal of Bilingual Education and Bilingualism*, *17*(1), 15–31.

de Jong, E. J., Yilmaz, T., & Marichal, N. (2019). A multilingualism-as-a-resource orientation in dual language education. *Theory into Practice*, *5*, 107–120.

DeMatthews, D., & Izquierdo, E. (2016). School leadership for dual language education: A social justice approach. *The Educational Forum*, *80*, 278–293.

DeMatthews, D., & Izquierdo, E. (2018). The importance of principals supporting dual language education: A social justice leadership framework. *Journal of Latinos and Education*, *17*(1), 53–70.

Escamilla, K., Olsen, L., & Slavick, J. (2022). Toward comprehensive effective literacy policy and instruction for English learner/emergent bilingual students. The National Committee on Effective Literacy. Retrieved from https://multilingualliteracy.org/

Feinauer, E., & Howard, E. (2014). Attending to the third goal: Cross-cultural competence and identity development in two-way immersion programs. *Journal of Immersion and Content-Based Language Education*, *2*(2), 257–272.

Freire, J. A., & Alemán, E. Jr. (2021). "Two schools within a school": Elitism, divisiveness, and intra-racial gentrification in a dual language strand. *Bilingual Research Journal*, *44*(2), 249–269.

García, O. (2009). *Bilingual education in the 21st century: A global perspective*. Blackwell.

Genesee, F. (2018). Taking stock: Lessons on dual language education. In M. B. Arias & M. Fee (Eds.), *Profiles of dual language education in the 21st century* (pp. 133–152). Multilingual Matters.

Goulah, J., & Soltero, S. (2015). Reshaping the mainstream education climate through bilingual-bicultural education. In Y. Freeman & D. Freeman (Eds.), *Research on preparing inservice teachers to work effectively with emergent bilinguals: Advances in research in teaching series* (pp. 177–203). Emerald Books.

Grosjean, F. (2021). *Life as a bilingual: Knowing and using two or more languages*. Cambridge University Press.

Heineke, A. J., & Davin, K. J. (2020). Prioritizing multilingualism in U.S. schools: States' policy journeys to enact the Seal of Biliteracy. *Educational Policy*, *34*, 619–643.

Hernández, S. (2017). Are they all language learners? Educational labeling and raciolinguistic identifying in a California middle school dual language program. *The CATESOL Journal*, *29*(1), 133–154.

Howard, E. R., & Sugarman, J. (2007). *Realizing the vision of two-way immersion: Fostering effective programs and classrooms*. Delta Systems.

Hunt, V. (2011). Learning from success stories: Leadership structures that support dual language programs over time in New York City. *International Journal of Bilingual Education and Bilingualism*, *14*(2), 187–206.

Krizman, J., Marian, V., Shook, A., Skoe, E., & Kraus, N. (2012). Subcortical encoding of sound is enhanced in bilinguals and relates to executive function advantages. *PNAS*, *109*(20), 877–881.

Lindholm-Leary, K (2001). *Dual language education*. Multilingual Matters.

Lindholm-Leary, K. (2012). Success and challenges in dual language education. *Theory into Practice*, *51*, 256–262.

Lindholm-Leary, K. (2014). Bilingual and biliteracy skills in young Spanish-speaking low-SES children: Impact of instructional language and primary language proficiency. *International Journal of Bilingual Education and Bilingualism*, 17(2), 144–159.

Lindholm-Leary, K. (2016). Bilingualism and academic achievement in children in dual language programs. In E. Nicoladis & S. Montanari (Eds.), *Bilingualism across the lifespan: Factors moderating language proficiency* (pp. 203–223). American Psychological Association.

Lindholm-Leary, K. J., & Block, N. (2010). Achievement in predominantly low-SES Hispanic dual language schools. *International Journal of Bilingual Education and Bilingualism*, *13*(1), 1–18.

Lindholm-Leary, K., & Borsato, G. (2005). Hispanic high schoolers and mathematics: Follow-up of students who had participated in two-way bilingual elementary programs. *Bilingual Research Journal*, *29*, 641–652.

Lindholm-Leary, K., & Borsato, G. (2006). Academic achievement. In F. Genesee, K. Lindholm-Leary, W. Saunders, & D. Christian (Eds.), *Educating English language learners* (pp. 176–221). Cambridge University Press.

Lindholm-Leary, K., & Hernández, A. (2011). Achievement and language proficiency of Latino students in dual language programmes: Native English speakers, fluent English/previous ELLs, and current ELLs. *Journal of Multilingual and Multicultural Development*, *32*, 531–545.

Mehisto, P. & Genesee, F. (2015). *Building bilingual education systems: Forces, mechanisms, and counterweights*. Cambridge University Press.

Menken, K. (2017). *Leadership in dual language bilingual education*. Center for Applied Linguistics.

Menken, K., & Solorza, C. (2015). Principals as linchpins in bilingual education: The need for prepared school leaders. *International Journal of Bilingual Education and Bilingualism*, *18*(6), 1–22.

Palmer, D., Cervantes-Soon, C., Dorner, L., & Heiman, D. (2019). Bilingualism, biliteracy, biculturalism, and critical consciousness for all: Proposing a fourth fundamental goal for two-way dual language education. *Theory into Practice*, *58*, 121–133.

Palmer, D., & Martínez, R. A. (2013). Teacher agency in bilingual spaces: A fresh look at preparing teachers to educate Latina/o bilingual children. *Review of Research in Education*, *37*, 269–298.

Pastor, M. (2013). Top 10 elements of social movements. University of Southern California Annenberg School for Communications and Journalism. Retrieved from: https://www.youtube.com/watch?v=o1H-gWZwRGs

Roque, R., Ferrin, S., Hite, J., & Randall, V. (2016). The unique skills and traits of principals in one-way and two-way dual immersion schools. *Foreign Language Annals*, *49*(4) 801–818.

Ruiz, R. (1984). Orientations in language planning. *Journal of the National Association for Bilingual Education*, *8*(2), 1–14.

Scanlan, M., Hunter, C., & Howard, E. R. (2019). *Culturally and linguistically responsive education: Designing networks that transform schools*. Harvard Education Press.

Scanlan, M., & López, F. (2012). ¡Vamos! How school leaders promote equity and excellence for bilingual students. *Educational Administration Quarterly*, *48*(4), 583–625.

Scanlan, M. & López, F. A. (2015). *Leadership for culturally and linguistically responsive schools*. Routledge.

Soltero, S. (2018). Dual language higher education: Post-secondary discipline-based bilingual immersion. In H. Knoerr, A. Weinberg, & C. Buchanan (Eds.), *Current issues in university-level immersion* (pp. 29–54). University of Ottawa Press.

Soltero, S. W. (2011). *Schoolwide approaches to educating ELLs: Creating linguistically and culturally responsive K–12 schools*. Heinemann.

Soltero, S. W. (2016). *Dual language education. Program design and implementation*. Heinemann.

Soltero, S. W. (2021). The building blocks of dual language education. *Multilingual Educator*, 45–49.

Souto-Manning, M., Madrigal, R., Malik, K., & Martell, J. (2016). Bridging languages, cultures, and worlds through culturally relevant leadership. In S. Long, M. Souto-Manning, & V. Vasquez (Eds.), *Courageous leadership in early childhood education: Taking a stand for social justice* (pp. 57–68). Teachers College Press.

Spillane, J. P. (2012). *Distributed leadership*. Jossey-Bass.

Steele, J., Slater, L., Zamarro, R. O., Miller, G., Li, T., & Burkhauser, J. (2018). Effects of dual-language immersion programs on student achievement: Evidence from lottery data. *American Educational Research Journal*, *54*(1), 282–306.

Stemler, S. E., Bebell, D., & Sonnabend, L. A. (2011). Using school mission statements for reflection and research. *Educational Administration Quarterly*, *47*(2), 383–420.

Tedick, D. J., & Björklund, S. (2014). Language immersion education: A research agenda for 2015 and beyond. *Journal of Immersion and Content-Based Language Education*, 2(2), 155–164.

Tedick, D., Christian, J., & Fortune, D. (2011). The future of immersion education: An invitation to dwell in possibilities. In D. J. Tedick, D. Christian, & T. W. Fortune (Eds.), *Immersion education. Practices, policies, and possibilities* (pp. 1–10). Multilingual Matters.

Tedick, D. J., & Lyster, R. (2019). *Scaffolding language development in immersion and dual language classrooms*. Routledge.

Thomas, W. P., & Collier, V. P. (2015). English learners in North Carolina dual language programs: Year 3 of study: School year 2009–2010. George Mason University.

Valdés, G. (1997). Dual-language immersion programs: A cautionary note concerning the education of language-minority students. *Harvard Educational Review*, *67*, 391–429.

Valdez, V. E., Freire, J. A., & Delavan, M. G. (2016). The gentrification of dual language education. *Urban Review*, *48*, 601–627.

Valero, W., & Makishima, P. (2019). Elgin, Illinois: An entire district goes dual. The journey of a district committed to culturally and logistically responsive instruction. In M. Scanlan, C. Hunter, & E. R. Howard (Eds.), *Culturally and linguistically responsive education: Designing networks that transform schools* (pp. 56–73). Harvard Education Press.

Yaden, B. (2019). Leveraging networks for coordinated professional development. In M. Scanlan, C. Hunter, & E. R. Howard (Eds.), *Culturally and linguistically responsive education: Designing networks that transform schools* (pp. 77–95). Harvard Education Press.

Zamudio, M., Russell, C., Ríos, F., & Bridgeman, J. (2011). *Critical race theory matters education and ideology*. Routledge.

Zeigler, K., & Camarota, S. A. (2019). *67.3 million in the United States spoke a foreign language at home in 2018*. Center for Immigration Studies. https://cis.org/Report

7

ENGLISH LEARNERS AND DUAL LANGUE LEARNERS IN THE EARLY YEARS

From Science to Policy and Practice

Eugene E. García

Introduction

One in four young children in the United States speaks a language in addition to English at home (Park et al., 2017). Throughout this chapter, the term *dual language learner* (DLL) is used to refer to children under the age of five who are exposed to more than one language in family, home, and primary care circumstances. The term *English learner* (EL) is used to refer to children enrolled in the PreK-12 educational system. The population of DLLs is a heterogeneous one, with hundreds of languages represented but with three in four DLLs speaking Spanish (Romo et al., 2018). In terms of geography, beginning in the 1990s, immigrant families and their DLL children dispersed in large numbers from concentrated enclaves in large cities and in the Southwest to nontraditional communities in the Southeast and the Rocky Mountain region, among other places (Kochhar et al., 2005; Romo et al., 2018).

We know from the existing science on multilingualism that young children can attain proficiency in more than one language (Bialystok, 2010; Genesee, 2010; Takanishi & Le Menestrel, 2017; Unsworth, 2016), and that DL programs in the early years can produce positive outcomes across multiple domains (García & Frede, 2010; Li et al., 2010; Reyes & Kleyn, 2010; Valentino & Reardon, 2015). Indeed, Cheung and Slavin (2012) found that English reading outcomes for Spanish-dominant DLLs were stronger (effect size = .21) for those in bilingual programs than those in English-only programs.

Yet, there is more that characterizes the early developmental contexts of DLLs than language alone. DLLs and their families vary widely in terms of race, ethnicity, socioeconomic status, immigrant generation, religion,

 DOI: 10.4324/9781003269076-11

country of origin, legal status, integration, social networks, and so on. Each of these factors, though not mutually exclusive, interacts with children's development. Although nine out of ten DLLs are born in the United States, most live with immigrant families in which at least one parent was born outside the United States; the early development of DLLs is inextricably related to the type of immigrant experiences their family has (Jensen & Bachmeier, 2015; Tobin et al., 2013). In short, the cultures, languages, and experiences of ELs and DLLs are highly diverse; moreover, they grow up in contexts that expose them to a number of risk factors (e.g., low levels of parental education, low family income, refugee status, homelessness) that can have a negative impact on their school success, especially when these disadvantages are compounded. However, this same population has significant assets including their bilingual skills, two-parent families, strong extended family and community supports, and positive attitudes toward education and educators.

Therefore, conceptually, it is significant to consider these various heterogeneous learning contexts for this important number of this U.S. population in educational venues. The conceptual framework shown in Figure 7.1 attempts to identify an important constellation of elements that must be considered in providing educational practice and policy that enable this

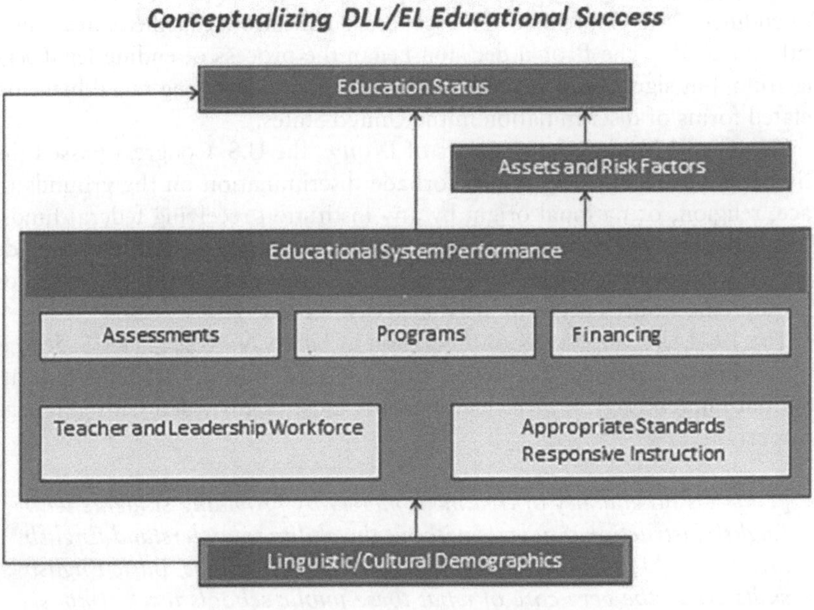

Figure 7.1 Conceptualizing DLL/El Educational Success

population of children and students to attain educational success. This conceptual framework is based on the most recent theoretical and empirical information related to the development and learning of this population (Takanishi & Le Menestrel, 2017). The framework can be used to comprehensively consider the multitude of variables that must be better understood when addressing the overall development and learning outcomes of DLLs. Maximizing opportunities for DLLs requires an understanding that language development is interdependent with the factors included in Figure 7.1 and an array of other institutional conditions and cultural practices (García & Ozturk, 2017).

Given the many ways that policy shapes the challenges and opportunities faced by DLLs and ELs (Takanishi & Le Menestrel, 2017), this chapter provides a brief historical overview of federal legislative and litigation history with a focus on DLLs.

Dual Language Learners and the Federal Courts

Understanding the legal status of children and students whose primary language is other than English and the U.S. federal courts requires specific initial attention to the courts' affirmative decisions regarding issues of equal protection in educational venues. In 1954, the U.S. Supreme Court, in the case of *Brown v. the Board of Education of Topeka, Kansas*, ruled that racial segregation in public schools was unconstitutional. Relying on the 14th Amendment, the Court held that "separate educational facilities are inherently unequal." The *Brown* decision began the process of ending legal segregation, but significantly, it altered the course of addressing racial bias and related forms of discrimination in the United States.

Significantly and in the shadows of *Brown*, the U.S. Congress passed the Civil Rights Act in 1964, which forbade discrimination on the grounds of race, religion, or national origin by any institution receiving federal funds. This broadened the scope of *Brown* and ultimately extended it to include language minorities under the national origin provision, setting the stage for the Supreme Court's decision in *Lau v. Nichols* in 1974.

The 1974 U.S. Supreme Court decision in *Lau v. Nichols* (414 US. 563) is the landmark statement of the rights of language-minority students indicating that limited English proficient students must be provided with language support:

> *[T]here is no equality of treatment merely by providing students with English instruction. Students without the ability to understand English are effectively foreclosed from any meaningful discourse. Basic English skills are at the very core of what these public schools teach. Imposition of a requirement that, before a child can effectively participate in*

> *the education program he must already have acquired those basic skills is to make a mockery of public education. We know that those who do not understand English are certain to find their classroom experiences wholly incomprehensible and in no way meaningful.* (p. 18)

This articulation of the rights of language-minority students prevails today. *Lau* does not stand for the proposition that children must receive a particular educational service, but instead that some form of effective educational programming must be available to "open the instruction" to language-minority students.

In a key Fifth Circuit decision of *Castañeda v. Pickard* (1981), the court interpreted Section 1703(f) of the Equal Educational Opportunities Act of 1974 as substantiating the holding of *Lau* that schools cannot ignore the special language needs of students (García, 2005). In this judgment, the court concluded that Congress did require districts to adopt an appropriate program, and that by creating a cause of action in federal court to enforce Section 1703(f), if left to federal judges the task of determining whether a given program is appropriate. The court noted that Congress had not provided guidance in that statute or in its brief legislative history on what it intended by selecting "appropriateness" as the operative standard. Continuing with clear reluctance and hesitancy, the court described a mode of analysis for a Section 1703(f) case:

1 The court will determine whether a district's program is "informed by an educational theory recognized as sound by some experts in the field or, at least, deemed a legitimate experimental strategy." The court explicitly declined to be an arbiter among competing theorists. The appropriate question is whether some justification exists, not the relative merits of competing alternatives.
2 The court will determine whether the district is implementing its program in a reasonably effective manner (e.g., adequate funding, qualified staffing).
3 The court will determine whether the program, after operating long enough to be a legitimate trial, produces results that indicate the language barriers are being overcome. A plan that is initially appropriate may have to be revised if expectations are not met or if the district's circumstances significantly change in such a way that the original plan is no longer sufficient (p. 73).

After *Castañeda*, it became legally possible to substantiate a violation of Section 1703(f), following from *Lau*, on three grounds: (a) the program providing special language services to eligible language-minority students is not based on sound educational theory; (b) the program is not being implemented in an effective manner; and (c) the program, after a period of "reasonable implementation," does not produce results that substantiate language barriers are being overcome so as to eliminate achievement gaps between bilingual and English-only speaking students. The "Castañeda Standard" with deference to "Lau" has become the most visible legal articulation of educational rights for ELs in public schools (Jiménez-Castellanos & García, 2017).

Legal Standing and DLLs

The previous discussion has highlighted the influential court initiatives influencing the educational services for language-minority students. The court opinions in particular have generated some understanding of a language-minority pupil's legal standing as it relates to the educational treatment received. At the national level, this legal standing stems from court opinions specifically interpreting Section 1703(f) of the 1974 U.S. Equal Educational Opportunities Act. The courts have consistently refused to invoke a corollary to the 14th Amendment to the U.S. Constitution with respect to educational treatment. Even so it is evident that litigation has increased (and is likely to continue) and has been an avenue of educational reform that has produced significant changes in educational programs for language-minority students. However, like almost all litigation, it has been a long (range of 4–13 years in court prior to an operational decision) and often highly complicated and resource-consuming enterprise. Nevertheless, several important conclusions regarding the responsibilities of educational agencies have been established. For articulation of these legal rights, see Roos (1984, 2020) and García and Ozturk (2017).

It is critical to note that none of these "rights" are relevant to DLLs in early childhood education (ECE) settings. Takanishi (2016) and Garcia and Ozturk (2017) have suggested that the same set of remedies relevant to ELs in public schools as defined by the courts are relevant to the millions of DLLs now in public ECE programs. DLLs presently enter early education learning opportunities that do not take into consideration their non-English-speaking background in the same way K-12 public schools are legally obligated to address. Moreover, federal funding through Title I does not directly mandate early education support for DLLs, although it does allow "permissive" support of PreK efforts. How does the right of language-minority children entering public learning environments begin only at kindergarten? Certainly, learning and development are now understood as contiguous from birth forward as well documented in the National Academy of Science, Engineering and Medicine report, How People Learn (NASM, 2017). And court adjudication has pointed out the need to address non-English proficiency as a way of "leveling the Playing field." Yet, DLLs are presently absent of any legal or civil right protection afforded older, public school, language-minority students.

DLLs and U.S. Federal Policy

The Federal Court's engagement in addressing educational equity related to ELs in the U.S. K-12 system has been highly influential in national-, state-, and local-level policy development, adoption and related educational practice. Since *Brown, Lau* and subsequent adjudication of the education responsibilities related to equity and ELs, the education, policy, and practice landscape for ELs has been significantly changed with regard to identification, program differentiation, and accountability (Takanishi & Le Menestrel, 2017). Yet, this changing landscape has not in and of itself proved to be the needed force in achieving a portfolio of equity results for ELs (Start with Equity: From the Early Years to the Early Grades, 2020). However, it must be noted that an effort related to federal or state court-related determination of DLL's "rights" to equal opportunity in early education venues aligned with those available in the K-12 educational sector would extend important policy attention to the growing number of DLLs.

The Elementary and Secondary Education Act and DLLs

Over the past 50 years, federal policies in particular have sought to support EL academic learning outcomes by addressing the reality that students with limited English proficiency face a significant barrier to mastery of subject matter content taught in English. Figure 7.2 summarizes the historical policy attention generated by federal court litigation and federal legislative actions related directly to those children and students who do not speak English as they enter formal educational environments in the United States. As Figure 7.2 indicates, policy attention to this population has been continuous since

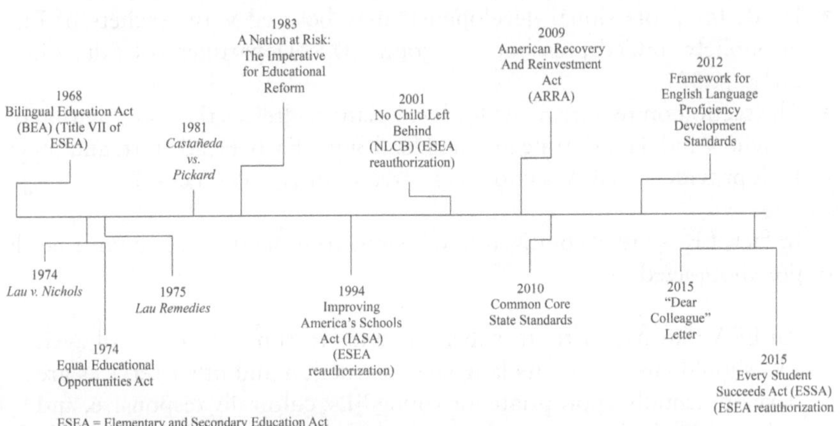

Figure 7.2 Education Policy Timeline

1968 into the present. It is only more recently, that ECE expansion has generated related policy-to-practice assumptions and expectations for DLLs.

Elementary and Secondary Education Act Reauthorization of 2015: Every Student Succeeds Act

The most recent reauthorization, in 2015, of the ESEA, known more prominently as the ESSA, went into effect on July 1, 2017 (Weise et al., 2019). While the 2015 reauthorization replaced the term *limited English proficient* with *EL*,[1] the state formulary grant structure introduced in the 2001 legislation remains the primary vehicle by which federal funds are allocated to support ELs, including the stipulation that 95% of the state award must flow to LEAs. However, the 5% reserved for state-level funding can be used to address a new requirement to establish and implement standardized statewide entrance and exit procedures, including assessing children who may be ELs within 30 days of enrollment (ESEA Section 3111(b)(2)(A)).[2]

Early Learning

While previous reauthorizations of ESEA permitted the use of Title III funds for ELs as young as three years of age, ESSA specifically promotes addressing young ELs in the following ways:

- The purpose section specifically calls out preschool teachers (ESEA Section 3102 [reauthorized as ESSA]).
- The section on subgrants to LEAs for ELs calls out "early childhood education programs" and "effective preschool ... language instruction educational programs" (ESEA Section 3115 [reauthorized as ESSA]).).
- Funds for professional development may be used with teachers of ELs in publicly funded preschool programs (U.S. Department of Education, 2016, p. 32).
- The section on requirements for local plans addresses the coordination of activities and data sharing among Head Start, Early Head Start, and other ECE providers (ESEA Section 3116 [reauthorized as ESSA]).).[3]

In fact, LEAs are encouraged to take into consideration the unique needs of preschool-aged ELs:

> An LEA that uses Title III subgrant funds to support preschool aged ELs should ensure that its language instruction and other services are developmentally appropriate for young ELs, culturally responsive, and reflective of the latest research on effective instruction for ELs in early learning programs and supportive of all ELs' needs. An LEA should

consider the developmental and language needs of children when determining which students may be served using Title III funds.

(U.S. Department of Education, 2016, p. 33)

Overall, federal policy—legislation and litigation—has emphasized a shift away from developing bilingual capacities and toward a focus on English language acquisition. Still, through reauthorizations of the ESEA, federal legislation continues to provide guidance as it relates to ELs and in 2015 specifically promoted a focus on young ELs (or DLLs) in preschool.

Educational Policy Advances for DLLs

Historically, the effort to serve the youngest population of non-English speakers in PreK has been a more local community and school district effort (Garcia, 1983; Garcia & Gonzalez, 1995). The Miami school district began such efforts as Cuban refugees arrived in substantial numbers in the 1960s. More recent early childhood DL efforts emerged in Santa Fe, Seattle, Albuquerque, Denver, and New York as these cities began to offer subsidized preschool experiences for their families (García & Ozturk, 2017).

At the local level, DL programs, beginning at pre-kindergarten levels, in the San Francisco School District, exemplify a truly responsive instruction option for these students. While most of the district programs offer instruction in Spanish and English, there are also DL programs which target Korean, Chinese and Tagalog. These efforts have three responsive goals: to help children to learn English and find success in U.S. schools; to help these children become competent in their own language without sacrificing their own success in school; and to promote linguistic and ethnic equity among the children, encouraging children to bridge the gaps between cultures and languages. Some states have moved directly to offer DL programming mirroring efforts at the local, district level.

Thirty-five state-funded preschool programs have policies specifically supporting DLLs and 34 states explicitly *permit* but do not require bilingual instruction (Children's Equity Project, 2020). Only Illinois explicitly requires bilingual instruction if there are 20 or more DLLs of the same home language. In addition:

- 14 states require monitoring of the quality of bilingual education;
- 17 states require an approved written plan for how programs will support DLLs;
- 19 state programs have policies for assessing children in their home language;
- 7 state programs require staff to have training or qualifications for working with DLLs;

- 33 state programs have a policy that specifies communicating with families of DLLs in home language for recruitment and outreach and/or program- or child-related issues.

Notably, 18 states had no policy supports related to preschool DLLs, specifically some states have taken the lead in providing DL programming, including California's Kindergarten Readiness Act of 2010 established transitional kindergarten (TK), allowing students who reach age five between September 2 and December 2 to receive an "age and developmentally appropriate" experience prior to entering kindergarten the following year. Since it has been implemented across the state, TK has been shown to significantly improve kindergarten readiness for California's students (Manship et al., 2015). However, a particular investigation was launched to assess TK benefits for DLLs—those eligible and participating students for TK who do not speak, read, write, or understand English well as a result of English not being their home language. This population of students makes up 33 % of the kindergarten population in California and represents a wide range of language groups, including Spanish, Vietnamese, Mandarin, Filipino, and Arabic with some two-thirds of these students identified as Latino (California Department of Education, 2016).

The American Institutes for Research (2010) provided the results of this statewide evaluation of TK. The findings are based on direct assessments of over 2000 DLL students in 20 school districts across California. The evaluation results indicate DL programs benefit DLLs in several developmental and learning domains:

- TK improves mathematics knowledge and problem-solving skills for DLL students, giving them almost a six-month advantage in problem-solving skills over EL students who did not attend TK.
- TK also improves literacy skills for DLL students, putting them ahead of their peers who did not attend TK by more than seven months at kindergarten entry.
- Participating in TK gives DL students a substantial boost in their English language development, including speaking skills, listening skills, and overall language proficiency. This benefit holds true for EL students from all language groups (American Institutes for Research, 2010).

In 2008, the Utah Senate passed the International Initiatives (Senate Bill 41), creating funding for Utah schools to begin Dual Language Immersion programs in English, Spanish, Portuguese, Chinese, French, and German. Beginning at the pre-kindergarten level, the Utah Dual Language Immersion Program uses a 50-50 model, in which students spend half of their school day in the target language and the other half-day in English. Most of the state's programs begin in first grade, with a few starting in PreK. All state-sponsored schools with Dual Language Immersion programs are required to implement the 50-50 model and use two teachers, one who instructs exclusively in the target language for half of the day and a second who teaches in English for the remainder of the day.

Regarding support for families of DLLs, in San Antonio, Texas, *AVANCE,* in Los Angeles, California, and *Abriendo Puertas* offer import family support services targeted at immigrant families. These programs serve Latino parents of DLLs from before the time of birth until the beginning of kindergarten. They delivered family support services and do so within culturally and linguistic respectful parameters, helping families adjust to immigrant circumstances through bilingual staff and programming. These efforts began with the basic premise that these families needed to be respected for all the assets they brought to the developmental processes and those cultural, social, linguistic, and cognitive assets were to be used to advance their own abilities to support and assist their children and families. And it worked, producing positive adult, child, and family outcomes. AVANCE and Abriendo Puertas are now a model for other family intervention programs that address DLL circumstances (García & Ozturk, 2017).

The field of ECE is amassing a body of science to inform policy and practice for DLLs, children who are learning two languages, in preschool through third grade. Three major categories of policy are considered most significant for DLLs and are addressed here: (a) access to preschool through third grade (PreK-3) services, (b) quality of PreK-3 services, including staff qualifications, and (c) standards and assessment used in PreK-3 settings. Each of these areas is multifaceted; they are interconnected and overlap.

The PreK-3 Landscape: Access to Services for DLLs

Since 2002, the National Institute for Early Education Research (NIEER) has collected information on state-funded preschool program policies. In recent years, they have added what information the states could provide on service to DLLs. Of the 53 state-funded preschool programs in 40 states and Washington, DC, only 22 collect data on the number of DLLs served.

Thus, doing an analysis of access and attendance in state PreK for DLLs is not possible. Recent analyses of national data on access and participation in early childhood center-based programs more broadly, including publicly supported childcare and other private providers, reveal that three- to four-year-old DLLs are less likely to participate in center-based programs than any other sub-group at that age. It seems likely that lack of access to quality programs is as important as factors such as income, parental education, and other family characteristics.

Quality of Services to the PreK-3 DLL Population

It is clear that there are cognitive and social benefits for children who attend high-quality preschool and growing evidence indicates that DLLs benefit more than others from effective preschool education. Factors influencing effectiveness of early education include class size, intensity and duration of the intervention, teacher qualifications, curriculum and fidelity of curriculum implementation, parental engagement and educational leadership.

The State Preschool Yearbook reports on a number of state policies regarding quality of services for DLLs in state-funded PreK. Of the 53 state-funded PreK programs include in the State Preschool Yearbook, 19 have no regulations specific to services for DLLs. While no regular means that state guidance is missing that might directly support specific services for DLLs, it also means that at least instruction in multiple languages is not prohibited. The majority of state programs expressly support/allow bilingual instruction and 19 allow monolingual home language instruction. Of significance, no state policies require English-only instruction. State policies for 20 of the programs require that a home language survey be administered but only 14 programs have policies that require that programs develop a systematic, written plan for how they will serve DLLs. Twenty-one programs require that information to parents be available in the home language and 17 require that bilingual staff be provided if children's home language is not English.

Landscape of Standards and Assessment for DLLs in PreK-3

Perhaps the biggest push toward an agenda of well-aligned and beneficial experiences for DLLs is the existence of an infrastructure that uniformly guides best practices and accountability. Levers here include well-developed standards and assessment practices that adequately and validly measure progress and inform practice. In addition, a compilation of information that also encompasses both policy and relevant resources could be helpful for systemic decision-making. What currently exists, however, is a set of well-intentioned but disjointed policies, each regulating different aspects of the landscape with little guidance on delivery for states. Standards pertaining to general academic progress for young DLLs fall into three major, distinct categories. These include individually developed state early learning standards (used in PreK and ECE settings), the Common Core State Standards (CCSS: used on K-12 settings), and for Head Start, the Child Development and Early Learning Standards (used on Head Start PreK settings). The National Center on Cultural and Linguistic Responsiveness (NCCLR) analyzed how state preschool standards address DLLs and found that only three states (CA, KY, and MA) have guidelines specifically for DLLs, nine states have sections for addressing DLLs within their guidelines, and eight states at least mention DLLs in the

Language and Literacy areas of their guidelines. The Common Core State Standards (CCSS), which are now adopted by 43 states, exclude any specific standards for DLLs and instead include guidelines for applying the standards to DLLs that basically describe DLLs as a heterogeneous group who should receive individualized "diagnosis" and instruction. They advise teachers to recognize that it is possible to achieve the standards for reading and literature, writing and research, language development, and speaking and listening without manifesting native-like control of conventions and vocabulary.

Another set of standards are those mandated by Title III for identification and intervention for English proficiency. Lack of cohesive standards for assessment of English proficiency is compounded by incoherent and, at times, ineffective, reclassification assessments to determine accurately who DLLs are, and when they are ready to exit support programs. Federal policy dictates through Title III that states develop or adopt English language proficiency standards and that an annual test of English proficiency be administered for DLLs in grades K-12. As part of its accountability provisions, the updated ESEA requires that states define criteria about progress in English, create English proficiency standards for performance, and set annually increasing performance targets for the population of DLLs meeting the criteria. The U.S. Department of Education released the National Evaluation of Title III Implementation Supplemental Report: Exploring Approaches to Setting English Language Proficiency Performance Criteria and Monitoring English Learner Progress in 2012 as means of support to state policy-makers in their efforts to generate empirically based standards and assessments to meet the Title III requirements. In large part, the release of this report acknowledges a gap between the goals of the legislation and states' capacity to adequately meet its provisions.

The World Class Instructional Design and Assessment (WIDA) consortium has begun to disentangle this problem by outlining standards, performance definitions, guiding principles for grades K-12, with PreK standards soon to come. Though the WIDA website reports that 36 states are currently members, it remains largely unclear how states are incorporating the resources created by the Consortium.

Potential Policy Levers to Enhance Access and Quality in PreK-3 Education for DLLs

In summary, there is a clear need for policies that specifically address DLLs' access to and the quality of their PreK-3 education experiences. Examples of such policies are the following:

- inclusion of preparing teachers to teach DLLs in certification requirements;
- adoption of the CEDS data standards and use of geo-mapping or other methods to ensure access to DLLs;

- inclusion of home language as an eligibility criterion for state PreK or offering universal access;
- using acceptable methods for identifying and placing DLLs in language development programs based on systematic and valid assessment of a child's proficiency in their home language and English;
- implementation of state-sponsored methods to improve and increase the opportunities teachers have for professional development specific to best practices for DLLs;
- program evaluation and monitoring that includes administration of classroom assessments of teacher supports for DLLs that are based on best practices;
- inclusion of DLL best practices as criteria in the state QRIS;
- specific policy guidance aimed to increase DL instruction in PreK-3 classrooms;
- requirement that programs and districts have DLL improvement plans and have developed continuity of education PreK-3;
- guidance and regulations that support language-minority parents' engagement in their child's learning.

Final Thoughts on a Research Agenda

An expanded research agenda will significantly build on the important work of the last two decades and can be of extreme usefulness for understanding and acting upon the educational early learning opportunities for DLLs. Research colleagues are asked to augment present research and theory acknowledging set of presuppositions:

1 Their "subjects" live in complex worlds that they inhabit, one of those is the school and others are constituted of families, neighborhoods, other social institutions (private, governmental, religious, peer oriented, etc.).
2 These same subjects are directly and indirectly influenced by their past experience in these and other organizations and the present action of various social entities.
3 Understanding the subjects and the social institutions and processes that influence the student requires the "tracking" of the perceptions, interactions, and changes of the student and the institutions over a reasonable period.
4 These subjects arrive at any intervention designed to support their development and learning with a wealth of cultural, linguistic, cognitive, and social resources upon which designed interventions can build upon.

This is not to say snapshot analyses of DLLs individually or collectively are not worthwhile. It is to suggest that the complexity of development and learning circumstances, coupled with their individual navigation through a diverse and multiple set of social circumstances, each changing over time, provide us with a much more in-depth, theoretical, and practice-rich understanding.

Considering what we now know about the lives of DLLs, two issues seem paramount in augmented research agenda in ECE practice and policy contexts: "what works best for who and why" and "maintenance of effects." Recommended as the basis of organizing future research, these two issues are addressed more specifically in the following critical questions:

- Which development and learning practices maximize benefits for DLLs and families with different characteristics under what types of circumstances? Why?
- Are gains sustained for children and families after the intervention experience?

Both questions consider the present conditions emerging in educational research strategies. The focus is on producing a knowledge base that can provide a foundation for ongoing program improvement and upgrading quality within educational partners, inside and outside of designed development and learning interventions. It is the lack of answers to the critical questions enunciated above that places services to DLL students in jeopardy of haphazard and highly politicized policy initiatives. The first question acknowledges the diversity and related understanding of the required flexibility of any designed intervention. Average outcomes of average programs, which were the aim of an earlier generation of studies, pose the risk of misleading findings and fail to provide the information needed to tailor services to identifiable subgroups of children and families. Developing strategies must respond to the differentiated information needs that must support quality improvements and to achieve the hoped-for societal benefits in moving toward highly specific practice and policy reforms. Put simply, "What works in El Paso may not work in Los Angeles, New York City or Miami." We are not only in need of "effective" or generic "best practices," but also rich contextual information about the interventions and those served by those interventions. The question, "Why?," implicates the need for an intellectual/theoretical foundation for the research as that research intersects with practices in the field. We need a set of theories or constructs that help us to better understand why some interventions work and others do not for the diverse populations being served. Such theories/constructs allow us more readily to adapt new interventions that are different than those we have studied.

The second question reflects issues that have come to the fore in the policy and research communities as a result of findings of socially meaningful, lasting gains for children who have participated in early learning programs. For example, English emphasis programs for Latino students generated significant inter-generation communication gaps that negatively affected children, parents, and grandparents (García & Ozturk, 2017). Attention to this type of social consequence has been sorely absent. Moreover, attention directed to issues related to lasting effects should not be interpreted to imply that any one intervention/strategy/program, by itself, would necessarily be responsible for producing long-term outcomes. On the contrary, the most plausible scenario is that the long-term outcomes are a product of the combined influences of the designed intervention experience, influences in the family, and follow-up actions of other community agencies that serve to extend or attenuate the effects. Even with these critical questions in mind and the importance of addressing them in augmented research, it is important to realize that policy- and practice-related research does require clarity in causal inference. In such research, it is the impact of policies and practices that are examined: Did this or that intervention work? Reforms, revisions, and add-ons to policies and practices are implemented to make a difference. While much of social science can avoid the troubled issues of the direction of causal effects, "reforms," or "ameliorative programs," cannot. Policy and practice research, and program evaluation in particular, for DLLs must have a commitment to causal inference, and a need to optimize the clarity of the inference. Description is not enough if practice and policy are to be harnessed in ways that support the development and learning of a growing and significant population of DLLs, nationally and internationally.

Notes

1 The legislation acknowledges the diversity of the EL population by calling out long-term ELs, immigrant ELs, and ELs with disabilities in reporting requirements.

2 The 2001 legislation specified that the 5% reserved for state-level activities could be used for planning, evaluation, administration, and interagency coordination; technical assistance to subgrantees; and recognition of subgrantees. This is also true for the 2015 legislation, which specifies that the technical assistance to subgrantees can be used for family engagement. The 2015 legislation also allows for state-level professional development to improve the teaching of ELs and state-level planning and direct administrative costs.

3 For further guidance regarding early learning programs and Title III, refer to the U.S. Department of Education (2016a, pp. 32–35).

References

American Institutes for Research (2010). *Evaluation of preschool for all (PFA) implementation in San Francisco County: Year 5 report*. First 5 San Francisco.

Bialystok, E. (2010). Global–local and trail-making tasks by monolingual and bilingual children: Beyond inhibition. *Developmental Psychology*, *46*(1), 93–105.

California, Proposition 227: English Language in Public Schools (1998).

California Department of Education (2016). Statewide enrollment by ethnicity with county data. http://bit.ly/2dxYeDC

Cheung, A. C., & Slavin, R. E. (2012). Effective reading programs for Spanish-dominant English language learners (ELLs) in the elementary grades: A synthesis of research. *Review of Educational Research*, *82*(4), 351–395.

Children's Equity Project (2020). *Start with equity*. Children's Equity Project and Bipartisan Policy Center.

García, E. (1983). *Early childhood bilingualism*. University of New Mexico Press.

García, E. E., & Frede, E. C. (2010). *Young English language learners: Current research and emerging directions for practice and policy*. Teachers College Press.

Garcia, E. E., & Gonzalez, R. (1995). Issues in systemic reform for culturally and linguistically diverse students. *Teachers College Record*, *96*(3), 1–14.

García, E. E., & Ozturk, M. (2017). *An asset-based approach to Latino education in the United States*. Routledge.

García, E. (2005). *Teaching and learning in two languages: Bilingualism and schooling in the United States*. Teachers College Press.

Genesee, F. (2010). Dual language development in preschool children. In E. E. García, & E. C. Frede (Eds.), *Young English language learners*. Teachers College Press.

Jensen, B., & Bachmeier, J. (2015). *A portrait of U.S. children of Central American origins and their educational opportunity*. MacArthur Foundation.

Jiménez-Castellanos, O., & García, E. (2017). Intersection of language, class, ethnicity, and policy: Toward disrupting inequality for English language learners. *Review of Research in Education*, *41*(1), 428–452. https://doi.org/10.3102/0091732X16688623

Kochhar, R., Suro, R., & Tafoya, S. (2005). The new Latino south: The context and consequences of rapid population growth. Pew Research Center. https://www.pewresearch.org/

Li, G., Edwards, P. A., & Gunderson, L. (2010). *Best practices in ELL instruction*. The Guilford Press.

Manship, K., Quick, H., Holod, A., Mills, N., Ogut, B., Chernoff, J. J., Blum, J., Hauser, A., Anthony, J., & Gonzalez, R. (2015). *Impact of California's transitional kindergarten program, 2013-14*. American Institutes for Research.

National Academies of Sciences, Engineering, and Medicine. (2017). *Training the future child health care workforce to improve the behavioral health of children, youth, and families*. Proceedings of a workshop. https://nam.edu/nasem-publications-round-up-may-2017/

Park, M., O'Toole, A., & Katsiaficas, C. (2017). *Dual language learners: A national demographic and policy profile*. Migration Policy Institute.

Reyes, S. A., & Kleyn, T. (2010). *Teaching in two languages: A guide for K–12 bilingual educators*. Corwin Press.

Romo, H. D., Thomas, K. J., & García, E. E. (2018). Changing demographics of dual language learners and English learners: Implications for school success. *Social Policy Report*, *31*(2), 1–35.

Roos, P. (1984). *Legal guidelines for bilingual administrators*. Society of Research in Child Development.

Roos, P. (2020). *Putting my mind and heart to educational equity*. Center for Applied Linguistics.

Takanishi, R. (2016). First things first!: Creating the new American primary school. Teachers College Press.

Takanishi, R., & Le Menestrel, S. (2017). *Promoting the educational success of children and youth learning English: Promising futures* (Report of the National

Academies of Sciences, Engineering, and Medicine). The National Academies Press.

Tobin, J., Adair, J. K., & Arzubiaga, A. (2013). *Children crossing borders: Immigrant parent and teacher perspectives on preschool for children of immigrants*. Russell Sage Foundation.

U.S. Department of Education. (2016). *Non-regulatory guidance: English learners and Title III of the Elementary and Secondary Education Act (ESEA), as amended by the Every Student Succeeds Act (ESSA)*. Author. https://www2.ed.gov/policy/elsec/leg/essa/essatitleiiiguidenglishlearners92016.pdf

Unsworth, S. (2016). Quantity and quality of language input in bilingual language development. In E. Nicoladis, & S. Montanari (Eds.), *Lifespan perspectives on bilingualism* (pp. 136–196). American Psychological Association.

Valentino, R. A., & Reardon, S. F. (2015). Effectiveness of four instructional programs designed to serve English learners: Variation by ethnicity and initial English proficiency. *Educational Evaluation and Policy Analysis*, *37*(4), 612–637.

Weise, A. M., Cuellar, D., & Garcia, E. E. (2019). Educational policy in the United States regarding bilinguals in early childhood education. In O. Saracho (Ed.), *The handbook of research on the education of young children*. Routledge/Taylor & Francis.

DLBE Outcomes

8

RECENTERING MULTIPLE MINORITIZED LANGUAGES IN DUAL LANGUAGE BILINGUAL EDUCATION

Trish Morita-Mullaney

Spanish dual language bilingual education (DLBE) programs represent the highest proportion of two-way programs in the United States (Center for Applied Linguistics, 2021). As Spanish is the second most spoken language in the United States among its K-12 students, and its development is seen as a marker of utility, it continues to be the most highly represented language of instruction (Pufahl & Rhodes, 2011). Yet, languages other than Spanish are represented throughout the U.S.' dual language models including Mandarin Chinese, Cantonese Chinese, Arabic, Hebrew, Japanese, Korean, Vietnamese, Hmong, Russian, Polish and Native American languages (Center for Applied Linguistics, 2021). Nearly all these program models bear the title of dual language or two-way, but such naming conventions are not understood nor used in the same way in all contexts. Dual language can denote a one-way immersion model with English majority speakers or dual simply denoting that two languages are used within instruction. Other programs may call themselves a DLBE program as they aspire to have a minoritized student constituency of a given target language, but fall short, as recruitment efforts often attract a higher proportion of English majority speakers (Morita-Mullaney & Chesnut, 2022).

For less commonly taught languages (LCTL), an important distinction arises for most of the languages discussed in this chapter. Many arise out of the fields of world language and heritage language revitalization. World language foci are largely funded by federal and/or state sources and may or may not include bilingual learners. Heritage language revitalization

DOI: 10.4324/9781003269076-13

programs are community based and thus, this bottom up approach informs different methods for teaching and rationale for identified content of focus. Some programs have origins within the field of bilingual education, but experienced significant erosion during the implementation of restrictive language policies as reinforced by U.S. federal educational accountability (Menken & Solorza, 2014) and are now making a comeback in the renovated format of DLBE.

In this chapter, I discuss four areas within LCTL. First, I discuss the foundations of a world language versus bilingual education models and its connections to DLBE. Second, I describe the representation of DLBE programs in languages other than Spanish and connect them to their policy foundations. Third, I discuss how such programs are regarded within language policy. Fourth, I detail the limited studies on the achievement outcomes of students in these LCTL DLBE programs. Lastly, I end with suggestions and talking points for the field of world and DLBE.

Intersecting Histories of World and Bilingual Education to Inform Dual Language Bilingual Education (DLBE) in Languages Other than Spanish

DLBE is an effort to bring together the two paradigms of world and bilingual education through its student constituency. Palmer (2009) describes that for language majority speakers, the purpose is an enrichment model of language education; whereas for designated-ELs (referenced hereafter as bilingual learners), the goal is language maintenance and development. This framing suggests a possible and likely power disequilibrium where bilingual learners get to keep their native language while language majority speakers get to gain a second language (Morita-Mullaney & Chesnut, 2022). This unevenness can be better understood by examining program type, purpose, constituency and language policy research, assisting in understanding such frameworks of DLBE in languages other than Spanish (Table 8.1). Beginning with the purposes of a dual language education, numerous scholars articulate different types of bilingual or dual language education programs (Abello-Contesse et al., 2013; Genesee et al., 2006).

Language Preservation/Reclamation Programs

This type of model is focused on languages that are risk of becoming moribund and are focused on language preservation and/or reclamation and is represented with in indigenous communities. Because many of these languages are at risk of loss, the student constituency is generally heritage speakers with limited to no proficiency in the language or native speakers with some to moderate degrees of proficiency.

Language Maintenance and Development Programs

The purpose of this model is to maintain and develop emergent bilingual students' native language and is generally transitional or short term in nature or development models, which are longer term. The only constituency in these programs are bilingual learners. The field often references this type of program as a bilingual education.

World Language Enrichment

This model is to introduce and develop a new target language to majority speakers and move them toward high levels of proficiency. The main constituency in this program model is language majority speakers and the focus is largely regarded as enrichment-oriented.

Dual Language Bilingual Education (DLBE)

DLBE is intended to center the needs and rights of bilingual students and families and is a form of bilingual education for them. For English majority students, its purposes are generally regarded as enrichment-oriented as they add a language to their repertoire. Blended with English majority students, the aims of this program are also cross cultural in nature as the embeddedness of the student constituency can lead to newer levels of understanding and connection across differences.

Within each of these four models, purposes and student constituencies, policies at the state and local level can also inform how such models are shaped from the top-down or the bottom-up. Drawing from the work of Kloss (1998) and Wiley (2007), they discuss a continuum of orientations within language planning and policy with a specified focus on minoritized speakers of languages other than English. *Promotion-oriented policies* are an explicit government agenda where federal or state resources are committed to advancing the use of the minority language(s). While the affordances for language preservation may be funded by governmental sources, such funding may be commissioned as a form of reparation due to historic restrictive policies and practices. *Tolerance-oriented* policies are laissez faire. There is no explicit nor active involvement of state governance in minoritized languages; thus, any action to implement languages other than English are decentralized to the local level, which can be community based and/or emancipatory in focus. *Restrictive-oriented* are policies, which moderate how, when and if the minority language can be used. Promotion- and restrictive-oriented policies are in large part, top-down, whereas tolerance-oriented policies are from the bottom-up, often incumbent upon local communities to take action in their local language planning.

Table 8.1 Program type, student constituency and state and local language policy

Name/type of dual language education	*Description*	*Student constituency*	*State and/or local language policy (Kloss, 1998; Wiley, 2007)*
Language preservation and/ or reclamation (Abello-Contesse, 2013)	Designed to reclaim and/ or preserve indigenous languages	Heritage and native speakers of indigenous languages	Promotion-oriented, tolerance-oriented
Language maintenance and development (Abello-Contesse, 2013)	Designed to maintain and develop students' native language for greater access to learning and positive identity formation	Native speakers of minoritized languages	Promotion-oriented, tolerance-oriented
World language enrichment (Abello-Contesse, 2013)	Designed to teach target language	Language majority students	Promotion-oriented
Dual language bilingual education (García, 2009; Genesee et al., 2006)	Designed to develop high levels of proficiency in target language and English	Language majority, language minoritized and world language students	Promotion-oriented, tolerance-oriented, restrictive-oriented

Drawing from the program type, student constituency and state and local language policies as detailed in Table 8.1, I now apply this matrix to DLBE programs in East Asian, Southeast Asian, Semitic and Native American languages. This analysis illuminates a continuum of policy positionings (restrictive to promotion oriented) of DLBE programs in languages other than Spanish.

East Asian Languages

Mandarin and Cantonese

Due in large part to the roles of Confucius Institutes (supported by the Chinese Ministry of Education) hosted at U.S. universities and world language initiatives including Language Flagships at universities and state Language

Roadmaps (The Indiana Language Roadmap, 2019; The Language Flagship, 2013; The Oregon Language Roadmap, 2007), the number of Mandarin-Chinese programs is proliferating (Koh et al., 2020; Sung & Tsai, 2019; Weise, 2014, 2021; Xiao, 2016). The Mandarin Immersion Parent's Council hosts a directory of programs on its website, quantifying a total of 342 programs throughout the United States, almost all of which have a 50/50 language allocation model. Proportionally, most are in California in medium-to-large cities, in close proximity to Chinese businesses (e.g. San Francisco Bay Area, greater Los Angeles area) and also where the density of Chinese or Chinese American families is larger, relative to the rest of the United States. The next most populous state is Utah, where there are 68 programs with none in private schools, 2 in charters and the majority hosted in public schools.

A closer look at the Mandarin immersion directory reveals a definitive pattern in the timing and location of implementation. Schools established prior to the 2000s are from the San Francisco, Bay Area with two in Portland, Oregon, one in New York and one in Maryland for a total of ten Mandarin immersion programs (Weise, 2021). Examining the period from 2000 to 2009, prior to the full implementation of the Language Flagships and Roadmaps, 43 Mandarin immersion programs are established throughout the country, most in large cities. From 2010 to 2015, another 161 programs were implemented in the United States, representing 23 states, including states with limited provisions of world and bilingual education including South Carolina and Missouri, newer immigrant gateway states (Hilburn, 2014). From 2015 to 2020, another 124 programs were established with projections for more schools beginning as far out as the 2024–2025 school years (Weise, 2021).

Less represented in the Chinese immersion programs is Cantonese. Cantonese is regarded as a more difficult language to master as its tonal attributes are regarded as more complicated (Sung & Tsai, 2019). In the case of San Francisco where there are five Cantonese dual language strands in five schools, leaders state that starting with Cantonese will result in trilingualism by the time children enter secondary school when Mandarin, the official language of China, will be introduced. "While most Chinese speakers in the world speak Mandarin, most Chinese speakers in San Francisco speak Cantonese, and well over 75% of the Chinese speakers in the SFUSD use Cantonese as the home language" (Chinese Immersion School at De Avila, 2021, p. 1). The proportion of Asian students attending these schools ranges from 48% to 67% and there is a moderate density of identified ELs of between 16% and 18%. The racial and ethnic subgroups, national origins and home languages are not disaggregated making it difficult to identify the precise portrait of the school.

Absent in the directory is the student constituency it serves, making it difficult to identify if the true moniker of DLBE is the case, but Lü's (2019) accounting attests to 84% of program models being one-way immersion models, mostly representing a world language constituency and secondarily, a heritage constituency. Thirty-one states have Mandarin or Cantonese programs among the 324 in the directory. Examining a representative sample of the 31 states' school websites for the dual program, promotional content or "About us" content suggests that the program is designed for English majority speakers as it fields questions about how to support your child in the learning of Chinese. Lastly, only a few actually use the term dual in the program name, most adopting the term immersion, consistent with Language Roadmaps which promote the naming convention of dual language immersion or DLI, demonstrating the mostly world language foundation (Abello-Contesse et al., 2013). While these models may present as being promotion oriented in their focus due to the teaching of Chinese, the constituency is less likely to be heritage or native Chinese-speaking students.

Japanese

Since immigration of the Japanese to the United States in the 1800s to Hawaii and the West Coast of the continental United States, Japanese was offered within community or Saturday schools. The first generation Issei from Japan grew increasingly concerned that their children were becoming too "Americanized" and set up such schools. At the onset of World War II, use of Japanese was seen as a threat to the national security given America's war on Japan, and many such schools were discouraged and/or shut down. During the internment of Japanese and Japanese Americans in incarceration camps, some Japanese language schools persisted within some of the camps, mostly because the Issei were fearful that they would be repatriated to Japan and their Americanized children were not be adequately prepared. Repatriation did occur for over 4,700 internees, more than half of whom were American citizens (Smithsonian National Museum of American History, 2021). During and post-World War II, the Issei and their children, the Nisei worked tirelessly to be ascribed as loyal Americans, or what the Japanese call *giri:* Do all actions at superior levels to prove one's loyalty (Sakamoto, 2012). This restrictive-policy past was pushed upon during the 1970s, when reparations for the incarceration were pushed and revitalization of Japanese was again promoted through weekend community schools (Doerr & Lee, 2010).

Concurrent with this time period is the economic boon of Japan and its increasing influence within the global economy. Japan America Societies, led by business owners from Japan, began to develop throughout the country, creating networks of support for Japanese companies wanting to do business in the United States and furnishing Japanese Saturday Schools for the children of executives bringing their young Japanese children to the United States for a one to three year period. Japanese parents wanted them to keep up with their studies as they would soon return to their home country of Japan.

The Center for Applied Linguistics documents 13 Japanese dual programs in the United States (2021). Of those reviewed, only one of the 13 discusses its student constituency. Schaumburg, Illinois' district, describes it as follows: "Dual Language and Immersion are programs of choice that are available for all students in District 54. Dual Language classes at the elementary level are composed of approximately 50% English or other language proficient students and 50% Spanish or Japanese-proficient students" (p. 1). In practice, however, the 50% that are regarded as the "native speakers" are mostly third- and fourth-generation Japanese heritage students.

Korean

Second-generation Korean youth are experiencing a rapid rate of language attrition relative to other minoritized languages (Au & Oh, 2009), due in part to families concerns about needing to excel in English and the Korean language not holding the same economic cache relative to Chinese Mandarin (Lee & Jeong, 2013). To address this language shift, community Korean programs have been established in churches and Korean DLI programs are growing throughout the United States. While most are concentrated in California's large cities (e.g. greater Los Angeles and San Francisco), a growing number are represented on the East Coast (Son, 2021). The Center for Applied Linguistics (2021) and the Korean Education Centers throughout the U.S. furnish directories and as of 2012, 12 such programs were identified throughout the United States (Lee & Jeong, 2013).

In review of the district websites, there is a combination of language allocations ranging from 50/50 at the onset to 100% at the beginning of the program model. Student constituencies are not often identified explicitly, but in review of the site's demographics, most are Asian students and many identify as heritage or second- or third-generation Koreans. Thus, there is a combination of heritage language development and native language maintenance and development goals.

Southeast Asian Languages

The circumstances of Southeast Asians have largely been through forced relocation as many sought amnesty in the United States following civil wars and strife within their countries. Their resettlement in the United States occurred in the 1970s and 1980s and following such adjustments, many community heritage schools developed, hosted in churches or religious settings and largely hosted by volunteers and donations (Tran, 2008). In this section, I discuss the development of Vietnamese and Hmong dual language programs throughout the United States, most of which began as heritage language community weekend schools with the aim of ethnic identity affirmation and transnational connections.

Vietnamese

After the Fall of Saigon in 1975 and resettlement in the United States, churches and temples served the purpose of providing housing and education to its newest refugees. An outcome of this support were community language schools, which focused on the development of Vietnamese in reading and writing as parents observed the attrition of Vietnamese once the children entered schools. In some parts of the country where the density of the Vietnamese was high, provisions of a language education were furnished in schools and some even bore the marker of bilingual education, yet in reality, they were transitional in nature and focused on quickly moving them into English with little to no explicit aim of bilingualism (García, 2009). As many of the Vietnamese pseudo bilingual programs were based in California where restrictive language policies were enforced through Proposition 227 from 1998 to 2016, many bilingual programs were dismantled rendering Vietnamese students to general education, sink-or-swim type contexts with English as a Second language models. California's Proposition 227 was countered with Proposition 58 in 2016, now making a bilingual education more possible, including a dual language education, yet the erosion from Proposition 227 has made this recovery slow.

In 2015, the first dual language program with a purposeful blending of Vietnamese heritage and native speakers was launched with a 50/50 language allocation (Villanueva, 2020). Because most Vietnamese students were now third-generation students, the focus has been on developing the literacy skills of the children to deepen family kinship (Fogle & King, 2013). With a blending of heritage and native speakers, Vietnamese dual language programs fall at the intersection of promotion oriented (policy) and reclamation and development (purposes).

Hmong

The Hmong community comes from the country of Laos, most by way of refugee camps in Thailand where they fled in the 1970s–1980s to escape the oppressive regime of their government. As ethnic minorities, they lived mostly in highland, rural communities where formal schooling was more limited. As the Hmong cooperated and served in a military capacity with the United States during a long-term CIA effort to prevent a communist takeover of the country, the United States sponsored the resettlement of the Hmong (Yau, 2005).

Based on the U.S. Census (2000), 84% of the Hmong live in Minnesota, Wisconsin and California. Thus, dual language programs in Hmong are represented in the Minneapolis, St. Paul area, Fresno, California and Madison, Wisconsin. Like Vietnamese programs, most are populated by heritage speakers who are third-generation speakers and have limited reading and writing proficiency in their heritage language (Cushing-Leubner, in press; Cushing-Leubner et al., in press). Although English majority speakers can be a part of the program, most are populated by heritage students of Hmong who have become English dominant.

Studies about parent's reasons for electing a dual language education include affirming their ethnic identities and remaining connected with their extended family members in Laos and Thailand (Pope, 2018; Vang, 2020). Vang (2020) found that first- and second-generation Hmong parents experienced an identity crisis as young children, which they argue could have been mitigated by having proficiency in English and Hmong. Thus, parents held aspirations that their children's proficiency in Hmong and English would avoid the ascription from the older Hmong community that they were "Mer" or "too Hmong" (p. 61). In short, families saw the dual language program's purpose as balancing and intersecting their children's dual identities. Like Vietnamese, most Hmong programs are now populated by heritage speakers. As an additive form of bilingual education, it is promotion oriented in its policy and holds reclamation and development as its purpose.

Semitic Languages

Arabic

The Middle East spans many countries, around 25, where Arabic is the official language. Such countries include Saudi Arabia, Yemen, Iraq and Qatar. Worldwide, there are over 466 million native speakers of Arabic. Arabic is also the language of the religious text for Islam, the Quran written in Quaranic or classical Arabic. Classical Arabic is emphasized within literacy (reading and writing), whereas Modern Standard Arabic is used more for speaking. Arabic speakers use these varieties interchangeably (Arab Academy, 2021).

Arabic is the fastest growing language in the world and is one of the fastest growing language programs at U.S. universities (Furman et al., 2010). Supported by the Qatar Foundation International and the U.S. Department of State, which have both economic and defense oriented interests, Arabic is demarked as a critical language. U.S. Language Flagships at six anchor universities aim to prepare undergraduate and graduate students with high levels of proficiency. Increasingly, Flagships are impacted in Language Roadmaps which include K-12 initiatives for language education. Four of the eight state roadmaps include provisions for developing and implementing Arabic programs throughout the United States (The Language Flagship, 2013).

Although the Qatar Foundation furnishes funding to many K-12 and higher education institutions (Qatar Foundation International, 2021) along with the U.S.' National Security Education Program (NSEP) education initiatives (National Security Education Program, 2021a, 2021b), most of the programs in the United States are one-way immersion models with less representation of Arabic native or heritage speakers. Zakharia (2016) found that "Despite this national interest in the Arabic language, instruction in U.S. schools has been faced with suspicion, controversy or staunch opposition, particularly where Arabic language programs have been developed by or for the Arabic-speaking community" (p. 144). Despite such opposition, Houston opened a two-way program with native Arabic and English speakers in 2015 with streams of protesters regarding the program as a terrorist endeavor (Mitchell, 2015). Upon closer look at their website and demographics, the bulk of students are English majority students with limited constitution of native Arabic speakers, making their aim of a 50/50 student constitution an aspiration versus a reality.

Arabic meets the criterion for being promotion oriented as defined by Kloss (1998) and Wiley (2007) as it receives state and federal level support for its implementation. Yet based on the United States and Middle East's economic and military history, such policy promotion does not immediately manifest into the same value at the local level as Arabic speakers can be regarded as a suspect class (Zakharia, 2016).

Hebrew

Hebrew day schools have long been hosted in congregations and/or private schools with the intent of language maintenance and development along with the affirmation and development of children's Jewish identities (Avni, 2012). Presently, there are 861 Hebrew Day Schools or *yeshivas* throughout the United States (Schick, 2014). The term "day" is used to differentiate them between schools that children attend only after school or on weekends and in most cases, that they are private entities. Dual language programs in Hebrew in public or charter schools are a relatively new phenomena where its oversight includes school and state level policies that define dual language more strictly based on student constitution and language allocation (Menken & Anvi, 2017).

Uniquely, U.S. Hebrew dual language programs in public schools serve the interests of making a previously tuition-bearing Hebrew education, free. In addition, it serves the purpose of changing the image of the school as evidenced in Menken and Anvi's (2017) study of Hebrew dual language school in New York. While supported by New York state and district dollars and policies to implement and develop dual language programs, making it promotion oriented, it is simultaneously restrictive as New York holds specific requirements for student constituencies and proportion of language use to earn the marker as a dual language program.

Slavic Languages

Slavic languages are inclusive of the languages of Russian, Polish, Czech, Bosnian/Croatian/Serbian, Macedonian and Bulgarian (Harvard University, 2021). Yet, representation of all these Slavic languages within dual language programs is scanter.

Russian

Russian dual language programs can be found in San Francisco, CA, Portland, OR, Northglenn, CO and Anchorage, AK. The population of the schools are largely English language majority students or speakers of languages other than Russian and English with some heritage speakers of Russian. Most programs hold the title of DLI, stating that most of its population are English majority speakers with some heritage speakers who were adopted from Russia and now live with American, English dominant parents. Russian is regarded as promotion-oriented as there is funding from two key federal sources, NSEP, and the National Security Agencies. Locally, there is a STARTALK program for critical languages out of Oregon where students can host artifacts of their Russian learning in a database, tracking their language progress and contributions over time.

As Russian programs receive federal funding for such language efforts, it is promotion oriented in nature, serving mostly an English-speaking clientele or languages other than English and Russian and for families adopting children transnationally from Russia. Its purpose is mostly focused on an English majority community where the primary focus is on the enrichment for their children's education. For Russian adoptees who may or may not have proficiency in Russian, parents identify the purpose of keeping them connected to their children's heritage and language learning is a mechanism to do so.

Polish

Polish dual language programs are a growing phenomenon in Chicago and New York City where historic immigrant populations have settled. Chicago is regarded as the most populace community of Poles outside of Poland proper and historic and newer immigrant Poles have been instrumental in shaping the political landscape of Chicago and Poland itself (Pacyga, 2005).

A more recent immigration from Poland occurred in the 1980s, often referenced as the "Solidarity" immigration as many fled due the imposition of martial law in their country. With three waves of immigration starting in the 1850s through the 1980s, many native and heritage Polish speakers collaborated and petitioned their school districts to begin a Polish dual language program. Polish families denoted their children's resistance to using Polish once they entered their English-medium schools and parents saw dual language as a means to encourage transnational identity and continued kinship with their extended family.

Although Polish is regarded as a critical language, it is not funded by the NSEP, like Russian. In the settings where Polish is being taught within a DLBE model, local districts support such efforts through state and local dollars making it promotion oriented, but to a lesser extent than programs that receive federal NSEP funding. It is also tolerance oriented as most of the support comes from Polish families, whose children are native or heritage speakers.

Native American Languages

As many Native American languages are moribund, efforts have been made to reclaim and revitalize for the present generations of native and heritage speakers with support from the U.S. Department of Education, U.S. Bureau of Indian Affairs, tribal councils, among others. Community language practices are central to the teaching of Native American languages. Importantly, McCarty and Wyman (2006) state that "Efforts to reverse language shift and revitalize languages are inherently intergenerational" (p. 280). To this end, McCarty, a scholar in Native American languages, references revitalization efforts as Native Language Immersion (McCarty, 2018), a naming convention founded through the implementation of the Native Language Immersion Student Achievement Act (2015) and an outcome of the previously instituted Native American Languages Act (NALA, 1990).

Arguments have been made that such models of revitalization are only focused on heritage speakers and that English majority speakers are absent from its classrooms, not making it a fully dual language program. Efforts from national organizations, such as Dual Language Education of New Mexico and their annual national conference, La Cosecha are challenging the boundaries set forth within dual language education to more fully represent varied approaches to teaching, language use and classroom constitution (Dual Language Education of New Mexico, 2021; Martinez & Haberman Lopez, 2020).

Native American dual-revitalization language education is promotion oriented in that it is supported at the national and state level and funds are allotted to support such efforts (Martinez & Haberman Lopez, 2020).

Yet this promotion follows a relatively recent history of subjugation and restrictive-oriented policies with the forcible and violent removal of Native children from their families to assimilate them linguistically and culturally (Spring, 2012). Seemingly, dual language education in Native American languages is reparation to heal these historic harms (Gándara & Orfield, 2012a; 2012b).

Limited Outcomes in Dual Language Programs Other Than Spanish

Extant data on the student achievement and bilingual outcomes of bilingual learners in DLBE programs are extremely limited. In a comprehensive review of the literature, most studies of DLBE in LCTL reference the students as "dual language learners", but not in the context of a dual language program. This lack of research is due in part to the short history of DLBE in LCTL. California, Arizona and Massachusetts where there is a longer history of bilingual programming, restrictive language policies have eroded many of the early beginnings of bilingual education, specifically designed and constituted for bilingual students. With the recent eradication and/or softening of these state policies, DLBE has become a more palatable mechanism for districts as it integrates various student groups and falls within the schema of the school choice movement (Bernstein et al., 2021; Delavan et al., 2022). Yet, due to their recency, little empirical research on student outcomes have been conducted.

The Elementary and Secondary Education Act's No Child Left Behind (2002) and newly reauthorized Every Student Succeeds Act (ESSA, 2015), the act governing K-12 U.S. education has affordances for bilingual education for bilingual learners, but such policies lean toward English as a priority (due in large part to testing accountability), leading to the dissolution of many bilingual programs throughout the U.S.' historic destination states (Menken & Solorza, 2014). With bilingual education's decline, the incline of DLBE programming materialized. Yet, in measuring the number of bilingual students actually benefitting from this student integrated model of language instruction, the number of bilingual students is proportionally lower than when bilingual education was more fully implemented.

Other potential reasons for lack of outcome-based data are because community-based, generative and tolerance-oriented approaches are driven from the bottom-up. Thus, particular linguistic communities have different ways of thinking about language maintenance, development and revitalization. The methods in which we traditionally regard measurement are thus, being reconfigured and reimagined within these more generative and tolerance-oriented contexts, yielding new definitions of student and community outcomes.

Conclusion and Discussion

Languages other than Spanish within DLBE originate from different foundations. Critical languages such as Arabic and Chinese-Mandarin mostly have economic and defense purposes. Both are top-down in its orientations, beginning with funding from departments of defense, the Chinese Ministry of Education and the Qatar International Foundation, impacting higher education through the establishment of university flagships to build advanced levels of language proficiency. From there, such efforts have trickled to the K-12 arena where DLBE could be a manifestation with a representation of students who are native or heritage speakers. Yet, such efforts have not fully materialized as most Chinese models are one-way programs (Sung, 2020; Zhang, 2020) and more newly minted Arabic programs aspire for a dual constituency but are most often populated by English majority students (Zakharia, 2016). Beginning with a top-down orientation with both federal and external foundation supports, such models are promotion oriented and are quickly increasing.

Participatory languages such as Vietnamese and Hmong, a community settled in the United States from the 1970s to the present, originate from community-based language programs, focusing on cultural and linguistic resources for children and families. Depending on the state context, Vietnamese or Hmong was then a part of transitional bilingual programs, yet the focus among most is on a quick transition to English with lower levels of the native language and meant to be short term. DLBE is a relatively newer manifestation for Vietnamese and Hmong, and its constituency often represents heritage and native speakers with greater numbers of heritage language students given that most are third-generation speakers, making such models bottom up. Funding can be used through federal (e.g. Title III) and state dollars to support such languages as a form of language education meeting the Castañeda v. Pickard standard (1981), but such languages fall in the policy mode of tolerance as they are decentralized to the local level.

Japanese and Korean can also be identified as participatory languages as many have similar origins in community language schools with Japanese dating back to the 1930s. With the increased economic interest in East Asia and the establishment of Japanese and Korean companies in the United States, increasingly such models have increasing business support. Such models in Japanese and Korean are regarded as community based and thus are bottom up, but also benefit from a promotion-oriented policy perspective as funds are coming from private corporations.

Russian and Polish are both regarded as critical languages, but the epistemic origins differ. Russian is regarded as top-down with federal and state funds for its induction, but most programs are one-way in nature with the inclusion of Russian adoptees whose parents want the program to recognize and honor their linguistic roots. Polish DLBE programs come more from the bottom-up in cities like Chicago and New York, where the long settled and newer immigrant community has reasons for heritage language revitalization to develop deeper ties with their extended Polish family.

The genesis of Native American revitalization programs is certainly participatory and emancipatory with such efforts taking place within and across tribal communities. Due to the colonial and violent subjugation of Native Americans by U.S.-sponsored public boarding schools, funding that is reparation-oriented is meeting the bottom-up revitalization efforts from the top-down. The policy is thus a newer nuance to Kloss (1998) and Wiley's (2007) work, suggesting that a history of restrictive language policies can move toward promotion-oriented approaches.

While Arabic is presently a promotion oriented, top-down and regarded as a critical language, Hebrew is a language with a history rooted in synagogues and congregations, funded and supported by the religion and private tuition. Hebrew, however, is now moving into the venue of public schools, where bilingual education has a long and contested history. In the case of New York City with higher proportions of Jewish students, DLBE funds can come from local or state dollars, yet it is contingent upon the school to meet the criterion of language allocation and student constituency in order to use such funds. Presently, Hebrew within DLBE has bounced between promotion and restrictive-oriented policies, showing the conditional positioning of Hebrew.

As DLBE has a focus on sociocultural competence and a newer pillar of critical consciousness (Cervantes-Soon et al., 2017), recognizing the disequilibrium of power that is present when varied linguistic, racial and ethnic constituencies are gathered is a needed area of inquiry and professional development in LCTL. Because DLBE is located in schools, which are institutional spaces, standardization is nearly always the focus. In review of the programs in LCTL, promotional websites and materials discuss language allocation, but not all explicitly discuss their student constituencies, making it difficult to identify if identified-ELs of the partner language are actually in the mix. This abstracting or backgrounding of bilingual learners demonstrates the subtle deselection of their eligibility and/or genuine inclusion in such program models (Morita-Mullaney & Chesnut, 2022), potentially yielding to more English majority students within such models in comparison to bilingual learners.

As a field of bilingual education and world language education, we would benefit from analyzing the history of our educational expertise and efforts. In review of the hundreds of websites that describe DLBE for languages other than Spanish, the personnel overseeing such program models may come from departments of world language, English learning, bilingual education or magnet schools; leadership that is grounded in different foundations of language learning and language policy. By illuminating the origins of each of these models, we can articulate their overlaps and fissures, yielding more specificity about what multilingualism means across varied types of speakers (e.g. world language, heritage or native speakers). Moreover, the world and bilingual disciplines need to examine language allocation, student constitution and language use (Menken & Anvi, 2017; Morita-Mullaney et al., 2020a, 2020b; Sánchez et al., 2018). Often framed as *debates* in our fields, we have to work beyond the binary of measuring or not measuring allocation, student audience and language use. Such simplicity will only keep our fields separate and unequal, ultimately further marginalizing bilingual youth and families of multiple minoritized languages and racial/ethnic identities.

References

Abello-Contesse, C., Chacón-Beltrán, R., Chandler, P. M., & López-Jiménez, M. D. (2013). *Bilingual and multilingual education in the 21st century: Building on experience*. Multilingual Matters.

American Council for International Education. (2021). *Canvass of dual language and immersion (DLI) programs in US public schools*. American Council for International Education.

Arab Academy. (2021). *Quranic Arabic vs. modern standard Arabic*. Retrieved from https://www.arabacademy.com/quranic-arabic-vs-modern-standard-arabic/

Au, T. K., & Oh, J. S. (2009). Korean as a heritage language. In P. Li, C. Lee, G. B. Simpson, & Y. Kim (Eds.), *Handbook of East Asian psycholinguistics, part III: Korean psycholinguistics* (pp. 268–275). Cambridge University Press.

Avni, S. (2012). Hebrew-only language policy in religious education. *Language Policy*, *11*(2), 169–188. https://doi.org/10.1007/s10993-011-9222-7

Bernstein, K. A., Alvarez, A., Chaparro, S., & Henderson, K. I. (2021). "We live in the age of choice": School administrators, school choice policies, and the shaping of dual language bilingual education. *Language Policy*, *20*(3), 383–412. https://doi.org/10.1007/s10993-021-09578-0

Castañeda v. Pickard, 648 F.2d 989 (1981).

Center for Applied Linguistics. (2021). *Dual language directory*. Retrieved from http://webapp.cal.org/duallanguage/

Cervantes-Soon, C. G., Dorner, L., Palmer, D., Heiman, D., Schwerdtfeger, R., & Choi, J. (2017). Combating inequalities in two-way language immersion programs: Toward critical consciousness in bilingual education spaces. *Review of Research in Education*, *41*, 403–427. https://doi.org/10.3102/0091732X17690120

Chinese Immersion School at De Avila. (2021). *Why Cantonese first?* Retrieved from https://www.sfusd.edu/school/chinese-immersion-school-cis-de-avila/about/why-cantonese-first

Cushing-Leubner, J. (in press). Politics of desire, policies of replacement: Race, empire, and worth(iness) in Hmong language education. *International Journal of Educational Research*.

Cushing-Leubner, J., Xiong-Lor, V., Vang, T., & Yang, P. (in press). Grappling with HMoob: Internal community dynamics for critical language pedagogy across Hmong language dialects. *Languages*.

Delavan, M.G, Freire, J. A., & Morita-Mullaney, T. (2022). Conscripted into thinking of scarce, selective, privatized, and precarious seats in dual language bilingual education: The choice discourse of mercenary exclusivity. *Current Issues in Language Planning*, 1–27. https://doi.org/10.1080/14664208.2022.2077032

Doerr, N., & Lee, K. (2010). Inheriting "Japanese-ness" diversely: Heritage practices at a weekend Japanese language school in the United States. *Critical Asian Studies*, *42*(2), 191–216. https://doi.org/10.1080/14672715.2010.486633

Dual Language Education of New Mexico. (2021). *Support for tribal communities*. Retrieved from https://www.dlenm.org/what-we-do/programmatic-support-and-resources/support-for-tribal-communities/

Every Student Succeeds Act, 20 U.S.C. § 6301 (2015). https://www.congress.gov/114/plaws/publ95/PLAW-114publ95.pdf

Fogle, L., & King, K. A. (2013). Child agency and language policy in transnational families. *Issues in Applied Linguistics*, *19*, 1–25. https://doi.org/10.5070/L4190005288

Furman, N., Goldberg, D., & Lusin, N. (2010). *Enrollments in languages other than English in United States institutions of higher education*. Modern Language Association of America.

Gándara, P., & Orfield, G. (2012a). Segregating Arizona's English learners: A return to the "Mexican Room"? *Teacher's College Record*, *114*(9), 1–27. https://doi.org/10.1177/016146811211400905

Gándara, P., & Orfield, G. (2012b). Why Arizona matters: The historical, legal and politcal contexts of Arizona's instructional policies and linguistic hegenomy. *Language Policy*, *11*. https://doi.org/10.1007/s10993-011-9227-2

García, O. (2009). *Bilingual education in the 21st century: A global perspective*. Wiley-Blackwell.

Genesee, F., Lindholm-Leary, K., Saunders, W. M., & Christian, D. (2006). *Educating English language learning: A synthesis of research evidence*. Cambridge University Press.

Harvard University. (2021). *What are the Slavic languages*? Retrieved from https://slavic.fas.harvard.edu/pages/what-are-slavic-languages#:~:text=Key%20to%20these%20peoples%20and,and%20Bulgarian%20to%20the%20south.

Hilburn, J. (2014). Challenges facing immigrant students beyond the linguistic domain in a new gateway state. *Urban Review*, *46*, 654–680. https://doi.org/10.1007/s11256-014-0273-x

Indiana Language Roadmap. (2019). *Indiana language roadmap: Building a more global Indiana*. Author. https://www.thelanguageflagship.org/sites/default/files/Indiana%20State%20Language%20Roadmap%20%282019%29.pdf

Kloss, H. (1998). *The American bilingual tradition*. Center for Applied Linguistics.

Koh, S. Y., Hoon, C. Y., & Haji-Othman, N. A. (2020). "Mandarin Fever" and Chinese language-learning in Brunei's middle schools: Discrepant discourses, multifaceted realities and institutional barriers. *Asian Studies Review*, *45*(4), 325–344. https://doi.org/10.1080/10357823.2020.1801577

Lee, J. S., & Jeong, E. (2013). Korean–English dual language immersion: Perspectives of students, parents and teachers. *Language, Culture and Curriculum*, *26*(1), 89–107. https://doi.org/10.1080/07908318.2013.765890

Lü, C. (2019). One-way immersion and Mandarin immersion in the United States. In C. Lü (Ed.), *Chinese literacy learning in an immersion program* (pp. 11–26). Palgrave Macmillan.

Martinez, R., & Haberman Lopez, M. J. (2020). *History of bilingual education in New Mexico: The shoulders we stand on*. New Mexico University Press.

McCarty, T. L. (2018). *Teaching the whole child: Language immersion and student achievement*. Retrieved from https://indiancountrytoday.com/archive/teaching-the-whole-child-language-immersion-and-student-achievement

McCarty, T. L., & Wyman, L. T. (2006). Indigenous youth and bilingualism—Theory, research, praxis. *Journal of Language, Identity & Education*, *8*(5), 279–290. https://doi.org/10.1080/15348450903305031

Menken, K., & Anvi, S. (2017). Challenging linguistic purism in dual language bilingual education: A case study of Hebrew in a New York City public middle school. *Annual Review of Applied Linguistics*, *37*, 185–202. https://doi.org/10.1017/S0267190517000149

Menken, K., & Solorza, C. (2014). No child left bilingual: Accountability and the elimination of bilingual education programs in New York city schools. *Educational Policy*, *28*(1), 96–125. https://doi.org/10.1177/0895904812468228

Mitchell, C. (2015). Districts diversify languages offered in dual-immersion. *Education Week*,. https://www.edweek.org/policy-politics/districts-diversify-languages-offered-in-dual-immersion/2015/09

Morita-Mullaney, T., & Chesnut, C. (2022). Equity traps in the deselection of English learners in dual language education: A collective case study of school principals. *NABE Journal of Research and Practice*, *12*(2), 49–68. https://doi.org/10.1080/26390043.2022.2079390

Morita-Mullaney, T., Renn, J., & Chiu, M. (2020a). Contesting math as the universal language: A longitudinal study of dual language bilingual education language allocation. *International Multilingual Research Journal*, *15*(1), 43–60. https://doi.org/10.1080/19313152.2020.1753930

Morita-Mullaney, T., Renn, J., & Chiu, M. (2020b). Obscuring equity in dual language bilingual education: A longitudinal study of emergent bilingual achievement, school course placements and grades. *TESOL Quarterly*, *54*(3), 685–718. https://doi.org/10.1080/19313152.2020.1753930

Morita-Mullaney, T., & Singh, M. (2019). Obscuring English learners from state accountability: The case of Indiana's language blind policies. *Educational Policy*, 1–25. https://doi.org/10.1177/0895904818823751

National Security Education Program. (2021a). *Critical languages*. Retrieved from https://www.nsep.gov/content/critical-languages

National Security Education Program. (2021b). *Grants to schools*. Retrieved from https://www.qfi.org/opportunities/grants-to-schools/

No Child Left Behind of 2001, P.L. 107-110, 20 U.S.C. § 6319 (2002).

Pacyga, D. A. (2005). *Polish immigrants and industrial Chicago: Workers on the south side, 1880–1922*. Retrieved from http://www.encyclopedia.chicagohistory.org/pages/982.html

Palmer, D. K. (2009). Middle-class English speakers in a two-way immersion bilingual classroom: "Everybody should be listening to Jonathan Right now…". *TESOL Quarterly*, *43*(2), 177–202. https://doi.org/10.1002/j.1545-7249.2009.tb00164.x

Pope, N. (2018). *Hmong parent choice in Hmong language programs in Central Valley California*. (Publication No. 10788699) [Doctoral dissertation, Mills College]. ProQuest Dissertations Publishing.

Pufahl, I., & Rhodes, N. C. (2011). Foreign language instruction in U.S. schools: Results of a national survey of elementary and secondary schools. *Foreign Language Annals*, *44*(2), 258–288. https://doi.org/10.1111/j.1944-9720.2011.01130.x

Qatar Foundation International. (2021). *Arabic dual language immersion project*. Retrieved from https://www.qfi.org/blog/arabic-dual-language-immersion-project/

Sakamoto, A. (2012). *Japanese and American cultural aspects of the Japanese American experience*. Paper presented at the Tateuchi Democracy Forum, Los Angeles, CA.

Sánchez, M. T., García, O., & Solorza, C. (2018). Reframing language allocation policy in dual language bilingual education. *Bilingual Research Journal*, *41*(1), 37–51. https://doi.org/10.1080/15235882.2017.1405098

Schick, M. (2014). *A census of Jewish Day schools in the United States – 2013–14*. Retrieved from http://avichai.org/knowledge_base/a-census-of-jewish-day-schools-in-the-united-states-2013-14-2014/

Smithsonian National Museum of American History. (2021). *A more perfect union*. Retrieved from https://amhistory.si.edu/perfectunion/non-flash/loyalty_expat.html

Son, M. (2021). *Choosing dual language bilingual education over English-only programs: A cultural-historical perspective of immigrant parents*. Teacher's College, Columbia University.

Spring, J. H. (2012). *Deculturalization and the struggle for equality: A brief history of the education of dominated cultures in the United States* (7th ed.). McGraw Hill.

Sung, K. Y. (2020). Parent satisfaction and one-way Mandarin Chinese dual-language programs in Utah. *Bilingual Research Journal*, *43*(4), 384–399. https://doi.org/10.1080/15235882.2020.1825540

Sung, K. Y., & Tsai, H. M. (2019). *Mandarin Chinese dual language immersion programs*. Multilingual Matters.

The Language Flagship. (2013). *The language flagship: Creating global professionals*. Retrieved from https://www.thelanguageflagship.org/content/language-roadmaps

The Oregon Language Roadmap. (2007). *Language roadmap for the 21st century*. RLanguage Roadmap: https://www.thelanguageflagship.org/sites/default/files/Oregon%20State%20Language%20Roadmap%20%282007%29.pdf

Tran, A. (2008). Vietnamese language education in the United States. *Language, Culture and Curriculum*:(3), 256–268. https://doi.org/10.1080/07908310802385923

Vang, C. (2020). *The language outcomes of Hmong dual-language immersion program* [Doctoral dissertation, Concordia University]. DigitalCommons@CSP.

Villanueva, S. (2020). *Parent motivation for enrollment and perceptions of a Vietnamese dual language immersion program: A qualitative study* (Publication No. 28152895) [Doctoral dissertation, University of California at Fullerton]. Proquest Dissertations Publishing.

Weise, E. (2014). *A parent's guide to mandarin immersion*. Chenery Street Press.

Weise, E. (2021). *Mandarin immersion school list*. Retrieved from https://miparents-council.org/full-mandarin-immersion-school-list/

Wiley, T. (2007). Accessing language rights in education: A brief history of U.S. Context. In O. Garcia & C. Baker (Eds.), *Bilingual education: An introductory reader* (pp. 89–109). Multilingual Matters.

Xiao, Y. (2016). Chinese education in the United States: Players and challenges. *Global Chinese*, 2(1), 23–50. https://doi.org/10.1515/glochi-2016-0002

Yau, J. (2005). *The foreign-born Hmong in the United States*. Retrieved from https://www.migrationpolicy.org/article/foreign-born-hmong-united-states

Zakharia, Z. (2016). Language, conflict, and migration: Situating Arabic bilingual community education in the United States. *International Journal of the Sociology of Language*, *237*, 139–160. https://doi.org/10.1515/ijsl-2015-0039

Zhang, B. (2020). Neoliberal multilingualism and "humanitarian connections": Discourses around parents' experiences with a Mandarin Chinese immersion school. *Language and Education*, *35*(1), 78–95. https://doi.org/10.1080/09500782.2020.1828451

9

ACADEMIC AND LANGUAGE OUTCOMES IN SPANISH-ENGLISH PROGRAMS

Elizabeth R. Howard, Manqian Zhao

Overview of Issue

The development of bilingualism and biliteracy is one of the three goals of dual language bilingual education (DLBE), and as such, there has been a considerable amount of research dedicated to the exploration of student outcomes in this area, as well as four past reviews of this research (Hopewell & Escamilla, 2014; Howard et al., 2003; Lindholm-Leary & Genesee, 2014; Lindholm-Leary & Howard, 2008). While past reviews have not been limited to the language and literacy outcomes of students in Spanish/English programs, the themes that have emerged from those reviews have largely been based on such programs because the majority of DLBE programs in the United States are Spanish/English programs. The following themes have been identified in the earlier reviews: (1) DLBE language and literacy outcomes that are ultimately comparable to or better than those of students in other programs, with the vast majority of these studies focusing on English attainment; (2) language and literacy development that is continuous for all DLBE students in both English and Spanish, but that differs by language and according to student and program characteristics; (3) cross-linguistic connections in language and literacy outcomes; and (4) the potential of specific pedagogical practices within DLBE programs to influence language and literacy outcomes.

As research in this area has continued to evolve, there have been shifts in guiding theories and methods to those that emphasize the holistic, interrelated nature of language and literacy development in the two languages, as well as the continuous rather than dichotomous bilingual proficiencies of entering students. Building on the findings of the previous reviews and

DOI: 10.4324/9781003269076-14

focusing on the research published within the past decade, this chapter seeks to address three main questions: (1) What are the language and literacy outcomes of DLBE students in Spanish-English programs, and how do they vary by student and program characteristics; (2) how does students' bilingualism manifest itself in language and literacy outcomes; and (3) how do pedagogical practices shape students' language and literacy outcomes? The chapter concludes with a discussion of implications and future questions to guide research, policy, and practice.

Main Findings from Current Empirical Research

Focusing on studies conducted over the past ten years, from 2011 to 2021, we conducted three searches of all publication types in order to capture a comprehensive body of relevant research. Our first search relied on a combined EBSCO-host search of the ERIC, PSYCInfo, MLA International, and Academic Host Premier databases. To increase the likelihood of capturing relevant literature from Spain and Latin America, we then carried out follow-up searches through Dialnet and HAPI. The search terms used in each database are in Table 9.1, along with the number of unique publications from each search.

The combined search resulted in a total initial database of 622 publications. We then carried out an inclusion/exclusion review, using the following criteria: the study had to have (1) included students enrolled in a Spanish/English DLBE program that extended at least through the elementary grades (i.e., no preschool-only sites) and (2) reported English and/or Spanish language and/or literacy outcomes. We independently rated the same 20 articles, resulting in .85 agreement. We reconciled the disagreements and further clarified our inclusion/exclusion criteria, then double-rated another 10 papers, increasing the overall inter-rater agreement to .9. We single-rated the remaining papers, yielding a total of 81 publications for potential inclusion. Given space limitations, we further restricted the sources to the 39 journal articles. The grade levels and methods employed in these studies are highlighted in Figures 9.1 and 9.2.

Finally, we reviewed and coded the articles for responses to the following three questions.

What Are the Language and Literacy Outcomes of DLBE Students in Spanish-English Programs, and How Do They Vary by Student and Program Characteristics?

The majority of studies addressed this first research question, which we further divided into three sub-questions to facilitate synthesis. The first sub-question addresses the topic broadly, the second considers how outcomes vary by home language profiles, and the third explores outcomes by program model.

Table 9.1 Overview of literature search

Database	*Tier 1 search terms (one at a time)*	*Tier 2 search terms*	*Tier 3 search terms (one at a time)*	*Total unique sources (n = 622)*
EBSCOhost (ERIC, PsycInfo, MLA, Academic Host Premier)	dual language two-way immersion TWI	Spanish	academic biliteracy reading achievement reading outcomes writing vocabulary development or vocabulary growth or vocabulary acquisition decoding spelling phonological awareness reading fluency oral language language outcomes cross-linguistic pedagogy or intervention or strategies (this was combined with a fourth line outcomes or impacts or effects)	494
Dialnet	*English*: dual language two-way immersion TWI *Spanish*: doble inmersión	*English*: Spanish *Spanish*: educación lectura escritura alfabetización bialfabetización vocabulario deletreo	*English*: academic biliteracy reading writing vocabulary decoding spelling phonological awareness cross-linguistic pedagogy interventions *Spanish*: n/a	107
HAPI	*English*: dual language two-way immersion *Spanish*: inmersión	n/a	n/a	21

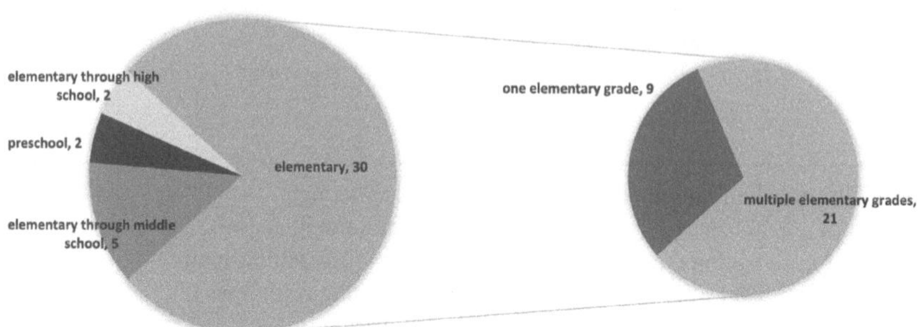

Figure 9.1 Breakdown of Included Studies by Grade Level

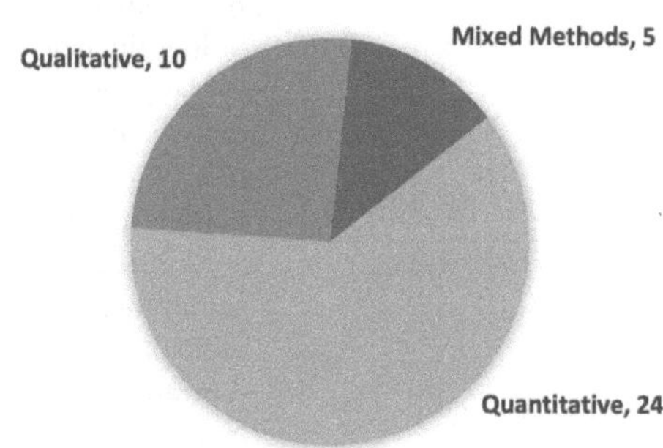

Figure 9.2 Breakdown of Included Studies by Methodology

What Are the Language and Literacy Outcomes of DLBE Students in Spanish-English Programs?

The papers summarized in this section provide insight about developmental trends as well as similarities and differences between English and Spanish performance. Four studies focused exclusively on Spanish outcomes, and all of them used measures that mapped onto ACTFL proficiency levels, thus facilitating comparison. As part of their study of DLBE programs in Portland, Oregon, Burkhauser et al. (2016) found that performance in reading and listening progressed from the Intermediate Mid level in fourth grade to Intermediate High (reading) or between Intermediate Mid and Intermediate High (listening) in eighth grade, while performance in speaking and writing progressed from a mean score between Novice High and Intermediate Low in fourth grade to Intermediate Mid in eighth grade.

Similarly, in a cross-sectional study of upper elementary and secondary students in Utah, Watzinger-Tharp et al. (2018) found that performance in listening and reading ranged from the lower sub-levels of Intermediate Mid in fourth grade to progressively higher sub-levels of Intermediate Mid in sixth grade and eighth grade, moving towards Intermediate High. Performance in speaking ranged from Intermediate Low in third grade to Intermediate Mid in fifth grade, and a higher sub-level of Intermediate Mid in eighth grade. In a later study, Watzinger-Tharp et al. (2021) found ongoing growth in all domains from the elementary into the secondary grades, reaching Intermediate Mid to Intermediate High in speaking by seventh grade and in the other three domains by eighth grade. Continued growth through grades 8 and 9 was difficult to assess because scores remained consistent at the top of the scale, but the authors noted that the program was successful in meeting its ninth-grade benchmark goal, since at least 80% of the students reached Intermediate High in listening and Intermediate Mid for the other three domains. Evidence of ongoing development in Spanish was likewise found in a longitudinal K-5 study of English home-language speakers in the Southeastern United States (Ruiz-Funes, 2020). This study focused specifically on oral Spanish proficiency and noted responses of increasing length and complexity in oral fluency, grammar, and vocabulary at each subsequent grade level. Scores in all three domains corresponded to Jr. Novice Low for kindergarteners, to Jr. Novice Mid for second graders, and to a range from Jr. Novice High to Jr. Intermediate Low (vocabulary) or Jr. Intermediate Mid (grammar and oral fluency) for fifth graders. Together, these studies provide evidence of DLBE students demonstrating ongoing growth and attainment of grade-level benchmarks in Spanish through the secondary grades.

Four additional studies explored the development of outcomes in both Spanish and English. First, Aguilar et al. (2020) examined English and Spanish academic language development cross-sectionally in grades 4–6, finding significantly higher mean performance in both languages at each subsequent grade level other than fourth- to fifth-grade Spanish. In the second study, Lucero (2018a) investigated microlevel (vocabulary and grammar) and macrolevel (story structure) performance in the oral narrative retelling of Spanish home-language students in grades K-2. For microlevel performance, students exhibited significant improvement in vocabulary performance in both languages, but not in grammar performance in either language. For macrolevel performance, students exhibited significant improvement only in English. The author discusses the possibility that the lack of significant improvement in Spanish macrostructure may indicate that there are not sufficient opportunities for Spanish discourse development, even in the context of DLBE. However, in a related cross-sectional study of K-2 Spanish home-language students, Lucero (2018b) found stronger macrostructure performance in Spanish than in English, stronger vocabulary performance in English than in Spanish, and no significant difference across languages for grammar. Additionally, the author found significant correlations between the two languages in macrostructure and vocabulary performance, but not for grammar performance. Finally, the author noted different biliteracy profiles across participating students, pointing to the need to explore student characteristics and the ways in which they may be associated with outcomes. In a longitudinal study of Spanish and English reading performance from second to fifth grade, Babino (2017) found progressively higher mean scores in both languages at each grade and similar patterns of progression in both languages, although these patterns varied across the two participating schools. Moreover, there were moderate to high positive correlations across languages at all time points, indicating that for many students, reading performance in one language is strongly related to reading performance in the other. Using the biliteracy zone guidelines developed by Escamilla et al. (2014), the author noted that approximately 85% of the fifth graders in both schools were within the biliteracy zone.

Self-report is another approach that has been used to explore similarities and differences in Spanish and English outcomes. In a study of fifth-grade Latinx students from Spanish-speaking homes in the Southwest, Babino and Stewart (2017) found differences in use of the two program languages, with English holding greater power. The students reported that their Spanish interactions were typically limited to those with Spanish monolinguals, that they were more likely to use hybridized language varieties in social situations, and that they had less confidence in their ability to use Spanish in academic situations. By contrast, they noted greater confidence in and need and preference for using English in both academic and social situations. Dworin (2011) found similar results in a study of five DLBE K-12 graduates from varying home-language and racial/ethnic backgrounds. While the five graduates reported that they did not use Spanish on a daily basis and that their Spanish was typically limited to carrying out specific functions with Spanish-dominant individuals, they all described themselves as bilingual and biliterate with the ability to use both languages as needed. The author therefore noted that while Spanish use was limited, their ongoing ability to carry out activities in both languages was a positive outcome, particularly given the anti-bilingual-education climate at the time in California. However, the author also expressed a concern about which students are given this opportunity, since the majority of Latinx students in the program were exited at the conclusion of elementary school and did not participate in college track courses at the high school. Thus, these two studies provide general support for students' overall ability to use the two languages but also raise concerns about the perpetual lower status and limited use of Spanish, as well as the extent to which DLBE programs are providing opportunities for Spanish home-language speakers and entering bilinguals to continue to develop proficiency in both languages.

How Do the Language and Literacy Outcomes of DLBE Students in Spanish-English Programs Vary by Home-Language Profiles?

The papers in this section explored Spanish and/or English outcomes of DLBE students and compared the performance of students by home-language profile. We present the results by language domain.

Language Proficiency. The studies in this section explored a number of sub-domains of language development, including vocabulary, listening and speaking, and academic language. Three studies addressed potential differences in vocabulary performance of DLBE students by home-language profile – one in Spanish, one in English, and one looking at both languages. Kuo et al. (2017) explored the development of Spanish vocabulary and morphological awareness of fourth-grade DLBE students in the Midwest and found that Spanish home-language students outperformed English home-language students on both high-frequency and low-frequency morphologically simple words, as well as on cognates, but the two groups performed comparably on morphologically complex words that involved knowledge of roots as well as derivational suffixes. In English, Esposito and Bauer (2019) compared the verbal comprehension (including vocabulary) of DLBE students and found that Spanish home-language students had significantly lower scores in kindergarten than English home-language speakers, but faster growth rates, indicating that they were moving in the direction of reaching parity, although their scores were still lower in fifth grade. Finally, Kalia et al. (2018) investigated the vocabulary development of DLBE students in both English and Spanish, finding that Spanish home-language speakers had significantly higher performance than English home-language speakers in Spanish, and that likewise, English home-language speakers had significantly higher scores on the English measure than Spanish home-language speakers. Together, these studies tend to corroborate earlier findings that students who speak the language of the assessment at home are likely to perform better than students who do not.

Three additional studies looked at language proficiency more broadly. Burkhauser et al. (2016) compared the oral language performance of Spanish home-language speakers in Portland, Oregon's Spanish immersion programs to the performance of all other students in the programs (primarily English home-language speakers). By fourth grade, the speaking scores of the two groups were the same, while there was a slight difference favoring Spanish home-language speakers in listening. By eighth grade, the outcomes had reversed, with a slight advantage in speaking for Spanish home-language students and a slightly lower score in listening. As these differences were minimal or non-existent at all time points, the overall trend indicated comparable performance in the two Spanish oral language domains across home-language groups. Looking at teacher-reported oral Spanish proficiency data for three subgroups of Latinx dual language (DL) students in grades 4–8 – current English learners (ELs), reclassified ELs, and students never classified as ELs – Lindholm-Leary and Hernandez (2011) found that reclassified ELs and current ELs had higher scores than never ELs, although all subgroups had high mean scores. Additionally, using self-reported oral proficiency data, the same study noted that the reclassified students had the highest scores for both Spanish and English. Finally, Aguilar et al. (2020) investigated the academic language development of DLBE students in the Northeast in grades 4–6 and found that English-proficient students scored significantly higher on both the English and Spanish measures of academic language than students classified as ELs (all of whom were Spanish home-language speakers). The authors note that this may have been a function of the fact that the English proficient group included reclassified ELs who were proficient in Spanish; additionally, a higher proportion of the EL group qualified for special education services. These somewhat conflicting findings point to the importance of considering how student populations are defined, what measures are used, and what analyses are carried out.

Reading. The four studies summarized in this section addressed reading fluency and reading comprehension. Taub et al. (2017) looked at the second language reading fluency of third graders in Florida and found that after controlling for pre-test scores, the English reading fluency of Spanish-dominant students was significantly higher than the Spanish reading fluency of English-dominant students. Burkhauser et al. (2016) looked at Spanish reading outcomes and found that the fourth-grade performance of Spanish home-language students was comparable to that of students who spoke other languages at home, but by eighth grade, the Spanish reading performance of Spanish home-language students was slightly lower. Lindholm-Leary and Hernandez (2011) found that reclassified EL Latinx students in grades 4–8 had the highest actual and self-reported reading scores in both Spanish and English compared to their current EL and never EL Latinx peers, although their English reading scores were not significantly higher than those of never ELs. Finally, Arteagoitia and Yen (2020) examined third- to fifth-grade reading trajectories of ever ELs and never ELs in Oregon and found no significant differences across the two groups in either initial status or growth rates in English reading, controlling for Spanish reading. However, they noted that controlling for English reading, ever ELs had significantly higher initial status but slower growth rates in Spanish than never ELs. It is somewhat challenging to synthesize the findings across these studies since they framed the outcomes and student groups in such different ways, but on the whole, they provide some insight into the ways in which the categorization of students and the inclusion of control variables may influence outcomes and point to the need for further investigation of these topics.

Writing. Three studies addressed writing outcomes. Burkhauser et al. (2016) found that Spanish home-language students slightly outperformed students from other home-language backgrounds in Spanish writing in fourth grade and maintained comparable performance through eighth grade. Howard and Neugebauer (2015) examined the second- to fifth-grade English and Spanish writing trajectories of students across a 5-point continuum of home-language profiles, from Spanish monolingual to varying levels of bilingualism to English monolingual (EM). The authors found that all students exhibited significant growth in writing ability in both languages that slowed over time. In English, students who spoke more English at home had significantly higher scores in second grade and continued to do so at fifth grade, but because the growth rate was faster for students who spoke more Spanish at home, this difference became smaller over time. In Spanish, however, students who spoke more Spanish at home had significantly higher scores in second grade, and this difference remained consistent over the four years. Finally, Neugebauer and Howard (2015) explored English and Spanish writing self-perceptions and narrative writing outcomes among fourth graders and found that English-dominant students rated their English writing ability significantly higher than Spanish-dominant students did. Conversely, there was not a significant difference between the two groups in their Spanish writing self-perception. Both language dominance and writing self-perception significantly predicted both English and Spanish writing outcomes, such that students with dominance in a language and higher self-perception scores for that language had higher predicted writing outcomes in that language. Together, the three studies indicate a positive relationship between home language and writing outcomes, whereby students from a home-language group are likely to have higher writing scores in that language.

How Do the Language and Literacy Outcomes of DLBE Students in Spanish-English Programs Vary by Program Characteristics?

The papers in this section compared the English and/or Spanish outcomes of DLBE students by program characteristics. The first section provides comparisons across DLBE programs (e.g., 90/10 vs. 50/50 or two-way vs.

one-way), and the second provides comparisons of DLBE programs to transitional bilingual education (TBE) and EM programs.

Comparing Outcomes across DLBE Models. Four studies explored potential differences in English and Spanish outcomes among DLBE students in 50/50 vs. 90/10 programs. Acosta et al. (2019) evaluated English literacy results among DLBE students classified as ELs in two elementary schools in the same district in California, one with a 50/50 program and the other with a 90/10 program. The authors found that higher percentages of students in the 90/10 program met or exceeded proficiency standards in English language arts, and higher percentages were also reclassified as former ELs and thus concluded that the 90/10 program is stronger for students classified as ELs because of their opportunity to first develop strong literacy abilities in their home language. Reaching the opposite conclusion, Berens et al. (2013) administered a series of English and Spanish literacy tasks to second- and third-grade students in one 50/50 program and one 90/10 program in two different locations. In Spanish, they found that students in 90/10 programs outperformed their peers in 50/50 programs on a Spanish oral proficiency assessment and all Spanish reading tasks – phonological awareness, decoding, irregular word reading and passage comprehension. However, English outcomes were more equivocal, with no program difference on the oral English proficiency assessment, but program differences on the English reading assessments such that 90/10 students performed better on the language-general tasks of phonological awareness and decoding, and 50/50 students performed better on the language-specific tasks of irregular word reading and passage comprehension. The authors concluded that with additional phonological training in the primary grades, 50/50 is the preferred model, as the simultaneous biliteracy development promotes deep processing of the subtle underlying differences in the two literacy systems.

Similarly, the research comparing Spanish outcomes in two-way vs. one-way programs has yielded equivocal findings. In a study of elementary students in one school district in Texas, Alvear (2019) found significantly higher growth in Spanish reading among K-3, Latinx, EL students in two-way than in one-way programs. A study by Watzinger-Tharp et al. (2018) of third- to sixth-grade students in one-way and two-way programs in Utah found limited long-term differences across program models. Although they found differences in growth rates in listening and speaking (but not reading), such that the performance of one-way students grew twice as fast as that of two-way students, mean scores for both program types by fifth grade (speaking) or sixth grade (listening and reading) were all at the Intermediate Mid level. In other words, one-way students (predominantly English home-language speakers) had considerably lower mean scores in Spanish speaking and listening performance in third and fourth grade, respectively, but caught up to their two-way peers by fifth grade (speaking) or sixth grade (listening). However, in a follow-up study, Watzinger-Tharp et al. (2021) found that the mean third-grade Spanish-speaking performance of Utah students in both two-way and one-way programs was Intermediate Low, but that by fifth grade, results diverged, such that two-way students on average progressed two sub-levels to the high range of Intermediate Mid, while one-way students progressed just one sub-level to the middle of Intermediate Mid, thus opening up this question to further exploration. Spanish reading and listening outcomes in the two programs were only assessed in grade 4, and at that point, there were no program differences in either domain. The authors noted the lack of program differences as surprising given the larger proportion of Spanish home-language speakers in the two-way program, and proposed that the lack of a difference may have related to increasing English dominance on the part of those children and/or the need for more targeted instructional strategies. Overall, the equivocal Spanish findings point to the need for more research on potential program model differences, particularly those that take into consideration differences in the student populations across models and that look at differences across language and literacy domains over time.

The two studies comparing English outcomes across two-way and one-way programs both found no difference across program models in the upper elementary or middle grades. In the same study cited in the preceding paragraph, Alvear (2019) found that by fifth grade, English reading outcomes were higher among two-way than one-way students, but not significantly so. Similarly, Steele et al. (2017) did not find a significant difference in the English reading development of third- to eighth-grade students in two-way vs. one-way programs in Portland, Oregon. They likewise found no significant differences in English reading between Spanish-English DLBE programs and programs in other languages; however, it is important to recognize that these two findings are highly collinear because all but one of the two-way programs were Spanish-English programs, and only one, one-way program was a Spanish-English program.

Comparing Outcomes in DLBE Programs to Outcomes in Other Programs. The majority of studies comparing DLBE outcomes to TBE or EM program outcomes have focused on English performance. We present the four studies providing Spanish literacy and language outcomes first. Starting with the youngest learners, Murphy (2014) compared the development of Spanish language and literacy skills among Latinx first and second graders in one school in the Northeast with both a DLBE and TBE program. Over the course of one school year, the author found significant growth in Spanish proficiency among students in both programs and at both grade levels, with the one advantage for DLBE second graders of significantly higher verbal expression. Nakamoto et al. (2012) compared the Spanish reading and oral language performance of Latinx ELs in DLBE, TBE, and EM programs across grades

K-3 within a single Texas district and found that the DLBE and TBE students consistently outperformed the EM students. Alvear (2019) compared the K-3 Spanish reading growth of Latinx ELs in two-way, one-way, and TBE programs and found that the growth of two-way students was slightly but not significantly greater than that of TBE students, while the growth of one-way students was significantly less than that of TBE students. Looking at older children from varying home-language backgrounds who participated in world language programs, Burkhauser et al. (2016) compared the eighth-grade Spanish outcomes of DLBE students with those who began taking Spanish as an elective in the upper elementary or middle school grades and found a considerable difference in mean performance, with DLBE students at the Intermediate Mid level and Spanish elective students at the Novice Mid level for all four language domains. As was noted in the previous section on differences across DLBE models, these differences in findings likely relate to differences in the home-language profiles, ages, and time of program entry of the comparison populations and warrant additional research. However, in general, they indicate that Spanish outcomes of DLBE students in the primary grades are usually comparable to those of TBE students and superior to those of students in traditional world language programs.

Results of English language and literacy outcome studies are mixed but follow previously established patterns of younger DLBE students demonstrating lower English outcomes than EM peers but older DLBE students demonstrating comparable or higher English outcomes than EM peers. First, Nakamoto et al. (2012) compared the English reading and oral language performance of Latinx ELs in DLBE, TBE, and EM programs across grades K-3 within a single Texas district and found that the EM students consistently outperformed the DLBE and TBE students. Similarly, Kalia et al. (2019) compared the English vocabulary and executive function of K-3 Latinx Spanish home-language students in a DLBE program to EMs in an EM program and found that the DLBE students had significantly smaller English vocabularies but significantly stronger executive function.

By contrast, Alvear (2019) compared the fifth-grade English reading performance of Latinx ELs in two-way, one-way, TBE programs, and EM program and found that the performance of both two-way and one-way students was significantly higher than that of TBE students, which in turn was significantly higher than that of EM students. Likewise, in a longitudinal study of third- to fifth-grade Spanish home-language students who were potentially at risk for reading difficulties, Neugebauer and Howard (2021) compared the fifth-grade English reading comprehension of Latinx Spanish home-language students in DLBE and EM programs. The authors found that there were no significant differences in fifth-grade English reading comprehension across the two program models, either for students who were at risk of experiencing English reading difficulties or those who were not. Given the limited research on students with learning difficulties in DLBE programs, this is an area that warrants further research.

Two studies carried out with English speakers indicate that this trend of lower English performance in the primary grades may vary by home-language profile. Kaushanskaya et al. (2014) compared outcomes among English home-language K-2 students in DLBE and EM programs and found no differences on non-linguistic task shifting or verbal short-term memory, but significant differences favoring DLBE students on English verbal working memory and word learning. Berens et al. (2013) compared the English language and literacy development of second- and third-grade English home-language speakers in 50/50, 90/10, and EM programs. The authors found comparable results in oral English proficiency, phonological awareness, and decoding; interestingly, however, they also found that 50/50 students outperformed both 90/10 and EM students in irregular word reading and passage comprehension.

Four studies included both Spanish-dominant and English-dominant students and had results that frequently varied by language domain or student population; however, on the whole, these studies typically found that students in DLBE programs performed comparably to or better than their peers in other programs. Esposito and Bauer (2019) compared the development of English verbal comprehension of Spanish home-language and English home-language students in DLBE and EM programs over grades K-5 and found no difference in initial status or rate of change based on program model. In the domains of English vocabulary and morphological awareness, Kuo et al. (2017) compared the English vocabulary and morphological awareness of fourth-grade Spanish home-language and English home-language DLBE students to English home-language students in EM programs. The authors found that the EM students performed comparably to their English home-language peers and better than their Spanish home-language peers in the DLBE program on a variety of measures other than cognates and morphologically complex words, which will be discussed further in the following section. Similarly, Kim et al. (2015) studied morphological awareness among fourth graders in a Spanish-English DLBE program in the Midwest, an EM program in the Midwest, and a Chinese-English DLBE program in Taiwan. The authors found that the Spanish home-language and English home-language students in the Spanish-English DLBE program outperformed the other students on measures of morphological awareness and also had the highest cognate scores. Finally, Lindholm-Leary and Hernandez (2011) found that the English reading performance of fourth- to eighth-grade Latinx DLBE students was comparable to or better than that of their peers in EM programs, and these findings also held for various subgroups, including never ELs, current ELs, and reclassified ELs. Thus, on the whole, the studies reviewed in this section provide evidence that English outcomes for both Spanish home-language and English home-language students in the upper elementary grades and beyond are comparable to or better than those of their peers in other programs.

How Does Students' Bilingualism Manifest Itself in Language and Literacy Outcomes?

A limited amount of research has explored ways in which DLBE students' bilingualism manifests itself in language and literacy outcomes, adding to a growing research base grounded in holistic bilingualism rather than monolingualism (e.g., Babino & Stewart, 2020). The research to date relates to three areas: cognate awareness, spelling, and translanguaging. First, two studies explored cognate awareness. Kuo et al. (2017) found that fourth-grade DLBE Spanish home-language students had higher Spanish cognate performance than their English home-language peers. Moreover, the DLBE students demonstrated equivalent (Spanish home-language) or stronger (English home-language) performance on English cognates and morphologically complex words than an EM comparison group, leading the authors to conclude that bilingual instructional approaches may confer advantages for the development of morphological awareness due to greater opportunities to develop cross-linguistic awareness and cross-language transfer. Similarly, Kim et al. (2015) studied morphological awareness among fourth graders in a Spanish-English DLBE program in the Midwest, an EM program in the Midwest, and a Chinese-English DLBE program in Taiwan. The authors noted that the Spanish DLBE teachers never provided explicit instruction about cognates, yet those students had the highest cognate scores and highest morphological awareness among all participants in the study, even higher than the Chinese immersion students whose teachers emphasized it. The authors hypothesized that Spanish ELs may spontaneously pick up on these vocabulary connections even without explicit instruction.

In the domain of spelling, two studies (Howard et al., 2012; Linan-Thompson et al., 2018) both found evidence of Spanish-influenced spelling errors in English spelling that decreased considerably over the course of second grade, and Howard et al. (2012) further noted that these errors were virtually non-existent by fourth grade. Linan-Thompson et al. (2018) emphasized that most errors related to vowel sounds and called for teachers to better understand these error types so as to create instructional approaches designed to address them. Howard et al. (2012) noted that not only did the Spanish-influenced spellings disappear over time without specific remediation, they also were only evidenced by a minority of students and did not have any long-term relationship to English reading, as second-grade cross-linguistic spelling errors did not significantly predict fourth-grade English reading outcomes. Both studies emphasized that this appears to be a developmental pattern for some Spanish-English bilinguals (including those from English home-language backgrounds) that does not typically persist beyond second grade.

Two other studies explored students' hybrid language use. First, using the framework created by Potowski (2007) to analyze the Spanish language use of DLBE students, Ruiz-Funes (2020) investigated the longitudinal Spanish oral language development of English home-language speakers from kindergarten through fifth grade. In kindergarten, the students did not provide any evidence of code-mixing, as they either did not answer the questions or responded with correct, one-word answers in Spanish. By second grade, the students were providing longer responses, in which a little more than half of the words were in Spanish. The Spanish words were typically high-frequency nouns related to the content of the prompts, while the English words were from a variety of grammatical classes and were used to fill in the ideas to provide a complete thought. Approximately two-thirds of the sentences incorporated intrasentential code-mixing. By fifth grade, the students' responses were yet longer and more complex, with about 75% of the words in Spanish, now from a variety of grammatical classes. Over half of the sentences continued to display intrasentential code-mixing. In a more naturalistic study, Alamillo et al. (2017) observed the language use of preschoolers in the first year of a DLBE program and noticed flexible and spontaneous translanguaging among the students. Specifically, students tended to respond in English, even when teachers spoke in Spanish. Additionally, the Spanish-dominant bilinguals were often responsive to the linguistic needs of their peers, switching to English or Spanish as needed to help other students participate in the conversation. Hence, these two studies provide two different profiles of hybrid language use: the first, one born of linguistic necessity by English home-language students who are still developing the necessary Spanish proficiency to carry out a conversation fully in Spanish; the second, a sociolinguistic portrait of students with the linguistic ability to use either or both languages and the social sophistication to understand when and how to make those shifts. Other recent studies have also looked at translanguaging in DLBE programs, but have done so as part of explorations of pedagogical approaches designed to promote it, and are therefore summarized in the subsequent section.

How Do Pedagogical Practices Shape Students' Language and Literacy Outcomes?

This final question was grounded in the small number of studies that explored the effects of specific instructional approaches within the context of DLBE. Seven of the eight studies focused on translanguaging. The one instructional study with a different focus was a preschool vocabulary intervention (Pollard-Durodola et al., 2021), which found a positive, significant correlation between teachers' beliefs that the intervention was effective and students' scores on standardized and researcher-developed English vocabulary measures.

Most of the translanguaging studies employed qualitative methodologies to explore the topic within a single classroom. Bauer et al. (2017) investigated peer writing support among kindergarten students in a Midwestern DLBE program, finding that the teacher's welcoming stance of students' linguistic and cultural practices enabled students to capably support one another in their writing. Osorio (2020), Clark (2020), and Esquivel (2020) carried out reading activities with first-, second-, and fifth-grade DLBE students, respectively, all using a culturally sustaining stance (and in the case of Esquivel [2020], a critical literacies stance as well), and all promoting the use of translanguaging to foster meaning-making and positive identity development as capable readers and writers.

Martínez-Álvarez et al. (2012) and Martínez-Álvarez (2017) likewise created responsive learning environments, emphasizing multimodal learning and hybrid language use that mirrored community varieties, but their studies also included comparison groups. Martínez-Álvarez et al. (2012) tested the efficacy of a fourth-grade integrated science and literacy curriculum that emphasized bilingual and metacognitive strategies to support reading comprehension, along with fieldwork and the use of photographs. While the authors did not find that students in the treatment group had a higher percentage of correct answers after controlling for guessing, they noted that qualitative responses demonstrated comprehension of the text. Martínez-Álvarez (2017) compared the language use and awareness of six- and seven-year-old students in a Northeast dual language after-school program that used hybrid, multimodal activities to that of peers who did not participate in the same instruction. The authors found that while both groups used hybrid language forms, most likely because it was a community norm, the students who received the targeted instruction did so more frequently and were able to use metacognitive strategies to discuss their language use. Finally, Esposito and Bauer (2019) compared EM and cross-linguistic instructional conditions within a dual language program at three grade levels, with the hypothesis that the monolingual condition would have better results because of instructional consistency. The results were mixed, in that the cross-linguistic condition had better results in first to second grade, when the lessons were highly contextualized, leading the authors to conclude that the contextualization plays a major role in making cross-linguistic instruction effective.

Summary of Findings

Before moving on to the implications and future directions, we summarize key findings below.

Consistent with earlier reviews, the studies reviewed for this chapter indicated that:

- DLBE students demonstrate continuous progress in language and literacy outcomes in both English and Spanish.
- There is a societal language effect, such that students tend towards English use, and the English performance of Spanish home-language speakers is stronger than the Spanish performance of English home-language speakers.
- There is a home-language effect, such that students who speak a language at home tend to perform better in that language than students who do not, although this trend tends to get reduced in upper grades, and sometimes goes away altogether, particularly in the case of reclassified ELs.
- There are equivocal findings for the studies investigating within-DLBE program effects, but the one study that compared Spanish attainment of 50/50 vs. 90/10 students did corroborate earlier findings of stronger Spanish performance among 90/10 students.
- Students in dual language programs typically perform as well as or better than students in other program models in both English and Spanish by the upper elementary or secondary grades.

New or more nuanced findings from this review indicate that:

- Outcomes vary by the specific language sub-domain; by student grade-level and biliteracy profile; by the ways in which the students are categorized (e.g., by home-language use, as first or second language speakers, according to past or present EL status, etc.); and by study methods.
- There was some evidence of students' bilingualism manifesting itself in certain areas, such as cognate awareness, spelling, and translanguaging. Conclusions from the various studies were equivocal about the extent to which this occurs spontaneously or requires explicit instruction to help students develop cross-linguistic awareness.
- There are some emerging positive findings about the effects of translanguaging pedagogy within the context of DLBE, but the studies with comparison groups demonstrated equivocal results that indicate potential differences with regard to specific constructs, contexts of learning, and grade levels.

Implications and Future Directions for DLBE

There are several key takeaways from the research presented in this chapter that can guide future research and inform policy and practice. First, there is need for further research on the effects of various DLBE program models on English and Spanish outcomes. The research to date is limited, typically small in scope, and has resulted in equivocal findings. Second, additional research is needed on the language and literacy attainment of various subpopulations, such as students with learning disabilities, newcomers, bilinguals with varying language profiles, and third-language speakers. Third, research is needed on the effects of pedagogical practices within DLBE rather than simply on the effects of DLBE itself as a pedagogical approach. In particular, given the increasing calls for translanguaging within DLBE programs, more research is needed to provide clearer guidance about how it would look within the context of DLBE and what the effects would be on the development of multiple varieties of English and Spanish for different types of students. Additionally, more research is needed to explore the use of explicit instruction that helps students make meaningful cross-linguistic connections. In both cases, larger scale studies with comparison groups would help the field pinpoint the extent to which outcomes relate to the instructional approach. Finally, given the number of Spanish-speaking countries in the world and the growing number of dual language programs within those countries, it would be helpful to see an international research base about language and literacy outcomes in Spanish-English programs. This would broaden our understanding of the ways in which social contexts and learner characteristics may influence program outcomes.

References

Acosta, J., Williams, J., & Hunt, I. (2019). Dual language program models and English language learners: An analysis of the literacy results from a 50/50 and a 90/10 model in two California schools. *Journal of Educational Issues*, *5*(2), 1–12.

Aguilar, G., Uccelli, P., & Galloway, E. P. (2020). Toward biliteracy: Unpacking the contribution of mid-adolescent dual language learners' Spanish and English academic language skills to English reading comprehension. *TESOL Quarterly: A Journal for Teachers of English to Speakers of Other Languages and of Standard English as a Second Dialect*, *54*(4), 1010–1036.

Alamillo, L., Yun, C., & Bennett, L. H. (2017). Translanguaging in a Reggio-inspired Spanish dual-language immersion programme. *Early Child Development & Care*, *187*(3), 469–486. https://doi.org/10.1080/03004430.2016.1236091

Alvear, S. A. (2019). The additive advantage and bilingual programs in a large urban school district. *American Educational Research Journal*, *56*(2), 477–513. https://doi.org/10.3102/0002831218800986

Arteagoitia, I., & Yen, S. J. (2020). Equity in representing literacy growth in dual language bilingual education for emerging bilingual students. *TESOL Quarterly*, *54*(3), 719–742. https://doi.org/10.1002/tesq.588

Babino, A. (2017). Same program, distinctive development: Exploring the biliteracy trajectories of two dual language schools. *Bilingual Research Journal*, *40*(2), 169–186. https://doi.org/10.1080/15235882.2017.1307290

Babino, A., & Stewart, M. A. (2017). "I like English better": Latino dual language students' investment in Spanish, English, and bilingualism. *Journal of Latinos & Education*, *16*(1), 18–29. https://doi.org/10.1080/15348431.2016.1179186

Babino, A., & Stewart, M. A. (2020). *Radicalizing literacies and languaging: A framework toward dismantling the mono-mainstream assumption*. Palgrave-Macmillan.

Bauer, E. B., Presiado, V., & Colomer, S. (2017). Writing through partnership: Fostering translanguaging in children who are emergent bilinguals. *Journal of Literacy Research*, *49*(1), 10–37.

Berens, M. S., Kovelman, I., & Petitto, L. (2013). Should bilingual children learn reading in two languages at the same time or in sequence? *Bilingual Research Journal*, *36*(1), 35–60.

Burkhauser, S., Steele, J. L., Li, J., Slater, R. O., Bacon, M., & Miller, T. (2016). Partner-language learning trajectories in dual-language immersion: Evidence from an urban district. *Foreign Language Annals*, *49*(3), 415–433.

Clark, A. (2020). Cultural relevance and linguistic flexibility in literature discussions with emergent bilingual children. *Bilingual Research Journal*, *43*(1), 50–70.

Dworin, J. (2011). Listening to graduates of a K–12 bilingual program: Language ideologies and literacy practices of former bilingual students. *GIST Education and Learning Research Journal*, *5*, 104–126.

Escamilla, K., Hopewell, S., Butvilofsky, S., Sparrow, W., Soltero-González, L., Ruiz-Figueroa, O., & Escamilla, M. (2014). *Biliteracy from the start: Literacy squared in action*. Caslon Publishing.

Esposito, A. G., & Bauer, P. J. (2019). From bench to classroom: Collaborating within a dual-language education model. *Grantee Submission*, *20*(2), 165–181.

Esquivel, J. (2020). Embodying critical literacy in a dual language classroom: Critical discourse analysis in a case study. *Critical Inquiry in Language Studies*, *17*(3), 206–227.

Hopewell, S., & Escamilla, K. (2014). Struggling reader or emerging biliterate student? Reevaluating the criteria for labeling emerging bilingual students as low achieving. *Journal of Literacy Research*, *46*(1), 68–89.

Howard, E. R., Green, J. D., & Arteagoitia, I. (2012). Can yu rid guat ay rot? A developmental investigation of cross-linguistic spelling errors among Spanish-English bilingual students. *Bilingual Research Journal*, *35*(2), 164–178.

Howard, E., & Neugebauer, S. (2015). Moving towards biliteracy: Varying paths of bilingual writers in two-way immersion programs. *Revista Miriada Hispanica*, *10*, 83–106.

Howard, E., Sugarman, J., & Christian, D. (2003). *Trends in two-way immersion education: A review of the research*. (Technical Report 63). Center for Research on the Education of Students Placed at Risk (CRESPAR).

Kalia, V., Daneri, M. P., & Wilbourn, M. P. (2019). Relations between vocabulary and executive functions in Spanish–English dual language learners. *Bilingualism: Language & Cognition*, 22(1), 1–14. https://doi.org/10.1017/S1366728917000463

Kalia, V., Lane, P. D., & Wilbourn, M. P. (2018). Cognitive control and phonological awareness in the acquisition of second language vocabulary within the Spanish-English dual immersion context. *Cognitive Development*, *48*, 176–189. https://doi.org/10.1016/j.cogdev.2018.08.010

Kaushanskaya, M., Gross, M., & Buac, M. (2014). Effects of classroom bilingualism on task-shifting, verbal memory, and word learning in children. *Developmental Science*, *17*(4), 564–583.

Kim, T. J., Kuo, L., Ramírez, G., Wu, S., Ku, Y., de Marin, S., Ball, A., & Eslami, Z. (2015). The relationship between bilingual experience and the development of morphological and morpho-syntactic awareness: A cross-linguistic study of classroom discourse. *Language Awareness*, 24(4), 332–354.

Kuo, L., Ramirez, G., de Marin, S., Kim, T., & Unal-Gezer, M. (2017). Bilingualism and morphological awareness: A study with children from general education and Spanish-English dual language programs. *Educational Psychology*, *37*(2), 94–111.

Linan-Thompson, S., Degollado, E. D., & Ingram, M. D. (2018). Spelling it out, one por uno: Patterns of emergent bilinguals in a dual language classroom. *TESOL Journal*, *9*(2), 330–347.

Lindholm-Leary, K., & Genesee, F. (2014). Student outcomes in one-way, two-way, and indigenous language immersion education. *Journal of Immersion and Content-Based Language Education*, *2*(2), 165–180.

Lindholm-Leary, K., & Hernandez, A. (2011). Achievement and language proficiency of Latino students in dual language programmes: Native English speakers, fluent English/previous ELLs, and current ELLs. *Journal of Multilingual and Multicultural Development*, *32*(6), 531–545.

Lindholm-Leary, K., & Howard, E. R. (2008). Language development and academic achievement in two-way immersion programs. In T. Fortune & D. Tedick (Eds.), *Pathways to multilingualism* (pp. 170–200). Multilingual Matters.

Lucero, A. (2018a). The development of bilingual narrative retelling among Spanish–English dual language learners over two years. *Language, Speech, and Hearing Services in Schools*, *49*(3), 607–621. https://doi.org/10.1044/2018_LSHSS-17-0152

Lucero, A. (2018b). Oral narrative retelling among emergent bilinguals in a dual language immersion program. *International Journal of Bilingual Education and Bilingualism*, *21*(2), 248–264.

Martínez-Álvarez, P. (2017). Language multiplicity and dynamism: Emergent bilinguals taking ownership of language use in a hybrid curricular space. *International Multilingual Research Journal*, *11*(4), 255–276.

Martínez-Álvarez, P., Bannan, B., & Peters-Burton, E. (2012). Effect of strategy instruction on fourth-grade dual language learners' ability to monitor their comprehension of scientific texts. *Bilingual Research Journal*, *35*(3), 331–349. https://doi.org/10.1080/15235882.2012.734005

Murphy, A. F. (2014). The effect of dual-language and transitional-bilingual education instructional models on Spanish proficiency for English language learners. *Bilingual Research Journal*, *37*(2), 182–194.

Nakamoto, J., Lindsey, K. A., & Manis, F. R. (2012). Development of reading skills from K–3 in Spanish-speaking English language learners following three programs of instruction. *Reading and Writing: An Interdisciplinary Journal*, *25*(2), 537–567.

Neugebauer, S. R., & Howard, E. R. (2015). Exploring associations among writing self-perceptions, writing abilities, and native language of English-Spanish two-way immersion students. *Bilingual Research Journal*, *38*(3), 313–335.

Neugebauer, S. R., & Howard, E. R. (2021). Exploring conceptions of reading risk and program-specific literacy outcomes for Spanish speakers in dual language and English-medium programs. Journal of Immersion and Content-Based Language Education, 9(2), 252–278.

Osorio, S. L. (2020). Building culturally and linguistically sustaining spaces for emergent bilinguals: Using read-alouds to promote translanguaging. *Reading Teacher*, 74(2), 127–135. https://doi.org/10.1002/trtr.1919

Pollard-Durodola, S., Gonzalez, J. E., Saenz, L., Soares, D., Davis, H. S., Resendez, N., & Zhu (2021). The social validity of content enriched shared book reading vocabulary instruction and preschool dlls' language outcomes. *Early Education and Development*. https://doi.org/10.1080/10409289.2021.1946761

Potowski, K. (2007). *Language and identity in a dual immersion school*. Multilingual Matters.

Ruiz-Funes, M. (2020). The development of oral ability in L2 Spanish by English-home language learners in a TWI program. *Foreign Language Annals*, *53*(1), 96–127.

Steele, J. L., Slater, R. O., Zamarro, G., Miller, T., Li, J., Burkhauser, S., & Bacon, M. (2017). Effects of dual-language immersion programs on student achievement: Evidence from lottery data. *American Educational Research Journal*, *54*(1_suppl), 282S–306S.

Taub, G. E., Sivo, S. A., & Puyana, O. E. (2017). Group differences between English and Spanish speakers' reading fluency growth in bilingual immersion education. *School Psychology Forum*, *11*(2), 45–51.

Watzinger-Tharp, J., Rubio, F., & Tharp, D. S. (2018). Linguistic performance of dual language immersion students. *Foreign Language Annals*, *51*(3), 575–595.

Watzinger-Tharp, J., Tharp, D. S., & Rubio, F. (2021). Sustaining dual language immersion: Partner language outcomes in a statewide program. *The Modern Language Journal*, *105*(1), 194–217. https://doi.org/10.1111/modl.12694

10

SOCIOCULTURAL COMPETENCE IN DUAL LANGUAGE BILINGUAL EDUCATION

A Literature Review of Student Outcomes

Erika Feinauer, Juan Freire, Kaila Willardson, Mallory Earl

Dual language bilingual education (DLBE) programs are unique because they have explicitly stated goals of sociocultural competence for their students (Howard et al., 2018; Lindholm-Leary, 2001). As the third goal of DLBE, however, sociocultural competence has not received the same level of attention or focus as have the other programmatic goals of bilingualism, biliteracy, and academic achievement across content areas in two languages (Feinauer & Howard, 2014; see Chapter 2 in this handbook). The lack of systematic attention to sociocultural competence has led to a lack of consensus or general understanding on behalf of scholars and practitioners alike as to what sociocultural outcomes might look like for students in DLBE programs.

The programmatic goal of sociocultural competence in DLBE is defined in the *Guiding Principles for Dual Language Education* (Howard et al., 2018) as encompassing "identity development, cross-cultural awareness, multicultural appreciation, [and] conflict-resolution strategies" (p. 60) and is necessarily broad. Because identity development is such an important part of sociocultural competence (Feinauer & Howard, 2014), and an important focus of study in its own right, there is another chapter dedicated to identity formation in DLBE in this handbook (see Chapter 23). Other aspects of sociocultural competence may include the knowledge, skills, dispositions, and

 DOI: 10.4324/9781003269076-15

behaviors that show knowledge of and appreciation for one's own culture as well as the culture of others. Positive attitudes toward language, bilingualism, and speakers of other languages are also an important part of sociocultural competence. Competency lists also often include empathy, perspective taking, tolerance for ambiguity, and meta-communication skills (Connerley & Pedersen, 2005; Deardorff, 2006; Sue, 2001). Sociocultural competence leads to observable behaviors, such as effective communication, behavioral flexibility and the formation of cross-group friendships (Byram & Wagner, 2018; Deardorff, 2006, 2011). As we discuss at the end of this chapter, recent work has suggested that an important aspect of sociocultural competence in DLBE programs is being aware of and attending explicitly to issues of power and oppression (Freire, 2020).

In this review, we cast the net broadly reviewing studies in DLBE programs with student outcomes related to any of the above-cited aspects of sociocultural competence. We present this work in a general chronological order, beginning in the 1960s, highlighting major trends and bodies of work that we considered crucial to understanding the evolution of work thus far on students' outcomes related to sociocultural competence in DLBE. Overall, this chapter highlights the increasing interest in this "third goal" of DLBE and underscores the need for further refinement and consensus around what is meant by sociocultural competence and what this might look like for students in DLBE programs.

The Early Years: Coral Way and the Canadian Studies

Maria Coady (2020) recently conducted important archival work to uncover student experiences and perspectives about their time at what is believed to be one of the first Spanish-English two-way bilingual education (TWBE) programs in the United States. The Coral Way program was opened in Miami, Florida in 1963 by Cuban refugees, to serve local Floridians alongside newly arrived Spanish-speaking Cuban children. Coady's (2020) research details many interesting and important aspects about this pioneering school, including information about sociocultural outcomes for the students who attended the school.

Coady (2020) found that both teachers and students reported cross-cultural friendships that formed as a result of the program. One teacher recalled that during play time, students "integrated well" and "played together" (p. 105). Poerschke, an English-dominant student, likewise shared that "most of my friends that I developed close relationships with were Spanish" (p. 106). A few former students at Coral Way shared how the sociocultural competencies they gained remained with them for years to come. One student pointed to how her experience at Coral Way helped her develop a sense of "cross-cultural dexterity" (p. 109), influencing her choice to later form friendships with people from various Latin American countries while in college. She also noted the instrumental value that bilingualism served in her life, as it helped her launch a successful career. Finally, multiple Latino students felt a sense of "identity affirmation" (p. 109) that helped them stay connected to their roots instead of becoming what one former student called "100% American" (p. 109). Although recently uncovered, these reports of sociocultural competencies from students in this early program re-emerge as relevant through the following decades, as DLBE programs evolved and expanded across the United States.

Some of the earliest research designed specifically to investigate sociocultural competence was carried out by Canadian psychologist Wallace Lambert and his colleagues at McGill University (Lambert, 1987; Lambert & Tucker, 1972). Over the course of several years, these scholars surveyed Canadian students across multiple grades in different French-English one-way world language immersion schools in Montreal, using Likert type measures as well as direct questioning. They found that these English-dominant Canadian students generally viewed French Europeans and French Canadians more favorably than did students who were not enrolled in French immersion programs. In his review, Lambert (1987) concluded that "immersion is more likely to foster more favorable attitude profiles toward the group whose language is being learned than is the case for children without immersion experience" (pp. 207–208). He also noted that the immersion experience did not lead to negative attitudes about one's own group but rather was likely to protect students from the negative biases of society around them.

Lambert's work led to the acceptance of a major tenet for researchers during this time which was that the language immersion setting, itself, was an intervention for promoting the development of sociocultural attitudes and competencies—specifically those of positive attitudes toward speakers of other languages (Lambert, 1987). Lambert (1987) called this the "immersion effect" (p. 204) claiming that interacting with students from different groups in DLBE programs, on its own, inherently led to the development of sociocultural competencies. He justified this assumption as …

> understandable if one realizes that the immersion pupils have virtually no social contact with French-speaking people other than that of their teacher. Thus, there is no social support to maintain personalized, favorable attitudes towards French people except for the contact pupils have with their French-speaking teacher. (p. 208)

Lambert concluded from his series of studies that personal interactions with speakers of minoritized languages led to positive attitudes toward them, and that student interaction with teachers, especially, seemed to affect students' views of cultural others, as the majority of teachers in these Canadian programs were from France.

The Amigos Program and the Oyster School

Lambert built on his work in the Canadian context as he shifted his focus to two-way bilingual education programs in the United States, working with Mary Cazabon in Cambridge, Massachusetts. They looked at a variety of student outcomes in the Amigos program, a 50-50 Spanish-English TWBE program implemented across two schools in Cambridge, with an explicit focus to "provide children with the opportunity to cultivate friendships with children from different ethnic backgrounds" (Cazabon et al., 1993, p. 2). Cazabon et al. (1993), Lambert and Cazabon (1994), and Cazabon et al. (1996) investigated a wide array of program outcomes for students in the Amigos program, including achievement, language data, and aspects of sociocultural competence. They used student surveys to assess attitudes toward language learning and becoming bilingual, as well as conducted sociograms to look at social-interactional friendship patterns.

Program evaluation reports produced from their work found that students across grades held positive attitudes toward becoming bilingual and bicultural, had an awareness of their language learning, and understood that bilingualism and biculturalism were important (Cazabon et al., 1993; Cazabon et al., 1996; Lambert & Cazabon, 1994). Sociometric data conducted in the Amigos program showed that students chose cross-cultural and cross-ethnic friendships more frequently the longer they were in the program. For example, students in the second grade tended to segregate into "ethnic hang-out spots" during recess and lunch (Cazabon et al., 1993, p. 22). Second-grade Anglo students also reported choosing other Anglo students to accompany them to after-school social settings, while African-American and Hispanic students stayed together. Cazabon et al. (1993) noted that these trends seemed to stem from the "own-group preferences of Anglo children" (p. 22). However, by third grade, researchers noted a decline in this pattern concluding that students in the Amigos program were in a "reciprocal appreciation network" (p. 22) as students were choosing friends in what they called a "color-blind random" fashion—especially when it came to choosing their best friends.

Survey questions about cross-cultural attitudes seem to support the sociometric data for upper elementary students as well. For example, when asked how comfortable they would feel if they "were born into a different ethnic household" (Lambert & Cazabon, 1994, p. 6), about half or more of the fourth-, fifth-, and sixth-grade Amigos students stated that they would be comfortable being born into a different ethnic household, though this was more true for the English-dominant students than for the

Spanish speakers. These students were also asked to choose whom they would most like to "sit next to, play games with, eat lunch with, [and] take home for a party", as well as to name their best friends (Cazabon et al., 1993, p. 6). Lambert and Cazabon reported that students expressed a clear preference for having friends across groups in the fifth and sixth grades (Lambert & Cazabon, 1994). Interestingly, Cazabon's dissertation work (2000) found that African-American and Latino students in the Amigos program reported higher levels of integrative motivation for becoming bilingual than did the European-American students, suggesting that the minoritized students in the program might "appreciate the fact that the two-way program brings minority racial and linguistic groups together to learn each others' language and culture" (2000, p. 92) in a way that the European Americans did not.

Around this time, important work was also being carried out by Rebecca Freeman (1996) at the Oyster Spanish-English TWBE program in Washington, D.C. The Oyster school was established to provide an alternative and equitable educational program for minoritized (mostly Latino) students in the Washington, D.C. area. The school made explicit attempts to align itself with guidelines of "exemplary practice", where sociocultural competencies were integrated into school culture in a "program-wide plan" that was "consistent at all grade levels" (Howard et al., 2018, p. 25). Freeman used ethnographic, observational, and discourse analysis methodology to examine student linguistic and academic outcomes, as well as what she called "cultural pluralism" at the school, referring mostly to student interactions and cross-group communication.

Freeman (1996) noted that students "seem[ed] to negotiate very well in their small groups, and they seem[ed] to expect and be able to accommodate diversity as they jointly construct[ed] meaning with each other through Spanish and English" (p. 578). According to Freeman, students seemed to be taking up the sociocultural competencies necessary to participate in critical conversations with diverse peers in classroom spaces. However, she also observed that, although all students at the Oyster school interacted frequently with one another during classroom instruction, student groups tended to segregate along racial and ethnic lines during lunch time, noting that students gravitated toward their own culture groups when they were not in structured time such as in the classroom. Freeman wrote that despite students frequently examining "problems of discrimination" within a classroom context, "their social interaction at school seem[ed] to correspond to racial, ethnic, or class lines in society" (p. 579).

Taken together, the Amigos and the Oyster studies' data on attitudes, these findings suggest that participation in this TWBE program may have promoted the development of internal aspects of sociocultural competence (positive attitudes and dispositions) but didn't translate fully into behavioral change, such as choosing students from different culture groups for social interaction during unstructured or social time.

A Focus on Student Attitudes across DLBE Programs

Sociocultural competence outcomes began receiving more systematic and cross-program attention as more research was carried out in DLBE programs in general at the beginning of the 21st century. Much of this work was carried out by Dr. Lindholm-Leary and her colleagues, who looked at what they called, "perceived psychosocial competence" (Lindholm, 1994, p. 189), which was largely a measure of self-esteem; "positive cross-cultural attitudes" (Lindholm, 1994; Lindholm-Leary, 2001; Lindholm-Leary & Block, 2010), generally defined as "student expectations and attitudes towards each other" (Lindholm, 1994, p. 192); and "cultural competence" (Lindholm-Leary, 2011), which was measured through students' self-reported knowledge of culture and comfortability interacting with other cultures. This work generally found that students expressed positive perceptions and attitudes toward themselves and toward the culturally, racially, and ethnically different students in their classroom. These scholars drew on Lambert (1987) in assuming an immersion effect was at play for the development of student sociocultural outcomes.

Lindholm (1994) specifically cited Allport's (1954) contact hypothesis, to posit that when majority and minority students had equal status and interacted with each other, such as they did in the TWBE programs she was studying, their expectations of and attitudes toward each other became positive. In this study (1994), she administered attitude surveys to third- and fourth-grade students in two Spanish-English DLBE programs in California. Students filled out self-rating instruments that examined student self-perception, using Harter's (1983) Self-Perception for Children measure, as well as cross-cultural attitudes, using the Cross-Cultural Language/Attitudes Scale (CLAS) developed by Lindholm-Leary herself (Lindholm, 1994). Students in the study scored high on measures of self-perception and cross-cultural attitudes—including positive attitudes toward other languages, and toward people speaking other languages. Lindholm-Leary (1994) concluded from this work that TWBE programs promote "positive psychosocial findings" for all students in the program, alongside bilingualism and academic achievement (p. 204).

Rolstad (1997) produced similar results with regard to the development of ethnic identification and cross-cultural attitudes for Latino and Filipino students in a highly diverse Korean-English TWBE program in Los Angeles, California. These students were already fluent in either Spanish or Tagalog, and they came to the program to learn a second and third language: Korean and English. Rolstad (1997) adapted surveys created by Lambert and Tucker

(1972) to create Bipolar Ethnic Attitudes Surveys (Rolstad, 1998), where students were asked to judge characteristics of different ethnic groups on a five-point adjective scale (e.g., tall vs. short). Students were each administered one survey about their own ethnic group, then three additional surveys for other ethnic groups, limited to Blacks, Whites, Koreans, and Latinos. The results of this study showed that these "third language students" (p. 43) reported viewing their own and other ethnic groups favorably. Importantly, the students in her study were not native speakers of either language of instruction at the school.

This early work was the springboard to the large-scale study Lindholm-Leary (2001) conducted in DLBE programs. This important study was carried out in 9 TWBE programs in California that served a total of 611 grade 3–8 students, inclusive of Hispanic, European-American and African-American students, examining student language learning, bilingualism, and achievement measures in math, science and social studies. As part of this study, Lindholm-Leary also collected student attitudinal data by administering a questionnaire, with each item scored using a Likert scale. She found that students in the programs she studied scored well on what she called "cross-cultural and integrative language attitudes" (p. 278). She also assessed student self-esteem and their beliefs about the benefits of bilingualism (p. 5). Lindholm-Leary reported consistently high ratings across these items for all students in the study, though there were some minor differences across programs and grades. She noted that "students did not differ in their cross-cultural and language attitudes according to gender, SES, or ethnicity, except that African American students consistently scored the lowest on every item" (p. 280). Similar findings emerged in Lindholm-Leary's (2011) work at one Cantonese and one Mandarin DLBE programs where she noted that "97% of TWI [two-way immersion] students reported feeling at least fairly comfortable" interacting with people with Chinese ancestry (p. 96). These studies supported the overall proposition that attending DLBE programs was beneficial for students in terms of their development of cross-cultural attitudes, positive attitudes toward self, positive attitudes toward speakers of other languages, and positive attitudes toward bilingualism.

Lindholm-Leary and Block (2010) extended this work by conducting studies in DLBE schools with predominantly Latino students and showed similar outcomes in terms of attitudes toward bilingualism and toward speakers of other languages. They carried out a set of two studies with fourth- to sixth-grade Latino students across two schools. The main focus of these studies was to examine how Latino students in DLBE programs fared in comparison to Latino students in English-only classrooms in terms of mathematics, English language, and Spanish language outcomes. However, they also administered a questionnaire to students that included items related to how students felt about acquiring a second language. Students were asked if they thought being bilingual would help them get along with others, if they would like to be friends with someone who mostly speaks a non-English language, and about playing with kids no matter what they looked like. Lindholm-Leary and Block found that DLBE students were "acquiring positive cross-cultural attitudes" (p. 54), in comparison to the English-only instructed Latino students because DLBE students' mean scores were high and positive on these questionnaire items, showing the effectiveness of DLBE programs in promoting positive attitudes for the Latino students who attended these programs.

In later work, Block (2011) conducted similar attitudinal research on the "third goal of dual-immersion education—biculturalism" (p. 129), looking at how participation in a Spanish-English DLBE program affected English-dominant Latino students' attitudes toward and perceptions of their Spanish-dominant Latino peers. In Block's work, tensions had historically existed between the Spanish- and English-dominant groups of Latino students in the study. He found that Latino students who participated in a DLBE program were more likely than their Latino peers in other programs to feel comfortable being friends with people who spoke a different language. His work suggested that attendance in DLBE programs supported the development of friendships across Latino student groups with varying levels of Spanish language proficiency—often an important and in this case distinguishing marker of group membership. Further, Latino students reported being more likely to enjoy "reading in Spanish and listening to music in Spanish" (p. 136), and, in general, being more likely to enjoy using Spanish and consuming Spanish literature and media.

Beyond Attitudes—A Closer Look at Student Outcomes in DLBE

As empirical work continued to be carried out examining sociocultural competence in DLBE, scholars began attending more carefully to how these programs differentially served the students who attended their programs, and the experiences of students in the DLBE context (Bearse & de Jong, 2008). Questions were posed about how intergroup contact and language learning experiences in DLBE programs might promote aspects of sociocultural competence differently for various student groups. Scholars began asking how the knowledge, skills, attitudes, and behaviors of these students would manifest differently depending on their positionality in the larger society, as well as within their schools and classrooms. Some of this work began to include multiple methodological approaches beyond the surveys and questionnaires that previous scholars had largely relied on for their work.

Bearse and de Jong (2008) collected both focus group interviews data as well as survey data from Anglo and Latino TWBE in grades 6–12 asking specifically about their attitudes toward and ideas about bilingualism and biculturalism. Although both groups expressed positive attitudes toward the TWBE program and toward bilingualism and biculturalism, differences emerged in the qualitative focus group data between the Anglo and Latino students. Bearse and de Jong (2008) noted that although Anglo students formed a "personal connection" with, and general appreciation of, their target (Latino) culture, they were less likely than their Latino peers to consider themselves as bicultural (p. 332). These Anglo students were also more likely to express an "instrumental" valuation of being bilingual by saying that they recognized it as important to help them get good jobs in the future (p. 335). In contrast, Latino students expressed the importance of being bilingual and bicultural because it connected them to their cultural identity and to their families.

Despite these differences, Bearse and de Jong (2008) also found that students in grades 6–12 from both groups reported gaining sociocultural competencies, such as cultural knowledge and open-mindedness, through their participation in the DLBE program and expressed positive attitudes toward being bilingual and having inter-ethnic friendships. For example, an Anglo tenth-grade female student remarked that "since we've been with kids of different cultures we're more acceptable of other cultures than maybe the mainstream kids" (p. 332). Another Anglo female stated she would not consider herself bicultural because "we've learned about it [culture] and stuff, but we haven't like experienced it" (p. 331), revealing her critical understanding of how her experience as a member of the majority culture was qualitatively different from that of her Latino classmates. A tenth-grade Latina reported valuing bilingualism, saying, "I remember how much I learned how to cherish both languages. I thank [the DLBE program] for bringing both Spanish-speaking and English-speaking great friends into my life" (p. 333). Both Anglo and Latino DLBE students noted the value of their cross-ethnic friendships and cited them as the reason why they chose to continue (rather than quit) their DLBE program as they entered secondary programs (Bearse & de Jong, 2008).

More recently, Butvilofsky and Gumina (2020) also conducted focus groups and collected student writing samples to similarly investigate student perceptions of bilingualism among students at a charter school on the Arizona-Mexican border. With the backdrop of Arizona's restrictive language education policies, this school sought to disrupt negative messaging toward bilingual students with an explicit focus on social justice that "centers students' identities and promotes critical thinking and revolutionary action" (p. 201). Findings revealed that students in the program expressed positive attitudes toward their bilingualism and biculturalism, specifically noting how being bilingual increased their social, symbolic, and economic capital. Students repeatedly reported awareness that their bilingualism allowed them to interact with people in ways that could lead to transformative action and expressed interest in leveraging their bilingual and bicultural abilities to transform the United States.

A small number of studies examined the question of how African-American students experience and acquire sociocultural competencies as a result of attending DLBE programs. For example, Anberg-Espinoza (2008) conducted interviews with fourth- to eighth-grade African-American students enrolled in a Spanish-English DLBE program in Northern California, reporting that students enjoyed strong friendships with students from various ethnic groups. Many students also positively mentioned that, through their participation in a DLBE program, they gained cultural knowledge about "Mexican and Latino culture", and a few students even mentioned learning about "Native American or Chinese cultures" as well. Students mentioned how much they enjoyed activities involving Black History Month, Afro-Brazilian Capoeira dance, and other cultural events, noting how such activities "helped other students under[stand] African American culture better" (p. 169). However, the students also expressed a desire to learn "hip-hop" and "African languages" in school, and they wished they could see more diverse cultures besides their own and Latino culture represented in the curriculum. Carrigo (2000) studied students in grades 4–6 who attended a K-8 DLBE school in Los Angeles, where 25% of the students were African American, 20% Anglo, and 50% Latino. She found that when students were asked whom they would like to invite to an after-school party, students chose peers from all ethnic groups represented at the school equally. There was also some positive evidence of "Black-White desegregation" (pp. 225–226) in social contexts outside of school, which is an important positive outcome for students in DLBE programs.

More recently, Bauer and Harrison (2015) interviewed nine parents of African-American students in kindergarten and first grade at one Spanish-English DLBE school in an urban low-income neighborhood that included African-American, Latino and White students. After two years, these parents reported that their children were making friends across linguistic and racial groups at the school, as well as in social interactions after school, and were demonstrating positive attitudes toward speaking Spanish and being bilingual. They noted, for example, that their children would voluntarily consume Spanish media, such as TV, and encouraged members of their family to learn Spanish alongside them. Of particular note was the finding that some students were developing a "critical stance" (p. 27) toward the notion of who could be a speaker of Spanish in the United States—recognizing that they could be part of that group if they so choose despite negative stereotypes and racist messages to the contrary. Many parents explicitly attributed these behaviors, attitudes, and shifts in perspective to attendance at the DLBE program, expressing gratitude that their children could connect with other children who were different from them and acquire a more global perspective as they participated in the program.

This work demonstrates the importance of attending to how African-American students develop sociocultural competence in DLBE settings. However, the stakes feel particularly high for this group of students, given that African American Vernacular English is often not valued as a standard dialect of English in DLBE program and African-American students often face negative raciolinguistic ideologies and stereotypes that can work against them (Palmer, 2010; Valdés, 2018). As Bauer and her colleagues have noted (Bauer & Harrison, 2015; Bauer et al., 2020), the lack of attention to African-American students in DLBE programs leaves a wide gap in the research literature, proving to be true as well for sociocultural competency outcomes (see Chapter 22 in this handbook).

Heritage Language Programs

During this time, more focused attention on heritage language programs emerged as an important part of the work on sociocultural competence for students in DLBE. Heritage language programs are unique in that they perform a specific, yet vital, function for students from Native communities in the United States (Fortune & Tedick, 2008), who continue to face linguistic and cultural discrimination (Rousseau & Dargent, 2019). Fortune and Tedick (2008) note that in addition to the strong focus on native language revitalization, these programs emphasize the development of students' understanding of the culture of the respective Native group. These programs often serve a similar purpose for Native students as the TWBE programs may serve for Latino students, in terms of promoting sociocultural competence that helps students remain connected to their cultural heritage and to their families (Bearse & de Jong, 2008; Luning & Yamauchi, 2010). Sociocultural competence that underpins these connections includes increased cultural knowledge, appreciation for self and one's cultural identity, as well as the acquisition of the heritage language and culture that facilitates cross-generational communication.

Sociocultural competence outcomes for students in these heritage DLBE programs are reflected in the unique role and mission of these schools. Hawaiian DLBE programs, for example, have roots in the Hawaiian Renaissance, which seeks to preserve Hawaiian culture and language and receive "reparations ... for the involvement in the United States with the illegal overthrow of the Hawaiian Kingdom in 1893" (Beyer, 2018, p. 58). These programs explicitly seek to preserve and elevate a culture and language that was marginalized and even banned after the overthrow of the Hawaiian monarchy (Luning & Yamauchi, 2010). The cultural and linguistic knowledge explicitly taught in these programs are specific to the culture, tradition, and languages of Hawai'i and act as important sociocultural competence outcomes for students in these programs. For example, at various Ka Papahana Kaiapuni public schools, located across five different Hawaiian islands, Luning and Yamauchi (2010) found that at these heritage TWBE programs "students learned about agriculture through working in taro patches, about science by testing the water in streams, and about Hawaiian history by visiting historic sites on neighboring islands" (p. 53). Interviews revealed that students valued the cultural emphasis of the program and felt that their participation had resulted in an increased connection to Hawaiian culture. Research concluded that students in these programs often taught their older family members what they had learned about Hawaiian culture, history, and language—promoting cross-generational communication and forging deep connections to their families and cultural heritage (Beyer, 2018; Luning & Yamauchi, 2010).

Research conducted by Lipka et al. (2007) similarly showed how sociocultural competence, taken up by students in one Yupiaq heritage language program in Alaska, served to strengthen community and family ties, often allowing students to interact with family members and communicate with their grandparents in their native languages. In this program, researchers, teachers, and community elders worked together to create a math curriculum based on tribal knowledge of how to make parkas. DLBE students learned from several elders who were invited to help demonstrate how they made patterns for their parkas, while the DLBE teacher used the knowledge from these elders to help the students create a geometry lesson that met academic standards of rigor and preserved students' culture. Lipka et al. noted that "although the project did not 'measure' students' increasing knowledge of Yupiaq language and culture, it is clear from the transcripts and the videotaped lesson that, in fact, these were occurring" (p. 111).

Discussion

This chapter reviewed scholarly work from the past 60 years that explored student's sociocultural competence outcomes in DLBE programs. Across the 45 articles reviewed for this chapter, sociocultural competence has largely been investigated in terms of student attitudes (toward each other, toward the partner language, and toward being bilingual) and cross-group friendship formation. Some work has attended to the acquisition of a culture associated with the partner language. We note a discernible shift over time among scholars from considering sociocultural competence emerging as an inevitable outcome of attending DLBE programs to an understanding that deliberate interventions are needed to support student development in this area. In the following sections, we will describe the main limitations in the research that emerged from our review and suggest scholarly work that would fill those identified gaps. We outline an agenda for future research that focuses on expanding notions of sociocultural competence to include more comprehensive theorization and conceptualization, as well as make a call for work that explicitly addresses issues of power and the needs of minoritized students in DLBE classrooms.

Future Directions for Research on Students' Sociocultural Competence Outcomes

Our review highlighted large gaps in the literature that require rigorous and purposeful attention. First, current research does not represent the diverse groups enrolled in DLBE programs. Out of the 45 articles reviewed for this chapter, 38 were in Spanish-English DLBE programs, while the remaining studies included two heritage languages programs, two French-English, one Korean-English program, and one Chinese-English. Given the rise of DLBE across the United States, and the diversity of languages other than Spanish being taught in these programs, there are clearly opportunities for students' sociocultural competence to be invested across an array of educational and linguistic contexts. As more diverse language programs are investigated, DLBE research can attend to how vernacular language use and language status impact students' sociocultural competence development (Alfaro & Bartolomé, 2017; Freire & Feinauer, 2022). There is a need for rigorous research studies in one-way developmental bilingual education programs and heritage language programs. These studies should center the experiences of minoritized students so that DLBE programs are better positioned to empower minoritized students with the knowledge, understanding, skills, and confidence to navigate the discrimination, injustice, and oppression they face. As there is often a greater commitment to culture on the part of students in a heritage DLBE program, sociocultural competence outcomes will likely differ for students in these programs. Additionally, it is crucial to understand how sociocultural competence is being taken up by students in the one-way immersion or world language programs, though we suggest this work be done with caution and with a deliberate focus on equity, access, and inclusion.

A second finding from our review is that sociocultural competence remains understudied and narrowly conceptualized—being operationalized primarily in terms of student attitudes and cross-cultural friendship formation. Missing from this research is what sociocultural competence looks like in practice: What are the knowledge, skills, practices, and behaviors that sociocultural competent students might display, embody, and enact? For example, what kinds of "conflict resolution strategies" (Howard et al., 2018, p. 60) might be employed by students who are socioculturally competent? What social and emotional competencies (empathy, perspective taking, and communication) are implicated in the development of sociocultural competence for students, and how should these competencies be taught, promoted, and then measured? Investigating these kinds of questions will widen the lens of inquiry on student outcomes and provide a more expansive body of empirical research to guide teachers and practitioners in supporting the development of sociocultural competencies among their students.

Based on our review, we have two main suggestions to address these current limitations and for expanding future scholarship on sociocultural competence in DLBE. First, we suggest broadening how sociocultural competence is conceptualized in terms of knowledge, skills and practices that students might exhibit as they develop these competencies. Scholars need to think together about what theoretical frameworks might underpin these competencies, and we offer some examples of theoretical work from other related fields of education as beginning points for these conversations. Second, we make an urgent call for attention to notions of equity and power relations in the broadening of definitions and conceptualizations of student's sociocultural competence outcomes. This includes looking more closely at how sociocultural competence is enacted in classrooms and the role of teachers in supporting the development of their students' sociocultural competence.

Expanding Understandings of Sociocultural Competence

As noted above, there remains a narrow conceptualization of what sociocultural competence outcomes look like for students in DLBE programs, limited in the current research literature mainly to student attitudes and cross-cultural friendship formation. Many questions remain about what sociocultural competence looks like and how it can be assessed. The narrow conceptualization of sociocultural competence that dominates current research can partially be attributed to a narrow set of theoretical lenses used to examine this outcome. We venture that by expanding the frame to include other lenses, new dimensions may become more evident. DLBE scholars can draw on theoretical frameworks and empirical work conducted in other fields to aid in expanding and deepening the construct of sociocultural competence (Parkes et al., 2009). For example, there is a vast body of work in the field of multicultural education that has had an impact internationally since the 1960s civil rights movement in the United States. Some of these include frameworks culturally relevant and culturally sustaining pedagogy (Ladson-Billings, 2014; Paris & Alim, 2014) that have helped highlight the different needs students from different racial and ethnic groups have in terms of developing sociocultural competence. These theories will help elevate the needs of minoritized students in the conversation of sociocultural competence and bring teachers more directly into the research conversations.

Related notions of intercultural competence from scholars in the fields of international education (Deardorff, 2006, 2011) and world languages (Byram & Wagner, 2018) have much to offer theoretically as well. For example, Deardorff (2006, 2011) proposes a process by which students develop internal and external aspects of intercultural competence by acquiring intercultural attitudes, knowledge, and skills—culminating in "effective and appropriate behavior and communication in intercultural situations" (Deardorff, 2011, p. 67). DLBE scholars should look closely, and empirically, at the student attitudes, knowledge, and skills implicated in this process. These constructs add granularity and specificity to the definitions and measurement of sociocultural competence and can help frame sociocultural competence from a developmental perspective—a much needed lens as DLBE programs serve a range of students across grades, ages, and developmental trajectories. Howard et al. (2020) have drawn on some of this work recently, incorporating the Council of Europe's competencies for democratic culture as a framework for sociocultural competence.

Additionally, there are new paradigms, such as transculturation, that may more accurately reflect the realities of how culture is enacted and contribute to a richer conceptualization of sociocultural competence (Babino & Stewart, 2020). Drawing on the work by Fernando Ortiz, Ofelia García (2011) discusses how using a transculturation lens can shift the focus from a bilingual/bicultural approach in transitional bilingual/bicultural programs to a multilingual/transcultural understanding in TWBE, thus allowing for a more authentic reflection of the fluidity and complexity of culture. While transculturation is still new to DLBE, this paradigm has the potential to challenge the cultural binary currently presented in DLBE, as critiqued by Freire (2020), and open possibilities to include the myriad cultures of minoritized communities in the United States and abroad.

Attending to Issues of Equity and Power in Sociocultural Outcomes

Issues of equity and power need to take center stage in the conceptualization of sociocultural competence and the study of student's sociocultural competence outcomes. We note that, for example, a focus on equity and power challenges the assumptions underpinning the "immersion effect" (Lambert, 1987), attributed solely to the diverse context of DLBE classrooms. Much of the early scholarship in DLBE was based on the assertion from Allport's (1954) contact hypothesis that interpersonal contact between two groups will promote tolerance and reduce prejudice. However, Allport noted a condition for this reduction in bias to when there is equal status among groups. Recent scholarship has highlighted the power dynamics present in many DLBE classrooms that preclude contexts where students share equal status and pointed to teachers as pivotal agents in promoting the development of sociocultural competence (González, 2020; Stolte, 2017). For example, in Freire's (2020) study about teachers' instructional efforts to meet the bicultural and sociopolitical conscious needs of students in a Spanish-English TWBE program, he asserted that sociocultural competencies are not automatically taken up by students as they become bilingual and biliterate, or as they are combined in classrooms with "balanced numbers of two linguistic groups of students" (p. 68). Rather, he wrote, "teaching in a non-English language can help, but it does not guarantee biculturalism" (p. 69).

Stolte (2017) has conducted similarly important work looking at the role of teachers and staff in DLBE programs in supporting and promoting student's sociocultural competence outcomes. She compared "cross-cultural learning" (p. 210) among students in two different Spanish-English TWBE schools—one where differences among students were de-emphasized by teachers and staff at the school, using a color-blind approach in their classrooms, while teachers at the other school openly discussed and highlighted differences between ethnic, racial, and religious groups, using "dynamic discourse of dissonance" (p. 210). Not surprisingly, all students at the first school reported feeling more uncomfortable discussing issues of race, and holding more biases toward "Muslims and Blacks" than the students at Sunset Elementary (p. 214), while students at this second school took up sociocultural competencies such as perspective taking, curiosity, cultural appreciation, and suspending judgment of culturally different other ways of living. We invite scholars to build on this work to explore and document the ways in which sociocultural competence can be leveraged to support the development of critical consciousness in students and vice-versa (see Chapters 2, 3, and 11 in this handbook).

We finish this chapter with a global call for an increase in scholarly work documenting the too often overlooked third goal of DLBE—students' sociocultural competence. There is a need for more empirical work looking at sociocultural competence from a variety of perspectives to expand understanding of this construct, and with careful attention to the lived and variable experiences of students in DLBE classrooms. Further, sociocultural competence needs to attend to issues of equity and power that disproportionately negatively impact minoritized groups, and for students in these programs to deliberately join in confronting and dismantling various types of oppression (Freire, 2020). We have provided some suggestions for beginning the work to fill these empirical gaps and look forward to future scholarship in this area that will undoubtedly strengthen DLBE programs and help provide a more equitable educational experience for their students.

References

Alfaro, C., & Bartolomé, L. (2017). Preparing ideologically clear bilingual teachers: Honoring working-class non-standard language use in the bilingual education classroom. *Issues in Teacher Education*, *26*(2), 11–34.

Allport, G. (1954). *The nature of prejudice*. Addison-Wesly.

Anberg-Espinoza, M. (2008). *Experiences and perspectives of African American students and their parents in a two-way Spanish immersion program*. [Doctoral Dissertation, the University of San Francisco]. USF Scholarship Repository. https://repository.usfca.edu/diss/155

Babino, A., & Stewart, M. A. (2020). *Radicalizing literacies and languaging*. Palgrave Macmillan.

Bauer, E., & Harrison, D. (December, 2015). Parental perspectives on dual language classrooms: The role of the African American parents. In P. Smith, & A. Kumi-Yeboah (Eds.), *Handbook of research on cross-cultural approaches to language and literacy development* (pp. 1–35). IGI Global.

Bauer, E., Colomor, S. E., & Wiemelt, J. (2020). Biliteracy of African American and Latinx kindergarten students in a dual-language program: Understanding students' translanguaging practices across informal assessments. *Urban Education*, *55*(3), 331–361.

Bearse, C., & de Jong, E. (2008). Cultural and linguistic investment: Adolescents in a secondary two-way immersion program. *Equity & Excellence in Education*, *41*(3), 325–340. https://doi.org/10.1080/10665680802174817

Beyer, C. K. (2018). Counter-hegemony in Hawai'i: The success of the Hawaiian language immersion movement. *American Educational History Journal*, *45*(2), 55–71.

Block, N. (2011). The impact of two-way dual-immersion programs on initially English-dominant Latino students' attitudes. *Bilingual Research Journal*, *34*(2), 125–141. https://doi.org/10.1080/15235882.2011.598059

Butvilofsky, S. A., & Gumina, D. (2020). The possibilities of bilingualism: Perceptions of bilingual learners in Arizona. *Bilingual Research Journal*, *43*(2), 196–211. https://doi.org/10.1080/15235882.2020.1781295

Byram, M., & Wagner, M. (2018). Making a difference: Language teaching for intercultural and international dialogue. *Foreign Language Annals*, *51*(1), 140–151. https://doi.org/10.1111/flan.12319

Carrigo, D. L. (2000). *Just how much English are they using? Teacher and student language distribution patterns, between Spanish and English, in upper-grade, two-way immersion Spanish classes*. Doctoral dissertation, Harvard University, Proquest Dissertations and Theses Global.

Cazabon, M. T. (2000). *The use of students' self-reporting in the evaluation of the 244 Amigos Two-Way language immersion program*. Doctoral dissertation, University of Massachusetts, Proquest Dissertations and Theses Global.

Cazabon, M. T., Nicolaids, E., & Lambert, W. E. (1996). Becoming bilingual in the Amigos two-way immersion program. National Center for Research on Education, Diversity, and Excellence.

Cazabon, M., Lambert, W. E., & Hall, G. (1993). Two-way bilingual education: A progress report on the Amigos program. National Center for Research on Cultural Diversity and Second Language Learning.

Coady, M. R. (2020). *The Coral Way bilingual program*. Multilingual Matters.

Connerley, M. L., & Pedersen, P. B. (2005). *Leadership in a diverse and multicultural environment: Developing awareness, knowledge, and skills*. Sage Publications.

Deardorff, D. K. (2006). Identification and assessment of intercultural competence as a student outcome of internationalization. *Journal of Studies in International Education, 10*(3), 241–266.

Deardorff, D. K. (2011). Assessing intercultural competence. *New Directions for Institutional Research, 2011*(149), 65–79.

Feinauer, E., & Howard, E. R. (2014). Attending to the third goal: Cross-cultural competencies and identity development in two-way immersion programs. *Journal of Immersion and Content-Based Language Education*, 2(2), 257–272. https://doi.org/10.1075/jicb.2.2.07fei

Fortune, T. W., & Tedick, D. J. (2008). One-way, two-way and indigenous immersion: A call for cross-fertilization. In T. W. Fortune, & D. J. Tedick (Eds.), *Pathways to multilingualism: Evolving perspectives on immersion education* (pp. 3–21). Multilingual Matters.

Freeman, R. D. (1996). Dual-language planning at oyster bilingual school: “It’s much more than a language”. *TESOL Quarterly, 30*(3), 557–582. https://www.jstor.org/stable/3587698

Freire, J. A. (2020). Promoting sociopolitical consciousness and bicultural goals of dual language education: The transformational dual language educational framework. *Journal of Language, Identity, and Education, 19*(1), 56–71.

Freire, J. A., & Feinauer, E. (2022). Vernacular Spanish as a promoter of critical consciousness in dual language bilingual education classrooms. *International Journal of Bilingual Education and Bilingualism, 25*(4), 1516–1529.

García, O. (2011). Lost in transculturation: The case of bilingual education in New York City. In M. Pütz, J. A. Fishman, & J. N. Aertselaer (Eds.), *Along the routes to power’: Explorations of empowerment through language* (pp. 157–178). De Gruyter Mouton.

González, V. (2020). *Beyond language: Critical and sustainable sociocultural competence in a dual language*. Doctoral dissertation, San Diego State University and Claremont Graduate University, Proquest Dissertations and Theses Global.

Harter, S. (1983). *Supplementary description of the Self-Perception Profile for Children: Revision of the Perceived Competence Scale for Children*. Unpublished manuscript, University of Denver.

Howard, E. R., Lindholm-Leary, K. J., Rogers, D., Olague, N., Medina, J., Kennedy, B., Sugarman, J., & Christian, D. (2018). *Guiding principles for dual language education* (3rd ed.). Center for Applied Linguistics.

Howard, E. R., Wagner, M., Bellara, A., Sada, E., Silva-Enos, S., & Galvez, D. (October 2020–September 2023). *Reimagining dual language education: Promoting equitable bilingualism and biliteracy outcomes through a focus on sociocultural competence*. Grant awarded by the U.S. Department of Education, Office of Postsecondary Education, International Research and Studies Grants.

Ladson-Billings, G. (2014). Culturally relevant pedagogy 2.0: Aka the remix. *Harvard Educational Review, 84*(1), 74–84.

Lambert, W. E., & Cazabon, M. (1994). Students’ views of the Amigos program. National Center for Research on Cultural Diversity and Second Language Learning.

Lambert, W. E. (1987). The effects of bilingual and bicultural experiences on children’s attitudes and social perspectives. In P. Homel, M. Palij, & D. Aaronson (Eds.), *Childhood bilingualism: Aspects of linguistic, cognitive, and social development* (pp. 197–221). Lawrence Erlbaum Associates, Inc.

Lambert, W. E., & Tucker, G. R. (1972). *Bilingual education of children: The St. Lambert Study*. Newbury House.

Lindholm, K. J. (1994). Promoting positive cross-cultural attitudes and perceived competence in culturally and linguistically diverse classrooms. In R. A. DeVillar, C. J. Faltis, & J. P. Cummins (Eds.), *Cultural diversity in schools: From rhetoric to practice* (pp. 189–206). State University of New York Press.

Lindholm-Leary, K., & Block, N. (2010). Achievement in predominantly low SES/ Hispanic dual language schools. *International Journal of Bilingual Education and Bilingualism*, *13*(1), 43–60. https://doi.org/10.1080/13670050902777546

Lindholm-Leary, K. J. (2011). Student outcomes in Chinese two-way immersion programs: Language proficiency, academic achievement, and student attitudes. In D. J. Tedick, D. Christian, & T. W. Fortune (Eds.), *Immersion education: Practices, policies, possibilities* (pp. 81–103). Multilingual Matters. https://doi.org/10.21832/9781847694041-008

Lindholm-Leary, K. J., (2001). Student outcomes: Attitudes. In N. Hornberger & C. Baker (Eds.), *Dual language education* (pp. 271–290). Multilingual Matters. https://doi.org/10.21832/9781853595332

Lipka, J., Sharp, N., Adams, B., & Sharp, F. (2007). Creating a third space for authentic bilingualism: Examples from math in a cultural context. *Journal of American Indian Education*, *46*(3), 94–115.

Luning, R. J. I., & Yamauchi, L. A. (2010). The influences of indigenous heritage language education on students and families in a hawaiian language immersion program. *Heritage Language Journal*, 7(2), 46–75. https://doi.org/10.46538/hlj.7.2.4

Palmer, D. (2010). Race, power, and equity in a multiethnic urban elementary school with a dual-language "strand" program. *Anthropology & Education Quarterly*, *41*, 94–114.

Paris, D., & Alim, H. S. (2014). What are we seeking to sustain through culturally sustaining pedagogy? A loving critique forward. *Harvard Educational Review*, *84*(1), 85–100.

Parkes, J., Ruth, T., Anberg-Espinoza, M., & de Jong, E. (2009). *Urgent research questions and issues in dual language education*. Dual Language Researcher Convocation Report.

Rolstad, K. (1997). Effects of two-way immersion on the ethnic identification of third language students: An exploratory study. *Bilingual Research Journal*, *21*(1), 43–63. https://doi.org/10.1080/15235882.1997.10815601

Rolstad, K. (1998). *Language minority children in a third language immersion context: Evidence for educational enrichment*. Doctoral dissertation, University of California, Proquest Dissertations and Theses Global.

Rousseau, S., & Dargent, E. (2019). The construction of Indigenous language rights in Peru: A language regime approach. *Journal of Politics in Latin America*, *11*(2), 161–180.

Stolte, L. (2017). Discussing dissonance: Color-blind collectivism and dynamic dissonance in two-way immersion contexts. *Bilingual Research Education Journal*, *40*(2), 205–221. https://doi.org/10.1080/15235882.2017.1310678

Sue, D. W.. (2001). Multidimensional facets of cultural competence. *Counseling Psychologist*, *29*, 790–821. https://doi.org/10.1177/0011000001296002

Valdés, G. (2018). Analyzing the curricularization of language in two-way immersion education: Restating two cautionary notes. *Bilingual Research Journal, 41*(4), 388–412.

11

CRITICAL CONSCIOUSNESS IN DUAL LANGUAGE BILINGUAL EDUCATION

A Literature Review of Students' Outcomes

Juan A. Freire, Erika Feinauer, Mallory Earl, Kaila Willardson

The development of critical/sociopolitical consciousness for students in dual language bilingual education (DLBE) classrooms has not received as much scholarly attention as other aspects of student learning in DLBE. The largest body of literature in DLBE students' outcomes has focused on academic achievement (Alvear, 2019; Collier & Thomas, 2017; Lindholm-Leary & Block, 2010; Steele et al., 2017) and bilingualism and biliteracy (Acosta et al., 2019; Genesee & Lindholm-Leary, 2013; Lindholm-Leary, 2016), with less attention to the goal of sociocultural competence in the literature (Feinauer & Howard, 2014; see Chapters 2 and 10 in this handbook).

In this chapter, we reviewed the literature on students' development of critical consciousness in dual language bilingual classrooms. First, we discuss critical consciousness in DLBE, including the importance of focusing on students' critical consciousness outcomes, and outline the different areas in which critical consciousness can be fostered. Second, we conduct a historical review of the empirical literature on students' critical consciousness outcomes in DLBE, highlighting the different areas of critical consciousness observed. We close with suggestions for future research, highlighting opportunities to fill the considerable gaps in the field to this point.

DOI: 10.4324/9781003269076-16

Critical Consciousness in Dual Language Bilingual Education

In his doctoral dissertation, J. A. Freire (2014) proposed sociopolitical (critical) consciousness as a fourth goal of DLBE. Other scholars, similarly, began publishing on this same topic (e.g. Alfaro & Bartolomé, 2017; Palmer et al., 2019; see Chapter 3 in this handbook). This literature – proposing critical consciousness as a fourth or foundational goal of DLBE – draws on Paulo Freire's (2005) idea of supporting students to read the word and the world to identify discrimination, injustice, and oppression. Reading the world, according to Freire (2005), empowers marginalized individuals to develop an understanding of their oppressive situation, move away from the margins, and resituate themselves in a position where they can advocate for themselves and others.

To date, the main focus of empirical studies on critical consciousness in DLBE has been on teachers' instructional practices, with little work focusing on students' outcomes. In this work, scholars have discussed ways for promoting the development of critical consciousness, such as calls for conscientization (Freire, 2021), the use of vernacular languages and translanguaging as tools for critical consciousness growth (Freire & Feinauer, 2022), acompañamiento (Heiman & Nuñez-Janes, 2021), caminatas (community walks) with teacher candidates (Heiman et al., 2021), and the actions of interrogating power, historicizing DLBE schools and communities, critically listening, and engaging with discomfort (Palmer et al., 2019; see Chapter 3 in this handbook).

Understanding students' outcomes in relation to critical consciousness is crucial considering the discrimination and oppression that minoritized students face, such as those that stem from racism, classism, citizenship differences, and the pressures of white hegemony, colonialism, imperialism, and neoliberalism. Alfaro and Bartolomé (2017) beautifully illustrate an example of how neoliberal ideologies are present in DLBE students and underscore the need to help students develop critical consciousness in the following vignette. Alfaro recounts how, during a visit to a Spanish-English bilingual/dual language school in Southern California, she interviewed a white, middle-class, native English-speaking, fourth-grade boy whose father was a well-known rancher in the area. When asked why he thought it was important to speak, read, and write Spanish, the young boy responded by saying, "I need to learn Spanish so when I grow up, I can tell the workers what to do" (p. 24). From a young age, this boy had internalized the neoliberal logic of learning Spanish for economic purposes and to exercise his inherited power and privilege as a white English-dominant male in society. He sought proficiency in Spanish in order to manage the Spanish-speaking laborers who would, presumably, work for him. His reason for learning Spanish was not based on a desire to advocate for or be an ally with the Spanish-speaking members of his community, nor did he seek to learn Spanish in order to identify, dismantle, or disrupt long-standing and visible inequities – or even to establish friendships with Spanish speakers. This vignette reveals the importance of systematically incorporating a critical stance in DLBE classrooms to promote students' critical consciousness outcomes that will help them question and dismantle such neoliberal ideologies. Otherwise, DLBE programs run the risk of setting students up to perpetuate power differentials, oppression, and a naïve consciousness.

We call for dual language bilingual programs to make explicit efforts to support students to develop critical consciousness. As illustrated later in this chapter, some schools with DLBE programs have been overt and clear about their intention to promote social change. For example, the Oyster Bilingual School, with a Spanish-English two-way bilingual education (TWBE) program, was explicit in its founding mission to address issues of discrimination and promote equity for all students (Freeman, 1998). Other examples include a Freirean-influenced Spanish-English DLBE school in the United States-Mexico border (Alfaro & Bartolomé, 2018) as well as Jackson Elementary School in Salt Lake City, which includes a Spanish-English two-way program strand within its school. Thanks to the support of the Adelante Partnership, Jackson Elementary was able to enact various social justice activities, including efforts to help students be aware of inequities and develop critical consciousness (Delgado Bernal & Alemán, 2017). These programs are all illustrative examples of ways schools can work to support students to develop critical consciousness in important ways. In our review of the literature, however, we also noted a lack of clarity around ways to think about critical consciousness outcomes in dual language bilingual students, including the different areas in which critical consciousness can be developed. For example, critical consciousness can be developed in multiple areas such as race, disability, language, gender, and class (socioeconomic status). Increased specificity is needed to help scholars and practitioners think about critical consciousness outcomes in their students in DLBE.

In our literature review, we noted students' critical consciousness outcomes in the areas of race, gender, immigration, class, and culture (See Table 11.1). We specifically refer to each one of the critical consciousness areas according to their respective construct: *critical race consciousness* includes concerns related to race and racism; *critical gender consciousness* encompasses concepts associated to gender representation and discrimination; *critical immigration consciousness* comprises themes such as immigration and deportation; *critical class consciousness* covers issues concerning poverty and neighborhood gentrification; and *critical cultural consciousness* includes topics related to the representation of minoritized individuals and their cultures. We found that referring to the specific areas of critical consciousness was helpful in organizing our review as we read about outcomes of students' critical consciousness. The consideration of any of these categories in students' outcomes is characterized often by intersectionality (see the topic of intersectionality in Chapter 14 of this handbook), which we acknowledge as we present and discuss each of the articles reviewed in this chapter. The historical review of the research is presented in the following section.

A Historical Overview of Students' Critical Consciousness Outcomes

In our literature review (through 2021), only 19 peer-reviewed journal articles focused on critical/sociopolitical consciousness in the classroom and 7 of those articles described students' outcomes of critical consciousness in dual language bilingual classrooms. Dissertations and book chapters were not included in this literature review. The findings of this chapter will follow a chronological order, starting with Freeman's (1996) and ending with J. A. Freire's (2020). Table 11.1 shows the list of journal articles reviewed in this chapter with contextual information from the research studies. The chronological focus highlights the gaps in the research as well as allows for a recognition of an emerging trend of work in this area. It is clear from our review that there has not been nearly enough scholarly work conducted and made available to understand how students develop critical consciousness in DLBE classrooms.

Table 11.1 Outcomes of students' critical consciousness development in the literature review

Author	*Program type*	*Language*	*Areas of critical consciousness development*
Freeman (1996)	Two-way	Spanish	• Critical race consciousness • Critical gender consciousness
Stolte (2017)	Two-way	Spanish	• Critical race consciousness • Critical immigration consciousness
Di Stefano and Camicia (2018)	Two-way	Spanish	• Critical immigration consciousness
Heiman and Yanes (2018); Heiman (2021)	Two-way	Spanish	• Critical race consciousness • Critical immigration consciousness • Critical class consciousness
Butvilofsky and Gumina (2020)	Two-way	Spanish	• Critical race consciousness • Critical cultural consciousness
Freire (2020)	Two-way	Spanish	• Critical race consciousness • Critical immigration consciousness

We use the language and terminology related to critical consciousness in describing student outcomes in our review – even when the authors of reviewed studies perhaps did not – in order to show how increased specificity can inform and help organize the nascent body of work on critical consciousness in DLBE. When applicable, we included examples in which students displayed understandings of, and/or engagement in, activism across the different studies. We have chosen to organize our review of the literature through a historical lens which reveals a gap in the literature after Freeman's study in the 1990s until the 2010s, when the proposal of establishing critical consciousness as the fourth goal of DLBE had already been introduced in the field (Freire, 2014, 2016).

1990s

1996 – Freeman

Rebecca Freeman (1996) was the first researcher who focused on students' outcomes in developing critical consciousness through DLBE education. She conducted her study at the Oyster Bilingual School, located in the Washington, D.C. area, which implements a Spanish-English TWBE program. This school started its operation in 1971 and is considered a pioneer school in DLBE. The school had an explicit mission to provide an alternative and equitable educational program for minoritized (mostly Latino) students.

Freeman's (1996) study focused on students' development as they gained increased understanding of discrimination with a focus on the development of critical race and gender consciousness, while also attending to student engagement in activism. Students' development of critical consciousness was supported by teachers' efforts and through school sponsored programs, such as the peer mediator program in which students were urged to talk about discrimination and to recognize it when it occurred. Increased awareness of discrimination led students to promote and engage in activism to counter the inequalities they observed happening around them.

Freeman (1996) noted how the principal at the Oyster Bilingual School reported implementing a school-wide curriculum that encouraged students to "identify discriminatory practices around them and develop strategies to combat such discrimination" (p. 573), with the support of parents, teachers, and administrators. For example, the school encouraged students "to think critically about how social groups [were] represented and evaluated relative to each other" (Freeman, 1998, p. 189). The school even went so far as to address racial injustice by hiring a conflict-resolution company to provide an intensive three-day bilingual training to address interracial and interethnic tensions, including aggression and violence at the school. In other words, the school made deliberate efforts to promote students' critical race consciousness, showing how supporting the development of any aspect of critical consciousness in DLBE must be through intentional action.

Freeman (1996) reported many ways that students at Oyster exhibited increased levels of critical race consciousness. She noted how they "learned to become peer mediators" to help improve racial tensions and racism (p. 574). She also described how they would recognize and "talk about discrimination and about solutions to problems of discrimination that they identifi[ied] both in and outside of school" (Freeman, 1998, p. 189). Students identified and discussed examples of discriminatory practices such as the "local and media treatment of groups in the racial riots that occurred in their neighborhood" (Freeman, 1996, p. 578).

Another discriminatory practice around which students gained critical consciousness was gender discrimination. Students were able to identify and discuss how the school curriculum did not fairly represent women. Once students identified inequitable practices and systems, they were able to craft creative solutions to discriminatory issues. For example, Freeman (1996) described how students wrote "stories in which they describe an alternative construction of reality with, for instance, women as heroes" (p. 578). DLBE students at this school also exhibited engagement in activism as an outgrowth of their critical consciousness, both through classroom activities and outside the classroom. For example, Freeman (1996) described how, after Oyster students identified problems, they would engage in the articulation of creative solutions, such as "circulate petitions and protest letters" (p. 578).

Freeman (1998) describes how students in one sixth-grade English class were taught to think critically about racism. During Black History Month, the sixth-grade teacher discussed a racist experience that affected Yvonne Braithwaite Burke at an all-white school when she was about the same age as the sixth graders. Burke is a Black former Attorney General of California and former Congresswoman in the United States. In the reading discussed in class, Burke recounts a field trip to a picnic at a whites-only park, and how this made her feel excluded and discriminated against as she was not allowed to participate in this school event. This institutional racist practice that hurt young Yvonne is related to the historical oppression experienced by African American individuals, as well as the great debt owed by the U.S. government of a genuine apology and reparations to the descendants of enslaved Blacks (Corlett, 2016; Ray & Perry, 2020).

Freeman (1998) writes about the ways students were led to develop critical consciousness and activism around racial injustice. For example, DLBE students at the Oyster School were given a homework assignment where they were tasked to write a response to the question: "How would you have felt and what would you have done if you were Yvonne Braithwaite Burke?" (p. 223). One Latina student showed her outrage over this racist event, providing an alternative proposed activity in her response. She wrote that "they could have had the picnic in a park where blacks WERE allowed" (p. 223). Freeman highlights the individual student's agency in which she "refuses an unfavorable position, and repositions herself favorably" (p. 225). In this way, this student shows increased critical race consciousness as she engaged in activism, showing her willingness to participate in and change the world around her. This student's activist plan included complaining to the teacher and the school principal, expressing her feelings about the incident and pointing out the injustice in her discussion with them. She further stated she would request at least an apology from the school. She also wrote that she would tell her parents if they did not apologize, even if they probably could not do something. She finished her response writing: "but at least I would know I had done the right thing" (p. 223). This last comment showed her increased critical race consciousness and her resultant willingness to engage in the world around her.

2010s to Present

2017 – Stolte

In this section, we present Stolte's (2017) important study that highlights the development of DLBE students' critical consciousness related to racism and immigration. Stolte (2017) conducted her research at two Spanish-English TWBE programs: Sunset Elementary and John Dewey Elementary. She studied students in a third-grade classroom at Sunset Elementary, noting how some students took up increased critical race consciousness. The third-grade teacher discussed the word *discrimination*, which led to a conversation addressing issues of racism. The students drew upon their personal experiences and knowledge gained from outside sources such as history, the news, interactions with peers, and family members' experiences to better understand that discrimination can mean "prejudice and structural racism against a range of marginalized groups" (p. 216).

The students at Sunset Elementary were able to expand their concept of discrimination to include both historical oppressions and modern-day prejudices. For example, students watched Martin Luther King's "I Have a Dream" speech and then responded to the prompt, "I have a dream that one day …" (Stolte, 2017, p. 216). Students' writing responses revealed that they were effective in using their own experiences and knowledge to critically engage with and respond to the inequality and discrimination they saw in the world. A young Latina girl, whose parents immigrated to the United States from Guatemala, expressed her personal dream of "let[ting] people come to the United States without visas because those people wait and wait and die alone without seeing their families" (p. 216). As documented in the literature, wait-times for some countries average between 7 and 23 years with "over 3.7 million petitions waitlisted in visa queues at U.S. consulates abroad" for family reunification and employment (Obinna, 2020). This young Latina student showed her critical immigration consciousness as she learned about the notion of discrimination.

This same student also wrote that she dreamed "they never again destroy churches or burn people" (p. 216). This young Latina's dream was presented in response to her classmate who shared an experience visiting the landmarks of the 16th Street Baptist Church bombing, a 1963 white supremacist/terrorist attack toward racialized people in the United States. This young girl used both a personal immigration experience of her own and a personal experience of a classmate to show her critical understanding of and increased empathy toward people affected by racial injustices. Other students also responded with dreams for their own concerns and concerns of their classmates. Stolte observed that "students frequently asked questions", and these questions often led to "gain[ing] new perspectives and, at times, increased acceptance" (p. 216). Stolte's work shows how classroom activities in DLBE can be leveraged to promote critical race consciousness in deliberate ways. This study also shows the intersectionality of race and immigration issues, promoting awareness of and critical consciousness development in both areas for students in this classroom.

2018 – Di Stefano and Camicia

Di Stefano and Camicia (2018) focused on the development of students' critical immigration consciousness, specifically in the United States. Their study took place in a Spanish-English TWBE school in the Northeast region of the United States, where Ms. Ramirez was the Spanish classroom teacher. Their research focused on observing Latino students designated as English learners. Findings revealed that these students gained a greater understanding of immigration issues and developed critical immigration consciousness through a student-led discussion, guided by Ms. Ramirez, soon after the 2016 presidential election. In a lesson reviewing the branches of power in the government, Ms. Ramirez asked a student about their thoughts on the new president. The student stated, "I think that Donald Trump is bad because he has been doing bad things, such as if parents are deported to their countries, their children will be adopted" (p. 11), a phenomenon that has been documented in the literature (Hall, 2011; Monico et al., 2019). Another student was also worried about immigration laws and expressed her worry of having to leave with her mom if she was deported. Ms. Ramirez then asked a student whose parents were born in the United States what she thinks about immigration and President Donald Trump. The student replied, "My opinion is that he is very bad because he says [...] that if people were not born here, they need to go back to their countries so they cannot stay in this school" (p. 11). These responses show how these DLBE students, regardless of their own immigration status, are engaging in critically thinking about the impact of injustices in the immigration system. They exhibited evidence of critical immigration consciousness, which disproportionately impacts many of the Latino communities that DLBE programs serve in the United States.

2018 – Heiman and Yanes; 2021 Heiman

A series of articles (Heiman, 2021; Heiman & Yanes, 2018), based on Heiman's (2017) dissertation study, highlight how students in one Spanish-English TWBE program in an urban setting in Texas came to critically reflect on racism, immigration, poverty, and neighborhood gentrification. Through these articles, we are introduced to Michelle, a Canadian-Latina teacher, who enacted a social justice-centered curriculum to promote critical consciousness among fourth- and fifth-grade students. Michelle also actively advocated for the Latino students and families whose neighborhood was in the process of undergoing major demographic changes through gentrification.

Findings in Heiman and Yanes' 2018 article highlight intersectionality in students' critical awareness around racial and immigration discrimination regarding citizenship and deportation. Their work shows how students were able to draw on school and community experiences to begin to understand the inequalities that are occurring in their own communities. Students' critical race and immigration consciousness were raised during one class, as Michelle read a document to her students about a girl whose family was in a Japanese internment camp. She followed the reading by asking her students to reflect on what might be a similar threat to national security inside and outside of the United States today. Many students replied with "Donald Trump!" while another student replied, "Syria, Afghanistan and terrorists" (p. 181). One student said, "America could be a threat to America. They could do more harm to themselves" (p. 181). Michelle then returned to the idea of Donald Trump and asked students why so many thought of him as a threat. One student said, "He's really racist", while another said, "He wants to put Mexicans back in Mexico and thinks they belong there" (p. 182). Michelle brought up the wall that Trump wants to build and asked the students their thoughts on it. Bradley, a student in the class, responded by saying, "I don't like it! My mom is Mexican. That's really rude!" and then another student asked a question, "If he sends people back ... Who gets to go back?" (p. 182). A student answered the question, "He would send the darker students back" (p. 182). Students made direct and critical connections between the history of Japanese internment, as presented by their teacher Michelle, and their current realities of living in a country and in communities where their own families face deportation and racial discrimination.

In Heiman's (2021) article, he focuses on how students' critical class consciousness is raised around issues of classism, and neighborhood gentrification intersecting with critical race consciousness. He returns to this elementary school to highlight how students are developing critical consciousness around classism, specifically related to urban gentrification – a very real experience for many students in the classroom and in the surrounding community. An extensive literature review by Pearman (2019) shows that "there is evidence that some aspects of the [neighborhood] gentrification process may be, at best, inconsequential and, at worst, potentially harmful to the academic achievement of children whose families have historically called these neighborhoods home" (p. 151). Michelle, the teacher mentioned earlier, invited a Latina mother – who had expressed feeling very at home in the school – to talk to her students about how gentrification pushed her out of the neighborhood due to a large rent raise. In response to this class visit, a middle-class white student reported:

> When Marisa's mother came it really helped me understand how it [gentrification] was driving people who lived in Austin out of Austin ... Like the houses, how they're getting so expensive cuz even apartments are, the prices of what houses used to be, ten years ago, it's just crazy how fast it's all just like gentrifying I guess.
>
> *(Heiman, 2021, pp. 72–73)*

A middle-class Latina student further reflected on the effects of gentrification, noting that "the only people who really came to our classroom and left, came and left, last year were Latinos and African Americans" (Heiman, 2021, p. 77). These two students were able to critically reflect on their own understanding of racial discrimination and classism by examining and reflecting on the phenomenon of neighborhood gentrification. They were able to connect neighborhood gentrification to their personal lives and communities because of the real-life testimonio given by a classmate's parent. Heiman's work shows how, through relevant discussion questions, the students developed critical race and class consciousness by making connections and developing understandings about how urban gentrification works and the ways racism is implicated in that process.

Heiman's studies point to how student critical consciousness can be promoted through deliberate, authentic, and relevant activities in DLBE classrooms – connecting student learning to students' lives outside the classroom. He writes that:

> Michelle's intentionality and commitment as a DLBE classroom teacher paid off as students' learning went beyond the classroom to an understanding of real-world problems, such as poverty and gentrification, issues that the students were experiencing first-hand in their communities. Notably, the students expressed an awareness of and appreciation for learning how to understand and think about issues related to class on a global scale. For example, one student noted: "Well, we didn't just learn like academics, we learned stuff that were real-world problems, things that aren't just happening in the U.S. but like across the world, like poverty, gentrification for instance, just many things that you don't get at a lot of schools, and many teachers don't teach".
>
> *(Heiman and Yanes, 2018, p. 182)*

These studies, based on Heiman's dissertation study, illustrate students' development of critical race and class consciousness by studying neighborhood gentrification. Students exhibited increased levels of critical consciousness due to their engagement with a curriculum of "humanizing pedagogies ... that acknowledge[d] the history of struggle and the humanity of every person in the community in ways that [were] personal, authentic, and relevant to the learners but that allow[ed] them to make connections to the larger society" (Palmer et al., 2019, p. 129).

2020 – Butvilofsky and Gumina

A study by Butvilofsky and Gumina (2020) also examined critical race and cultural consciousness displayed by students at a Spanish-English DLBE school. This study was carried out at Mexicayotl Academy, a charter school in Nogales, Arizona on the United States/Mexico border. Overall 98% of the students at this school were Latino, 50% of them designated as English learners, and 15% of the students crossed the United States/Mexico border each day to attend school. All of the students who were observed for the study were Mexican and spoke Spanish. Issues of racism and cultural discrimination toward Latinos in the United States were especially salient for these students. Their study focused on how, during a history lesson, students in the Spanish-English DLBE school became more critically aware of racism, deficit ideologies with regard to Mexican culture, and the resultant need for activism. The history lesson, focused on the students' Mexican ancestors, led to a wider discussion about racism, where students articulated their developing critical understandings of how the "wider sociopolitical context marginalizes and has negative perceptions toward Chicanos and Mexicans" (p. 205). One Mexican student stated,

> A veces piensan que los mexicanos no servimos para nada. Y sinceramente no pienso lo mismo. Los mexicanos son muy trabajadores, y que quieren seguir adelante (sometimes they think that Mexicans are not good at anything. And sincerely, I don't think the same. Mexicans are hard workers, and they want to get ahead). (p. 205)

Another student similarly stated,

> Lo que tú haces como Mexicano Americano puede influir a las opiniones de la gente especialmente en estos tiempos han sido víctimas del racismo causadas por Donald Trump (What you do as a Mexican American can influence people's opinions, especially in these times where they have been victims of racism caused by Donald Trump). (p. 205)

These same students felt the need to act for change and equality because of how the school "supported their academic and cultural development" (Butvilofsky & Gumina, 2020, p. 205). One student specifically appreciated the pedagogies used in the DLBE school, noting that the discussions in their classroom, "in reality helps us think about our community ... and about what is going on around the world, and why we should care about it and why we should take action when things occur" (p. 205). This student comment reveals the awareness and appreciation students have about the development of their own critical consciousness, the role that deliberate pedagogies in the DLBE classroom play in this development, and the need to take action. Further, the school culture and environment prompted these students to feel the need and desire to take action in their community and to invite change – thus leading directly to activism for social justice.

2020 – Freire

Based on his doctoral dissertation published in 2014, Freire (2020) highlights the development of students' critical consciousness about the intersection between racism and immigration. He also reveals student understandings of activism in a fifth-grade class at a Spanish-English TWBE program in Utah. Ms. Wilson, a Latina immigrant teacher, found success working with a small group of Latina students. She taught a lesson based on the book *Let's Talk About Racism* and introduced the topic of racism in her discussion, asking students what they could do, as Latinas, about racism.

In response to the discussion prompt, students brought up the difficulty for their parents in finding work, given their undocumented status. This showed their understanding of how racism intersects with other critical topics such as immigration and citizenship. For example, one student noted how a man let her dad work even though he didn't have papers. Another student added that their dad worked in landscaping but also didn't have papers. These responses were used by the students to describe these events as an exception to what was normally experienced in their communities. By citing the undocumented status of their parents, in response to a conversation about racism, these students were making connections about the intersectionality between racial discrimination and immigration status in relation to the persistent systemic discrimination against undocumented individuals in the labor market, mainly racialized immigrant individuals (Aranda & Vaquera, 2015). Ms. Wilson continued to prompt this discussion by asking the students if it was fair for employers to treat their employees differently if they come from another country. One student said no, "because it was unfair" (p. 66). Another student stated, "we should all be treated equally" (p. 66). These students' responses showed a critical consciousness of, and resistance to, the marginalization of undocumented individuals in the labor market. In this dialogue, the students were able to "recognize, understand, and critique current social inequities" for undocumented communities in the United States (p. 67).

In relation to discrimination, the teacher commented, "If you are victims of such treatment. If your dad is a victim of such treatment at his workplace, he has to go and report it, talk, and fight it. Why? Because that isn't being just. We can all experience racism: Colombians, Venezuelans, Mexicans. But there's no reason for us to shut our mouths" (p. 67). The students were encouraged to take up activism by fighting for justice, combating racism, and advocating for themselves and their families. They were also encouraged to be aware of the social inequities around them and to report them when they were seen. Students engaged in the process of developing critical consciousness of the inequities they saw in the world and began to understand how they can fight against them to create a better world. The students expressed their agreement, saying that "we need to speak up" and "fight" (p. 67).

Discussion

Our review of the literature suggests that the field of DLBE is still in its infancy in examining and conducting research documenting student outcomes in critical consciousness development. However, this chapter further demonstrates that the little literature that does exist has mainly focused on promoting learning in the categories of race, class, language, and immigration, with racism being discussed most widely and the rest of the topics being more limited. Students need to learn about various social justice issues that go beyond these larger categories and the lack of empirical work to review suggests that critical consciousness, in terms of students' outcomes, are not being attended to in DLBE classrooms in ways that combat the rising inequities predicted by Valdés (1997). We hope to see future empirical work addressing other areas of critical consciousness beyond those discussed in this chapter.

Despite a body of DLBE research addressing the perspectives and experiences of minoritized students on equity issues in the area of language (Babino & Stewart, 2017; Ballinger & Lyster, 2011; Gerena, 2010; Hadi-Tabassum, 2006; Oliveira et al., 2020), children are rarely given the opportunity to develop critical consciousness in this area or learn about language discrimination. Scholarly work should address how DLBE students view various dimensions of language, language practices and language ideologies. For example, students might connect how students with "foreign" accents are perceived in racialized ways, as they learn English, as compared to how white students are treated when they speak a minoritized language with an accent. These understandings can then be extended (and hopefully dismantled) to how individuals with accents are viewed in the larger society. Similarly, attention to the minoritized students' entire language repertoire can also help DLBE students identify inequities in how their languages are perceived and represented in society. Freire and Feinauer (2022) proposed that use and discussion of different language varieties and translanguaging in the DLBE classroom can and should promote students' critical consciousness.

While our review of the literature shows some attention to students' outcomes on immigration topics, there is little work specifically addressing undocumented populations, as well as transnationally mobile students who are often overrepresented in DLBE classrooms in the United States. Alemán et al. (2013)[1] highlight the experience of Alvaro, a third-grade DLBE student at Jackson Elementary, who expressed his frustration and fear that he and his family could be deported due to their citizenship status as undocumented in the United States. He stated to an Adelante Partnership representative during an activity that "I hate living here ... at least in Guatemala we can walk outside in the streets" (p. 330). This student was aware of the unjust immigration system and the reality of deportation, yet his reality was not taken up in his DLBE classroom as an important social justice issue. His teachers seemed unaware of his reality as an undocumented student, although it was clearly a huge preoccupation and worry for him, as well as being an important social justice issue related to the ongoing immigration into the United States.

It is problematic when students' knowledge (or funds of knowledge) on this, and other issues, are not explicitly discussed or reflected in DLBE classrooms and curriculum. The public education system has historically and systematically ignored minoritized students as holders and creators of knowledge (Delgado Bernal, 2002). In ways like Alvaro, minoritized DLBE students bring knowledge and critical consciousness to the DLBE classroom, acquired in their homes and communities. However, this knowledge and critical consciousness continues to be ignored and marginalized – despite the stated intentions of DLBE teachers and programs. Future work and teaching in DLBE classrooms need to explicitly acknowledge the experiences and expertise of the minoritized students in their classrooms in ways that not only help these students feel welcome and empowered, but also help all DLBE students understand the cruel realities experienced by many immigrants and the systematic history of deportation by the United States (Goodman, 2021; Kubrin et al., 2012). These efforts include supporting DLBE students to engage in activism, either to advocate for themselves and their communities as undocumented or to serve as allies for such individuals.

In our review, we noticed that students' outcomes in the DLBE classroom only focused on issues affecting those in the United States. We find this U.S.-centric nationalistic approach problematic. All students in the public educational system should learn about issues affecting other countries, especially the heritage countries of students represented in the classroom. This is essential in a DLBE setting since learning a language and a culture needs to go hand in hand with issues affecting the countries where the partner language is spoken. DLBE instruction needs to help students understand other countries and promote those countries from an asset-based and equity perspective. While we acknowledge the urgent need to address social justice issues in the United States, future work needs to focus on racialized DLBE students' heritage countries, as well as countries where the partner language is spoken. Learning about other countries can help students develop cultural knowledge and incorporate the mastery of geography and main facts of various countries, especially those associated with the partner language. This is especially relevant since for the most part U.S. schools poorly prepare students in the area of global geography (Bednarz et al., 2013; Passow, 2017). While learning about other countries and their geography is related to meeting the sociocultural competence goal, the development of critical consciousness will focus on helping students identify and understand inequities affecting those countries. For example, students will learn about racism and the sources of poverty and oppression in relation to the impacts of neoliberalism and the economic hitmen coercing countries with lower level of privilege, which ensure their subjugation to the interests of powerful hegemonic countries who control the global resources (Perkins, 2004). These conversations can help students develop critical consciousness regarding a U.S. imperialist approach and combat a U.S. superiority sentiment and deficit perspectives toward other countries.

Activism, understood as the action of working toward bringing social change, is an essential component of critical consciousness. In our review, we noted teachers inviting students to engage in activism and students taking up these ideas. However, none of the cited studies were about students engaging in a specific activist activity. This raises questions about how activism is taught and enacted as part of DLBE programs. DLBE programs should regularly involve their stakeholders, including their students, in activism activities connected to the critical consciousness raising efforts that are being enacted in classrooms. Scholars and educators might investigate the ways DLBE students take up these social justice and equity initiatives by engaging in activism. The lack of evidence of activities, itself, among DLBE students makes a concerning case for the need to continue advancing the proposal of critical consciousness as a fourth or foundational goal.

When considering the goal of critical consciousness, it is imperative to consider how this goal relates and interacts with the goals of academic achievement, bilingualism/biliteracy, and sociocultural competence. Dual language bilingual programs must concern themselves with teaching social justice issues and enacting equity perspectives to support an overarching mission of confronting social inequities and transforming power imbalances through social justice initiatives. Research is needed that documents ongoing efforts and ways in which critical consciousness can be leveraged to help students also meet the other stated goals of DLBE, such as academic achievement and bilingualism/biliteracy goals, but especially how the sociocultural competence of students is implicated in the development of critical consciousness. Much more attention needs to be paid to the intersection of these student outcomes with an eye toward developing curricula and pedagogies that promote these important outcomes for students in DLBE programs.

Note

1 This study was not included in our literature review because it is a book chapter and our review focused on peer-reviewed journal articles.

References

Acosta, J., Williams, J., III & Hunt, B. (2019). Dual language program models and English language learners: An analysis of the literacy results from a 50/50 and a 90/10 model in two California schools. *Journal of Educational Issues*, *5*(2), 1–12.

Alemán, E. Jr, Delgado Bernal, D., & Mendoza, S. (2013). Critical race methodological tensions: Nepantla in our community-based praxis. In M. Lynn, & A. D. Dixson (Eds.), *Handbook of critical race theory in education* (pp. 325–338). Routledge.

Alfaro, C. A., & Bartolomé, L. (2018). Preparing ideologically clear bilingual teachers to recognize linguistic geniuses. In B. R. Berriz, A. C. Wager, & V. M. Poey (Eds.), *Art as a way of talking for emergent bilingual youth* (pp. 44–59). Routledge.

Alfaro, C., & Bartolomé, L. I. (2017). Preparing ideologically clear bilingual teachers: Honoring working-class non-standard language use in the bilingual education classroom. *Issues in Teacher Education*, *26*(2), 11–34.

Alvear, S. A. (2019). The additive advantage and bilingual programs in a large urban school district. *American Educational Research Journal*, *56*(2), 1–37.

Aranda, E., & Vaquera, E. (2015). Racism, the immigration enforcement regime, and the implications for racial inequality in the lives of undocumented young adults. *Sociology of Race and Ethnicity*, *1*(1), 88–104.

Babino, A., & Stewart, M. A. (2017). "I like English better": Latino dual language students' investment in Spanish, English, and bilingualism. *Journal of Latinos and Education*, *16*(1), 18–29.

Ballinger, S., & Lyster, R. (2011). Student and teacher oral language use in a two-way Spanish/English immersion school. *Language Teaching Resource*, *15*(3), 289–306.

Bednarz, S. W., Heffron, S., & Huynh, N. T. (2013). *A road map for 21st century geography education research* (A report from the Geography Education Research Committee of the Road Map for 21st Century Geography Education Project). Association of American Geographers.

Butvilofsky, S. A., & Gumina, D. (2020). The possibilities of bilingualism: Perceptions of bilingual learners in Arizona. *Bilingual Research Journal*, *43*(2), 196–211.

Collier, V. P., & Thomas, W. P. (2017). Validating the power of bilingual schooling: Thirty-two years of large-scale, longitudinal research. *Annual Review of Applied Linguistics*, *37*, 203–217.

Corlett, J. A. (2016). U.S. reparations to descendants of enslaved Blacks in the U.S. *Africology: The Journal of Pan African Studies*, *9*(5), 15–34.

Delgado Bernal, D. (2002). Critical race theory, Latino critical theory, and critical raced-gendered epistemologies: Recognizing students of color as holders and creators of knowledge. *Qualitative Inquiry*, *8*(1), 105–126.

Delgado Bernal, D., & Alemán, E. Jr (2017). *Transforming educational pathways for Chicana/o students: A critical race feminista praxis*. Teachers College Press.

Di Stefano, M., & Camicia, S. P. (2018). Transnational civic education and emergent bilinguals in a dual language setting. *Education Sciences*, *8*(128), 1–22.

Feinauer, E., & Howard, E. R. (2014). Attending to the third goal: Cross-cultural competencies and identity development in two-way immersion programs. *Journal of Immersion and Content-Based Language Education*, 2(2), 257–272. https://doi.org/10.1075/jicb.2.2.07fei

Freeman, R. D. (1996). Dual-language planning at Oyster Bilingual School: "It's much more than language". *TESOL Quarterly*, *30*, 557–582.

Freeman, R. D. (1998). *Bilingual education and social change*. Multilingual Matters.

Freire, J. A. (2016). Nepantleras/os and their teachers in dual language education: Developing sociopolitical consciousness to contest language education policies. *Association of Mexican American Educators Journal*, *10*(1), 36–52.

Freire, J. A. (2020). Promoting sociopolitical consciousness and bicultural goals of dual language education: The transformational dual language educational framework. *Journal of Language, Identity, and Education*, *19*(1), 56–71.

Freire, J. A. (2021). Conscientization calls: A white dual language educator's development of sociopolitical consciousness and commitment to social justice. *Education and Urban Society*, *53*(2), 231–248.

Freire, P. (2005). *Pedagogy of the oppressed*. Continuum.

Freire, J. A., & Feinauer, E. (2022). Vernacular Spanish as a promoter of critical consciousness in dual language bilingual education. *International Journal of Bilingual Education and Bilingualism*, *25*(4), 1516–1529.

Freire, J. A. (2014). *Spanish-English dual language teacher beliefs and practices on culturally relevant pedagogy in a collaborative action research process* (Publication No. AAI3672850) [Doctoral dissertation, University of Utah]. ProQuest Dissertations Publishing.

Genesee, F., & Lindholm-Leary, K. (2013). Two case studies of content-based language education. *Journal of Immersion and Content-Based Language Education*, *1*(1), 3–33.

Gerena, L. (2010). Student attitudes toward biliteracy in a dual immersion program. *The Reading Matrix*, *10*(1), 55–78.

Goodman, A. (2021). *The deportation machine: America's long history of expelling immigrants*. Princeton University Press.

Hadi-Tabassum, S. (2006). *Language, space, and power: A critical look at bilingual education*. Multilingual Matters.

Hall, E. (2011). Where are my children… and my rights? Parental rights termination as a consequence of deportation. *Duke Law Journal*, *60*(6), 1459–1503.

Heiman, D. (2021). "So, is gentrification good or bad?": One teacher's implementation of the fourth goal in her TWBE classroom. *Anthropology & Education*, *52*(1), 63–81.

Heiman, D., Bybee, E. R., Rodríguez, H. M., & Urrieta, L. (2021). "Era como si esas casas no encajaban con la comunidad": Caminatas with futurxs maestrxs bilingües in a gentrifying Latinx community. *Journal of Language, Identity & Education*, *20*(1), 30–44.

Heiman, D., & Nuñez-Janes, M. (2021). "Research shows that I am here for them": Acompañamiento as language policy activism in times of TWBE gentrification. *Language Policy*, *20*(3), 491–515.

Heiman, D., & Yanes, M. (2018). Centering the fourth pillar in times of TWBE gentrification: "Spanish, love and content, not in that order". *International Multilingual Research Journal*, *12*(3), 173–187.

Heiman, D. B. (2017). *Two-way immersion, gentrification, and critical pedagogy: Teaching against the neoliberal logic*. Doctoral dissertation, University of Texas. Proquest Dissertations and Theses Global.

Kubrin, C. E., Zatz, M. S., & Martínez, R. (2012). *Punishing immigrants: Policy, politics, and injustice*. NYU Press.

Lindholm-Leary, K. (2016). Bilingualism and academic achievement in children in dual language programs. In E. Nicoladis, & S. Montanari (Eds.), *Bilingualism across the lifespan: Factors moderating language proficiency* (pp. 203–223). APA Books.

Lindholm-Leary, K. J., & Block, N. C. (2010). Achievement in predominantly low SES/Hispanic dual language schools. *International Journal of Bilingual Education and Bilingualism*, *13*(1), 43–60.

Monico, C., Rotabi, K. S., & Lee, J. (2019). Forced child–family separations in the southwestern U.S. border under the "Zero-tolerance" policy: Preventing human rights violations and child abduction into adoption (part 1). *Journal of Human Rights and Social Work*, *4*(3), 164–179. https://doi.org/10.1007/s41134-019-0089-4

Obinna, D. N. (2020). Wait-times, visa queues and uncertainty: The barriers to American legal migration. *Migration and Development*, *9*(3), 390–410.

Oliveira, G., Lima Becker, M., & Chang-Bacon, C. K. (2020). "Eu sei, i know": Equity and immigrant experience in a Portuguese-English dual language bilingual education program. *TESOL Quarterly*, *54*(3), 572–598.

Palmer, D. K., Cervantes-Soon, C., Dorner, L., & Heiman, D. (2019). Bilingualism, biliteracy, biculturalism, and critical consciousness for all: Proposing a fourth fundamental goal for two-way dual language education. *Theory into Practice*, *58*(2), 121–133.

Passow, M. J. (2017). What's wrong and what's right with geography education in the USA? *Revista Espinhaço*, *6*(1), 41–49.

Pearman, F. A. (2019). Gentrification and academic achievement. A review of recent research. *Review of Educational Research*, *89*(1), 125–165.

Perkins, J. (2004). *Confessions of an economic hitman*. Berrett-Koehler Publishers.

Ray, R., & Perry, A. (April, 2020). Why we need reparations for Black Americans. Policy 2020 Brookings: Big Ideas. Retrieved from https://www.brookings.edu/policy2020

Steele, J. L., Slater, R., Zamarro, G., Miller, T., Li, J., Burkhauser, S., & Bacon, M. (2017). Effects of dual-language immersion programs on student achievement. *American Educational Research Journal*, *54*(1_suppl), 282S–306S.

Stolte, L. (2017). Discussing dissonance: Color-blind collectivism and dynamic dissonance in two-way immersion contexts. *Bilingual Research Education Journal*, *40*(2), 205–221.

Valdés, G. (1997). Dual-language immersion programs: A cautionary note concerning the education of language-minority students. *Harvard Educational Review*, *67*(3), 391–430.

SECTION II

Key Issues and Trends

Social Justice Issues

12

GENTRIFICATION OF DUAL LANGUAGE BILINGUAL EDUCATION

Defining Types, Historical Evidence, and Alternatives

M. Garrett Delavan

Introduction

Overview

This chapter lays out the principal scholarly arguments and evidence produced suggesting that dual language bilingual education (DLBE) is undergoing various forms of *gentrification*, that is, that privileged families are increasingly occupying its physical and discursive spaces in ways that push out the original beneficiaries of this type of public education. Starting with Guadalupe Valdés' (1997) cautionary tale, scholars and educators in the field of DLBE have increasingly grown concerned about how privileged students and families—most frequently the White, middle-class populations who begin programs as monolingual English speakers—have gentrified DLBE in different ways. With the publication of Valdez et al.'s (2016) article, *The gentrification of dual language education*, the field found a name to refer to the increasing penetration of bilingual education (BE) spaces by the interests and children of linguistically, racially, and economically privileged populations. Since then, a growing number of scholars have used this term in their work, which has been and can be applied beyond the original debate in the field around demographic gentrification of two-way programs to include other forms of inequity that resemble the metaphor of urban gentrification.

First, this chapter reviews and categorizes research since 1996 on how DLBE is being mainstreamed and popularized with discourses and pedagogical choices that appeal to simplistic models of integration and the interests

DOI: 10.4324/9781003269076-19

of stakeholders with racial, economic, linguistic, and migration-status privilege. These discourses and practices are often driven by economic and defense initiatives, and the increased normalization of educational "choice" programs. Second, the chapter fills a gap in the literature by clearly laying out historical evidence that prior to this recent shift, BE throughout U.S. history had overwhelmingly served proficient or "heritage" speakers of the partner language—the maintenance and heritage constituencies of DLBE—rather than the world language (WL) constituency, the English-dominant stakeholders without an ethnic connection to the partner language. Finally, the chapter makes an optimistic call for research and action on ways that DLBE can offer a truer form of racial and economic integration.

The Essence of the Gentrification Argument: For Whom Were the Pre- and Post-Boom?

A useful way to summarize a critical or non-naïve approach to DLBE or language planning and policy in general is with the question, "Who plans what for whom and how?" (Cooper, 1989, p. 31). Delavan and Freire (2010) raised the concept of the rapid increase in DLBE programs in the 21st century in North America, asking "for whom is this boom?" A handy tool for discussing equity among such whoms is to speak of DLBE as having three constituencies (Delavan et al., 2017): (1) a *maintenance (or development) constituency* of families seeking to use schooling to help with sustaining their child's use of a home language other than English (LOTE), children and families who are often relatively new learners of English but often fully bilingual, (2) a *heritage constituency* of families seeking to regain or revitalize a language in the family or student's ethnic past, or (3) a *WL constituency* adding a new language to their repertoire that they have no ethnic connection to.

Two-way programs are an attempt to serve all three of these groups simultaneously but in more simplistic, binary terms. The scholarly conversation on the gentrification of DLBE—though it used other metaphors at the time—was originally focused on the politics of two-way immersion (TWI)'s two language groups—English-dominant students versus partner-language-dominant or bilingual students. Scholars of education both within and beyond language education often cite two-way DLBE as a shining example of racial integration. For example, writing about equity for all subdisciplines in perhaps the most respected generalist journal in the field of North American P-12 education, Thompson (2013) lauded two-way DL programs as a promising means of giving students designated as English learners access to effective instruction without excessive segregation from other students. She argued that DL is one program option that can balance negative equality (identical treatment) with positive equality, i.e., that "all people are moral equals but that differential treatment is what equality demands" in many cases (p. 1251). Gándara (2021) has consistently articulated a similar vision for two-way DLBE as a positive force for desegregating schools for the benefit of immigrant and other marginalized communities. Scholars participating in gentrification critiques generally see the integration goal as well intentioned in the abstract but not fully reflective of what is happening in actual DLBE programs and classrooms. De Jong and Howard (2009) were among the first to argue explicitly that integration via two-way DLBE is not automatic. Others have drawn on the concept of *interest convergence* to explain how joining forces with privileged groups offers as many problems as it does possibilities (Burns, 2017; Freire et al., 2017; Morales & Maravilla, 2019; Shannon, 2011).

Typology of Critiques of Gentrification and Simplistic Promises of Integration

Delavan et al. (2021a) in their introduction to a special issue on the topic of DLBE gentrification offer a chronological literature review that traces the evolution of gentrification-style critiques of DLBE policy and practice and the eventual diversification of the critique into multiple forms of gentrification worthy of study and in need of amelioration. Rather than repeat such a chronology, let me simply present a more typology-based review here of what the field has offered. Under the three main types of gentrification identified—demographic, discursive/ideological, and programmatic—I will list the major themes then discuss them and provide some fresh analysis on themes that merit deeper attention from scholars.

Demographic Gentrification

Inequitable Exchange Critique

The first type of demographic gentrification critique on the list dates back at least to Valdés (1997) and is perhaps her most insightful and powerful contribution: the extent to which the knowledge of the proficient speakers in the partner language in two-way DLBE is being exploited or mined by privileged peers without reciprocal benefits in the other direction. She argues English-dominant Whites will benefit from the linguistic and cultural modeling they receive from their peers in ways that their modeling of English will never equally benefit Latina/o/x students (who can learn English and the dominant culture on their own and whose Spanish will never seem as impressive to the dominant culture).

Inequitable Educator Attention Critique

Inequitable educator attention toward privileged students and parents in DLBE has been documented by many scholars. Amrein and Peña (2000) offered one of the first empirical analyses of this dynamic. Palmer's (2010) research has gained a large profile deepening the critique and corroborating earlier studies, including one study with the stark title, "Middle-class English speakers in a two-way immersion bilingual classroom: 'Everybody should be listening to Jonathan right now'" (Palmer, 2009). Oliveira et al. (2020) recently pioneered found that Brazilian immigrant students in a Portuguese DLBE program "did not enjoy the attention and support that their English-dominant peers experienced" (p. 572). Although the oversized power and influence of privileged parents in DLBE programs emerges as a theme of many studies, it has been the primary focus of several pieces from earlier work by Dorner (2011) and Shannon (2011) to recent work by Valdés (2021).

Inequitable Program Access and Demographics

Program access and demographic inequities have been a focus of studies such as Palmer's (2010) documentation of overrepresentation of Whites in DLBE strand programs and Scanlan and Palmer's (2009) documentation of the push out of students designated as having special needs. Henderson (2019) demonstrates that these patterns of exclusivity continue to plague DLBE. Freire and Alemán (2021) found a "push out of racialized students with a darker skin tone, lower English proficiency, lower SES, non-citizenship status, low academic performance, behavioral issues, and/or disability" and yet open "doors for more privileged racialized students," which they termed intra-racial gentrification to signal that White students need not be present in a program for gentrifying processes to occur (p. 253).

Of particular note and hardly acknowledged in the United States is the critique of the gentrification of program demographics in Canada that emerged strongly in 2008. That is when data began to emerge suggesting that French one-way world/foreign language immersion for Anglophone students, which had long been the most common form of DLBE in Canada, was tending to function as a form of exclusionary tracking that served and benefitted privileged students and families more than others. Dissimilar in many ways to processes in the U.S. context, this first wave of gentrification critique in Canada focused on inequitable access among students of the same racial and linguistic positionality, White families dominant in English. Evidence emerged that the overt and subtle forms of exclusion were based on special needs designation, socioeconomic status, gender, academic ability, and behavior (Willms, 2008). Dan Gardner (2008), a journalist in Vancouver, passionately called his nation out on the hidden-in-plain-sight findings of Willms (2008) in the province of New Brunswick:

> Everyone knows why French immersion is so popular among the ambitious parents who drive high-end SUVs, serve on school committees and draft detailed plans for getting their children into Harvard.

> It's because immersion is the elite stream [track]. The good kids are in immersion. ... The rude word for this process is "culling." Immersion is tough. Kids who struggle are culled. Slow kids are culled. Troubled kids. Poor kids who come to school with empty stomachs. Disabled kids who need teaching assistants. All the kids who could burden teachers and drag the class down and annoy the ambitious parents of future Harvard alumni. Forget national unity. Making kids bilingual for the good of the country is as dead as Trudeau. Job prospects? That's the reason most parents give when researchers ask why they choose immersion, but I think that's what we say in polite company. Chinese or Spanish would look much better on the résumés ... It's about the streaming [tracking].

The accusation here is stark: DLBE's attractiveness may have more to do with its exclusivity than its language results per se. The following year White parents in the province of Ontario protested to their school board over such patterns of inequitable access (Rushowy, 2009).

Program Placement Inequities and Gentrification of a Program's Neighborhood

Studies citing inequities over program placement and the literal gentrification of the neighborhoods where programs were situated have grown steadily over time. Morales and Rao (2015) and Valdez et al. (2016) found that privileged neighborhoods were receiving an inequitable share of new DLBE programs in Illinois and Utah, respectively. Inequities resulting from the gentrification of the neighborhoods and cities surrounding programs were key themes in many recent studies (Chaparro, 2017; García-Mateus, 2020; Flores & Chaparro, 2018; Heiman, 2017, 2021; Heiman & Murakami, 2019), including a study of a bilingual school for the deaf in a town in Mexico being gentrified by White expats, several of whom have taken over administrating the school (Kasun et al., 2021).

Discursive or Ideological Gentrification

From Equity-Heritage toward Neoliberalism, Human Capital, and Globalization Framings

The concept of discursive or ideological gentrification generally refers to the way patterns of talk, text, images, and other communicative modalities can reinforce the interests of more privileged newcomers to DLBE even when demographic gentrification is absent. For instance, the relatively sudden turn toward neoliberal, human capital, and globalization framings of

DLBE has been critiqued as working to privilege already privileged students increasingly taking advantage of the boom in programs and working against the interests of marginalized communities in DLBE. Freeman (1996) in her ethnographic study of the early and longstanding DLBE program at Oyster Bilingual School in Washington, DC—which was conducted for her 1993 dissertation—pioneered this critique when she observed that in

> Oyster's historical overview and in my interviews with Senor Estevez, the arguments presented in support of the bilingual program focused on economic and security benefits to the community rather than on the benefits of bilingual education or any moral commitment to equal educational opportunities for the native Spanish-speaking students. (p. 569)

Over the next two decades, Petrovic (2005), Varghese and Park (2010), and Cervantes-Soon (2014) all cautioned that BE was taking a risky bet that neoliberal marketability of its programs would save it from its longstanding foes in English hegemony, White supremacy, and xenophobia/nativism. Valdez et al. (2016) offered the idea of *market( )ability* to read new DLBE policy discourses that were silencing a prior equity-heritage framework beneath one of globalized human capital. News media text and imagery (Hamann & Catalano, 2021; Lu & Catalano, 2015) as well as state promotional materials tended to corroborate this interpretation (Freire et al., 2017). Flores and García (2017) contrasted the pros and cons of the older basement programs—which, although marginalized, constituted a space of self-determination for mostly working-class Latina/o/x students and teachers—with the newly marketable "boutique" two-way programs where that autonomy was now largely surrendered. Delavan, Freire & Valdez (2021b) analyzed the DLBE boom in terms of its capitalistic mass production of new programs, mass marketing to "mainstream" families, and mass displacement of equity-heritage interests. Zheng (2021) broke new ground beyond the traditional focus of Spanish-English programs by bringing a critique of neoliberal multiculturalism strongly to findings to a one-way WL Mandarin program. Meanwhile, Bernstein et al. (2021) found that the neoliberal politics of the school choice movement were at the center of the competitive, gentrifying thinking of administrators on planning DLBE programs in Arizona, California, and Texas.

From Advocacy or Student-Focused toward Technical or Language-Focused Framing

A related discursive turn documented by many DLBE scholars was away from an advocacy or student-focused approach to BE toward a purely technical or language-focused approach. Flores (2013) critiques a purely technical approach to bilingual and DLBE, arguing that in an attempt to defend

BE from political backlash, far too many scholars and practitioners have deemphasized "political critique" and "community empowerment" in favor of a "technocratic and cognitive understanding" of BE and "a focus on bureaucratic regulations" and depoliticized curricula (p. 273). He builds on Grinberg and Saavedra's (2000) claim that as it became a field of university study, bilingual and English as a Second Language education "formulated itself as a palatable co-optation within the mainstream political and ideological agenda" (p. 437) and thus lost its radical purpose to transform education by decentering English and its associated cultural implications. In Flores (2016), similar phenomena are elaborated as a conflict between *race radical* approaches to BE that emerged from Chicano movements in the United States and an institutionalization of BE driven by liberal multiculturalism and an ideology of problematic, standardized measures of language proficiency, achievement, and cognitive ability.

The technical, cognitive, and institutionalized approach to DLBE can be critiqued as well as language-centered rather than student-centered. Flores and García (2017) write,

> Whereas, from its early U.S. beginnings, bilingual education had focused on more effective teaching of language-minoritized children, [TWI] programs were modeled after Canadian immersion programs and were geared toward the teaching of two languages by separating languages strictly and following an immersion pedagogy. The difference between teaching children bilingually and teaching two languages lies at the heart of the change that took place almost surreptitiously at this time. (p. 25)

As I interpret it, what also fits into this type of gentrification critique are the observations that naming DLBE programs evolved from "bilingual" and toward the term "dual" (García & Kleifgen, 2010) because they worked to sanitize or abstract the naming of the learning away from the students associated with it (non-White bilinguals) toward the two named languages associated with it. Most recently, Avni and Menken (2021) found in a new middle school Hebrew-English program in New York City a hyper focus on language rather than culture and religion that could have ameliorated the racialized divisions among students.

Competition to Be the Spokespeople between the Fields of Bilingual Education and World Language Education

DLBE lies at the intersection of the fields of BE and foreign or WL education, which sets it up as a contested space where those two fields vie to control narratives and be seen as the experts worthy of consulting on all matters

DLBE. Cervantes-Soon (2014) produced perhaps the earliest clear articulation of a shift in balance of power where the WL field was gaining more ownership over DLBE than BE.

> For TWI programs to become a reality, they must be attractive enough to politicians and parents of the dominant group ... [via] marketing strategies such as emphasizing a strong academic focus, selecting campuses in desirable locations, and framing TWI as a form of "gifted education." In North Carolina, mostly for practical reasons but very likely also as a strategy to present TWI as an enrichment program, it is the field of World Language Education ... that has taken the lead in the promotion of dual-language education, ... reif[ying] a neoliberal ideology that can lead to an easy disregard of equity issues. (p. 70) I wish to point to the danger of throwing out the baby with the bath water in trying to establish TWI on a clean slate through WL [education], separate from past equity efforts in the fields of bilingual education and ESL. (p. 72)

This articulation was built on by Valdez et al. (2016) when they argued,

> A new globalized human capital discursive climate is leading policymakers and more privileged parents to envision DL as a necessary educational enrichment (foreign language education) ... [amid] the receding influence of the bilingual education field as a megaphone of counterhegemonic equity/heritage discourses ... [Thus] we argue that a larger educational struggle over access to enrichment education—and the capital it provides—appears to be incorporating language education as its next battlefront. (p. 620)

Other scholars' references to these two foundational articulations of the DLBE gentrification critique often omit how centrally they placed the factor of the balance of power between BE and WL.

Fortunately, inequitable discourses or ideologies are resisted as much as they are accepted, and the field has begun to generate more studies of the ideology work of successfully resistant teachers and programs (Heiman, 2021; Heiman & Nuñez-Janes, 2021; Heiman & Yanes, 2018).

Programmatic Gentrification

Language Allocation and Separation Policies

The term programmatic gentrification emerged from a study that traced references to language allocation/separation in U.S. state policies, suggesting the need to name the phenomenon of *fiftyfication*, that is, the privileging the 50:50 model over other language allocation ratios and programs seeking to decenter ratios in favor of an embrace of translanguaging (Freire & Delavan, 2021). Yet such considerations were clearly already part of earlier studies that had observed either declines or rises in the prevalence of BE program types and their gentrification-like implications (Delavan et al., 2021a).

Closure of Transitional BE and One-Way Developmental BE and Rise of Two-Way Immersion and One-Way WL

Program types particularly beneficial to or targeted primarily to language-minoritized students have tended to disappear over time in the United States. The aftermath of New York's de facto departure from forms of BE that were not two-way (Menken & Solorza, 2014) and California's 1999 de jure departure from BE (Linton & Franklin, 2010; Wentworth et al., 2010) have received ample attention in this regard. Even the good news, however, of the dismantling of California's 1999 restriction on all program besides two-way via Proposition 58 in 2016 has been critiqued for again resorting to problematic discourse frames such as neoliberalism (Flores, 2020; Katznelson & Bernstein, 2017) that do not significantly alter a BE landscape still thoroughly moving in a gentrified direction. It is two-way programs, not other types, that are continuing to grow in California in the absence of any de jure programmatic ban.

Rise in State-Level Planning, Including Emulation of the Utah Model

A rise in state-level DLBE policymaking—as opposed to merely district- or school-level—has been highlighted either explicitly or implicitly in several studies as a key factor in programmatic DLBE gentrification patterns. The state-level bans in California in 1999, Arizona in 2000, and Massachusetts in 2002 (Menken, 2013) were clearly gentrifying in that two-way programs or one-way WL programs were generally made the only forms of BE that were allowed. Yet this turn-of-the-century moment of backlash also prompted much of the thinking critiqued above (for instance, Petrovic, 2005) that amounted in essence to self-censorship by the DLBE field or capitulation to the new gentrified landscape. Despite critiquing their closure, BE scholars largely stopped advocating explicitly for building *new* BE programs of any type besides the same two-way programs permitted by the bans, though they clearly did advocate starting them in marginalized rather than privileged neighborhoods. Research on the Utah Model brought this state-level planning surge and power grab to the foreground and how it was being met with some resistance (Freire et al., 2021). Subsequent studies have documented the emulation of the Utah Model—including the highly explicit state-levelness of it—by other states (Freire et al., 2022; Morita-Mullaney et al., 2020). The roots of the Utah Model, however, lie in the Canadian model (discussed earlier) and in the insufficiently discussed *North Carolina model*, which is arguably an ironic counterexample to an overall pattern of gentrification of DLBE in the United States. Cervantes-Soon (2014) writes,

> In contrast to other regions of the country with a longer presence of bilingual education, dual-language immersion in North Carolina did not emerge as an attempt to achieve educational equity for language-minority students. Instead, its existence originated about 25 years ago [1989] with a **state initiative** ... [that] developed program implementation criteria, guidelines, and curriculum standards and provided professional development. As the Latin@ population began to grow in unprecedented numbers, a few progressive educational leaders saw TWI education as a logical and viable approach to address the needs of language-minority students. María Petrea, a Latina principal, established the first Spanish-English TWI program in 1997 ... [T]oday out of the 77 programs available, 26 are TWI. (pp. 68–69, bold type added)

North Carolina's state-model DLBE programs were 75% WL-constituency-only at about the same time as Utah's were 82%, yet unlike North Carolina, Utah started as a majority two-way space with a few transitional BE programs as well (Valdez et al., 2016, p. 618). In other words, North Carolina could only be argued to be gentrifying rather than de-gentrifying programmatically if one were to argue that its early 1990s program boom and state policy were a gentrifying development for U.S. BE as a whole. To help draw that overall picture, I turn next to quantifying BE participation rates in the United States as a whole, which the literature has thus far failed to do.

Assessing the Three Constituencies' Participation in U.S. Bilingual Education Reveals a Past with Few World Language Constituency Students

Gentrification critiques tend to start from a reading of history that sees BE in the United States as having been a space primarily used to serve the heritage and maintenance constituencies, and that after the DLBE boom in the 2000s, the WL constituency reasserted a kind of demographic, discursive, and programmatic land rush or gold rush into this minoritized space. A quantitative look at evidence of participation rates in the literature and archival sources supports this interpretation of history despite exceptions to the overall trend in spaces like North Carolina.

Evidence that Helps Quantify Constituencies across Time

Ovando (2003) discusses that from the 1700s to the 1880s large new immigrant communities had private and public schools. Supported by laws that authorized BE in the 19th century, immigrant communities provided BE in their schools using their heritage language. Around 1900, there was a peak in the first heyday of BE in the United States when approximately 4% of U.S. elementary school students were enrolled in bilingual German programs (by far the most common type of program) that offered all or part of their instruction in German. The main beneficiaries of these programs were ethnic Germans from German-speaking homes, that is, maintenance and heritage constituents. San Miguel and Valencia (1998) contend that before the arrival of White Europeans to the Southwest, in the 1848s–1890s Mexicans had established schools that promoted literacy and culture, which grew in number after the Mexican American War. These programs transitioned from mainly teaching the heritage language to a form of one-way BE for Spanish-speaking communities in the Southwest decades, long before the WL constituency participated for the first time via the first two-way program at Coral Way in Florida in 1963. Similarly, New York City schools were piloting bilingual instruction for Spanish-dominant Puerto Rican students at least as early as the early 1960s, and experimentation in Florida with Spanish-dominant Cubans preceded the decision to institute a two-way model at Coral Way (Blanton, 2004; Coady, 2019). Blanton (2004) describes how early research on and piloting of BE in Texas started around 1964 and concerned itself exclusively with one-way programs for Spanish speakers.

French immersion debuted in Canada in 1963 and had its origins not in preservation of French as a home language but in the strategies of English-dominant middle-class families in Quebec to gain entry into the dominant French-speaking community. Yet such DLBE programs in the United States designed exclusively or primarily for the WL constituency dated back only to 1974–1975 and grew slowly since then in the 20th century in contrast to TWI and forms of BE designed solely for linguistically minoritized communities (Lenker & Rhodes, 2007).

> Until 1999, schools offering foreign language immersion programs outnumbered those offering two-way immersion programs, but that balance has shifted [between 2000 and 2006]. … The surge in two-way programs can be explained in part by changes in the policy context for bilingual education and the growing interest, at state and local levels,

> in two-way immersion as a program that addresses the needs of both English language learners and native English speakers. Both bilingual education programs and foreign language immersion programs have been transformed into two-way programs by integrating the two student populations being served.
>
> *(Lenker & Rhodes, 2007, p. 6)*

Yet even apart from this "surge in two-way programs," the total number of students in one-way developmental BE, transitional BE, and other types of BE at that same time dwarfs the WL constituency's rate of participation.

Prior to Ron Unz's political victories around the year 2000, there were thousands of short-term and long-term BE programs—most developing bilingualism and biliteracy in both English and a locally valued language as well as contributing to academic achievement for multilingual students—spread across many states in the United States, including California, Texas, New York, Washington, Arizona, and Illinois. Several of these states had large BE enrollments because of laws that mandated programs be created when a school reached a certain number of eligible students with the same home language. Table 12.1 shows the results of my archival-evidence-based

Table 12.1 Estimated ratio of language-minoritized to language-majoritized students at peak levels of participation in bilingual education in the U.S. in the late 1990s

	BE enrollments of English-Learner-designated students	*WL-constituency enrollments*
California	410,000	
Texas	296,550	
New York	176,000	
Washington	66,000	
Arizona	11,000	
Illinois	114,402	
Total language-minoritized	**1,073,952**	
CAL's estimated number of two-way programs (converted to students estimating 150 students per program)		200 programs = 30,000
CAL's estimated number of foreign language immersion programs (converted to students estimating 300 students per program)		275 programs = 82,500
Total language-majoritized		**112,500**
Ratio of minoritized to majoritized = 9.5:1		

Note: Estimate is based on states with large bilingual programs and available data (Bergeson et al., 2000; Center for Applied Linguistics, 2010; Evergreen Freedom Foundation, n.d.; Illinois State Board of Education, 2012; Lenker & Rhodes, 2007; Peralta, 2000; Rossell, 2003, 2009).

analysis of those states' peak years of BE enrollments prior to the recent decline of transitional BE amid the DLBE boom of the 2000s and 2010s. Available evidence in the cited documents indicates these programs offered services to over a million English-learner-designated students at the end of the 1990s (Bergeson et al., 2000; Evergreen Freedom Foundation, n.d.; Illinois State Board of Education, 2012; Peralta, 2000; Rossell, 2003, 2009). Compare this number with the 475 DLBE programs at that time (Center for Applied Linguistics, 2010; Lenker & Rhodes, 2007) involving what is likely to be 112,500 English-privileged students. At the turn of the last century, English-learner-designated students benefitting from BE appear to have outnumbered English-privileged students by a factor of nine to one.

Two Example Contexts where WL was the Gentrifying Newcomer

Two example DLBE contexts that emerged later than Spanish programs in the United States—Chinese and French—corroborate this overall quantified history by demonstrating how DLBE emerged first as an equity-heritage-framed intervention rather than a tool for the WL constituency. For example, the first public Chinese DLBE program in the United States was at San Francisco Unified School District's West Portal Elementary in 1984, begun by a group of parents seeking to maintain their families' linguistic heritage and form a one-way developmental DLBE program (Tucker, 2009). The next public program, also Cantonese rather than Mandarin, was a two-way program that emerged in the same district in 1995 and was named in honor of the first Chinese-American teacher in San Francisco's public schools, Alice Fong Yu (http://www.afypa.org/ourSchool.html). Mandarin-English programs had a more elitist origin because several of the earliest were at private schools. According to Weise (2013, 2019), the first Mandarin DLBE program emerged in San Francisco and sought to serve heritage learners, opening 1981 as a private school still operating as the Chinese American International School (https://www.cais.org); it sought to be two-way but consistently has had more English-dominant students, though many of Chinese heritage. The next private programs began in the Bay Area in 1991 and 1996, and the first public program began in Potomac, Maryland in 1996, with two other public programs following in 1998, Shuang Wen School in New York City's Chinatown—a clear effort to center the maintenance and heritage constituencies—and Woodstock Elementary in Portland, Oregon (Weise, 2013, 2019). After 2006, Mandarin programs boomed with federal support driven by post-9/11 national security policy and Cantonese programs have lagged far behind.

As a second example, Louisiana stakeholders instituted its first phase of French immersion programs primarily to preserve bilingualism among the

Cajun community there. These equity-heritage purposes led Louisiana to have the largest number of French programs of any state for several decades (CITE). Kristmanson and Dicks (2014) write,

> The original student FI [French Immersion] population in Louisiana, mainly comprised of families who had cultural connections to the French language, has since expanded due to increased interest in immersion. In particular, over the last 20 years, immersion programs have seen a growth in the enrollment numbers of African-American children, many if not most from low socioeconomic backgrounds.

What this example indicates is that the politics of the expansion of constituencies served by DLBE is complex in that it also involves possibilities for equitable integration of diverse groups of students, a theme I will now turn to by way of conclusion.

Conclusion

The evidence cited and reported in this chapter favors the view that the vast majority of BE programs in the United States—and the earliest ones—began with the purposes of serving (at least in part) language-minoritized populations for the purposes of maintaining bilingualism or using instruction in students' first language to create an equitable pathway to success in an English-dominated educational system, what has been termed the *equity-heritage framework* for bilingual and immersion education (Valdez et al., 2016). This demographic influx of the WL constituency into DLBE that the United States has experienced since the turn of the century is complex and sometimes does appear to involve mutually beneficial integration rather than gentrification, for example, when DLBE programs involve significant populations who are historically marginalized racially and economically despite being English-privileged.

All students should be welcomed in DLBE programs of some kind, yet the presence of the most racially and economically privileged students will be gentrifying to DLBE as a whole unless those engaged in DLBE planning seek to actively recruit and serve language-minoritized communities. These communities have a logical right to continue to access and benefit from educational forms that once belonged largely to them. Indeed, the keys to ameliorating the gentrifying effects—rather than more equitably *diversifying* effects—of the influx of more varied linguistic positionalities into BE lie perhaps in primarily combatting discursive and programmatic gentrification. Toward this end, I briefly considered classifying patterns of inequitable attention in DLBE as a discursive rather than a demographic issue. After all, today's identity categories across which inequities operate are ultimately less important than the need to resist the persistence of inequalities among ever-evolving identities.

A truer form of racial and economic integration is surely possible through DLBE despite it not being an automatic outcome of diversifying the participants and increasing the number of programs. To counter programmatic gentrification, we need to advocate for flexible policy that allows for locally crafted programs and varied program models in DLBE (Delavan et al., 2021b). To counter discursive or ideological gentrification is a taller order because it is a matter of engaging beyond the DLBE field with the larger movements for social and ecological justice in the work we do, raising critical consciousness and agency within DLBE schools, teacher preparation programs, and the communities they serve (Alfaro, 2019; Delavan, 2020; Flores & Chaparro, 2018), which is work that happens to center on multilingualism but should hardly be confined to multilingualism. In fact, the literature reviewed in this chapter shows that language teaching is proving to be more harmful when confined so narrowly to language alone—this myopia can leave DLBE professionals naively unaware of who gains more from the language exchanges we facilitate. Part of our work should be to continually ask our students, colleagues, and policymakers why gentrification-like processes are so baked into our society and how they think we could change that.

References

Alfaro, C. (2019). Preparing critically conscious dual-language teachers: Recognizing and interrupting dominant ideologies. *Theory into Practice*, *58*(2), 194–203.

Amrein, A., & Peña, R. A. (2000). Asymmetry in dual language practice: Assessing imbalance in a program promoting equality. *Education Policy Analysis Archives*, *8*(8), 1–17.

Avni, S., & Menken, K. (2021). Hebrew dual language bilingual education: The intersection of race, language and religion. In N. Subtirelu, N. Flores, & A. Tseng (Eds.), *Bilingualism for all? Raciolinguistic perspectives on dual language education*. Multilingual Matters.

Bergeson, T., Mayo, C. L., Wise, B. J., Gomez, R., Malagon, H., & Bylsma, P. (2000). *Educating limited-English-proficient students in Washington state*. Retrieved from http://www.capaa.wa.gov/about/study2K.pdf

Bernstein, K. A., Alvarez, A., Chaparro, S., & Henderson, K. I. (2021). "We live in the age of choice": School administrators, school choice policies, and the shaping of dual language bilingual education. *Language Policy*, *20*(3), 1–30.

Blanton, C. K. (2004). *The strange career of bilingual education in Texas, 1836-1981*. Texas A&M University Press.

Burns, M. (2017). "Compromises that we make": Whiteness in the dual language context. *Bilingual Research Journal*, *40*(4), 339–352.

Center for Applied Linguistics (2010). *Growth of TWI programs, 1962-present*. Retrieved from http://www.cal.org/twi/directory/twigrow.htm

Cervantes-Soon, C. G. (2014). A critical look at dual language immersion in the new Latin@ diaspora. *Bilingual Research Journal*, *37*(1), 64–82.

Chaparro, S. (2017). *Language and the gentrifying city: An ethnographic study of a two-way immersion program in an urban public school.* (Doctoral dissertation).
Coady, M. R. (2019). *The coral way bilingual program*. Multilingual Matters.
Cooper, R. L. (1989). *Language planning and social change*. Cambridge University Press.
De Jong, E. J., & Howard, E. (2009). Integration in two-way immersion education: Equalising linguistic benefits for all students. *International Journal of Bilingual Education and Bilingualism*, *12*(1), 81–99. https://doi.org/10.1080/13670050802149531
Delavan, M. G. (2020). Earth democracy as empowerment for TESOL students and educators: Though the crisis speaks English, Englishes can become a commons language of sustainability. In J. Goulah, & J. Katunich (Eds.), *TESOL and sustainability: New perspectives on English language teaching in the Anthropocene Era* (pp. 19–40). Bloomsbury Press.
Delavan, G., & Freire, J. A. (2010, October). *Utah's dual language immersion boom: Is it listening to cultural differences or reinforcing differences in power?* [Paper presentation]. Annual meeting of the American Educational Studies Association (AESA). Denver, CO, United States.
Delavan, G. M., Freire, J. A., & Menken, K. (2021a). Editorial introduction: A historical overview of the expanding critique (s) of the gentrification of dual language bilingual education. *Language Policy*, *29*(3), 1–23.
Delavan, M. G., Freire, J. A., & Valdez, V. E. (2021b). The intersectionality of neoliberal classing with raciolinguistic marginalization in state dual language policy: A call for locally crafted programs. In N. Subtirelu, N. Flores, & A. Tseng (Eds.), *Bilingualism for all? Raciolinguistic perspectives on dual language education.* Multilingual Matters.
Delavan, M. G., Valdez, V. E., & Freire, J. A. (2017). Language as whose resource? When global economics usurp the local equity potentials of dual language education. *International Multilingual Research Journal*, *11*(2), 86–100. https://doi.org/10.1080/19313152.2016.1204890
Dorner, L. M. (2011). Contested communities in a debate over dual-language education: The import of "public" values on public policies. *Educational Policy*, *25*(4), 577–613.
Evergreen Freedom Foundation (n.d.). *Bilingual education: Removing the barriers. School directors' handbook*. http://www.myfreedomfoundation.com/pdfs/education_directors_handbook3.pdf
Flores, N. (2013). Silencing the subaltern: Nation-state/colonial governmentality and bilingual education in the United States. *Critical Inquiry in Language Studies*, *10*(4), 263–287.
Flores, N. (2016). A tale of two visions: Hegemonic whiteness and bilingual education. *Educational Policy*, *30*(1), 13–38.
Flores, N. (2020). Producing national and neoliberal subjects: Bilingual education and governmentality in the United States. In L. M. Rojo, & A. D. Percio (Eds.), *Language and neoliberal governmentality* (pp. 49–68). Routledge.
Flores, N., & Chaparro, S. (2018). What counts as language education policy? Developing a materialist anti-racist approach to language activism. *Language Policy*, *17*(3), 365–384.
Flores, N., & García, O. (2017). A critical review of bilingual education in the United States: From basements and pride to boutiques and profit. *Annual Review of Applied Linguistics*, *37*, 14–29. https://doi.org/10.1017/S0267190517000162

Freeman, R. D. (1996). Dual-language planning at Oyster Bilingual School: "It's much more than language". *TESOL Quarterly*, *30*(3), 557–582.

Freire, J. A., & Alemán Jr, E. (2021). "Two schools within a school": Elitism, divisiveness, and intra-racial gentrification in a dual language strand. *Bilingual Research Journal*, *44*(2), 249–269.

Freire, J. A., & Delavan, M. G. (2021). The fiftyfication of dual language education: One-size-fits-all language allocation's "equality" and "practicality" eclipsing a history of equity. *Language Policy*, *20*(3), 351–381.

Freire, J. A., Delavan, M. G., & Valdez, V. E. (2021). Grassroots resistance and activism to one- size-fits-all policies by dual language schools en comunidades latinas. *International Journal of Bilingual Education and Bilingualism*. https://doi.org/10.1080/13670050.2021.1874868

Freire, J. A., Gambrell, J., Kasun, G. S., Dorner, L. M., & Cervantes-Soon, C. (2022). The expropriation of dual language bilingual education: Deconstructing neoliberalism, whitestreaming, and English-hegemony. *International Multilingual Research Journal*, *16*(1), 27–46.

Freire, J. A., Valdez, V. E., & Delavan, M. G. (2017). The (dis) inclusion of Latina/o interests from Utah's dual language education boom. *Journal of Latinos and Education*, *16*(4), 276–289.

Gándara, P. (2021). The gentrification of two-way dual language programs: A commentary. *Language Policy*, *20*(3), 525–530.

García, O., & Kleifgen, J. (2010). *Educating emergent bilinguals: Policies, programs and practices for English language learners*. Teachers College Press.

García-Mateus, S. (2020). Bilingual student perspectives about language expertise in a gentrifying two-way immersion program. *International Journal of Bilingual Education and Bilingualism*. Advance Online Publication. https://doi.org/10.1080/13670050.2020.1797627

Gardner, D. (2008, July 26). French immersion is education for the elite. *The Vancouver Sun*. http://www2.canada.com/vancouversun/news/editorial/story.html?id=144196bf-8a12-47e8-8109-b7be65a7bb9b

Grinberg, J., & Saavedra, E. R. (2000). The constitution of bilingual/ESL education as a disciplinary practice: Genealogical explorations. *Review of Educational Research*, *70*(4), 419–441.

Hamann, E. T., & Catalano, T. (2021). Picturing dual language and gentrification: An analysis of visual media and their connection to language policy. *Language Policy*, *20*(3), 1–22.

Heiman, D. (2021). "So, is gentrification good or bad?": One teacher's implementation of the fourth goal in her TWBE classroom. *Anthropology & Education*, *52*(1), 63–81.

Heiman, D., & Murakami, E. (2019). "It was like a magnet to bring people in": School administrators' responses to the gentrification of a two-way bilingual education (TWBE) program in central Texas. *Journal of School Leadership*, *29*(6), 454–472.

Heiman, D., & Nuñez-Janes, M. (2021). "Research shows that I am here for them": Acompañamiento as language policy activism in times of TWBE gentrification. *Language Policy*, *20*(3), 1–25.

Heiman, D., & Yanes, M. (2018). Centering the fourth pillar in times of TWBE gentrification: "Spanish, love, content, not in that order". *International Multilingual Research Journal*, *12*(3), 173–187.

Heiman, D. B. (2017). *Two-way immersion, gentrification, and critical pedagogy: Teaching against the neoliberal logic* [Doctoral dissertation, The University of

Texas at Austin]. The University of Texas at Austin, Texas Scholar Works. https://repositories.lib.utexas.edu/handle/2152/61911

Henderson, K. L. (2019). The danger of the dual-language enrichment narrative: Educator discourses constructing exclusionary participation structures in bilingual education. *Critical Inquiry in Language Studies*, *16*(3), 155–177.

Illinois State Board of Education (2012). *Data analysis and accountability, bilingual: Annual reports*. http://www.isbe.state.il.us/research/htmls/bilingual.htm

Kasun, G. S., Scott, J., Kaneria, A. J., & Delavan, M. G. (2021). North American coloniality and decoloniality: Transnational tensions in a Mexican deaf bilingual school. *Bilingual Research Journal*, *44*(1), 74–89.

Katznelson, N., & Bernstein, K. (2017). Rebranding bilingualism: The shifting discourses of language education policy in California's 2016 election. *Linguistics and Education*, *40*, 11–26.

Kristmanson, P., & Dicks, J. (2014). Looking in the one-way mirror: Reflections on the changing face (s) of immersion in North America and beyond. *Journal of Immersion and Content-Based Language Education*, 2(2), 273–287.

Lenker, A., & Rhodes, N. (2007). *Foreign language immersion programs: Features and trends over thirty-five years*. Center for Applied Linguistics.

Linton, A., & Franklin, R. C. (2010). Bilingualism for the children: Dual-language programs under restrictive language policies. In P. Gándara, & M. Hopkins (Eds.), *Forbidden language* (pp. 175–191). Teachers College Press.

Lu, J., & Catalano, T. (2015). Let them learn English: Reader response to media discourse about dual language education. *International Journal of Language Studies*, 9(2), 1–26.

Menken, K. (2013). Restrictive language education policies and emergent bilingual youth: A perfect storm with imperfect outcomes. *Theory Into Practice*, *52*(3), 160–168.

Menken, K., & Solorza, C. (2014). No child left bilingual: Accountability and the elimination of bilingual education programs in New York City schools. *Educational Policy*, *28*(1), 96–125.

Miguel, G. S. Jr, & Valencia, R. (1998). From the Treaty of Guadalupe Hidalgo to Hopwood: The educational plight and struggle of Mexican Americans in the Southwest. *Harvard Educational Review*, *68*(3), 353–413.

Morales, P. Z., & Maravilla, J. V. (2019). The problems and possibilities of interest convergence in a dual language school. *Theory Into Practice*, *58*(2), 145–153.

Morales, P. Z., & Rao, A. B. (2015, September 28). *How ideology and cultural capital shape the distribution of Illinois' bilingual education programs*. Teachers College Record (ID Number: 18139).

Morita-Mullaney, T., Renn, J., & Chiu, M. M. (2020). Obscuring equity in dual language bilingual education: A longitudinal study of emergent bilingual achievement, course placements, and grades. *TESOL Quarterly*, *54*(3), 685–718.

Oliveira, G., Lima Becker, M., & Chang-Bacon, C. K. (2020). "Eu sei, I know": Equity and immigrant experience in a Portuguese English dual language bilingual education program. *TESOL Quarterly*, *54*(3), 572–598.

Ovando, C. J. (2003). Bilingual education in the United States: Historical development and current issues. *Bilingual Research Journal*, *27*(1), 1–24.

Palmer, D. (2010). Race, power, and equity in a multiethnic urban elementary school with a dual-language "strand" program. *Anthropology & Education*, *41*(1), 94–114.

Palmer, D. K. (2009). Middle-class English speakers in a two-way immersion bilingual classroom: "Everybody should be listening to Jonathan right now". *TESOL Quarterly*, *43*(2), 177–202.

Peralta, M. O. (2000). *Some facts about proposition 203 and bilingual education in Arizona.* http://azbilingualed.org/AZ%20Hist-ALEC/some_facts_about_proposition_203.htm

Petrovic, J. E. (2005). The conservative restoration and neoliberal defenses of bilingual education. *Language Policy*, *4*, 395–416.

Rossell, C. H. (2003). The near end of bilingual education in the wake of California's prop 227. *Education Next*, *4*(3). http://educationnext.org/the-near-end-of-bilingual-education/

Rossell, C. (2009). *Does Bilingual Education Work? The Case of Texas.* Texas Public Policy Foundation. www.texaspolicy.com/pdf/2009-09-RR01-bilingual-rossell.pdf

Rushowy, K. (2009, March). *French immersion debate: Oakville parents claim French immersion bias.* http://www.parentcentral.ca/parent/article/606543

Scanlan, M., & Palmer, D. (2009). Race, power, and (in)equity within two-way immersion settings. *Urban Review*, *41*, 391–415.

Shannon, S. (2011). Bicultural parent engagement: Advocacy and empowerment. In E. Olivos, O. Jiménez-Castellanos, & A. M. Ochoa (Eds.), *Bicultural parent engagement: Advocacy and empowerment* (pp. 83–102). Teachers College Press.

Thompson, K. D. (2013). Is separate always unequal? A philosophical examination of ideas of equality in key cases regarding racial and linguistic minorities in education. *American Educational Research Journal*, *50*(6), 1249–1278.

Tucker, J. (2009, September 26). West Portal immersion program still thriving. *San Francisco Gate.* https://www.sfgate.com/education/article/West-Portal-immersion-program-still-thriving-3215601.php

Valdés, G. (1997). Dual-language immersion programs: A cautionary note concerning the education of language-minority students. *Harvard Educational Review*, *67*(3), 391–430.

Valdés, G. (2021). "Verde is not the word for green in Spanish": The problematic arrogance of monolingual, powerful parents. *Language Policy*, *20*(3), 517–523.

Valdez, V. E., Delavan, G., & Freire, J. A. (2016). The marketing of dual language education policy in Utah print media. *Educational Policy*, *30*(6), 849–883. https://doi.org/10.1177/0895904814556750

Valdez, V. E., Freire, J. A., & Delavan, M. G. (2016). The gentrification of dual language education. *Urban Review*, *48*(4), 601–627. https://doi.org/10.1007/s11256-016-0370-0

Varghese, M. M., & Park, C. (2010). Going global: Can dual-language programs save bilingual education? *Journal of Latinos and Education*, *9*(1), 78–80.

Weise, E. (2013, June 6). *The nation's oldest public Mandarin immersion program.* Blog post. https://miparentscouncil.org/2019/06/16/the-state-of-mandarin-immersion-in-the-united-states-june-2019/

Weise, E. (2019, June 16). *The State of Mandarin Immersion in the United States: June 2019.* Blog post. https://miparentscouncil.org/2013/06/06/the-nations-oldest-mandarin-immersion-program/

Wentworth, L., Pellegrin, N., Thompson, K., & Hakuta, K. (2010). Proposition 227 in California: A long-term appraisal of its impact on English learner student achievement. In P. Gándara, & M. Hopkins (Eds.), *Forbidden language: English learners and restrictive language policies* (pp. 37–49). Teachers College Press.

Willms, J. D. (2008). *The case for universal French immersion.* https://policyoptions.irpp.org/magazines/quebec-1608-2008/the-case-for-universal-french-instruction/

Zheng, B. (2021). Neoliberal multilingualism and "humanitarian connections": Discourses around parents' experiences with a Mandarin Chinese immersion school. *Language & Education*, *35*(1), 78–95.

13

A LITERATURE REVIEW OF RACIOLINGUISTICS IN DUAL-LANGUAGE BILINGUAL EDUCATION

A Call for Conceptualizing Racialization

Laura C. Chávez-Moreno

In this chapter, I review empirical research on dual-language bilingual education (DLBE) that uses a raciolinguistic lens. The question guiding the review is: *How is a raciolinguistics lens being used by scholars researching DLBE?* The chapter starts with an overview of a raciolinguistics lens. I then describe the search for and analysis of the studies. Next, I present the 16 reviewed articles by highlighting how education researchers utilize and understand a raciolinguistic lens in their study. I then discuss the trends across the included research studies (a majority focus on: language/linguistic inquiries; who benefits from DLBE) and I offer possible future research inquiries. I argue that research employing a raciolinguistic lens would do well to define or conceptualize "race,"[1] including viewing Latinx[2] (the focus group of nine of the studies) as a racialized group, not an ethnic label. To conclude, I share implications for research and suggest possible future research directions for the United States and abroad.

Overview

The legacies of racial discrimination influence people's access to and the quality of schooling—which includes DLBE. Many DLBE programs/schools aim to serve students from racialized and language-minoritized groups, and this, coupled with society's unjust conditions, motivates some scholars to research questions about racism in bilingual education and about the bilingual

 DOI: 10.4324/9781003269076-20

schooling of students from underserved communities. An emerging framework that scholars employ to consider race and language in DLBE research is a raciolinguistic lens.

Flores and Rosa (2015) coined *raciolinguistic ideologies* to theorize about seeing the speaker's racialized group (e.g., Latina) as an important factor of how the listener (e.g., a teacher) evaluates the speaker's language appropriateness. Flores and Rosa claim that even when Latinxs (and more broadly, racialized people) use academic language, they will be heard by White-mainstream-English speakers (and others adopting standards of whiteness) as having inappropriate academic language since Latinxs are negatively racialized and speakers of stigmatized language varieties. Extending this idea of inappropriate language because of a speaker's racialized group, Rosa (2016) drew from raciolinguistics to theorize *languagelessness*, that is, Latinxs are not fully proficient/knowledgeable of either Spanish or English. These theorizations suggest that raciolinguistic ideologies influence people's evaluations of others and themselves and impact their decisions, with negative consequences for racialized people.

Since their introduction of the term, Flores and Rosa have extended the concept of raciolinguistic ideologies to theorize about the oppressive societal ideas that relate to language and race. For example, Rosa and Flores (2017) note that raciolinguistics also concerns the creation of the subject position—how language and race "co-naturalize" each other (for more components of a raciolinguistic perspective, see Flores et al., 2020b). Other scholars have extended the idea of raciolinguistics to focus on how people use language to racialize others and to shape ideas about race (e.g., Alim et al., 2016). Accordingly, scholars have conceptualized a raciolinguistic lens in different ways, with some using the lens to contribute insights into how language forms racialized categories, that is, delineating the boundaries of a particular racialized group.

The different conceptualizations of raciolinguistics lead to my questions: How is a raciolinguistics lens being used by scholars researching DLBE? How is DLBE research that draws from raciolinguistics contributing to understanding the racialization[3] of groups?

With the emergence of a raciolinguistic lens, a literature review focused on how scholars are using and understanding this lens in research on DLBE would help the field notice trends and possible directions for future research.

Literature Search and Analysis

I searched six databases (EBSCO, JSTOR, Project Muse, SAGE, Taylor & Francis, and Wiley) with the key words "raciolinguistic" AND "dual language" OR "two way" (search completed December 2021) for peer-reviewed articles of empirical research. The literature review sought to include qualitative, quantitative, and mixed-methods research, and also U.S.-focused and international work; however, the articles that met the inclusion criteria are U.S.-based and all qualitative-based studies (except one). The 16 articles included in the literature review are marked with an asterisk (*) in the reference list.

For my analysis, I read all the articles in their entirety, but I concentrated my analytic notes on how each article's theoretical-framework section describes a raciolinguistics lens and on how authors attended to racialization (or described "race"). I also noted how authors used raciolinguistics, where relevant/explicit, to inform their research study and discuss their findings and conclusions. In the findings section, I discuss all the included articles by highlighting relevant information that may be common in or may diverge from the group.

Findings

I organized the 16 articles into three groups (however, some articles overlap into another group[s]). The first group ($n = 9$) presents studies that centered linguistic research, language ideologies, and/or general issues about DLBE. The articles in the second group ($n = 4$) centered questions about accessibility. The third group ($n = 3$) describes studies that also or primarily theorized about racial ideologies.

Group 1: Centering Linguistic Research and/or Language Ideologies

Nine of the articles nestled raciolinguistic ideologies within linguistic research and/or language ideologies. For example, Bauer and colleagues (2020) examined an African-American student's bilingual/biliterate identity development in regard to language ideologies. The authors referred to "raciolinguistic ideologies to describe the conflation of race and language" (p. 685) in that identity is (re)created through linguistic practices. Considering the imposition of identity labels, Chaparro (2019) mentions language ideologies and language socialization along with raciolinguistic ideologies. She notes that for Latinx children "Spanish and its ties to students' ethnolinguistic identities as Latinx is complex and affects students' use of Spanish and classroom experiences" (p. 2). Through her study in elementary-level DLBE, Chaparro develops her theorization of *raciolinguistic socialization*, which recognizes race and class as "consequential in the evaluations of children's language development" (p. 2).

Ascenzi-Moreno and Seltzer (2021) used a critical translingual approach along with the frameworks translanguaging and raciolinguistic ideologies to center language ideologies. According to the authors, a raciolinguistic lens helps "point out how the language and literacy practices of emergent bilinguals of color are particularly stigmatized and misperceived" (p. 3). They analyzed teacher discourse to understand the ideologies guiding elementary-level teachers' assessments of emergent bilinguals of color as readers. Two of the four teachers taught in a French/English dual-language program; the others were English-as-a-new-language teachers. Regardless of the context, the researchers found that "assessments negatively shape teachers' perceptions of *all* emergent bilinguals as readers," and, importantly, assessments "*further* marginalized emergent bilinguals of color" (p. 13, italics added).

Other articles that focused on language/linguistic questions and evaluating racialized speakers include Briceño and colleagues (2018). Briceño and colleagues drew from linguistic ideologies and raciolinguistic ideologies to highlight the challenge of "objective" assessment of language performance. They demonstrated that potential teachers' internalized raciolinguistic beliefs (e.g., undervaluing their bilingualism/Spanish) discouraged them from seeing themselves as qualified to be bilingual teachers. The authors suggest that pre-service teachers should learn about sociolinguistic and raciolinguistic ideologies to promote their becoming bilingual-education teachers. In another study, these same authors (Rodríguez-Mojica et al., 2019) used autoethnographies to interrogate who is linguistically qualified to prepare bilingual teachers. They highlight the raciolinguistic ideology of positioning racialized Others as having inferior/incorrect language varieties and they call for teacher educators to learn about ideologies and develop their critical consciousness.

Along with Bauer and colleagues' (2020) aforementioned study, three other articles considered Black students in elementary-level DLBE. Frieson and Scalise (2021) used a raciolinguistic lens to identify colonialization and racism as positioning Black Americans' languaging as not worthy of being an "'official' instructional language in DLBE" (p. 216). This consequently frames the Black body/speaker as deficient and "uneducated." Using this lens, the authors examined Black children's language repertoires and how they challenged/conformed to policies promoting rigid language separation, with specific attention to how students reaffirmed their linguistic practices. In another study, Frieson (2021) similarly drew from a raciolinguistic lens to study Black children's languaging in biliteracy centros (small-group instruction stations). In an article focused on Black girls' literacies and counter-narratives, Presiado and Frieson (2021) connected raciolinguistics to Black girl literacies and translanguaging frameworks to show how two Black girls resisted oppressive raciolinguistic ideologies like languagelessness.

Examining a family with a child in a middle-school DLBE program, Hernandez (2017) used a raciolinguistic lens to connect deficit ideologies to the family's struggles with the program. Despite the program describing all students as "language learners" (including White Spanish learners), policies and practices did not attenuate the perceived languagelessness and the negativity of the deficit label of "English learner" given to Latinx students, thus disadvantaging these students compared to the White Spanish learners.

Group 2: Centering Questions about Accessibility

Along with language ideologies, four articles also focused their inquiry on questions about accessibility to and who benefits from DLBE. For example, Alonso and Le (2020) report on a participatory action research (PAR) project where the authors collaborated with middle-school students to explore students' perspectives regarding bilingualism. They also examined how the DLBE model could best be implemented in their school, which did not offer bilingual education. The research team specifically focused on the dual-language model because New York City was expanding DLBE. The authors mention a raciolinguistic lens as part of their theoretical framework on critical post-structuralist approaches to language. They describe how the lens shows that raciolinguistic ideologies benefited White-monolingual speakers and allows a focus on "how the language practices of minoritized communities are racialized" (p. 4). The authors conclude that the PAR project affected the implementation of the school's DLBE by including *all* students in the school (instead of certain students).

Sun and Wang (2023) employed a quantitative-text-analysis method and critical discourse analysis to examine the webpages of over 200 DLBE programs in a southern U.S. state with a growing Latinx population. The authors used a raciolinguistic lens for a linguistic analysis focused on language, race, and power. They drew from this lens to reveal ideologies and power relations between dominant and minoritized languages and found that the interests of language minoritized children were largely ignored.

Wall and colleagues (2022) examined the school institutional processes that inhibited working-class Latinx families and Black families from accessing DLBE. They used a raciolinguistic theoretical framework to understand the "intertwined nature of race and language ... on ideologies and social hierarchies" (p. 2). They found that the raciolinguistic ideology of valuing White speakers' English inhibited Black families and working-class English-dominant Latinxs from accessing DLBE.

Moving from centering language ideologies, Flores and McAuliffe (2020) completed a case study of efforts to expand DLBE in some predominantly Latinx, high-poverty Philadelphia schools. They offer a "raciolinguistic perspective on bilingual education" (p. 2) that examines how "language and race intersect in the maintenance of social inequalities even within efforts to promote bilingual education" (p. 2). Flores and McAuliffe emphasize a materialist framing of race, meaning racialization processes emerged from "the exploitation and genocide of racialized communities in service of the capitalist need for raw materials from colonized lands" (p. 2). They show

how the historical segregation and poverty that affects Latinxs also prevents DLBE programs from being successfully implemented and improving the educational outcomes of students.

Group 3: Theorizing Racial Ideologies

Three studies departed from the others in their attention to their conceptualization of race and/or racialization. Flores and colleagues (2020a) examined how elementary-level teachers in a DLBE K-8 school made sense of Latinx students whose first language is English and are simultaneously labeled English learners. By drawing from a social view of bilingualism and a biliteracy framework, the authors argue that the teachers made sense of Latinx students through discourses of languagelessness that constructed the *raciolinguistic category*: "English-dominant English leaner."

Chávez-Moreno (2022) coupled raciolinguistic ideologies with racist ideologies to examine middle- and high-school-level teachers' assessments of their Latinx youth. I explained the conceptualization of race that guided my study and noted that Latinxs are a racialized group delineated by an assumed Spanish-language connection (a conceptualization I problematize; 2021b). I found, like Flores and colleagues (2020a), that teachers made sense of Latinx adolescents through discourses of languagelessness and racist ideologies. I argued that teachers believed that DLBE was "inherently culturally relevant" because DLBE provided Latinxs with Spanish-language/biliteracy schooling. However, this belief prevented teachers from seriously considering how the program could enhance youths' critical-racial consciousness.

Martinez Negrette (2020) focused on how a DLBE kindergarten classroom socially constructed ideas about race, ethnicity, and bilingualism/languaging and how young children perceived these ideas. Negrette describes that the Spanish-language Latina teacher experienced a "'darkening' process" (p. 10) because of her Spanish use. Negrette shows how the program staff's language practices and interactions influenced the children's ideas about constructing "people as inferior/superior, normal/deviant, insider/outsider" (p. 11). Notably, in a rare example of the author being explicit about how they conceptualize race and ethnicity, Negrette described Latinx as an ethnic label—a "category referring to 'cultural practices and outlooks of a community, which identifies them as a distinctive social group'" (p. 13).

The next section answers the review's questions and highlights other trends across the included research studies.

Discussion

For this review, I asked: *How is a raciolinguistics lens being used by scholars researching DLBE? How is DLBE research that draws from raciolinguistics contributing to understanding the racialization of groups?*

Scholars mostly used raciolinguistics to contribute insights about language ideologies concerning racialized Others, for example, to mark, examine, and challenge deficit views. Considering that Rosa and Flores (2017) note that raciolinguistics also concerns the creation of the subject position, using a raciolinguistic lens to offer theorizations about how language ideologies and racialization co-naturalize the category of a racialized group could yield a fruitful future line of inquiry.

In order to engage in such a project, scholars would do well to clearly conceptualize certain terms. A needed intervention for scholars interested in using a raciolinguistic lens is to distinguish between ethnicity and race, especially when using a framework said to be about "race and language." To spotlight some of the issues that emerge from not clarifying the distinction, I next discuss viewing Latinx as a racialized group versus an ethnic group. Starting with race, social and basic science scholars have shown a biological concept of race to be erroneous; instead they advance the idea that racialized groups are socially constructed (e.g., Omi & Winant, 2015). Race (i.e., racialized groups) was invented to oppress and have whiteness reign supreme in a racial hierarchy by creating social categories, sorting people into those categories, and dehumanizing individuals by, for example, erasing the distinctions between people's cultural practices (ethnicity). Social science has found that ideas and boundaries about racialized categories shift according to context, time, and space and that what delineates and amalgamates a particular racialized group is different; for example, the group cohesion may be based on histories of slavery and land theft (Molina et al., 2019).

Work that refers to these ideas and the consequences of racialization should, I suggest, conceptualize Latinxs as a racialized group—not an ethnicity, the varied cultural practices of the people in the group (Chávez-Moreno, 2021b). The alternative—thinking of "Latinx" as an ethnic group—leads to essentializing the cultural practices of U.S. people who originate from geographically diverse (and nation-state delineated) places such as California, Cuba, Colombia, and Central America. That is, designating Latinxs as an ethnicity reinforces the work of race by erasing variations in people's cultural practices.

The Latinx racialized group's boundaries have been problematically delineated based on a supposed connection that comes from the Spanish language (or assuming one should have these connections even if they do not; Chávez-Moreno, 2021b). To address this problematic social construction, I have argued for not defining Latinxs based on Spanish language/bilingualism and instead conceptualizing Latinx as a racialized group that has suffered from *multiple colonialisms*, which includes Spanish colonialism, American colonialism, *and* American imperialism.[4] By conceptualizing Latinxs with this description, we underscore race's teleology and the histories that this racialized group shares without ignoring that they may have different cultural practices (just as, e.g., Asian and Black folks have). For scholars using raciolinguistics in DLBE research, I submit that acknowledging that Latinxs suffer from the histories of multiple colonialisms serves to define the racialized group Latinx. Doing so specifies the distinctions and can lead to comparisons between Latinxs and other racialized groups, which can advance understandings about how language and race co-naturalize the category of a racialized group.

The aforementioned trend in the articles' use and emphasis of raciolinguistics being on language not on race may relate to which journals published this research, which may also point to the authors' orientation/training. This trend results in the development of theoretical frameworks being focused on understanding questions about language, leaving race, and racialization as undertheorized social constructs.

To conceptualize "race" in a study, some in the bilingual-education field may turn to critical race theory (CRT). In the reviewed articles, five studies used or mentioned CRT or its associated constructs (e.g., intersectionality, whiteness as property, counterstories) to highlight race issues and/or support their methodology (Chaparro, 2019; Martinez Negrette, 2020; Presiado & Frieson, 2021; Rodríguez-Mojica et al., 2019; Wall et al., 2022). However, I note that utilizing a CRT framework may not yield a robust conceptualization of race. Education race scholars have argued that CRT in education undertheorizes race (Leonardo, 2013) and lacks a racial theory (Cabrera, 2018). Scholars who find this argument convincing and are interested in examining the intersection of race and language may do well to look beyond CRT for theories that help conceptualize race and racialization. Considering sociological theories and other social science and/or humanities theories may prove productive (e.g., Enriquez, 2019; Lewis et al., 2019; Molina et al., 2019). I suggest other possible directions for future research in the next section.

Implications and Future Directions

Among other implications, the reviewed studies highlight the need for practitioners and youth to learn about raciolinguistic ideologies. Scholars suggested that learning about such ideologies would help develop the critical consciousness needed to challenge oppressive practices and ideologies. This is an important contribution of this literature, and teacher education programs and practitioner professional development should seriously consider how to help teachers and youth learn about these ideologies. Future research that focuses on this level of analysis could provide implications that would help prepare practitioners to engage thoughtfully in this undertaking.

As is the trend in bilingual-education research (Chávez-Moreno, 2020, 2021a), most of the studies situated in classrooms/schools took place in the elementary level (9 out of 12). The field would benefit from studies employing a raciolinguistic lens to examine interactions and/or experiences in secondary-level DLBE classroom/school contexts. Additionally, research is needed that centers particular racialized groups, for example, Black adolescents. This research could, for example, provide empirically based information about how secondary-level DLBE can attend to these students' experiences.

Some authors connected their raciolinguistic framework to colonization (e.g., Flores & McAuliffe, 2020; Frieson & Scalise, 2021), a much needed intervention in DLBE research. Employing a raciolinguistic lens along with theories on colonization and/or imperialism could illuminate future studies that focus on Indigenous-language DLBE, a context missing in the literature. The literature also points to the need for DLBE research to explicitly incorporate thinking about imperialism, and to conceptualize it as distinct from colonialism, especially when focusing on immigrant populations or teachers of immigrants (Chávez-Moreno, 2021c; Motha, 2014).

For future DLBE research that is set in and/or that wishes to compare transnational contexts, researchers should be careful to clearly conceptualize "race," given that place, space, and time all affect racialization. Indeed, a person who is considered Black (or any other racial category) in one context may not have the same racial categorization in another context. Considering the aforementioned ideas about racialization, the need to clearly conceptualize and contextualize the term "race" not only relates to future studies wanting to offer international comparisons but also to studies in a U.S. context.

Returning to what a raciolinguistic lens offers, Flores and Rosa (2017) note that raciolinguistics also concerns the creation of the subject position—how language and race co-naturalize the category of a racialized group. This aspect of the framework would serve well as a focus in future studies that use a raciolinguistic lens to explore how schooling interconnects language and race to form racialized group categories. Given many DLBE classrooms have a racially diverse student composition, future research could use raciolinguistics to connect racialization to language and then examine how DLBE engages in the process of delineating racialized group's boundaries.

Conclusion

The 16 empirical research articles on DLBE that use a raciolinguistic lens have provided important contributions for the education field. Future research would do well to present the major conceptualization of "race" guiding the work and explain distinctions with other concepts (i.e., ethnicity) under analysis in the study. Given a raciolinguistic lens is an emerging framework in the study of DLBE, future research can continue to contribute important insights on how racialization and language intersect to affect the education experiences and opportunities of students and their communities.

Notes

1 I use "race" in quotations in specific places to highlight its use as a term. I do not suggest using the quotations to signal the social constructedness of race, given so many other social constructs exist (e.g., gender) and adding quotations to all social constructs would clutter a text.

2 I use Latinx as inclusive of Latina/Latino/Latinx/Latine and to challenge gender binaries and to X-out the "Latin" because of its European reference; however, I use an author's term when appropriate. The term "Latinxs" refers to people who reside in the United States and have suffered from multiple colonialisms, as I describe in this chapter and elsewhere (Chávez-Moreno, 2021b). Thus, I conceptualize differently the terms "Latinxs" (those who live in the United States) and "Latin Americans" (those living in Latin American countries).

3 Racialization refers to the process of socially constructing racialized groups by delineating their boundaries compared to other racialized groups (thus, is different from racial discrimination or individuals' racial identities or racial identity development).

4 By pointing to Spanish colonialism and seeing Latinx as emerging from "Spanish speaking/Hispanic," the Latinx category excludes Spanish immigrants and/or people living in the United States who come from Spain's ex-colonies. Although some argue convincingly for Latinx to not only refer to people from hispanophone countries, I leave this discussion for a future piece.

References

Alim, H. S., Rickford, J. R., & Ball, A. F. (Eds.). (2016). *Raciolinguistics: How language shapes our ideas about race*. Oxford University Press.

*Alonso, L., & Le, K. (2020). The language warriors: Transcending ideologies on bilingualism in education. *Action Research*. https://doi.org/10.1177/1476750320931155

*Ascenzi-Moreno, L., & Seltzer, K. (2021). Always at the Bottom: Ideologies in assessment of emergent bilinguals. *Journal of Literacy Research*. https://doi.org/10.1177/1086296X211052255

*Bauer, E., Cárdenas-Curiel, L., & Ponzio, C. (2020). "You can talk in Espagñol!": An ethnographic case study of an African-American emergent bilingual and biliterate identity. *Reading Psychology*, *41*(7), 680–711.

*Briceño, A., Rodríguez-Mojica, C., & Muñoz-Muñoz, E. (2018). From English learner to Spanish learner: Raciolinguistic beliefs that influence heritage Spanish speaking teacher candidates. *Language & Education*, *32*(3), 212–226. https://doi.org/10.1080/09500782.2018.1429464

Cabrera, N. L. (2018). Where is the racial theory in critical race theory?: A constructive criticism of the Crits. *Review of Higher Education*, *42*(1), 209–233.

*Chaparro, S. (2019). "But mom! I'm not a Spanish boy": Raciolinguistic socialization in a two-way immersion bilingual program. *Linguistics and Education*, *50*, 1–12.

Chávez-Moreno, L. C. (2020). Researching Latinxs, racism, and white supremacy in bilingual education: A literature review. *Critical Inquiry in Language Studies*, *17*(2), 101–120. https://doi.org/10.1080/15427587.2019.1624966

Chávez-Moreno, L. C. (2021a). Dual language as white property: Examining a secondary bilingual-education program and Latinx equity. *American Educational Research Journal*, *58*(6), 1107–1141. https://doi.org/10.3102/00028312211052508

Chávez-Moreno, L. C. (2021b). The problem with Latinx as a racial construct vis-à-vis language and bilingualism: Toward recognizing multiple colonialisms in the racialization of Latinidad. In E. G. Murillo Jr., et al. (Eds.), *Handbook of latinos & education: Theory, research, and practice* (2nd ed., pp. 164–180). Routledge.

Chávez-Moreno, L. C. (2021c). U.S. Empire and an immigrant's counternarrative: Conceptualizing imperial privilege. *Journal of Teacher Education*, 72(2), 209–222. https://doi.org/10.1177/0022487120919928

*Chávez-Moreno, L. C. (2022). Racist and raciolinguistic teacher ideologies: When bilingual education is "inherently culturally relevant" for Latinxs. *Urban Review*, *54*, 554–575. https://doi.org/10.1007/s11256-021-00628-9

Enriquez, L. E. (2019). Border-hopping Mexicans, law-abiding Asians, and racialized illegality: Analyzing undocumented college students experiences through a relational lens. In *Relational formations of race* (pp. 257–277). University of California Press.

*Flores, N., & McAuliffe, L. (2020). 'In other schools you can plan it that way': A raciolinguistic perspective on dual-language education. *International Journal of Bilingual Education and Bilingualism*, 1–14. https://doi.org/10.1080/13670050.2020.1760200

*Flores, N., Phuong, J., & Venegas, K. M. (2020a). "Technically an EL": The production of raciolinguistic categories in a dual language school. *TESOL Quarterly*, *54*(3), 629–651.

Flores, N., & Rosa, J. (2015). Undoing appropriateness: Raciolinguistic ideologies and language diversity in education. *Harvard Educational Review*, *85*(2), 149–171.

Flores, N., Tseng, A., & Subtirelu, N. (Eds.). (2020b). *Bilingualism for all?: Raciolinguistic perspectives on dual-language education in the United States*. Multilingual Matters.

*Frieson, B. L. (2021). Remixin' and flowin' in centros: Exploring the biliteracy practices of Black language speakers in an elementary two-way immersion bilingual program. *Race Ethnicity and Education*, 1–21. https://doi.org/10.1080/13613324.2021.1890568

*Frieson, B. L., & Scalise, M. (2021). Linguistic artistry and flexibility in dual-language bilingual classrooms: Young Black children's language and literacy practices. *Bilingual Research Journal*, *44*(2), 213–230.

*Hernandez, S. J. (2017). Are they all language learners?: Educational labeling and raciolinguistic identifying in a California middle school dual-language program. *CATESOL Journal*, *29*(1), 133–154.

Leonardo, Z. (2013). *Race frameworks: A multidimensional theory of racism and education*. Teachers College Press.

Lewis, A. E., Hagerman, M. A., & Forman, T. A. (2019). The sociology of race and racism: Key concepts, contributions & debates. *Equity & Excellence in Education*, *52*(1), 29–46.

Molina, N., HoSang, D., & Gutiérrez, R. (Eds.). (2019). *Relational formations of race: Theory, method, and practice*. University of California Press.

Motha, S. (2014). *Race, empire, and English-language teaching: Creating responsible and ethical anti-racist practice*. Teachers College Press.

Martinez Negrette, G. (2020). 'You don't speak Spanish in the cafeteria': An intersectional analysis of language and social constructions in a kindergarten dual language immersion class. *International Journal of Bilingual Education and Bilingualism*, 1–17. https://doi.org/10.1080/13670050.2020.1767536

Omi, M., & Winant, H. (2015). *Racial formation in the United States* (3rd ed.). Routledge.

*Presiado, V. E., & Frieson, B. L. (2021). "Make sure you see this": Counter-narratives of multilingual black Girls' language and literacy practices. *Literacy Research: Theory, Method, and Practice*, *70*(1), 388–407. https://doi.org/10.1177/23813377211038264

*Rodríguez-Mojica, C., Briceño, A., & Muñoz-Muñoz, E. R. (2019). Combating linguistic hegemony: Preparing and sustaining bilingual teacher educators in the United States. *Teacher Education Quarterly*, *46*(3), 57–78.

Rosa, J. (2016). Standardization, racialization, languagelessness: Raciolinguistic ideologies across communicative contexts. *Journal of Linguistic Anthropology*, *26*(2), 162–183. https://doi.org/10.1111/jola.12116

Rosa, J., & Flores, N. (2017). Unsettling race and language: Toward a raciolinguistic perspective. *Language in Society*, 1–27. https://doi.org/10.1017/S0047404517000562

*Sun, W., & Wang, X. (2023). A raciolinguistic analysis of the neoliberal promotion of dual language education in a new Latinx South state. *Discourse: Studies in the Cultural Politics of Education*, *44*, 61–75.

*Wall, D. J., Greer, E., & Palmer, D. K. (2022). Exploring institutional processes in a district-wide dual language program: Who is it for? Who is left out? *Journal of Latinos & Education*, *21*(1), 87–102. https://doi.org/10.1080/15348431.2019.1613996

14

NAMED, UNNAMED, AND CODED OPPRESSIONS

Applying Intersectionality to Dual Language Bilingual Education Programs

Alexandra Babino

Introduction

As DLBE educators and researchers, part of our conscientization call (Freire, 2020) is to name problems, tensions, and contradictions in DLBE settings so that we may act on them. This allows DLBE stakeholders to fulfill the two-part definition of Paolo Freire's (1970) critical consciousnesses: problem-posing and acting. One such problem brought to the field's collective consciousnesses is how emergent bilinguals (EBs) are many times treated as a homogenous group in the research literature, when in reality EBs include many heterogenous peoples with distinct sociocultural realities and educational experiences. The study and application of intersectional analyses can be one way to address the enduring call to realize the action-component of critical, or sociopolitical, consciousness so that DLBE programs may garner greater equity in the pursuit of social justice. In service of this aim, the three questions that guide this theoretical literature review are: (a) What is intersectionality, and how is it relevant to DLBE? (b) How has intersectionality (not) been explored in the DLBE literature? and (c) How can intersectional analyses foster socially just DLBE programs moving forward? This chapter is organized by the three research questions with the major themes in the research.

Positioning the Construct

History and Definitions

With variable definitions and uses across the social science literature (Salem, 2018), intersectionality is said to be traveling theory (Said, 1983) birthed

DOI: 10.4324/9781003269076-21

from critical legal studies, Black feminism, and Third World liberation movements that later was taken up by feminism as a whole before moving to the Global South and then the Global North. Thus, according to Brochin (2018), while "Crenshaw is credited for introducing the term [intersectionality], Black and Chicana feminists were writing intersectional theory without using the term to describe similar concerns about identity politics, location, racism, and power" (Anzaldúa, 1987; Collins, 2008). In this time, some say that intersectionality has become an overused, misused, and co-opted framework by the neoliberalization of the academy (Bilge, 2013; Salem, 2018). In turn, tracing its (mis)use sheds light on its productive explanatory power in critiquing liberalism as well as its potential to work toward liberatory educational policy in DLBE programs—instead of functioning as a vapid buzzword (Robert & Yu, 2018).

With this in mind, intersectionality has been described as a theory, a metaphor (Brochin, 2018; Crenshaw, 1989, 1991; Tefera et al., 2018), a radical ontology (Bilge, 2013), a practice (Nash, 2011), and an analytic tool (Collins & Bilge, 2016) "for explaining how social divisions of race, gender, age, and citizen status, among others, position people differential in the world, especially in relation to global social inequality" (p. 13). It further critiques single lens analyses of social material inequalities by simultaneously highlighting the role of power across multiple institutions in complex, dynamic, layered relationship in oppressing/privileging people in historical social contexts. Table 14.1 displays how multiple systems position and assign people's social identities across numerable axes of oppression/privilege in the United States.

Key Distinctions

From its inception, an enduring emphasis in intersectional analyses centers on marginalizing *systems* rather than marginalized *individuals* (Crenshaw, 1991; Godfrey & Burson, 2018). This is a critical consideration to both the current and aspirational nature of intersectionality: it "is not *only* asserting a theoretical sophisticated approach to so-called difference but an *ethical* approach as well, one that is *deeply attentive* to the social world" (Nash, 2017, p. 127, emphasis mine). Another fundamental tenet of intersectionality is that the systems and subsequent positionings simultaneously intersect and reinforce one another to shape one's experiences and identities in uniquely consequential ways (Chaparro, 2019; Crenshaw, 1991); that is, it creates a layered assemblage of minoritized and majoritized positionings and identities that are fused and inseparable with distinct experiences at these intersections. Hill Collins (2008) further explores how systems can simultaneously oppress *and* privilege certain groups at the same time. Thus, the systems and positionings do not operate in discrete impermeable categories, but rather

Table 14.1 Group identities across relations of power

Minoritized/Oppressed group	*Oppression*	*Dominant/Majority group*
Peoples of Color	Racism	White
Poor, working class, middle class[1]	Classism	Owning class
Women, transgender, genderqueer	Sexism	(cis)men
Gays, lesbians, bisexuals, two-spirit	Heterosexism	Heterosexuals
Muslims, Buddhists, Jews, Hindus, and other non-Christian groups	Religious oppression, anti-Semitism	Christians
People with disabilities	Ableism	Able-bodied
"Too" old or "too" young	Ageism	Young adult
Unattractive according to European standards: short, dark, fat	Lookism	Attractive according to European standards: tall, fair, thin
(Im)migrants (perceived)	Nationalism/ Nativism	Citizens (perceived)
Indigenous peoples	Colonialism	White settlers
Speakers of non-standardized language varieties	Linguicism	"Standardized" speakers
Racialized speakers of English and all other languages	English hegemony	"Standardized" English speakers

Source: Adapted from Sensoy and DiAngelo (2017).[1]

on a continuum of privilege/oppression (Bucholtz & Hall, 2005). A person may simply (not) be a part of the white-dominant group or racialized group but also can exist in degrees toward and from the white-dominant group. An additional key consideration is that interlocking systems position and create identities that are negotiated across contexts in a dynamic relationship between how people and systems *see and treat* people as well as how people *assert themselves* to be (Compton-Lilly et al., 2017; Martinez Negrette, 2020).

Affordances of Intersectionality in DLBE

Perhaps the prime affordance of intersectionality as a theory and analytical tool is how it resolutely rejects the ideology of pathology for those that are multiply minoritized (Souto-Manning & Rabadi-Raol, 2018). In doing so, it shifts the focus of pathology onto the interconnected social systems instead of people in these systems. It further elucidates the nature of learning contexts for historically and multiply minoritized students (Martinez Negrette, 2020) as being multiple, interconnected, and dynamic over history. Especially in relation to DLBE, it has the potential to highlight the unique interaction of linguicism, racism, nativism, and classism on EBs' schooling experiences, thereby humanizing students and their realities that are often invisibilized; it provides opportunity to reveal not only multiple oppressions, but also multiple privileges, mixed privileges, and oppressions as well as liminality (García-Mateus et al., 2020; Pugach et al., 2019). Thus, the multiple lenses afforded by intersectionality illuminate with fine gradation intragroup differences between EBs typically treated as a (mostly) homogenous group. In particular, it can illumine the qualitative differences of myriad structural positionings, including how marginalized EBs can actually be further marginalized by the very programs seeking to provide equitable practices through the singular lens of language. Ultimately, with fine-grained illumination of the problems, there arises the possibility that the redressing the problems also be fine-grained.

Mining the Field

I began by locating key texts on intersectionality, including Crenshaw's (1989, 1991) germinal articles and Hill Collins and Bilge's (2016) comprehensive book. Afterward, I used the search terms "intersectionality" and "bilingual education" and "intersectionality" along with "dual language" in EBSCO Host and ERIC to explore publications from 1990 to 2021. From past study, I knew that works employing critical race theory (CRT), Latino Critical Race Theory (LatCrit), and raciolinguistic framings also applied intersectional analyses without always using the term. This led to using the additional search terms "CRT", "LatCrit", "raciolingusitics", and "nepantla/nepantleras" with variations of "DLBE" using the same publication period. Like Pugach et al. (2019) surmise, there were comparably few studies that explicitly drew on intersectionality as a framework or analytic tool; out of over 100 articles, 45 articles addressed intersectionality in some way, 35 of which expressed a direct connection to the theory or analysis. The following three sections delineate those oppressions that are named (employed), unnamed (yet to be employed), and/or coded (obscured) in the DLBE research.

Named Oppressions

In this review, only 35 studies explicitly addressed intersectionality in DLBE programs in some way. Thus, in the discussion of how intersectionality has (not) been applied to DLBE programs, I find it necessary to contextualize these findings in relation to the *amount* of representation in the literature, as well as the *ways* intersectionality has (yet) been addressed. Twenty-two articles employed intersectionality as a *framework*, five explored intersectional *positionings and/or identities*, four articles explored intersectionality as a *framework on intersectional identities*, and finally another four made brief mention of intersectionality as part of making a greater argument (see Figure 14.1).

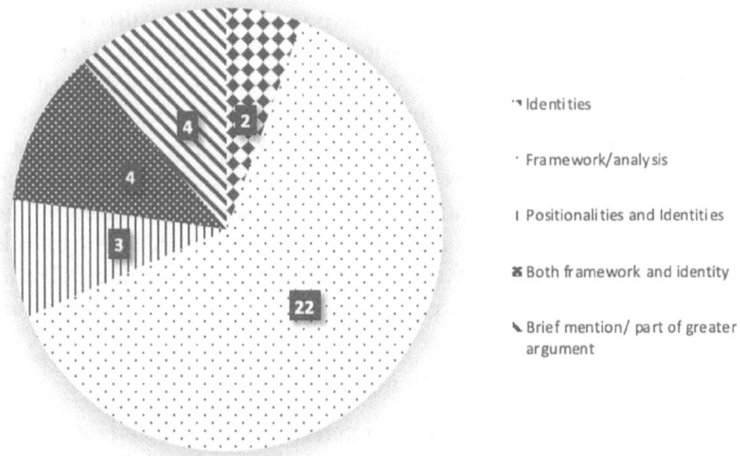

Figure 14.1 Ways Intersectionality is Explored

The remaining ten articles show threads of conceptual connections to intersectionality through the study of LatCrit (Morales & Maravilla, 2019; Talamantes, 2021), nepantla (Aguilar-Valdez et al., 2013; de la Piedra & Araujo, 2012; Palmer, 2018; Venegas-Weber, 2018), and raciolinguistics (Bauer et al., 2020; Chaparro, 2019; Cioè-Peña, 2021; García-Mateus, 2020). With their foci on linguicism, racism, and nativism (LatCrit), language, culture, gender, colonialism, and nationalism (nepantla) and race, language, and other intersections (raciolinguistics), these related theoritizations range from directly taking up intersectional frames and analyses (like LatCrit and raciolinguistics) to indirectly employing intersectionality (like nepantla).

Figures 14.2 and 14.3 further illustrate how intersectionality is currently employed in the DLBE literature by first representing which and how often social dimensions (and their subordinating systems) are discussed and then illustrating in what ways these intersecting phenomena are explored in the DLBE literature to date.

While taking a single-axis analysis of social systems is antithetical to intersectional approaches, I examine how often each lens is explored in DLBE programs to reveal which social systems have been addressed to what degree in the literature. Figure 14.2 illustrates how language and race predominate discussions of intersectionality, followed by immigration status, class, ethnicity, and culture. Since language development is one of the prime goals of DLBE programs, the first finding is not surprising. In comparison to other

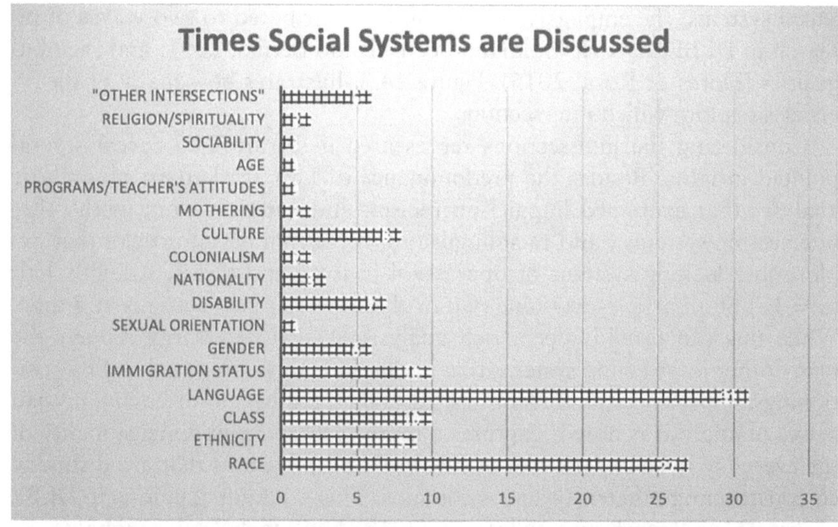

Figure 14.2 Social Systems Explored

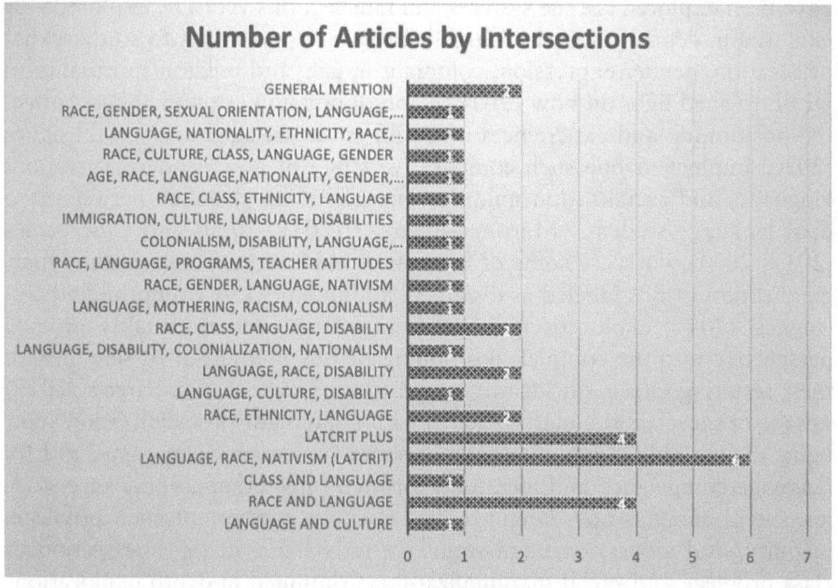

Figure 14.3 Number of Articles by Intersections

social systems, the emphasis on race may be attributed to two waves of research in DLBE: LatCrit (Solórzano & Delgado Bernal, 2001) and raciolingusitics (Flores & Rosa, 2015). Figure 14.3 illustrates how many of the 35 articles explore which intersections.

Considering the intersections represented in Figure 14.3 reveal several pointed insights. Besides the predominance of LatCrit, LatCrit plus (those analyses that examined linguicism, racism, and nativism along with other intersecting systems), and raciolingusitics, is the number of articles that explore interlocking systems of oppression in twos and threes. Roughly half ($n = 17$) of all articles examine two or three overlapping systems at a time. While this can provide deep, rich analysis, it also necessarily ignores the many other intersecting systems that are inextricably connected to EBs positionings, experiences, and identities. Arguably, the benefit of having myriad lenses of analysis is how it captures a more accurate multidimensionality of the everyday lived experiences of EBs in DLBE programs that are distinctly co-constructing differently across contexts. This is a finding unique to DLBE programs, as Pugach and colleagues (2019) find much intersectionality research in education inadvertently reifies and dehumanizes students by only studying overlapping systems of subordination in "threes".

Unnamed

Perhaps just as important as considering which systems and intersections have been explored are the systems and intersections yet to be explored—or explored in depth. Figure 14.2 highlights ripe opportunities to study sexual orientation, gender expression, colonialism, age, and religion/spirituality in DLBE to shed light on how privilege and oppression at these nexuses affect the positioning and experiences of DLBE students. Salerno and colleagues (2020) implement one such comparative study of how gender expression, language, and racialization uniquely interact in the dialogue between two dual language students. Martínez-Álvarez's (2019, 2020) and Cioè Peña's (2017, 2021) work are some of the first to explore the compounding marginalization of EBs labeled as dis/abled; additionally Lily Compton and colleagues' (2017) exploration of age, immigration, and spirituality provide perspective into the complex positioning of EBs in and out of school with their resulting effects on identity negotiation. Likewise, Chaparro's (2019) uptake of raceclass (Leonardo, 2012) with raciolinguistic socialization spotlights the variable expectations teachers and students have in regard to EB's language competence and identities; through three ethnographic case studies, she illuminates how language and raceclass further entrench privilege, inequity, and anxiety through simultaneously living at the intersection of class privilege and racial marginalization. Continued in-depth explorations in addition to LatCrit's linguicism, racism and nativism and raciolinguistics' race and language through the development of the fourth tenet of a raciolinguistic perspective are also fertile foci for study.

Coded

Coded oppressions refer to those that are named as one system yet hide another. A prime example is calling a school or culture "urban", when in reality it's referring to students racialized as People of Color (POC). The field of bilingual education—and DLBE programs in particular—also have these codes, such as "everybody" being a code for "white students" (Cervantes-Soon et al., 2020) and "culture" being a code for "race" (Chávez-Moreno, 2020). Chávez-Moreno (2020) reminds bilingual scholars of how the discussion on Latinx students' (under)achievement is addressed in schools: far too often the racialization processes and their impact on Latinx bilingual achievement are obfuscated by the discussion of culture. That is, culture has become a more palatable gloss for race/racism in whitestream schools and scholarship (Urrieta, 2009). Subsequently, the actual root influences on educational inequities for EBs remain silenced and unaddressed. In the 35 articles that explicitly explored intersectionality, culture was mentioned 8 times, language/linguicism was mentioned 31 times, and race was mentioned 27 times.

While these numbers may seem like language and race are expressly examined at a greater rate than culture and other subordinating systems, I must foreground two points: first, the publication date range for the articles under examination is only from 2013 to 2021—19 of which were published from 2019 to 2021. To put it bluntly, the explicit study of racialization and how it intersects with other oppressive/privileging systems is relatively recent in DLBE. Second, while racialization appears to be a major lens in intersectional analyses, this is deviation from the greater norm in DLBE research that uses "culture" and "language" as a gloss for race (Chávez-Moreno, 2020; Flores, 2016). In my estimation, the eight articles that mention culture (or put another way, don't mention race) at all are vestiges of bilingual education's dominant history that obscures issues of racialization under the guise of language and culture.

Looking Forward

In this review of the literature, I aimed to name and explain how intersectional analyses have unique contributions to the study of DLBE programs, specifically in how researcher-practitioners might employ this work as part of their conscientization call. While there are some studies that explicitly examine intersectionality in DLBE programs in terms of linguicism, racism, and nativism, other examinations of intersectionality have been wholly unnamed, yet to be explored. Others are camouflaged by discussions of language and/or culture. Thus, in line with Tefera et al. (2018), I conclude that explicit intersectional lenses are nascent in DLBE research, with much potential for continued collective examination. Others' (and my own) compulsion to examine inequities through intersectional analyses is fueled from the belief that intersectionality calls attention to the differences that make a difference, and who does(n't) experience the "astounding effectiveness" of DLBE (Collier & Thomas, 2004, p. 1). Inspired by Kimberlé Crenshaw (1991)'s prescient assessment in regard to Women of Color, I argue that who decides which differences matter in DLBE has the power to formulate (in) equitable policies with these differences in mind. Whiteness and other marginalizing systems routinely have the power to determine whether the intersectional differences of racialized EBs (or any other minoritized group) will be included into fundamental program policies. In turn, at best, DLBE programs' work toward equity is significantly mitigated for those living and learning at multiple nexuses of subordination. It also erases the particular assemblages of privilege and oppression like those Latinxs simultaneously living liminally across several axes, like between classes, races, ethnicities, languages, and spiritualities (myself included). At worst, DLBE programs effectively reproduce the status quo of transversal power relations. The purposeful use of multiple lenses in intersectionality animates a precision that is potentially humanizing to EBs; as researchers strive to illuminate and honor the full personhood and agency of its communities, equally precise policies and pedagogies are made possible.

To work toward these goals, I culminate this chapter with several recommendations. First, like Pugach and colleagues (2019), I propose that future explorations of intersectionality in DLBE programs critically consider the intersections studied: whether exploring these convergences in "threes" to provide deep understanding of a few dimensions or examining intersections beyond "threes" to more accurately acknowledge myriad inextricable assemblages. Each set of lenses has their theoretical nuances that may better inform our practice. As part of this, I also believe that examining liminal positionings and identities among EBs to be a fruitful point of exploration; by taking what's been learned from theorizations like nepantla, transfronterizo, and multicrit scholars, DLBE researchers may engender more rich and robust understandings of positionings that change over time and space—especially as much of the intersectionality research in DLBE programs focus on how EBs are multiply minoritized or multiply privileged. In fact, Babino and Stewart (2020) found liminality across several axes of oppression to be a potential privilege afforded to three of their four participants. Finally, as DLBE researchers expand their intersectional lenses on what is researched, I suggest DLBE researchers also expand upon their intersectional reflexivity throughout the research process; researchers should also move beyond reflecting on their positionalities in "threes". In concert with the extant research on intersectionality, these practices may poise the field to not only better understand the lives of EBs in DLBE programs but more importantly catalyze greater precision in equitable praxis.

Note

1 While Sensoy and DiAngelo (2017) consider the middle class to be minoritized, in the context of U.S. education I am of the belief that the middle class with its worldviews and experiences is significantly different enough from the "poor" and "working class" to be considered a primarily majoritized group.

References

Aguilar-Valdez, J. R., LópezLeiva, C. A., Roberts-Harris, D., Torres-Velásquez, D., Lobo, G., & Westby, C. (2013). Ciencia en Nepantla: The journey of Nepantler@ s in science learning and teaching. *Cultural Studies of Science Education*, *8*(4), 821–858. https://doi.org/10.1007/s11422-013-9512-9

Anzaldúa, G. (1987). *Borderlands/la frontera: The new mestiza.* Aunt Lute Books.

Babino, A., & Stewart, M. A. (2020). *Radicalizing literacies and languaging: A framework toward dismantling the mono-mainstream assumption.* Palgrave-MacMillan.

Bauer, E., Cárdenas-Curiel, L., & Ponzio, C. (2020). "You can talk in espagñol!": An ethnographic case study of an African-American emergent bilingual and biliterate identity. *Reading Psychology*, *41*(7), 680–711. https://doi.org/10.1080/02702711.2020.1783136

Bilge, S. (2013). Intersectionality undone: Saving intersectionality from feminist intersectionality studies. *Du Bois Review: Social Science Research on Race*, *10*(2), 405–424. https://doi.org/10.1017/S1742058X13000283

Brochin, C. (2018). Assembled identities and intersectional advocacy in literacy research. *Literacy Research: Theory, Method, and Practice*, *67*(1), 164–179. https://doi.org/10.1177/2381336918786890

Bucholtz, M., & Hall, K. (2005). Identity and interaction: A sociocultural linguistic approach. *Discourse Studies*, *7*(4–5), 585–614. https://doi.org/10.1177/1461445605054407

Cervantes-Soon, C., Gambrell, J., Kasun, G. S., Sun, W., Freire, J. A., & Dorner, L. M. (2020). "Everybody wants a choice" in dual language education of el Nuevo Sur: Whiteness as the gloss for everybody in media discourses of multilingual education. *Journal of Language, Identity & Education*, 1–17. https://doi.org/10.1080/15348458.2020.1753201

Chaparro, S. E. (2019). But mom! I'm not a Spanish boy: Raciolinguistic socialization in a two-way immersion bilingual program. *Linguistics and Education*, *50*, 1–12. https://doi.org/10.1016/j.linged.2019.01.003

Chávez-Moreno, L. C. (2020). Researching Latinxs, racism, and white supremacy in bilingual education: A literature review. *Critical Inquiry in Language Studies*, *17*(2), 101–120. https://doi.org/10.1080/15427587.2019.1624966

Cioè-Peña, M. (2017). The intersectional gap: How bilingual students in the United States are excluded from inclusion. *International Journal of Inclusive Education*, *21*(9), 906–919. https://doi.org/10.1080/13603116.2017.1296032

Cioè-Peña, M. (2021). Raciolinguistics and the education of emergent bilinguals labeled as disabled. *The Urban Review*, *53*(3), 443–469. https://doi.org/10.1007/s11256-020-00581-z

Collier, V. P., & Thomas, W. P. (2004). The astounding effectiveness of dual language education for all. *NABE Journal of Research and Practice*, 2(1), 1–20.

Collins, P. H. (2008). Reply to commentaries: Black sexual politics revisited. *Studies in Gender and Sexuality*, 9(1), 68–85. https://doi.org/10.1080/15240650701759292

Collins, P. H., & Bilge, S. (2016). *Intersectionality*. Polity Press.

Compton-Lilly, C., Papoi, K., Venegas, P., Hamman, L., & Schwabenbauer, B. (2017). Intersectional identity negotiation: The case of young immigrant children. *Journal of Literacy Research*, *49*(1), 115–140. https://doi.org/10.1177/1086296X16683421

Crenshaw, K. (1989). Demarginalizing the intersection of race and sex: A black feminist critique of antidiscrimination doctrine, feminist theory and antiracist politics. *University of Chicago Legal Forum*, 139–167.

Crenshaw, K. (1991). Mapping the margins: Intersectionality, identity politics, and violence against women of color. *Stanford Law Review*, *43*, 1241–1299.

de la Piedra, M. T., & Araujo, B. E. (2012). Literacies crossing borders: Transfronterizo literacy practices of students in a dual language program on the USA–Mexico border. *Language and Intercultural Communication*, *12*(3), 214–229. https://doi.org/10.1080/14708477.2012.667416

Flores, N. (2016). A tale of two visions: Hegemonic whiteness and bilingual education. *Educational Policy*, *30*(1), 13–38. https://doi.org/10.1177/0895904815616482

Flores, N., & Rosa, J. (2015). Undoing appropriateness: Raciolinguistic ideologies and language diversity in education. *Harvard Educational Review*, *85*(2), 149–171. https://doi.org/10.17763/0017-8055.85.2.149

Freire, J. A. (2020). Conscientization calls: A white dual language educator's development of sociopolitical consciousness and commitment to social justice. *Education and Urban Society*, *53*(2), 231–248. https://doi.org/10.1177/0013124520928608

Freire, P. (1970). *Pedagogy of the oppressed*. Continuum.

García-Mateus, S. (2020). Bilingual student perspectives about language expertise in a gentrifying two-way immersion program. *International Journal of Bilingual Education and Bilingualism*, 1–16. https://doi.org/10.1080/13670050.2020.1797627

Godfrey, E. B., & Burson, E. (2018). Interrogating the intersections: How intersectional perspectives can inform developmental scholarship on critical consciousness. In C. E. Santos, & R. B. Toomey (Eds.), Envisioning the *integration of an intersectional lens in developmental science. New directions for child and adolescent development* (pp. 17–38). Wiley.

Leonardo, Z. (2012). The race for class: Reflections on a critical raceclass theory of education. *Educational Studies*, *48*(5), 427–449. https://doi.org/10.1080/00131946.2012.715831

Martínez-Álvarez, P. (2019). Dis/ability labels and emergent bilingual children: Current research and new possibilities to grow as bilingual and biliterate learners. *Race Ethnicity and Education*, 22(2), 174–193. https://doi.org/10.1080/13613324.2018.1538120

Martínez-Álvarez, P. (2020). Essential constructs in the preparation of inclusive bilingual education teachers: Mediation, agency, and collectivity. *Bilingual Research Journal*, *43*(3), 304–322. https://doi.org/10.1080/15235882.2020.1802367

Morales, P. Z., & Maravilla, J. V. (2019). The problems and possibilities of interest convergence in a dual language school. *Theory Into Practice*, *58*(2), 145–153. https://doi.org/10.1080/00405841.2019.1569377

Nash, J. C. (2011). Home truths on intersectionality. *Yale JL & Feminism*, *23*, 445.
Nash, J. C. (2017). Intersectionality and its discontents. *American Quarterly*, *69*(1), 117–129.
Martinez Negrette, G. (2020). 'You don't speak Spanish in the cafeteria': An intersectional analysis of language and social constructions in a kindergarten dual language immersion class. *International Journal of Bilingual Education and Bilingualism*, 1–17. https://doi.org/10.1080/13670050.2020.1767536
Palmer, D. K. (2018). Introduction to the special issue: Teacher agency and "pedagogies of hope" for bilingual learners (in a brave new world). *International Multilingual Research Journal*, *12*(3), 143–144. https://doi.org/10.1080/19313152.2018.1474624
Pugach, M. C., Gomez-Najarro, J., & Matewos, A. M. (2019). A review of identity in research on social justice in teacher education: What role for intersectionality? *Journal of Teacher Education*, *70*(3), 206–218. https://doi.org/10.1177/0022487118760567
Robert, S. A., & Yu, M. (2018). Intersectionality in transnational education policy research. *Review of Research in Education*, *42*(1), 93–121. https://doi.org/10.3102/0091732X18759305
Said, E. (1983). Traveling theory. In E. Said (Ed.), *The world, the text, and the critic* (pp. 226–47). Harvard University Press.
Salem, S. (2018). Intersectionality and its discontents: Intersectionality as traveling theory. *European Journal of Women's Studies*, *25*(4), 403–418. https://doi.org/10.1177/1350506816643999
Salerno, A. S., Kibler, A. K., & Hardigree, C. N. (2020). 'I'll be the hero': how adolescents negotiate intersectional identities within a high school dual-language program. *International Journal of Bilingual Education and Bilingualism*, 1–14. https://doi.org/10.1080/13670050.2020.1784086
Sensoy, O., & DiAngelo, R. (2017). *Is everyone really equal?: An introduction to key concepts in social justice education*. Teachers College Press.
Solórzano, D. G., & Delgado Bernal, D. (2001). Examining transformational resistance through a critical race and LatCrit theory framework: Chicana and Chicano students in an urban context. *Urban Education*, *36*(3), 308–342. https://doi.org/10.1177/0042085901363002
Souto-Manning, M., & Rabadi-Raol, A. (2018). (Re)centering quality in early childhood education: Toward intersectional justice for minoritized children. *Review of Research in Education*, *42*(1), 203–225. https://doi.org/10.3102/0091732X18759550
Talamantes, M. D. R. (2021). A critical classroom study of language oppression: Manuel and Malena's testimonios, "Sentía como que yo no valía nada… se reían de mí". *Journal of Latinos and Education*, 1–22. https://doi.org/10.1080/15348431.2021.1880412
Tefera, A. A., Powers, J. M., & Fischman, G. E. (2018). Intersectionality in education: A conceptual aspiration and research imperative. *Review of Research in Education*, *42*(1), vii–xvii. https://doi.org/10.3102/0091732X18768504
Urrieta, L. (2009). *Working from within: Chicana and Chicano activist educators in whitestream schools*. University of Arizona Press.
Venegas-Weber, P. (2018). Teaching and knowing in nepantla: "I wanted them to realize that, that is being bilingual". *International Multilingual Research Journal*, *12*(3), 160–172. https://doi.org/10.1080/19313152.2018.1474622

Programmatic Issues

15

ASSESSMENT, ACCOUNTABILITY AND CULTURE

Key Issues and Trends in Dual Language Bilingual Education

Saúl I. Maldonado

Informed by research literature, this chapter analyzes key assessment issues and accountability trends in dual language bilingual education (DLBE) programs in the United States. Unlike heritage and one-way developmental and "foreign" language programs, the existence of DLBE programs is dependent upon the participation of students minoritized by their cultural and English-language backgrounds (Flores & García, 2017). DLBE programs in the United States are designed and implemented to develop students' "academic achievement, bilingualism and biliteracy, and sociocultural competence" (Howard et al., 2018) through "content-based instruction, using the [partner] language at least 50% of the time for at least 5 years" (Fitzsimmons-Doolan et al., 2017, p. 704). DLBE programs implemented with fidelity require that minoritized students are not systematically excluded or neglected. The interdependence of DLBE programs and culturally and linguistically minoritized students requires an explicit consideration of how societal discourses influence policymaking decisions and resource allocations. de Jong (2013) recommends assimilationist and pluralist categorizations as discursive frames to analyze how DLBE program stakeholders define views of bilinguals and bilingualism as well as policy and practice goals. Specifically, DLBE program stakeholders require pluralist framing to determine the appropriateness and effectiveness of assessment practices and accountability policies (Georges et al., 2019). This chapter synthesizes the research literature on assessment practices and accountability trends in DLBE and proposes pedagogical assessment knowledge, dispositions and

DOI: 10.4324/9781003269076-23

skills as a conceptual model for DLBE assessment practices and accountability policies.

Assessment Practices

Researchers, teacher educators and community members interested in the assessment practices of DLBE programs are encouraged to consider the relationship between language, literacy, achievement and culture, as well as the alignment and consistency between formative and summative assessment as key issues. Additionally, it is important to consider bilingual students' achievement in concert with student and familial educational aspirations and expectations as well as community contexts. Neglecting or excluding such considerations promotes narrow definitions of effective assessment practices in DLBE programs.

Language, Literacy, Achievement and Culture

DLBE programs require a comprehensive and dynamic approach for determining bilingual students' achievement that encompasses learning content, languages and culture in concert (Georges et al., 2019). Maldonado et al. (2018) developed and shared a classroom observation protocol and coding matrix with tables and figures for DLBE program stakeholders to assess curricular and instructional indicators of students' exposure and dosage to explicit learning objectives for: (a) content, (b) acquisition of languages, (c) biliteracy development and (d) standards for cultural competency. Moreover, measures of DLBE students' content achievement require complementary communication of the critical factor of time (e.g., years in program) as well as explicit consideration of the relationship between the languages of instruction and the languages of assessment. Content-area achievement measures for DLBE students without five years of program participation are likely to be inconclusive information of bilingual students' learning.

Alignment and Consistency of Formative and Summative Assessment

Salkind (2006) suggests there are five purposes for assessment: selection, placement, diagnosis, testing hypotheses and classification. Although educators use both formative and summative assessments for diagnostic decision-making, "automatically generated interpretations should be used with care in diagnostic settings, because they may not take into account other relevant information about the individual" (AERA, APA, NCME, 2014, p. 119). DLBE programs collect formative assessment information *for* students' learning as well as summative information *of* students' learning. Summative achievement measures of what students know and are able to do, such as standardized tests and high-stakes exams, require an intentional consideration of alignment and consistency with formative assessment measures that describe to what extent DLBE programs provided students with appropriate opportunities-to-learn (OTL) across dimensions of language, literacy and culture as detailed by the *Standards for Educational and Psychological Testing* (AERA, APA, NCME, 2014). Maldonado and Andrade (2018) describe how OTL is an appropriate framework for simultaneously interpreting summative achievement measures as well as accounting for students' contextual experiences and characteristics. OTL accounts for DLBE programs' curricular fidelity, supportive learning services and expenditures as well as teachers' DLBE qualifications and formative assessment practices across languages, biliteracy and sociocultural competence. Alignment and consistency of formative and summative assessment in DLBE programs includes proportional collection of assessment data, such as students' fluency and literacy, between partner-language and English, as well as explicit summative assessment expectations in both languages across all content areas. DLBE programs are responsible for the alignment and consistency of the bilingual formative assessment practices that students experience across all content areas and a comprehensive bilingual summative assessment system. In contrast, a monolingual summative assessment system for determining what students know and are able to do in a few content areas is an inappropriate DLBE information system.

Achievement and Aspirations

Formative assessment and summative achievement measures of students' learning are often interpreted without contextualization of students' motivations as well as their self-efficacy beliefs and attitudes (Abedi & Gándara, 2006; Ing & Nylund-Gibson, 2013). Students' self-efficacy as well as educational and career aspirations influence achievement as well as socioeconomic mobility (Bandura, 1993; Sewell et al., 1969). Georges et al. (2019) developed a survey for all students in a Spanish/English DBLE program that measured enjoyment, utility and importance of content-area learning and found "a significant association between students' self-efficacy" and scores on summative achievement measures (p. 176). Without accounting for DLBE students' self-efficacy beliefs and attitudes, formative and summative assessment measures of achievement are to be interpreted with critical caution and reservations.

Familial Expectations and Community Contexts

Students' educational aspirations are associated with their family caregivers' educational expectations as well as the material realities of communities' socioeconomic contexts (Bohon et al., 2006; Kao & Tienda, 1995).

An association exists between students' achievement and their mother's reading proficiency as well as family members' participation in literacy programs (Come & Fredericks, 1995; Sastry & Pebly, 2010). Students' achievement is influenced by familial expectations, such as supervision of students' homework (Kralovec & Buell, 2001) as well as students' participation in extracurricular school clubs and community activities (Flores-Gonzalez, 2005; Gibson et al., 2004). Formative and summative assessment practices require regular collection of family caregiver information to analyze relationships between DLBE students' achievement, their familial expectations and their participation in learning environments situated in community contexts.

Accountability Trends

Researchers, teacher educators and community members interested in the accountability trends of DLBE programs are encouraged to consider the relationship between accountability, bilingualism and biliteracy, as well as the appropriateness and alignment of data collection and decision-making, and the importance of multiple measures for program effectiveness.

Accountability, Bilingualism and Biliteracy

Interpretations of DLBE programs' accountability data require explicit consideration of how programs account for the variability of languages of instruction as well as anticipated time for acquisition of languages, such as students' years in program (Lindholm-Leary, 2012). Additionally, attentiveness to how accountability measures, such as summative standardized tests, prioritizes or neglects bilingualism is indicative of programs' perceptions of language prestige and power. Soltero (2016) and Hopewell et al. (2016) have suggested authentic and performance-based bilingual outcomes are more appropriate indicators for program improvement considerations than state-level accountability data of students' English language fluency and literacy for designation purposes in non-DLBE programs. DLBE programs require designing and implementing a progress monitoring system that includes information from accountability benchmarks and measures that communicate how emergent bilinguals from diverse language and literacy backgrounds become classified as bilingual and biliterate (Escamilla, 2006; Soltero, 2016). Georges et al. (2019) found an associative correlation between DLBE students' summative achievement and "self-identification as bilingual and biliterate" (p. 177). Moreover, accountability data in DLBE programs must examine the limitations of both categorical and continuous measures of biliteracy, as well as the confoundedness of biliteracy and English language proficiency (Proctor & Silverman, 2011). Hopewell and colleagues (2016) suggest "creating an assessment trajectory that requires that students in biliteracy programs be assessed in two languages and that these assessments be interpreted together" (p. 91).

Appropriateness of Data Collection and Decision-Making

Narrow measures of federal and state accountability data are insufficient and ineffective for complex systems like DLBE programs. Field (2011) describes broadening measures of accountability in local level DLBE programs as continuous data sources "Grounded in contextual information, framed by learning goals, standards and benchmarks, and tied to curriculum and instruction" (p. 22). DLBE programs collect many forms of student, educator and family caregiver data that are internal to the functioning of classrooms, schools and communities but often disconnected from decision-making processes and policies for external accountability (Gottlieb & Nguyen, 2007). Additionally, data collected for accountability purposes requires explicit considerations of which persons are invited, and supported, for determining consequential validity. How results from accountability data are used and associated with social consequences for students, educators, schools and communities is a key trend in understanding the design and implementation of educational policy (Brewer et al., 2014). Persons influential in decision-making processes and policies must interrogate how disaggregating accountability data (e.g., socioeconomically and racially-ethnically) is inclusive and appropriate for all linguistic and cultural groups. In particular, students from Indigenous Mesoamerican cultural groups are often ignored in DLBE programs' accountability data and such neglect perpetuates cultural and linguistic erasure as well as exacerbates inaccessibility to resources (Maldonado et al., 2018). Although DLBE programs are designed for the cultural and linguistic integration of students from diverse cultural groups, persons responsible for associating consequential decisions with accountability data require explicit reminders that diversity and equity are distinctive lenses for interpreting results.

Multiple Measures of Program Effectiveness

Exclusively using student measures of bilingualism, biliteracy and sociocultural competence to evaluate DLBE programs' effectiveness is inappropriate. Castañeda v. Pickard (1981) determined program effectiveness as interdependent with adequate resources and appropriate pedagogy in languages as well as content areas (Ovando, 2003). Furthermore, DLBE programs have agency and collective action opportunities in responding to federal and state accountability requirements "by developing pedagogically sound, well-implemented dual language programs with authentic accountability systems that rely on multiple measures of student learning" (Field, 2011, p. 32).

A comprehensive accountability system measures students' development of biliteracy and achievement in content areas, development of bilingualism across dimensions of listening, speaking, reading and writing, and development of sociocultural competence. An authentic accountability system regularly reports analyses of students' developments in bilingualism, biliteracy and sociocultural competence to students, families, educators and community members to determine whether DLBE program resources are adequate and if existing pedagogy is appropriate for meeting language, content and cultural learning goals.

Multiple measures of DLBE programs' effectiveness include quality, fidelity, exposure, dosage, responsiveness and differentiation (Maldonado et al., 2018). Several evaluative tools for self-determining which measures of program effectiveness are most appropriate for local accountability policies and practices are available to persons in DLBE programs (Gottlieb & Nguyen, 2007; Howard et al., 2003a, 2003b, 2018; Lindholm-Leary & Hargett, 2006). Gottlieb and Nguyen (2007) recommend using a pivotal portfolio approach to balance and distribute accountability across formative assessment in DLBE classrooms, school district measures of achievement and state as well as federal measures of accountability. A pivotal portfolio follows students throughout their participation in DLBE programs and integrates educators' evidence of student achievement "in multiple targeted academic subjects and other areas of learning" and comparable assessment data "for students across classes in the program and across programs in the district" (Gottlieb & Nguyen, 2007; p. 79).

In addition to adequate resources and effective implementation, interpreting accountability data from DLBE programs requires explicit consideration of how systemic inequities influence the understanding and implementation of language policy and planning specifically in relation to orientations of language status and prestige (Wiley & García, 2016). One way to analyze the language status orientations of DLBE programs is the advocacy for "heteroglossic language ideologies that build on the dynamic bilingualism of emergent bilingual students," including translanguaging (Flores & Schissel, 2014). Another way to analyze the language status orientations of DLBE programs is the social positioning of white racial privilege, socioeconomic wealth and English-language fluency and literacy, including gentrification (Heiman & Yanes, 2018; Valdez et al., 2016). Language status orientations may also be analyzed in DLBE educators' ideological stances and pedagogical practices that continue, as well as counter, cultural hegemony via racial-ethnic neutrality, social class formation and gender inequities (Alfaro & Bartolomé, 2017; Henderson, 2017). Combined, language status orientations and educators' ideological stances are important resource and pedagogy accountability measures to consider in relation to the Castañeda v. Pickard (1981) legislation for determining the appropriateness and effectiveness of DLBE programs.

Pedagogical Assessment Dispositions, Knowledge and Skills

The interdependence between assessment, accountability and culture extends beyond PK-12 DLBE programs to institutions of higher education. Bilingual teacher preparation programs prepare educators with the appropriate pedagogical qualifications for developing and implementing assessment practices in compliance with state standards, policies and procedures. Higher education faculty are responsible for developing bilingual teachers' community agency as well as "ideological clarity on concepts such as [cultural] hegemony, critical consciousness and equity" (Georges et al., 2019, p. 166).

Assessment practices and accountability trends of DLBE programs interrelate with educators' higher education preparation in pedagogical assessment knowledge, dispositions and skills (Alfaro et al., 2018; Bunch, 2013). Bilingual teacher preparation programs are encouraged to develop educators' assessment practices and accountability perspectives across dimensions of knowledge, dispositions and skills. Pedagogical assessment knowledge refers to the use and decision-making associated with assessment tools, instruments and systems. Pedagogical assessment dispositions refer to the ideological stances that value dynamic bilingualism and pluralist analytic discursive frames (Alfaro, 2019). Pedagogical assessment skills refer to the contextually appropriate and culturally responsible measurement and monitoring practices across curriculum, instruction and assessment in two or more languages (Machado-Casas et al., 2022; Maldonado & Machado-Casas, 2019).

Pedagogical assessment knowledge contributes to how fairness in assessment and accountability is created and sustained in services, programs and systems. DLBE educators require assessment knowledge in frameworks such as OTL to structure synergistic learning experiences for students across formative assessment and summative achievement measures. Particularly, knowledge of content, construct and consequential validity provides DLBE educators with useful information to advocate for fairness in assessment practices (Basterra et al., 2011). Educators' knowledge of validity in assessment improves learning experiences and achievement for students from specific cultural and linguistic groups learning in particular DLBE programs.

Pedagogical assessment dispositions contribute to how culture in assessment and accountability is prioritized. In addition to assessment knowledge, such as measurement error and construct relevance, DLBE educators require assessment dispositions informed by frameworks such as cultural validity in assessment (Solano-Flores, 2011) to prioritize contextual appropriateness and cultural responsibility throughout all assessment practices and accountability policies. Particularly, dispositions conscientious of students' self-efficacy as well as family and community contexts provide DLBE educators with pluralist ideological stances. Educators' dispositions of pluralism in assessment and achievement improve learning experiences for culturally and linguistically minoritized students in DLBE programs.

Pedagogical assessment skills contribute to how bilingualism, biliteracy and sociocultural competence is designed, implemented and monitored in services, programs and systems. DLBE educators require assessment skills informed by dynamic bilingualism (García & Wei, 2014) and language status orientations to design, modify and use assessment tools, instruments, processes and systems. Particularly, pedagogical assessment skills in monitoring students' development of biliteracy in listening, speaking, reading and writing, across content areas, provide DLBE educators with valuable experiences for data use. Educators' use of customized bilingual assessment tools and instruments improves progress monitoring processes and systems and, most importantly, improves learning experiences for all DLBE students (Machado-Casas et al., 2022).

Pedagogical Assessment Practices and Program Accountability Policies

Baca (2021) suggests administrators are also responsible for interrogating the validity, and identifying the limitations, of accountability processes and decisions in DLBE programs. Assessment practices and accountability policies in DLBE programs require actionable information for language policy and planning decisions that are perceptive of prestige and power determinations. Furthermore, DLBE programs using assessment, accountability and culture information to analyze their program's appropriateness and effectiveness are reminded that such measures may be inappropriate and ineffective for other DLBE programs, as well as unintentionally harmful. DLBE administrators are encouraged to develop and sustain additive internal processes and policies for accountability that celebrate the unique journey of each program's development of appropriateness and achievement. Researchers and teacher educators are encouraged to contribute services, programs and systems to support practitioners (including administrators) and policymakers in developing and sustaining community agency and critical consciousness at all levels of DLBE, particularly in relation to assessment practices and accountability trends.

References

Abedi, J., & Gándara, P. (2006). Performance of English language learners as a subgroup in large-scale assessment: Interaction of research and policy. *Educational Measurement: Issues and Practice*, *25*, 36–46. https://doi.org/10.1111/j.1745-3992.2006.00077

Alfaro, C. (2019). Preparing critically conscious dual language teachers: Recognizing and interrupting dominant ideologies. Reimaging dual language education in the U.S. *Theory Into Practice*, *58*(2), 194–203.

Alfaro, C., & Bartolomé, L. (2017). Preparing ideologically clear bilingual teachers: Honoring working-class non-standard language use in the bilingual education classroom. *Issues in Teacher Education*, *26*(2), 11–34.

Alfaro, C., Cadiero-Kaplan, K., & Ochoa, A. M. (2018). Teacher education and Latino emergent bilinguals: Knowledge, dispositions and skills for critically conscious pedagogy. In P. C. Ramírez, C. J. Faltis, & E. J. de Jong (Eds.), *Learning from emergent bilingual Latinx learners in K-12*. Routledge.

American Educational Research Association, American Psychological Association, & National Council on Measurement in Education (Eds.). (2014). *Standards for educational and psychological testing*. American Educational Research Association.

Baca, E. (2021). From compliance to resistance: Administrator perspectives on implementing structured English immersion and dual language bilingual education programs. *International Journal of Bilingual Education and Bilingualism*. https://doi.org/10.1080/13670050.2021.1943303

Bandura, A. (1993). Perceived self-efficacy in cognitive development and functioning. *Educational Psychologist*, *28*(2), 117–148. Advance online publication. https://doi.org/10.1207/s15326985ep2802_3

Basterra, M. D. R., Trumbull, E., & Solano-Flores, G. (2011). *Cultural validity in assessment: Addressing linguistic and cultural diversity*. Routledge.

Bohon, S. A., Johnson, M. K., & Gorman, B. K. (2006). College aspirations and expectations among Latino adolescents in the United States. *Social Problems*, *53*(2), 207–225. https://doi.org/10.1525/sp.2006.53.2.207

Brewer, C., Knoeppel, R. C., & Lindle, J. C. (2014). Consequential validity of accountability policy: Public understanding of assessments. *Educational Policy*, *29*(5), 711–745. https://doi.org/10.1177/0895904813518099

Bunch, G. C. (2013). Pedagogical language knowledge: Preparing mainstream teachers for English learners in the new standards era. *Review of Research in Education*, *37*, 298–341.

Come, B., & Fredericks, A. D. (1995). Family literacy in urban schools: Meeting the needs of at-risk children. *Reading Teacher*, *48*(7), 566–570.

de Jong, E. J. (2013). Policy discourses and U.S. language in education policies. *Peabody Journal of Education*, *88*, 98–111. https://doi.org/10.1080/0161956X.2013.752310

Escamilla, K. (2006). Semilingualism applied to the literacy behaviors of Spanish-speaking emerging bilinguals: Bi-illiteracy or emerging biliteracy? *Teachers College Record*, *108*(11), 2329–2353.

Field, R. F. (2011). Competing discourses about education and accountability for ELLs/bilingual learners: Dual language educators as agents for change. *Journal of Multilingual Education Research*, *2*(3), 9–34. http://fordham.bepress.com/jmer/vol2/iss1/3

Fitzsimmons-Doolan, S., Palmer, D., & Henderson, K. (2017). Educator language ideologies and a top-down dual language program. *International Journal of Bilingual Education and Bilingualism*, *20*(6), 704–721. https://doi.org/10.1080/13670050.2015.1071776

Flores, N., & García, O. (2017). A critical review of bilingual education in the United States: From basements and pride to boutiques and profit. *Annual of Applied Linguistics*, *37*, 14–29.

Flores-Gonzalez, N. (2005). Popularity versus respect: School structure, peer groups and Latino academic achievement. *International Journal of Qualitative Studies in Education*, *18*(5), 625–642. https://doi.org/10.1080/09518390500224945

Flores, N., & Schissel, J. L. (2014). Dynamic bilingualism as the norm: Envisioning a heteroglossic approach to standards-based reform. *TESOL Quarterly*, *48*(3), 454–479. https://doi.org/10.1002/tesq.182

García, O., & Wei, L. (2014). *Translanguaging: Language, bilingualism, and education*. Palgrave Macmillan Pivot.

Georges, A., Maldonado, S. I., & Uppal, H. K. (2019). Learning content, language and culture: The academic achievement, aspirations, and social experiences of eighth grade dual immersion students. *NABE Journal of Research and Practice*, *9*(3–4), 166–180.

Gibson, M. A., Bejínez, L. F., Hidalgo, N., & Rolón, C. (2004). Belonging and school participation: Lessons from a migrant student club. In M. Gibson, P. Gándara, & J. P. Koyama (Eds.), *School connections: U.S. Mexican youth, peers, and school achievement* (pp. 129–149). Teachers College Press.

Gottlieb, M., & Nguyen, D. (2007). *Assessment and accountability in language education programs: A guide for administrators and teachers*. Caslon.

Heiman, D., & Yanes, M. (2018). Centering the fourth pillar in times of TWBE gentrification: "Spanish, love, content, not in that order". *International Multilingual Research Journal*, *12*(3), 173–187. https://doi.org/10.1080/19313152.2018.1474064

Henderson, K. I. (2017). Teacher language ideologies mediating classroom-level language policy in the implementation of dual language bilingual education. *Linguistics and Education*, *42*, 21–33. https://doi.org/10.1016/j.linged.2017.08.003

Hopewell, S., Butvilofsky, S., & Escamilla, K. (2016). Complementing the common core with holistic biliteracy. *The Journal of Education*, *196*(2), 89–98.

Howard, E. R., Lindholm-Leary, D., Rogers, D., Olague, N., Medina, J., Kennedy, B., Sugarman, J., & Christian, D. (2018). *Guiding principles for dual language education* (3rd ed.). Center for Applied Linguistics.

Howard, E. R., Olague, N., & Rogers, D. (2003a). *The dual language program planner: A guide for designing and implementing dual language programs*. Center for Research on Education, Diversity & Excellence.

Howard, E. R., Sugarman, J., & Christian, D. (2003b). *Trends in two-way immersion education: A review of the research* (Report No. 63). Center for Research on the Education of Students Placed at Risk.

Ing, M., & Nylund-Gibson, K. (2013). Linking early science and mathematics attitudes to long-term science, technology, engineering, and mathematics career attainment: Latent class analysis with proximal and distal outcomes. *Educational Research and Evaluation*, *19*, 510–524. https://doi.org/10.1080/13803611.2013.806218

Kao, G., & Tienda, M. (1995). Optimism and achievement: The educational performance of immigrant youth. *Social Science Quarterly*, *76*(1), 1–19.

Kralovec, E., & Buell, J. (2001). *The end of homework: How homework disrupts families, overburdens children, and limits learning*. Beacon Press.

Lindholm-Leary, K. (2012). Success and challenges in dual language education. *Theory Into Practice*, *51*, 256–262. https://doi.org/10.1080/00405841.2012.726053

Lindholm-Leary, K., & Hargett, G. (2006). *Evaluator's toolkit for dual language programs*. Center for Applied Linguistics.

Machado-Casas, M., Maldonado, S. I., & Flores, B. B. (2022). *Assessment and evaluation in bilingual education*. Peter Lang. https://www.peterlang.com/document/1140567

Maldonado, S. I., & Andrade, R. J. (2018). After the press release on mathematics achievement: The alignment of formative assessments and summative standardized tests for students from minoritized language backgrounds. *Revista de Sociología de la Educación, 11*(3), 421–432.

Maldonado, S. I., Georges, A., Puglisi, J., & Hernandez, M. M. (2018). Partnership pathways in a two-way bilingual immersion program: From evaluation to constructing capacity. *NABE Perspectives, 41*(2), 13–19.

Maldonado, S. I., & Machado-Casas, M. (2019). Sustaining the sociopolitical spirit of bilingual education: Assessment practices and evaluative policies for students minoritized by national background and English-language proficiency. In S. Keengwe, & G. Onchwari (Eds.), *Handbook of research on assessment practices and pedagogical models for immigrant students* (pp. 1–17). IGI Global.

Ovando, C. J. (2003). Bilingual education in the United States: Historical development and current issues. *Bilingual Research Journal, 27*(1), 1–24. https://doi.org/10.1080/15235882.2003.10162589

Proctor, C. P., & Silverman, R. D. (2011). Confounds in assessing the association between biliteracy and English-language proficiency. *Educational Researcher, 40*(2), 62–64.

Sastry, N., & Pebly, A. (2010). Family and neighborhood sources of socioeconomic inequality in children's achievement. *Demography, 47*(3), 777–800. https://doi.org/10.1353/dem.0.0114

Salkind, N. J. (2006). *Tests & measurement for people who (think they) hate tests & measurement*. Sage.

Sewell, W. H., Haller, A. O., & Portes, A. (1969). The educational and early career attainment process. *American Sociological Review, 34*, 82–93. https://doi.org/10.2307/2092789

Solano-Flores, G. (2011). Assessing the cultural validity of assessment practices. In M. D. R. Basterra, E. Trumbull, & G. Solano-Flores (Eds.), *Cultural validity in assessment: Addressing linguistic and cultural diversity* (pp. 3–21). Routledge.

Soltero, S. (2016). *Dual language education: Program design and implementation*. Heinemann.

Valdez, V. E., Freire, J. A., & Delavan, M. (2016). The gentrification of dual language education. *The Urban Review, 48*, 601–627. https://doi.org/10.1007/s11256-016-0370-0

Wiley, T. G., & García, O. (2016). Language policy and planning in language education: Legacies, consequences, and possibilities. *The Modern Language Journal, 100*(Supplement 2016), 48–63.

16

LANGUAGE IDEOLOGY

The Driver of Inclusive Education

Xochitl Archey

Overview of the Issue: The Inclusion Mandate and the Framing of Difference

Presently, in the United States, 19.74% of Emergent Bilinguals (EBs) are believed to have a (dis)ability (U.S. Department of Education, 2019) – the fastest growing population in the United States (Council of the Great City Schools, 2019). The Individuals with Disabilities Education Act (IDEA) (2004) promises to safeguard the inclusive education of these students, in part, through the Least Restrictive Environment (LRE) mandate. Some of the least restrictive educational settings, such as the general education classroom, have steadily seen an increase of EBs with (dis)abilities. As of 2019, 60.52% of EBs with (dis)abilities participated in the general education classroom for at least 80% or more of the instructional day, 22% for 40%–79% of the time, and 16% for less than 40% of the time (U.S. Department of Education, 2019). The other percent of the time is sometimes spent receiving special education and related services in learning centers/resource rooms. Other times, it is remedial English language development (ELD) that is taught through pull-outs. And yet, other times, inclusion (broadly understood) is a non-existent practice in the education of EBs with (dis)abilities. And so, we continue to see that "good policy ideas frequently come to grief when put into the context of a specific set of circumstances at the local level" (Gallagher et al., 1995, p. 372).

The exclusion of EBs with (dis)abilities from DLBE is routinely pointed out in the research (Archey, 2019; Cioè-Peña, 2020) with statements such as "special education students [are] not immersion material" (Palmer, 2010, p. 103). Statements such as these are "powerful [demonstrations] that

 DOI: 10.4324/9781003269076-24

(dis)ability continues to operate as a racialized barrier to equity" (Gillborn et al., 2016, p. 52). This beckons us to consider, not just the physical manifestations of segregation or isolation such as fragmented instruction, but also the occult forms of such (Cioè-Peña, 2017): linguistic assimilation, language discreteness/purity, and notions of languagelessness.

Through time, language-minoritized students (e.g., EBs) have been barred from educational inclusion for unfounded reasons like homogeneity movements (e.g., World War I) (Highham, 1975), xenophobic ideologies prohibiting the once accepted teaching of bilingualism (e.g., German instruction for German-speaking children), monies funding the teaching of English to *aliens* and *native illiterates* (as cited in Olneck, 2005), government-speared abduction and separation of children from their families into English-only schools, punishment for not speaking English at school (e.g., The Indian Boarding School Policies) (Truth and Healing Commission on Indian Boarding School Policies Act, 2011), and assimilation ideologies that shorten the time that EBs spent in home language-supported classrooms before moving to English-only classrooms (e.g., Proposition 227 The English for the Children Act) (California Department of Education, 2006; Mora, 2016). Ability-minoritized students (e.g., students with (dis)abilities) have also experienced barriers to inclusive education such as criminalizing the ability to enroll students with (dis)abilities in public schools (e.g., North Carolina prior to 1969) (Wright & Wright, 2016), federal court case rulings stating that minor benefits from inclusion at an extraordinary cost do not merit the inclusion of students with (dis)abilities (e.g., 1987 A.W. v. Northwest School District court case) (Blankenship et al., 2007), racist political motivations for upholding the intellectual superiority of English speakers, and the deficit-ideologies that continue to propagate myths and discourage parents from enrolling their children in DLBE (Cioè-Peña, 2020) and thus, ignoring the linguistic realities of students' home and community contexts.

Much of the segregation and integration, whether apparent through physical structures or intangible ideologies, stem from a judgment on *difference*. This *difference*, often powered by ideologies of atavism, biological essentialism is used to "justify discrimination, exclusion, and violence against marginalized populations" (Valentine, 2022, p. 338). In this way, ableism and racism operate jointly and borrow from each other, intensifying notions of normality and, by default, *difference*.

In the section that follows, I continue to raise the issue of inclusion within issues concerning DLBE. Inclusion is reimagined, no longer from a deficit lens, but as a shift that dismantles and rejects deficit-based ideologies and embraces *difference* as a social responsibility (Braunsteiner & Mariano-Lapidus, 2014). Each of the questions is addressed in turn by drawing on the current literature.

Standing on the Shoulders of Those That Came before Us: A Review

Despite the growing movements towards inclusion in education, many continue to subscribe to status quo frameworks of inclusion through a deficit lens (Archey, 2021) and thereby perpetuate notions of linguistic assimilation, xenophobia, inflexible language arrangements, silent agenda of admission selectivity (Somers, 2017), language discreteness (Piller & Takahashi, 2011), and the theoretically unsound expectation to master the majority language first (Mady & Turnbull, 2010). These language ideologies are barriers to recruitment to-, access to-, and inclusion of EBs with (dis)abilities in DLBE (UnidosUS, 2021) and are often based on myths and misinterpretations (Archey, 2021; Byers-Heinlein & Lee-Williams, 2013).

Indeed, there has been an ideological problem with how *difference* is conceptualized in ways that cause a threat to inclusive education. Language and ability differences are entangled in a complex web of lies about language assimilation, language purity, and languagelessness ideologies. The interconnectedness between educational programming and issues of power and social control exacerbates the manifestation of these deficit-based language ideologies in DLBE.

I borrow from the work of Annamma et al. (2013) on Disability Studies in Education (DSE) and Critical Race Theory (CRT) – *DisCrit* – to explore the intersectional identities of EBs with (dis)abilities in DLBE and the work of Minow (1985) on the *Difference Dilemma* to center inclusion for a bilingual special education context.

Annamma et al. (2013) provide a platform to engage in the intersectional conversations of race and (dis)ability. Seven tenets are proposed as part of the framework. Throughout, the tenets ask us to make shifts. We begin by recognizing the intersectionality of identities (race and disability) and upholding marginalized voices. We are prompted to acknowledge the social power in defining the labels and recognize the impact these have on students' self-worth. A key dimension of DisCrit is to identify how legal systems have worked to perpetuate the legalization of (dis)ability and race problems through structures that reproduce and uphold racism and ableism. The structures are often upheld through benevolent racism – prejudice hidden in superficial positive statements or structures or interest convergence – a practice that uses marginalized communities when in the best interests of the dominant communities (White, able-bodied). This framework pushes us to think about EBs with (dis)abilities as students experiencing intersectional forms of oppression (Kangas, 2017).

Minow (1985) revisits bilingual and special education legislation (e.g., court cases) to ideologically deconstruct inclusion. From such, three approaches to dismantling the *difference dilemma* are presented here. First, programs cannot operate in the singular or separate constructs (e.g., monocultural, monolingual, unicentric assessment practices, academic skills v. language acquisition, identify v. accomplishment, the right to special education and related services v. the right to bilingual education). Similarly, people cannot be defined in dichotomies. "Categories that take the form of dichotomies-same and different, normal and handicapped, English proficient and not English proficient-especially obscure the variety and range of characteristics that more aptly describe experience" (Minow, 1985, p. 203). Second, deficit-based ideologies are often linked to stigmatizing expressions of sameness and difference and equality and inequality. Equality is not sameness and inequality is not difference. Being different and equal can co-exist in systems that push us to relate across differences and forge relational structures in where "difference no longer belongs to the one child who is called *different*, but instead to the relationship between the two children []. They are both different from each other, whatever the proficiencies or deficiencies used to characterize each" (Minow, 1985, p. 204).

Let us circle back to DLBE as a platform for building off of the work of Annamma et al. (2013) and Minow (1985). First, DLBE aims to disrupt language dominance (Cummins, 2000). This allows us to envision structures where dichotomies of student identity, worth, languages are dismantled and value is not just talked about but also institutionalized. Second, home language goals and supports (e.g., Individualized Education Plan [IEP]) have a greater role in DLBE than in traditional English-only programs where child-family communication is often disrupted (Cartledge & Kourea, 2008). This gives us a platform to rethink the relational aspect of education and shift the responsibility of inclusion to everyone, not just those who have been *labeled*. Third, in DLBE, students' languages are (more readily) viewed as strengths throughout the IEP process (Archey, 2020. When IEPs are reconceptualized as safeguards of inclusion, goals then encompass both a need to learn in mainstream American English and the home language – not just mere translated versions of English goals written in *Spanish* (Archey, 2020). This is a space to reexamine the practices we take and implications of such when we categorize EBs with (dis)abilities as *different*. These are opportunities for DLBE.

To conceptualize these opportunities for DLBE further, the sections that follow extend a review of the literature and an examination of language ideologies.

Language Ideologies: An Examination

While the social inclusion agenda has been widely adopted, social inclusion policies are often blind to the ways in which language proficiency and language ideologies mediate social inclusion in linguistically

> diverse societies. If language is written into social inclusion policies, it is often done in a top-down manner informed by linguistic ideologies of monolingualism and linguistic discreteness rather than an informed understanding of the realities of communication in linguistically diverse societies.
>
> *Piller and Takahashi (2011)*

Earlier, I mentioned that educational purposes are often conceived for political purposes, to promote not only educational but societal goals and thus, inclusive education reflects social inclusion. Behind every societal goal lies an ideology that permeates and trickles down into our schools. In language programming, the "perceived prestige of a language influences how a program grows and develops" (Polanco & Luft de Baker, 2018, p. 427). In bilingual settings, language ideologies are intertwined with the notions of power (Zentella, 2005). Due to this interconnectedness, language ideologies play an important role in deciding who is included or excluded as a legitimate member of language programs. Ideologies help individuals construct meaning and make sense of experiences. This means that we need to turn inward to understand how we conceive of inclusion in DLBE. Let us take a closer look at the language ideologies driving educational programming for EBs with (dis)abilities.

Linguistic Assimilation

Bourdieu (1982) reminds us that language is not merely a method of communication but a mechanism of power to legitimize. In the programming of education for EBs with (dis)abilities, we have often seen the legitimization of English being upheld through pull-out and push-in ELD programs – in which the language of instruction is English with goals to linguistically assimilate into English and the consequential erasure of home language(s). Although linguistic assimilation can occur gradually as language maintenance is lost (Mendoza, 2019), schools are often sites where assimilation is exacerbated. These programs are very much connected with the idea that to learn English (or the mainstream language albeit not necessarily the national language) is directly related to increased social inclusion (benevolent racism). From the literature, we know that assimilation is a false solution to inclusion – it does not reduce inequality or marginality. Through time, we have seen assimilation as an attempt to erase the differences in language, abilities, beliefs, culture, behavior resulting in devastating loss of cultural knowledge and identity.

We are reminded that linguistic assimilation is not only happening in ELD programs. Bilingual programs are not exempt from feeding into assimilation ideology (Mijares & Relaño Pastor, 2011). Take for instance the early-exit transitional model where students start by learning in their home language, but slowly transition into English (Kim et al., 2015). The late-exit bilingual model follows a more gradual transition, but ultimately the goal remains to transition students from their home language to English (Ovando, 2003) during which time they are in classes with only dominant speakers of the same language throughout the day (Ovando, 2003). These programs can be said to *work* because the goal is to temporarily solve the *problem* of schooling EBs with (dis)abilities. That is, teaching them in a language they understand – their home language for the time being – but ultimately face a much greater challenge when transitioning into the *target* language (English) (Mijares & Relaño Pastor, 2011). In DLBE (two-way immersion), one of the most promising components is also one of its most limiting conditions; biliteracy. In this case, linguistic assimilation into the "academic" (often egregiously referred to "proper" or "correct") version of a home language (e.g., Spanish). Thereby, negating their linguistic-semiotic, cultural, and historical repertoires (García et al., 2021).

Whether it is an ELD program, transitional, developmental program, or DLBE, the denial of inclusion may be manifesting through linguistic segregation or isolation. And yet, EBs with (dis)abilities have an increased need for language skills to strengthen their community networks because segregation and isolation are often already part of the experiences of people with (dis)abilities. The preoccupation with linguistic assimilation (often disguised as integration) has grown language programs that focus on transitioning EBs with (dis)abilities as quickly as possible to the *target* language (English) and/or completing barring them from a DLBE (Ovando, 2003; Yağmur & Extra, 2011). These misconceptions of language and how language functions for EBs with (dis)abilities are often a reflection of biases that are "grounded in the student's racial, ethnic, linguistic, and dis/abled identity" (Cioè-Peña, 2021).

Language Discreteness/Purity

Building from the previous section, assimilation does not only manifest in the erasure of a home language and assimilation into the *dominant* language. Accordingly, assimilation also surfaces in specific language norms where EBs with (dis)abilities are asked to learn the *proper* version of their home languages. Inflexible language practices are far too often implemented with such conviction, that linguistic diversity, for instance *Spanglish*, is frequently viewed as having "deformed elements of vocabulary and grammar from both Spanish and English" (Royal Spanish Academy as cited in Garsd, 2012). A study on teacher attitudes revealed that preconceived notions on language purity are still upheld among pre-service teachers, despite courses on multiculturalism (Kozel, 2007). This exposes how deeply rooted harmful ideologies of the past continue to permeate in different niches of the educational system and society at large. However, it is important to remember that ideological clarity has the potential to transcend despite deep-seeded systems that work towards models of assimilation (Bartolomé, 2006). Macedo et al. (2003) state that assimilation-based ideologies are enacted in restrictive language policies – this type of exclusion has monolingual underpinnings. When bilingualism is associated with monolingualism, the linguistic repertoires of EBs with (dis)abilities are constructed as a problem.

In language purity approaches (e.g., often adopted by DLBE), when the *incorrect* language is used, students' behavior can be dangerously misrepresented as disruptive (e.g., showing *no respect* for classroom norms). The problem, in this case, can be *fixed* by speaking in the *correct* language. This ritualization of monolingual languages in bilingual programs continues to evoke the same deficit-ideologies as "English-only movements" as they creep into students' interactions and ways of learning that legitimize only one language. These practices are not inclusive of students' linguistic repertoires.

Garcia (2009) highlights the complexity of how languages interplay. In practice, Garcia (2009) suggests that individuals do not have divisive or compartmentalized languages, but rather a unified automatic language processing system (the notion of transglossia). Studies on neuroimaging support the idea that as bilinguals acquire more proficiency, the language network becomes one – there is no separation of languages in the brain (Abutalebi, 2008). This idea of language interrelationship (one communication network) is an accurate description of the fluid and dynamic role languages play in society (Otheguy et al., 2019). In inclusive classrooms, languages can and often do work together for learning. This concept is called translanguaging. Translanguaging (trawsieithua) was first used by Cen Williams in 1996 to describe a dynamic process by which information comes through in one language and is, then, used in another language to output a product (Garcia & Kleifgen, 2010). There are many cognitive processing strategies like the input/output approach that support EBs with (dis)abilities in DLBE by allowing one language to be used for the input of information and another for the output – both working together (e.g., read in one language, discuss in another). This is not just an inclusive pedagogical practice, but it also allows students to use their full linguistic repertoires to make meaning (Baker, 2011). Translanguaging highlights students' linguistic strengths instead of just seeing one language or another (García & Otheguy, 2020) or two monolinguals in one person (Baker, 2011). This hybrid and simultaneous use of languages (translanguaging) is better aligned with a globalized world in which languages are interrelated. From the literature, we know that acquiring two languages simultaneously is not detrimental to the language proficiency of children (Baker, 2011; De Houwer, 2009), rather proving to be cognitively, culturally, communicatively, and academically beneficial (Baker, 2011) and yet, the "cognitive overload" of learning two languages is often used as an excuse to exclude EBs with (dis)abilities from DLBE (Archey, 2021).

Language Rights and Languagelessness

Foundationally, schools are often thought of as leveling grounds that provide students of diverse language profiles and abilities the opportunities to learn the *codes of power* that can support their *success*. However, "schools often compete to recruit 'value adding' students" and exclude "those students who add 'negative value'" (Ball, 2008, p. 187). The silent agenda of selectivity (Apsel, 2012) is a covert access criteria set forth to exclude already marginalized student groups (e.g., EBs with (dis)abilities) (Eurydice, 2017).

One of the concerns surrounding EBs with (dis)abilities is the acquisition of language proficiency. EBs with (dis)abilities enter public schools with a language other than the *target* language (English) and often with a disability that can affect the sequence of how they develop language. Typically, schools do not see this group as *value adding* students.

While access to bilingual programs is open to everyone, marginalized students and their families often experience this as a false choice. Educational researchers have questioned the access to bilingual education in the context of inclusion. The first critique centers on language rights. Many additive bilingual programs have not physically existed in lower socioeconomic status (SES) communities. Given that many EBs with (dis)abilities come from families experiencing a lower SES (Kieffer, 2010), it is important to question the nature of inclusion in systems in which native speakers of the language (often Spanish) do not have access to bilingual education programs (e.g., redlining) and/or quality bilingual education programs. The literature on language rights serves as a warning that "threatens to position bilingual education as the next wave of inequitably distributed enrichment education" (gentrification) that gives access to "White, English-dominant majority and those without an ethnic connection to the [non-English] language" (Freire et al., 2016; Palmer, 2010). The lack of governing structures to guide and demand recruitment of EBs with (dis)abilities into DLBE is a barrier to honoring the linguistic and cultural maintenance rights of these students.

While redlining and gentrification continue to be issues that threaten bilingual education, through legislation such as Proposition 58 bilingual education is increasingly becoming the environment of choice for many families. Advocates of inclusive DLBE continue to caution against the misguided beliefs that play a role in the exclusion of EBs with (dis)abilities in DLBE (Archey, 2020; Genesee, 2007; Mady, 2012; Somers, 2017). Rosa (2016) gives us the term *languagelessness*. I use this term to frame the misguided but often used justification for denying bilingual education access to EBs with (dis)abilities. Discourses that racialize EBs with (dis)abilities center them as deficient – that is, languageless (Flores et al., 2020). Misguided consequences lead to exclusion from DLBE (e.g., enrollment and participation in DLBE with lack of support, enrollment in a DLBE school but no participation in a DLBE classroom, complete exclusion from DLBE).

The notion of *languagelessness* discourages families from enrolling their children in bilingual programs on the false premise that students' competences in either language is insufficient, therefore making a bilingual education too difficult (Hernandez, 2017; Mady & Turnbull, 2010; Mijares & Relaño Pastor, 2011). For EBs with (dis)abilities, we know that the equal balance of languages is a false and dangerous assumption. Rarely do individuals have equal proficiency levels of both languages, the concept of *languagelessness* is false (Baker, 2011). For EBs with (dis)abilities, we know that DLBE helps counter the disruption of child-family communication (Cartledge & Kourea, 2008) and that these students benefit academically and socially from bilingual education (Bialystok, 2015; Bialystok & Poarch, 2014; Blanchett et al., 2009). We also know that there is a current shift in the theoretical underpinnings of how we are coming to understand bilingualism and the acquisition of such. As Larsen-Freeman (2013) points out, the end state of the acquisition of another language has evolved from cognitivist theories (native-like mastery, complete acquisition of languages, two discrete language systems that are kept separate in use) to socially oriented understandings in which the linguistic repertoires grow and change to meet communicative needs without an endpoint. Misguided beliefs, while unintentional in some cases, result in the gatekeeping of some of the most effective bilingual models (e.g., DLBE) and the continued segregation and racialization of students (Tsokalidou, 2015).

Ideologies, policies, and practices centered around giving the privileged more privilege most benefit students with four types of privilege: White racial privilege, English privilege, ability privilege, and wealth. Liasidou (2012) reminds us that addressing the multiplicity of factors that *handicap* students means a reconfiguring, "redistributing, and [re]focusing of resources for groups of students who are entangled in a complex web of social and educational disadvantages" (p. 177).

An Introspective Reflection on Language Ideologies: Moving Forward

Inclusion in education means that we also think beyond the physical spaces and towards an examination of the ideologies and stories we tell ourselves about EBs with (dis)abilities, language, and inclusion. In the section that follows, I reposition inclusion within the context of DLBE by visiting a language affirming ideology – structural ideology.

When education stakeholders embrace structural ideology, they recognize that achieving equity means dismantling barriers. Educational barriers can be entirely traced to structural systems in and out of schools (Gorski, 2016). This means, we cannot just want or believe in inclusion but rather move forward with actionable steps. For example, more educators with background from – or knowledge in – the communities they serve. More educators with dual expertise in bilingual *and* special education. More curricular attention to the development of bilingualism and biliteracy in connection with bicultural identity. Good conversations can begin with identification and reframing of practices, such as norms, expectations, judgments that only or mostly serve dominant, privileged groups (Minow, 1985). Close attention should also refocus on the (un)intentional messages we send through the goals, programming, culture, recruitment, support systems. EBs with (dis)abilities can often fall victims to beliefs of inadequacy leading to "shedding [of] their home language[s]" (Migliarini & Cioè-Peña, 2022, p. 17).

The chapter opened with an overview of the issue with *difference* to contextualize how ideological shifts impact EBs with (dis)abilities. I then presented dominant language ideologies permeating bilingual educational spaces. At this point, I ask that we take on a structural lens and consider the issues more deeply by asking ourselves to reflect on our own complicity:

- Who is recruited for DLBE?
- Who has access to DLBE?
- How can DLBE be inclusive through structural and language affirming ideologies?

These reflective questions are posed because inclusion cannot arise from bias (Scanlan, 2011). I underscore the importance of awareness in understanding how ideologies of language have considerable power in impacting the lives of students. Specifically, this is a call for DLBE to examine the inclusion of the language community, the cultural climate (including identity and representation in curricula), internal and external organizational structures, and the role and input of informal and formal education stakeholders (including families) in shaping DLBE. I also echo the messages of advocates for educating EBs with (dis)abilities in DLBE by stating that this is a shared responsibility, and that the dedication of teacher preparation programs is equally needed in preparing pre-service and in-service educators (Kangas, 2017, 2018).

A moment of pause to underscore the need for strong preparation of teachers in bilingual special education. Often, these fields appear to work in silos with different processes and goals (Martínez-Álvarez, 2019), but education today looks very different and acknowledging this intersection may lead to established bilingual special education credentialing programs that prepare teachers to recognize and address students' unique languages and ability needs (Farrand & Deeg, 2021). Unification of the special education and bilingual education practices, in part, needs to confront deficit ideology – EBs with (dis)abilities are fully capable of success in DLBE.

I conclude this section with a reminder that "no set of curricular or pedagogical strategies can turn a classroom led by a teacher with a deficit view into an equitable learning space" (Gorski, 2016). Advocacy for inclusion is not easy, but it is important. Views on how to move forward can be challenging, often controversial. Surfacing and contesting the nature of language ideologies that drive bilingual models can be a viable path. We ask that bilingual leaders (educators, administrators, families, researchers, policy-makers, advocates, students, language communities) break away from the grip of monolingual, assimilation, language discreteness and purity, and languagelessness notions and make efforts to center conversations about inclusion using guides such as the Index for Inclusion (Vaughan, 2010) and the points extended below.

1 Assimilation operates from a standpoint that equates differences to deficiencies. Being different does not equal deficient. When we let our implicit biases compare EBs with (dis)abilities to monolingual students or students with (dis)abilities to their typically developing counterparts, we narrow their humanity and standardize the image of what it means to be a learner with varied and intersecting identities – an unfair comparison.
2 Language discreteness/purity is based on social expectations that work to maintain language power and control. Translanguaging is a natural part of being bilingual – often supporting students in making deeper and more meaningful connections to learning.
3 Languagelessness is a dangerous notion. The concept devalues our EBs with (dis)abilities. If some level of language proficiency has not been reached, it is important to look towards the sociopolitical and edupolitical conditions.

Lastly, as the *edupolitical* landscape slowly moves away from upholding spaces of segregation and into spaces of integration, we must continue to push forward into the utopian – if we cannot imagine it, we will never take steps towards achieving it: "Yes" to inclusion, but more so "yes" to spaces of belonging. There is no better place to do this work than in DLBE.

References

Abutalebi, J. (2008). Neural aspects of second language representation and language control. *Science Direct: Acta Psychologica*, *12*(8), 466–478.

Annamma, S. A., Connor, D., & Ferri, B. A. (2013). Dis/ability critical race studies (DisCrit): Theorizing at the intersections of race and dis/ability. *Race Ethnicity and Education*, *16*(1). https://doi.org/10.1080/13613324.2012.730511

Apsel, C. (2012). Coping with CLIL: Dropouts from CLIL streams in Germany. *International CLIL Research Journal, 1*(4), 47–56.
Archey, X. (2019). The living document of intentionality: Critically transforming access and equity for English learners with special needs. *The Multilingual Educator*, 28–31.
Archey, X. (2020). Individualized education plans (IEPs) in a dual language bilingual education context. *The Multilingual Educator*, 21–23.
Archey, X. (2021). *Myths and facts about children with (dis)abilities in bilingual education*. Multilingual Educator. California Association for Bilingual Education (CABE).
Baker, C. (2011). *Foundations of bilingual education and bilingualism*. Multilingual Matters.
Ball, S. (2008) The legacy of ERA, privatization and the policy ratchet. *Educational Management, Administration and Leadership, 36*(2), 185–199.
Bartolomé, L. (2006). The struggle for language rights: Naming and interrogating the colonial legacy of "English Only." *Human Architecture: Journal of the Sociology of Self-Knowledge, 4*, 25–32.
Bialystok, E. (2015). Bilingualism and the development of executive function: The role of attention. *Child Development Perspectives, 9*(2), 117–121. https://doi.org/10.1111/cdep.12116
Bialystok, E., & Poarch, G. (2014). Language experience changes language and cognitive ability. *Zeitschrift Für Erziehungswissenschaft, 14*(3), 433–446.
Blanchett, W. J., Klingner, J. K., & Harry, B. (2009). The intersection of race, culture, language, and disability: Implications for urban education. *Urban Education, 44*(4), 389–409.
Blankenship, T., Boone, T., & Fore, C. (2007). Inclusion and placement decisions for students with special needs: A historical analysis of relevant statutory and case law. *Electronic Journal of Inclusive Education, 2*(1), 1–10.
Bourdieu, P. (1982). *Language and symbolic power*. Harvard University Press.
Braunsteiner, M. L., & Mariano-Lapidus, S. (2014). A perspective on inclusion: Challenges for the future. *Global Education Review, 1*(1), 32–43.
Byers-Heinlein, K., & Lee-Williams, C. (2013). Bilingualism in early years: What the science says. *Learning Landscape, 7*(1), 95–112.
California Department of Education. (2006). *Effects of the implementation of proposition 227 on the education of English learners, K-12: Findings from a five-year evaluation*. American Institutes for Research and WestED. https://www.wested.org/online_pubs/227Reportb.pdf
Cartledge, G., & Kourea, L. (2008). Culturally responsive classrooms for culturally diverse students with and at risk for disabilities. *Council for Exceptional Children, 74*(3), 351–371.
Cioè-Peña, M. (2017). The intersectional gap: How bilingual students in the United States are excluded from inclusion. *International Journal of Inclusive Education*. http://dx.doi.org/10.1080/13603116.2017.1296032
Cioè-Peña, M. (2020). Raciolinguistics and the education of emergent bilinguals labeled as disabled. *The Urban Review, 53*(3), 443–469. https://doi.org/10.1007/s11256-020-00581-z
Council of the Great City Schools. (2019). *Annual report 2018–2019*. https://www.cgcs.org/Page/866
Cummins, J. (2000). *Language, power, and pedagogy: Bilingual children in the crossfire*. Multilingual Matters.

De Houwer, A. (2009). *Bilingual first language acquisition.* Multilingual Matters. https://doi.org/10.21832/9781847691507
Eurydice. (2017). *Key data on teaching languages at school in Europe – 2017 edition* [Eurydice report]. European Union https://webgate.ec.europa.eu/fpfis/mwikis/eurydice/images/0/06/KDL_2017_internet.pdf
Farrand, K. M., & Deeg, M. T. (2021). Implementing co-teaching with paraprofessionals to provide pre-kindergarten students with special rights access to dual language. *The British Journal of Special Education*, *48*(3), 282–300. https://doi.org/10.1111/1467-8578.12364
Flores, N., Phuong, J., & Venegas, K. M. (2020). Technically an EL: The production of raciolinguistic categories in a dual language school. *TESOL Quarterly*, *54*(3), 62–651.
Freire, J. A., Valdez, V., & Delavan, M. G. (2016). The (dis)inclusion of Latina/o interests from Utah's dual language education boom. *Journal of Latinos and Education*, *16*(4), 276–289. https://doi.org/10.1080/15348431.2016.1229617
Gallagher, J., Desimone, L., & Porter, F. (1995). Lessons learned from implementation of the IEP: Applications to the IFSP. *Topics Early Childhood Special Education (TECSE)*, *15*(3), 353–378.
Garcia, O. (2009). *Bilingual education in the 21st century: A global perspective.* Wiley Blackwell.
Garcia, O., & Kleifgen, J. A. (2010). *Educating emergent bilinguals: Policies, programs, and practices for English language learners.* Teachers College Press.
García, O., Flores, N., Seltzer, K., Wei, L., Otheguy, R., & Rosa, J. (2021). Rejecting abyssal thinking in the language and education of racialized bilinguals: A manifesto. *Critical Inquiry in Language Studies.* https://doi.org/10.1080/15427587.2021.1935957
García, O. & Otheguy, R. (2020). Plurilingualism and translanguaging: Commonalities and divergences. *International Journal of Bilingual Education and Bilingualism*, *23*(1) 17–35. http://doi/org 10.1080/13670050.2019.1598932
Garsd, J. (2012). Puedes believe it? Spanglish gets in el dictionary. National Public Radio (NPR).
Genesee, F. (2007). French immersion and at-risk students: A review of research evidence. *The Canadian Modern Language Review*, *63*(5), 655–687.
Gillborn, C. D., Ferri, B., & Annamma, S. (2016). *DisCrit: Disability studies and critical race theory in education.* Teacher's College Press.
Gorski, P. C. (2016). Poverty and the ideological imperative: A call to unhook from deficit and grit ideology and to strive for structural ideology in teacher education. *Journal of Education for Teaching*, *42*(4), 378–386. http://doi.org/10.1080/02607476.2016.1215546
Hernandez, S. (2017). Are they all language learners?: Educational labeling and raciolinguistic identifying in a California middle school dual language program. *The CATESOL Journal*, *29*(1), 133–154.
Higham, J. (1975). *Send these to me: Jews and other immigrants in urban America* (1st ed). Atheneum.
Individuals with Disabilities Education Act (IDEA). (2004). Public Law 108-446, 20 U.S.C §1400 et seq.
Kangas, S. E. (2017). That's where the rubber meets the road: The intersection of special education and dual language education. *Teachers College Record*, *119*, 1–36.
Kangas, S. E. (2018). Why working apart doesn't work at all: Special education and English learner collaborations. *Intervention in School and Clinic (ISC)*, *54*(1), 31–39. https://doi.org/10.1177/1053451218762469

Kieffer, M. J. (2010). Socioeconomic status, English proficiency, and late-emerging reading difficulties. *Educational Researcher*, *3*(6), 484–486.

Kim, Y. K., Hutchison, L. A., & Winsler, A. (2015). Bilingual education in the United States: An historical overview and examination of two-way immersion. *Educational Review*, *67*(2), 236–252.

Kozel, S. (2007). *Exploring pre-service teachers' sense of responsibility for multiculturalism and diversity: Scale construction and construct validation* [Electronic thesis]. https://etd.ohiolink.edu/

Larsen-Freeman, D. (2013). *The standards and second language development: A complexity theory perspective*. Paper presented at the TESOL.

Liasidou, A. (2012). Inclusive education and critical pedagogy at the intersections of disability, race, gender, and class. *Journal for Critical Education Policy Studies (JCEPS)*, 168–185.

Macedo, D., Dendrinos, B., & Gounari, P. (2003). *The hegemony of English*. Paradigm.

Mady, C. (2012). Inclusion of English language learners in French as a second official language classes: Teacher knowledge and beliefs. *International Journal of Multilingualism*, *9*(1), 1–14.

Mady, C., & Turnbull, M. (2010). Learning French as a second official language: Reserved for anglophones? *Canadian Journal of Educational Administration and Policy*, *99*, 1–23.

Martínez-Álvarez, P. (2019; Online First). Redistribution of labor to prepare teachers to work in inclusive bilingual classrooms. *Urban Education*. https://doi.org/10.1177/0042085919873697

Mendoza, S. (2019). Bilingual education: Segmented assimilation or selective acculturation. *Journal on English Language Teaching*, *9*(3), 1–5.

Migliarini, V., & Cioè-Peña, M. (2022). Performing the good (im)migrant: Inclusion and expectations of linguistic assimilation. *International Journal of Inclusive Education*. https://doi.org/10.1080/13603116.2022.2112770

Mijares, L., & Relaño Pastor, A. M. (2011). Language programs at Villababel High: Rethinking ideologies of social inclusion. *International Journal of Bilingual Education and Bilingualism*, *14*(4), 427–442. https://doi.org/10.1080/13670050.2011.573066

Minow, M. (1985). Learning to live with the dilemma of difference: Bilingual special education. *Law and Contemporary Problems*, *48*(2), 157–211.

Mora, J. K. (2016). *The California multilingual education act 2016* [PowerPoint slides]. http://moramodules.com/blog/ca-multilingual-education-act-2016

Olneck, M. R. (2005). Americanization, U.S. In M. C. Horowitz (Ed.), *New dictionary of the history of ideas* (pp. 1–7). Charles Scribner's Sons.

Otheguy, R., García, O., & Reid, W. (2019). A translanguaging view of the linguistic system of bilinguals. *Applied Linguistics Review*, *10*(4), 625–651. https://doi.org/10.1515/applirev-2018-0020

Ovando, C. J. (2003). Bilingual education in the United States: Historical development and current issues. *Bilingual Research Journal*, *24*(1), 1–24.

Palmer, D. (2010). Race, power, and equity in a multiethnic urban elementary school with a dual language strand program. *Anthropology & Education Quarterly*, *41*(1), 94–114.

Piller, I., & Takahashi, K. (2011). Linguistic diversity and social inclusion. *International Journal of Bilingual Education and Bilingualism*, *14*(4), 371–381. https://doi.org/10.1080/13670050.2011.573062

Polanco, P., & Luft de Baker, D. (2018). Transitional bilingual education and two-way immersion programs: Comparison of reading outcomes for English learners in the United States. *Athens Journal of Education*, *5*(4), 423–444. https://doi.org/10.30958/aje.5-4-5

Rosa, J. D. (2016). Standardization, racialization, languagelessness: Raciolinguistic ideologies across communicative contexts. *Journal of Linguistic Anthropology*, *24*. https://doi.org/10.1111/jola.12116

Scanlan, M. (2011). How school leaders can accent inclusion for bilingual students, families, and communities. *Multicultural Education*, *18*(2), 5–9.

Somers, T. (2017). Content and language integrated learning and the inclusion of immigrant minority language students: A research review. *International Review of Education*, *63*, 495–520. https://doi.org/10.1007/s11159-017-9651-4

Truth and Healing Commission on Indian Boarding School Policies Act, KAT21A37 111, 111th Cong. (2011). https://www.warren.senate.gov/imo/media/doc/Truth%20and%20Healing%20Commission_9.30.21_FINAL.pdf

Tsokalidou, R. (2015). Bilingualism otherwise: Research approaches towards language contact issues and inclusion of bilingual children in the Greek school. In E. Tressou, S. Mitakidou, & P. Karagianni (Eds.), *Roma inclusion-international and Greek experiences. Complexities of inclusion* (pp. 164–177). Copy City.

U.S. Department of Education. (2019). *IDEA section 618 data products: Static tables*. https://www2.ed.gov/programs/osepidea/618-data/static-tables/index.html

UnidosUS. (2021). *English learners with disabilities are excluded from the learning programs that could help them most* [Progress report: Defending equal access to quality education]. https://www.unidosus.org/progress-report/english-learners-with-disabilities-excluded-from-learning-programs/

Valentine, D. (2022). Racialized disablement and the need for conceptual analysis of "racial health disparities." *Bioethics*, *36*(3), 336–345. https://doi.org/10.1111/bioe.12979

Vaughan, M. (2010). An index for inclusion. *European Journal of Special Needs Education*, *17*(2), 197–201. https://doi.org/10.1080/08856250210139316

Wright, P. W. D., & Wright, P. D. (2016). History of special education law. In P. W. D. Wright, & P. D. Wright (Eds.), *Wrightslaw: Special education law* (2nd ed., pp. 11–16). Harbor House Law Press.

Yağmur, K., & Extra, G. (2011). Urban multilingualism in Europe: Educational responses to increasing diversity. *Journal of Pragmatics*, *43*(5), 1185–1194.

Zentella, A. C. (2005). *Building on strength: Language and literacy in Latino families and communities*. Teachers College Press/California Association for Bilingual Education.

17

DUAL LANGUAGE DEAF EDUCATION

Shifting to Multilingual Multimodal Concepts

Patrick Graham, Christopher Kurz

Brief History of Dual Language Deaf Education

Dual language[1] Deaf education in the United States received its formal beginning in the early 19th century, especially when Lydia Huntley started to teach Alice Cogswell in her mainstreamed classroom using written and signed languages (Sayers & Gates, 2008) and Thomas H. Gallaudet, an American clergyman, brought Laurent Clerc, a Deaf French teacher at the National School in Paris, to the United States in 1816, in hopes of teaching deaf children how to read, write, and communicate (Greenwald, 2021). At the time, the National School, founded by Charles-Michel Abbé de l'Epée in 1760, promoted the use of dual language in the classrooms where students learned Old French Sign Language and written French.

The American School for the Deaf (ASD) opened on April 15, 1817. Clerc and Gallaudet adopted the National School policy for instruction, which emphasized the importance of using sign language and written language as the dual language of instruction. The policy allowed teachers and students to use American Sign Language (ASL) and written English in their classroom to discuss subjects such as mathematics, science, and English. ASL is a creolized language imported and developed from different sign languages (i.e., imported Old French Sign Language, British Sign Language, Native ASLs, Martha's Vineyard Sign Language, Maritime Sign Language, and local and home signs) (Kurz et al., 2021; Power, 2022). By 1850, more than 15 new schools for the deaf employed ASL and English as the dual languages of pedagogy. Within 50 years of the ASD founding, a national college for the deaf was established to serve Deaf students who wished to pursue higher education as they were turned away from hearing colleges in the country

DOI: 10.4324/9781003269076-25

(Greenwald, 2021). The college followed the dual language model where their students used ASL and English in the classroom.

Since the beginning of deaf education, there have been debates among professionals who worked with deaf and hard of hearing (DHH) children on languages and modalities for teaching DHH children (Greenwald, 2021). The 1880 International Congress for Education of the Deaf in Milan, Italy passed resolutions that spoken communication should be the primary approach in teaching DHH children and sign language was banned from the classroom (Leeson & van den Bogaerde, 2020). This gradually led to a monolingual approach in academic buildings, which impacted deaf education in the United States for many years. Sign language, however, was maintained in segregated schools for the deaf, dormitories, and vocational buildings where deaf teachers were reassigned to teach and those students who did not do well in oral classrooms were placed. It was not until a decade after the 1954 Brown v. Board of Education case decision for racial desegregation that the U.S. Congress commissioned a national report on deaf education (now known as the Babbidge Report), that called for the inclusion of signs in the academic classroom (Babbidge, 1965).

Coupled with the publication on sign language structure and dictionary in the early 1960s, ASL was gradually accepted by the public as a language that had its own syntax and linguistic structure, although deaf professionals have described sign languages through the linguistics lens since the beginning of deaf education (see Barnard, 1835 for example). Numerous studies have been undertaken in the field of sign language research that continue to provide empirical evidence of ASL, and its varieties and dialects, including Black ASL (see McCaskill et al., 2011) and Plains Indian Sign Languages (see Davis & McKay-Cody, 2010). Since then, dialogue surrounding dual language programming for DHH children gradually increased.

The past five decades have seen the emergence of modern dual language programming for deaf children and its evolution to include multilingual and multicultural perspectives in the United States and around the world. Research showed the effectiveness of bilingual education in Scandinavian countries (Mahshie, 1995) and that the instruction based only in English has miserably failed deaf students (Drawgow, 1993; Johnson et al., 1989). Moving the blame away from DHH students and their parents, educators began to develop programs that reflected six core principles that unlock the accessibility to the curriculum for DHH children, and they include the need for awareness and acceptance of ASL and Deaf culture as a deaf identity, early use of ASL and access to literacy, use of ASL as a language of instruction, inclusion of Deaf role models in providing natural linguistic experiences, dual language competencies and high expectations of qualified teachers, and the need for parental support, especially when adjusting to different modalities (Johnson et al., 1989).

In 1974, Barbara Kannapell proposed a new direction in deaf education that ASL should be used in the classroom as the first language of DHH children and English as a second language. In the same vein, the Center for ASL/English Bilingual Education Resource (CAEBER) advocated for the utilization of both ASL and English models in the classroom, centering on two principles:

1 Deaf bilingual students are given equal opportunity to learn the same challenging content and acquire skill levels that are recommended for all students.
2 Proficiency in American Sign Language (ASL) and English is promoted for all deaf students because bilingualism enhances cognitive, social, and linguistic growth, as well as our understanding of diverse multicultural groups in the Deaf and Hearing cultures (Nover et al., 2002).

One major discussion related to dual language programming for DHH students was time allocation for instruction in each language (Nover et al., 2002). While there were varying dual language approaches that were implemented during the time, the popular approach was that DHH youngest learners (ages 0–5) start in full ASL immersive environments where they would be exposed to signing models/teachers on a daily basis to build background knowledge, and then gradually introduced to English with ASL support. Fingerspelling, sandwiching (signing, fingerspelling), and chaining (signing, fingerspelling, drawing, reading) are a few methods of associating ASL concepts and English concepts. Eventually, the learners are provided opportunities to integrate language and content instruction in both languages. In the past few years, the concept of lesson time allocation for using dual language has been gradually deemphasized as we shift to focus more on embracing learners' language uses and preferences to express their understanding clearly during lessons (Henner & Robinson, 2021).

While each state has its own Preschool to 12 English Language Arts learning standards, deaf education often needs to modify these standards and lessons to focus on dual language instruction to teach ELA concepts. Many ELA learning standards are developed without any considerations of bilingualism where students use two languages on a daily basis. The K-12 ASL Content Standards for DHH students were developed and adopted by many schools for the deaf in the past decade, and as of this writing, no empirical research was published related to DHH students and their ASL standards. As of this writing, there is no other standard for DHH students to learn their sign language in other countries.

Main Findings on Dual Language Deaf Education

Since this time, there has been extensive research on different learning impacts of bilingual education for DHH children, research has focused on linguistic acquisition, bilingualism, cultural outcomes as well as pedagogical strategies. Multilingual deaf education is defined as the practice of using two or more languages as the primary languages of curriculum, instruction, and assessment (Valdés, Poza, & Brooks, 2015). Kurz et al. (2021) define dual language modalities as the channels by which communication happens. These channels can be visual/manual, auditory/oral, and tactile, among others. Not all modalities are linguistic, they can be expressed through different mediums (e.g., arts, kinesthetics, visuals, and interactions). Consideration should include the concept of a semiotic repertoire as explained by Kusters et al. (2017), wherein people combine multiple modalities for the purpose of ensuring positive communication environments with a variety of language-support partners.

Language Acquisition and Development

Deaf children have capabilities to acquire and develop two or more languages as evidenced in studies involving Deaf children of signing Deaf parents (Geeslin, 2007) and recent brain studies (Goodwin et al., 2021). If with the right conditions, Deaf children follow similar language milestones as their hearing peers (Graham & Shuler-Krause, 2020; Lange et al., 2013). Deaf children of signing Deaf parents are likely to meet the milestones as expected as they have continual access to languages at an early age, although they are learning two languages at the same time (Clark et al., 2020; Spellun et al., 2022). They arrive at Kindergarten ready to learn as they have background knowledge, language foundations, and social interaction skills (Clark et al., 2020; Meinzen-Derr et al., 2020). With the knowledge and skills, they are able to learn advanced concepts without difficulties, including processes involving theory of mind concepts (see Courtin, 2010).

Without continual exposure to any type of language in early childhood years, deaf students arrive at school without being prepared to learn (Krizter, 2009). Some of them are language deprived as they did not have an opportunity to develop language and build background knowledge (Gulati, 2018; Hall, 2017). For those students, it would mean they have to learn new languages and, at the same time, the curriculum while they catch up with filling up the knowledge gap. This can impact both academic and social skills. It is important to encourage development of a natural visual language as the first language to support the second language (Hall et al., 2019; Humphries et al., 2014).

Empirical studies on dual education of DHH students in Scandinavian countries (i.e., Norway, Sweden, and Denmark) show positive literacy development in DHH students (Bagga-Gupta, 2004; Svartholm, 2010; Swanwick et al., 2014). Studies also show that adding sign language and Deaf teachers to the classroom does not adversely affect literacy development in DHH students in Hong Kong (Wong et al., 2021).

Additionally, studies have shown the relationship between bilingual pedagogies and academic growth. There is a key longitudinal study that involves reading and mathematics achievement growth over a number of years. Lange et al. (2013) examined reading and mathematics academic growth of DHH students in a school for the deaf that consistently follows an ASL-English bilingual model. Their longitudinal study findings showed the gradual increase of academic scores as measured using the Northwest Evaluation Association's Measure of Academic Progress (NWEA) assessment and compared with a normed group of grade-level hearing students was initially slower in the early grades, and after a period time, the scores eventually picked up and the DHH students outperformed the comparison group of hearing students in the later grades. In the study, DHH students picked up the growth pace in mathematics earlier than reading, which indicates that it takes time to learn a new language, and they still outperformed the comparison group. This longitudinal study is critical in that it shows consistent dual language planning takes time to show its significant impact on student learning.

When looking at dual language programs in deaf education, we need to reframe these programs as multilingual, multimodal, and multicultural. Their use of their home languages should be honored in schools (Musyoka & Adeoye, 2020). Educational professionals in multilingual Deaf education programs should be expected to have language fluency, and techniques and tools to tap the diverse languages, cultures, resources, and creativity of Deaf communities and Deaf students, in order to support learning in the classroom. School language planning policy for Deaf students should embrace multilingual, multimodal, and multicultural approaches to foster cognitive, social, and linguistic growth in Deaf children. There is still much work to be done in developing teaching strategies to support dual language deaf learners in the classroom, especially when it comes to pragmatic and social language.

Bilingual Pedagogies

There are different pedagogical strategies available to teachers in classrooms, but not many of them are visually or culturally appropriate for DHH students. These strategies include chaining, sandwiching, and codeswitching. Teachers can use these strategies to help bridge the two languages and create a full concept of the topic at hand. Sandwiching is one of the most used strategies in deaf education classrooms. When teachers try to define the word, they would first sign the word, then fingerspell the English word, and then show the sign again (Quinto-Pozos & Reynolds, 2012). For example, the person would sign the word "WITH" and then fingerspell W-I-T-H and then follow the fingerspelled English word with the ASL sign again. This allows the student to see the difference between ASL and English and shows them what the word may look like in print.

The other approach is "chaining," in which the teacher may point at the word, then give the sign for the word, and then fingerspell the word (Swanwick, 2016a). This will support the reading process for the student and create connections between the multiple modalities (e.g., signed, fingerspelled, print, and drawing). Chaining can also be used to teach spoken language, in which the teacher may sign the word, then show the word in spoken language, and then fingerspell the word. There are multiple ways to show sandwiching and chaining, but the emphasis remains the same, to have the student associate new words and concepts in both languages.

Codeswitching is the other bilingual strategy in which the teacher can go from one language to another language to support the student's acquisition of knowledge. Andrews and Rusher (2010) define "codeswitching from a sociolinguistic perspective is the switching or changing from one language to another" (p. 411). Teachers and their Deaf students use all of the languages in their linguistic repertoire to advance or develop literacy (Swanwick, 2016b). For example, Black Deaf students in the United States may navigate between Black ASL and English to communicate ideas. Smith and Ramsey (2004) found that deaf teachers use codeswitching practices, including chaining and sandwiching, more than hearing teachers in the classroom. There needs to be more research in this area for deaf students in using dual languages in the classroom to develop literacy skills.

Conclusion and Redefining Dual Language in Deaf Education

Bimodal bilingual learning for deaf children certainly involves different linguistic, cognitive, and social factors (Kannapell, 1974; Swanwick, 2016a). As discussed in this chapter, we see a gradually growing number of empirical studies in dual education for DHH children. While it is important to include epistemological studies of deaf people about the way of knowing and navigation in the world, we need careful attention to include diverse individuals and school variables in future empirical studies, such as best practices of caregivers' partnership and involvement in supporting multilingual, multimodal, and multicultural education of DHH students. We acknowledge that there are multiple variables that affect the impact of dual language instruction on deaf children's academic learning, socio-emotional learning, and skills learning. While quantitative empirical studies often ask for comparisons between groups, they can mislead the public about deaf students' learning capabilities when compared to their hearing peer group (Scott et al., 2021). Since Deaf students come to schools from homes that use languages other than ASL and English (e.g., BASL, Spanish), we encourage more future in-depth studies on multilingual, multicultural, and multimodal instruction in dual language deaf education, especially their impact on deaf children's cognitive processes and knowledge, social and personal identities, and language fluency.

It is also important to note that teacher preparation and instructional practices in dual language education should be examined to determine best practices in supporting DHH students.

Note

1 Dual Program Deaf Education is defined as a form of multilingual education in which DHH students are taught literacy and content in two languages (i.e., American Sign Language and English). We acknowledge there are other languages that are included and used in deaf education, such as Black American Sign Language, Plains Indian Sign Language, Pro-Tactile Sign Language, Mexican Sign Language, or any other sign languages that are used primarily at DHH students' homes and communities. The current deaf education has language development standards for English language and American Sign Language.

References

Andrews, J. F., & Rusher, M. (2010). Codeswitching techniques: Evidence-based instructional practices for the ASL/English bilingual classroom. *American Annals of the Deaf, 155*(4), 407–424.

Babbidge, H. (1965). *Education of the deaf in the United States: Report of the advisory committee on education of the deaf*. U.S. Government Printing Office.

Bagga-Gupta, S. (2004). *Literacies and deaf education: A theoretical analysis of the international and Swedish literature*. Myndigheten för skolutveckling.

Barnard, F. A. P. (1835). Existing state of the art of instructing the deaf and dumb. *Literary and Theological Review*, 2(7), 367–398.

Clark, M. D., Baker, S., & Simms, L. (2020). A culture of assessment: A bioecological systems approach for early and continuous assessment of deaf infants and children. *Psychology in the Schools, 57*(3), 443–458.

Courtin, C. (2010). A critical period for the acquisition of a theory of mind. In G. Mather, & D. Napoli (Eds.), *Deaf around the World* (pp. 184–193). Oxford University Press.

Davis, J. E., & McKay-Cody, M. (2010). Signed languages of American Indian communities: Considerations for interpreting work and research. In R. L. McKee, & J. E. Davis (Eds.), *Interpreting in Multilingual, Multicultural Contexts* (pp. 119–157). Gallaudet University Press.

Drasgow, E. (1993). Bilingual/bicultural deaf education: An overview. *Sign Language Studies, 80*(1), 243–266.

Geeslin, J. D. III (2007). Deaf bilingual education: A comparison of the academic performance of deaf children of deaf parents and deaf children of hearing parents [Doctoral dissertation, Indiana University].

Goodwin, C., Carrigan, E., Walker, K., & Coppola, M. (2021). Language not auditory experience is related to parent-reported executive functioning in preschool-aged deaf and hard-of-hearing children. *Child Development*. https://doi.org/10.1111/cdev.13677

Graham, P. J., & Shuler-Krause, E. (2020). Building strong foundations for educational achievement: Language assessments in early childhood education for deaf and hard of hearing children. *Psychology in the Schools, 57*(3), 418–425.

Greenwald, B. H. (2021). Two centuries of deaf education and deaf agency in the United States. In C. Enns, J. Henner, & M. McQuiarrie (Eds.), *Discussing bilingualism in deaf children: Essays in honor of Robert Hoffmeister* (pp. 3–16). Routledge.

Gulati, S. (2018). Language deprivation syndrome. In N. S. Glickman, & W. C. Hall (Eds.), *Language deprivation and deaf mental health* (pp. 24–53). Routledge.

Hall, W. C. (2017). What you don't know can hurt you: The risk of language deprivation by impairing sign language development in deaf children. *Maternal and Child Health Journal*, *21*(5), 961–965.

Hall, M. L., Hall, W. C., & Caselli, N. K. (2019). Deaf children need language, not (just) speech. *First Language*, *39*(4), 367–395.

Henner, J., & Robinson, O. (2021). *Unsettling languages, unruly bodyminds: Imaging a crip linguistics*. https://psyarxiv.com/7bzaw

Humphries, T., Kushalnagar, P., Mathur, G., Napoli, D. J., Padden, C., Pollard, R., Rathmann, C., & Smith, S. (2014). What medical education can do to ensure robust language development in deaf children. *Medical Science Educator*, *24*(4), 409–419.

Johnson, R., Liddell, S., & Erting, C. (1989). *Unlocking the curriculum: Principles for achieving access in deaf education.* Gallaudet Research Institute Working Paper No. 89–3.

Kannapell, B. (1974). Bilingual education: A new direction in the education of the deaf. *The Deaf American*, *26*(10), 9–15.

Kritzer, K. L. (2009). Barely started and already left behind: A descriptive analysis of the mathematics ability demonstrated by young deaf children. *Journal of Deaf Studies and Deaf Education*, *14*(4), 409–421.

A. Kusters, M. De Meulder, & D. O'Brien (Eds.). (2017). Innovations in deaf studies: Critically mapping the field. *Innovations in deaf studies: The role of deaf scholars* (pp. 1–53). Oxford University Press.

Kurz, C., Golos, D., Kuntze, M., Henner, J., & Scott, J. (2021). *Guidelines for multilingual deaf education teacher preparation programs*. Gallaudet University Press.

Lange, C. M., Lane-Outlaw, S., Lange, W. E., & Sherwood, D. L. (2013). American Sign Language/English bilingual model: A longitudinal study of academic growth. *Journal of Deaf Studies and Deaf Education*, *18*(4), 532–544.

Leeson, L., & van den Bogaerde, B. (2020). (What we don't know about) Sign languages in higher education in Europe: Mapping policy and practice to an analytical framework. *Sociolinguistica*, *34*(1), 31–56.

Mahshie, S. N. (1995). *Educating deaf children bilingually: With insights and applications from Sweden and Denmark*. Harris Communication.

McCaskill, C., Lucas, C., Bayley, R., & Hill, J. (2011). *The hidden treasure of Black ASL: Its history and structure*. Gallaudet University Press.

Meinzen-Derr, J., Wiley, S., Grove, W., Altaye, M., Gaffney, M., Satterfield-Nash, A., … & Boyle, C. (2020). Kindergarten readiness in children who are deaf or hard of hearing who received early intervention. *Pediatrics*, *146*(4), 1–9.

Musyoka, M. M., & Adeoye, S. O. (2021). Designing an inclusive culturally competent classroom for immigrant deaf students in the United States. In K. Sprott, J. O'Connor Jr., & C. Msengi (Eds.), *Designing culturally competent Programming for PK-20 classrooms* (pp. 180–197). IGI Global.

Nover, S. M., Andrews, J. F., Everhart, V. S., & Bradford, M. (2002). *Star Schools' USDLC Engaged Learning Project No. 5 ASL/English bilingual staff development project in Deaf Education Staff Development in ASL/English Bilingual Instruction for Deaf Students: Evaluation and impact study*. New Mexico School for the Deaf, 1997–2002.

Power, J. M. (2022) Historical linguistics of sign languages: Progress and problems. *Frontiers in Psychology*, *13*, 818753. https://doi.org/10.3389/fpsyg.2022.818753

Quinto-Pozos, D., & Reynolds, W. (2012). ASL discourse strategies: Chaining and connecting-explaining across audiences. *Sign Language Studies*, *12*(2), 211–235.

Sayers, E. E., & Gates, D. (2008). Lydia Huntley Sigourney and the beginnings of American deaf education in Hartford: It takes a village. *Sign Language Studies*, *8*(4), 369–411.

Scott, J. A., Dostal, H. M., & Lane-Outlaw, S. (2021). A call for a diversity of perspectives in deaf education research: A response to Mayer and Trezek (2020). *American Annals of the Deaf*, *166*(1), 49–61.

Smith, D. H., & Ramsey, C. L. (2004). Classroom discourse practices of a deaf teacher using American Sign Language. *Sign Language Studies*, *5*(1), 39–62.

Spellun, A., Shearer, E., Fitzpatrick, K., Salamy, N., Landsman, R., Wiley, S., & Augustyn, M. (2022). The importance of accessible language for development in deaf and Hard of hearing children. *Journal of Developmental & Behavioral Pediatrics*, *43*(4), 240–244.

Svartholm, K. (2010). Bilingual education for deaf children in Sweden. *International Journal of Bilingual Education and Bilingualism*, *13*(2), 159–174.

Swanwick, R. (2016a). Deaf children's bimodal bilingualism and education. *Language Teaching*, *49*(1), 1–34.

Swanwick, R. (2016b) Scaffolding learning through classroom talk: The role of translanguaging. In: M Marschark, and P.E. Spencer (Eds.), *The Oxford handbook of deaf studies in language*. Oxford University Press.

Swanwick, R., Hendar, O., Dammeyer, J., Kristoffersen, A. E., Salter, J., & Simonsen, E. (2014). Shifting contexts and practices in sign bilingual education in northern Europe. M. Marschark, G. Tang, & H. Knoors (Eds.), *Bilingualism and bilingual deaf education* (pp. 292–310). Oxford University Press.

Valdés, G., Poza, L., & Brooks, M. D. (2015). Language acquisition in bilingual education. W. E. Wright, S. Boun, & O. García (Eds.), *The handbook of bilingual and multilingual education* (pp. 56–74). John Wiley & Sons, Inc.

Wong, F., Tang, G., Li, Q., & Yiu, C. K. M. (2021). Literacy learning of deaf and hearing preschoolers in a sign bilingual, coenrollment setting in Hong Kong. *American Annals of the Deaf*, *166*(4), 527–553.

18

K-12 SCHOOL FUNDING, DUAL LANGUAGE/ BILINGUAL EDUCATION

An Overview

Oscar Jimenez-Castellanos, Irina Okhremtchouk

Introduction

In this chapter, we focus on the topic of K-12 funding related to dual language and bilingual education (DLBE). This area has been insufficiently researched thus far yet we believe that funding is fundamental to accomplishing any goals set out by bilingual advocates and educators. Through this contribution to the handbook, we provide an overview of salient issues in school finance concerning bilingual/dual language programs and the different roles federal, state, and local agencies play in funding English language learner (ELL) services and programs.

As we begin this discussion, it is important to remember that ELLs and language minority student population as a whole is the fastest growing segment of the K-12 demographic (USDE, 2020). However, these students also represent one of the most neglected populations within the system (Poza et al., 2021). Despite the many efforts to address the needs of language minority and ELL students, there has been meager progress toward closing the many equity gaps that currently exist between ELLs and their English-only counterparts (Gándara, 2018).

Additionally, we are living in a moment where bilingual education is making somewhat of a resurgence, and dual language programs continue to increase across the nation; albeit primarily in middle-class neighborhoods (Valdez et al., 2016). Interestingly, this development coincides with ELL students most of whom are not enrolled in a bilingual or dual language program, and at a time for increased calls for funding in K-12 education momentarily ameliorated through stimulus federal funding during the COVID pandemic.

 DOI: 10.4324/9781003269076-26

Origins and Evolution of Federal Funding for Dual Language/Bilingual Education

It is important to acknowledge that the United States has had tensions with language rights and language identity since its inception (Crawford, 1995). While language rights were granted to some, others have been excluded. More specifically, the privilege of maintaining heritage language, just like anything else, was afforded to the White English-speaking majority. The same rights were not extended to non-English speaking or multi-lingual communities. Instead, acculturation into a mainstream dominant culture and the English language were imposed (Wiley, 2004). As a consequence, the language rights struggle we see today is not a new phenomenon but rather a carryover from our country's xenophobic past.

Bilingualism and bilingual education were not institutionalized on the federal level until the National Defense Act of 1958 which funded the teaching and learning of foreign languages to support the nation's geopolitical agenda around at the time perceived national defense needs. The 1968 Title VII–Bilingual Education Act (BEA) in the Elementary and Secondary Education Act of 1965 for the first time established federal funds earmarked to fund programs serving language minority students in K-12.

Initially, Title VII provided only 7.5 million in supplemental funds to support 76 programs across the nation during the initial year. The funding encouraged instruction in the English language and multicultural awareness not bilingual programs (Hakuta, 2011). While the BEA did not explicitly mandate bilingual education, it did provide an opportunity for the nation's school districts to use the federal funds to develop bilingual programs. Therefore, the federal government's official policy supported a transitional bilingual education model instead of a maintenance model. Notably, the passing of Title VII enabled several states to pass their own bilingual education acts to provide additional state funding and support for bilingual education and/or students learning English as a second language (Jiménez-Castellanos, 2010a, 2010b).

It was not until after the U.S. Supreme Court *Lau v. Nichols* (1974) ruling, which stated that language was a fundamental right and that schools needed to address the language needs of language minority children, did the monetary support for bilingual education began to increase. Then *Castañeda* (1981), a federal fifth circuit court of appeals ruling, provided several general guidelines for bilingual education programs. Importantly, *Castañeda* established a three-prong test for a bilingual program: Unfortunately, states and districts were never able to implement an effective bilingual program as outlined by *Castañeda* due to many reasons, including the lack of necessary resources (Jiménez-Castellanos et al., 2022).

Starting in 1981, Reagan federalism gave the states more powers, therefore curtailing any national movement for expanding bilingual education and other federal programs. However, a significant change occurred in 2001 with the authorization of the No Child Left Behind Act that replaced Title VII Bilingual Education Act with Title III—Office of English Language Acquisition promoting English learning instead of any bilingual approach to serve language minority students; thus, implicitly circumscribing federal funding designated for bilingual education that includes primary language instruction in the heritage language. The Every Student Succeeds Act (ESSA) has continued a similar policy toward Bilingual/Dual Language Education but has opened up more grant opportunities to support Dual Language programs and teacher professional development.

State Funding: Different Funding Approaches

Different funding approaches inevitably impact and, at times, disrupt equitable implementation of DBLE programs. Since ELL students are often on the receiving end of DBLE education, understanding constitutional and legal obligations of funding practices across states as these relate to funding ELL students is a good place to start. The *Serrano* (1971) and *Rodriguez* (1973) school finance cases challenged both the federal and state constitutions' obligation to fund public schools regardless of the property wealth of the school district (Kiracofe & Weiler, in press). Ultimately, this federal argument was denied in the *Rodriguez* case in a 5-4 U.S. Supreme Court decision. Thus, it is the responsibility and obligation of the state to provide and fund their K-12 education system. Still the *Serrano* case became the first successful school finance litigation against an individual state (i.e., California). Since then, over 40 states have faced lawsuits for unconstitutional state funding mechanisms with the majority ruling in favor of the plaintiffs (Rebell, 2022). In addition, individual states began to provide additional funds for special populations, ELLs included (Jiménez-Castellanos et al., 2021). As of 2021, 48 out of the 50 states provide some additional funding for ELLs. The only two states that do not provide supplemental funding for ELLs are Mississippi and Montana (Education Commission of the States [ECS], October 2021).

There are four primary mechanisms that ELLs are funded. First, most states provide funding through the state funding formula or categorical programs. About half of states in this category provide a flat weight—either an additional percentage or flat dollar amount—for each identified student, regardless of their level of language proficiency or the types of services offered. The second most common approach is a multiple weight system, which allocates funding based on the amount of time spent in ELL classification, based on proficiency levels, or based on the concentration of ELLs in a district. The third and a much less popular approach is a resource-based allocation, which allocates funding based on specific resources provided to ELLs. This approach used in only a handful of states, e.g., Washington, Virginia,

Tennessee, Wyoming, and Illinois. The fourth approach is a reimbursement. This approach is used by only one state, Wisconsin, which reimburses districts for all or a portion of their spending once costs are accrued (ECS, October 2021).

The vast majority of the above-mentioned state funding mechanisms are structured to allocate funds per pupil and not on the basis of funding a specific program. Thus, the ELL student and not a specific bilingual program generates the additional funding in most cases. Additionally, these supplemental resources vary considerably across the nation's states (Verstegen, 2011). From states not providing ELL supplemental resources (Montana and Mississippi) to meager weights (e.g., Utah's weight of .025 per ELL among other states providing a weight of .10 or below) to states assigning weights between .20 and .50, which is the majority of states, all the way to doubling the amount of supplemental funding per ELL (New York, Georgia, and Maryland) (ESC, October 2021).

Notwithstanding, there are only five states that specifically allocate funds in their state-funding mechanism for bilingual and/or dual language programs (Connecticut, Texas, Washington, Indiana, and New Mexico) (ECS, October 2021). Albeit, each of the three states funds their bilingual program differently as shown below.

Connecticut

Uses a hybrid model. First, an additional flat weight of .25 is applied to the number of ELL pupils. Second, a categorical state grant of $1.9 million (2021–2022) for bilingual education. The amount is subject to state legislative approval on a yearly basis. Connecticut does not specify a particular type of bilingual education.

Texas

Uses a multiple student weights approach. The first weight is .10 for a student of limited English proficiency. The second weight of .15 for students of limited English proficiency in bilingual education program using a dual language immersion. The third weight of .05 for any other student using a dual language immersion. This is the only funding mechanism that explicitly targets dual language programs yet the additional allocation is extremely low.

Washington

Uses a resource-based allocation approach. It allocates additional funds based on the number of enrolled students in transitional bilingual programs. The additional funding is required to cover an extra 4.7780 hours of instruction per week for students in grades K-6, and an extra 6.7780 hours of extra instruction per week for students in grades 7–12. Thus, providing funding for a ratio of 15 transitional bilingual instruction program students per teacher. It is unclear if another type of bilingual model, such as a dual language program, would receive funding given that a transitional bilingual program is highlighted in their formula.

Indiana

Bilingual-bicultural programs are funded by categorical grants with a set annual amount capped at $300 per pupil in 2021–2022 academic school year. The funding distribution is not automatically generated and requires district application to receive funds. In 2021–2022, 27.5 million were available to fund such programs.

New Mexico

Similar to Texas, New Mexico uses weights to fund Bilingual Multicultural Education Programs Units across state's districts. However, unlike Texas where multiple student weights are employed, New Mexico's allocations are based on the flat weight approach of an additional .50 per pupil.

Further, several states are prioritizing the development of dual language programs; however, such programmatic developments appear to focus on predominantly English-only speakers. To this end, Boyle et al. (2015) found that "six states—Delaware, Georgia, Indiana, Kentucky, Oregon, and Utah—offered funds specifically to support the development of dual language programs. In these states, the funds tend to be administered through the world languages office, rather than a state EL/bilingual education or Title III office, and they tend to be used for one-way foreign language programs (for predominantly English speakers) and two-way dual language programs" (p. 90). The amounts ranged across states from $10,000 per school to $100,000 per school.

Inadequate State Funding

Despite the efforts, the literature shows that states are not adequately funding ELL students to support grade-level attainment (Boyle et al., 2015; Gándara & Rumberger, 2008) and, by default, are not prioritizing ELLs' needs through programs such as DLBE. In fact, often funding is based more on political and budgetary considerations than based on the actual costs needed (Baker, 2003); this includes funding bilingual/dual language education or supporting ELL students to meet state standards. Put differently, the funding allocated to serve ELLs in bilingual programs or other programs is not based on the empirical evidence from a cost study, but instead on legislatively predetermined revenue and political negotiations.

Costing out studies is a useful tool to determine the true cost of education. These studies are utilized by researchers, state legislators, and the courts to determine the base cost and marginal costs of providing an adequate education to the general public-school population (Odden & Picus, 2019). However, the current costing out literature is scarce, in considering the needs of ELLs. For example, Jiménez-Castellanos and Topper (2012) conducted a thorough review of the ELL cost study literature. Of the 70 empirical studies reviewed, only 4 focused specifically on ELLs. This review provides an insight into the ways in which ELL students are considered—or not considered—in costing out studies. Although each of the costing out methodologies accounted for ELLs in some way, the level of consideration and detail varied substantially across methodologies. In addition, there are several important patterns evident in the cost study literature:

1 States are not allocating sufficient funds to adequately educate the general K–12 population,
2 ELLs are inconsistently addressed across the cost study literature, and
3 Current costing out methods need to be adapted to better account for the diverse and complex needs of the ELL student population.

The four costing out studies with a specific focus on ELLs include as follows: (1) Arizona Department of Education (2001); (2) Gándara and Rumberger (2008); (3) Multicultural Education Training and Advocacy, Inc. (META) (2008); (4) National Conference of State Legislatures (2005). The two, one conducted in California (Gándara & Rumberger, 2008) and the second conducted in New York (META, 2008), serve as better examples of how costing out studies could be modified to focus on the programmatic needs of ELL students in particular because they do begin to discuss issues of bilingual programs, including dual language programs albeit without enough details or nuance.

Together, these studies can serve as essential references in developing a framework for future cost studies and, more importantly, how much it takes to address ELLs' needs adequately through dual language programs. Given that language minority students are the fastest growing school-age population in the nation, the states would benefit from refining their resource estimates for this segment of the student population in dual language programs.

District and School Level Supplemental Funding

One of the central aims of K-12 supplemental programs is to maximize students' potential for success. Therefore, the intent behind supplemental funds, at least in theory, is to provide services and programs that are designed to address the needs of otherwise underrepresented and marginalized students (Okhremtchouk, 2017). As mentioned earlier in this chapter, the passage of key federal and state legislation since 1968 as well as the case law that followed helped secure funding streams for language minority and ELL students. However, the impact on ELLs' educational and life trajectories has not improved much despite supplemental programs securing extra funds for earmarked services.

To this end, reports consistently reflect that ELLs often receive a lower quality education than their English-only counterparts (Gándara & Rumberger, 2008; Jiménez-Castellanos & Okhremtchouk, 2013). Furthermore, these students continue to be burdened with high-stakes tests and subjected to culturally deficient curricula and, more often than not, do not have access to primary language supports or qualified teachers skilled in addressing these students' needs (Abedi, 2008; Okhremtchouk & Sellu, 2019). Therefore, and as evident, the educational system continues to fail this student population. In the following sections, we attempt to address many layers of the system's role in influencing supplemental services and programs for ELLs.

The Role of Home Language Survey and Classification in Funding

Irrespective of placement, e.g., mainstream, English Language Development, or Dual Language/Bilingual programs, all language minority students are first subjected to an identification process. Likewise, the *initial trigger* for supplemental funding of any type is student identification by means of the Home Language Survey (HLS)—an instrument widely used across the nation's public-school districts in all 50 states (Salerno & Andrei, 2021). The use of the HLS is also widely criticized as a poor substitute for other, more accurate measures of determining proficiency in the English language (Bailey & Carroll, 2015). Nonetheless, the HLS serves as the first point of contact between parents and schools. The HLS exclusively relies on the parental self-report data at the time of student enrollment. If a parent indicates a language other than English, a child is subjected to identification processes through standardized assessment and/or teacher evaluation and later classification. After standardized language testing is administered, the process leads to one of two classifications. A student is either classified[1] ELL group becomes entitled to supplemental services and, by default, ELL classification serves as a trigger to initiate supplemental funding since ELL funding is typically allocated based on enrollment (Okhremtchouk, 2011).

Identification, classification, and reclassification practices for language minority students are key levers that directly influence supplemental funding generated for ELLs based on a state's per pupil allocation and, therefore, directly impact students' access to supplemental programs, including that of Dual Language/Bilingual programs. These classification/reclassification practices are complicated and flawed due to many contributing factors, such as parental self-reported data on HLS, a lack of consistent data across school districts, the absence of uniform classification criteria, student mobility, among other issues (see Okhremtchouk, 2014; Okhremtchouk et al., 2018). As a result, nation's school districts vary considerably with respect to whom they consider ELL and how well they identify and monitor ELLs. That is, in some districts, a student may be identified as ELL and in other districts, the same student may not be due to a lack of uniform criteria for classification or a district's capacity to monitor, or a combination of these two factors. Over-reporting or underreporting the number of ELLs affects how much money districts receive to serve this group of students (Tanenbaum et al., 2012) and certainly adds to the variation in funding across districts to address ELL students' needs through programs such as DLBE (Okhremtchouk, 2011; Tanenbaum et al., 2012).

The Use of Federal, State, and Local Funds

In this section, we focus on four salient issues regarding how federal, state, and local funds are used that merit some discussion (Jiménez-Castellanos, 2017). First, the current levels of supplemental funding are insufficient to fund programs and services for ELLs, federal funds in particular. Second, there is a pervasive deficit thinking mentality in how funds are used to serve ELLs. Third, there is a lack of transparency and accountability in how funds are used within a district. And fourth, supplemental ELL funds are frequently misused and used in ineffective ways.

The federal government plays an important yet limited role in education. For the vast majority of the nation's school districts, federal dollars represent less than 12% (roughly 8.3% on average) of their total revenue (U.S. Department of Education, 2014). And, most of the federal allocation is earmarked for low-income students, where Title III funds (ELL dollars) are just a small fraction of federal allotment. Title III appropriations have not changed significantly nor adjusted for inflation since the passage of NCLB in 2002 (Williams, 2020). While the ELL population continues to grow rapidly across the nation, the Title III appropriations have increased slightly in total appropriations from 664 million in 2002 to 737 million in 2020 (Williams, 2020). Currently, averaging approximately $150 per pupil, depending on the state—the amount varies considerably from state to state due to how ELLs are accounted for from $86 to $457 per pupil (Tanenbaum et al., 2012; Williams, 2020). In fact, the current per pupil Title III amount represents a decline in allocation since 2002. Regrettably, the federal dollars continue to have a marginal impact on language minority/ELL services (Jiménez-Castellanos, 2010a, 2010b; Jiménez-Castellanos & Okhremtchouk, 2013).

A second issue is the way ELLs are negatively perceived as learners. It is unfortunate that our educational system, whether implicitly or explicitly, has low expectations of ELLs and views them from a deficit perspective (Valencia, 2010). Furthermore, these perceptions have a profound impact not only on the learning outcomes for the students but also on the worth schools and districts assign to this student population and their potential for achievement. To this end, ELL students' language, heritage, and culture are seen as impediments or "problems" to academic learning (García, 2006). Ironically, such perceptions directly influence decisions schools and districts make about how to spend the supplemental resources generated by this very student population (Jiménez-Castellanos, 2010a, 2010b). As a result, these decisions habitually lead to subpar learning environments and low-rigor curricula designed to compensate or remediate for the students' perceived deficiencies (Jiménez-Castellanos, 2012).

The third salient issue related to ELL funding is the lack of transparency and accountability with respect to expenditures (Jiménez-Castellanos, 2017). Although school districts are recipients and therefore stewards of the money allocated by the state and federal governments, they are often seen as a "black box" because there is minimal public transparency on how they expend funds earmarked to address ELL needs (Jiménez-Castellanos, 2010a, 2010b). This lack of transparency is evident within and across schools and school districts, and even more so in how these supplemental dollars trickle down (or not) to the student level (Roza, 2008). And, although ELL funds are earmarked as entitlement dollars based on the number of students in ELL classification, local decision-making around expanding these funds is not entitlement-based (Jiménez-Castellanos & Okhremtchouk, 2013). That is, the priorities concerning services are not tied to individualized needs or plans as would be in the case of other entitlement programs, such as Special Education. Instead, ELL funds are often lumped to provide widespread services without considering individual or even group student characteristics. All the while, the students continue to generate additional funds for their district/school based on per pupil allotments (Jiménez-Castellanos & Topper, 2012).

The fourth salient issue is the inappropriate and ineffective use of ELL supplemental resources. Although studies are limited on the actual school site expenditures of ELL funds, the existing reports describe often sporadic school site decision-making for expenditures due to budgetary deadlines and lack of funding among other factors which lead to supplanting of funds, all while missing the mark entirely on much-needed direct services to the students (Jiménez-Castellanos & Okhremtchouk, 2013). For instance, the schools use monies on remedial type of services such as test preparation or low-rigor interventions and personnel (paraprofessional or teachers aid) that do not make a significant difference.

In particular, Title III supplemental resources tend to be ineffective because these funds are often not used on bilingual/dual language programs since the majority of ELLs are not provided access to these programs (Valdez et al., 2016), and the meager federal funding thresholds for ELLs (Williams, 2020). The stark reality of inadequate funding coupled with compliance-focused obligations naturally diverts funds further away from ELL students, habitually resulting in Title III funding never even reaching the school level. Often the focus is on "keeping the system operational" as compared to narrowing down the best services to address ELL needs (Jiménez-Castellanos & Okhremtchouk, 2013). Districts use Title III funds on direct administrative costs, teacher professional development, and other centralized/district-level services such as monitoring compliance requirements (Jiménez-Castellanos & Okhremtchouk, 2013; Tanenbaum et al., 2012).

Recommendations for Future Research

Dual Language Bilingual Education and Programs

Much research is needed in K-12 finance in general, but especially in the area of DLBE. Unfortunately, school finance literature centering on language minority students, including those receiving DLBE, has been scant at best. Moreover, a handful of existing studies are either limited in scope or dated. This said, we can learn from these scholarly works to determine the path forward. Below we outline two areas.

The first area that must be tackled is that of adequacy. Extant literature shows that states are not adequately funding ELL students to support grade-level attainment (see Boyle et al., 2015; Gándara & Rumberger, 2008). However, studies on the subject of funding concerning adequacy for ELL and DLBE programs are far and few in between. More studies on the actual costs to address the needs of students enrolled in ELL and DLBE programs will help create an evidence-based platform that both scholars and practitioners can use to advocate on behalf of the DLBE programs and language minority students enrolled in these programs. The four costing out studies with a specific focus cost (see Arizona Department of Education, 2001; Gándara & Rumberger, 2008; META, 2008; National Conference of State Legislatures, 2005) serve as an essential reference; yet, more research and up to date research is needed to determine the actual cost of funding ELL and DBLE programs.

The second area is that of quality—namely, addressing how funding for ELL and DBLE programs is being utilized and managed? This question is fundamental since, more often than not, earmarked funding for language minority students is based on political and budgetary considerations than meeting student needs through instruction and programs that value student language and heritage, such as DLBE programs. Currently, there are only a handful of studies that look into expenditures and investments (see Jiménez-Castellanos & Okhremtchouk, 2013; Okhremtchouk & Jiménez-Castellanos, 2018); therefore, the field could certainly benefit from more empirical research in this area. Put differently, without a clear understanding of where the funds are invested and whether these funds address students' needs, the field will not be able to determine the true cost of supporting quality ELL and DBLE programs.

Note

1 Terminology varies from state to state but the usual designation/term for language minority students who are deemed initially proficient in the English language is either IFEP (Initially Fluent English Proficient) or FEP (Fluent English Proficient).

References

Abedi, J. (2008). Classification system for English language learners: Issues and recommendations. *Educational Measurement: Issues and Practice*, *27*(3), 17–31.

Arizona Department of Education (2001). *English acquisition program cost study—Phases I through IV*. Phoenix.

Bailey, A. L., & Carroll, P. E. (2015). Assessment of English language learners in the era of new academic content standards. *Review of Research in Education*, *39*(1), 253–294.

Baker, B. D. (2003). State policy influences on the internal allocation of school district resources: Evidence from the common core of data. *Journal of Education Finance*, *29*(1), 1–24.

Boyle, A., August, D., Tabaku, L., Cole, S., & Simpson-Baird, A. (2015). *Dual language education programs: Current state policies and practices*. United States Department of Education.

Crawford, J. (1995). *Bilingual education: History, politics, theory and practice*. Bilingual Education Services.

Education Commission of the States [ECS] (October, 2021). *50-State comparison: K-12 and special education funding: English learner funding*. https://reports.ecs.org/comparisons/k-12-and-special-education-funding-05

Gándara, P. (2018). *Immigrant students: Our kids, our future*. Retrieved from https://learningpolicyinstitute.org/blog/immigrant-students-our-kids-our-future

Gándara, P., & Rumberger, R. W. (2008). Defining an adequate education for English learners. *Education Finance and Policy*, *3*(1), 130–148.

García, O. (2006). Equity's elephant in the room. Multilingual children in the U.S. are being penalized by current education policies. *TC Today*, *31*(1), 40.

Hakuta, K. (2011). Educating language minority students and affirming their equal rights. *Research and Practical Perspectives*, *40*(4), 163–174.

Jiménez-Castellanos, O. (2010a). Relationship between educational resources and school achievement: A mixed method intra-district analysis. *The Urban Review*, *42*(4), 351–371. https://doi.org/10.1007/s11256-010-0166-6

Jiménez-Castellanos, O. (2010b). School finance and English language learners: A legislative perspective. *Association of Mexican-American Educators Journal*, *4*(1), 12–21.
Jiménez-Castellanos, O. (2012). Revisiting the Coleman Report: Deficit ideologies and Federal compensatory funding in low-income Latino school communities. *Association of Mexican-American Educators Journal*, *6*(2), 48–55. https://amaejournal.utsa.edu/index.php/amae/article/view/113
Jiménez-Castellanos, O. (2017). English language learner education finance scholarship: An introduction to the special issue. *Education Policy Analysis Archives*, *25*(14), 1–13.
Jiménez-Castellanos, O., Garcia, E., & Rodriguez-Mojica, C. (2022). Editorial introduction: Revisiting and (re)imagining Castañeda v. Pickard through critical lenses. *Language Policy*, *21*(3), 295–303.
Jiménez-Castellanos, O., Kelly, M., & Carranza, L. (2021). Pre and post Serrano: Systemic racism, school funding disparities and Mexican-American communities. *Education Law and Policy Review*, *6*(1), 49–72.
Jiménez-Castellanos, O., & Okhremtchouk, I. (2013). K-12 categorical entitlement funding for English language learners in California: An intradistrict case study. *Educational Considerations*, *40*(2), 27–33.
Jiménez-Castellanos, O., & Topper, A. (2012). The cost of providing an adequate education to English language learners: A review of the literature. *Review of Educational Research*, *82*(2), 179–232.
Kiracofe, C., & Weiler, S. (2022). Surfing the Waves: An examination of school funding litigation from *Serrano v. Priest* to *Cook v. Raimondo* and the possible transition to the Fourth Wave. *BYU Education and Law Journal*, 2022(1). https://scholarsarchive.byu.edu/byu_elj/vol2022/iss1/5
Multicultural Education Training and Advocacy, Inc. (2008). *Getting it right: Ensuring a quality education for English language learners in New York*. Prepared by the New York Immigration Coalition. http://72.34.53.249/˜thenyic/sites/default/files/NYIC_ELLBRIEF_FINAL.pdf
National Conference of State Legislatures. (2005). *Arizona English language learner cost study*. Prepared for the Arizona Legislative Council. http://www.schoolfunding.info/states/az/AZ-NCSLenglanglearn2005.pdf
Odden, A. R., & Picus, L. O. (2019). *School finance: A policy perspective* (6th ed.). McGraw-Hill.
Okhremtchouk, I. S. (2014). Classifying language-minority students: A closer look at individual student data. *Bilingual Research Journal*, *37*(3), 327–348.
Okhremtchouk, I. S. (2017). The politics of schools and money: Building awareness about channeling practices for supplemental resource allocations to serve English language learners. *Education Policy Analysis Archives*, *25*(17), 1–25.
Okhremtchouk, I. S., & Jimenez-Castellanos, O. (2018). The Obama Administration American Recovery and Reinvestment Act and Local School Board Politics. *Journal of Cases in Educational Leadership*, *21*(4), 67–85. https://doi.org/10.1177/1555458918762259
Okhremtchouk, I., Levine-Smith, J., & Clark, A. T. (2018). The web of reclassification for English language learners: A cyclical journey waiting to be interrupted: Discussion of realities, challenges, and opportunities. *Educational Leadership and Administration: Teaching and Program Development*, *29(1)*, 1–13.
Okhremtchouk, I. S., & Sellu, G. S. (2019). Teacher readiness to work with English language learners: Arizona Context. *Teacher Educator*, *54*(2), 125–144.
Okhremtchouk, I. S. (2011). *Disjointed continuity: Classification practices for language minority students and implications: A case study* [Doctoral dissertation, University of California, Davis].

Poza, L.E., García, O., & Jiménez-Castellanos, Ó. (2021). After Castañeda: A glotopolítica perspective and educational dignity paradigm to educate racialized bilinguals. *Language Policy*, 1–24. https://doi.org/10.1007/s10993-021-09606-z

Rebell, M. (2022). State courts and education finance: Past present and future. *BYU Education and Law Journal*, *2022*(1), 1–74. https://scholarsarchive.byu.edu/byu_elj/vol2022/iss1/7

Roza, M. (2008). *Allocation anatomy: How district policies that deploy resources can support (or undermine) district reform strategies*. University of Washington.

Salerno, A. S., & Andrei, E. (2021). Inconsistencies in English learner identification: An inventory of how home language surveys across U.S. states screen multilingual students. *AERA Open*.

Tanenbaum, C., Boyle, A., Soga, K., Le Floch, K., Golden, L., Petroccia, M., Toplitz, M., Taylor, J., & O'Day, J. (2012). *National evaluation of title III implementation: Report on state and local implementation*. US Department of Education. https://files.eric.ed.gov/fulltext/ED531982.pdf

U.S. Department of Education (USDE), National Center for Education Statistics, Common Core of Data (CCD). "Local Education Agency Universe Survey," 2018–19. See *Digest of Education Statistics 2020*, table 204.20.

U.S. Department of education. (2014). *10 Facts about K-12 education funding*. https://www2.ed.gov/about/overview/fed/10facts/index.html

Valdez, V., Freire, J. A., & Delavan, G. (2016). The gentrification of dual language education. *Urban Review: Issues and Ideas in Public Education*, *48*(4), 601–627.

Valencia, R. (2010). *Dismantling contemporary deficit thinking*. Routledge.

Verstegen, D. A. (2011). Public education finance systems in the United States and funding policies for populations with special educational needs. *Education Policy Analysis Archives*, *19*, 21.

Wiley, T. G. (2004). Language policy and English-only. In E. Finegan, & J. R. Rickford (Eds.), *Language in the USA: Perspectives for the twenty-first century* (pp. 319–338). Cambridge University Press.

Williams, C. P. (2020, March 31). *The case for expanding federal funding for English learners*. The Century Foundation. https://tcf.org/content/commentary/case-expanding-federal-funding-english-learners/

19

INCREASING BILINGUAL TEACHER PATHWAYS TO ADDRESS THE SURGE OF DUAL LANGUAGE BILINGUAL EDUCATION PROGRAMS

Sera J. Hernández

Introduction

Teacher shortages across a variety of subject matters and instructional levels are widespread in the United States and documented since state-level teacher data have been collected and reported to the federal government. These "teacher shortage areas" refer to "area[s] of specific grade, subject matter or discipline classification, or a geographic area[s] in which the Secretary determines that there is an inadequate supply of elementary or secondary school teachers" (U.S. Department of Education, 2017, p. 3). Teacher shortages are usually highest in areas such as foreign/world language education and special education, as well as in particular geographical locations in the country, like California, Alaska, Hawaii, New Mexico, and Arizona (Murphy et al., 2003).

Because the recent surge of dual language bilingual education programs requires a qualified teacher force to meet this historical moment, this chapter is guided by the following questions: What documentation do we have of a bilingual teacher shortage? What policies have led us to this historical moment in bilingual teacher education? What have been some short-term remedies for the bilingual teacher shortage? What bilingual teaching credential pathways exist and which are most promising? What are the implications of the bilingual teacher shortage and bilingual teacher pathways?

DOI: 10.4324/9781003269076-27

What Documentation Do We Have of a Bilingual Teacher Shortage?

Teacher shortages in general are largely due to growing enrollments in some parts of the country, class size reduction policies in certain states, and teacher turnover through retirements and pre-retirement attrition (e.g., organizational restructuring, teacher job dissatisfaction, upward job mobility) (Murphy et al., 2003). There is ample research on teachers of color (Achinstein et al., 2010) and minoritized educators in general, groups through which bilingual teachers tend to identify. Over the last 25 years, minoritized teachers were more likely to leave the profession than their non-minoritized peers (Ingersoll et al., 2019; Simon & Johnson, 2015), often due to less desirable organizational conditions. Yet, little attention is focused on where minoritized teachers are employed, what happens to them once they have secured teaching positions, and the role of school organization in teacher retention (Ingersoll et al., 2019).

A shortage of bilingual teachers to work in bilingual classrooms or with bilingual students has been documented for decades (U.S. Department of Education, 2017) and is currently a leading factor impeding effective dual language implementation (Collier & Thomas, 2017). A recent report identified more than 3,600 dual language education (DLE) programs across the United States (Roberts, 2021), with 44 states reporting dual language programs. California, Texas, New York, Utah, and North Carolina account for almost 60 percent of all dual language programs, and Spanish programs account for about 80 percent of all programs followed by Chinese (8.6 percent) and French (5.0 percent) (Roberts, 2021). California was the first state in the United States to pass progressive language policy initiatives across the last several years and state level analyses indicate that the bilingual teacher shortage is only growing (Carver-Thomas & Darling-Hammond, 2017; Ramos Harris & Sandoval-González, 2017). For example, DLE grew from 229 schools in 2011 to 407 in 2017 (California Department of Education, 2018); thus, the need for credentialed bilingual teachers is rising rapidly. Unfortunately, as noted by Carver-Thomas and Darling-Hammond (2017), "At just 700 new bilingual teachers in 2015–16, California authorizes fewer than half the number of new bilingual teachers than it did when bilingual education hiring was at its peak in the mid-1990s" (p. VI). The trend is moving upwards quickly, as the California Department of Education (2019) has more recently documented 747 schools in the state that have a dual language program, and the totals do not include other types of bilingual education in program models that also need credentialed bilingual teachers. Fifty-three percent of districts in California that were surveyed after Proposition 58 passed reported a shortage of bilingual teachers and 86 percent that planned to expand their bilingual offerings reported that a shortage of teachers would be a massive obstacle to program implementation (Ramos Harris & Sandoval-González, 2017). This creates a predicament for states with additive bilingual education policies like California where dual language programming is rapidly expanding, and we lack a comprehensive investigation of the current bilingual teacher shortage. A recent case study in Texas (Kennedy, 2020) identified three factors that contributed to the state's shortage of qualified bilingual educators: (1) the growth in the racialized bilingual student population, (2) the need for a highly specialized skill set for bilingual teachers, and (3) challenges in bilingual teacher pathways. And because attrition has a huge impact on the bilingual teacher shortage, it warrants further consideration. Specifically, retaining current bilingual teachers requires that we document and ameliorate additional burdens bilingual teachers face on the job (e.g., the invisible work of translating and creating curriculum materials in languages other than English) (Amanti, 2019).

What Policies Have Led Us to This Historical Moment in Bilingual Teacher Education?

Rare in the reports on teacher shortages across the country are explanations for how and why we have a shortage of bilingual teachers. The sociopolitical and linguistic landscape of PreK-12 education in the United States has always been highly politicized, largely shaped by ideologies in assimilationist or pluralist approaches (Schmidt, 2000). The United States has historically ebbed and flowed between language suppression and language tolerance, influenced by immigration, wars, and other historical events (Baker & Wright, 2017). Studies of language policies point to the hegemonic English-only educational language policies that have codified monolingualism as the societal norm. The sociopolitical landscape in this country determines, in many ways, which populations get to become bilingual or maintain their bilingualism. An investment in the bilingualism and biliteracy of PreK-12 students is only a more recent trend, and limited only to states with progressive language policies, such as California, Colorado, and Massachusetts. Even with such policies, the distribution of who benefits by this investment has been noted across race and class (Cervantes-Soon et al., 2017; Hernández, 2017; Valdés, 2018; Valdez et al., 2016).

Building on Ladson-Billings' concept of educational debt (2006), the country's historic, and in most places, current disinvestment in the bilingualism and biliteracy of racialized immigrant communities has contributed to linguistic and cultural loss. Educational reform efforts that ignore this and other racio-ethnic inequities and social class conditions likely undermine progressive efforts. Critical scholars denounce educational policies or practices that ascribe educational or societal change to the individual level solely, without examining social conditions involved in the sustaining of power dynamics and relationships across groups (Anyon, 2005). This is true for dual language programming where its gentrification is heavily documented (Valdez et al., 2016), and the language and culture of racialized immigrant communities that are not valued in the United States are marketed to more privileged others in the name of *multilingualism for all.* While the additive language policy approaches in some states may mitigate the damage of restrictive language policies tied to the U.S. linguistic and cultural debt to some extent, we cannot ignore the inequities that continue to be perpetuated in dual language programming.

What Have Been Some Short-Term Remedies for the Bilingual Teacher Shortage?

Where there is a discrepancy between the number of bilingual teaching positions and the availability of locally credentialed candidates to fill the vacancies across the nation (e.g., Carver-Thomas & Darling-Hammond, 2017; Cervantes-Soon et al., 2021), some districts rely on short-term remedies, such as hiring substitute teachers, teachers without certification, and/or outsource international teachers who speak the non-English target language (Cervantes-Soon, 2014). Outsourcing teachers in U.S. schools is not a new phenomenon. According to the American Federation of Teachers (2009):

> Unwilling or unable to address the root causes of a growing teacher shortage, public school systems around the country have begun importing teachers to meet their staffing needs. Overseas-trained teachers are being recruited from nearly all corners of the globe and are being placed primarily in hard-to-staff inner-city or very rural schools teaching the hard-to-fill disciplines of math, science and special education. Despite being highly qualified teachers in their own countries, many migrant teachers struggle with the very different challenges of America's schools. Moreover, they are ripe for exploitation by for-profit recruiters who have found yet another way to extract private profit from a public system. (p. 7)

In the dual language context, the reliance on international Spanish-speaking teacher recruitment is on the rise, partly due to the lack of local bilingual educators licensed and ready for the classroom (Cervantes-Soon, 2014; Dorner et al., 2021). Dunn (2013, p. 4) argues that recruiting teachers from other counties is offered "as both a solution to the shortage and as a way to provide students of color with more world exposure." These teachers are often not from the countries of origin of their racialized bilingual students and are not always supported to work with U.S. students. Studies have highlighted how international teachers often lack the knowledge of the sociopolitical context of U.S. schooling, particularly as it affects historically minoritized students and racialized bilinguals (Dunn, 2013). Dorner and colleagues (2021) noted that though international teachers shared "culture and language to some extent with their TLLs [transnational language learners], many teachers reinforced hegemonic social hierarchies through the establishment of a colonial difference" where "the cultural and linguistic practices of the dominant group (including the highly-educated, international Spanish-speaking teachers) were connected to intellectual potential, while low income, minoritized students were framed as unfit or undeserving of TWBE [two way bilingual education]" (p. 341). This recruitment practice is also indicative of a larger neoliberal approach (Cervantes-Soon et al., 2021) that puts money into the pockets of recruiting agencies and largely serves the interests of white children and families at the expense of racialized and linguistically minoritized populations (Dorner et al., 2021). Additionally, these teachers, who are usually working in the United States with a temporary visa, face the risk of abusive practices, and the practice ignores the underlying issues for teacher shortages in the United States (American Federation of Teachers, 2009).

What Bilingual Teaching Credential Pathways Exist and Which Are Most Promising?

Multiple pathways can and should be available for future bilingual teachers to support with transitions to the teaching field and to avoid band-aid approaches to systemic issues. Creating career pathways such as "Grow Your Own" (GYO) programs, for example, are growing in popularity nationwide where local high school students and community members are recruited to become teachers (Sutcher et al., 2016). GYO pathways include four-year college programs and other paraprofessional and post-baccalaureate options for individuals who have the desire to return to their communities or communities with similar demographics to become teachers (Valenzuela, 2016). GYO efforts have generated mixed results (Kennedy, 2020) as credentialing obstacles remain steady, such as the quantity and nature of certification exams (i.e., costly, culturally biased) required of bilingual teacher candidates (Hernández & Alfaro, 2019; Kennedy, 2020).

Residency models are also a viable option for placing bilingual teacher candidates "into paid, yearlong apprenticeships with expert mentor teachers while the candidates complete tightly linked credential and master's degree coursework with partnering universities. In exchange, candidates pledge to teach in the district for 3–5 years" (Sutcher et al., 2016, p. 8).

In a report by Californians Together, a nonprofit advocacy group for "English learners" in the state, over 7,000 teachers were identified as ready to teach in bilingual classrooms with additional support (Ramos Harris

& Sandoval-González, 2017). Many of these teachers earned their bilingual credential before Proposition 227 passed or did not earn the bilingual authorization when they were credentialed despite their bilingualism. Providing a pathway for existing bilingual teachers in English-only classrooms to earn a bilingual credential or update the knowledge, skills, and dispositions through professional development of teachers with a bilingual credential who have not been teaching in bilingual programs is another way to address the need. As such, micro-credentials (MCs) are becoming more popular across the United States to address high-need areas in education, like bilingual education (Tooley & Hood, 2021). MCs are similar to digital badges earned to demonstrate in-demand skills and knowledge, and that specifically "offer teachers opportunities to document their formal and informal learning ... [through] work samples, videos, and other artifacts to make public what they have mastered and accomplished with their students and colleagues ... and assessed against established rubrics" (Barnett et al., 2016, p. 36). Los Angeles Unified School District, for example, has a DLE MC Program that prepares educators to work with bilingual learners through a hybrid program of 105 hours of coursework that includes multiple artifacts demonstrating their learning as applied to their educational context (LAUSD, n.d.). Evidence of application in classroom practice is a key characteristic of MCs and this approach "can help attract and retain highly talented teachers by formally assessing and recognizing previously unrecognized skills and providing opportunities for increased responsibilities related to those skills, along with compensation in line with those responsibilities" (Tooley & Hood, 2021, p. 44).

There are additional recommendations to increase the bilingual teacher workforce, such as creating pathways for bilingual paraprofessionals to earn a bilingual credential, build awareness for the teaching field for students who graduate high school with a Seal of Biliteracy, and create regional cohort partnerships such as higher education institutions with county offices of education that can facilitate a pathway to the bilingual credential with support (Ramos Harris & Sandoval-González, 2017). The need for high-retention pathways into the teaching force, that is "teachers [that] will spend lasting teaching careers in those [high-need] fields and locations" (Sutcher et al., 2016, p. 8), is a critical issue. If the turnover rate for teachers remains high, often due to feeling ill-prepared, experiencing high levels of burnout, or low salary, the shortage for teachers in general, and bilingual teachers in particular, will persist.

What Are the Implications of the Bilingual Teacher Shortage and Bilingual Teacher Pathways?

There are myriad challenges to the bilingual teacher shortage and no silver bullet to undo the historic disinvestment in the bilingualism and biliteracy of PreK-12 students in the United States. Some pathways have demonstrated promise in recruiting and retaining teachers. We can learn from the policy recommendations for general teacher shortages, while acknowledging the unique reality for bilingual teachers. For example, teacher retention can be supported by well-designed mentoring and induction programs and improvement in teaching conditions (e.g., providing mentor teachers, common planning and collaboration time with other teachers) (Sutcher et al., 2019). But Valenzuela (2016) reminds us that there is no one way to build pathways for teachers and that context matters. At a policy level, a focus on retaining existing bilingual teachers is just as critical as recruiting teachers when there is a shortage (Sutcher et al., 2016). Strong teacher education programs must be accessible (Sutcher et al., 2016), particularly to teacher candidates who are bilingual, who are often first-generation college graduates from low-income backgrounds. And because bilingual teachers tend to be from historically minoritized communities, similar issues must be considered such as reducing costs for credentialing programs (Bristol, 2016). Research suggests that making teacher preparation programs affordable, such as through forgivable loans and scholarships with a commitment to serve in high-need areas, will assist with critical shortages (Sutcher et al., 2016).

Only focusing on a bilingual teacher shortage "moves us toward short-term solutions that are unlikely to address the long-term underlying problem" which is "the historical, economic, sociopolitical, and moral decisions and policies that characterize our society [that] have created an education debt" (Ladson-Billings, 2006, pp. 4–5). The United States has inflicted assimilationist and erasure projects for centuries (Grande, 2004) and decades of English-only policies cannot be quickly undone. To start, we can shift our focus to the neoliberal systems that reproduce "capital" for the privileged and "debt" for the historically minoritized in our society in general, and in schools in particular. The irreparable harm to thousands of linguistically minoritized students who have experienced their schooling under these restrictive language policies (Alfaro, 2018; Gándara & Hopkins, 2010) is documented and directly contributes to the perpetual bilingual teacher shortage (Briceño et al., 2018). It is irrefutable that the bilingual teacher shortage is a material consequence of this disinvestment.

Lastly, it is essential that dual language educators and researchers understand the sociohistorical and political context of the bilingual teacher shortage. It is a national dilemma that many bilingual teacher candidates have experienced being language learners in their K-12 schooling in English-only programs to then later be positioned as Spanish learners at the university level because their literacy skills in both languages were never invested in within their schooling experiences (Briceño et al., 2018). All stakeholders nationwide must promote initiatives that invest in bilingual PreK-12 students and bilingual teachers. Bilingual teacher candidates with a language policy knowledge base understand their own role in contributing to the reproduction or transformation of schooling practices. We must center equity for racialized bilinguals and infuse critical consciousness into the fabric of our teacher education programs, for both bilingual and monolingual educators. By addressing head on a deep understanding of history based on a "generational consciousness" from "a culturally and community–anchored standpoint" (Valenzuela, 2016, p. 5), we can increase the likelihood that English-only hegemony and linguicism can at least be mitigated, if not avoided. We must not lose sight of who gets to be/stay bilingual in the United States, consider how educational policies perpetuate status quo power dynamics between English and other languages, and contribute to efforts that strive to mitigate the bilingual teacher shortage by redressing the linguistic and cultural loss experienced by countless minoritized communities through a strategic historical disinvestment at a federal and state policy level.

In addition to ramping up bilingual teacher pathways and other recruitment initiatives, we must commit to "viewing the roots of shortages as an organizational and occupational design issue, implying the need for a different arrangement, better built for those who do the work of teaching" (Ingersoll et al., 2019, p. 33). The success of dual language programming and quality educational experiences for racialized bilinguals depends on our ability to meet this historical moment.

References

Achinstein, B., Ogawa, R. T., Sexton, D., & Freitas, C. (2010). Retaining teachers of color: A pressing problem and a potential strategy for "hard-to-staff" schools. *Review of Educational Research*, *80*(1), 71–107.

Alfaro, C. (2018). The sociopolitical struggle and promise of bilingual teacher education: Past, present and future. *Bilingual Research Journal*, *41*(4), 413–427.

Amanti, C. (2019). The (invisible) work of dual language bilingual education teachers. *Bilingual Research Journal*, 42(4), 455–470.

American Federation of Teachers (2009). *Importing educators: Causes and consequences of international teacher recruitment.* Author. Retrieved on December 1, 2021, from https://www.aft.org/sites/default/files/importingeducators_2009.pdf

Anyon, J. (2005). What "counts" as educational policy? Notes toward a new paradigm. *Harvard Educational Review*, *75*(1), 65–88.

Baker, C., & Wright, W. E. (2017). *Foundations of bilingual education and bilingualism* (6th ed.). Multilingual Matters.

Barnett, B., Airhart, K. M., & Byrd, P. A. (2016). Microcredentials: Teacher learning transformed. *Phi Delta Kappan*, *98*(3), 34–40.

Briceño, A., Rodriguez-Mojica, C., & Muñoz-Muñoz, E. (2018). From English learner to Spanish learner: Raciolinguistic beliefs that influence heritage Spanish speaking teacher candidates. *Language and Education*, 32(3), 212–226.

Bristol, T. J. (2016). The troubling shortage of Latino and Black teachers—and what to do about it. *Valerie Strauss' Answer Sheet column in the Washington*

Post. Retrieved on June 10, 2016 from https://www.washingtonpost.com/news/answersheet/wp/2016/05/15/the-troublingshortage-of-latino-and-black-teachers-and-what-to-do-about-it/

California Department of Education (2018). *Global California 2030*. Retrieved on March 3, 2020 from https://www.cde.ca.gov/eo/in/documents/globalca2030report.pdf

California Department of Education (2019). *List of schools offering multilingual programs*. Retrieved on March 3, 2020 from https://www.cde.ca.gov/sp/el/er/multilingualedu.asp

Carver-Thomas, D., & Darling-Hammond, L. (2017). *Addressing California's growing teacher shortage: 2017 Update*. Learning Policy Institute.

Cervantes-Soon, C. G. (2014). A critical look at dual language immersion in the new Latin@ diaspora. *Bilingual Research Journal*, *37*, 64–82. https://doi.org/10.1080/15235882.2014.893267

Cervantes-Soon, C. G., Dorner, L., Palmer, D., Heiman, D., Schwerdtfeger, R., & Choi, J. (2017). Combating inequalities in two-way language immersion programs: Toward critical consciousness in bilingual education spaces. *Review of Research in Education*, *41*, 403–427.

Cervantes-Soon, C. G., Gambrell, J., Kasun, G. S., Sun, W., Freire, J. A., & Dorner, L. M. (2021). "Everybody wants a choice" in dual language education of el nuevo sur: Whiteness as the gloss for everybody in media discourses of multilingual education. *Journal of Language, Identity & Education*, *20*(6), 394–410. https://doi.org/10.1080/15348458.2020.1753201

Collier, V., & Thomas, W. (2017). Validating the power of bilingual schooling: Thirty-two years of large-scale, longitudinal research. *Annual Review of Applied Linguistics*, *37*, 203–217.

Dorner, L. M., Cervantes-Soon, C. G., Heiman, D., & Palmer, D. (2021). "Now it's all upper-class parents who are checking out schools": Gentrification as coloniality in the enactment of two-way bilingual education policies. *Language Policy*, *20*, 323–349. https://doi.org/10.1007/s10993-021-09580-6

Dunn, A. H. (2013). *Teachers without borders?: The hidden consequences of international teachers in U.S. schools*. Teachers College Press.

Gándara, P., & Hopkins, M. (2010). *Forbidden language: English learners and restrictive language policies*. Teachers College Press.

Grande, S. (2004). *Red pedagogy: Native American social and political thought*. Rowman and Littlefield.

Hernández, S. (2017). Are they all language learners?: Educational labeling and raciolinguistic identifying in a middle school dual language program. *CATESOL Journal*, *29*(1), 133–154.

Hernández, A. M., & Alfaro, C. (2019): Naming and confronting the challenges of bilingual teacher preparation: A dilemma for dual language education in California–lessons learned. *NABE Journal of Research and Practice*, 1–16. https://doi.org/10.1080/26390043.2019.1653053

Ingersoll, R., May, H., & Collins, G. (2019). Recruitment, employment, retention and the minority teacher shortage. *Education Policy Analysis Archives*, *27*(37). http://dx.doi.org/10.14507/epaa.27.3714

Kennedy, B. A. (2020). The bilingual teacher shortage in one Texas school district: Practitioner perspectives. *Journal of Latinos and Education*, *19*, 338–354.

Ladson-Billings, G. (2006). From the achievement gap to the education debt: Understanding achievement in U.S. schools. *Educational Researcher*, *35*(7), 3–12.

LAUSD (n.d.). *Overview dual language education micro-credential (2021-2022)*. https://docs.google.com/document/d/10ZjcwDEEeo4wfY-hAGLDisdrHZSm-v6ohD9th7RtW5ZA/edit

Murphy, P., DeArmond, M., & Guin, K. (2003). A national crisis or localized problems? Getting perspective on the scope and scale of the teacher shortage. *Education Policy Analysis Archives*, *11*(23). http://epaa.asu.edu/epaa/v11n23/

Ramos Harris, V., & Sandoval-González, A. (2017). Unveiling California's growing bilingual teacher shortage: Addressing the urgent shortage, and aligning the workforce to advances in pedagogy and practice in bilingual education. *Californians Together*. Retrieved on December 1, 2021 from https://californianstogether.app.box.com/s/aowa6abuqltyql3kokfhpbru93h00ull

Roberts, G. (2021). *Canvass of dual language and immersion (DLI) programs in U.S. public schools*. American Councils Research Center.

Schmidt, R. (2000). *Language policy and identity politics in the United States*. Temple University Press.

Simon, N., & Johnson, S. M. (2015). Teacher turnover in high-poverty schools: What we know and can do. *Teachers College Record*, *117*(3), 1–36. https://doi.org/10.1177/016146811511700305

Sutcher, L., Darling-Hammond, L., & Carver-Thomas, D. (2016). *A coming crisis in teaching? Teacher supply, demand, and shortages in the U.S.* Learning Policy Institute. https://learningpolicyinstitute.org/product/coming-crisis-teaching

Sutcher, L., Darling-Hammond, L., & Carver-Thomas, D. (2019). Understanding teacher shortages: An analysis of teacher supply and demand in the United States. *Education Policy Analysis Archives*, *27*(35). http://dx.doi.org/10.14507/epaa.27.3696

Tooley, M., & Hood, J. (2021). Harnessing Micro-credentials for teacher growth: A national review of early best practices. *New America*. Retrieved on December 1, 2021 from newamerica.org/education-policy/reports/harnessing-micro-credentials-teacher-growth/

U.S. Department of Education (2017). *Teacher shortage areas nationwide listing 1990–1991 through 2017–2018*. TSA Nationwide Listing Comprehensive Compendium. Retrieved on December 1, 2021 from https://www2.ed.gov/about/offices/list/ope/pol/bteachershortageareasreport201718.pdf

Valdés, G. (2018). Analyzing the curricularization of language in two-way immersion education: Restating two cautionary notes. *Bilingual Research Journal*, *41*(4), 388–412.

Valdez, V. E., Freire, J. A., & Delavan, M. (2016). The gentrification of dual language education. *Urban Review*, *48*, 601.

A. Valenzuela (Ed.). (2016). *Growing critically conscious teachers: A social justice curriculum for educators of Latino/a youth*. Teachers College Press.

20

THE SEAL OF BILITERACY AND DUAL LANGUAGE BILINGUAL EDUCATION

Amy J. Heineke, Kristin J. Davin, Joe Elliott

Overview of the Seal of Biliteracy

The Seal of Biliteracy (SoBL) is a recognition bestowed to students in the United States for demonstrating proficiency in two or more languages prior to high-school graduation. This language education policy attaches to legislation or educational code at the state level, with 49 states and the District of Columbia having passed iterations of the SoBL from 2011 to 2022 (Davin & Heineke, 2022; Heineke & Davin, 2020). Originating in California and spreading across the United States, the SoBL movement shares focus on promoting students' biliteracy with varying policy nuances across states. For example, state-level SoBL policies vary by (a) tiers and titles of the recognition, (b) levels of language proficiency to achieve the recognition, (c) approved assessments to demonstrate proficiency, and (d) involvement of schools outside the public sector (Davin & Heineke, 2017). These policy nuances influence implementation on the ground, including the interaction with bilingual programming.

Over the past decade of its existence, the SoBL has straddled bilingual and world-language education, though its origins lie in bilingual education. The initiative began in California in the early 2000s when bilingual educators and advocates sought to push back against Proposition 227, which largely eradicated bilingual education for students labeled as English learners (ELs; Olsen, 2020), referred to in this chapter as *emergent bilingual learners* (EBLs; García, 2009). Recognizing the detrimental effects of the policy that mandated English immersion in place of bilingual education, stakeholders envisioned the SoBL as a mechanism to promote students' home and heritage language development. Nonetheless, as the movement took hold across

DOI: 10.4324/9781003269076-28

California and the United States, the emphasis shifted from home languages to world languages, with the SoBL often housed in secondary world-language programs and awarded to English-dominant world-language students (Subtirelu et al., 2019).

This chapter probes the central themes related to bilingual education in the current literature on the SoBL. We organize the literature review around layers of language policy, including (a) macro-level policy design, (b) meso-level implementation in districts and schools, and (c) micro-level impact on students in bilingual programming. The following questions guide our literature review: How have stakeholders crafted SoBL policies in relation to bilingual education? In what ways have local educators implemented the SoBL to connect to bilingual education? How does SoBL implementation involve and influence bilingual students? Implications follow discussion of key themes from the literature, centering on the need for state and local efforts to explicitly connect to dual-language bilingual education spanning kindergarten through 12th grade (K-12) schools in addition to secondary world-language programs.

Key Themes from the Existing Literature

Focus on Policy

The SoBL movement is typified by state-level policies, which have been independently crafted by state legislators and educational advocates utilizing guidelines collaboratively drafted by national language organizations including the American Council on the Teaching of Foreign Languages (ACTFL), National Association for Bilingual Education (NABE), and TESOL International (ACTFL et al., 2020). As individual states have enacted and implemented various iterations of SoBL policies, large-scale research has explored how states' policies vary and connect to bilingual education in distinct ways. Early research documented various iterations of state SoBL policies and how nuances influenced who received the recognition (Davin & Heineke, 2017). SoBL policies have consistently been designed as assessment-oriented recognitions, meaning students must demonstrate proficiency on state-approved assessments. But in early years of the SoBL movement, proficiency assessments included commonly taught languages, such as French, German, and Spanish, and often excluded hundreds of heritage languages used by U.S. students. Whereas some states sought equity via clauses allowing alternative assessments, others maintained focus on common world languages and subsequently marginalized heritage language learners (Heineke & Davin, 2020).

When considering how state SoBL policies connect to bilingual education, the availability of proficiency assessments in multiple languages was not the only cause for concern. Another study (Heineke et al., 2018) probed policies' framing of EBLs, as well as issues of equity and access. Researchers found that most states did not explicitly mention EBLs in SoBL policies, instead using discourse related to elite bilingualism in a globalizing world. Equity issues often emerged from testing requirements, including the conundrum of *double testing* where EBLs needed to pass additional tests beyond those required of English-dominant students. Some states also set EBLs up at a disadvantage with the timing of required assessments, such as EBLs in Florida having to demonstrate English proficiency in 10th grade, while non-EBLs could demonstrate proficiency in their second language through 12th grade. Authors asserted that these policy nuances could result in inequities in recognizing EBLs' biliteracy and privileged English-dominant students in world-language coursework.

Researchers have also studied policy enactment in individual states, informing how sociocultural context influences linkages between the SoBL and bilingual education. Take, for example, the context of Georgia, where stakeholders framed policy around world-language education to gain support from conservative state legislators who rallied around global competitiveness (Jansa & Brezicha, 2017). With the defined focus on world language in the state's SoBL policy and additional award requirements for EBLs, implementation remained centered on secondary world language rather than bilingual education. But this differed from Minnesota, where stakeholders focused on world language in their policy but strategically promoted equity for heritage language learners and EBLs (Okraski et al., 2020). Here, policy makers included clauses to (a) expand assessments in less commonly taught languages, (b) remove double testing requirements for EBLs, (c) allow multiple opportunities to demonstrate proficiency, and (d) provide pathways to receive college credit. These choices opened doors for local stakeholders to attach SoBL efforts to home- and heritage language instruction.

Distinct from states centering policy around world-language education, Massachusetts integrated dual-language bilingual education from the start. Like the original advocacy work in California, Massachusetts stakeholders sought to challenge the prevalence of monolingual programming emergent from legislation that had previously limited bilingual education (Olsen, 2020; Sherf et al., 2020). Sherf and colleagues (2020) documented state-level efforts of world-language, dual-language, and EL educational organizations. This coalition collaborated across language-education models by creating guidelines, standards, assessments, and tools for districts to pilot the SoBL, such as portfolio assessments to measure language proficiencies. In addition to efforts in local settings, the group advocated for SoBL legislation to state lawmakers and community members. Even after legislation passed, the coalition lobbied for changes including pathway awards to recognize elementary and middle-school students progressing along the pathway to proficiency and equitable assessment options for EBLs.

Focus on Schools

Distinctions in state-level policies have influenced local implementation, as educators worked within state guidelines to recognize students using predefined criteria (Davin & Heineke, 2017). Nonetheless, stakeholders in local settings have exercised agency in implementation that can support or deter from dual-language bilingual education regardless of the initial intent of state legislation. Consider the findings from one study of California districts implementing the SoBL following passage of the state's 2011 legislation (DeLeon & Lavadenz, 2020). Despite the state's policy emphasis on EBLs' biliteracy with pathway options spanning K-12, SoBL efforts centered on high-school world-language teaching with few districts tracking participation or ensuring equitable access for EBLs. Researchers noted the lack of connection between SoBL efforts and dual-language bilingual programs in elementary schools.

Early implementation efforts have also been documented in Washington, the sixth state to pass SoBL legislation in 2014, where state administrators and local educators sought to build upon students' linguistic assets while fostering bilingualism as a valuable lifelong skill (Burnet, 2020; Heineke et al., 2019). In a study of four districts spanning rural and suburban contexts, Burnet (2020) investigated how superintendents, language coordinators, teachers, and data managers made decisions while implementing the SoBL. Conducted in 2015–2016 when anti-immigrant sentiments ran high during the presidential campaign, the study found that educators negotiated challenges and opportunities of the SoBL, focusing on benefits for heritage language learners and EBLs. Even though efforts centered in world-language departments, the state's use of competency-based credits allowed districts to use assessments in home and heritage languages to award world-language credit toward high-school graduation. In this way, this unique nuance in Washington's SoBL policy enhanced equity efforts for EBLs among local educators.

As policy implementation has evolved over time, local educators across contexts have increasingly used the SoBL to enhance dual-language bilingual education. Findings from a study of six districts that awarded the SoBL with high frequency indicated how local educators connect the SoBL to bilingual programming and recognize heritage language learners (Heineke & Davin, 2021). Researchers pinpointed states with well-established SoBL policies and invited leaders from top districts in each state in terms of numbers of SoBL recognitions to share their approach to implementation. In all six districts spanning five states, educators looked beyond secondary world-language programs to ground the SoBL in K-12 bilingual education, seeing the initiative as a medium to elevate, celebrate, and extend bilingual programming. With the connection to bilingual education from the outset of implementation, stakeholders made decisions to expand recognition among EBLs and heritage language learners, such as increasing options for testing, paying for SoBL assessments, and expanding biliteracy programming.

Purposeful attention to EBLs has not only occurred at the district level. Studies led by teacher-researchers in schools have demonstrated how classroom- and school-level decisions enhance equity in SoBL implementation. Focused on one high school in Los Angeles, Castro (2020) captured educators' efforts to use the SoBL to disrupt deficit thinking and actions toward EBLs. Despite obstruction by the principal, two instructional coaches persisted in advocacy efforts to extend the SoBL across the school, particularly to EBLs. In another study situated in a high school in rural Florida, Marichal and colleagues (2021) documented one teacher's plight to implement the SoBL to shift prevalent deficit-based thinking and subtractive bilingual education. In a community facing challenges related to migratory work and limited access to resources such as reliable transportation, the teacher sought to support EBLs by advocating for bilingualism schoolwide and creating an advanced placement course in Spanish to help EBLs earn the SoBL. Due to one teacher's efforts, EBLs felt increased pride in their bilingualism and recommended the course to peers.

Focus on Students

Whether at the state, district, school, or classroom level, stakeholders' decisions influence the recognition of heritage language learners and EBLs. Subtirelu and colleagues (2019) provided a birds-eye view of participating districts and SoBL recipients to investigate potential inequities in implementation. One component of their multifaceted research design involved analysis of student demographics within participating school districts in California. Findings revealed that districts with high percentages of English-dominant students were more likely to participate in the SoBL, revealing the potential for perpetuating elite bilingualism rather than recognizing the developing language competencies of heritage language learners and EBLs. Further, districts with high percentages of Black and Asian students were less likely to participate in the SoBL, raising concerns about racial disparities in award distribution. Researchers' analysis of promotional and policy materials uncovered the centering of SoBL efforts in world-language programs, which prompted important implications regarding the need to prioritize the bilingualism of EBLs and immigrant-origin students through bilingual and heritage language education. Situated in the trailblazing state that initiated the SoBL to promote EBLs' biliteracy, this study solidified the importance of critically probing ongoing efforts for equity and access across students, programs, and communities.

Another state-level study has provided insight into how an explicit lens on dual-language bilingual education influenced students receiving the SoBL. Hancock and colleagues (2020) explored SoBL implementation in North Carolina in relation to the State Board of Education's commitment to increase dual-language programs across the state. Authors were interested in how North Carolina incentivized school districts to create dual-language programs and award the SoBL, including which student groups had opportunity and access. Researchers found that the number of SoBL recipients increased as a result of this explicit lens on dual-language bilingual education. The state initiative accelerated growth of dual-language programs beyond original predictions, and 5 of 13 school districts with large populations of EBLs graduated significant numbers of SoBL recipients. In this way, the state's explicit priority on dual-language education helped bolster programs and SoBL implementation in North Carolina.

Another important sub-theme in the literature has involved students sharing perspectives on the SoBL, situating adolescents as agentive participants making decisions around their developing biliteracies. Colomer and Chang-Bacon (2020) investigated the perspectives of three White and three Latinx students who earned the SoBL prior to graduating from a Spanish-English dual-language program in Oregon. With limited research focused on the SoBL in dual-language programs, the researchers sought to understand how students experienced biliteracy as a part of this K-12 program. Students shared insights on merging language and culture, articulating biliteracy as a process of learning language and literacy in two languages paired with the development of cultural competence. Participants described their experiences as culturally and linguistically affirming, asserting access to more diverse perspectives and materials than those provided in traditional curricula outside of the dual-language program. Some students perceived tangible benefits to achieving biliteracy, such as enhanced employment marketability, whereas others recognized inequitable access to dual-language programming.

Other studies have explored why or why not students chose to pursue the SoBL (Davin, 2021; Davin & Heineke, 2018). Though not situated in dual-language programs, these studies have contributed to the field of bilingual education as stakeholders seek to understand why or why not EBLs pursue the SoBL. In one study of three Illinois districts (Davin & Heineke, 2018), researchers found that heritage language learners and EBLs not enrolled in world-language programs did not consistently know about the SoBL or assessment opportunities to demonstrate biliteracy. Another study involved 26 high-school students in Minnesota (Davin, 2021) to investigate current and former EBLs' decisions to take proficiency assessments in their home languages for the SoBL. Whereas some students saw these assessments as a form of resistance toward English monolingualism, others saw them as indexes of heritage language abilities and gatekeepers of future success. Many described lacking confidence in their heritage language abilities, even those who had access to heritage language coursework. External pressures also influenced decisions, as families espoused beliefs toward language maintenance or English assimilation, demonstrating the complexity of decision-making around the SoBL.

Implications and Future Directions for DLBE

Currently adopted in 49 states and the District of Columbia, the SoBL has potential to enhance language education across the United States, though still a nascent area of research in its decade of existence. Originating from grassroots efforts in California, the SoBL emerged as a legislative mechanism to promote the biliteracy development of EBLs amidst policy restrictions to bilingual education (Olsen, 2020). Nonetheless, as the initiative has been adopted and implemented in state and local contexts, that original focus has not remained intact across contexts (Davin & Heineke, 2017). Variation exists in state policy, local implementation, and student outcomes with disparate connections to bilingual education. These variations have sometimes resulted in inequitable distribution of the SoBL by school district, home language, and institutional label (e.g., EL; Subtirelu et al., 2019). Skewed implementation has reinforced critiques that the initiative has benefited the elite bilingualism of White, English-dominant students rather than home and heritage language development among immigrant- and indigenous-origin students (Schwedhelm & King, 2019; Subtirelu, 2020; Valdés, 2020).

Merging SoBL efforts with dual-language bilingual education might begin to respond to these critiques. We recommend stakeholders expand SoBL implementation to include bilingual education, striking balance between bilingual and world-language education. At the state level, lawmakers, administrators, leaders, and advocates should consider revisions to SoBL policies to widen the framing of legislation beyond world-language learning and embrace the value of maintaining home and heritage languages (Heineke et al., 2018; Subtirelu et al., 2019). Nuanced policy requirements can be revised to match this inclusive goal and ensure equity for heritage language learners and EBLs, including those who use less commonly taught languages.

At the local level, SoBL implementation should involve educators with expertise spanning language education contexts and student populations, including world language, bilingual education, and EBLs (Davin & Heineke, 2022). Multiple voices shape implementation, subsequently enriching implementational efforts and nurturing equitable access to biliteracy programming, assessments, and recognition. But collaboration should also extend beyond K-12 schools. Community language schools can serve as valuable partners to promote, support, and assess heritage languages (Borowczyk, 2019). Universities can utilize the SoBL for world-language placement and credit, as well as serve as post-secondary locales to extend biliteracy development beyond K-12 settings (Alfaro et al., 2022; Davin & Heineke, 2022). As a part of these collaborative efforts, stakeholders should meaningfully engage students in SoBL implementational planning and language programming to promote their agency, language competencies, and cultural identities (Colomer & Chang-Bacon, 2020; Davin, 2021).

Research on the SoBL in dual-language bilingual education is currently limited. One dearth in the literature involves SoBL pathway programs, where students receive recognition for their developing biliteracy in elementary and middle schools. Many states and districts have been working to design and implement pathway recognition, and future research could support efforts to infuse the SoBL into K-12 bilingual education. Another area ripe for research lies in SoBL implementation in dual-language programs in high-school settings. As bilingual programs extend into secondary settings in districts across the United States, research can help elucidate how the SoBL initiative might support these efforts by encouraging longitudinal enrollment and providing teachers with ongoing data on language proficiency. Research might also probe how high schools with dual-language programs maintain balance in implementing the SoBL alongside world-language departments to provide equitable access for all learners. Finally, future research might explore the efficacy of using the SoBL to develop pipelines of bilingual teachers, seeking to create actionable steps for school and university stakeholders to recruit, prepare, and license bilingual teachers in response to the teacher shortage that currently plagues U.S. schools.

References

Alfaro, C., Barton, R., & Castro, A. (2022). Lengthening the language line: University Global Seal of Biliteracy. *Multilingual Educator*, Spring, 15–19. https://www.gocabe.org/wp-content/uploads/2022/04/ME-2022-Revised.pdf

American Council on the Teaching of Foreign Languages, Modern Language Association, National Association for Bilingual Education, National Association of English Learner Program Administrators, National Council of State Supervisors for Languages, SealofBiliteracy.org and Californians Together, & TESOL International Association. (2020). *Guidelines for implementing the Seal of Biliteracy* (Joint report). https://sealofbiliteracy.org/doc/sobl-guidelines-2020-final.pdf

Borowczyk, M. (2019). Credentialing heritage: The role of community language schools in implementing the Seal of Biliteracy. *Foreign Language Annals*, *53*, 28–47.

Burnet, M. M. (2020). Signed, sealed, delivered: District-level adoption of the Washington state Seal of Biliteracy. In A. J. Heineke, & K. J. Davin (Eds.), *The Seal of Biliteracy: Case studies and considerations for policy implementation* (pp. 105–122). Information Age.

Castro, A. (2020). Validating the linguistic strengths of English learners: Los Angeles Unified School District's implementation of the Seal of Biliteracy. In A. J. Heineke, & K. J. Davin (Eds.), *The Seal of Biliteracy: Case studies and considerations for policy implementation* (pp. 123–140). Information Age.

Colomer, S. E., & Chang-Bacon, C. K. (2020). Seal of Biliteracy graduates get critical: Incorporating critical biliteracies in dual-language programs and beyond. *Journal of Adolescent and Adult Literacy*, *63*(4), 379–389. https://doi.org/10.1002/jaal.1017

Davin, K. J. (2021). Critical language testing: Factors influencing students' decisions to (not) pursue the Seal of Biliteracy. *Harvard Educational Review*, *91*(2), 179–203. https://doi.org/10.17763/1943-5045-91.2.179

Davin, K. J., & Heineke, A. J. (2017). The Seal of Biliteracy: Variations in policy and outcomes. *Foreign Language Annals*, *50*(3), 486–499. https://doi.org/10.1111/flan.12279

Davin, K. J., & Heineke, A. J. (2018). The Seal of Biliteracy: Adding students' voices to the conversation. *Bilingual Research Journal*, *41*, 312–328. https://doi.org/10.1080/15235882.2018.1481896

Davin, K. J., & Heineke, A. J. (2022). *Promoting multilingualism in schools: A framework for implementing the Seal of Biliteracy*. ACTFL.

DeLeon, T. M., & Lavadenz, M. (2020). The new ecology of biliteracy in California: A study of the early implementation of the Seal of Biliteracy. In A. J. Heineke, & K. J. Davin (Eds.), *The Seal of Biliteracy: Case studies and considerations for policy implementation* (pp. 49–66). Information Age.

García, O. (2009). *Bilingual education in the 21st century: A global perspective*. Wiley-Blackwell.

Hancock, C. R., Davin, K. J., Williams, J. A. III, & Lewis, C. W. (2020). Global initiatives in North Carolina: The impact on culturally and linguistically diverse learners. *Dimension*, 132–150. https://eric.ed.gov/?id=EJ1249862

Heineke, A. J., & Davin, K. J. (2020). Prioritizing multilingualism in U.S. schools: States' policy journeys to enact the Seal of Biliteracy. *Educational Policy*, *34*, 619–643. https://doi.org/10.1177/0895904818802099

Heineke, A. J., & Davin, K. J. (2021). Implementing the Seal of Biliteracy: A multiple case study of six high-awarding districts. *Modern Language Journal*, *105*(2), 395–411. https://doi.org/10.1111/modl.12708

Heineke, A. J., Davin, K. J., & Bedford, A. (2018). The Seal of Biliteracy: Considering equity and access for English learners. *Education Policy Analysis Archives*, *26*(99). https://doi.org/10.14507/epaa.26.3825

Heineke, A. J., Davin, K., & Dávila, A. (2019). Promoting multilingual communities, schools, and students: A closer look at the Seal of Biliteracy in Washington state. *TESOL Journal*, *10*, 1–5. https://doi.org/10.1002/tesj.451

Jansa, T., & Brezicha, K. (2017). The Georgia Seal of Biliteracy: Exploring the nexus of politics and language education. *Dimension*, *45*, 32–48. https://scholarworks.gsu.edu/eps_facpub/27/

Marichal, N., Rosario Roldán, A., & Coady, M. (2021). "My language learners seemed like ghosts": A rural teacher's transformational journey implementing the Seal of Biliteracy. *Rural Educator*, *42*(1), 52–56. https://doi.org/10.35608/ruraled.v42i1.1180

Okraski, C. V., Hancock, C. R., & Davin, K. J. (2020). An innovative approach to the Seal of Biliteracy in Minnesota. In A. J. Heineke, & K. J. Davin (Eds.), *The Seal of Biliteracy: Case studies and considerations for policy implementation* (pp. 67–82). Information Age.

Olsen, L. (2020). The history of the movement: Enacting the state Seal of Biliteracy in the state of California. In A. J. Heineke, & K. J. Davin (Eds.), *The Seal of Biliteracy: Case studies and considerations for policy implementation* (pp. 17–34). Information Age.

Schwedhelm, M. C., & King, K. A. (2019). The neoliberal logic of the state seals of biliteracy. *Foreign Language Annals*, *2020*, 1–16. https://doi.org/10.1111/flan.12438

Sherf, N. L., Hardy, P. R., & Solórzano, H. (2020). A collaborative model for Seal of Biliteracy implementation in the Massachusetts pilot program. In A. J. Heineke, & K. J. Davin (Eds.), *The Seal of Biliteracy: Case studies and considerations for policy implementation* (pp. 85–104). Information Age.

Subtirelu, N. (2020). Raciolinguistic ideology, the Seal of Biliteracy, and the politics of language education. In A. J. Heineke, & K. J. Davin (Eds.), *The Seal of Biliteracy: Case studies and considerations for policy implementation* (pp. 161–176). Information Age.

Subtirelu, N. C., Borowczyk, M., Thorson Hernández, R., & Venezia, F. (2019). Recognizing whose bilingualism? A critical policy analysis of the Seal of Biliteracy. *Modern Language Journal*, *103*(2), 371–390. https://doi.org/10.1111/modl.12556

Valdés, G. (2020). The future of the Seal of Biliteracy: Issues of equity and inclusion. In A. J. Heineke, & K. J. Davin (Eds.), *The Seal of Biliteracy: Case studies and considerations for policy implementation* (pp. 177–204). Information Age.

Racial/Ethnic Groups

21

INDIGENOUS REVITALIZATION-IMMERSION EDUCATION IN NATIVE AMERICAN SETTINGS

Teresa L. McCarty, Sjana Baker

Introduction

Dual-language bilingual education in Native American settings encompasses immense linguistic, cultural, and organizational diversity and unique pedagogical goals. We focus on what is now the United States, though these programs are part of a worldwide network of Indigenous school-community initiatives.[1] Native Peoples in the United States share a history of colonization in which compulsory schooling in the colonial language was a prime instrument of intended identity erasure and territorial dispossession. The effects have been Indigenous-language loss and enduring education disparities. As noted by Lumbee scholar Bryan McKinley Jones Brayboy and Māori scholar Margaret J. Maaka (2015), on every academic indicator, "Indigenous students are suffering" (p. 65). Hence, the combined goals of contemporary Indigenous-language programs are reclaiming ancestral languages and cultural practices and producing academic outcomes equal to with or surpassing mainstream programs (National Coalition of Native American Language Schools and Programs [NCNALSP], 2022).

Indigenous Peoples in the United States Include 564 federally recognized American Indian and Alaska Native nations and Native Hawaiians. Of the 381 languages other than English spoken in the United States, 169 (44%) are Native American languages (U.S. Census Bureau, 2011). All are endangered, as traditional intergenerational language socialization processes have been disrupted by colonization. In addition, there are many "sleeping" languages with no current speakers which may be reawakened

DOI: 10.4324/9781003269076-30

through community-driven language revitalization (Leonard, 2011). Yet most Native students attend public schools with few if any Indigenous teachers and little if any Native-language and culture support (Rampey et al., 2021).

Given these conditions, one promising educational innovation is Indigenous-language immersion (ILI), also called Indigenous revitalization-immersion (McIvor & McCarty, 2016; see also García, 2009). In contrast to two-way dual-language immersion (e.g., Spanish-English programs in the United States) and one-way elite/enrichment immersion (e.g., French immersion for Anglophone students in Canada), ILI is one-way and designed for Indigenous-language revitalization (Tedick et al., 2011). As Indigenous scholars Mary Hermes and Keiki Kawaiʻaeʻa (2014) point out, "nearly all involved" in ILI programs – teachers, students, and parents – "are *heritage language learners themselves*" (p. 305). Also unlike elite one-way immersion, ILI students represent economically and socially minoritized communities for whom there is minimal heritage-language support. Noting that Indigenous-language education does not "fit the standard model of a 'dual language school,'" the National Coalition of Native American Language Schools and Programs (NCNALSP) describes ILI as a "unique pathway" to "high proficiency and literacy in English," in which the Indigenous language is taught as primary and English as auxiliary (2022, para. 6).

Contemporary Native American ILI programs have their roots in coterminous movements in the United States, Canada, and Pacific. One "tap root" movement is Mohawk (Kanien'kehá:ka) in what is now southeastern Canada and the northeastern U.S. Mohawk language and culture schools emerged in the 1970s in response to state/provincial policies that excluded Indigenous languages and cultural content in school (White, 2015; Wilson et al., 2022). As Mohawk scholar Louellyn White writes, Mohawk language reclamation began with community members united in "a determination to keep Mohawk culture alive" (2015, p. 56).

During this same period, a Hawaiian "renaissance" took root in Hawaiʻi, as awareness grew among the youth of the illegal U.S. overthrow of the Hawaiian Monarchy and subsequent Hawaiian-language bans (Wilson et al., 2022). The renaissance led to a 1978 state constitutional amendment establishing Hawaiian as co-official with English. With support from Māori language activists in Aotearoa/New Zealand (Hawaiian and Māori are related Austronesian languages and there are longstanding connections between the two Peoples), a small group of Hawaiian families established ʻAha Pūnana Leo, Hawaiian-medium "language nest" preschools. "By then, the population that spoke Hawaiian had been reduced primarily to elders born before 1920" (Wilson et al., 2022, p. 246). The Pūnana Leo preschools paved the way for Hawaiian-medium tracks and full immersion preK-12 public schools (Warner, 2001; Wilson & Kamanā, 2001, 2011).

The Hawaiian and Māori language movements, as well as earlier Navajo community-controlled schools, influenced the establishment in 1986 of the first Navajo (Dinė) immersion program at Fort Defiance, Arizona within the Navajo Nation. As program cofounders Marie Arviso and Wayne Holm wrote of this program in its infancy, "we wanted to help ... children experience success in school *through* Navajo" (2001, p. 205). By 2004, the program had evolved into a K-8 school, Tséhootsooí Diné Bi'ólta' (TDB, The Navajo School at the Meadow between the Rocks). The school continues today as a public K-5 Navajo (Diné) immersion school.

These early ILI programs are part of international movements for content-based dual-language instruction (Wilson et al., 2022). In 2022, there were 27 Hawaiian-medium schools and hundreds of ILI programs serving American Indian and Alaska Native learners, pre-K through adult, throughout the United States. As NCNALSP Vice President Nāmaka Rawlins observes, ILI "has become a viable path for education" (McCarty et al., 2021, p. 340).

In the remainder of this chapter, we present findings from research on Indigenous revitalization-immersion education across four cross-cutting themes: (1) academic parity and equity; (2) family-community engagement; (3) language and culture reclamation; and (4) new language-learning tools, spaces, and places. We conclude with a discussion of ongoing challenges and future prospects for research, policy, and practice.

Theme 1: Academic Parity and Equity

Writing in 2013, the sociolinguist Stephen May noted the "relative invisibility in *pedagogical* discussions of [Indigenous] immersion education" (May, 2013, p. 35). May's earlier work with Richard Hill and Māori scholar Sarah Tiakiwai (May et al., 2004) had established the benefits for Māori students of "Level 1" immersion in which 90%–100% of content instruction is carried out in the Indigenous language. Achieving these outcomes, May, Hill, and Tiakiwai stressed, requires a minimum of six years of at least 50% immersion at the primary level, a finding consistent with international research, and an "active commitment to equality and positive teacher-student and student-student relationships" (p. 133).

Empirical research on ILI supports these findings. In 2012, Windwalker Corporation and the Center for Applied Linguistics published "an exhaustive search of published and unpublished materials" on American Indian/Alaska Native immersion (Windwalker Corporation & Center for Applied Linguistics, 2012, p. 1). This report cites outcomes of improved academic achievement, enhanced proficiency in the Indigenous language and English, and the development of cultural pride and "school success," measured by strong student attendance, parent involvement, and teacher evaluations (p. 7). In 2011, Teresa McCarty reported a meta-review of research on the role of Native American language(s) and cultural content in Native students' academic achievement (McCarty, 2011). This analysis highlights the benefits of "strong and long" Indigenous-language and culture instruction – programs equivalent to May et al.'s (2004) Level 1 immersion – with robust culturally based content. In addition to improvements in English-medium and locally designed assessments, "strong and long" programs are associated with improved attendance and college-going rates "and enhanced teacher-student and school-community relations" (p. 15).

Several key cases exemplify these outcomes. In northern Arizona, the trilingual K-5 Spanish-English/Navajo-English Puente de Hózhǫ́ (Bridge of Beauty) School has been recognized for consistently "outperforming comparable peers in monolingual English programs" (McCarty, 2011, p. 10). Equally important are teachers' and administrators' reports of "enhanced student motivation and the engagement of parents and the local community" (McCarty, 2011, p. 10; Fillerup, 2011). The early Tséhootsooí Diné Bi'ólta' program produced "[s]ome of the best [student] writing in the school" and the highest math performance (Arviso & Holm, 2001, p. 211). A subsequent study showed that TDB students continued to outperform peers in nonimmersion classrooms on local and state assessments of English reading and math, while developing strong Navajo oral language and literacy skills (Johnson & Legatz, 2006). The preK-12 Nāwahīokalani'ōpu'u (Nāwahī) Laboratory School, which teaches all subjects (including English) through Hawaiian, has a consistent 100% graduation rate and an 80% college-going rate and has attained topmost ratings on state-mandated tests (Wilson & Kamanā, 2011). Hermes and Kawai'ae'a (2014) describe ILI at Nāwahī "as a family commitment to quality education through the revitalization of Hawaiian for today and generations of tomorrow" (pp. 315–316).

Equally significant are the pedagogies underlying these outcomes. In a two-year New Mexico-wide study of promising practices for Native students, Indigenous scholars Theodore Jojola, Tiffany Lee, and their associates (2010) correlated such outcomes with kinship-based pedagogies that cultivate family-like relationships of mutual respect and reciprocity, link subject matter to community and place, and engage students in social justice projects so they can, in one teacher's words, "develop tools to positively change their communities" (Jojola et al., 2010, p. 46). To better understand these pedagogies, we turn to the role of families and communities in ILI schooling.

Theme 2: Family and Community Engagement

Family and community engagement is a hallmark of ILI schooling. "Language immersion methods require knowledge of the cultural community and necessitate relationship building between schools and communities," states Lee (2016, p. 102). According to Native Hawaiian scholar-activist Noelani

Iokepa-Guerrero (2016), ILI brings together older and younger generations to learn together by creating curriculum, taking language classes, and volunteering. Many ILI programs offer language classes for parents and caregivers who are second-language learners, so they can support children's language learning at home. "These family language-learning opportunities have enabled more families to use Hawaiian in the home and community"; parents report a "greater sense of community," says Iokepa-Guerrero, and "that their family is more involved in their child's education" (p. 241).

We illustrate these processes with data from a 2016 to 2023 U.S.-wide, multi-method, multi-university study of ILI schooling at eight well-established ILI schools.[2] In preliminary analyses of the study's qualitative data, McCarty et al. (2021) describe a pattern whereby ILI teachers, their children, and extended family members are united for the purpose of language and culture revitalization. Parents regularly volunteer at ILI schools, helping maintain school facilities, assisting with fund-raising, and contributing to other needed tasks. "I feel like it keeps us more close-knit as parents," a father with two children at an ILI school stated. A grandmother whose children and grandchildren attended the ILI school where she works described it as "a big extended family." Because ILI students move as a cohort through grade levels, children and families tend to bond. "For me," said a parent with multiple children at an ILI school, "this school feels more like a family than [an] ... institution" (McCarty et al., 2022). By its very nature, ILI constructs a communal school culture – a family-like setting of care, responsibility, and mutual support. As a result, explains Iokepa-Guerrero (2016), "individuals grow as a community, supporting one another for the greater purpose of perpetuating the language and culture" (2016, p. 41).

Extensive empirical research documents the benefits to student learning of strong school-parent-community engagement (Education Northwest, 2018). These benefits have feedback loops to other aspects of students' academic, linguistic, cultural, and social-emotional well-being. "Families are the primary contexts in which Indigenous children learn who they are, Indigenous ways of knowing, and what is expected of them," say Indigenous scholars Megan Bang, Charlene Montaño Nolan, and Nikki McDaid-Morgan (2018, p. 2). ILI builds these mechanisms into the fiber of students', teachers', and family members' experiences through "a collaborative model [of] community and school relationships" (Lee, 2016, p. 102).

Theme 3: Language and Culture Reclamation

Now entering its fifth decade, the ILI movement has produced thousands of new speakers of Native American languages. In Hawai'i, a state in which there were fewer than 50 child speakers in 1983, the numbers of child speakers have grown to approximately 4,000, the majority of whom have been educated in Hawaiian-medium schools (Iokepa-Guerrero, 2016). U.S.-wide, the number of speakers of Hawaiian is estimated at 10,000–24,000 (Hermes & Kawai'ae'a, 2014). While linguistic enumeration is problematic (Moore et al., 2010), research makes clear there are many more "new speakers" of Native American languages of all ages and varying proficiencies, the majority of whom have a connection to school- and/or community-based revitalization-immersion programs.

These are vital linguistic outcomes. But ILI programs seek more than linguistic or academic outcomes alone. Culture is "a central driving force" in these programs (Hermes & Kawai'ae'a, 2014, p. 315), and the goal of strengthening learners' cultural knowledge, identity, and pride is paramount. As Native Hawaiian scholar-activist Kauanoe Kamanā emphasizes: "When we think about language, we think about culture. ... so we're not really talking about language methodology but instead the reestablishment of Hawaiian identity ...." (Hermes & Kawai'ae'a, 2014, p. 315). Mohawk scholar-activist Louellyn White states: "Our journey of language reclamation goes beyond the mechanisms of language as communication and honors the ways that language encapsulates culture and identity" (McCarty et al., 2018, p. 167).

Findings from the U.S.-wide ILI study above illuminate how ILI fosters these language-culture connections. Land- and waters-based learning is a key practice in ILI schools. Outdoor classrooms – gardens where traditional crops are cultivated, woodlands, and waterways – are prominent teaching-learning settings, and animal, plant, and earth care are integral to these schools' curricula. These are hands-on, language- and culture-rich environments in which students learn the histories and features of their homeplace and the values and practices of responsibility, earth care, and being in relationship with the more-than-human world (Bang et al., 2015; McCarty et al., 2022). All of this envelopes science, social studies, and language arts. Further, as one ILI teacher related, through these experiences students grow "stronger in heart and mind," knowing "who they are and what their self-identity is" (McCarty et al., 2021, p. 348).

Ethnographic case studies amplify these themes. White (2015), for example, describes an Indigenous approach to holistic education at Akwesasne Freedom School modeled after a pine tree, in which "the language acts as the trunk of the tree, a vital lifeline to all the branches," including Mohawk "dances, songs, and ceremonial knowledge and practice" (p. 80). At the top of the metaphoric tree is "positive identity formation depicted as becoming 'fully Mohawk' or a whole human being" (2015, p. 82). In an ethnographic account of a Hawaiian culture-based secondary school, Hālau Kū Māna, Native Hawaiian scholar Noelani Goodyear-Ka'ōpua (2013) describes land- and waters-based aloha 'āina projects such as kalo cultivation "focused on the community's cultural wealth"; in these projects, students learn language while also working against hegemonic deficit notions about drawing sustenance from the land (pp. 139–140). In a qualitative study of the Native American Community Academy, a language- and culture-based public charter school in Albuquerque, New Mexico, Lee and McCarty (2017) describe a Lakota language teacher's assessment methods, which focus not simply on language proficiency, but also on students' demonstrations of "respect, compassion, and helpful behavior with others, ... attributes associated with Native language practices" (p. 67).

These learnings and teachings fostered by ILI are deeply culture-based. Such education practices "go beyond the classroom," Nāmaka Rawlins points out, and "fill the character [of] our children and the expectation we have for them" (McCarty et al., 2021, p. 348).

Theme 4: New Language-Learning Tools, Spaces, and Places

In 2001, Arapaho scholar-activist Stephen Greymorning reported on the success of an innovative language revitalization initiative, the dubbing of the Walt Disney movie *Bambi* into Arapaho. "Young Arapaho children have been said to watch the video repeatedly and have learned some of the speaking parts of their favorite characters," Greymorning wrote (2001, p. 295). As the linguist Tracey McHenry observed, "A primary way of asserting utility and value and an orientation toward the future in today's world is the skillful use of technology" (2002, pp. 107–108).

Since that time, research and practice on technology for Indigenous-language learning have grown exponentially. In 2006, linguist Susan Penfield and Indigenous colleagues Phillip Cash Cash, Candace Galla, Tracy Williams, and Depree ShadowWalker published one of the first training manuals for technology-enhanced Indigenous language revitalization, reminding readers that "technology ... has *always* been brought to bear on linguistic work with Indigenous languages," often by outside linguists for extractive purposes (Penfield et al., 2006, p. 11). The difference today, they argue, is that advanced multimedia technologies are being repurposed by Indigenous Peoples for language reclamation.

For example, recent work by Hermes and Ojibwe community members uses Indigenous production processes for language learning outside the classroom and the creation of non-school-based teaching materials. The project, described by Hermes et al. (2012), involved Ojibwe movie camps that included over 45 community members over four years "to playfully re-create everyday spoken language situations" (p. 393). Smaller gatherings were held throughout the year to extend the summer camp accomplishments. "One of our hopes in this project," write Hermes et al. (2012), is to "use technology to design materials that can propel a 'quantum leap' in Indigenous language learning. ... Repurposing technological tools for language revitalization opened new spaces for the integration of Indigenous epistemologies and axiologies in learning materials" (pp. 387, 395–396). In another project, Hermes and Kendall King (2013) describe how two urban Ojibwe families used self-guided multimedia software designed to provide a "naturalistic, simulated language-immersion experience" over eight weeks in their homes (p. 128). The analysis shows how families incorporated the software in face-to-face interactions within existing family dynamics – a potential "jumpstart" to offline language use (p. 141; see also Hermes & King, 2019).

Revitalization-immersion is increasingly taking place in the virtual world. The COVID-19 pandemic, which disproportionately impacted Indigenous nations, has heightened the need for technology-mediated language learning and research on its affordances. One of the few recent studies of remote Indigenous-language learning was undertaken by Sjana Baker (Anishinaabe) with Anishinaabemowin (the Anishinaabe language, also known as Ojibwemowin) among learners of all ages in a northern Michigan Anishinaabe nation (Baker, 2021, 2022). The studies took place when virtual learning was not completely new but nonetheless not completely familiar to most study participants. Data included observations of online classes over three months and in-depth videotaped interviews with language learners and teachers of varying ages. How has COVID-19 impacted Indigenous language classes formerly held in person? What are the benefits and challenges of online/virtual learning platforms, creative platforms for materials development, music and video software, and social media messaging and posts?

Participants agreed that the benefits outweighed the limitations. For instance, online classes brought Anishinaabemowin into family homes in ways that had not been possible when classes were held in person. Online classes afforded the opportunity to adapt technology for traditional cultural practices such as storytelling, and "to better ourselves and give future generations the chance to learn their language" – an expression of Anishinaabe sovereignty (Baker, 2022, p. 4). This is a "full circle moment," writes Baker, "because language was originally taught in the home and it is returning home now" (2002, p. 3).

These findings accentuate the crucial role of new technologies in Indigenous-language education. As Native Hawaiian scholar-activist Candace Kaleimamoowahinekapu Galla (2016) states, "[I]t is difficult to imagine the survival of Indigenous languages in the twenty-first century without the intervention of digital technology," especially for youth (p. 1). Baker's (2021, 2022) studies affirm that technology opens new possibilities for intergenerational language learning; technology has the potential "to bring together youth, who are digital natives ... and elders, who are language and cultural knowledge holders" in collaborative language learning and teaching (Galla, 2016, p. 9).

Challenges and Future Prospects for Research, Policy, and Practice

Achieving academic parity and equity, healing the traumas of colonial schooling, reclaiming Indigenous languages and cultural practices, and adapting traditional language acquisition processes to new contexts (schools and online platforms) are complex, time-intensive, and fraught endeavors. In this chapter, we have highlighted *some* of the ways these projects are being carried out through Indigenous revitalization-immersion education. As Hermes et al. (2012) observe, this is "passionate, political, and deeply personal" work for "Native people who are acutely aware that the federal government's attempted genocide was the direct cause of Indigenous language loss" (p. 383). The foregoing analysis has shown that these are not merely education "reforms," but rather larger projects aimed at promoting the holistic well-being of Indigenous children, families, communities, and nations – "projects of survivance" (Goodyear-Ka'ōpua, 2013, p. 5).

This work brings a multitude of challenges, including "overcoming the historical effects of suppression of Indigenous languages in their homelands" (NCNALSP, 2022, para. 7). This requires applying a critical, anticolonial, antiracist lens to this work. This history also means that first-language speakers are increasingly elderly and teachers are typically Indigenous-language learners. There is no other country from which to recruit new teachers; they must come from their home communities and nations. Nor are there large, well-funded curriculum production entities such as are available for colonial languages. Developing a sustainable cadre of language teachers and teaching materials is a long-term, ground-up effort.

The economic challenges are massive due to chasms of wealth disparity. Federal and state support is meager. And, there are ideological challenges, described by Hermes and Kawai'ae'a as the "pull" between mainstream Western education with overwhelming federal, state, and public support, and anticolonial approaches that promote Indigenous languages, knowledges, and desired futures. More research is needed on how these challenges are being addressed, and the implications for language education policy and practice. Concrete, significant public support, including federal and state resources, is urgently needed.

Despite the challenges, the revitalization-immersion movement continues to grow, aided by Indigenous organizations such as the NCNALSP and by hard-fought legislation crafted by Indigenous practitioners, scholars, and allies. The latter include the 1990 Native American Languages Act (Public Law 101-477), the 2006 Esther Martinez Native American Languages Preservation Act (Public Law 109-394), and the 2007 United Nations *Declaration on the Rights of Indigenous Peoples.*

Indigenous-language revitalization-immersion is an expression of the inherent sovereignty of Indigenous Peoples. While much remains to be done, the movement has planted the seeds and birthed the fruits of linguistic and educational self-determination.

Notes

1 We use the term Native American to refer to American Indian, Alaska Native, and Native Hawaiian Peoples in what is now the United States. We also use Native and Indigenous to refer to Native American Peoples, languages, lands, and to Indigenous Peoples in other parts of the world.

2 The *Indigenous-Language Immersion and Native American Student Achievement Study* is funded by the Spencer Foundation (Grant Award No. 201700054). Principal investigators are Teresa L. McCarty, Tiffany S. Lee, Sheilah E. Nicholas, and Michael Seltzer.

References

Arviso, M., & Holm, W. (2001). Tséhootsooídi Ólta'gi Diné bizaad bíhoo'aah: A Navajo immersion program at Fort Defiance, Arizona. In L. Hinton, & K. Hale (Eds.), *The green book of language revitalization in practice* (pp. 203–215). Academic Press.

Baker, S. (2022). Anishinaabemowin and technology. Master's thesis, University of California, Los Angeles, American Indian Studies.

Baker, S. (2021). Remote Indigenous language learning: Exploring the impacts of the COVID-19 pandemic on community language classes. Unpublished MS.

Bang, M., Marin, A., Medin, D., & Washinawatok, K. (2015). Learning by observing, pitching in, and being in relations in the natural world. In M. Correa-Chávez, R. Mejia-Arauz, & B. Rogoff (Eds.), *Children learn by observing and contributing to family and community endeavors* (pp. 303–313). Elsevier.

Bang, M., Montaño Nolan, C., & McDaid-Morgan, N. (2018). Indigenous family engagement: Strong families, strong nations. In E.A. McKinley, & L.T. Smith (Eds.), *Handbook of Indigenous education.* https://doi.org/10.1007/978-981-10-1839-8_74-1

Brayboy, B. McK. J., & Maaka, M. (2015). K-12 achievement for Indigenous students. *Journal of American Indian Education*, *54*(1), 63–98.

Education Northwest. (2018). *What the research says on engaging Native families.* Retrieved on May 20, 2022 from https://educationnorthwest.org/resources/what-research-says=engaging-native-families

Fillerup, M. (2011). Building a "bridge of beauty": A preliminary report on promising practices in Native language and culture teaching at Puente de Hózhǫ́ Trilingual Magnet School. In M. E. Romero, S. J. Ortiz, T. L. McCarty, & R. Chen (Eds.), *Indigenous languages across the generations: Strengthening families and communities* (pp. 145–164). Arizona State University Center for Indian Education.

Galla, C. K. (2016). Indigenous language revitalization, promotion, and education: Function of digital technology. *Computer Assisted Language Learning.* http://dx.doi.org/10.1080/09588221.2016.1166137

García, O. (2009). *Bilingual education in the 21st century: A global perspective.* Wiley-Blackwell.

Goodyear-Ka'ōpua, N. (2013). *The seeds we planted: Portraits of a Native Hawaiian charter school.* University of Minnesota Press.

Greymorning, S. (2001). Reflections on the Arapaho Language Project, or when Bambi spoke Arapaho and other tales of Arapaho Language revitalization efforts. In L. Hinton & K. Hale (Eds.), *The green book of language revitalization in practice* (pp. 287–297). Academic Press.

Hermes, M., & Kawai'ae'a, K. (2014). Revitalizing Indigenous languages through Indigenous immersion education. *Journal of Immersion and Content-Based Language Education*, *2*(2), 303–322.

Hermes, M., & King, K. A. (2013). Ojibwe language revitalization, multimedia technology, and family language learning. *Language Learning and Technology*, *17*(1), 125–144.

Hermes, M., & King, K. A. (2019). Task-based language learning for Ojibwe: A case study of two intermediate adult language learners. In T. L. McCarty, S. E. Nicholas, & G. Wigglesworth (Eds.), *A world of Indigenous languages: Politics, pedagogies and prospects for language reclamation* (pp. 134–152). Multilingual Matters.

Hermes, M., Bang, M., & Marin, M. (2012). Designing Indigenous language revitalization. *Harvard Educational Review*, *82*(3), 381–402.

Iokepa-Guerrero, N. (2016). Revitalization programs and impacts in the USA and Canada. In S. M. Coronel-Molina, & T. L. McCarty (Eds.), *Indigenous language revitalization in the Americas* (pp. 227–246). Routledge.

Johnson, F. T., & Legatz, J. (2006). Tséhootsooí Diné Bi'ólta' [Fort Defiance Navajo Immersion School]. *Journal of American Indian Education*, *45*(2), 26–33.

Jojola, T., Lee, T. S., …, & Singer, B. (2010). *Indian education in New Mexico, 2025*. New Mexico Public Education Department and Eight Northern Indian Pueblos Council, Inc.

Lee, T. S. (2016). The home-school-community interface in language revitalization in the USA and Canada. In S. M. Coronel-Molina, & T. L. McCarty (Eds.), *Indigenous language revitalization in the Americas* (pp. 99–115). Routledge.

Lee, T. S., & McCarty, T. L. (2017). Upholding Indigenous education sovereignty through critical culturally sustaining/revitalizing pedagogy. In D. Paris & H. S. Alim (Eds.), *Culturally sustaining pedagogies: Teaching and learning for justice in a changing world* (pp. 61–82). Teachers College Press.

Leonard, W. Y. (2011). Challenging "extinction" through modern Miami language practices. *American Indian Culture and Research Journal*, *35*(2), 135–160.

May, S. (2013). Indigenous immersion education: International developments. *Journal of Immersion and Content-Based Language Education*, *1*(1), 34–69.

May, S., Hill, R., & Tiakiwai, S. (2004). *Bilingual/immersion education: Indicators of good practice*. Ministry of Education.

McCarty, T. L. (2011). *State of the field: The role of Native languages and cultures in American Indian, Alaska Native, and Native Hawaiian student achievement*. Arizona State University Center for Indian Education.

McCarty, T. L., Lee, T. S., Noguera, J., Yepa, W., & Nicholas, S. E. (2022). "You should know the name of the wind where you live" – Relationality and relational accountability in Indigenous-language education. *Comparative Education Review*, *66*(3), 417–441.

McCarty, T. L., Nicholas, S. E., Chew, K., Diaz, N., Leonard, W. Y., & White, L. (2018). Hear our languages, hear our voices: Storywork as theory and praxis in Indigenous-language reclamation. *Daedalus, Journal of the American Academy of Arts and Sciences*, *147*(2), 160–172.

McCarty, T. L., Noguera, J., Lee, T. S., & Nicholas, S. E. (2021). "A viable path for education" – Indigenous-language immersion and sustainable self-determination. *Journal of Language, Identity, and Education*, *20*(5), 340–354.

McHenry, T. (2002). Words as big as the screen: Native American languages and the internet. *Language Learning and Technology*, *6*(2), 102–115. https://dx.doi.org/10125/25164

McIvor, O., & McCarty, T. L. (2016). Indigenous bilingual and revitalization-immersion education in Canada and the USA. In O. García & A. Lin (Eds.), *Bilingual and multilingual education, Encyclopedia of language and education*. Doi:10.1007/978-3-319-02324-3_34-1.

Moore, R. E., Pietikäinen, S., & Blommaert, J. (2010). Counting the losses: Numbers as the language of endangerment. *Sociolinguistic Studies*, *4*(1), 1–26.

National Coalition of Native American Language Schools and Programs (NCNALSP). (2022). *Frequently asked questions*. Retrieved on May 15, 2022 from http://www.ncnalsp.org/faq

Penfield, S. D., Cash Cash, P., Galla, C. K., Williams, T., & ShadowWalker, D. (2006). *Technology-enhanced language revitalization*. Arizona Board of Regents.

Rampey, B. D., Faircloth, S. C., Whorton, R. P., & Deaton, J. (2021). *National Indian Education Study 2019* (NCES 2021-018). U.S. Department of Education.

Tedick, D. J., Christian, D., & Fortune, T. W. (2011). The future of immersion education: An invitation to "dwell in possibility. In D. J. Tedick, D. Christian, & T. W. Fortune (Eds.), *Immersion education: Practices, policies, possibilities* (pp. 1–10). Multilingual Matters.

U.S. Census Bureau. (2011). *Native North American languages spoken at home in the United States and Puerto Rico: 2006–2010*. American Community Survey Briefs. U.S. Department of Commerce.

Warner, S. N. (2001). The movement to revitalize Hawaiian language and culture. In L. Hinton & K. Hale (Eds.), *The green book of language revitalization in practice* (pp. 133–144). Academic Press.

White, L. (2015). *Free to be Mohawk: Indigenous education at the Akwesasne Freedom School*. University of Oklahoma Press.

Wilson, W. H., & Kamanā, K. (2001). Mai loko mai o ka 'i'ini: Proceeding from a dream": The 'Aha Pūnana Leo connection in Hawaiian language revitalization. In L. Hinton, & K. Hale (Eds.), *The green book of language revitalization in practice* (pp. 147–176). Academic Press.

Wilson, W. H., & Kamanā, K. (2011). Insights from Indigenous language immersion in Hawai'i. In D. J. Tedick, D. Christian, & T. W. Fortune (Eds.), *Immersion education: Practices, policies, possibilities* (pp. 36–57). Multilingual Matters.

Wilson, W. H., DeCaire, R., Gonzalez, B. N., & McCarty, T. L. (2022). Progress, challenges, and trajectories for Indigenous language content-based instruction in the United States and Canada. *Journal of Immersion and Content-Based Language Education*, *10*(2), 343–373.

Windwalker Corporation & Center for Applied Linguistics (2012). *In-depth literature review of American Indian and Alaska Native language immersion programs*. Report submitted to the U.S. Office of Indian Education. Windwalker Corp.

22

TOWARD A CRITICAL MULTIDIMENSIONAL PEDAGOGY FOR MULTILINGUAL BLACK LEARNERS

Christina L. Dobbs, Eurydice Bouchereau Bauer

Despite a large and growing number of Black multilingual learners (BMLs) in schools, research literature that focuses on this population of students in dual language education settings is scarce. Given this scarcity, this chapter will review what is known about BMLs in dual language education settings to argue for more research on BMLs in order to better design dual language settings that center their full intersectional identities. This synthesis highlights the need for a critical and intersectional approach to supporting the academic achievement and identity development of BMLs.

The Population of Black Multilingual Learners

It can be difficult to discern particulars about the population of BMLs, due to a lack of consistent data over time that breaks down groups by language status, race, and other demographic factors. According to the U.S. Office of English Language Acquisition (2021), in 2017–18, 4.2% of English learners in K-12 identified as Black (*n* = 223,893 students), and 2.9% of students who identify as Black were classified English learners. They note that the most common countries of origin for foreign-born students were Haiti (17%), Ethiopia (8.2%), Nigeria (7.3%), Kenya (6.7%), and the Dominican Republic (6.2%). The languages spoken by Black English learners (ELs) most commonly are Spanish (30.6%), Haitian (13.1%), French (11.1%), and Swahili (8%).

Additionally, data about Black immigrants to the United States can inform our understandings of BMLs. As of 2015, 3.8 million Black immigrants

 DOI: 10.4324/9781003269076-31

were living in the United States, which is quadruple the number in 1980, and this growth has continued (Anderson, 2015; Romo et al., 2018; Zong & Batalova, 2016). Black immigrants who come to the U.S. voluntarily have increased by 2,000% from the mid-1960s to the 2010s (Anderson, 2015), making these groups one of the fastest growing populations of U.S. immigrants (Capps et al., 2001; Romo et al., 2018).

It is also known that, in the United States, English learners with African and Caribbean origins are a growing group (Romo et. al., 2018). Approximately half of the population of Black immigrants to the United States are from the Caribbean, with the largest share of 18% from Jamaica and 15% from Haiti (Anderson, 2015). Much of the growth in the Black immigrant population is driven by immigrants from Africa, with virtually all of this growth drawn from countries in sub-Saharan Africa; of the population of Black population born outside the United States, Africans comprise 36% up from 24% in 2000 and 7% in 1980. Anderson (2015) also points to the large numbers of Black immigrants from countries using primarily Spanish: the Dominican Republic, Mexico, Cuba, and Panama among them, and 11% of the foreign-born Black U.S. population identify as Hispanic. The South African literature, from which some of the research about BMLs is drawn, also points toward a broad diversity of learners from different linguistic backgrounds (Vandeyar & Catalano, 2020).

Despite the size of the population of BMLs and their unique needs, this group is often invisible in the research literature due to a common tendency to disaggregate data based on only one demographic dimension (Awokoya & Clark, 2008; Harry & Klingner, 2006), and this simple sorting often folds BMLs into a broader group of Black students or English learners. This invisibility erases the unique needs of a group whose specific experiences require attentiveness to a range of intersecting elements of marginalization.

Black Multilingual Learners in Dual Language Education Settings

We begin with the body of research about BMLs, which while small provides important insights into this population of students. A key study by Palmer (2007) uncovered patterns in a dual language two-way immersion program focused on Spanish/English in a 90:10 model. First, the two-way immersion school second grade that was studied did not enroll many Black students in the dual language program, and given the school's general focus on English, the Spanish language was marginalized except in the dual language classrooms. This English-dominant environment created a need for highly qualified bilingual teachers and organizational moves to counter discourses that continued to position English as central.

An ethnographic study conducted in a South African urban primary school sought to understand how the dual language approach was functioning when students were learning in English and either Sesotho or isiZulu depending on their home language (Sekhukhune, 2015). The study pointed to the complexity of language use in the classroom, as students used multiple languages, including English and a range of languages connected to Sesotho and isiZulu, and therefore the need to support parents/caregivers in being confident using first languages with students outside school and to prepare teachers for this sort of language diversity (Alfaro, 2019). This pattern was also shown to be true in a study of secondary schools in South Africa, with teachers reporting they felt differing degrees of comfort delivering instruction in English vs. in Afrikaans (Mpisi, 2010).

Two-way immersion bilingual programs, which often enroll first-language English speakers in the United States as well as users of another language, often do not enroll Black students, opting instead to reserve space for users of White mainstream English (Palmer, 2010), despite the fact that evidence shows that Black students can excel in dual language programs (Holobow et al., 1991; Lightbown, 2007). A study of nine African-American parents of students enrolled in an early elementary Spanish-English two-way dual language program found that parents placed a high value on language as capital that would provide opportunities for students later in life, though they also felt tensions around learning Spanish in a demographically shifting community (Bauer & Harrison, 2015).

These patterns in existing literature point toward the potential of dual language instructional settings to engage BMLs in learning multiple languages while attending to complex biliterate/bilingual identities being developed. The prior research also highlights the need for the effective preparation of teachers to support BMLs and create learning spaces that allow students to utilize all of their language resources to support their learning.

Intersections of Identity and Language for Black Multilingual Learners in DLE Programs

A study with elementary BL users in a Spanish-English two-way immersion program showed that students used language from across their repertoires, and they often resisted attempts to push them toward using White mainstream English as the standardized classroom form (Frieson, 2021). However, because two-way immersion programs tend to separate the two languages, focusing on one teacher delivering instruction in a target language and another focused on White mainstream English, Black language users often encounter the erasure of their language as monolingual ideologies are promoted in each space.

An ethnographic study of an African-American student's bilingual and biliterate identity development followed a student enrolled in a Spanish-English two-way dual language program (using a language allocation model that varied across grades) from kindergarten to fifth grade (Bauer, Cárdenas-Curiel, & Ponzio, 2020). The study showed a shifting bilingual/biliterate identity for the student, who felt excited about learning Spanish early but later she began to reject Spanish in more explicit ways, as English-dominant speakers in her class also began to be less invested in Spanish leading to conflicts between classmates that were racialized.

Studies also show complex linguistic practices used by BMLs in dual language classrooms, only some of which are acknowledged or sanctioned by schools. A case study of six students enrolled in a Spanish-English two-way dual language kindergarten (in a 90:10 allocation) included several Black multilinguals, some who used English primarily at home and others who used Spanish (Bauer, Colomer, & Wiemelt, 2020). A wordless picture book retelling task revealed the fluid and dynamic ways that students used language to tell rich stories in ways that are often missed by traditional literacy assessments. Another study showed similar patterns and found kindergarten and first-grade BMLs translanguaging to push back against the rigid language allocation policies in their Spanish/English dual language program (Frieson & Scalise, 2021), a pattern also seen in a South African primary school (Ncoko et al., 2000).

However, teachers can make instructional moves that value the rich linguistic repertoires of students in ways that encourage translanguaging. One study in a two-way Spanish-English dual language kindergarten classroom used a system called buddy pairs, a paired talk structure, which allowed student participants to take risks, translanguage, and write more in Spanish (Bauer et al., 2017). This pattern of translanguaging as a supportive practice for BMLs held true in a university setting, in a multilingual tutoring system to ensure that speakers of a range of languages received course information in English or Afrikaans as well as their first language (du Plessis, 2014). These sorts of approaches encourage translanguaging, and their impact on BMLs should be studied in more contexts.

Perspectives on the Complexity of the School Experiences of Black Multilingual Learners

Research has also used critical race theory (CRT) to dissect the complex lived experiences of BMLs. These studies, while sometimes conducted outside dual language settings, push the field to consider how intersectional identities are experienced by BMLs. Given that prior work has demonstrated the potential for dual language programs to replicate similar harms to students as in other settings (Frieson, 2022), research from a range of settings is useful here to understand how intersectionally supportive dual language contexts could be built.

There is a wealth of research that documents an 'achievement gap' wherein Black and Brown students are shown to be 'behind' White and Asian students (see Shapiro, 2014 for a discussion). A study of African refugee students documented their frustration at being perceived as lacking education when they first arrived in the United States and the systematic focus on proving their knowledge using standardized tests that rely solely on English (Shapiro, 2014). These deficit discourses seldom look closely at identity beyond basic racial classification, and BMLs can provide a counterexample to this common narrative. A study of school achievement of U.S. BMLs showed that they outperform their multilingual peers of other races on standardized assessments (Shockley, 2021). The author suggested that the rarity of breaking down demographics beyond inclusion of only race or language status masks this pattern and reinforces a problematic narrative of student achievement.

Studies of BMLs in dual- and single-language education settings demonstrate that these students continually grapple with and negotiate interconnected and complex identities simultaneously, continually constructing identities of their own, even as their identities are co-constructed by others. A study of Somali teens revealed students grappling with facets of identity having to do with language and race, but also culture, religion, and identities as refugees (Bigelow, 2010). Research about BMLs in Canada revealed similar patterns of struggle against discourses that frame them as 'at risk' (Dei, 2008; West-Burns & Murray, 2016); this embrace of multilingualism is key for dual language programs to avoid marginalizing BMLs.

A study of former refugee students in a New England refugee resettlement community highlights many key discourses that can harm BMLs. The study explored the impact of deficit discourses on these students who left school to protest racism in response to interracial tensions in the school (Shapiro, 2014). The students described their experience as being treated as though all African students are the same, and the unfair spotlighting of African students and their achievement, despite the fact that other groups were not subject to this same singling-out. They described being perceived as intellectually inferior, illiterate, and having fewer educational experiences as other students, regardless of their actual prior education, a pattern demonstrated in other studies as well (See Bigelow, 2010).

Additionally, studies of BMLs point to the hegemonic centrality of English as an academic goal for these students, at times to the exclusion of other sorts of content and skills. A study of two fifth grade African immigrants, fluent in French and Lingala and educated in French prior to coming to America, revealed a pattern wherein ESL teachers focused primarily on developing English skills, at the expense of exposure to other content such as math or science (Somé-Guiébré, 2016). Other studies also point toward the positioning of English as a key lever for opportunity to advance academically across various educational settings (du Plessis, 2014), leading to key questions around broad discourses about language and race that are often surrounding, and in some cases, even espoused by, BMLs and how these hierarchies might be unlearned.

Another study that documents a counterstory of a Black mother whose child was marginalized in a U.S. dual language program (an English/Spanish program embedded within a broader English-focused school), in a space that recruited White and Latinx students to participate with no focus at all on recruiting Black children, despite the fact that approximately a third of the school's students were Black (Blanton et al., 2021). At this site, as is the case in dual language programs that can disproportionately serve privileged students and families (Valdez et al., 2016), White families asserted their Whiteness as property, as CRT describes, to access the dual language instructional space in high numbers, creating a space wherein the mother had to advocate for her Black child in the dual language program and causing her to feel a sense of racial battle fatigue (See Smith, 2004), an accumulation of stress experienced by marginalized people in spaces wherein racial aggressions are experienced regularly. It is clear that dual language education programs that do not attend to and centralize the full humanity of BMLs run the risk of doing harm to those students (Frieson, 2022).

Mitchell (2013) used CRT to explore 100 studies of secondary multilingual learners to uncover what she terms 'majoritarian' stories that play an important role in how decisions were made about educating multilingual learners. The majoritarian stories uncovered included two relevant to this discussion: first that English is all that matters, and second, that there is no story about race. Given how many multilingual learners in U.S. schools are students of color (80% of immigrant students) (Suárez-Orozco et al., 2009), it is problematic to refuse to focus on race when discussing this population of students. This means that initiatives and their resulting policies such as 'English for the Children,' a campaign that was successful in abolishing dual language education in California, Arizona, and Massachusetts are not viewed as racist because they are positioned such that there is no story of race to explore and English is the only language that matters (Mitchell, 2013). The sanitized, non-racialized versions of these stories persist, despite evidence that demonstrates the key role of racism in passing these initiatives (Arellano-Houchin et al., 2001; Cline et al., 2004). The ban on bilingual education in California was repealed in 2016 and in Massachusetts in 2017, while Arizona's stands as of this writing (Mitchell, 2019), but the pattern of erasure of the discussion of race and racism in efforts to rebuild dual language education in these states seems to continue as new policies are being made.

Discourses of schooling that easily position the 'social defaults' of Whiteness or monolingualism (often with English) atop a hierarchy of priorities are doubly harmful to students who are neither White nor monolingual.

These sorts of discourses too often position BMLs as outsiders who are meant to assimilate as quickly as possible into English and to ignore these students' racialized experiences (McKinney, 2010). These discourses of dominant English monolingualism are exacerbated by new discourses that position African migrants, in particular, as a new model minority in the United States, an idea that certainly perpetuates anti-Blackness (Smith, 2020; Ukpokodu, 2018).

Toward a Critical Multidimensional Pedagogy

BMLs often find themselves in spaces dedicated both to the hegemony of English and to anti-Blackness (Darder, 2012; Macedo et al., 2015). As a result, they face intersecting forms of oppression and schooling that deny various elements of their lived experience. But if we consider what is known about BMLs in dual language programs, it seems possible that dual language instruction that is delivered by highly qualified and critically conscious teachers (Alfaro, 2019) and that attends purposefully to both race and linguistic identity can support BMLs in having positive identity development as well as successful academic achievement and heritage language maintenance.

But in order to foster these positive outcomes, instruction will need to take a critical stance in helping students deconstruct the messages that surround them about their linguistic and racial experiences. Smith (2019), a researcher who studies BMLs and teachers, calls for a transraciolinguistic approach to instruction for BMLs. This approach is focused on the complex personhood of students whose race and language both shape their experiences of the world and should be honored in school in ways that retain that personhood. This approach is supported by instructional settings that support students in using all of their language resources in ways that are authentic and fluid and do not reinforce dominant English hegemony, while affirming student identity (Davila, 2019).

The population of BMLs is understudied, and therefore future research would do well to ensure that data are disaggregated by both race and language status, as well as focusing specifically on the wide range of groups of Black multilingual students. Students who are immigrants from the African continent have different needs than those from Afro-Latinx communities, just to name two examples of the broad diversity of BMLs. We call here for more research dedicated to specific groups of BMLs to better inform our knowledge base about how to best support their development and build dual language educational settings that will serve them in ways that support multilingual language development and positive racial identity development, all while supporting students in acquiring content knowledge and skills to support their goals.

References

Alfaro, C. (2019). Preparing critically conscious dual-language teachers: Recognizing and interrupting dominant ideologies. *Theory into Practice*, *58*, 194–203.

Anderson, M. (2015). *A rising share of the US black population is foreign born; 9 percent are immigrants*. Pew Research Center.

Arellano-Houchin, A., Flamenco, C., Merlos, M., & Segura, L. (2001). Has California's passage of Proposition 227 made a difference in the way we teach? *The Urban Review*, *33*(3), 221–235.

Awokoya, J. T., & Clark, C. (2008). Demystifying cultural theories and practices: Locating black immigrant experiences in teacher education research. *Multicultural Education*, *16*(2), 49–58.

Bauer, E. B., Cárdenas-Curiel, L., & Ponzio, C. (2020). "You can talk in Espagñol!": An ethnographic case study of an African-American emergent bilingual and biliterate identity. *Reading Psychology*, *41*(7), 680–711.

Bauer, E. B., & Harrison, D. (2015). Parental perspectives on dual language classrooms: The role of the African American parents. In P. Smith, & A. Kumi-Yeboah (Eds.), *Handbook of research on cross-cultural approaches to language and literacy development* (pp. 139–157). IGI Global.

Bauer, E. B., Colomer, S., & Wiemelt, J. (2020). Biliteracy of African Americans and Latinas/os in a kindergarten dual language program: Understanding students' translanguaging practices across informal assessments. *Urban Education*, *55*(3), 331–361.

Bauer, E. B., Presiado, V., & Colomer, S. (2017). Writing through partnership: Fostering translanguaging in children who are emergent bilinguals. *Journal of Literacy Research*, *49*(1), 10–37.

Bigelow, M. H. (2010). *Mogadishu on the Mississippi: Language, racialized identity, and education in a new land*. Wiley.

Blanton, A., Kasun, G. S., Gambrell, J. A., & Espinosa, Z. (2021). A Black mother's counterstory to the Brown-White binary in dual language education: Toward disrupting dual language as White property. *Language Policy*, *20*, 463–487.

Capps, R., McCabe, K., & Fix, M. (2001). *New streams: Black African migration to the United States*. Migration Policy Institute. https://www.migrationpolicy.org/research/new-streams-black-african-migration-united-states

Cline, Z., Necochea, J., & Rios, F. (2004). The tyranny of democracy: Deconstructing the passage of racist propositions. *Journal of Latinos and Education*, *3*(2), 67–85.

Darder, A. (2012). *Culture and power in the classroom: Educational foundations for the schooling of bicultural students*. Paradigm.

Davila, L. T. (2019). Multilingualism and identity: Articulating 'African-ness' in an American high school. *Race, Ethnicity & Education*, *22*(5), 634–646.

Dei, G. J. S. (2008). Schooling as community: Race, schooling, and the education of African youth. *Journal of Black Studies*, *38*(3), 346–366.

du Plessis, S. (2014). Peer tutoring during language code-switching lectures as a teaching strategy in multilingual classes. *South African Journal of Higher Education*, *28*(4), 1194–1215.

Frieson, B. L. & Scales, M (2021). Linguistic artistry and flexibility in dual-language bilingual classrooms: Young Black children's language and literacy practices. Bilingual Research Journal, *44*(2), 213–230. https://doi.org/10.1080/15235882.2021.1942323

Frieson, B. L. (2021). Remixin' and flowin' in centros: Exploring the biliteracy practices of Black language speakers in an elementary two-way immersion bilingual program. *Race, Ethnicity and Education*. https://doi.org/10.1080/13613324.2021.1890568

Frieson, B. (2022). "It's like they don't see us at all": A critical race theory critique of dual language bilingual education for Black children. *Annual Review of Applied Linguistics*, *42*, 47–54.

Harry, B., & Klingner, J. (2006). *Why are so many minority students in special education? Understanding race and disability in schools*. Teachers College Press.

Holobow, N., Genesee, F., & Lambert, W. (1991). The effectiveness of a foreign language immersion program for children from different ethnic and social class backgrounds: Report 2. *Applied Psycholinguistics*, *12*, 171–198.

Lightbown, P. (2007). Fair trade: Two-way bilingual education. *Estudios de Lingüística inglesa aplicada*, *7*, 9–34.

Macedo, D., Dendrinos, B., & Gounari, P. (2015). *Hegemony of English*. Routledge.

McKinney, C. (2010). Schooling in black and white: Assimilationist discourses and subversive identity performances in desegregated South African girls' school. *Race, Ethnicity and Education*, *13*(2), 191–207.

Mitchell, K. (2013). Race, difference, meritocracy, and English: Majoritarian stories in the education of secondary multilingual learners. *Race, Ethnicity and Education*, *16*(3), 339–364.

Mitchell, C. (2019, October 30). 'English-only' laws in education on verge of extinction. *Education Week*, *39*(11), 1.

Mpisi, A. S. (2010). *The scholastic experience of Black learners in multicultural FET schools in the northern Cape*. Unpublished doctoral dissertation. University of the Free State.

Ncoko, S. O. S., Osman, R., & Cockcroft, K. (2000). Codeswitching among multilingual learners in primary schools in South Africa: An exploratory study. *International Journal of Bilingual Education and Bilingualism*, *3*(4), 225–241.

Office of English Language Acquisition (2021). *English learners who are Black [fact sheet]*. US Department of Education, Office of English Language Acquisition.

Palmer, D. (2007). A dual immersion strand programme in California: Carrying out the promise of dual-language education in an English-dominant context. *International Journal of Bilingual Education and Bilingualism*, *10*(6), 752–768.

Palmer, D. (2010). Race, power, and equity in a multiethnic urban elementary school with a dual-language "strand" program. *Anthropology & Education Quarterly*, *41*(1), 94–114.

Romo, H. D., Thomas, K. J. A., & García, E. E. (2018). Changing demographics of dual language learners and English learners: Implications for school success. *SRCD Social Policy Report*, *31*(2), 1–35.

Sekhukhune, C. D. (2015). The narrative of dual medium in a multilingual context of a Black urban area in grade R. *International Journal of Educational Development in Africa*, *2*(1), 70–83.

Shapiro, S. (2014). "Words that you said got bigger": English language learners' lived experiences of deficit discourse. *Research in the Teaching of English*, *48*(4), 386–406.

Shockley, E. T. (2021). Expanding the narrative of the Black-White gap in education research: Black English learners as a counterexample. *Journal of Negro Education*, *90*(1), 7–25.

Smith, W. A. (2004). Black faculty coping with racial battle fatigue: The campus racial climate in a post-civil rights era. In D. Cleveland (Ed.), *A long way to go: Conversations about race by African American faculty and graduate students* (pp. 171–190). Peter Lang.

Smith, P. (2019). (Re)positioning in the Englishes and (English) literacies of a black immigrant youth: Towards a *transraciolinguistic* approach. *Theory into Practice, 58*, 292–303.

Smith, P. (2020). Silencing invisibility: Toward a framework for Black immigrant literacies. *Teachers College Record, 122*(13), 1–42.

Somé-Guiébré, E. (2016). Mainstreaming English language learners: Does it promote or hinder literacy development? *English Language Teaching, 9*(1), 33–40.

Suárez-Orozco, C., Pimental, A., & Martin, M. (2009). The significance of relationships: Academic engagement and achievement among newcomer immigrant youth. *Teachers College Record, 111*(3), 712–749.

Ukpokodu, O. M. (2018). African immigrants, the "new model minority": Examining the reality in U.S. K–12 schools. *The Urban Review, 50*, 60–96.

Valdez, V. E., Freire, J. A., & Delavan, M. G. (2016). The gentrification of dual language education. *Urban Review, 48*(4), 601–627.

Vandeyar, S., & Catalano, T. (2020). Language and identity: Multilingual immigrant learners of South Africa. *Language Matters, 51*(2), 106–128.

West-Burns, N., & Murray, K. (2016). Critical practitioner inquiries: Re-framing marginalized spaces for Black students. *Perspectives on Urban Education, 13*(1), 60–64.

Zong, J., & Batalova, J. (2016). Caribbean immigrants to the United States in 2014. *Migration Information Source*. https://www.migrationpolicy.org/article/caribbean-immigrants-united-states-2014

SECTION III

School-Based Practices

Student Relationships

23

IDENTITY CONSTRUCTION AND STUDENTS IN DLBE CLASSROOMS

Suzanne García-Mateus, Idalia Nuñez, Luis Urrieta

> Until I can take pride in my language, I cannot take pride in myself. Until I can accept as legitimate Chicano Texas Spanish, Tex-Mex and all the other languages I speak, I cannot accept the legitimacy of myself. Until I am free to write bilingually and to switch codes without having always to translate, while I still have to speak English or Spanish when I would rather speak Spanglish, and as long as I have to accommodate the English speakers rather than having them accommodate me, my tongue will be illegitimate.
>
> *(Anzaldúa, 1987, p. 81)*

Overview of an Issue: Identity Construction in DLBE School Contexts

Across the United States and wherever im/migrants settle internationally, students are asked to acquire the un/official language. Part of acquiring the language of power includes taking on a challenge to their identity and, for many students, the process can mean losing a sense of their cultural pride and academic competency (Fillmore, 2000; Relaño-Pastor, 2007; Valenzuela, 1999). When students lose a sense of who they are culturally and linguistically, they are also likely to have trouble connecting and communicating with their parents and extended family members (Surrain, 2021). Additionally, academic success for im/migrant communities is closely linked with ethnic, cultural, and linguistic pride (Nieto, 2000). Schools have the capacity to create programs that center on the cultural identities of *all* students.

DOI: 10.4324/9781003269076-34

We see cultural identity as including students' multilingual, multicultural, racial backgrounds and other identities. In fact, studies have shown that schools that center on the cultural backgrounds of minoritized students tend to have greater student academic success (Bartlett & García, 2011). One such model, the dual language bilingual education (hereafter DLBE) is ideal for students who speak a heritage language because it centers on bilingualism, biculturalism, and biliteracy for *all* children. In the United States, the majority of DLBE programs have a Spanish/English focus. The DLBE model includes both students for whom Spanish, Chinese, Vietnamese, Hmong, French, and others are their heritage languages and students for whom the minoritized language is not part of their cultural heritage. For non-heritage speakers, the DLBE program offers the opportunity to learn a second language and empathize with members of a cultural and linguistic community they would have likely not interacted with in school. For heritage speakers, this same experience has manifested in ways where (bilingual) students of Color (BSoC) are required to share their cultural and linguistic wealth (Yosso, 2005) with the promise of sustaining it for academic success.

DLBE programs also converge with the interest and investment of white[1] families to raise bilingual children. This interest in raising bilingual children through a dual language program, like the two-way immersion bilingual education (hereafter TWBE) model, is one of the main reasons why these programs grew in popularity in the United States (Cervantes-Soon et al., 2017; Flores, Phuong, & Venegas, 2020; Pimentel et al., 2008; Valdés, 1997). Parents/families from white and upper-middle-class backgrounds advocate for dual language education in the United States to promote the cognitive and economic benefits of bilingualism. In gentrifying neighborhoods, white parents/families also specifically advocate for integration in order to foster an openness, interest, awareness, and empathy towards other cultural and ethnic groups (Shange, 2019; Stillman, 2012). Families of Color who choose to have their children in a DLBE program do so in the interest of sustaining family relationships, to nurture cultural pride and develop a sense of investment in speaking Spanish (Nuñez & García-Mateus, 2021; Olivos & Lucero, 2020). Despite having a significant role in sustaining their children's language practices, im/migrant families' multilingualism is often framed as a problem (Ruiz, 1984), and as a result, education policy requires that their language practices be monitored through yearly language assessments until they are deemed "fluent" in English (Hernández, 2017). White parents' interest in bilingualism converges with also promoting an additive approach to bilingual education for language-minoritized students, the crux of the matter is that People of Color have been advocating for equitable educational programs for their children for decades (Castañeda v. Pickard, 1981; Hernández et al., 2022; Lau v. Nichols, 1974; Mendez v. Westminster, 1946; Valdez et al., 2016).

Teachers play a crucial part in creating equitable and socially just DLBE schools. Teachers have the capacity to position students and co-construct positive identities as language learners (García-Mateus & Palmer, 2017), in addition to creating spaces in the classroom to interrogate power structures that can otherwise deem students from marginalized backgrounds as deficient (Flores, Phuong, & Venegas, 2020; Freire, 2016; Freire & Valdez, 2017; Heiman & Yanes, 2018; Palmer et al., 2019). In the DLBE classroom, where children are drawing from their linguistic repertoire as bilingual learners, the co-construction of identity intersects with students' ethnic, racial, cultural, gendered, social class, and language backgrounds. To continue to promote DLBE programs as a way to bring culturally and linguistically diverse students together to become bilingual, bicultural, and biliterate, DLBE advocates must prioritize children of Color experiences, interests, and multiple identities, as front and center.

In this chapter, we explore how cultural identities have been conceptualized in DLBE schools and examine empirical research to broadly describe topics such as the development of positive cross-cultural attitudes, language learning experiences, and cultural identities (Bearse & de Jong, 2008; García, 2009; García-Mateus & Palmer, 2017; Martínez et al., 2017; Palmer, 2008; Palmer & Martínez, 2013; Pimentel et al., 2008; Reyes & Vallone, 2007). We highlight how pressing issues, such as undocumented immigration (García-Mateus, 2020a, 2020b), anti-black racism (Cervantes-Soon, Degollado, & Nuñez, 2020), gendered roles (Caldas, 2018), the gentrification of DLBE (Valdez et al., 2016), among others, have only emphasized the urgency in weaving identity construction across the established DLBE goals. As a concept, identity construction is relevant in and through students' academic success, bilingual and biliteracy development, sociocultural competence, and in becoming critically conscious. This chapter reframes DLBE to include, as Reyes and Vallone urged, a *critical* approach, which includes the co-construction of identity and centers on the experiences, identities, and knowledge of students from marginalized backgrounds.

The following sections will describe research trends and discuss central themes as they relate to studies examining identity in DLBE programs. We begin with a focus on literature that describes how teachers have both the capacity and potential to position students in TWBE programs as they co-construct their identities. The section on critical literacy responds to Reyes and Vallone's urgent call about centering the identities of Latinx[2] students by validating their (multi)literacy practices and aligning them with a school-based curriculum. The third section focuses on how we are (re)imagining the goals of DLBE, which includes integrating identity across the goals as the basis for additive programs, like the two-way bilingual education model, which brings together students who speak the dominant language and students of Color who speak a minoritized language. As scholars with interdisciplinary expertise in identity, (bilingual) education, and multiliteracy and as former bilingual educators in K-12 settings, we reflect on the intersectionality of race, language, and power and offer future directions for teachers, parents, scholars, and administrators. Lastly, we discuss implications of including the co-construction of identity in the field of (bilingual) education and in teacher education programs and future directions in terms of DLBE implementation, research, education, and language policy.

Cultural Identities as a Broader Conceptual Tool in DLBE

Identity is a concept that we define broadly as self-understandings, especially those with strong emotional resonances, often marked with culturally produced and socially constructed identity labels (Holland et al., 2001; Núñez & Urrieta, 2020; Urrieta, 2007). Identities are relational, often revolving around social positionings (Davies & Harré, 1990), interpersonal relations, internal dialogues, and "figuring" out our cultural worlds (Holland et al., 2001). Identities are social products deeply connected to subject formation and power, often creating "en-'trap'-ments", often via labels, that maintain and support boundaries of inclusion, but most importantly of exclusion from particular points of access (Urrieta & Noblit, 2018). We recognize that culture is a contested and problematic concept, especially in its relationship to anthropology (Borofsky et al., 2001; González, 1999). However, we concur that culture maintains value as an analytic, especially in relation to identity and identification. We understand cultures as complex, dynamic, and nuanced, historically produced repertoires of practices for participation, that, according to Gutiérrez and Rogoff (2003), endure or change for communities over time and which are embedded within intra- and inter-diverse, sociopolitical landscapes of power. We, therefore, define cultural identities as self and collective understandings of belonging, or membership to particular groups that co-produce shared practices in relation to other identifiable groups or groupings (Urrieta, 2013; Urrieta & Noblit, 2018). Cultural identities are learned ways of knowing, ways of being, and ways of doing in the world, which attend to the nuances and complexities of intersectional experiences. Cultural identities also link shared experiences through learned repertoires of practice for participating in collective communities with different degrees of individual and collective competencies (Gutiérrez & Rogoff, 2003; Urrieta, 2013). As a broader conceptual tool, we use cultural identity to encompass critical elements that impact and/or influence identity construction which includes many of those researched by DLBE scholars, including academic achievement, language and literacy learning, the development of positive cross-cultural attitudes, and the crucial role of teachers in positioning students to co-construct identity (Bartlett & García, 2011; García-Mateus, 2020a, 2020b; García-Mateus & Palmer, 2017; Zúñiga et al., 2017).

Further, we draw on this concept to delve into the salient themes and issues related to that address identity in DLBE.

Teacher Agency, Positionality, and Students' Co-Construction of Identity

Research on schools serving BSoC has demonstrated how teachers have the potential and agency to position students' cultural identities and language practices in positive ways (Alfaro & Bartolomé, 2017; Bartlett & García, 2011; Cervantes-Soon, 2018; García-Mateus, 2020a, 2020b; Palmer, 2007; Palmer & Martínez, 2013; Urrieta, 2007; Zúñiga et al., 2017). For DLBE, specifically, bilingual teachers are language arbiters in their classrooms who have the power to make decisions about how language policies are interpreted and how language(s) are positioned, used, learned, and experienced in the classroom (Hernández et al., 2022; Hornberger & Johnson, 2007).

Palmer (2008), for example, examined teachers' roles in positioning students (half English dominant and half Spanish dominant and Latinx) in a Spanish/English two-way immersion program to co-construct their identities (i.e., academic and multilingual) during classroom dialogue about content-area instruction. While she highlighted the pivotal role teachers play in opening up spaces in the classroom for *all* students' voices to be heard, she also recognized that "... it may be overly ambitious to expect students to carry their nascent academic identities outside their classroom doors, at least while they are in the classroom under the tutelage of their teacher, the equitable learning environment she has helped create for them will facilitate their development of skills and confidence" (p. 21). In other words, teachers have the agency to position children in ways that can allow them to positively interact with their classmates despite the difference in their backgrounds or language practices. A teacher's influence can be limited, however, to their own classroom if the extended school community does not share this same approach to teaching and learning. It is, therefore, imperative that the entire school community embrace inclusivity and the critical work of identity construction with BSoC.

Bartlett and García's (2011) ethnographic study of a newcomer (mostly students from the Dominican Republic) high school in New York City also offers insight into the interplay between identity construction and academic achievement, even though it did not take place in a DLBE program. Teachers at Luperon High School engaged in translanguaging practices to teach students in different content areas. Over a four-year span, the students at Luperon were successful in passing the standardized assessments needed to graduate. Barlett and García attributed a translanguaging pedagogical approach (see Chapter 28 in this handbook), placing value on the students' multicultural identities, and the co-construction of positive academic and multilingual identities and experiences, to an increase in the number of students passing standardized exams and graduating from Luperon High School. This and previous studies emphasize the importance of teachers' purposeful social positioning of students to co-construct identity for academic success and cultural pride (Caldas, 2018; DePalma, 2010; Fitts, 2009; García & Wei, 2014; García et al., 2017; García-Mateus, 2020a, 2020b; Palmer et al., 2014). Even though academic achievement and positive multilingual identities are important indicators of student success, literature centering on the experiences of students of Color has shifted to prioritize a social justice lens as a means to offer *all* students a transformative learning experience (Caldas, 2018; García-Mateus, 2020a, 2020b; Heiman & Yanes, 2018).

Reyes and Vallone (2007) urged scholars, practitioners, and administrators to consider how "Past and current research on two-way programs focuses on the linguistic and/or academic achievement of children in immersion programs rather than on what involvement in such programs means to the participants. Such studies ask if children are becoming bilingual and if they are achieving academically, but they do not ask what it means to children to become bilingual, bicultural, and bi-literate" (p. 1). In a special issue of the *International Journal of Bilingual Education and Bilingualism,* Hamman-Ortiz and Palmer (2020) and contributors highlight the importance of how Latinx BSoC take up their bilingual identities across an array of DLBE programs. The bilingual student perspectives revealed that while DLBE is supposed to be additive, students of Color can be perceived by their peers and teachers in deficit ways and receive subtractive schooling experiences (Chaparro, 2019; de Jong et al., 2020; García-Mateus, 2020a, 2020b). Bilingual students of Color are aware of the inequities they experience, especially when their teachers play critical roles in creating dialogue in the classroom about how DLBE programs do or don't reflect their cultural identities (Adams, 2015; Adams & Busey, 2017; de Jong et al., 2020; García-Mateus, 2020a, 2020b; Heiman & Yanes, 2018; Malsbary, 2014; Martínez, 2017; Mortimer & Dolsa, 2020; Salerno et al., 2020). Studies that examine teachers' roles in navigating DLBE programs demonstrate that when identity is interwoven with the work of developing *sociocultural competence and critical consciousness,* it can be just as, if not more important as becoming bilingual. Part of socially positioning students to co-construct their multiple identities in positive ways includes teachers drawing from their own identities to inform their teaching. Awareness of how to socially position students includes teachers' ability to connect to their students' backgrounds to incorporate the cultural identities of young BSoC into their work as practitioners.

A growing body of research focused on identity and the teaching of BSoC includes the emphasis of teachers drawing from their own cultural backgrounds to inform their teaching practices (Alfaro, 2008; Alfaro & Bartolomé, 2017; Cervantes-Soon, 2018; Cervantes-Soon & Carrillo, 2016; Espinoza et al., 2021; Nuñez et al., 2020; Palmer & García-Mateus, 2023; Urrieta, 2007). Cervantes-Soon (2018), for example, examines the urgent need for practitioners working with BSoC to draw from their borderland experiences and cultural identities to shape transformative pedagogical frameworks and practices. Similar to how Nuñez and García-Mateus (2021) described Mexican Madres raising bilingual children, borderland experiences refer to "… people on the margins [who draw on their lived experiences] to transcend the limitations set by physical and metaphorical borders" (p. 4). When teachers mindfully incorporate their backgrounds into the curriculum, they have the potential to create spaces in the classroom to center on the experiences, knowledge, and identities of students from marginalized backgrounds. Cervantes-Soon (2014) and colleagues (e.g., Cervantes-Soon et al., 2017; Heiman & Yanes, 2018; Palmer et al., 2019) who have critically examined two-way dual language programs have proposed more critical approaches with a social justice lens such as teaching through an authentic caring approach (Valenzuela, 1999), building convivencia (Villenas, 2005), and incorporating drama-based pedagogy to foment advocacy by bilingual educators (Caldas, 2017). For example, in Caldas' study, predominately Latinx preservice bilingual teachers in a university course used drama-based pedagogy to practice having conversations with their field-based teacher about pressing issues encountered in their classroom with young BSoC. Critical strategies that *take action* to co-construct meaning about social inequities are especially important in gentrifying DLBE programs, which can otherwise further marginalize the identities of BSoC.

Research focused on teachers' agency to position students to co-construct identity includes examples that give us hope but also highlight how the concept of identity is a critical thread in the teaching and learning of BSoC. One proven way to effectively address identity is through multicultural children's literature, which can supplement all content areas (i.e., math, science, language arts). In fact, the notion of identity is a central component of high-quality multicultural children's books because the books reflect the lived experiences and realities of children from culturally and linguistically diverse backgrounds.

Critical (Bi)literacies in DLBE to Empower Students' Identities

In 2007, Reyes and Vallone urged the field of bilingual education to focus their attention on students' critical (bi)literacy knowledge and practices as integral to their cultural and linguistic identity. Critical (bi)literacies were grounded on Freire's conceptualization of reading and writing the word and the world in and through language (Freire & Macedo, 2005). Bilingual students of

Color traversing the discourses of multiple nation-states, immigration, racialization, linguistic violence, among other systems of oppression, have nuanced understandings of how the world works and how their intersectional identities can and are perceived across spaces (Nuñez & Urrieta, 2021). This awareness is a *consciousness* that recognizes systems of oppression and inequities that allow individuals to engage in *praxis* by strategically utilizing language and literacy knowledge to embody resistance and/or agency (Freire, 1970). In turn, critical consciousness can shift students' and teachers' perspectives from positioning certain cultural identities as deficit to understanding the roots of deficit discourses and how they impact students and communities differently.

Colomer and Chang-Bacon (2020) interviewed graduated high school students that were in a Spanish/English two-way dual language program. In their work, they found that students' narrations of the meaning of biliteracy challenged the ways in which biliteracy was implemented through their schooling experiences. The authors argued that critical biliteracies with bilingual students should anchor efforts aimed at exploring issues at the "intersection of languages, literacies, culture, power, and race in U.S. contexts" (p. 387). Esquivel (2020) also documented the critical literacies of Latinx bilingual students in a Spanish/English two-way dual language school on the Texas borderlands and examined how literacy instruction through critical content generated discussions and understandings about Latinx communities in the United States. Specifically, Esquivel conducted critical discourse analysis during a literacy activity where the teacher used the book, *Harvesting Hope: The Story of César Chávez* (Krull, 2003) to help her Latinx bilingual students understand the racial and economic inequities experienced by Mexican workers. The critical literacy activities allowed the students to engage bilingually in discussions about inequities typically experienced by Mexican communities and use writing to strengthen their arguments about various social issues such as racism and the exploitation of Mexican workers. These critical (bi)literacy activities historicized the agency and resistance of communities of Color and, thus, empowered the identities of BSoC by learning of their community's histories. Martínez-Roldán's (2003) study also documented how narratives during literature discussions in a second-grade bilingual classroom supported a Latina student, Isabela, to draw on her storytelling funds of knowledge and construct her identity. Through the text selections and discussions in the classroom, Isabela shared stories about herself, her family, and their experiences. Isabela used storytelling both to showcase her bilingual academic skills and identity and to socially construct her linguistic and cultural identity. In discussing *Pepita talks twice/Pepita habla dos veces* by Ofelia Dumas Lachtman (2006), Isabela was able to use her bilingualism and narratives to share about the discrimination she faced when she only knew Spanish and other students laughed at her. The book prompted her critical awareness of linguistic discrimination and provided her space to position herself proudly as a Spanish speaker, as a bilingual, and as a Mexican.

Freire (2016) and Palmer et al. (2019) expand on the role of critical consciousness which has been explored and recognized as the fourth goal of dual language education. For Palmer and colleagues, critical consciousness is about being able to "talk, deeply listen, and 'read the world' (Freire, 1970) in multiple languages" (p. 129). Freire and Feinauer (2020) add, "Critical consciousness also provide students anti-hegemonic tools against the artificial dominant ideology" (p. 9) about linguistic hierarchies or "standard" language forms such as enacting translanguaging. These understandings are beyond reading and understanding critically how the world(s) function, it is also about writing-taking action. For example, Durán (2017) documented how bilingual students in a kindergarten, bilingual classroom made decisions about their writing and their language choices. In their work, students initially translanguaged by writing in English and translating to Spanish, but eventually some students moved their writing to only Spanish because they were aware of their parents/families' linguistic identities. Instead of writing in English or translating English into Spanish, the students felt empowered to act by making critical decisions as writers and prioritizing their families' language over the use of English. In a similar study, Osorio (2018) discusses how critical literacy helped BSoC discuss topics related to im/migrant communities, deportation, and the racist discourse of former President Trump. Through conversations and culturally relevant children's literature, students opened up to their peers and teacher about their fears of family members' deportation, and their awareness of various family members' im/migration status. The students used bilingual writing to compose letters to the former president challenging his assumptions, policies, and damaging discourses by offering anti-racist perspectives and humanizing solutions to societal problems. Their actions resulted from the critical (bi) literacies and perspectives the students embraced about their identities in their DLBE experience.

These studies outline how dual language spaces serving multiple cultural and linguistic communities can be spaces designed with the potential to intentionally challenge the status quo, curriculum, racist ideologies, and social/ structural inequities through critical (bi)literacies. These studies show how critical (bi)literacy activities that combine culturally relevant multilingual books, critical discussions with dynamic languaging, and the use of writing and talk to share stories and challenge inequities can cultivate strong cultural and linguistic identities in BSoC. More importantly, the studies show the pivotal role of bilingual teachers as arbiters with the agency to make decisions about how the dual language program design works in favor or against students.

Bilingualism for Whom?: Proposing Identity Construction Across the Goals

When Guadalupe Valdés (1997) published a cautionary note for scholars and advocates of the TWBE program, she motioned the use of a critical lens in the (re)design and implementation model that integrates a diverse group of students. Qualitative studies of DLBE continue to ask the unresolved question, *bilingualism for whom* (Flores, Tseng, & Subtirelu, 2020; Pimentel et al., 2008)? The DLBE model requires that students from the dominant language and students who speak a minoritized language come together with the goal of becoming bilingual, bicultural, and biliterate. Classrooms across the United States, especially in gentrifying neighborhoods, usually include students from an upper-middle-class, English-speaking, and white background and students from a Spanish-speaking, Latinx background. Reyes and Vallone (2007) emphasized, "For linguistic majority children in two-way classrooms, learning a minority language may be foundational to promoting positive cross-cultural attitudes" and adds, "for linguistic minority children, developing and/or maintaining a minority (heritage) language may be foundational to promoting positive identity construction" (p. 5). In other words, identity construction should be central to the goals of bilingualism, biliteracy, and biculturalism in DLBE spaces. We argue that by infusing *identity construction* across the goals, DLBE has the potential to affirm students' cultural identities while attending to dismantling inequitable structures. If a critical approach to DLBE programs is not centered, do supposedly "additive" bilingual programs end up becoming subtractive schooling experiences for bilingual Latinx students? In such cases, the question remains: *¿quiénes ganan* (Pimentel et al., 2008)?

For students of Color who speak minoritized languages, bilingualism, biliteracy, and biculturalism are ways of knowing and being in the world – it is who they are, not a choice. These ways of knowing and being in the world align with views of bi/multilingualism as living organisms characterized by organized structures that grow and adapt according to the context in which they developed. Such practices and knowledge cannot be parsed out into discrete, isolated components, but rather they come together to build a synchronous platform for ongoing, dynamic identity construction in DLBE spaces (see Figure 23.1).

While academic success, bilingualism, biliteracy, biculturalism, and sociocultural competence are the established goals of DLBE, critical scholarship (Cervantes-Soon, Degollado, & Nuñez, 2020; Freire, 2020; García-Mateus, 2016, 2020a, 2020b; García-Mateus & Palmer, 2017; Palmer et al., 2019) highlights the need to infuse the work of identity and conscious raising across the goals while interrogating the processes, curriculum, and practices involved in the experiences of bilingual students of Color. In 2014, Feinauer and Howard also highlighted the role of positive cross-cultural attitudes and behaviors,

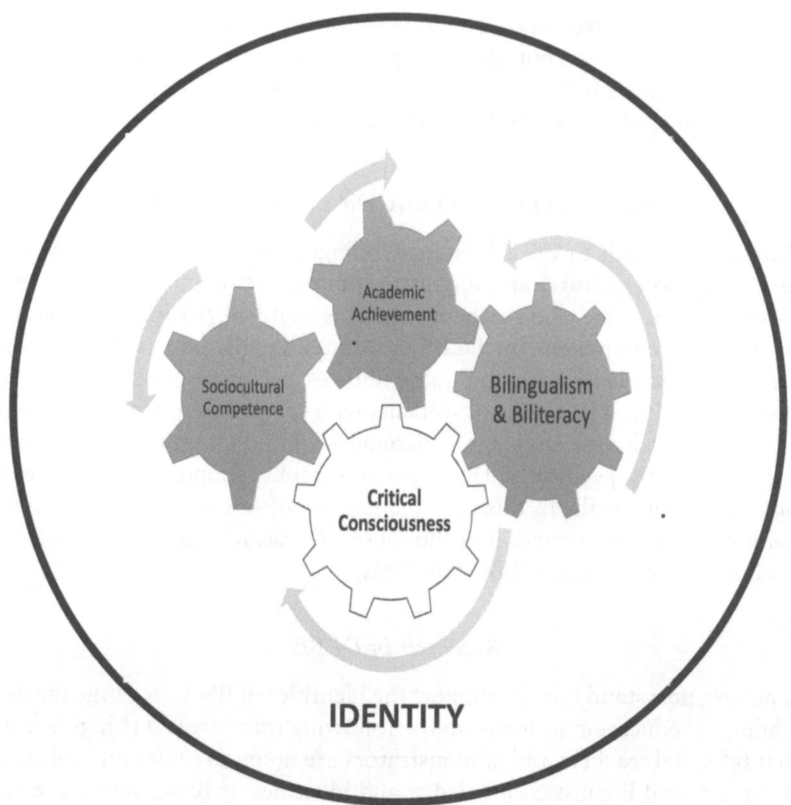

Figure 23.1 Identity Central to DLBE Goals

high self-esteem, cross-cultural awareness as important to supporting students' self-understandings and "how they make sense of who they are in relation to other social and cultural groups, as well as in relation to the majority culture or culture of power within a society" (p. 267). Raising critical consciousness is an essential component of DLBE programs in co/constructing identities of emergent bilinguals (Cervantes-Soon et al., 2017). Critical consciousness can support teachers and students in identifying the power dynamics present and how they function across dual language programs and impact students' lives (Alfaro, 2019; Palmer et al., 2019). When students engage in critical thinking and conversations about cultural differences, they are more likely to co-construct positive identities (García-Mateus & Palmer, 2017).

We assert that the focus on identity must take place across the un/official goals of DLBE to make these programs more equitable and just for BSoC, who need to see themselves, their culture, and their language represented in affirming and positive ways. The journey of being and becoming bilingual is by no means perfect, but affirming positive identities is a step in the right direction towards equity, justice, and from a place of love (Heiman & Yanes, 2018) for *all* students served by DLBE programs.

Implications and Future Directions for DLBE

DLBE and the goals towards biliteracy, bilingualism, and biculturalism serving two or more cultural and linguistic communities compel us to continuously seek to examine who are these programs really supporting academically. For us, a key component for DLBE is to intentionally and critically design curriculum and plan instruction that embraces, celebrates, and critically empowers the cultural identities of students who speak minoritized language(s) (i.e., Spanish, Chinese languages, Vietnamese, Hmong) represented in these programs. More specifically, DLBE programs must support the identities of BSoC across the goals. In this next section, we offer suggestions for how to position identity construction at the center of research, policy, and practice that informs and defines DLBE programs.

Research in DLBE

To better understand how to support the identities of BSoC, we urge the field of bilingual education to focus on the following three areas: (1) highlighting what bilingual teachers and administrators are doing to center and celebrate the culture and linguistic knowledge and identities of BSoC across the curriculum and the culture of the school both in U.S. and international contexts; (2) identifying the conditions and supports that DLBE teachers still need to better understand how to support the identities of BSoC; and (3) documenting how students' and families' perspectives, practices, and identities are impacted over time by DLBE programs and their efforts to promote equity for bilingual students of Color.

Research in DLBE should expand beyond the theoretical and physical boundaries of the U.S. context in order to learn from programs that decenter Euro-centric approaches to teaching and learning. Research is also needed that examines the co-construction of identity across the goals and in various elementary and secondary settings. For example, studies focused on a specific content area (i.e., language arts, art, math, social studies, science) can consider the implications of how students' identities are being shaped across the goals, how (*all*) teachers draw from their identity to inform their pedagogy, and how *all* students are making sense of their own identities as participants in DLBE programs. We have described how previous and emerging research has demonstrated that identity matters in all aspects of teaching and learning, especially with students of Color. It is critical that we braid the concept of identity through the four goals of DLBE in order to (re)imagine and (re)design programs, outside of the white gaze (Flores & Rosa, 2015; Morrison, 1994), in ways that center marginalized students' knowledges, experiences, and interests. Last but not least, we are making a call for more research on identity in DLBE contexts that focus on other minoritized languages (i.e., Chinese languages, Indigenous languages) and in various racial/ethnic communities.

Policy and Bilingual Education

Reconfigurations of bilingual programs' practices and curriculums over time have not been enough to support students who speak minoritized languages. Bilingual students of Color continue to be at a disadvantage when compared to their white counterparts. This happens when teaching and learning experiences do not center on the identities and practices of marginalized students. As Nuñez and Palmer (2017) explain, this work requires intentional efforts from those involved, especially teachers and administrators. Policy plays a key role in centering and calling into action equity goals that should be part of bilingual education (Flores & Chaparro, 2018). Specifically, for DLBE programs, policies should dictate how language, curriculum, and instruction are implemented in bilingual classrooms (Fitzsimmons-Doolan et al., 2015; Zúñiga et al., 2017). Policies around these areas should encourage teachers and administrators to (re)conceptualize and implement bilingual and biliteracy education from a critical perspective (Colomer & Chang-Bacon, 2020; Reyes & Vallone, 2007). Bilingual education would subsequently not simply be about maintaining home languages, but instead about sustaining and empowering the cultural identities and knowledge of bilingual students of Color.

Implications for education and language policy at the national and local level, both in the United States and internationally, should include the critical perspectives about bi/multilingualism of families of Color and from im/migrant backgrounds (Nuñez & García-Mateus, 2021). Bilingual education advocates can urge their representatives to change local and national policies (Avineri et al., 2016; García-Mateus et al., 2021) to center on the multilingual and multicultural identities of students of Color. This sort of advocacy work is especially critical in the United States where the multilingualism and cultural identities of racialized im/migrant groups are constantly under surveillance through language assessments, deficit labeling, and subtractive schooling experiences (Nuñez, 2021; Valenzuela, 2002).

Bilingual Teacher Education

Alongside research and policy efforts focusing on identity, we address the implications for bilingual teacher education programs and teacher educators.

Bilingual teacher education programs are significant in ensuring preservice bilingual teachers develop the critical awareness and understanding about how policies, curriculum, and practices shape the experiences and identities of BSoC. Teacher education programs should prioritize self-reflection on preservice teachers' identities in order for them to understand why developing strong and positive student identities is critical to being successful in academic settings, and the role of teachers in that dynamic and ongoing process (Alfaro, this volume; Nuñez et al., 2020; Palmer, 2018). We also urge teacher educators to cultivate critical discussions and include content and experiences in their preparation programs to help preservice teachers recognize and disrupt deficit views of the cultural identities of BSoC, subtractive approaches to language learning, and inequitable policies and practices that target BSoC (Heiman & Urrieta, 2019). More importantly, supporting preservice teachers in seeing and understanding how these issues are longstanding in the schooling of BSoC and the impact these have on their cultural and academic identities. Encouraging preservice teachers to engage in this work has the potential to positively influence their pedagogical decisions in ways that will ultimately also support their future bilingual students in DLBE and other bilingual academic settings.

K-12 Bilingual Education Teachers

In the area of K-12 teaching and learning, it is critical for DLBE teachers to also center on the identities of BSoC and their communities. It is particularly important for this learning to involve historicizing and deconstructing the social, institutional, and structural inequities found in DLBE programs and local communities in ways that center on the lived experiences of BSoC; learning about the histories of struggle, resistance, and agency of communities of Color; and embracing and empowering BSoC by positioning them as cultural and linguistic experts in the classroom. Bilingual educators should incorporate literature that reflects the practices and identities of students, cultivate an environment of critical listening (Heiman & Yanes, 2018) and dialogue (Palmer et al., 2019), and guide students' voices, writings, and actions towards creating positive change. Focusing on these areas will empower students' voices and identities in the process of becoming bilingual, biliterate, and bicultural and can also foster critical understanding, consciousness, and engagement in all students served by DLBE.

Lastly, we want to add that as scholars of Color and as parents who are raising bilingual children who are/have been enrolled in DLBE, we are deeply invested in supporting and improving the education offered to BSoC. The research on DLBE continues to show us how BSoC (which includes our own children) and their identities have never been at the forefront of the work that happens in bilingual education programs, yet these programs were imagined and created for them. Not centering on their histories, language practices, and cultural knowledge has had serious social and academic implications (i.e., disengagement with schooling, low self-esteem, poor academic performance, grade-level retention, dropping out of school) (Tillman et al., 2006) that have been witnessed even in "additive" bilingual academic settings. If we do not deliberately work to center on our BSoC and communities, we will continue to reproduce and enable the social and academic inequities that have sustained the dominant white-culture. And, in that case, the question would remain, *¿Quienes ganan?*, and we add, *¿y por qué?*

Notes

1 The authors use a lowercase "w" for the label white to problematize and challenge representations of white supremacy in society and in school settings.
2 We use the term "Latinx" as a challenge to gender binaries and to embrace gender inclusivity with respect to human diversity and dignity. Latinx also unsettles the gendered binaries of language ideologies, culture, and sex-gender norms.

References

Adams, M. (2015). *Math identities information: Latin@ students tell their math stories* (Unpublished doctoral dissertation). University of Texas–Austin.

Adams, M., & Busey, C. (2017). "They want to erase that past": Examining race and Afro-Latin@ identity with bilingual elementary students. *Social Studies and the Young Learner*, *30*(1), 13–18.

Alfaro, C. (2008). Teacher education examining beliefs, orientations, ideologies & practices. In L. Bartolome (Ed.), *Ideologies in education: Unmasking the trap of teacher neutrality* (pp. 231–241). Peter Lang.

Alfaro, C. (2019). Preparing critically conscious dual language teachers: Recognizing and interrupting dominant ideologies. *Reimaging Dual Language Education in the U.S. Theory into Practice Journal*, *58*(2), 194–203.

Alfaro, C., & Bartolomé, L. (2017). Preparing ideologically clear bilingual teachers: Honoring working-class non-standard language use in the bilingual education classroom. *Issues in Teacher Education*, *26*(2), 11–34.

Anzaldúa, G. (1987). *Borderlands/La Frontera: The New Mestiza*. Lute Books.

Avineri, N., Blum, S. D., García-Mateus, S., & Zentella, A. C. (2016). Save California residents from a language drought: Vote 'yes' this fall. *The Huffington Post* [Online News]. http://www.huffingtonpost.com/american-anthropological-association/save-ca-residents-from-a_b_11387726.html

Bartlett, L., & García, O. (2011). *Additive schooling in subtractive times: Bilingual education and Dominican youth in the heights*. Vanderbilt University Press.

Bearse, C., & de Jong, E. J. (2008). Cultural and linguistic investment: Adolescents in a secondary two-way immersion program. *Equity & Excellence in Education*, *41*(3), 325–340.

Borofsky, R., Barth, F., Shweder, R. A., Rodseth, L., & Stolzenberg, N. M. (2001). When: A conversation about culture. *American Anthropologist*, *103*(2), 432–446.

Caldas, B. (2017). Shifting discourses in teacher education: Performing the advocate bilingual teacher. *Arts Education Policy Review*, *118*(4), 190–201.

Caldas, B. (2018). Juxtaposing William and Graciela: Exploring gender nonconformity through drama-based pedagogy in a dual-language classroom. *TESOL Journal*. https://doi.org/10.1002/tesj.420

Castañeda v. Pickard, 648 F.2d 989, 1006–07 (5th Cir. 1981).

Cervantes-Soon, C., Degollado, E. D., & Nuñez, I. (2020). The black and brown struggle for agency: African American and Latinx children's plight to bilingualism. In N. Flores, A. P. A. Tseng, & A. P. N. Subtirelu (Eds.), *Bilingualism for all?: Raciolinguistic perspectives on dual language education in the United States*. Multilingual Matters.

Cervantes-Soon, C. G. (2014). A critical look at dual language immersion in the new Latin@ diaspora. *Bilingual Research Journal*, *37*(1), 64–82.

Cervantes-Soon, C. G. (2018). Using a Xicana feminist framework in bilingual teacher preparation: Toward an anticolonial path. *The Urban Review*, *50*(5), 857–888.

Cervantes-Soon, C. G., & Carrillo, J. F. (2016). Toward a pedagogy of border thinking: Building on Latin@ students' subaltern knowledge. *The High School Journal*, *99*(4), 282–301.

Cervantes-Soon, C. G., Dorner, L., Palmer, D., Heiman, D., Schwerdtfeger, R., & Choi, J. (2017). Combating inequalities in two-way language immersion programs: Toward critical consciousness in bilingual education spaces. *Review of Research in Education*, *41*(1), 403–427.

Chaparro, S. E. (2019). "But mom! I'm not a Spanish boy": Raciolinguistic socialization in a two-way immersion bilingual program. *Linguistics and Education*, *50*, 1–12.

Colomer, S. E., & Chang-Bacon, C. K. (2020). Seal of biliteracy graduates get critical: Incorporating critical biliteracies in dual-language programs and beyond. *Journal of Adolescent & Adult Literacy*, *63*(4), 379–389.

Davies, B., & Harré, R. (1990). Positioning: The discursive production of selves. *Journal for the Theory of Social Behaviour*, *20*(1), 43–63.

de Jong, E., Coulter, Z., & Tsai, M. (2020). Two-say bilingual education programs and sense of belonging: Perspectives from middle school students. *International Journal of Bilingual Education and Bilingualism*, *26*(1), 84–96.

DePalma, R. (2010). *Language use in the two-way classroom: Lessons from a Spanish-English bilingual kindergarten* (Vol. 76). Multilingual Matters.

Durán, L. (2017). Audience and young bilingual writers: Building on strengths. *Journal of Literacy Research*, *49*(1), 92–114.

Espinoza, K., Nuñez, I., & Degollado, D. E. (2021). "This is what my kids see every day": Bilingual pre-service teachers embracing funds of knowledge through border thinking. *Pedagogy, Journal of Language, Identity & Education*, *20*(1), 4–17.

Esquivel, J. (2020). Embodying critical literacy in a dual language classroom: Critical discourse analysis in a case study. *Critical Inquiry in Language Studies*, *17*(3), 206–227.

Feinauer, E., & Howard, E. R. (2014). Attending to the third goal: Cross-cultural competence and identity development in two-way immersion programs. *Journal of Immersion and Content-Based Language Education*, 2(2), 257–272.

Fillmore, L. W. (2000). Loss of family languages: Should educators be concerned? *Theory into Practice*, *39*(4), 203–210.

Fitts, S. (2009). Exploring third space in a dual-language setting: Opportunities and challenges. *Journal of Latinos and Education*, *8*(2), 87–104.

Fitzsimmons-Doolan, S., Palmer, D., & Henderson, K. (2015). Educator language ideologies and a top-down dual language program. *International Journal of Bilingual Education and Bilingualism*, *20*(6), 704–721. https://doi.org/10.1080/13670050.2015.1071776

Flores, N., & Chaparro, S. (2018). What counts as language education policy? Developing a materialist anti-racist approach to language activism. *Language Policy*, *17*, 365–384.

Flores, N., & Rosa, J. (2015). Undoing appropriateness: Raciolinguistic ideologies and language diversity in education. *Harvard Educational Review*, *85*(2), 149–171.

Flores, N., Phuong, J., & Venegas, K. M. (2020). "Technically an EL": The production of raciolinguistic categories in a dual language school. *TESOL Quarterly*, *54*(3), 629–651.

Flores, N., Tseng, A., & Subtirelu, N. (2020). *Bilingualism for all? Raciolinguistic perspectives on dual language education in the United States*. Multilingual Matters.

Freire, J. A. (2016). Nepantleras/os and their teachers in dual language education: Developing sociopolitical consciousness to contest language education policies. *Association of Mexican American Educators Journal*, *10*(1), 36–52.

Freire, J. A. (2020). Promoting sociopolitical consciousness and bicultural goals of dual language education: The transformational dual language educational framework. *Journal of Language, Identity & Education*, *19*(1), 56–71. https://doi.org/10.1080/15348458.2019.1672174

Freire, J. A., & Feinauer, E. (2020). Vernacular Spanish as a promoter of critical consciousness in dual language bilingual education classrooms. *International Journal of Bilingual Education and Bilingualism*, *25*(4), 1516–1529.

Freire, J. A., & Valdez, V. E. (2017). Dual language teachers' stated barriers to implementation of culturally relevant pedagogy. *Bilingual Research Journal*, *40*(1), 55–69.

Freire, P. (1970). *Pedagogy of the oppressed*. Herder & Herder.

Freire, P., & Macedo, D. (2005). *Literacy: Reading the word and the world*. Routledge.

García, O. (2009). *Bilingual education in the 21st century: A global perspective*. Wiley/Blackwell.

García, O., & Wei, L. (2014). *Translanguaging: Language, bilingualism and education*. Palgrave Macmillan.

García, O., Johnson, S., & Seltzer, K. (2017). *The translanguaging classroom: Leveraging student bilingualism for learning*. Caslon.

García-Mateus, S. (2016). *"She was born speaking English and Spanish!" co-constructing identities and exploring children's bilingual language practices in a two-way immersion program in central Texas* [Doctoral dissertation].

García-Mateus, S. (2020a). "Yeah, things are rough in Mexico. Remember we talked about hard times?" Process drama and a teachers role in critically engaging students to dialogue about social inequities in a dual language classroom. *The Urban Review*. https://doi.org/10.1007/s11256-020-00555-1

García-Mateus, S. (2020b). Bilingual student perspectives about language expertise in a gentrifying two-way immersion program. *International Journal of Bilingual Education and Bilingualism*. https://doi.org/10.1080/13670050.2020.1797627

García-Mateus, S., & Palmer, D. (2017). Translanguaging pedagogies for positive identities in two-way dual language bilingual education. *Journal of Language,*

Identity & Education, *16*(4), 245–255. https://doi.org/10.1080/15348458.2017.1329016

García-Mateus, S., Wong, J. W., & Chaparro, S. (2021). A critical perspective on the educational labeling of multilingual students in the United States. *American Association for Applied Linguistics*. https://assets.noviams.com/novi-file-uploads/aaal/AAAL_Briefs/2021/Labelling_Brief_FinalApproved_10_24_21_.pdf

González, N. (1999). What will we do when culture does not exist anymore? *Anthropology & Education Quarterly*, *30*(4), 431–435.

Gutiérrez, K. D., & Rogoff, B. (2003). Cultural ways of learning: Individual traits or repertoires of practice. *Educational Researcher*, *32*(5), 19–25.

Hamman-Ortiz, L., & Palmer, D. (2020). Identity and two-way bilingual education: Considering student perspectives: Introduction to the special issue. *International Journal of Bilingual Education and Bilingualism*, *26*(1), 1–6.

Heiman, D., & Urrieta, L. Jr (2019). La cuarta meta de la educación bilingüe y la pedagogía crítica en los mundos figurados de la preparación de futurxs maestrxs bilingües. *Bilingual Review/Revista Bilingüe*, *34*(1), 36–56.

Heiman, D., & Yanes, M. (2018). Centering the fourth pillar in times of TWBE gentrification: "Spanish, love, content," not in that order". *International Multilingual Research Journal*, *12*(3), 173–187.

Hernández, S. J. (2017). Are they all language learners? Educational labeling and raciolinguistic identifying in a California middle school dual language program. *The CATESOL Journal*, *29*(1), 133–154.

Hernández, S. J., Alfaro, C., & Martell, M. A. N. (2022). Bilingual teacher educators as language policy agents: A critical language policy perspective of the Castañeda v. Pickard case and the bilingual teacher shortage. *Language Policy*, *21*(3), 381–403.

Holland, D., Lachiotte, Jr, W. S., Skinner, D., & Cain, C. (2001). *Identity and agency in cultural worlds*. Harvard University Press.

Hornberger, N. H., & Johnson, D. C. (2007). Slicing the onion ethnographically: Layers and spaces in multilingual language education policy and practice. *TESOL Quarterly*, *41*(3), 509–532.

Krull, K. (2003). *Harvesting hope: The story of Cesar Chavez*. Houghton Mifflin Harcourt.

Lachtman, O. D. (2006). *Pepita talks twice/Pepita habla dos veces* (A. P. DeLange, Illustrator). Arte Publico Press.

Lau v. Nichols, 414 U.S. 563 (1974).

Malsbary, C. (2014). "Will this hell never end?" Substantiating and resisting race-language policies in a multilingual high school. *Anthropology & Education Quarterly*. https://doi.org/10.1111/aeq.12076

Martínez, D. (2017). Imagining a language of solidarity for Black and Latinx youth in English language arts classrooms. *English Education*, *49*(2), 179–196.

Martínez, R. A., Durán, L., & Hikida, M. (2017). Becoming "Spanish learners": Identity and interaction among multilingual children in a Spanish-English dual language classroom. *International Multilingual Research Journal*, *11*(3), 167–183.

Martínez-Roldán, C. M. (2003). Building worlds and identities: A case study of the role of narratives in bilingual literature discussions. *Research in the Teaching of English*, *37*(4), 491–526.

Mendez v. Westminster, 64 F. Supp. 544 (S.D. Cal. 1946).

Morrison, T. (1994). *The bluest eye*. Plume Book.

Mortimer, K., & Dolsa, G. (2020). Ongoing emergence: Borderland high school DLBE students' self-identifications as lingual people. *International Journal of Bilingual Education and Bilingualism*, *26*(1), 7–19.

Nieto, S. (2000). Placing equity front and center: Some thoughts on transforming teacher education for a new century. *Journal of Teacher Education*, *51*(3), 180–187.

Nuñez, I. (2021). "Because we have to speak English at school": Transfronterizx children translanguaging identity to cross the academic border. *Research in the Teaching of English*, *56*(1), 10–32.

Nuñez, I., & García-Mateus, S. (2021). Ruptures of possibilities: Mexican origin mothers as critical translanguaging pedagogues. *Association of Mexican American Educators Journal*, *15*(3), 107–125.

Nuñez, I., & Palmer, D. (2017). Who will be bilingual? A critical discourse analysis of a Spanish-English bilingual pair. *Critical Inquiry in Language Studies*, *14*(4), 294–319.

Nuñez, I., & Urrieta, L. Jr (2021). Transfronterizo children's literacies of surveillance and the cultural production of border crossing identities on the US–Mexico border. *Anthropology & Education Quarterly*, *52*(1), 21–41.

Nuñez, I., Villareal, D., & DeJulio, S. (2020). Sustaining bilingual–biliterate identities: Latinx preservice teachers' narrative representations of bilingualism and biliteracy across time and space. *Journal of Teacher Education*, *72*(4), 419–430.

Olivos, E. M., & Lucero, A. (2020). Latino parents in dual language immersion programs: Why are they so satisfied? *International Journal of Bilingual Education and Bilingualism*, *23*(10), 1211–1224.

Osorio, S. L. (2018). No room for silence: The impact of the 2016 presidential race on a second-grade dual-language (Spanish-English) classroom. *Occasional Paper Series*, *39*(4), 1–13.

Palmer, D. (2007). A dual immersion strand programme in California: Carrying out the promise of dual language education in an English-dominant context. *International Journal of Bilingual Education and Bilingualism*, *10*(6), 752–768.

Palmer, D., & García-Mateus, S. (2023). *Gentrification and bilingual education: A Texas TWBE school across seven years*. Edited Volume, Lexington Books.

Palmer, D., & Martínez, R. A. (2013). Teacher agency in bilingual spaces a fresh look at preparing teachers to educate Latina/o bilingual children. *Review of Research in Education*, *37*(1), 269–297.

Palmer, D. K. (2008). Building and destroying students' 'academic identities': The power of discourse in a two-way immersion classroom. *International Journal of Qualitative Studies in Education*, *21*(6), 647–667.

Palmer, D. K. (2018). *Teacher leadership for social change in bilingual and bicultural education*. Multilingual Matters.

Palmer, D. K., Cervantes-Soon, C., Dorner, L., & Heiman, D. (2019). Bilingualism, biliteracy, biculturalism, and critical consciousness for all: Proposing a fourth fundamental goal for two-way dual language education. *Theory Into Practice*, *58*(2), 121–133.

Palmer, D. K., Martínez, R. A., Mateus, S. G., & Henderson, K. (2014). Reframing the debate on language separation: Toward a vision for translanguaging pedagogies in the dual language classroom. *The Modern Language Journal*, *98*(3), 757–772.

Pimentel, C., Soto, L. D., Pimentel, O., & Urrieta, L. Jr (2008). The dual language dualism:¿ Quiénes ganan? Texas *Association for Bilingual Education Journal*, *10*, 200–223.

Relaño-Pastor, A. (2007). Competing language ideologies in a bilingual/bicultural after-school program in Southern California. *Journal of Latinos and Education*, *7*, 4–24. https://doi.org/10.1080/15348430701693366

Reyes, & Vallone (2007). Toward an expanded understanding of two-way bilingual immersion education: Constructing identity through a critical additive/bicultural pedagogy. *Multicultural Perspectives*, 9(3), 3–11.
Ruiz, R. (1984). Orientations in language planning. *NABE Journal*, 8(2), 15–34.
Salerno, A., Kibler, A., & Hardigree, C. (2020). "I'll be the hero": How adolescents negotiate intersectional identities within a high school dual-language program. *International Journal of Bilingual Education and Bilingualism*, 26(1), 20–33.
Shange, S. (2019). *Progressive dystopia: Abolition, antiblackness, and schooling in San Francisco*. Duke University Press.
Stillman, J. B. (2012). *Gentrification and schools: The process of integration when whites reverse flight*. Palgrave MacMillan.
Surrain, S. (2021). Spanish at home, English at school': How perceptions of bilingualism shape family language policies among Spanish-speaking parents of preschoolers. *International Journal of Bilingual Education and Bilingualism*, 24(8), 1163–1177.
Tillman, K. H., Guo, G., & Harris, K. M. (2006). Grade retention among immigrant children. *Social Science Research*, 35, 129–156.
Urrieta, L. (2007). Identity production in figured worlds: How some Mexican Americans become Chicana/o activist educators. *The Urban Review*, 39(2), 117–144.
Urrieta, L. Jr (2013). Familia and comunidad-based saberes: Learning in an Indigenous heritage community. *Anthropology & Education Quarterly*, 44(3), 320–335.
Urrieta, L., & Noblit, G. W. (Eds.). (2018). *Cultural constructions of identity: Meta-ethnography and theory*. Oxford University Press.
Valdés, G. (1997). Dual-language immersion programs: A cautionary note concerning the education of language-minority students. *Harvard Educational Review*, 67(3), 391–429.
Valdez, V., Freire, J. A., & Delavan, G. (2016). The gentrification of dual language education. *The Urban Review*, 48(4), 601–627.
Valenzuela, A. (1999). *Subtractive schooling*. State University of New York Press.
Valenzuela, A. (2002). Reflections on the subtractive underpinnings of education research and policy. *Journal of Teacher Education*, 53(3), 235–241.
Villenas, S. A. (2005). Latina literacies in convivencia: Communal spaces of teaching and learning. *Anthropology & Education Quarterly*, 36(3), 273–277.
Yosso, T. J. (2005). Whose culture has capital? A critical race theory discussion of community cultural wealth. *Race Ethnicity and Education*, 8(1), 69–91.
Zúñiga, C. E., Henderson, K. I., & Palmer, D. K. (2017). Language policy toward equity: How bilingual teachers use policy mandates to their own ends. *Language and Education*, 32(1), 60–76. https://doi.org/10.1080/09500782.2017.1349792

24

FULFILLING POTENTIAL AND INTERROGATING ASSUMPTIONS OF INTEGRATION

Examining Intergroup Relations in Dual Language Bilingual Education

Melinda Martin-Beltrán, Amanda Cataneo

While schools around the world bring together students from diverse backgrounds, dual-language bilingual education (DLBE) programs are distinct in the way that intergroup relations are integral to the core educational goals of developing bilingualism, bi/multi-literacies, and sociocultural competence. Although DLBE is used in this volume to describe several different types of programs, for the purposes of this chapter, we focus on two-way bilingual programs that are explicitly designed to integrate students with different linguistic backgrounds. As we discuss in this chapter, language differences intersect with differences in race, ethnicity, culture, and socioeconomic status among other factors that remind us that DLBE is about "much more than language" (Freeman, 1996). In the first section of this chapter, we briefly discuss the socio-historical context of intergroup relations in DLBE and scholarly work that has theorized intergroup relations. We discuss how the lens of critical consciousness can complement optimal conditions for intergroup relations, proposed by intergroup contact theory. In the four sections that follow, we review and synthesize empirical studies in DLBE as they relate to four conditions for intergroup relations through the lens of critical consciousness. In the final section of this chapter, we offer implications for future research and practice concerning relations among diverse stakeholders in DLBE.

DOI: 10.4324/9781003269076-35

Intergroup Relations: Theory and Socio-historical Context

Schools are complex social contexts that reflect and resist the legacies of settler colonialism, capitalism, assimilation, and segregation that have promoted White supremacy and reinforced hierarchies based on race, class, language, and immigration status, among other factors (Chávez-Moreno, 2020). Facing these challenges, DLBE has been proposed as an approach that could lead to societal change, improve intergroup relations, reduce discrimination, and support multilingualism (Baker, 2003; Cummins, 1995). Rooted in the Civil Rights movements in the 1960s, advocates for the educational rights of language-minoritized students helped to pass the Bilingual Education Act (Flores & García, 2017; Fránquiz et al., 2019). DLBE/Two-way immersion emerged as a bilingual education model to address a growing "concern for the prolonged student segregation of minority language speakers...[and] the need for authentic interaction between native speakers of English and native speakers of a partner language for the purpose of developing stronger language and literacy skills in both languages and for achieving better sociocultural integration and intergroup relationships" (de Jong, 2016, p. 7).

Some DLBE programs became part of broader desegregation plans as educators continue to grapple with inequalities that reflect a history of *de jure* and *de facto* segregation in U.S. schools and society (e.g., *Mendez* case and *Brown* case, see Moll, 2010; Morales & Razfar, 2016). Orfield and Ee (2015, p. 67) document, "the consensus of nearly 60 years of social science research on the harms of school segregation is that racially and socioeconomically isolated schools are strongly related to an array of factors that limit educational opportunities and outcomes." Scholars caution that integration should not be confused with assimilation to dominant societal norms, but instead DLBE should create a liberating space for students and educators to re-imagine norms that break away from the constraints of hegemonic Whiteness (Arias, 2007; Flores, 2016; Stolte, 2017). Research from around the globe has highlighted the potential of DLBE programs to integrate students and improve relations across linguistic and culturally diverse populations (Frankenberg et al., 2019; Gándara & Aldana, 2014; Hertz-Lazarowitz et al., 2008; Sandberg, 2015; Tankersley, 2001; Wright & Tropp, 2005). However, questions remain about *how* school stakeholders integrate and whether integration allows positive intergroup relations to develop (Ee, 2020; Muro, 2016). Scholars acknowledge that desegregation does not solve all educational inequalities, which are deeply entrenched in society, nor does integrating students necessarily lead to better intergroup relations (Schofield, 2006; Schofield & Eurich-Fulcer, 2004). However, an extensive body of theoretical and empirical research suggests that intergroup contact can reduce intergroup prejudice if certain conditions are present (Orfield & Lee, 2005; Pettigrew & Tropp, 2006).

Intergroup Contact Theory: Optimal Conditions and Challenges

Research investigating intergroup relations has been guided by intergroup contact theory (Allport, 1954; Brown & Hewstone, 2005; Pettigrew & Tropp, 2006, 2013), a well-established theory in social psychology and sociology (Schofield, 2006; Wright & Tropp, 2005). A meta-analysis of 515 studies (Pettigrew & Tropp, 2006) demonstrated that intergroup contact typically reduces intergroup prejudice with facilitating conditions (Orfield & Ee, 2015). Allport's (1954) intergroup contact theory proposed *four optimal conditions* that are necessary to produce positive intergroup relations: (1) common goals, (2) equal status, (3) collaboration, and (4) institutional support/authority sanction. First, group members need to understand they share (and are working together toward) common goals. Second, all group members need to be recognized as having "equal status" in the specific context (e.g., power to participate equally within class activity). The third condition is to create a collaborative (non-competitive) context that cultivates supportive relationships and emphasizes interdependence, requiring group members to rely on each other to achieve the shared goals. Fourth, institutions (e.g., schools) and authority figures (e.g., teachers, principals, policy makers) need to support and explicitly demonstrate that they value positive intergroup relations (e.g., establishing rules/structures that support the other three conditions). It is not within the scope of this chapter to analyze the shortcomings of the definitions of the *optimal conditions*; instead, we examine the complexity of these conditions across DLBE contexts.

Intergroup contact theory has been critiqued for over-simplifying the definition of "group membership" when, in fact, individuals are often members of several groups that have fluid boundaries (Bell et al., 2021; Ghavami et al., 2020). In discussing group salience (Bigler & Liben, 2007; Stolte, 2017), intergroup contact theory often reifies dichotomous relations (Black *or* White, Spanish-speaker *or* English-speaker) rather than recognizing intersectional and multi-faceted identities that are more representative of multilingual communities. While intergroup contact research has examined a wide range of groups defined by race, ethnicity, class, gender identity, sexual orientation, and religion (Pettigrew & Tropp, 2006); DLBE research has often narrowly focused on groups defined by "language." Recent research has moved away from static or dichotomous definitions of "groups" in DLBE programs and instead recognizes that group boundaries are not fixed, and stakeholders identify with multiple, intersectional identities that extend beyond the school context (e.g., de Jong, 2016; Poza, 2019a).

Understanding Intergroup Relations through Critical Consciousness

While much research suggests that DLBE programs have the potential to create the ideal conditions for positive intergroup relations; a growing body of research sheds light on the challenges to sustain these conditions. Building on previous scholarship, we argue that our field needs to reconceptualize these *optimal conditions* for intergroup contact through a lens of critical consciousness (Cervantes-Soon et al., 2017; Palmer et al., 2019) to make visible the ways that intergroup relations in DLBE contexts reproduce and/or resist social hierarchies and relationships that extend beyond the classroom.

A rich body of scholarship has argued that critical consciousness (Cervantes-Soon et al., 2017; Freire, 1970) should be the foundation of DLBE programs. Because critical consciousness involves analyzing the role of power and societal relations, this lens is key to understanding intergroup relations and equity in DLBE. Critical consciousness offers a lens to acknowledge and interrogate histories of intergroup contact built upon exploitation rather than cooperation and reveals the problematic nature of interest convergence (Bell, 1980) when DLBE programs may prioritize the goals of White, middle-class stakeholders over the goals of Black, Indigenous, People of Color stakeholders. Palmer and colleagues (2019) argue that critical consciousness as a core goal "will better maintain a focus on equity and fulfill [DLBE programs'] potential to support a more integrated and socially just society" (pp. 122–123). Palmer et al. (2019) describe four elements of critical consciousness as continuously interrogating power, historicizing schools, critical listening, and engaging with discomfort, which we argue have consequences for intergroup relations. There is no space in this chapter to review the deep and broad scholarship of critical consciousness rooted in the work of Paulo Freire (1970); instead, we focus on the theoretical tenets of critical consciousness (described in Palmer et al., 2019) as we discuss common themes across DLBE research. In the four sections that follow, we review empirical studies in DLBE as they relate to each optimal condition for intergroup relations through the lens of critical consciousness. We acknowledge that several studies span across the themes; thus, we discuss studies on multiple levels across the sections.

Common Goals, Competing Agendas, or Interest Convergence?

This section reviews DLBE research that has investigated issues related to the first *optimal condition* for intergroup relations: *common goals* for students. When promoting the DLBE program to policy makers, educators, and parents, DLBE programs explicitly name three central goals (or Pillars) for "all students": (1) bilingualism/biliteracy, (2) academic achievement, (3) sociocultural competence (Christian et al., 2000; Howard et al., 2018). The lens of critical consciousness offers a way to interrogate how these goals work for different groups of students in different socio-historical contexts.

Several studies have called into question whether DLBE goals are "shared" across diverse stakeholders (Cervantes-Soon et al., 2017; Chávez-Moreno, 2020). In her cautionary note, Valdés (1997) warned of competing agendas and raised concerns that the goals and needs of minoritized students are likely to be marginalized in DLBE contexts and may reproduce "the place of the powerful and powerless in wider society" (p. 393). The theoretical rationale for DLBE draws from two different bodies of research: (1) bilingual education focusing on quality education for language-minority students who benefit from mobilizing their home languages for school learning; (2) foreign language immersion primarily focusing on second language acquisition (SLA) for language-majority students (see Christian, 1996; Cloud et al., 2000; Lindholm-Leary, 2001; Valdés, 1997, 2018). SLA research emphasized that interaction among so-called "native speakers" and "non-native speakers" is beneficial for language acquisition (Mackey & Goo, 2007); however, more recent research problematizes the categories of "native" or "non-native" and suggests that interaction among all kinds of learners expands opportunities for language development (de Jong et al., 2019).

de Jong and Howard (2009) examined the issue of student integration and the shared goal of bilingualism and biliteracy. Citing SLA research, they explain that DLBE seems to be "optimally suited to provide the ideal context for second language development" (p. 85); yet they warn that, "without conscious attention to those issues that arise as a result of native and non-native speaker student integration, the foreign language needs of native English speakers and the bilingual needs of minority language speakers can easily become dueling rather than mutually reinforcing agendas" (p. 92).

A growing body of research has questioned whether bilingualism is a *shared goal,* when bilingual community practices and classroom practices aiming to support bilingualism may look very different for different groups (e.g., racialized multilinguals or students who use "non-standard" language varieties have different goals than students from monolingual dominant communities) (Flores et al., 2020; Hamman, 2018; Morales & Razfar, 2016). de Jong and Howard (2009) echo Valdés's (1997, 2018) concern when they write, "in the absence of a bilingual perspective that takes into consideration issues of differential language status and language acquisition contexts, TWI classrooms may fail to optimize language learning opportunities for all students, particularly for language minority students" (p. 81).

Several studies have demonstrated how societal discourses and structural inequalities are related to how DLBE program goals are framed by stakeholders (Bernstein et al., 2020; Chaparro, 2020; Flores et al., 2020). Bernstein et al. (2020) document how DLBE stakeholders generally share the goal to counter the "language as problem" orientation (Ruiz, 1984); there is disagreement about how to frame DLBE as a right or resource. Bernstein et al. (2020) identify two predominant "dueling discourses" framing DLBE: "equity/social justice" and "instrumentalism neoliberalism" (p. 656), which frame DLBE goals in ways that are conflicting rather than unifying. The equity/social justice framing of DLBE emerged out of collective political movements for racial, linguistic, and civil rights (Flores, 2016). In contrast, the instrumentalism/neoliberalism framing narrowed the goals of bilingual education "from a means for social, cultural, and political change to a tool for language acquisition" (Bernstein et al., 2020, p. 658) linked to individual profit and globalization (Cervantes-Soon, 2014; Flores & Chaparro, 2018; Flores & García, 2017; Delavan et al., 2017; Petrovic, 2005). The predominance of the "instrumentalist/neoliberal" framing of goals, as DLBE programs expand and gentrify (Heiman & Yanes, 2018; Valdez et al., 2016), aligns with the theory of *interest convergence* (Bell, 1980), which argues that policy changes that aim to increase racial integration and equity often only occur when affluent, White populations perceive that such policies will benefit them. Several studies (Muro, 2016; Pearson et al., 2015) have found evidence of interest convergence when DLBE programs promote the goals of the dominant group (e.g., second language proficiency for White, English-speaking students), while benefits for minoritized students are framed as a "by-product" (Cervantes-Soon et al., 2017; Flores & McAuliffe, 2022; Petrovic, 2005). DLBE goals are often framed as "magnet programs" as part of voluntary desegregation (Ee, 2020); however, implementing DLBE to prevent "White flight" (Senesac, 2002; Valdés, 1997) raises "questions about the ethics of using linguistic-minority students as a tool to lure in white families" (Burns, 2017, p. 339).

Sociocultural competence, the third DLBE goal, arguably connects the most strongly with intergroup relations yet is the least emphasized in both research and practice. Several studies suggest that if educators attended to the often-overlooked third goal, intergroup relations could improve (Cervantes-Soon, 2017; Feinauer & Howard, 2014; Feinauer & Whiting, 2014; Freire, 2020). Ee (2020) argues that integration in DLBE must be a school-wide commitment requiring participation from multiple stakeholders (students, educators, families). Rather than assuming common goals are a given condition; educators, researchers, students, and families could benefit from engaging in critical listening (a key element of critical consciousness) to understand how diverse stakeholders make sense of DLBE goals in order to co-(re)construct goals that are meaningful across groups.

Striving for Equal Status and Confronting Race-, Class-, and Language-Based Hierarchies

This section reviews research that has investigated issues related to the second *optimal condition*: equal status. DLBE program design calls for a deliberate effort to equalize status among diverse groups; however, research suggests that DLBE may not do enough to counter the societal status differences among groups related to language, race, and class. DLBE models promote "equal" or "balanced" conditions in terms of instructional time and populations defined by language (Feinauer & Howard, 2014). In the early years of DLBE, student populations were defined dichotomously as language-majority (e.g., "native" English speakers) and language-minority ("native" Spanish speakers) (Christian, 1996; Tedick, 2014). More recent research has challenged dichotomous definitions of "groups" and recognized multiple and intersectional identities within heterogeneous populations (e.g., de Jong, 2016; Poza, 2019a).

DLBE programs' use of a minoritized language for teaching and learning can provide a clear affirmation of the status of the non-dominant language (Cummins, 1989; Donitsa-Schmidt et al., 2004; Lambert & Cazabon, 1994), which has been shown to contribute to positive intergroup conditions (Donitsa-Schmidt et al., 2004; Tankersley, 2001; Wright & Tropp, 2005). Tankersley (2001) described how a Macedonian/Albanian dual-language program built community between language groups, increased students' "cross-ethnic" friendships and respect for two languages yet still struggled with language status among groups with a long history of ethnic conflict.

Many studies have found that DLBE schools in the United States reproduce language status differences reinforcing English hegemony (Babino & Stewart, 2018; Hamman-Ortiz, 2020; Hernández, 2015; Lucero, 2015; Palmer, 2009; Pratt & Ernst-Slavit, 2019), rather than centering language practices from racialized, multilingual communities. Creating conditions for "equal status" of language practices has proven to be particularly challenging in a context in which the hegemony of English is embedded in students', teachers', and families' beliefs about access to status, resources, and educational opportunities (Dorner, 2010; Fitts, 2006; Lee & Jeong, 2013; Lucero, 2015). Several studies have documented the way that the unequal status of minoritized languages impacts the status of the students in the classroom who are perceived as minority-language speakers (Oliveira et al., 2020; Palmer, 2009; Stolte, 2017). Research has found that institutional labels and misconceptions of language proficiency affect student status and participation in classrooms (Amrein & Peña, 2000; Coyoca & Lee, 2009; Martin-Beltrán, 2010a; Palmer, 2008, 2009).

Linguistic purism that devalues certain language varieties or multilingual language practices (e.g., translanguaging) may also result in stigmatization of minoritized and racialized students (García & Wei, 2014; Martínez et al., 2015; Valdés, 2018). In early DLBE research, status related to race and class remained largely invisible; however, recent scholarship (Frieson & Scalise, 2021; Martinez Negrette, 2021) explores the experiences of Black students in DLBE programs pointing to a need for further research. Applying the lens of raciolinguistics (Flores & Rosa, 2015; Flores et al., 2020), several studies have shed light on how racialization is tied to the perceived status of language varieties and multilingual communities, which has consequences for educational equity and intergroup relations. Raciolinguistic ideologies perpetuate unequal power relations, which (without critical language awareness) may reproduce rather than resist racial and linguistic stratification of groups in the classroom. More critical research is needed to understand how to implement anti-racist pedagogies (Baker-Bell, 2020; Flores, 2017) in DLBE programs and to disrupt asymmetrical power relations to reconstruct "equal status" among stakeholders.

Synthesizing a comprehensive body of research that has revealed inequalities in DLBE, Cervantes-Soon et al. (2017) write, "The socioeconomic, racial, and ethnic disparities and wide range of cultural identities between and within ethnic/linguistic groups have important implications for social relations in TWI classrooms, often leading to segregation along linguistic, racial, ethnic, and class lines" (Amrein & Peña, 2000; Feinauer & Whiting, 2014; Fitts, 2006; Hernández, 2015; Muro, 2016) (p. 416). While DLBE cannot escape the sociopolitical and historical context that has perpetuated the stratification of groups by race, language, and class (and other dominant, colonizing ideologies), research has suggested that acknowledging the power dynamics and "fostering cross-cultural relations could change these power asymmetries within these classrooms" (Cervantes-Soon et al., 2017, p. 416). DLBE contexts need to do more to give "conscious attention to group status differences" (de Jong, 2006, p. 39). Using critical consciousness to interrogate these differences, educators can transform longstanding inequities (Heiman & Yanes, 2018; Oliveira et al., 2020).

de Jong and Howard (2009) suggest that DLBE must do more to raise awareness of language status issues related to historical, political, and social societal patterns, which aligns with subsequent research on critical language awareness (Cervantes-Soon et al., 2017; Nuñez, 2021). Research also suggests that DLBE programs need to increase access to and promote the value of minoritized languages. Several researchers have argued that the construction of status occurs in moment-to-moment interactions, and both teachers and students have power to challenge the status quo through translanguaging practices and positionings that offer opportunities for more students to be recognized as multilingual experts (Lee et al., 2008; Martin-Beltrán, 2010a, 2013, 2014; Martínez et al., 2015; Nuñez, 2021; Palmer, 2009; Palmer et al., 2014). For example, as students and teachers interact, they may reclaim or resist the status-laden label of "language learner" to construct a more democratic space where all students are expanding their linguistic repertoire in different ways. These student and teacher interactions are related to the third condition, *intergroup cooperation*, the focus of the next section.

Cooperation, Interdependence, and Critical Listening

This section reviews research that has investigated issues related to the third *optimal condition*, which stipulates that a context or activity should be cooperative (encouraging collaboration over competition) and should support positive relationships. A critical consciousness lens reveals the importance of *embracing discomfort* and *critical listening* in cooperative activities to build empathy and "meaningful and transformative connection … and attending, sharing, caring, reciprocity and responsivity toward others" (Palmer et al., 2019, p. 126).

DLBE guiding principles suggest that programs should be designed so that students will meaningfully interact, cooperate, and learn from other students to expand their linguistic repertoire (Christian, 1996; de Jong, 2016; de Jong & Howard, 2009; Howard et al., 2018). Research rooted in sociocultural theory has shown that peer interaction can afford opportunities for multilingual learners to practice language together, to negotiate for meaning, to engage in knowledge construction, and to expand students' multilingual repertoire (García, 2009; Gutiérrez, 2008; Martin-Beltrán, 2009, 2010b, 2014; 2017; Martin-Jones, 2000). Research on collaborative learning (Cohen & Lotan, 1997) has argued that educators need to deliberately plan "group-worthy" tasks that require interdependence and offer multiple ways for students to show competence (Lotan, 2003, p. 72).

Studies investigating the collaborative nature of interactions in DLBE contexts have revealed how students can co-construct a "Third space" (Gutiérrez et al., 1999) where they can expand collective linguistic repertoire to co-construct collaborative bilingual interactional spaces (Lee et al., 2008; Martin-Beltrán, 2009, 2010b, 2013). Angelova et al. (2006) and Pacheco and Hamilton (2020) noted how students across language groups supported each other's learning. Gort (2008) documented the ways that hybrid language practices affirmed student collaboration. Similarly, Poza (2019a) found that DLBE students demonstrated an openness and voluntary inclusion of peers across linguistic and cultural backgrounds and used translanguaging (García & Wei, 2014) to forge bonds and alliances. On the other hand, studies have documented DLBE students using their language skills to exclude, distance, or elevate their status (Lucero, 2015; Oliveira et al., 2020; Poza, 2019a). For example, English-dominant students, mostly from white, middle-class backgrounds, felt a certain pride or giftedness in their bilingualism (Hamman-Ortiz, 2020), whereas Spanish-dominant students from predominantly Latinx families perceived their bilingualism as related to the obligatory expectation to learn English (Colomer & Chang-Bacon, 2020).

Several studies focusing on peer interactions in DLBE contexts have suggested that language brokering among peers may facilitate participation and peer collaboration (Coyoca & Lee, 2009). However, other studies have found that language brokering negatively affects student dynamics (Lee et al., 2011), and brokering is often inequitable in DLBE classrooms where Spanish-dominant bilinguals are regularly required to translate for struggling English speakers in Spanish-medium instruction; yet English speakers rarely reciprocated the language brokering during English-medium instruction (Palmer, 2008; Palmer et al., 2014). DeNicolo's (2010) study revealed that Spanish-dominant bilingual students often acted as "language warriors" (p. 234) advocating for their marginalized monolingual Spanish-dominant peers while also supporting English-dominant peers; yet bilingual students' cooperative problem solving, mediation, and advocacy often went unrecognized.

Decades of research have shown that DLBE students tend to have more positive cross-cultural attitudes and value intergroup interactions with classmates from different linguistic and cultural backgrounds (Bearse & de Jong, 2008; Cazabon et al., 1993; Donitsa-Schmidt et al., 2004; Hausman-Kelly, 2001; Lindholm-Leary, 2012, 2016; Tankersley, 2001). Survey and interview-based research have documented that positive cross-cultural attitudes are long-term (extending into high school) and are more prevalent among students in DLBE programs than other educational models (de Jong & Bearse, 2011; Lindholm-Leary & Borsato, 2001; Lindholm-Leary & Genesee, 2014; Lindholm-Leary & Howard, 2008). Feinauer and Howard note that, "while general trends of positive cross-cultural attitudes tend to be consistent across subgroups, there are also some differences, with Latino, Spanish-speaking students being more likely to affirm the importance of TWI and the resulting opportunities for extended Spanish language and literacy development to be central to their identity" (Gerena, 2010; Lindholm-Leary & Ferrante, 2005, as cited in Feinauer & Howard, 2014, p. 259). In Colomer and Chang-Bacon's (2020) study among DLBE graduates in the Pacific Northwest, they found that the benefits of the Seal of Biliteracy and DLBE programs were often unevenly distributed across Latinx and White participants, yet their findings revealed opportunities for community building. For example, they found that one Latinx participant credited his family's participation in the DLBE program for the stronger bond between his family and a White family, who invited each other's children into their homes.

Intergroup contact theory posits that "friendship invokes many of the optimal conditions for positive contact effects: it typically involves cooperation and common goals as well as repeated equal-status contact over an extended period and across varied settings" (Pettigrew et al., 2011, p. 276). Several studies have found that participation in out-of-school activities is often segregated following linguistic, racial, and socioeconomic lines, reinforcing in-group friendships (Ee, 2018; Hausman-Kelly, 2001; Valdés, 1997). Feinauer and Whiting (2014) found that students self-segregated when they had some degree of choice about peer associations. Ee (2018) documented that students in a 50/50 Korean/English DLBE program in California were more likely to get along with students from the same racial background. Research has documented that in-group friendships and affinity groups are developmentally important for minoritized youth (e.g., Carter, 2007; Ghavami et al., 2020; Tatum, 1997), thus raising questions about how or *if* educators should deliberately integrate students. More research is needed to understand how students in DLBE programs form, rebuff, and/or sustain friendships with peers from distinct linguistic, racial, cultural, and socioeconomic backgrounds and what consequences this has for students' learning and social development.

Institutional Support and Interrogating Power

In this section, we review research that has investigated issues related to the fourth optimal condition, *institutional support*, which is when institutions (e.g., schools, districts) and authority figures (e.g., teachers, principals, policy makers) explicitly demonstrate that they value positive intergroup relations (e.g., by modeling and establishing rules/structures that support the previous three conditions). Per the DLBE Guiding Principles, institutional support takes form in program design, curriculum, and instruction that support the three core goals. While many DLBE programs strive for equity and diversity by using a lottery-based admission system to balance student populations (usually based on home language without regard to race or socioeconomic diversity); research has found that choice programs may create less inclusive contexts (Stolte, 2017).

Educators need "an in-depth understanding of varying levels of power dynamics around race, ethnicity, language, and immigration history" to develop and demonstrate a long-term commitment and support system for DLBE stakeholders (Ee, 2020, p. 14). Research has found that teachers offer institutional support to promote equitable intergroup relations (Heiman, 2021; Poza, 2019b), yet they face larger institutional constraints, such as program viability (Lucero, 2015) and standardized testing that reify inequitable systems. For example, Oliveira et al. (2020) found that teachers prioritized the needs of English-speaking students, fearing the loss of their DLBE program.

Together with institutional labels and policies that racialize and minoritize students, teacher discourse (how teachers talk about intergroup differences) has important consequences for intergroup relations. Stolte (2017) argues that "there may be a link between the diversity and contact conditions in a context and how people talk about difference" (p. 207). Indeed, several studies have found that the ways students are discursively positioned (e.g., as helper, expert) have the power to further marginalize or amplify minoritized voices (Chaparro, 2019; Palmer, 2009; Martin-Beltrán, 2010a, Oliveira et al., 2020). Stolte's (2017) comparative case study of two DLBE Spanish/ English programs found that the teachers' distinct discourses around cultural differences (colorblind vs. dissonance) impact student's cross-cultural attitudes toward students, with specific consequences for students such as Black or Muslim students, who have been overlooked in many DLBE programs.

Although teachers' conscious efforts can create better conditions for intergroup relations, research notes that without a societal shift or more radical transformation, dominant societal discourses promulgating inequity will prevail (Cervantes-Soon et al., 2017; Freeman, 1996; Palmer, 2008). Outside of the classroom, teachers must be able to advocate for the needs of all their students, without the fear of reprisal or program dissolution (Oliveira et al., 2020). Educators cannot do the work of promoting positive intergroup relations alone; they need allies inside and outside of institutions who are also interrogating power and disrupting disparities.

Conclusion and Implications

This chapter has called attention to research investigating intergroup relations, which sits at the nexus of DLBE goals of bilingualism, academic achievement, and sociocultural competence. Much research and policy have discussed intergroup relations from an instrumentalist orientation (Bernstein et al., 2020) that foregrounds the benefits of integration for language learning and overlooks the potential of DLBE to transform social relations and disrupt racial, linguistic, and class-based hierarchies that have consequences for educational equity (Flores, 2016). By connecting intergroup contact theory with research grounded in critical consciousness, this chapter shed light on how intergroup relations are fostered or constrained in DLBE contexts and raises questions about the potential to promote equitable relations and increase intercultural awareness. Together, this research suggests that DLBE program stakeholders need to engage in dialogue to strategize policies and practices to: (1) co-construct understanding of shared goals while historicizing and acknowledging distinct goals for different groups, (2) promote equal status among DLBE stakeholders and interrogate hierarchies of language, race, and class, (3) elevate collaboration and interdependence among groups that requires critical listening and embracing discomfort, (4) demonstrate institutional support by modeling positive intergroup relations and interrogating institutional power structures that undermine optimal conditions for positive and equitable intergroup relations.

Working toward positive intergroup relations in DLBE calls for changes in teacher preparation, curriculum, pedagogies, admission processes, and school connections with and among families. Using a lens of critical consciousness, teacher education programs must historicize DLBE and address how teachers can transform DLBE classrooms into spaces where all stakeholders can interrogate power, critically listen, and engage with discomfort (Heiman & Yanes, 2018). Future need to consider how teachers are prepared to foster positive intergroup relations in DLBE and to scrutinize their practices using the critical analytic framework described in this chapter.

As we look to the future of DLBE, educators and researchers need to center the voices of diverse youth who are reconstructing and expanding how groups are defined, embracing intersectional identities, interrogating power structures, engaging in anti-racist activism, and offering counternarratives to dominant discourses of previous generations. Future research is needed to problematize the relevance of "groups" in DLBE programs to acknowledge the ways that groups and identities are fluid and overlapping (Bell et al., 2021; de Jong, 2016; Poza, 2019a). Questions remain about how social constructions of language, race, ethnicity, socioeconomic status, gender, and other identities affect intergroup relations both inside and outside of DLBE classrooms. More research is needed to understand pedagogical practices teachers can use to mediate encounters between minoritized and dominant groups to promote greater equity and resist-hegemonic ideologies that privilege dominant groups. Humanizing and participatory action research that involves diverse stakeholders in communities (beyond traditional education/research institutions) can offer new perspectives to deepen and shift the field's understanding of intergroup relations.

We look forward to future research and practice to investigate and implement the complex conditions that foster human connections across differences in DLBE. It is our hope that through the continued commitment of research and practice, scholars, teachers, parents, and students in the DLBE community can work together to help DLBE reach its full transformative potential.

References

Allport, G. W. (1954). *The nature of prejudice*. Addison Wesley.

Amrein, A., & Peña, R. A. (2000). Asymmetry in dual language practice: Assessing imbalance in a program promoting equality Audrey Amrein Arizona State University. *Education Policy Analysis Archives*, *8*, 08.

Angelova, M., Gunawardena, D., & Volk, D. (2006). Peer teaching and learning: Co-constructing language in a dual language first grade. *Language and Education*, *20*(3), 173–190.

Arias, B. (2007). School desegregation, linguistic segregation and access to English for Latino students. *Journal of Educational Controversy*, *2*(1), 7.

Babino, A., & Stewart, M. A. (2018). Remodeling dual language programs: Teachers enact agency as critically conscious language policy makers. *Bilingual Research Journal*, *41*(3), 272–297.

Baker, C. (2003). 6. Education as a site of language contact. *Annual Review of Applied Linguistics*, *23*, 95–112.

Baker-Bell, A. (2020). Dismantling anti-black linguistic racism in English language arts classrooms: Toward an anti-racist black language pedagogy. *Theory into Practice*, *59*(1), 8–21.

Bearse, C., & de Jong, E. J. (2008). Cultural and linguistic investment: Adolescents in a secondary two-way immersion program. *Equity & Excellence in Education*, *41*(3), 325–340.

Bell, D. A. Jr (1980). Brown v. Board of Education and the interest-convergence dilemma. *Harvard Law Review*, *93*(3), 518–533.

Bell, A. N., Smith, D. S., & Juvonen, J. (2021). Interpersonal attitudes toward cross-ethnic peers in diverse middle schools: Implications for intergroup attitudes. *Group Processes & Intergroup Relations*, *24*(1), 88–107.

Bernstein, K. A., Katznelson, N., Amezcua, A., Mohamed, S., & Alvarado, S. L. (2020). Equity/social justice, instrumentalism/neoliberalism: Dueling discourses of dual language in principals' talk about their programs. *TESOL Quarterly*, *54*(3), 652–684.

Bigler, R. S., & Liben, L. S. (2007). Developmental intergroup theory: Explaining and reducing children's social stereotyping and prejudice. *Current Directions in Psychological Science*, *16*(3), 162–166.

Brown, R., & Hewstone, M. (2005). An integrative theory of intergroup contact. *Advances in Experimental Social Psychology*, *37*, 255–343.

Burns, M. (2017). "Compromises that we make": Whiteness in the dual language context. *Bilingual Research Journal*, *40*(4), 339–352.

Carter, D. J. (2007). Why the Black kids sit together at the stairs: The role of identity-affirming counter-spaces in a predominantly White high school. *The Journal of Negro Education*, *76*(4), 542–554.

Cazabon, M., Lambert, W. E., & Hall, G. (1993). *Two-way bilingual education: A progress report on the Amigos program*. National Center for Research on Cultural Diversity and Second Language Learning.

Cervantes-Soon, C. G. (2014). A critical look at dual language immersion in the new Latin@ diaspora. *Bilingual Research Journal*, *37*(1), 64–82.

Cervantes-Soon, C. G., Dorner, L., Palmer, D., Heiman, D., Schwerdtfeger, R., & Choi, J. (2017). Combating inequalities in two-way language immersion programs: Toward critical consciousness in bilingual education spaces. *Review of Research in Education*, *41*(1), 403–427.

Chaparro, S. (2020). School, parents, and communities: Leading parallel lives in a two-way immersion program. *International Multilingual Research Journal*, *14*(1), 41–57.

Chaparro, S. E. (2019). But mom! I'm not a Spanish boy: Raciolinguistic socialization in a two-way immersion bilingual program. *Linguistics and Education*, *50*, 1–12.

Chávez-Moreno, L. C. (2020). Researching Latinxs, racism, and white supremacy in bilingual education: A literature review. *Critical Inquiry in Language Studies*, *17*(2), 101–120.

Christian, D. (1996). Two-way immersion education: Students learning through two languages. *The Modern Language Journal*, *80*(1), 66–76.

Christian, D., Howard, E. R., & Loeb, M. I. (2000). Bilingualism for all: Two-way immersion education in the United States. *Theory into Practice*, *39*(4), 258–266.

Cloud, N., Genesee, F., & Hamayan, E. (2000). *Dual language instruction: A handbook for enriched education*. Heinle & Heinle.

Cohen, E. G., & Lotan, R. A. (1997). *Working for equity in heterogeneous classrooms: Sociological theory in practice*. Teachers College Press.

Colomer, S. E., & Chang-Bacon, C. K. (2020). Seal of biliteracy graduates get critical: Incorporating critical biliteracies in dual-language programs and beyond. *Journal of Adolescent & Adult Literacy*, *63*(4), 379–389.

Coyoca, A. M., & Lee, J. S. (2009). A typology of language-brokering events in dual-language immersion classrooms. *Bilingual Research Journal*, *32*(3), 260–279.
Cummins, J. (1989). Language and literacy acquisition in bilingual contexts. *Journal of Multilingual & Multicultural Development*, *10*(1), 17–31.
Cummins, J. (1995). Bilingual education and anti-racist education. In C. Baker, & O. Garcia (Eds.), *Policy and Practice in Bilingual Education: Extending the Foundations* (pp. 63–69). Multilingual Matters Limited.
de Jong, E. J. (2006). Integrated bilingual education: An alternative approach. *Bilingual Research Journal*, *30*(1), 23–44.
de Jong, E. J. (2016). Two-way immersion for the next generation: Models, policies, and principles. *International Multilingual Research Journal*, *10*(1), 6–16.
de Jong, E. J., & Bearse, C. I. (2011). The same outcomes for all? High-school students reflect on their two-way immersion program experiences. In D. Tedick, D. Christian, & T. Williams Fortune (Eds.), *Immersion education* (pp. 104–122). Multilingual Matters.
de Jong, E. J., & Howard, E. (2009). Integration in two-way immersion education: Equalising linguistic benefits for all students. *International Journal of Bilingual Education and Bilingualism*, *12*(1), 81–99. https://doi.org/10.1080/13670050802149531
de Jong, E. J., Yilmaz, T., & Marichal, N. (2019). A multilingualism-as-a-resource orientation in dual language education. *Theory into Practice*, *58*(2), 107–120.
Delavan, M. G., Valdez, V. E., & Freire, J. A. (2017). Language as whose resource?: When global economics usurp the local equity potentials of dual language education. *International Multilingual Research Journal*, *11*(2), 86–100.
DeNicolo, C. P. (2010). What language counts in literature discussion? Exploring linguistic mediation in an English language arts classroom. *Bilingual Research Journal*, *33*(2), 220–240.
Donitsa-Schmidt, S., Inbar, O., & Shohamy, E. (2004). The effects of teaching spoken Arabic on students' attitudes and motivation in Israel. *The Modern Language Journal*, *88*(2), 217–228.
Dorner, L. M. (2010). English and Spanish 'para un futuro' – or just English? Immigrant family perspectives on two-way immersion. *International Journal of Bilingual Education and Bilingualism*, *13*(3), 303–323.
Ee, J. (2018). Exploring Korean dual language immersion programs in the United States: Parents' reasons for enrolling their children. *International Journal of Bilingual Education and Bilingualism*, *21*(6), 690–709.
Ee, J. (2020). Are parents satisfied with integrated classrooms?: Exploring integration in dual language programs. *International Journal of Bilingual Education and Bilingualism*, 1–17.
Feinauer, E., & Howard, E. R. (2014). Attending to the third goal: Cross-cultural competence and identity development in two-way immersion programs. *Journal of Immersion and Content-Based Language Education*, 2(2), 257–272.
Feinauer, E., & Whiting, E. F. (2014). Home language and literacy practices of parents at one Spanish-English two-way immersion charter school. *Bilingual Research Journal*, *37*(2), 142–163.
Fitts, S. (2006). Reconstructing the status quo: Linguistic interaction in a dual-language school. *Bilingual Research Journal*, *30*(2), 337–365.
Flores, N. (2016). A tale of two visions: Hegemonic whiteness and bilingual education. *Educational Policy*, *30*(1), 13–38.
Flores, N. (2017). Developing a materialist anti-racist approach to language activism. *Multilingua*, *36*(5), 565–570.

Flores, N., & Chaparro, S. (2018). What counts as language education policy? Developing a materialist anti-racist approach to language activism. *Language Policy, 17*(3), 365–384.

Flores, N., & García, O. (2017). A critical review of bilingual education in the United States: From basements and pride to boutiques and profit. *Annual Review of Applied Linguistics, 37*, 14–29.

Flores, N., & McAuliffe, L. (2022). 'In other schools you can plan it that way': A raciolinguistic perspective on dual language education. *International Journal of Bilingual Education and Bilingualism, 25*(4), 1349–1362.

Flores, N., Phuong, J., & Venegas, K. M. (2020). "Technically an EL": The production of raciolinguistic categories in a dual language school. *Tesol Quarterly, 54*(3), 629–651.

Flores, N., & Rosa, J. (2015). Undoing appropriateness: Raciolinguistic ideologies and language diversity in education. *Harvard Educational Review, 85*(2), 149–171.

Frankenberg, E., Ee, J., Ayscue, J., & Orfield, G.. 2019. Harming our Common Future: America's Segregated Schools 65 Years after Brown. The Civil Rights Project at UCLA. https://cloudfront.escholarship.org/dist/prd/content/qt23j1b9nv/qt23j1b9nv.pdf.

Fránquiz, M. E., Leija, M. G., & Salinas, C. S. (2019). Challenging damaging ideologies: Are dual language education practices addressing learners' linguistic rights? *Theory into Practice, 58*(2), 134–144.

Freeman, R. D. (1996). Dual-language planning at Oyster Bilingual School: "It's much More than language". *TESOL Quarterly, 30*(3), 557–582.

Freire, J. A. (2020). Promoting sociopolitical consciousness and bicultural goals of dual language education: The transformational dual language educational framework. *Journal of Language, Identity and Education, 19*(1), 56–71. https://doi.org/10.1080/15348458.2019.1672174

Freire, P. (1970). *Pedagogy of the oppressed*. Continuum Books.

Frieson, B. L., & Scalise, M. (2021). Linguistic artistry and flexibility in dual-language bilingual classrooms: Young Black children's language and literacy practices. *Bilingual Research Journal, 44*(2), 213–230.

Gándara, P. C., & Aldana, U. S. (2014). Who's segregated now? Latinos, language, and the future of integrated schools. *Educational Administration Quarterly, 50*(5), 735–748.

García, O. (2009). Education, multilingualism and translanguaging in the 21st century. In T. Skutnabb-Kangas, R. Phillipson, A. K. Mohanty, & M. Panda (Eds.), *Social justice through multilingual education* (pp. 140–158). Multilingual Matters.

García, O., & Wei, L. (2014). *Translanguaging: Language, bilingualism and education*. Palgrave Pivot.

Gerena, L. (2010). Student attitudes toward biliteracy in a dual immersion program. *Reading, 10*(1), 55–78.

Ghavami, N., Kogachi, K., & Graham, S. (2020). How racial/ethnic diversity in urban schools shapes intergroup relations and well-being: Unpacking intersectionality and multiple identities perspectives. *Frontiers in Psychology, 11*, 3133.

Gort, M. (2008). "You give me idea!": Collaborative strides toward bilingualism, biliteracy, and cross-cultural understanding in a two-way partial immersion program. *Multicultural Perspectives, 10*(4), 192–200.

Gutiérrez, K. D. (2008). Developing a sociocritical literacy in the third space. *Reading Research Quarterly, 43*(2), 148–164.

Gutiérrez, K. D., Baquedano-López, P., & Tejeda, C. (1999). Rethinking diversity: Hybridity and hybrid language practices in the third space. *Mind, Culture, and Activity*, *6*(4), 286–303.

Hamman, L. (2018). *Reframing the language separation debate: Language, identity, and ideology in two-way immersion*. The University of Wisconsin-Madison.

Hamman-Ortiz, L. (2020). Becoming bilingual in two-way immersion: Patterns of investment in a second-grade classroom. *International Journal of Bilingual Education and Bilingualism*, *26*(1), 69–83.

Hausman-Kelly, T. A. (2001). *"You thought I was a stranger": Cross-cultural integration in a two-way bilingual classroom*. Teachers College, Columbia University.

Heiman, D. (2021). "So, is gentrification good or bad?": One Teacher's implementation of the fourth goal in her TWBE classroom. *Anthropology & Education Quarterly*, *52*(1), 63–81.

Heiman, D., & Yanes, M. (2018). Centering the fourth pillar in times of TWBE gentrification: "Spanish, love, content, not in that order". *International Multilingual Research Journal*, *12*(3), 173–187.

Hernández, A. M. (2015). Language status in two-way bilingual immersion: The dynamics between English and Spanish in peer interaction. *Journal of Immersion and Content-Based Language Education*, *3*, 102–126.

Hertz-Lazarowitz, R., Mor-Sommerfeld, A., Zelniker, T., & Azaiza, F. (2008). From ethnic segregation to bilingual education: What can bilingual education do for the future of the Israeli Society? *Journal for Critical Education Policy Studies*, *6*(2), 1–15.

Howard, E. R., Lindholm-Leary, D., Rogers, D., Olague, N., Medina, J., Kennedy, B., Sugarman, J., & Christian, D. (2018). *Guiding principles for dual language education* (3rd ed.). Center for Applied Linguistics.

Lambert, W. E., & Cazabon, M. (1994). Students' Views of the Amigos Program. Research Report No. 11.

Lee, J. S., Hill-Bonnet, L., & Gillispie, J. (2008). Learning in two languages: Interactional spaces for becoming bilingual speakers. *International Journal of Bilingual Education and Bilingualism*, *11*(1), 75–94.

Lee, J. S., Hill-Bonnet, L., & Raley, J. (2011). Examining the effects of language brokering on student identities and learning opportunities in dual immersion classrooms. *Journal of Language, Identity & Education*, *10*(5), 306–326.

Lee, J. S., & Jeong, E. (2013). Korean–English dual language immersion: Perspectives of students, parents and teachers. *Language, Culture and Curriculum*, *26*(1), 89–107.

Lindholm-Leary, K. (2001). *Dual language education* (Vol. 28). Multilingual Matters.

Lindholm-Leary, K. (2012). Success and challenges in dual language education. *Theory into Practice*, *51*(4), 256–262.

Lindholm-Leary, K. (2016). Students' perceptions of bilingualism in Spanish and Mandarin dual language programs. *International Multilingual Research Journal*, *10*(1), 59–70.

Lindholm-Leary, K. J., & Borsato, G. (2001). *Impact of two-way bilingual elementary programs on Students' attitudes toward school and college*. CREDE.

Lindholm-Leary, K. J. & Ferrante, A. (2005.) Follow-up Study of Middle School Two-Way Students. In F. Salili, & R. Hoosain (Eds.), *Language in Multicultural Education* (pp. 157–179). Information Age Publishing.

Lindholm-Leary, K., & Genesee, F. (2014). Student outcomes in one-way, two-way, and indigenous language immersion education. *Journal of Immersion and Content-Based Language Education*, *2*(2), 165–180.

Lindholm-Leary, K., & Howard, E. R. (2008). Language development and academic achievement in two-way immersion programs. In D. Tedick, & T. Williams Fortune (Eds.), *Pathways to multilingualism* (pp. 177–200). Multilingual Matters.

Lotan, R. A. (2003). Group-worthy tasks. *Educational Leadership*, *60*(6), 72–75.

Lucero, A. (2015). Who's Holding El Marcador? Peer Linguistic mediation gone awry in a dual language classroom. *Journal of Language, Identity & Education*, *14*(4), 219–236. https://doi-org.proxy-um.researchport.umd.edu/10.1080/15348458.2015.1070571

Mackey, A., & Goo, J. (2007). Interaction research in SLA: A meta-analysis and research synthesis. In A. Mackey (Ed.), *Conversational interaction in second language acquisition: A collection of empirical studies* (pp. 407–451). Oxford University Press.

Martin-Beltrán, M. (2009). Cultivating space for the language boomerang: The interplay of two languages as academic resources. *English Teaching: Practice and Critique*, *8*(2), 25–53.

Martin-Beltrán, M. (2010a). Positioning proficiency: How students and teachers (de) construct language proficiency at school. *Linguistics and Education*, *21*(4), 257–281.

Martin-Beltrán, M. (2010b). The two-way language bridge: Co-constructing bilingual language learning opportunities. *The Modern Language Journal*, *94*(2), 254–277.

Martin-Beltrán, M. (2013). "I don't feel as embarrassed because we're all learning": Discursive positioning among adolescents becoming multilingual. *International Journal of Educational Research*, *62*, 152–161.

Martin-Beltrán, M. (2014). "What do you want to say?": How adolescents use translanguaging to expand learning opportunities. *International Multilingual Journal*, *8*(3), 208–230.

Martin-Beltrán, M. (2017). Exploring peer interaction among multilingual youth: New possibilities and challenges for language and literacy learning. *International Multilingual Research Journal*. https://doi.org/10.1080/19313152.2017.1328968

Martínez, R. A., Hikida, M., & Durán, L. (2015). Unpacking ideologies of linguistic purism: How dual language teachers make sense of everyday translanguaging. *International Multilingual Research Journal*, *9*(1), 26–42.

Martinez Negrette, G. (2021). 'He looks like a monster': Kindergarten children, racial perceptions, and systems of socialization in dual language education. *Race Ethnicity and Education*, 1–19.

Martin-Jones, M. (2000). Bilingual classroom interaction: A review of recent research. *Language Teaching*, *33*, 1–9.

Moll, L. C. (2010). Mobilizing culture, language, and educational practices: Fulfilling the promises of Mendez and Brown. *Educational Researcher*, *39*(6), 451–460.

Morales, P. Z., & Razfar, A. (2016). Advancing integration through bilingualism for all. *School Integration Matters: Research-Based Strategies to Advance Equity*, 135–144.

Muro, J. A. (2016). "Oil and water"? Latino-white relations and symbolic integration in a changing California. *Sociology of Race and Ethnicity*, *2*(4), 516–530.

Nuñez, I. (2021). 'Siento que el inglés esta tumbando mi español': A transfronteriza child's embodied critical language awareness. *International Journal of Bilingual Education and Bilingualism*, *25*(7), 2608–2620.

Oliveira, G., Lima Becker, M., & Chang-Bacon, C. K. (2020). "Eu sei, I know": Equity and immigrant experience in a Portuguese-English dual language bilingual education program. *TESOL Quarterly*, *54*(3), 572–598.

Orfield, G., & Ee, J., 2015. Connecticut school integration: Moving forward as the northeast retreats. *The Civil Rights Project at UCLA*. https://civilrightsproject.ucla.edu/research/k-12-education/integration-and-diversity/connecticut-school-integration-moving-forward-as-the-northeast-retreats

Orfield, G., & Lee, C. (2005). Why segregation matters: Poverty and educational inequality. *Civil Rights Project at Harvard University*.

Pacheco, M., & Hamilton, C. (2020). Bilanguaging love: Latina/o/x bilingual students' subjectivities and sensitivities in dual language immersion contexts. *TESOL Quarterly*, *54*(3), 548–571.

Palmer, D. K. (2008). Building and destroying students' 'academic identities': The power of discourse in a two-way immersion classroom. *International Journal of Qualitative Studies in Education*, *21*(6), 647–667.

Palmer, D. K. (2009). Middle-class English speakers in a two-way immersion bilingual classroom: "Everybody should be listening to Jonathan right now...". *TESOL Quarterly*, *43*(2), 177–202.

Palmer, D. K., Cervantes-Soon, C., Dorner, L., & Heiman, D. (2019). Bilingualism, biliteracy, biculturalism, and critical consciousness for all: Proposing a fourth fundamental goal for two-way dual language education. *Theory into Practice*, *58*(2), 121–133.

Palmer, D. K., Martínez, R. A., Mateus, S. G., & Henderson, K. (2014). Reframing the debate on language separation: Toward a vision for translanguaging pedagogies in the dual language classroom. *The Modern Language Journal*, *98*(3), 757–772.

Pearson, T., Wolgemuth, J. R., & Colomer, S. E. (2015). Spiral of decline or "beacon of hope:" Stories of school choice in a dual language school. *Education Policy Analysis Archives*, 23. http://epaa.asu.edu/ojs/article/view/1524/1559

Petrovic, J. E. (2005). The conservative restoration and neoliberal defenses of bilingual education. *Language Policy*, *4*, 395–416.

Pettigrew, T. F., & Tropp, L. R. (2006). A meta-analytic test of intergroup contact theory. *Journal of Personality and Social Psychology*, *90*(5), 751.

Pettigrew, T. F., & Tropp, L. R. (2013). *When groups meet: The dynamics of intergroup contact*. Psychology Press.

Pettigrew, T. F., Tropp, L. R., Wagner, U., & Christ, O. (2011). Recent advances in intergroup contact theory. *International Journal of Intercultural Relations*, *35*(3), 271–280.

Poza, L. E. (2019a). "Los dos son mi idioma": Translanguaging, identity, and social relationships among bilingual youth. *Journal of Language, Identity & Education*, *18*(2), 92–109.

Poza, L. E. (2019b). "Where the true power resides": Student translanguaging and supportive teacher dispositions. *Bilingual Research Journal*, *42*(4), 408–431.

Pratt, K. L., & Ernst-Slavit, G. (2019). Equity perspectives and restrictionist policies: Tensions in dual language bilingual education. *Bilingual Research Journal*, *42*(3), 356–374.

Ruiz, R. (1984). Orientations in language planning. *NABE journal*, *8*(2), 15–34.

Sandberg, Y. (2015). CLIL interaction challenges: Genre and translanguaging as pedagogic tools? In C. Gitsaki, & T. Alexiou (Eds.), *Current issues in Second/Foreign language teaching and teacher development: Research and practice*, 212–227. Cambridge Scholars Publishing.

Schofield, J. W. (2006). *Migration background, minority-group membership, and academic achievement research: Research evidence from social, educational, and developmental psychology*. Social Science Research Center.

Schofield, J. W., & Eurich-Fulcer, R. (2004). When and how school desegregation improves intergroup relations. In M. B. Brewer, & M. Hewstone (Eds.), *Applied social psychology* (pp. 186–205). Blackwell Publishing.

Senesac, B. V. K. (2002). Two-way bilingual immersion: A portrait of quality schooling. *Bilingual Research Journal*, *26*(1), 85–101.

Stolte, L. (2017). Discussing difference: Color-blind collectivism and dynamic dissonance in two-way immersion contexts. *Bilingual Research Journal*, *40*(2), 205–221.

Tankersley, D. (2001). Bombs or bilingual programmes?: Dual-language immersion, transformative education and community building in Macedonia. *International Journal of Bilingual Education and Bilingualism*, *4*(2), 107–124.

Tatum, B. D. (1997). Why are all the Black kids sitting in the cafeteria? And other conversations about race. *Basic Books*.

Tedick, D. J. (2014). Language immersion education: A research agenda for 2015 and beyond. *Journal of Immersion and Content-Based Language Education*, *2*(2), 155–164. https://doi.org/10.1075/jicb.2.2.00int

Valdés, G. (1997). The teaching of Spanish to bilingual Spanish-speaking students: Outstanding issues and unanswered questions. In M. C. Colombi, F. X. Alarcón, & H. Mifflin (Eds.), *La enseñanza del español a hispanohablantes: Praxis y teoría* (pp. 8–44). Foreign Language Study.

Valdés, G. (2018). Analyzing the curricularization of language in two-way immersion education: Restating two cautionary notes. *Bilingual Research Journal*, *41*(4), 388–412.

Valdez, V. E., Delavan, G., & Freire, J. A. (2016). The marketing of dual language education policy in Utah print media. *Educational Policy*, *30*(6), 849–883.

Wright, S. C., & Tropp, L. R. (2005). Language and intergroup contact: Investigating the impact of bilingual instruction on children's intergroup attitudes. *Group Processes & Intergroup Relations*, *8*(3), 309–328.

Pedagogical Issues

25

TRANSLANGUAGING IN DUAL LANGUAGE BILINGUAL EDUCATION IN THE UNITED STATES

Framings, Research, and Possibilities

Maite T. Sánchez[1]

Translanguaging

The language practices of racialized bilinguals have historically been studied from a monoglossic, named language perspective. This perspective posits the fluid practices common in bilingual households as an impure—and inferior—linguistic practice in need of remediation (Flores & Schissel, 2014; García, 2009) that has roots in colonial understandings of language (García et al., 2021). Named languages with strict boundaries are "inventions" to dominate and minoritize other groups (Makoni & Pennycook, 2007). Languages, as well as race and gender, are colonial productions, constructed to subjugate the colonized (Mignolo, 2000). This process continues today through the hierarchization of race and knowledge systems such as language (Quijano, 2000). This ensuing "coloniality" is what is at the root of the colonial matrix of power (Mignolo, 2000) and why language practices other than those of dominant groups have been restricted in schools.

The term "translanguaging" was first coined by Cen Williams (in Welsh) and translated into English by Baker (2001) to refer to pedagogical practices in which Welsh and English were used for different activities and purposes (i.e., reading in one language, writing in another). This term resonated with scholars who had been studying the language practices and education of racialized bilinguals and who were questioning the monoglossic framing of their language practices (García, 2009). The "trans" prefix provided the framework to expand the languaging of bilinguals as transcending named

 DOI: 10.4324/9781003269076-37

language boundaries (García & Wei, 2014; Otheguy et al., 2015, 2019; Wei, 2011). Translanguaging is a decolonial project, starting not from named languages but from the languaging practices of racialized bilinguals (García & Alvis, 2019), and always as a political act (Flores, 2014). Translanguaging has developed into a "practical theory of language" (Wei, 2018).

Translanguaging theory has had much impact in the ways we theorize pedagogical practices (see, for example, CUNY-NYSIEB [City University of New York-New York State Initiative on Emergent Bilinguals], 2021; García et al., 2017). Vogel and García (2017) posit three premises of translanguaging for pedagogy: (1) translanguaging maintains that bilinguals select and deploy features from a *unitary linguistic/semiotic repertoire* in order to communicate; (2) translanguaging takes up a perspective on bi/multilingualism that privileges *speakers' own dynamic linguistic and semiotic practices* above the named languages of nations and states; and (3) translanguaging recognizes the *material effects of socially constructed named language* categories and structuralist language ideologies, especially for racialized speakers. These premises all together challenge traditional understandings of additive bilingualism and center the language/semiotic practices of individuals and communities that have been labeled "non-standard" and in need of remediation.

The understandings of translanguaging theory and its pedagogical practices have challenged the original conceptualization of dual language (DL) programs in the United States, as language programs simply teaching "English" and the "Language other than English" (LOTE). These programs were constructed to develop additive bilingualism, that is, the addition of two separate named languages (Sánchez et al., 2018). Despite the material effects that named languages have always had, the two languages of bilinguals have no psycholinguistic reality in their minds. Bilingual speakers select features and meanings from a unitary repertoire, from a network that is interconnected and always emergent (Otheguy et al., 2015, 2019).

Dual Language Programs and Translanguaging

The term "two-way immersion" first appeared in the United States to describe a type of bilingual education program that was modeled after Canadian immersion programs for majority English-speaking students in Quebec (Genesee, 1987). At a time of retrenchment away from the bilingual education struggles of activists during the civil rights movement, "two-way" or "dual language" programs that included language majority children were introduced and promoted in the late 1990s (Lindholm-Leary, 2001). With the "dual" label, the word "bilingual" that was tied to the struggles on behalf of the socio-economic improvement of language-minoritized populations was silenced (Crawford, 2000; García, 2009). Scholars working with the Center for Applied Linguistics (CAL) consolidated the term "two-way dual language" or "two-way immersion" and created their first iteration of their Guiding Principles in the late 2000s (Howard et al., 2007). Those guidelines called for approximately half of the students to be "native speakers of English" and the other half as "native speakers of the partner language" (p. 1), and for students to be taught each language in monolingual environments through immersion methods. Instruction in English and the LOTE would alternate by week, day, time of day, and/or academic subject.

Early on, Guadalupe Valdés warned that DL education moved away from meeting the needs of racialized bilinguals (Valdés, 1997). Translanguaging as a theory of bilingual languaging and learning has provided ways to open up spaces (Wei, 2011) in DL classrooms where students can leverage their entire repertoire of knowledge and meanings (García & Lin, 2017; Sánchez et al., 2018; see also chapters in Sánchez & García, 2022). Sánchez and colleagues (2018) incorporated the "bilingual" label into the "dual language education" one (as "dual language bilingual education" or DLBE) to reclaim the bilingualism of students and that translanguaging is always present in those classrooms. But translanguaging in DLBE classrooms has also faced much opposition and criticism, especially from some teachers, school administrators, and district leaders who follow the guidelines for strict language separation. Some scholars have also been critical of adopting translanguaging stances and practices in DLBE classrooms (see, for example, Fortune & Tedick, 2019; Guerrero, 2021).

In the last decade, scholars have started to empirically study how translanguaging functions in DLBE classrooms. In the next section, I present the results of a literature review on empirical studies on translanguaging in United States. DLBE classrooms published in scholarly journals between 2014 and October 2021.

Translanguaging in Empirical Studies of Dual Language Bilingual Programs

Through One Search and Google Scholar, I conducted a literature search on empirical studies published in scholarly journals related to "translanguaging" in "dual language," "dual immersion," "two-way," and "one-way" pre-school to high school classrooms in the United States. I also expanded the search for additional journal articles by going directly to the webpages of journals that published at least two articles on translanguaging in DLBE programs through the original search. I acknowledge that there might be other journal articles that do not explicitly mention the terms "translanguaging" and "dual language," although they implicitly study these concepts. In addition, and to limit the scope of the study, I didn't include empirical articles published outside of the United States, or those published in edited books (see, for example, Fu et al., 2019; García & Kleyn, 2016; Wright et al., 2015). I recognize that the way in which I have carried out this review may have resulted in important omissions. Expanding the literature review to include these publications is important for future work.

Between 2014 and October 2021, I found 28 empirical journal articles that fit the search criteria. Table 25.1 presents each of the articles reviewed, organized by year of publication, from oldest to most recent, their context and their methods.

"Tabling" Complexity

The exercise of putting the information from the 28 empirical studies reviewed into Table 25.1 form clearly revealed the complexity of the label "dual language." In the United States, most DL programs were originally conceived as being two-way, with half of the population being language majority, and the other half racialized bilinguals. When analyzing the authors' descriptions of the programs, I noted that the labels and categories used for these programs are faulty, always leaking. Most students in these programs are racialized bilinguals who fall along all points of the bilingual continuum for the different tasks in which they *do* language. Despite the difficulties, and for this analysis, I used the label "one-way, developmental" when the authors described the students in the classroom as "primarily" students who were in some way connected to the group that spoke the LOTE (approximately 80% or more). I used the label "one-way, majority" when the studies included only white students from higher socio-economic status primarily without family connections to the LOTE. I kept the label "two-way," when the programs had a complexity of race, language, and socio-economic status, and not simply two categories of students. Some of these programs had more white students from affluent families than students with family connections to the LOTE, whereas other classrooms studied had more Latinx students, with different language practices and socio-economic status. Also important to note is that there is only one study on high schools. While the programs studied were called "dual language," they only included one to two courses taught in Spanish.

Another complexity that I noted is that even though all classrooms studied had a designated language policy with a "target language" of instruction, and DLBE teachers were sometimes designated as teachers of one language or another (see Columns 4 and 5), there is much translanguaging that occurs. This is important, for it shows how translanguaging can work alongside dual language allocation policies, so that instructional spaces for each language are respected, albeit with flexibility. This suppleness allows a targeted response to the different desires and needs of the students (Sánchez et al., 2018).

Table 25.1 Context and methods. Empirical journal articles on translanguaging in U.S. dual language bilingual programs (2014 to October 2021)

	The study context			*The study methods*	
Authors and year	*Type of program designation* and students served**	*Grade level(s) and teacher(s)*	*Language(s) of instruction per teacher and type of classroom***	*Target language(s) and subjects of instruction for study*	*Design and data sources (+, ++)*
Durán and Palmer (2014)	Spanish/English One-way, developmental [Formal label: "two-way"] 80% Latinx students Others primary white affluent	First grade Two bilingual co-teachers Latinas	Both languages Co-teaching	English & Spanish First half: different subjects, second half: literacy	Qualitative Classroom data+ primarily on four focal students++, and teacher interview
Esquinca et al. (2014)	Spanish/English One-way, developmental Students primarily Latinx transfronterixs	Fourth grade One bilingual teacher Latina	Both languages Self-contained	Spanish Science	Qualitative Classroom data and artifacts and student artifacts
Garza and Langman (2014)	Spanish/English One-way, developmental Students of Mexican origin, all but two	Fifth grade One bilingual Teacher Latina	Both languages Self-contained	English (Science) and Spanish (Social Studies)	Qualitative Classroom data and teacher interviews
Palmer et al. (2014)	Spanish/English Two-way More white students than Latinx	Pre-K and first grade Two bilingual teachers Latinas	Both languages each Self-contained	English and Spanish Different subjects	Qualitative Classroom data+ and artifacts and teachers' interviews

(*Continued*)

Table 25.1 (Continued)

	The study context			*The study methods*	
Authors and year	*Type of program designation* and students served**	*Grade level(s) and teacher(s)*	*Language(s) of instruction per teacher and type of classroom***	*Target language(s) and subjects of instruction for study*	*Design and data sources (+, ++)*
Gort and Sembiante (2015)	Spanish/English One-way developmental 100% Latinx students, mixed SES	Pre-school Three bilingual teachers (one lead, and two co-teachers) Latinas	Lead teacher, both languages (depending on week); other teachers, one language Co-teaching	English and Spanish Literacy	Qualitative Classroom data+
Henderson and Palmer (2015)	Spanish/English One-way, developmental [Formal label: "two-way"] From 1 to 4 English speakers in each class	Third grade (two classrooms) Two bilingual teachers One white and one Latina	One language each; white teacher (English); Latina teacher (Spanish) Type of classrooms: no information	English and Spanish (depending on teacher) Language arts	Qualitative Classroom data, teacher planning meetings, and interviews
Martínez et al. (2015)	Spanish/English One-way, developmental 78% Latinx students, primarily low SES	K/first and first/second Two bilingual teachers One white One Latina	Both languages each Self-contained	English and Spanish Different subjects	Qualitative Classroom data+ and teacher interviews

(*Continued*)

Table 25.1 (Continued)

	The study context			*The study methods*	
Authors and year	*Type of program designation* and students served**	*Grade level(s) and teacher(s)*	*Language(s) of instruction per teacher and type of classroom***	*Target language(s) and subjects of instruction for study*	*Design and data sources (+, ++)*
Pontier and Gort (2016)	Spanish/English One-way, developmental All but one Latinx students	Pre-school Two bilingual co-teachers	One language each Co-teaching	English and Spanish (depending on teacher) Literacy	Qualitative Classroom data+ and artifacts
Alamillo et al. (2017)	Spanish/English No information on students in the classroom, except for focal students, all Latinx	Pre-school One bilingual teacher Latina	One language Type of classroom: co-teaching	Spanish Free play, teacher-led events, and communal mealtime	Qualitative Classroom data+ primarily on four focal students' interactions++, teacher think-aloud reflections, and interviews
Bauer et al. (2017)	Spanish/English Two-way Approx. 50% Spanish-dominant and 50% English-dominant Primarily African American, with low SES	Kindergarten One bilingual teacher Latina	Both languages Self-contained	Spanish Morning message, read-aloud, and writing activities	Qualitative Classroom data+ and two focal students' writing samples++

(Continued)

Table 25.1 (Continued)

	The study context			*The study methods*	
Authors and year	*Type of program designation* and students served**	*Grade level(s) and teacher(s)*	*Language(s) of instruction per teacher and type of classroom***	*Target language(s) and subjects of instruction for study*	*Design and data sources (+, ++)*
García-Mateus and Palmer (2017)	Spanish/English Two-way Balanced in home languages	First grade One bilingual teacher Latina	Both languages Self-contained	Spanish Social Studies	Qualitative Classroom data+ of four focal students++, teacher, and focal students' interviews
Bauer et al. (2018)	Spanish/English Two-way 60% Latinx and 40% non-Latinx Primarily African American, with low SES	Kindergarten One bilingual teacher Latina	Both languages Self-contained	Spanish Literacy (but data collection not during instructional time)	Mixed methods Teachers' interview, and two informal assessments with six focal students++
Garza and Arreguín-Anderson (2018)	Spanish/English One-way, developmental All Latinx	Fourth grade One bilingual teacher Latina	Both languages Self-contained	Spanish Science	Qualitative Classroom data+

(*Continued*)

Table 25.1 (Continued)

	The study context			*The study methods*	
Authors and year	*Type of program designation* and students served**	*Grade level(s) and teacher(s)*	*Language(s) of instruction per teacher and type of classroom***	*Target language(s) and subjects of instruction for study*	*Design and data sources (+, ++)*
Hamman (2018)	Spanish/English Two-way Approx. 50% Spanish-dominant and 50% English-dominant	Second grade One bilingual teacher Latina	Both languages Self-contained	English (Science and Social Studies) and Spanish (literacy and math) Different subjects	Qualitative Classroom data+ and teacher interviews (with video-elicitation)
Henderson and Ingram (2018)	Spanish/English One-way, developmental All Latinx, started as "Spanish dominant"	Third grade One bilingual teacher white	Both languages Self-contained	English and Spanish Different subjects	Mixed methods Classroom data+, student artifacts, language ideology survey, and teacher interviews
Mortimer (2018)	Spanish/English Programs were called "dual language," but most courses were in English with 1–2 courses offered in Spanish Most students were Latinx	Two elementary schools and two high schools Unknown number of teachers	No information available	English and Spanish Did not specify subjects	Qualitative Classroom data+ teachers interview with them

(*Continued*)

Table 25.1 (Continued)

	The study context			*The study methods*	
Authors and year	*Type of program designation* and students served**	*Grade level(s) and teacher(s)*	*Language(s) of instruction per teacher and type of classroom***	*Target language(s) and subjects of instruction for study*	*Design and data sources (+, ++)*
Poza (2018)	Spanish/English Two-way 72% Latinx students	Fifth grade One bilingual teacher Latino	One language Type of classroom: no information	Spanish Science	Qualitative Classroom data+
Poza (2019)	Spanish/English Two-way Approx. 50% Latinx	Fifth grade (two classrooms) One bilingual teacher Latino	One language Type of classroom: no information	Spanish Language Arts and Science	Qualitative Classroom data+, and teacher and students' interviews
Pratt and Ernst-Slavit (2019)	Spanish/English Two-way 40% of students spoke Spanish at home	Third grade One bilingual teacher Latina	One language Type of classroom: no information	Spanish Literacy	Qualitative Classroom data+ and observations of teacher activities during after school events
Somerville and Faltis (2019)	Spanish/English Two-way 50% had a Spanish-speaking parent	Fourth grade One bilingual teacher Latina	Both languages Self-contained	Spanish Social Studies and Math	Qualitative Classroom data+ primarily on three focal students++, and interviews with teacher, focal students and principal

(*Continued*)

Table 25.1 (Continued)

	The study context			*The study methods*	
Authors and year	*Type of program designation* and students served**	*Grade level(s) and teacher(s)*	*Language(s) of instruction per teacher and type of classroom***	*Target language(s) and subjects of instruction for study*	*Design and data sources (+, ++)*
Zheng (2019)	Mandarin/English One-way, majority [Formal label: "Chinese Immersion"] All except two students had no connection with Chinese	Fourth/fifth grade One bilingual teacher Chinese	One language Type of classroom: side-by-side	Mandarin	Qualitative Classroom data, student artifacts, conversations with teacher, interview with students and parents
Licona and Kelly (2020)	Spanish/English Two-way 35% were non-Latinx, mostly African Americans, others Latinx	Seventh grade (two classrooms) One bilingual teacher Latina	One language Type of classroom: no information	Spanish Science	Qualitative Classroom data+
de Jong et al. (2021)	Spanish/English One-way developmental [Formal label: "two-way"] 79% reported using only Spanish or both English and Spanish at home	Sixth–eighth grades No information on teachers	N/A	Spanish	Mixed methods Student survey and small group interviews++

(*Continued*)

Table 25.1 (Continued)

	The study context			*The study methods*	
Authors and year	*Type of program designation* and students served**	*Grade level(s) and teacher(s)*	*Language(s) of instruction per teacher and type of classroom***	*Target language(s) and subjects of instruction for study*	*Design and data sources (+, ++)*
Du (2021)	Mandarin/English One-way, majority Private school with primarily English speakers	Fourth grade One bilingual teacher Chinese	One language Type of classroom: no information	Mandarin Math and Science	Mixed methods For three focal students++: classroom data and student artifacts, interviews, developmental reading assessment (DRA2) results and Chinese midterm exam
Frieson (2021)	Spanish/English Two-way 50% Latinx and almost 50% African American students	K and first grades Two bilingual teachers Latinas	Both languages Self-contained	Spanish Literacy	Qualitative Classroom data+ primarily for five focal students++ (African American), interviews and conversations with teachers, parents, and focal students, and informational materials about the dual language program

(*Continued*)

Table 25.1 (Continued)

	The study context			*The study methods*	
Authors and year	*Type of program designation* and students served**	*Grade level(s) and teacher(s)*	*Language(s) of instruction per teacher and type of classroom***	*Target language(s) and subjects of instruction for study*	*Design and data sources (+, ++)*
Frieson and Scalise (2021)	Spanish/English Two-way Almost 50% African American students and 17% Latinx	K and first grades Two bilingual teachers Latinas	Both languages Self-contained	Spanish Literacy	Qualitative Classroom data+ primarily on two focal students (African American), and teacher's interviews
Infante and Licona (2021)	Spanish/English One-way developmental Majority Latinx	Seventh grade (two classrooms) One bilingual teacher Latina	Both languages Type of classroom: no information	English and Spanish Science	Qualitative Classroom data+

(*Continued*)

Table 25.1 (Continued)

	The study context			*The study methods*	
Authors and year	*Type of program designation* and students served**	*Grade level(s) and teacher(s)*	*Language(s) of instruction per teacher and type of classroom***	*Target language(s) and subjects of instruction for study*	*Design and data sources (+, ++)*
Tian (2021)	Mandarin/English Primarily English-dominant students or heritage speakers of Chinese that spoke primarily English, and from higher SES	Third grade One bilingual teacher Chinese from Taiwan	One language Type of classroom: side-by-side	Mandarin Language Arts	Qualitative Classroom data+ and artifacts, researcher-teacher planning meetings and artifacts, with the teacher and 12 focal students' artifacts

* Program designation: one-way developmental (primarily for racialized bilinguals), one-way majority or two-way (for both racialized and majority students).

**Type of classroom: "self-contained" (same teacher is designated to teach in both languages, although in different instructional spaces), "co-teaching" (two or more teachers teaching together in the classroom, usually each is designated a language) "side-by-side" (different teacher in charge of instructing in the other language, English, in most of the studies) or "no information (the study didn't provide details on who was responsible of teaching the language not studied).

+Data sources: classroom data may include field notes as well video and/or audio recordings.

++Focal students: when the analysis solely focuses on a handful of focal students.

The Contexts and Methods for Studying Translanguaging in Dual Language Bilingual Education

The contexts of the DLBE programs studied and the methods that researchers employed in their studies and displayed in Table 25.1 provide a perspective on how translanguaging in DLBE has been studied. Below is an overview of salient issues related to the context and methods of the 28 journal articles reviewed.

Language

Of the 28 articles reviewed, 25 were Spanish/English programs, and 3 were Mandarin/English (see Column 2). This is consistent with the overwhelming number of Spanish/English bilingual programs in the United States compared to those which teach in LOTEs other than Spanish.

All classrooms studied had a designated language policy with a "target language" of instruction (see Column 5) although translanguaging was occurring during the process of learning and teaching. Of the 24 articles focusing on classroom-based data in Spanish/English DLBE programs, 13 collected data during "Spanish" designated target of instruction and 11 during both designated. The three studies in Mandarin/English programs focused on "Chinese" designated time. None of the articles collected data solely during the "English" designated time.

When data was collected during both English and Spanish time, the studies did report the presence of translanguaging during English instructional time. Translanguaging in this case was purely a scaffold for students labeled "English language learners" and those who had recently arrived in the United States. Despite our advances with translanguaging pedagogical practices, English still seems to be more protected than the LOTE, pointing to monoglossic nationalistic tendencies and the hegemony of English even in DLBE classrooms. Some critics of translanguaging might point to this finding and think that whereas the English space is protected, the space for the LOTE is not. Even though we must continue to push against monoglossic assumptions in English language teaching, we also must acknowledge and support racialized students' translanguaging in those spaces because it can transform their minoritized subjectivities that make them ashamed of the dynamic bilingual practices of their homes, families, and communities.

Grade Levels and Subjects

It was not surprising that 86% of the studies (24) were at the elementary level, pre-school to fifth grade (see Column 3) and focused on leveraging translanguaging in the teaching of language and literacy. Most children labeled "English language learners" who qualify for dual language programs have been born in the United States. Of the eight studies that took place in fourth and fifth grades, half focused on how translanguaging was used in the context of teaching science, math, social studies and/or multiple subjects. This points to the fact that language is the conduit to knowledge and understandings of all subject matter. Translanguaging is not simply a matter of language; it is a matter of knowledge and understandings. There are very few DLBE programs designed for immigrant adolescents in the United States, and this shows also in the limited research available on them (two studies at the middle school level and one at the high school one).

Teachers

The bilingual teachers in the Spanish/English DLBE programs were Latinas for the most part (see Column 3). In two of the studies there was one Latina bilingual teacher designated as the "Spanish" teacher, and one white bilingual teacher, designated as the "English" teacher. This is a growing phenomenon in the United States, where some schools recruit Anglo bilingual teachers in their DL programs to model bilingualism for the students who are not yet bilingual. In one study the sole bilingual teacher was white and working with Latinx students. The bilingual teachers in the Chinese/English DLBE programs were all Chinese.

Teachers in these studies teach in either one language solely or in two languages (see Column 4). In more than half of the Spanish/English classrooms studied (13 of the 24), individual teachers imparted instruction in all subjects, all day, and delivered instruction bilingually, even if they were expected to act monolingually in each space according to the language allocation policy of the school This number could be higher given that eight of the studies did not provide information on whether the same teacher was responsible for teaching subjects in English or if it was a different teacher doing so. In the three Mandarin/English programs, the teachers were expected to teach in Mandarin. Two of the classrooms studied followed a side-by-side model, with another teacher being in charge of English instruction. The third study didn't include this information.

Four of the Spanish/English classrooms in which two or more teachers were involved had a co-teaching model, that is, there was more than one teacher in the same classroom who used only one language in teaching. This is a privileged form of bilingual teaching, prevalent especially in pre-schools and in integrated co-teaching for children with dis/abilities. This co-teaching model also can have strict language allocation policies, as in the case of one pre-school classroom studied, there were three teachers—a lead teacher who changed language of instruction every week, and two co-teachers with designated languages of instruction.

What is instructive here is to realize that despite the ethnicity/race/language profile of bilingual teachers, and despite whether they teach monolingually in one language or in two separate languages, translanguaging was present among all these teachers and in classrooms that were both self-contained and/or side-by-side or that followed a co-teaching model.

Students

The labeling of students that attend DLBE programs is problematic (García & Kleifgen, 2018). Students that attend DLBE programs tend to receive labels like "English dominant" or "Spanish/Chinese/LOTE dominant" and some are also labeled "English language learners." These name tags don't reflect the complexity of bilingual development. Students' language practices develop over time. And the labels are often created through standardized assessments that do not in any way reflect the dynamic ways in which bilingual students *do* language. These labels have provoked much criticism among several of the authors of the studies included (i.e., Alamillo et al., 2017; Durán & Palmer, 2014; Hamman, 2018; Henderson & Palmer, 2015; Palmer et al., 2014; Pontier & Gort, 2016; Poza, 2018). Researchers problematized the categorization of students, pointing to the ways in which students engage in doing language and translanguaging differently, depending on tasks, subject, interest, and interlocutors. I have done my best to try to identify the students' characteristics (see Column 2).

In 11 of the 28 programs studied, the majority of students were of Latinx origin, meaning that in their households either themselves or their family members spoke Spanish and had cultural connections to Spanish-speaking Latin American countries (see Column 2 under the "one-way, developmental" label). Some of these programs had Latinx students of mixed socio-economic status; other Latinx students were from the neighboring community. In the rest of the officially designated Spanish/English "two-way" classrooms, there was a complexity of race, language, and socio-economic status, and not simply two categories of students. Some of these programs had more white students from affluent families than students with family connections to the LOTE, whereas other classrooms studied had more Latinx students, with different language practices and socio-economic.

It is also instructive to realize that as DL programs have grown throughout the country, the growing language-minoritized population has made increasing use of them to their benefit. The three Mandarin/English DLBE programs served primarily white students from higher socio-economic status primarily without family connections to the LOTE. These programs were officially designated as "two-way" because they were not allowed to exclude language-minoritized students. However, despite the designation of "two-way," these programs served the white majority with economic means and were instruments of a neoliberal globalized economy to make majority English-speaking children bilingual (Flores & García, 2017).

It is interesting to note that bilingual scholars have become interested in the anti-blackness of many DL programs (Chávez-Moreno, 2019; Cioè-Peña, 2022) and have increasingly sought to study the presence of African American students in such programs. Four studies have all looked at DLBE classrooms in which Latinx and African American students interact using features from their language repertoire that do not simply reproduce those of white monolinguals, but that reflect the practices of racialized people who usually reside in proximity. The turn to studying Latinx and Black students learning together in DLBE classrooms does not in any way indicate a proliferation of African Americans in these classrooms. On the contrary, Black students remain rare. But scholars today have greater interest in ensuring that these spaces do not simply reproduce white monolingual monoglossic practices but include the great range of linguistic practices, the translanguaging, with which people, including African Americans, language.

The Research Design and Data Collection

All studies used qualitative research methods, with all but two using extended data collection in classrooms (from weeks to months) (see Column 6). Data collected included field notes, audio/video recording, interviews with teachers and/or students, and/or classroom/instructional artifacts. Three studies also included quantitative measures, including data from surveys, informal assessments, midterm exams or Developmental Reading Assessment (DRA2) results. Ten studies focused exclusively on the analysis of student work and/or student interactions. Missing from this table are student scores on standardized tests, an important and telling omission from the methodology of all studies in this review. This points to the greater attention of translanguaging scholars to transformations in the classroom than to numerical changes in student academic scores and the "achievement gap." The emphasis of these scholars is on providing greater equity, and an education that is more socially and cognitively just.

Now that I have provided descriptive background on the 28 studies included in this review, I will analyze these studies *jointly* to better understand how translanguaging spaces within the rigid language allocation of DL are enacted in those classrooms, their benefits for students, as well as some challenges and tensions.

Enacting Translanguaging within the Classrooms Language Allocation Policies

We learn much from these studies about the context of DLBE classrooms in which translanguaging is being leveraged in one way or another. Despite the focus on translanguaging, all the articles included demonstrate the importance of a language allocation policy, albeit with flexibility. Within spaces that had been allocated to one or another language, translanguaging was occurring during the process of learning and teaching.

In most of these studies, the teachers validated their students' translanguaging even if the teacher's input continued to be in the "target language" of instruction. For example, during play time in a first-grade classroom in Durán and Palmer's study, students' translanguaging was the norm, whereas the teachers observed the language of instruction of the "day" or "time." However, educators responded to translanguaging in a natural way, encouraged it, and validated it. In 11 studies, the teachers' support of students' translanguaging was a conscious decision, reflecting their translanguaging stance and heteroglossic ideologies. These teachers decided purposefully not to enforce the strict language separation of DL programs. For example, Alamillo et al. (2017) studied a pre-school classroom that was designed for the teacher to follow the students' languaging, rather than following strictly the language of instruction. Although the bilingual Latina teacher was originally skeptical of the approach, she changed her mind after seeing evidence of the students' bilingual development over the course of a year. In the study by Garza and Langman, the fifth-grade bilingual Latina teacher stated explicitly that she didn't want to force students to perform in the language of the subject because she wanted to support their bilingual identities. Following the Sánchez and colleagues (2018) translanguaging allocation framework, Tian and the third-grade teacher in the Mandarin/English DLBE program co-designed lessons based on translanguaging, focusing on its use to document and assess what students knew, to scaffold instruction for individual students, and to transform subjectivities of inferiority among emergent bilingual students.

Sometimes, however, the teachers' ideologies supported very strict language separation. They made it explicit that the students were not to use the other language in the classroom. And yet, translanguaging was forever present among the students. For example, in Pratt and Ernst-Slavit, a third-grade teacher acted as language police, primarily during Spanish instruction. Students also took on that role and policed each other while the teacher wasn't around. And yet, the students understood that it was translanguaging that was supporting their understanding of the content.

Benefits of Translanguaging in Dual Language Bilingual Classrooms

All of the articles studied mentioned the benefits of translanguaging in the process of learning and teaching in DLBE classrooms. I consider three of these benefits below: (1) to support the students' content knowledge and understandings; (2) to validate their identities; and (3) to develop and sustain their bilingualism, biliteracy, and multilingual awareness.

Support of Students' Content Knowledge and Understandings

Over half of the articles (15) provided evidence that translanguaging in DLBE classrooms supported students' content knowledge and understandings. For example, translanguaging practices were important for the transfronterizx fourth graders in a border city in Texas in the study by Esquinca and colleagues. Whereas the teacher communicated primarily in the target language of instruction, English, her transfronterizx students used translanguaging to make sense of the science lesson on molecular structure.

Licona and Kelly studied two seventh-grade science classrooms taught by one teacher who thought of translanguaging as the norm. The teacher provided materials to students in both English and Spanish, and they were free to engage with them in the language(s) of their choice. The authors noted that translanguaging positioned students as competent members of the classrooms' scientific communities and allowed them to engage in dialogues to learn how evidence is used in scientific argument.

Validation of Bilingual Identities

Almost half of the articles (13) found evidence that translanguaging in DLBE created bilingual classroom communities that supported the building of students' bilingual identities. For example, Palmer and colleagues studied a pre-K and first-grade classrooms where the Latina bilingual teachers, through their translanguaging practices, became models of dynamic bilingualism for their students. They also found evidence that the teachers created a classroom community where they positioned children as competent bilinguals regardless of the children's actual language performances.

Gort and Sembiante studied a pre-school classroom in which a Latina bilingual teacher served as the "language model," alternating between English and Spanish each week, and two Latina co-teachers taught in one of the two languages always. While at times each teacher was consistent with the language policy role that they had been assigned, their linguistic performances, during other times, were more flexible. Their translanguaging appeared to be influenced by the nature of their co-teaching partnerships, the function or purpose of their interaction, and the teachers' perceptions of the children's language preferences and unique developmental needs. Together, they created a bilingual classroom in which teachers and students recognized, validated, and expressed their bilingual identities.

Developing and Sustaining Bilingualism, Biliteracy and Multilingual Awareness

Eleven studies highlighted ways in which translanguaging supported their students' languaging and literacies performances and/or biliteracies development, including their metalinguistic awareness. In Bauer et al.'s (2017) study, for example, the teacher strategically paired an African American girl and a Latino kindergarten boy to support each other's emergent bilingual writing. The researchers data analyses showed that the classroom's acceptance of translanguaging encouraged their collaborative negotiation of their writing during their multilingual discussions.

Henderson and Ingram (2018) study highlights a white bilingual teacher's translanguaging moves to support the development of the students' metalinguistic awareness. The teacher brought attention to linguistic features of Spanish, English, and to features associated with varieties of Spanish and English. They found that these pedagogical practices supported their students' critical metalinguistic awareness, especially when they sung bilingual songs and explained jokes, found the hidden word (word roots), explained word etymologies, and discussed linguistic variation.

Tensions and Challenges of Translanguaging in Dual Language Bilingual Classrooms

Although all 28 studies highlighted ways in which translanguaging in DLBE programs supported their students, several of them also raised tensions that they encountered and challenges that translanguaging posed. I describe below the two major tensions and challenges that the studies identified: (1) enacting translanguaging while maintaining the hegemony of named languages, especially English; and (2) underrepresenting the heteroglossic/translanguaging practices of African American and other racialized bilingual students.

Maintaining the Hegemony of English and Named Languages

The monoglossic ideologies of bilingualism and of language separation expectation are still very engrained in many of the teachers in the studies. Whereas students' translanguaging may be acceptable, and despite many teachers making their own translanguaging explicit, some of them still gave a message that translanguaging is not necessarily appropriate, transmitting ideologies of language purism. For example, one of the two teachers that Martínez et al. studied was a white bilingual teacher in a self-contained kindergarten/first-grade DLBE classroom. The researchers observed many instances of students' oral translanguaging in her classroom, as well as a few instances in which the teacher herself engaged in translanguaging. While the teacher commented being "a big fan" (p. 31) of her students' oral translanguaging, she stated that she expected her students to keep Spanish and English separated in their writing in order for them to develop academic registers in each language. The authors reflected that whereas the teacher held monoglossic ideologies (García, 2009), her intention was to provide opportunities for them to develop Spanish. They noted: "[A]lthough some of her views on language mixing echo dominant language ideologies of linguistic purism, her perspective on promoting and sustaining Spanish can be seen as counterhegemonic" (p. 35).

Two of the studies in Mandarin/English DLBE programs addressed concerns about the protection and maintenance of the LOTE. As I have noted, the three studies in Mandarin/English bilingual classrooms primarily included English-speaking white students. The authors and the teachers in the study by Zheng and Tian found that the hegemony of English was still prevalent in the classrooms and wondered how Chinese instruction could be enhanced, even if translanguaging pedagogy was to be at the center of instruction. Tian found that opening translanguaging spaces in a third-grade Mandarin Language Arts classroom enabled students to more fully demonstrate their content proficiency and develop bilingual and biliteracy abilities, and metalinguistic awareness. Yet, when given a choice of language, the language majority students tended to use more English. The author cautioned that when using translanguaging pedagogical practices, there needs to be awareness of how to use it purposefully and strategically so that students would want to use the LOTE.

Not all studies demonstrated this concern about translanguaging in relationship to the "maintenance" and protection of the LOTE. For example, the teacher in a fourth-grade math and science Mandarin/English DLBE classroom in Du's study did not find an issue with the protection of the Chinese language because "without translanguaging, the linguistic challenges [given their different proficiency levels in Mandarin] would affect the students' learning" (p. 7). Gort and Sembiante also challenged the question of English hegemony in bilingual programs in the pre-school classroom that they studied. The co-teachers sometimes performed monolingually according to their designated roles, but sometimes were more flexible with their languaging to meet young children's developing experiences. It seems that with very young children in pre-school there is less concern with the protection of the LOTE or of the hegemony of English than with older students. This has to do with the fact that very young children are developing linguistically as simultaneous bilinguals, while at the same time absorbing concepts of early literacy, numeracy, and understandings of the world. For that complex task, it is better to meet them conceptually and linguistically where they are, as emergent bilinguals who are still drawing from a young linguistic/semiotic repertoire (Ascenzi-Moreno et al., 2022). Suggesting that bilingual students perform language in monolingual ways only accentuates their deficiency in comparison to monolingual bodies who perform language in monolingual contexts and countries. Translanguaging precisely sustains the language practices of bilinguals in ways that are theirs, valid, and authentic.

Hamman wondered how DLBE teachers enacting translanguaging pedagogy could pay more attention to counterbalancing the hegemony of English. She studied a second-grade two-way bilingual classroom with approximately the same number of students with Latinx backgrounds (that is, who started the bilingual program designated as "Spanish dominant") and students with white families of higher socio-economic status. The bilingual program had more instructional time in Spanish, and the translanguaging pedagogy enacted in those classrooms helped students with their metalinguistic awareness and biliteracy development. However, Hamman found that white English speakers tended to use more translanguaging in Spanish spaces, whereas in the English spaces, Latinx students didn't, unless prompted by the teacher. Hamman suggested the term "critical translanguaging" space, suggesting that teachers need to understand how translanguaging pedagogy, without the teacher's critical implementation, may reproduce the hegemony of English.

Underrepresentation of African American and Other Racialized Students' Language Practices

The complexity of students' language practices is many times made invisible in DL programs, hid under the categorical label to which they are assigned. However, influenced by the study of raciolinguistic ideologies (Flores & Rosa, 2015; Rosa & Flores, 2017), some scholars have turned their attention to how African American students, as well as other racialized bilingual/bidialectal students engage in translanguaging practices in DL classrooms. The study of African American language has traditionally focused on the variety known as Black English or African American Vernacular English (Rickford, 1999), and of their bidialectism. Translanguaging problematizes not only external constructions of named languages, but also of named language varieties. African Americans, as well as many other racialized students who are described as "bidialectal" engage in translanguaging. Taking the *internal perspective* advocated for by W. E. du Bois (1903) when he talked about "lifting the veil," African Americans and other racialized students, just like bilingual students, select features from their unitary repertoire. Their languaging performances fall along all points of the bilingual continuum, with some exhibiting more features of what is called "Black English," and some less.

Frieson and Scalise, and Frieson followed African American children (and classmates that interacted with them) in a kindergarten and first-grade classrooms in a Spanish/English DLBE program serving primarily racialized bilinguals (African American and Latinx). The children were chosen purposefully because they spoke what are considered a white mainstream English variety and a Black language variety and were learning Spanish in the program. Frieson and Scalise found that during interactions with peers, African American children "actively resisted Spanish/English binaries by employing translanguaging practices through classroom talk and academic tasks that normalized Black Language in DLBE bilingual classrooms across racialized and linguistic identities" (p. 13). Frieson highlights that translanguaging in DLBE has the potential to support the biliteracy practices of Black American children by honoring all their language practices and literacies.

A translanguaging lens brings into focus the heteroglossic aspects of the languaging of African Americans and other racialized students (for example, of students who also language with Indigenous languages of Latin America) and disrupts the monoglossic representations of English. English has been constructed matching the way in which white monolinguals with power use language. By drawing tight boundaries around white monolingual middle-class ways of using language, aspects of languaging that go beyond those borders are assigned as "dialects" or "varieties." Translanguaging enables us to reimagine the use of English by all, colonized and colonizers, from the perspective of the speaker, rather than from its rigid construction to colonize, racialize and dominate racial/ethnic/linguistic minoritized and Indigenous people, and build nation-states with powerful global economies that subjugate those who are less powerful.

The Possibilities of Translanguaging and the Camino that We Need to Andar

It is clear from the empirical evidence of the studies reviewed in this chapter that students' translanguaging is a reality in DLBE classrooms. Teachers leverage racialized bilingual students' dynamic language practices, their translanguaging, regardless of strict language allocation policies, grade levels, types of teachers and classrooms, types of programs, or types of students.

The studies included in this review have shown different benefits of translanguaging in DLBE, including supporting students' content knowledge and understandings, validating bilingual identities, and developing and sustaining bilingualism, biliteracy, and multilingual awareness. These benefits resemble the purposes of translanguaging in education posited by García and Wei (2014) and García et al. (2017)—to support students in meaning making, in expanding their language practices, and in enacting their creativity and criticality. The studies reviewed have also highlighted the potential of translanguaging in DL education as a political act (Flores, 2014), disrupting their strict language allocation policies, and their exclusion of racialized bilinguals. In challenging the superiority and academic value of the languaging of white monolingual middle-class people, translanguaging in education can provide a measure of social and cognitive justice (García & Wei, 2014; García et al., 2017), particularly on behalf of the most numerous racialized bilingual group in the country—Latinx (Sánchez & García, 2022).

The hegemony of English in U.S. schools persists, even in DLBE. Translanguaging has the potential to disrupt this hegemony. By being inclusive of the languaging of racialized minorities, translanguaging theory can also disrupt the monoglossic ways in which English has been "invented" and academic English validated as the only source of knowledge (Alfaro, 2019). DLBE classrooms have validated other languages, in these studies, Spanish and Chinese. Translanguaging theory also disrupts the monoglossic ways in which we understand those LOTEs, taking into account the ways they are spoken in bilingual communities, the "everyday language" (Martínez & Mejía, 2020) of Latinx and Chinese people. Translanguaging theory opens the door to recognize the diversity of languaging in those communities, including the great many speakers of Indigenous languages among Latinx communities, and of other languages (officially called "varieties" of Mandarin) among Chinese communities.

While there is much evidence of the importance of translanguaging in DLBE, there is much to uncover about the transformational power (or the potential) of translanguaging in such programs. Empirical educational research is an iterative process. As researchers unpack translanguaging in DLBE classrooms, the dissemination of these studies may inspire other teachers to enact some of those practices in their classrooms, or to bring them to the surface, instead of engaging in translanguaging an escondidas (Sánchez & García, 2022). To move forward the transformational potential of translanguaging, DLBE teachers and researchers need to pay particular attention to the different ways in which teachers' translanguaging stance and their translanguaging pedagogy can further support the disruption of the hegemony of named languages, and in particular of English. They also need to enact, and study, larger culturally responsive and sustaining education approaches to contextualize the social-cultural-political teaching and learning processes (Muhammad, 2020). While some studies published in edited volumes are starting to show ways in which translanguaging spaces have been central to combat the gentrification of DL education (i.e., Heiman et al., 2022; Poza & Stites, 2022), this is an area that needs further investigation.

The studies included here offer a path to transform DLBE from programs that teach languages to programs that educate racialized bilingual students and improve their unequal position in society. As Antonio Machado wrote: "caminante no hay camino, se hace camino al andar." This paper is a call for researchers, in collaboration with DLBE teachers, to keep opening and shaping the path, as well as highlighting the transformative translanguaging spaces in DLBE classrooms that are already offering caminos.

Note

1 I would like to thank Ofelia García for the invaluable feedback she provided to this manuscript.

References

Alamillo, L., Yun, C., & Bennett, L. H. (2017). Translanguaging in a Reggio-inspired Spanish dual-language immersion programme. *Early Childhood Development and Care*, *187*(3–4), 469–486. https://doi.org/10.1080/03004430.2016.1236091

Alfaro, C. (2019). Preparing critically conscious dual language teachers: Recognizing and interrupting dominant ideologies. Reimaging dual language education in the U.S. *Theory Into Practice Journal*, *58*(2), 194–203.

Ascenzi-Moreno, L., Espinosa, C., & Lehner-Quam, A. (2022). Move, play, language: A translanguaged, multimodal approach to literacies with young emergent bilinguals. In S. Brown, & S. Hao (Eds.), *Multimodal literacies with young emergent bilinguals: Beyond print-centric practices* (pp. 117–130). Multilingual Matters.

Baker, C. (2001). *Foundations of bilingual education and bilingualism* (3rd ed.). Multilingual Matters.

Bauer, E. B., Colomer, S. E., & Wiemelt, J. (2018). Biliteracy of African American and Latinx kindergarten students in a dual-language program: Understanding students' translanguaging practices across informal assessments. *Urban Education*, *55*(3), 331–361. https://doi.org/10.1177/0042085918789743

Bauer, E., Presiado, V., & Colomer, S. (2017). Writing through partnership: Fostering translanguaging in children who are emergent bilinguals. *Journal of Literacy Research*, *49*(1), 10–37. https://doi.org/10.1177/1086296X16683417

Chávez-Moreno, L. C. (2019). Researching Latinxs, racism, and white supremacy in bilingual education: A literature review. *Critical Inquiry in Language Studies*, *17*(2), 101–120. https://doi.org/10.1080/15427587.2019.1624966

Cioè-Peña, M. (2022). The master's tools will never dismantle the master's school: Interrogating settler colonial logics in language education. *Annual Review of Applied Linguistics*, *42*, 25–33.

Crawford, J. (2000). *At war with diversity. U.S. language policy in an age of anxiety*. Multilingual Matters.

CUNY-NYSIEB (City University of New York-New York State Initiative on Emergent Bilinguals) (Eds.). (2021). *Translanguaging and transformative teaching for emergent bilingual students. Lessons from the CUNY-NYSIEB project*. Routledge.

de Jong, E. J., Coulter, Z., & Tsai, M. (2021). Two-way bilingual education programs and sense of belonging: Perspectives from middle school students. *International Journal of Bilingual Education and Bilingualism*. https://doi.org/10.1080/13670050.2020.1783635

Du, X. (2021). Translanguaging practices of students in science and math classes in a Chinese/English dual language bilingual program. *Applied Linguistics Review*. https://doi.org/10.1515/applirev-2021-0019Du

du Bois, W. E. (1903). *The souls of black folk*. A.C. McClurg & Co.

Durán, L., & Palmer, D. (2014). Pluralist discourses of bilingualism and translanguaging talk in classrooms. *Journal of Early Childhood Literacy*, *14*(3), 367–388. https://doi.org/10.1177/1468798413497386

Esquinca, A., Araujo, B., & de la Piedra, M. T. (2014). Meaning making and translanguaging in a two-way dual-language program on the U.S.-Mexico Border. *Bilingual Research Journal*, *37*(2), 164–181. https://doi.org/10.1080/15235882.2014.934970

Flores, N., & García, O. (2017). A critical review of bilingual education in the United States: From basements and pride to boutiques and profit. *Annual Review of Applied Linguistics*, *37*, 14–29. https://doi.org/10.1017/S0267190517000162

Flores, N., & Rosa, J. (2015). Undoing appropriateness: Raciolinguistic ideologies and language diversity in education. *Harvard Education Review*, *85*(2), 149–171. https://doi.org/10.17763/0017-8055.85.2.149

Flores, N. (2014). Let's not forget that translanguaging is a political act. *The Educational Linguist*. Blog (July 19, 2014). https://educationallinguist.wordpress.com/2014/07/19/lets-not-forget-that-translanguaging-is-a-political-act/

Flores, N., & Schissel, J. L. (2014). Dynamic bilingualism as the norm: Envisioning a heteroglossic approach to standards-based reform. *TESOL Quarterly*, *48*(3), 454–479. https://doi.org/10.1002/tesq.182

Fortune, T. W., & Tedick, D. J. (2019). Context matter. Translanguaging and language immersion in the U.S. and Canada. In M. Haneda, & H. Nassaji (Eds.), *Perspectives on language as action* (pp. 27–44). Multilingual Matters.

Frieson, B. L. (2021). Remixin' and flowin' in centros: Exploring the biliteracy practices of Black language speakers in an elementary two-way immersion bilingual program. *Race, Ethnicity and Education*, *25*(4), 585–605.

Frieson, B. L., & Scalise, M. (2021). Linguistic artistry and flexibility in dual-language bilingual classrooms: Young Black children's language and literacy practices. *Bilingual Research Journal*, *44*(2), 213–230. https://doi.org/10.1080/15235882.2021.1942323

Fu, D., Hadjioannou, X., & Zhou, X. (2019). *Translanguaging for emergent bilinguals. Inclusive teaching in the linguistically diverse classroom*. Teachers College Press.

García, O. (2009). *Bilingual education in the 21st century: A global perspective*. Wiley/Blackwell.

García, O., & Alvis, J. (2019). The decoloniality of language and translanguaging: Latinx knowledge-production. *Journal of Postcolonial Linguistics*, *1*, 26–40.

García, O., & Kleifgen, J. (2018). *Educating emergent bilinguals: Policies, programs and practices for English learners* (2nd ed.). Teachers College Press.

García, O., & Kleyn, T. (Eds.) (2016). *Translanguaging with multilingual students: Learning from classroom moments*. Routledge.

García, O., & Lin, A. M. Y. (2017). Translanguaging in bilingual education. In: O. García, A. Lin, & S. May (Eds), *Bilingual and multilingual Education. Encyclopedia of language and education* (3rd ed.). Springer. https://doi.org/10.1007/978-3-319-02258-1_9

García, O., & Wei, L. (2014). *Translanguaging: Language, bilingualism and education*. Palgrave Macmillan Pivot.

García, O., Flores, N., Seltzer, K., Li, W., Otheguy, R., & Rosa, J. (2021). Rejecting abyssal thinking in the language and education of racialized bilinguals: A manifesto. *Critical Inquiry in Language Studies*, *18*(3), 203–228. https://doi.org/10.1080/15427587.2021.1935957

García, O., Johnson, S. I., & Seltzer, K. (2017). *The translanguaging classroom: Leveraging student bilingualism for learning*. Caslon.

García-Mateus, S., & Palmer, D. (2017). Translanguaging pedagogies for positive identities in two-way dual language bilingual education. *Journal of Language, Identity, and Education*, *16*(4), 245–255. https://doi.org/10.1080/15348458.2017.1329016

Garza, E., & Arreguín-Anderson, M. (2018). Translanguaging: Developing scientific inquiry in a dual language classroom. *Bilingual Research Journal*, *41*(2), 101–116. https://doi.org/10.1080/15235882.2018.1451790

Garza, A., & Langman, J. (2014). Translanguaging in a Latin@ bilingual community: Negotiations and mediations in a dual-language classroom. *Association of Mexican American Educators Journal*, *8*(1), 37–49. https://amaejournal.utsa.edu/index.php/amae/article/view/151

Genesee, F. (1987). *Learning through two languages: Studies of immersion and bilingual education*. Newbury House Publishers.

Gort, M., & Sembiante, S. F. (2015). Navigating hybridized language learning spaces through translanguaging pedagogy: Dual language preschool teachers' languaging practices in support of emergent bilingual children's performance of academic discourse. *International Multilingual Research Journal*, *9*(1), 7–25. https://doi.org/10.1080/19313152.2014.981775

Guerrero, M. (2021). Gauging the adequacy of translanguaging allocation policy in two-way immersion programs in the U.S. *Journal of Latinos and Education*. https://doi.org/10.1080/15348431.2021.1971086

Hamman, L. (2018). Translanguaging and positioning in two-way dual language classrooms: A case for criticality. *Language and Education*, *32*(1), 21–42. https://doi.org/10.1080/09500782.2017.1384006

Heiman, D., Cervantes-Soon, C. G., & Hurie, A. H. (2022). 'Well good para quién?': Disrupting two-way bilingual education gentrification and reclaiming space through a critical translanguaging pedagogy. In M. T. Sánchez, & O. García (Eds.), *Transformative translanguaging espacios: Latinx students and their teachers rompiendo fronteras sin miedo* (pp. 47–70). Multilingual Matters.

Henderson, K. I., & Ingram, M. (2018). "'Mister, you're writing in Spanglish': Fostering spaces for meaning making and metalinguistic connections through teacher translanguaging shifts in the bilingual classroom. *Bilingual Research Journal*, *41*(3), 253–271. https://doi.org/10.1080/15235882.2018.1481894

Henderson, K. I., & Palmer, D. K. (2015). Teacher and student language practices and ideologies in a third-grade two-way dual language program implementation. *International Multilingual Research Journal*, *9*(2), 75–92. https://doi.org/10.1080/19313152.2015.1016827

Howard, E. R., Christina, D., Lindholm-Leary, K., & Sugarman, J. (2007). *Guiding principles for dual language education*. Center for Applied Linguistics.

Infante, P., & Licona, P. R. (2021). Translanguaging as pedagogy: Developing learner scientific discursive practices in a bilingual middle school science classroom. *International Journal of Bilingual Education and Bilingualism*, *24*(7), 913–926. https://doi.org/10.1080/13670050.2018.1526885

Wei, L. (2011). Moment analysis and translanguaging space: Discursive construction of identities by multilingual Chinese youth in Britain. *Journal of Pragmatics*, *43*(5), 1222–1235. https://doi.org/10.1016/j.pragma.2010.07.035

Wei, L. (2018). Translanguaging as a practical theory of language. *Applied Linguistics*, *39*(1), 9–30. https://doi.org/10.1093/applin/amx039

Licona, P. R., & Kelly, G. J. (2020). Translanguaging in a middle school science classroom: Constructing scientific arguments in English and Spanish. *Cultural Studies of Science Education*, *15*, 485–510.

Lindholm-Leary, K. J. (2001). *Dual language education*. Multilingual Matters.

Makoni, S., & Pennycook, A. (2007). *Disinventing and reconstituting language*. Multilingual Matters.

Martínez, R. A., & Mejía, A. F. (2020). Looking closely and listening carefully: A sociocultural approach to understanding the complexity of Latina/o/x students' everyday language. *Theory Into Practice*, *59*(1), 53–63. https://doi.org/10.1080/00405841.2019.1665414

Martínez, R. A., Hikida, M., & Durán, L. (2015). Unpacking ideologies of linguistic purism: How dual language teachers make sense of everyday translanguaging. *International Multilingual Research Journal*, *9*, 26–42. https://doi.org/10.1080/19313152.2014.977712

Mignolo, W. (2000). *Local histories/global designs: Essays on the coloniality of power, subaltern knowledges and border thinking*. Princeton University Press.

Mortimer, K. (2018). The hegemony of language separation: Discontents en programas de lenguaje dual en Paraguay and El Paso. *Association of Mexican American Educators Journal*, *12*(2), 121–152. https://doi.org/10.24974/amae.12.2.397

Muhammad, G. (2020). *Cultivating genius: An equity framework for culturally and historically responsive literacy*. Scholastic Teaching Resources.

Otheguy, R., García, O., & Reid, W. (2015). Clarifying translanguaging and deconstructing named languages: A perspective from linguistics. *Applied Linguistics Review*, *6*(3), 281–307. https://doi.org/10.1515/applirev-2015-0014

Otheguy, R., García, O., & Reid, W. (2019). A translanguaging view of the linguistic system of bilinguals. *Applied Linguistics Review*, *10*(4), 625–651. https://doi.org/10.1515/applirev-2018-0020

Palmer, D. K., Martínez, R. A., Mateus, S. G., & Henderson, K. H. (2014). Reframing the debate on language separation: Toward a vision for translanguaging pedagogies in the dual language classroom. *The Modern Language Journal*, *98*(3), 757–772. https://doi.org/10.1111/j.1540-4781.2014.12121.x

Pontier, R., & Gort, M. (2016). Coordinated translanguaging pedagogy as distributed cognition: A case study of two dual language bilingual education preschool coteachers' languaging practices during shared book readings. *International Multilingual Research Journal*, *10*(2), 89–106. https://doi.org/10.1080/19313152.2016.1150732

Poza, L. (2019). "Where the true power resides": Student translanguaging and supportive teacher dispositions. *Bilingual Research Journal*, *42*(4), 408–431. https://doi.org/10.1080/15235882.2019.1682717

Poza, L. E. (2018). The language of ciencia: Translanguaging and learning in a bilingual science classroom. *International Journal of Bilingual Education and Bilingualism*, *21*(1), 1–19. https://doi.org/10.1080/13670050.2015.1125849

Poza, L. E., & Stites, A. (2022). 'They are going to forget about us': Translanguaging and student agency in a gentrifying neighborhood. In M. T. Sánchez, & O. García (Eds.), *Transformative translanguaging espacios: Latinx students and their teachers rompiendo fronteras sin miedo* (pp. 71–91). Multilingual Matters.

Pratt, K. L., & Ernst-Slavit, G. (2019). Equity perspectives and restrictionist policies: Tensions in dual language bilingual education. *Bilingual Research Journal*, *42*(3), 356–374. https://doi.org/10.1080/15235882.2019.1647900

Quijano, A. (2000). Coloniality of power, ethnocentrism, and Latin America. *Nepantla*, *1*(3), 533–580.

Rickford, J. R. (1999). *African American vernacular English. Features, evaluation, educational implications*. Blackwell.

Rosa, J., & Flores, N. (2017). Unsettling race and language: Toward a raciolinguistic perspective. *Language in Society*, *46*(5), 621–647. https://doi.org/10.1017/S0047404517000562

Sánchez, M. T., & García, O. (2022). *Transformative translanguaging espacios. Latinx students and their teachers rompiendo fronteras sin miedo*. Multilingual Matters.

Sánchez, M. T., García, O., & Solorza, C. (2018). Reframing language allocation policy in dual language bilingual education. *Bilingual Research Journal*, *41*(1), 37–51. https://doi.org/10.1080/15235882.2017.1405098

Somerville, J., & Faltis, C. (2019). Dual languaging as strategy and translanguaging as tactic in two-way dual language programs. *Theory into Practice*, *58*(2), 164–175. https://doi.org/10.1080/00405841.2019.1569380

Tian, Z. (2021). Translanguaging design in a third grade Chinese language arts class. *Applied Linguistics Review*. https://doi.org/10.1515/applirev-2021-0024

Valdés, B. (1997). Dual-language immersion programs: A cautionary note concerning the education of language-minority students. *Harvard Educational Review*, *67*(3), 391–430. https://doi.org/10.17763/haer.67.3.n5q175qp86120948

Vogel, S., & García, O. (2017). Translanguaging. In *Oxford research encyclopedia of education*. Oxford University Press. https://doi.org/10.1093/acrefore/9780190264093.013.181

Wright, W. E., Boun, S., & García, O. (Eds.) (2015). *The handbook of bilingual and multilingual education*. Wiley/Blackwell.

Zheng, B. (2019). Translanguaging in a Chinese immersion classroom: An ecological examination of instructional discourses. *International Journal of Bilingual Education and Bilingualism*, *24*(9), 1324–1339. https://doi.org/10.1080/13670050.2018.1561642

26

ON CURRICULUM AND PEDAGOGY IN DUAL LANGUAGE BILINGUAL EDUCATION

Rebecca Blum-Martinez, Lily Wong Fillmore

Introduction

In this chapter, we consider the choice and use of curriculum materials in DLBE programs and discuss their influence on instructional practices and potential outcomes. Despite compelling evidence that the choice of instructional materials can have an outsized influence on student learning outcomes (Chingos & Whitehurst, 2012; Steiner, 2018), curriculum is seldom viewed as a central concern or issue in discussions of dual language and bilingual education. The most frequently cited goals of DLBE programs are high levels of bilingualism, biliteracy, sociocultural competence, and academic achievement both in English and the partner languages. The curriculum, what teachers teach and what students learn in school, is critical to these goals, and yet the issues and problems related to their choice, development and use are not given the attention they deserve in discussions of DLBE programs, in the professional preparation of teachers, or in fact, in the evaluation of program effectiveness (Polikoff, 2018).

Any discussion of curriculum for DLBE must reflect its goals but also recognize the contretemps that exists in the society over the school's curriculum. The lack of agreement is striking but perhaps not unexpected given the decentralized control over the school's curriculum. In the United States, curricular decisions are made at the state and local levels for public school programs rather than at the national level. Politics, religion, and cultural biases have from time to time and place to place made curricular decision-making a fraught process. The question of race relations in the United States is of critical importance for an understanding of how racism has shaped public policy and the role it plays in dividing the society. It is a topic that has raised deep

DOI: 10.4324/9781003269076-38

divisions in discussions of curriculum at school board meetings at the state and local level, much as have questions of teaching evolution, ethnic studies, or sex education at other times and places (Underwood, 2019). This decentralized system can result in rather substantial differences in what is covered in schools across the country, and in learning outcomes for students. Considerations of DLBE curricula must begin with that reality since it is as likely as any of a school's programs to be affected by the prevailing socio-political zeitgeist which exploits divisions that have long existed in our society—race, ethnicity, religion, language, culture, and economic circumstances.

In addition to local and state-based differences, federal legislation and efforts also shape DLBE curriculum. The accountability systems that accompanied the 2001 Elementary and Secondary Education re-authorization (also known as the No Child Left Behind Act or NCLB), for example, privileged and prioritized reading and mathematics at the cost of other subjects, including science and social studies (Dee et al., 2010; Pederson, 2007). Time and attention to subjects that were not assessed under NCLB were cut, and the cuts were most acute for students such as English learners who were deemed unlikely to perform well on the critical assessments. It is within these contested policy contexts that DLBE educators make curricular decisions. The sections below address linguistic and cultural considerations in curricular decision-making.

Linguistic Considerations

Two key issues emerge when considering materials, curriculum, and pedagogical approaches in two languages in DLBE programs: translation equivalencies and structural differences between languages.

Curricular Materials in DLBE: Availability and Equivalences

The questions DLBE program planners must consider are these: Are curricular materials—student texts and instructional guides such as scope and sequence of activities—available in the partner language for the subjects to be taught in that language? Do they meet grade level standards for the state? Is the content of those materials consistent with the subject matter expectations for the grade level? The solution some schools have resorted to when appropriate curricular materials in the partner language are unavailable has been to translate English materials into the partner language (Gonzales, personal communication). Translation, however, raises some serious questions and challenges. Translation implies equivalence between languages. But while two languages may express similar ideas, writers for each language use its unique lexical, grammatical, and cultural resources to express these ideas. There may be no equivalent of an English word or phrasal expression in the partner language. For example, "struggle" has no equivalent in Spanish. To translate this sentence, "Students may struggle with this concept," into Spanish, the translator would have to apprehend its meaning and know how it would be appropriately expressed in the context in which it is to appear: *Los estudiantes podrán tener dificultades con este concepto*. Pragmatically, idioms and expressions that are based on particular cultural understandings may also present difficulties, i.e., "ballpark figure" or *vergüenza ajena* (to be embarrassed for someone) (Madolo, 2021).

Translating children's literature requires specialization (Edwards & Ngwaru, 2011). Translating for children is more difficult "because of the need to take into consideration the fluent child reader or the adult reading to the child .... Translators therefore need to take account of features that affect the rhythmic totality of performance, including sentence length, punctuation, page openings and turnings" (Edward & Ngwaru, 2011, p. 594). Often, when texts are translated directly the result is "poor literary quality for all readers" because of "Awkward dialogue, misuse of words and overgeneralization of the [Spanish] language" (Naidoo & Lopez-Robertson, 2007).

Similarly, translations of informational texts are not a simple matter of translating key terms but require familiarity with the specific disciplinary register (Al-Samdi, 2022; Fang & Schleppegrell, 2010; Shanahan & Shanahan, 2008). Translations of scientific/informational texts may be difficult when texts focused on recent technological or scientific discoveries or practices may not yet have an equivalent terminology in the partner language (Al-Samdi, 2022). Ramirez et al. (2018) analyzed the academic language structures of authentic and translated Spanish academic texts using a Systemic Functional Linguistic analysis of two third-grade science texts focused on "matter." One was a translation of an English textbook (what the authors called the mirror text), the other was a textbook written in Spanish and used in Venezuela and Colombia. Although each text began with an introduction asking students to consider what "matter" is while seeking an interpersonal connection with the student, in the following pages, the focus of the texts diverged. In the case of the mirror text, following the English version, the interpersonal connections were further emphasized and students were asked to think about reading for a purpose. The Spanish text was more concerned with building disciplinary knowledge. Further analyses revealed stark differences in language complexity. While the mirror text included simple sentences, "*La materia puede tener diferentes colores* (Matter can be different colors)," the Spanish text, focused on further describing matter: *Las sustancias de origen natural provienen de la naturaleza, y a su vez, pueden ser: de origen animal, como la lana y la seda; de origen vegetal como la madera y el corcho; y de origen mineral, como las rocas* ("Substances of natural origin originate from nature, and in turn, these can be: of animal origin, such as wool and silk; of vegetal origin, such as wood and cork; and of mineral origin, such as rocks" p. 307). The sentence from the Spanish text follows the Spanish convention of lengthy sentence construction by utilizing *y a su vez* as the conjunction of two independent clauses. Rather than using the simple *Y*, *a su vez* (in turn) is added signaling greater formality. The second clause further describes the first by giving examples of types of matter, animal, vegetable, or mineral through prepositional phrases (*de origen animal*). This is an example of the ways Spanish is used to discuss science concepts different from English.

Finally, a common practice in dual language Spanish/English programs is to teach the cognates and false cognates in each language. However, while a particular word or phrase may have a cognate, it does not mean both words are used in the same way. Pérez Blanco (2018) found that while "certainly" and *ciertamente* are cognates, they were used differently in persuasive writing in newspaper articles. "Certainly" was used consistently and widely indicating the author's commitment to his/her opinion. Instead of *ciertamente, sin duda* or *desde luego* were used in ways similar to the use of "certainly."

In short, in order to convey ideas or intended messages of the original, the translator faces problems that go beyond language and deal with aesthetic and sociocultural communication of nuance and sense in conveying the feelings, the context, and the viewpoints expressed in the original, in other words a sense-to-sense translation (p. 119). … [A]ccurate translations require that a translator have a high level of proficiency in both languages, content knowledge, extensive cultural knowledge of both languages and expertise in translation (Lambert, 1986; Baker, 1997 and Toury 1995 cited in Daniel & Rentsch, 2009).

Language, Orthographies, and Literacy Instruction in DLBE

Among the central aims of DLBE programs is the development of high levels of proficiency in language and literacy in English and a partner language. DLBE educators working with literacy development in English and a partner language soon discover that each language presents teachers and students with unique challenges for teaching and learning. Many dual language programs base their curriculum on the standards adopted by their state. These standards, however, are designed for English monolingual schooling and on the knowledge and skills students need for successful participation in an English-speaking world. Research in various languages focused on literacy development demonstrate that the scope and sequence followed in English literacy does not map onto other languages (Beeman & Urow, 2013; Daniels & Rentsch, 2009; Escamilla et al., 2014; Ferreiro & Teberosky, 2003; Maamouri, 2018), and a linear scope and sequence may not be appropriate for literacy development in all languages. The section below considers the orthographies of the three most frequent partner languages: Spanish, Arabic, and Chinese and contrast these with English. At one end is Spanish with its highly regular sound and symbol correspondences, and its relatively simple syllable structure, at the other is Arabic with its shape-shifting symbols and its reliance on a written language variety which most readers must learn as a second language to understand the texts they read. A look at the challenges posed by the writing systems of these languages in addition to the familiar hurdles presented by English to beginning readers may help DLBE educators choose curricular materials and instructional strategies to facilitate dual language literacy instruction.

Approaches and materials for teaching beginning literacy depend on the language and writing system[1] in question. Alphabetic writing systems, such as the Latin-based script used for English and most other European countries,[2] use symbols to represent consonants and vowels in a language are said to be easier to learn to read than logographic systems (e.g., Chinese) in which symbols represent morphemes or words, or syllabaries in which symbols represent syllables. Learning to read in Chinese involves learning thousands of separate "characters," each representing a different morpheme or word; it is said that readers must know some 2000–3000 characters to read a newspaper. In contrast, 27 letters are used to represent the 22 phonemes (5 vowels and 17 consonants) that encode all the words in Mexican Spanish (Pineda et al., 2004). Languages differ in that regard: English uses 26 letters to represent its 44 phonemes (20 vowel and 24 consonant sounds, although the exact number depends on dialectal variation in English), so letters do not map simply onto sounds in the language, a situation that adds up to a degree of opacity and complexity in the orthographic system for the reader. How the sounds in a language combine to form syllables and morphemes in the language can add to the complexity in the language. Thus, the task of learning to read in a language varies, depending on the specific features of the orthographic system, the sound system of the language, and the way sounds are used in the language to represent meanings and words. The beginning reader must learn to associate symbols with sounds, and the more straightforward and regular the match between sound and symbol, the easier it is to learn to access the words they encode (Grainger & Ziegler, 2011).

Learning to read in some languages appears to be easier than in others, and research suggests that orthographic transparency and morphological-syllabic complexity are important factors (Borleffs et al., 2017). In a large transnational study of the acquisition of foundational literacy skills in 12 European orthographies, children from most of the countries included in the study were accurate and fluent in decoding before the end of their first year in school (Seymour et al., 2003). Writing systems differ in the challenge presented to readers, which is sometimes characterized in terms of "orthographic depth," which refers to "the reliability of print-to-speech correspondences" (Schmalz et al., 2015). Children found it easier to learn to read in languages with simple syllable structures and orthographies that the researchers describe as orthographically "shallow" or transparent (e.g., Finnish, Greek, and Spanish) than they did in languages with complex syllable structures and orthographies that were "deep" or opaque (e.g., Danish, French, and English). English was found to present the greatest difficulty to children, and they made the slowest progress in learning to decode and to read. Indeed, that finding should not surprise educators in the United States where, despite compulsory schooling for children between ages 5 and 14–17 (depending on the state), 52% of all adults (ages 16–65)[3] have below basic literacy skills (i.e., they are functionally illiterate)[4] or read at a basic level of literacy.[5]

English

English is described as having a deep orthography since the same spelling pattern can have multiple pronunciations as "ough" does in words such as "cough," "tough," "though," "through," "bough," "bought," or a given pronunciation [sō] can have multiple spellings as in "sew," "so," and "sow." Why, in fact, is the initial letter in "so" pronounced [s] as in "so" and not [ʃ] as in "sure" or "sugar"? English orthography is decodable but there are many irregularities stemming from sound changes that have occurred in the language historically. Pronunciations changed, but spellings did not. Historical contacts with languages such as Latin, Norse, German, and French left their traces on English. The complexities in English orthography stem in part from its not having a language academy as do French, Spanish, Dutch, and other European languages which conduct regular review and reforms of spelling to avoid inconsistencies between spelling and pronunciation that accrue as languages change over time (Fillmore & Snow, 2018). English has been notoriously conservative in its writing system and has held firmly to its spelling peculiarities despite notable efforts at spelling reform over the past several centuries by thinkers and writers such as Noah Webster, Benjamin Franklin, George Bernard Shaw, and Mark Twain.

Spanish

In sharp contrast to the orthographic challenges of English is the consistency and regularity of Spanish orthography, which mostly follows straightforward spelling and pronunciation rules. Vowels in Spanish are sometimes described as "pure" because their pronunciations remain the same, no matter what letters precede or follow them in the syllable. There are in addition to the 5 simple vowels, 13 diphthongs or vowel combinations, as in aula, *hay, reina, piano, ciudad, tierra, fue, fui, agua*, etc. However, because there are more letters than sounds in Spanish, some sounds are represented by more than one letter: e.g., The initial sounds in *llegar* and *yendo* are both pronounced [ˈɟ͡ʝ], although spelled by *ll* in the first, and *y* in the second. Other cases include *c* and *s* in *ciento* (hundred) and *siento* (I feel), and c and z as in *casar* (to marry) and *cazar* (to hunt) both of which are pronounced [ka-**sar**].[6] Another departure from full transparency is the case of *h*, which is always silent or not pronounced as we see in *hablar*, *hermano*, and *hijo*. In addition, *u* is sometimes silent in diphthongs with *i* or *e̲* as in words such as guisantes, and portugués when preceded by *g*. In contrast to English where reading instruction begins with a focus on the consonants, the Spanish reading instruction begins with the vowels. Once children learn the sounds that each vowel makes, vowels can be paired with consonants to make syllables and words. It is notable that the confusions presented by Spanish orthography tend to show up in writing rather than in reading. Children learn to decode readily enough once they learn the sound and symbol correspondences, but errors in spelling such as "ase" for *hace*, *sierto* for *cierto*, and *ayar* for *hallar* suggest that the problems posed by the orthography affect encoding more than they do decoding. Initial literacy begins with learning to write words and through writing, children discover phonological rules (Beeman & Urow, 2013; Daniels & Rentsch, 2009; Escamilla et al., 2014; Ferreiro & Teberosky, 2003).

Arabic

Compared to Spanish, Arabic lies at the other end of the orthographic scale of depth and challenges for children learning to read. Arabic script can be characterized as an *abjad* or consonant-based writing system, with vowel sounds indicated by diacritics—markings written above or below consonant symbols. Various of the 28 consonant symbols are rather similar in shape, and children are sometimes confused by the subtle marks that differentiate them (Maamouri, 2018). Further complicating matters, the consonant symbols change in shape, depending on whether they appear in initial, medial, or final position in words, and learners must learn multiple forms for each letter. In addition to the shape-shifting characteristics of its symbols, Arabic is written in a continuous line without punctuation, which can cause further difficulties for students who are not familiar with the variants of each letter. The complexities of this venerable and widely used script would make reading instruction a daunting enough task, but it is further complicated by the fact that Arabic is spoken in 27 countries and in each country, there are many spoken varieties. Bridging all these countries and language varieties is one written language, Modern Standard Arabic (MSA), which is for most speakers of Arabic a new language to be learned along with and through literacy. MSA can differ phonologically, lexically, and syntactically from the Arabic children already speak, which can present difficulties for children learning to decode and understand what they read depending on the distance between the variety of Arabic they speak and MSA (Assiri, personal communication). Speakers of Arabic dialects must learn both the language, MSA, and its orthography in order to decode and to understand what they are reading, which Maamouri describes as the challenge in initial Arabic literacy instruction:

> Because the Arabic reader needs to understand in order to read, the Arabic reading process seems to have completely reversed what is usually the norm in other languages, where people read in order to understand.
> *(op. cit. pp. 8–9)*

From this brief look at Arabic orthography and literacy instruction, it appears that the reality of Arabic dialects must be considered before a scope and sequence of literacy development can be devised for Arabic-English dual language programs. In program planning, educators would have to find ways to teach MSA as a new language to students who speak various dialects of Arabic, and to teach the intricacies of its orthographic system (Saiegh-Haddad & Ziv, 2008). They would have to find and obtain materials that support the acquisition of Arabic language and literacy, much of which come from Egypt or Lebanon (Assiri, personal communication). In addition, each Arabic-speaking country has produced its own textbooks and literacy materials, although some such materials may not be usable because they include sayings from the Prophet Mohammed and religious content (Assiri, personal communication) which are not allowed in U.S. public schools.

Chinese

Chinese, with its thousands of symbols to be learned, may appear to be off the charts in any discussion of orthographic complexity but, as unwieldy a writing system as it is, it was a practical solution given the considerable linguistic diversity that has long existed in China. Although the languages of China are collectively referred to as "Chinese dialects," that designation is not accurate, since "dialects" suggest mutually intelligible forms of a given language. For example, Mandarin, Shanghainese, and Cantonese are often called "Chinese dialects" although speakers of those languages cannot readily understand one another. What is collectively called Chinese includes as many as seven to ten different languages, each with numerous dialects (Ramsey, 1987). The orthography for Chinese is logographic or logosyllabic, a system by which words or syllables are represented by unique pictographic glyphs or "characters."[7] Being logographic rather than alphabetic, Chinese writing works across the various "dialects" because the symbols represent words and not sounds. For example, 语 denotes "language" and can be "read" as *waá, hua, yu, gho,* or *lengua*, for that matter. Thus, the writing system serves as a bridge across languages and dialects. Word order differences sometimes require minor adjustments, but readers come to regard them as aspects of written language. The writing system most closely follows Mandarin, the language spoken in the northern region of China, and Mandarin was established early in the 20th century as the lingua franca (*Guoyu*, *Hanyu*, or *Putonghua*) of China. A noteworthy aspect of Chinese phonology is tone—the use of pitch variation as a phonological feature. For example, the syllable "ma," spoken with a level tone *mā*, is the word for *mother.* The level tone is just one of four tones (level, rising, turn tone, and falling) in Mandarin.[8] Thus, the same syllable, "ma," can, depending on tone, express four different words: *mā (mother)*, *mǎ (horse)*, *má* ("hemp"), *mà (scold)*. Chinese reading and writing comprise a daunting system to learn because of the sheer number of symbols in use, and in their complexity of form.[9] Each character is formed by "strokes" or marks. The simplest is the left-to-right horizontal stroke representing *yi*, "one." The average number of strokes is estimated to be from 9 to 12 strokes. There has been since the mid-20th century, the promulgation of simplified characters to facilitate literacy development in China (Yang & Wang, 2019). Traditional characters have been simplified and streamlined by requiring fewer strokes in their formation, which are meant to make them easier to write and to remember.[10] However, they are hardly fewer in overall number: there are tens of thousands of characters in use, but it is estimated that only the 2000 most frequently used words are simplified. That such a system is even learnable by normal human children has been attributed to the enduring cultural values and beliefs that undergird teaching practices, and the social norms that guide children's learning behaviors (Yang et al., 2006).

Children learn to read and write at the same time, at the rate of about 6 or 7 per day early on, starting with relatively simple characters initially (Hanley et al., 1999; Tan et al., 2005). Each character is learned by rote, which entails learning how to form the character in a prescribed manner on graph paper and keeping each character within the boundaries of a frame. The strokes that make up a character are ordered, top to bottom, left to right, horizontal strokes first then vertical ones, right to left diagonals are written before left-to-right ones, and in the case of enclosed characters, there are rules for the order in which the frames are written and closed.[11] Stroke order is engrained in learners early on, and readers can tell when they have not been observed—they appear almost like misspellings to the astute reader.[12] This might seem like a mind-boggling task: rote learning to read and write separate characters for each word in the language, and doing so in a strict order and precise manner, but children manage the task handily enough for the system to work. In learning to write Chinese characters, children are encouraged to practice by tracing them with a finger on the palm of their hand, thereby developing kinetic memory of how characters look and are formed.

Materials produced for the teaching overseas children to read and write in Chinese were commissioned by the Overseas Chinese Affairs Office of the State Council of the People's Republic of China in 1997.[13] Course materials include textbooks and teacher guides and are designed to teach basic literacy with the help of pinyin. The Asia Society also provides support for DLBE educators (Asia Society, 2006, 2012, 2016).

To conclude, linguistic (orthography, phonology) factors need to be considered as DLBE educators make curricular and instructional decisions for their programs. Since literacy instruction takes place in English and the partner language, the orthographic challenges presented by each language must be identified and evaluated in planning and the staging of instruction.

Cultural Considerations

The Guiding Principles for Dual Language Programs (Howard et al., 2018) highlight two goals for DLBE regarding curriculum and culture: "The curriculum promotes appreciation of multiculturalism and linguistic diversity," and "The curriculum is culturally responsive and representative of the cultural and linguistic backgrounds of students" (p. 42). These goals acknowledge the inextricable connection between language and culture and advocate for the consideration of culture, multiculturalism, and culturally responsiveness in the curriculum. Any discussion of culturally relevant materials or a culturally responsive curriculum must begin with a consideration of what is meant by culture and which aspects of culture are to be incorporated into the curriculum. Culture has many meanings, but the one that is most germane to this discussion is culture as a dynamic process by which members, who are connected by language, geographic location, social class, religion, or other shared bonds, both receive and construct a common set of values, traditions, worldviews, and social and political relationships (Nieto & Bode, 2018, p. 171). Rogoff (2003, p. 11) has shown that culture is not just what people do, it also includes relational patterns, orientations towards interdependence and autonomy, expectations during developmental transitions, and ways of thinking with the specific tools, technologies, and cultural institutions.

An important step in identifying materials that reflect the cultural values and aesthetics of the partner language is confronting the business-as-usual American school ethos where language and cultural differences are sometimes neither understood or valued. Boykin (1994), as cited by Gay (2000, p. 9), points out that culture, as it is embodied in the practices and mindsets of schools and many educators, is regarded as universal and completely natural:

> "there has always been a profound and inescapable cultural fabric of the schooling process in America" (p. 244). This "cultural fabric," primarily of European and middle-class origins, is so deeply ingrained

> in the structures, ethos, programs, and etiquette of schools that it is considered simply the "normal" and "right" thing to do.
>
> *(Boykin, 1994)*

Too often these "normal" structures and cultural practices are then applied to the partner language as efforts to achieve parity between English and the partner language, whether or not they reflect the cultural values of the partner language. An example of this can be seen in Spanish-English dual language programs holding "spelling bees" in Spanish, following a long-standing American school tradition. Spelling is a special challenge in English stemming from its often, non-transparent writing system with historical changes, loan words, and irregular spellings (Okrent, 2021). As has been discussed above, spelling in Spanish, by comparison, is less a challenge given its orthographic transparency. Spelling-bees in Spanish might appear to be an effort at achieving parity between the languages, but in fact, they demonstrate the power of the "cultural fabric" being imposed on another language and culture.

Instead, schools may ask, what are some of the "public display" practices that are valued in children's home cultures? What are the customs in schools in Spanish-speaking countries? Poetry recitals in which students dramatically recite Spanish language poetry either individually or chorally have been a tradition in many schools in Latin America (Engelbrecht, personal communication; Garcia, 2022; Secretaría de Educación Pública, 2016). This practice requires students to commit poetry to memory and recite poems publicly, often chorally, thereby celebrating the beauty of the Spanish language and highlighting the importance of this genre within various Spanish-speaking cultures. Moreover, some of the greatest literary figures in the Spanish-speaking world have written poetry for children, and these poems are included in children's language arts texts.[14] At a dual language high school in Albuquerque, a poetry recital for the community resulted in an overwhelming attendance by parents and family members.[15] In order to make this community presentation, teachers had to know Spanish poetry so that they could guide students in reading, studying, and memorizing selected Spanish language poetry.

Another key resource for culturally relevant curriculum and materials is the use of authentic texts. These texts can provide students with models of language appropriate to the rhythms, expressions, structures, and traditions of that culture. Finding models for that language is not only critical to children's language growth in both oral and written forms, they also introduce themes and worldviews of the speakers of that language (Escamilla et al., 2014; Secretaría de educación de México). A story taken from the recommended reading list for first grade by the Puerto Rico Department of Education provides an example of the benefits of an authentic text. *El Flamboyán Amarillo* written by Puerto Rican award winning author, Georgina Lázaro (2004) eulogizes this beautiful tree, iconic to Puerto Rico and found in many tropical areas and countries. In the story, a boy walks with his mother in the countryside and sees a yellow *flamboyán* tree.[16] He collects seeds from this tree, takes them home, and plants them in a pot. The seeds sprout, and one of them eventually grows into a tiny tree. The boy plants the seedling tree in the ground, waters, and cares for it, and over time, boy and tree grow tall and older. When the tree finally matures and blooms, the boy (and the reader) is surprised that the tree's flowers are not the golden yellow of the parent tree, but are a flamboyant red, thus inviting the reader to learn about the genetic traits of that tree. Through rhyme, rhythm and metaphor, this narrative poem invites the readers to reflect on the many cultural themes it touches on: a mother's role as first teacher, the miracle of nature, and our responsibility for caring for the gifts nature bestows on us. Moreover, the language in the text is wonderfully evocative of the beauty of nature, the beauty of the island, and the appreciation of that beauty by the boy and his mother.

The language in this text can serve as a model for teaching children about figurative expressions and rhyming patterns. It can also lead to many lively and stimulating conversations about the flora and fauna of the tropics where many children's families may be from. Teachers can tap into the funds of knowledge (Gonzalez et al., 2005) of the children and their families about silviculture or other agricultural knowledge. In the poem, the mother teaches the boy about planting and caring for seeds. Children can discuss what their mothers or extended family members have taught them and be reminded that learning can happen everywhere, not just at school, thus elevating the expertise of family and community members.

Equally important is to utilize culturally responsive materials in the English language arts program. For example, Morren López et al. (2015) discuss the increased participation of students who read *Sylvia and Aki*, a story about a Mexican American family who come to live on a farm formerly owned by a Japanese family, who have been sent to an internment camp. Pratt et al. (2021) analyzed the themes presented in children's literature that had won the Pura Belpré prize, given to "Latino Latina authors and illustrators whose works best portrays, affirms and celebrates the Latino cultural experience in an outstanding work of literature for children and youth" by the American Library Association.[17] The researchers found that the two most common themes were interdependence and resourcefulness. They argue that the inclusion of children's literature that positions students as capable and affirms their experiences can change the power dynamics in classrooms (Feinauer & Howard, 2014; Freire, 2020).

Unfortunately, teachers do not always have the time or knowledge to address the scarcity of readily available authentic partner materials and, as a result, resort to the translated version of an English text. For example, rather than selecting an authentic text in Spanish, a publisher may translate Oliver Twist, or Charlotte's Web into Spanish (Gomez-Najarro, 2020). These texts in translation cannot serve as authentic models of language, nor can they reflect the richness and diversity of the cultural worlds of the students' backgrounds and heritage. What can Oliver Twist teach students about the history and complexities of challenges individuals have struggled with in Latin America, or those faced by Latinx communities in the United States? What can Charlotte's Web teach students about interdependence, or resilience as it is experienced in Latinx families and communities? The argument here is not about the value of this literature, rather about the choice to use translations without consideration of the goal of sociocultural competence.

A culturally responsive curriculum must include all subjects, science, social studies, math, and fine arts. Much attention has been paid to including culturally responsive material in English Language Arts. Less attention is given to other subjects. For example, most history or social studies textbooks are oriented to the study of European immigration, but seldom include the immigration of Asians or Latinos. When the latter groups are referenced, they are likely characterized as problematic. It is critical to include the many contributions communities of color have made, as these more closely reflect the majority of students in DLBE programs. In U.S. history textbooks, pioneers may be highlighted in the western movement while the cost of this movement to Indigenous people is barely mentioned. Commonly ignored is the long history of Hispanic/Latinx communities in the Southwest. The result of such biases in textbooks materials is that many DLBE students are unlikely to find themselves reflected in those texts. Moreover, the message conveyed is that these regions, communities, and people are unimportant.

Summary: In order for students to develop sociocultural competence, it is critical that culture be considered and integrated when developing and identifying materials for use in DLBE. Authentic texts in the partner language provide important models for robust language development. Additionally, authentic texts represent the values, processes, and concepts that are central to a specific culture, assisting students in developing their cultural knowledge. Cultural considerations should be applied in all subject areas.

In closing, the success of any instructional program or approach depends ultimately on what happens in the classrooms where teachers and students come together for teaching and learning. That extended relationship is the pedagogical context in which skills, content, and attitudes towards knowledge and learning are, or are not, developed in students. At its very essence, pedagogy is about the relationship between teachers and students, and how what is said and done influences the learning of content, skills, and habits of mind as set out in a curriculum. This relationship is critical. How teachers regard the languages, cultures, and worldviews children bring from their homes to school—whether they respect them and try to organize their programs of teaching and learning in ways that promote full intellectual, social, and cultural inclusion, or not, is critical to the outcome—for DLBE as an educational approach and for students, alike.

Research Recommendations

The examination of the differences between English and three of the most commonly spoken languages by students highlights the need for greater research in these orthographic differences and in the learning trajectories of literacy in partner languages. The complexities of non-equivalence and translations especially in school-based texts demonstrate the need for scholars to investigate these issues as well. Research on the role of materials and curricula in dual language programs is a critical need. Presently, publishers have an oversized role in determining what gets taught in these programs. Specialists in diverse cultures, children's literature, and school-based subject matter, and who are expert in the partner languages are needed to examine the conventions and expectations in the oral and written discourses of the partner languages. As well, an investigation of the efficacy of different instructional strategies aimed at assisting students in discovery of how language works in the complex texts would assist dual language educators and those who develop academic materials.

Notes

1 There are four other alphabetic writing systems used in Europe: Cyrillic, Greek, Armenian, and Georgian.
2 See Omniglot, an online encyclopedia of writing systems and languages for a handy overview of types of orthographies used across the world https://omniglot.com/writing/types.htm
3 Adult Literacy in the United States. Fast Facts. U.S. Department of Education, National Center for Educational Statistics https://nces.ed.gov/fastfacts/display.asp?id=69
4 Overall, 19% of adults score at or below the most basic level, "1," on the 4 point scale.
5 Overall, 33% of adults score at level "2" on a 4 point scale.
6 It should be noted that this discussion of pronunciation is based on Mexican Spanish. There are many varieties of Spanish spoken in the Americas and they are as different from one another as they are from Iberian Spanish, i.e., Spanish in Spain.
7 Asia Society https://asiasociety.org/china-learning-initiatives/chinese-writing
8 Cantonese has six tones and Taishanese, the Yue language spoken in the Taishan region of Guangdong Province, has nine tones.
9 Estimates of how many Chinese characters are in current use (i.e., excluding archaic words) vary rather greatly, but most online sources suggest around 80,000. It is said that it takes knowledge of around 20,000 to read a newspaper.
10 Character simplification tends to make characters more abstract and therefore more difficult to analyze, according to one expert educator, Christinia Cheung. Personal communication, February 9, 2022.
11 https://en.wikipedia.org/wiki/Written_Chinese
12 https://en.wikipedia.org/wiki/Stroke_order
13 www.chinaqw.com
14 In the first-grade Spanish language arts text from the Mexican Secretaria de Educación, the following authors are included: Octavio Paz, Julio Cortazar, Nicolás

Guillén, Rosario Castellanos, Federico García Lorca, and Nezahualcóyotl. https://www.conaliteg.sep.gob.mx
15 May, 2017, Atrisco Heritage High School, Albuquerque Public Schools.
16 For an oral reading of this text: https://www.youtube.com/watch?v=M0X-CBuJ_P0
17 https://www.ala.org/alsc/awardsgrants/bookmedia/belpre

References

Al-Samdi, H. M. (2022). Challenges in translating scientific texts: Problems and reasons. *Journal of Language Teaching and Research*, *13*(3), 550–560. https://doi.org/10.17507/jltr.1303.11

Asia Society. (2006). *Creating a Chinese language program in your school*. Author. https://asiasociety.org/files/Creating%20a%20Chinese%20language%20Program%20in%20Your%20School.pdf

Asia Society. (2012). *Chinese language learning in the early grades: A handbook of resources and best practices for Mandarin immersion*. Author. https://asiasociety.org/files/chinese-earlylanguage.pdf

Asia Society. (2016). *Developing initial literacy in Chinese*. Author. https://asiasociety.org/files/uploads/522files/2016-celin-brief-developing-initial-literacy-in-chinese.pdf

Beeman, K., & Urow, C. (2103). *Teaching for biliteracy. Strengthening bridges between languages*. Caslon Publishing.

Borleffs, E., Maassen, B. A., Lyytinen, H., & Zwarts, F. (2017). Measuring orthographic transparency and morphological-syllabic complexity in alphabetic orthographies: A narrative review. *Reading and Writing*, *30*(8), 1617–1638.

Boykin, A. W. (1994). The sociocultural context of schooling for African American children. A proactive deep structural analysis. In E. Hollins (Ed.), *Formulating a knowledge base for teaching culturally diverse learners* (pp. 233–245). Association for Supervision and Curriculum Development.

Chingos, M. M., & Whitehurst, G. J. (2012). *Choosing blindly: Instructional materials, teacher effectiveness, and the common core*. Brookings.

Daniels, M., & Rentsch, V. (2009). Collaboration and discovery: A pilot study of leveling criteria for books written in Spanish for K-3 grade. In *Literacy issues during changing times. A call to action. College reading association yearbook* (Vol. 30). College Reading Association, University of Texas at Arlington.

Dee, T. S., Jacob, B. A., Hoxby, C. M., & Ladd, H. F. (2010). The Impact of No Child Left Behind on Students, Teachers, and Schools [with Comments and Discussion]. Brookings Papers on Economic Activity, 149–207. http://www.jstor.org/stable/41012846

Edwards, V., & Ngwaru, J. M. (2011). African language publishing for children in South Africa: Challenges for translators. *International Journal of Bilingual Education and Bilingualism*, *14*(5), 589–602. https://doi.org/10.1080/13670050.2011.558618

Escamilla, K., Hopewell, S., Butvilofsky, S., Sparrow, W., Soltero-González, L., Ruiz-Figueroa, O., & Escamilla, M. (2014). *Biliteracy from the start. Literacy squared in action*. Caslon Publishing.

Fang, Z., & Schleppegrell, M. J. (2010). Disciplinary literacies across content areas: Supporting secondary reading through functional language analysis. *Journal of Adolescent and Adult Literacy*, *53*(7). https://doi.org/10.1598/JAAL.53.7.6

Feinauer, E, & Howard, E. (2014). Cross-cultural competence and identity development in two-way immersion programs. *Journal of Immersion and Content-Based Language Education*, 2(2). https://doi.org/10.1075/jicb.2.2.07fei

Ferreiro, E., & Teberosky, A. (2003). *Los sistemas de escritura en el desarrollo del niño*. Siglo Veintiuno Editores.

Fillmore, L. W., & Snow, C. E. (2018). What teachers need to know about language. In *What teachers need to know about language* (2nd ed., pp. 8–51). Multilingual Matters.

Freire, J. A. (2020). Promoting sociopolitical consciousness and bicultural goals of dual language education: The transformational dual language education framework. *Journal of Language, Identity, & Education*, *19*(1), 56–71. https://doi.org/10.1080/15348458.2019.1672174

Garcia, O. (2022). *Be cha-cha-chá: Stepping back to step forward*. National Association for Bilingual Education.

Gay, G. (2000). *Culturally responsive teaching: Theory, research and practice*. Teachers College Press.

Gomez-Najarro, J. (2020). Children's intersecting identities matter: Beyond rabbits and princesses in the common core book exemplars. *Children's Literature in Education*, 51, 392–410. https://doi.org/10.1007/s10583-019-09390-9

Gonzalez, N., Moll, L. C., & Amanti, C. (2005). *Funds of knowledge: Theorizing practices in households, communities and classrooms*. Lawrence Erlbaum Associates.

Grainger, J., & Ziegler, J. C. (2011). A dual-route approach to orthographic processing. *Frontiers in Psychology*, *2011*(2), 1–13. https://doi.org/10.3389/fpsyg.2011.00054

Hanley, J. R., Tzeng, O., & Huang, H.-S. (1999). Learning to read Chinese. In M. Harris, & G. Hatano (Eds.), *Learning to read and write: A cross-linguistic perspective* (pp. 173–195). Cambridge University Press.

Howard, E. R., Lindholm-Leary, K. J., Rogers, D., Olague, N., Medina, J., Kennedy, B., Sugarman, J., & Christian, D. (2018). *Guiding principles for dual language education* (3rd ed.). Center for Applied Linguistics.

Lázaro, G. (2004). *El flamboyán amarillo*. Lectorum Publications Inc. https://okvirtuallibrary.overdrive.com/media/1332448

Maamouri, M. (2018). Arabic literacy. Lemma 11. *Encyclopedia of Arabic Language and Linguistics*. https://referenceworks.brillonline.com/search?s.f.s2_parent=s.f.book.encyclopedia-of-arabic-language-and-linguistics&s.au=%22Mohamed+Maamouri%22&s.q=maamouri

Madolo, Y. (2021). Strategies utilised in translating children's stories from English into isiXhosa. *South African Journal of African Languages*, *41*(1), 76–82. https://doi.org/10.1080/02572117.2021.1902144

Morren López, M., Ynostroza, A., Fránquiz, M. E., & Cárdenas Curiel, L. (2015). Cultural artifacts: Using *Sylvia* and *Aki* for opening up authoring spaces. *Bilingual Research Journal*, *38*(2), 190–206. https://doi.org/10.1080/15235882.2015.1068243

Naidoo, J. C., & Lopez-Robertson, J. (2007). Descubriendo el sabor: Spanish bilingual book publishing and cultural authenticity. *Multicultural Review*, *16*(4), 24–38.

Nieto, S., & Bode, P. (2018). *Affirming diversity: The sociopolitical context of multicultural education* (7th ed.). Pearson.

Okrent, A. (2021). *Highly irregular: Why tough, through, and dough don't rhyme—And other oddities of the English language*. Oxford Scholarship Online. https://doi.org/10.1093/oso/9780197539408.001.0001

Pederson, P.D., (2007). What is measured is treasured: The impact of the no child left behind act on nonassessed subjects. *The Clearing House: A Journal of Educational Strategies, Issues and Ideas*, *80*(6), 287–291. https://doi.org/10.3200/TCHS.80.6.287-291

Pérez Blanco, M. (2018). The Discourse functions of certainly and its Spanish counterparts in journalistic opinion discourse. *Revista Española de Lingüística Aplicada/ Spanish Journal of Applied Linguistics*, *31*(2), 520–549. https://doi.org/10.1075/resla.16026.per

Pineda, L. A., Pineda, L. V., Cuétara, J., Castellanos, H., & López, I. (2004, November). DIMEx100: A new phonetic and speech corpus for Mexican Spanish. In *Ibero-American conference on artificial intelligence* (pp. 974–983). Springer.

Polikoff, M. (2018). *The challenges of curriculum materials as a reform lever* (Evidence Speaks Report, Vol. 2, #58. June 28, 2018).

Pratt, K. L., Puzio, K., & Lee, Y.-H. (2021). "¡Olé!" Locating capital and community cultural wealth within multicultural children's literature. *Journal of Latinos and Education*, *20*(1), 48–61. https://doi.org/10.1080/15348431.2018.1540350

Ramirez, A., Sembiante, S. F., & de Oliveira, L. C. (2018). Translated science textbooks in dual language programs: A comparative English- Spanish functional linguistic analysis. *Bilingual Research Journal*, *41*(3), 298–311. https://doi.org/10.1080/15235882.2018.1494061

Ramsey, S. R. (1987). *The languages of China*. Princeton University Press.

Rogoff, B. (2003). *The cultural nature of human development*. Oxford University Press.

Saiegh-Haddad, E., & Ziv, M. (2008). Early literacy in Arabic: An intervention study among Israeli Palestinian kindergartners. *Applied Psycholinguistics*. https://doi.org/10.1017/S0142716408080193

Schmalz, X., Marinus, E., Coltheart, M., & Castles, A. (2015). Getting to the bottom of orthographic depth. *Psychonomic Bulletin & Review*, *22*(6), 1614–1629.

Secretaría de Educación de México. Comisión nacional de libros de texto gratuitos. https://www.conaliteg.sep.gob.mx

Secretaría de Educación de México. https://www.gob.mx/cms/uploads/docs/Propuesta-Curricular-baja.pdf

Secretaría de Educación Pública. (2016). *Propuesta Curricular Para La Educación Obligatoria*. https://www.gob.mx/cms/uploads/docs/Propuesta-Curricular-baja.pdf

Seymour, P. H., Aro, M., & Erskine, J. M., Collaboration with COST Action A8 Network (2003). Foundation literacy acquisition in European orthographies. *British Journal of Psychology*, *94*(2), 143–174.

Shanahan, T., & Shanahan, C. (2008). Teaching disciplinary literacy to adolescents: Rethinking content area literacy. *Harvard Educational Review*, *78*(1), 40–59.

Steiner, D. (2018). Materials matter. *The Learning Professional*, *39*(6), 24.

Tan, L. H., Spinks, J. A., Eden, G. F., Perfetti, C. A., & Siok, W. T. (2005). Reading depends on writing, in Chinese. *Proceedings of the National Academy of Sciences of the United States of America*, *102*(24), 8781–8785. https://doi.org/10.1073/pnas.0503523102

Underwood, J. (2019). Under the law: The legal balancing act over public school curriculum. *Phi Delta Kappan*, *100*(6), 74–75.

Yang, R. & Wang, W. (2018). Categorical perception of Chinese characters by simplified and traditional Chinese readers. *Reading and Writing*, *31*. https:doi.org/10.1007/s11145-018-9832-y

Yang, B., Zheng, W., & Li, M. (2006). *Chinese view of learning and implications for developing human resources*. https://files.eric.ed.gov/fulltext/ED492822.pdf

27
CURRICULUM ISSUES IN DLBE

Ester J. de Jong, Zach Coulter

Introduction

The *Guiding Principles for Dual Language Education* (GPDLE) unequivocally assert that "having curriculum and materials in both languages is an absolute necessity so that students have the opportunity to develop a full range of proficiency, both linguistic and cultural, in both languages" (Howard et al., 2018, p. 34). Despite the centrality of curriculum, classroom-based dual language bilingual education (DLBE) research has focused more on pedagogical approaches and discursive moves that shape the learning experiences of students in DLBE than how teachers plan and coordinate the development of specific content and language competencies. In this chapter, we use the Curriculum Strand in the *GPDLE* as a starting point for discussion of curricular issues that have emerged in the context of DLBE. After a brief overview of the Curriculum Strands, the chapter considers the role of vertical and horizontal curricular integration and the emphasis on standards-based instruction. The chapter concludes with directions for research.

Curriculum in DLBE: Principles and Key Points

The Curriculum Strand in the GPDLE document (Howard et al., 2018) identifies three key elements (principles) related to curriculum development and implementation in dual language bilingual education (DLBE) programs: (a) the program has a process for developing and revising a high-quality curriculum, (b) the curriculum is standards-based and promotes attainment of the three core goals of dual language education, and (c) the curriculum effectively integrates technology to deepen and enhance

DOI: 10.4324/9781003269076-39

learning. For each principle, the GPDLE document identifies key points that should guide quality program implementation. These key points are supported by general educational research as well as research in bilingual education settings (Howard et al., 2018). Given space constraints, the focus of this chapter will be on the first two principles (e.g., Mercuri & Musanti, 2018). Whereas the first principle focuses on coordination and alignment, the second curriculum principle emphasizes standards-based instruction that reflects linguistically and culturally relevant content and materials in both languages.

Related to the first Curriculum Strand principle (high-quality curriculum), the five key points stress the need for (a) a curriculum development and implementation plan; (b) building on a general and a bilingual learner research base; (c) adaptability of the curriculum to student, program, and community needs; (d) coordination with support services; and (e) coordination within and across grade levels. The first three key points acknowledge that curriculum and curriculum materials are often designed for a generalized, often monolingual, audience and this requires teachers to make changes and adaptations in response to their specific, local, contexts. The last two key points underscore the integrated nature of learning and the importance of providing student with a comprehensive, coherent, and interdisciplinary learning experience.

Six key points undergird the second principle that refers to the importance that DLBE programs implement a standards-based curriculum aligned with program goals. Effective DLBE programs use a curriculum approach that (a) meets or exceeds district, state, or national content standards; (b) reflects standards-based scope and sequences for language and literacy development in both languages of instruction; (c) promotes equal status of both languages; (d) promotes appreciation of multiculturalism and linguistic diversity; (e) is culturally responsive and representative of the cultural and linguistic backgrounds of all students; and (f) articulates measurable learning outcomes. Collectively, these key points stress DLBE curriculum alignment with state and national standards while simultaneously centering culturally and linguistically responsive practices in ways that explicitly support language and student status equalization (de Jong & Howard, 2009).

Curricular Integration

The first principle considers the planned integration of various DLBE curriculum components at the program and classroom level. Vertical curriculum planning involves the coordination of learning from grade level to grade level, including managing transitions from elementary to secondary school levels. Horizontal integration refers to grade-level curriculum integration, that is how DLBE teachers, including special program teachers, explicitly plan for connections between instruction in both languages to ensure a coherent learning experience for DLBE students.

Vertical Program Coordination

Vertical planning includes program-level decisions about language allocation across the grade levels in support of program goals. The GPDLE calls for an explicit language allocation planning document that outlines how the partner languages are to be used, at different grade levels, for which subjects, and how much time in each subject. Kennedy (2019, p. 12) notes, "an effective DLI language allocation plan provides a clear structure for balancing instruction in the two program languages to ensure that grade-level curriculum is addressed with equal rigor through each program language." Vertical curriculum articulation is needed to ensure that proficiency goals are reached. As a general guideline, DLBE programs provide a minimum of 50% of instruction in the minoritized partner language. Some programs start with most of the instruction in the minoritized language (80%–90%) and gradually increase instruction to English to reach 50%–50% in the upper elementary/early middle school grades (see also Chapter 5 by Wright and Choi for different DLBE program models and language distribution). Since most DLBE programs begin in the elementary grades, articulation into secondary school is important to sustain bilingual development. Rubio (2018) presents Utah's Language Road Map as an example of one state's K-16 articulated language continuum.

Although the need for vertical articulation has been identified, there is little research on such planning efforts within the field of DLBE (for a recent review of foreign or second language program articulation research, see Lord & Isabelli-García, 2014; for an example of middle to high school world language articulation efforts, see Greenman & Hansen, 2019). Merritt (2011) documents a case where students in a two-way immersion elementary education program transitioned to a world language program in a secondary school. Merritt found that the teachers' views and instructional practices differed significantly between the two-way immersion (TWI) and the world language teachers. For example, although the TWI teachers valued bilingual expertise of minoritized language speakers, the world language teachers positioned these students negatively and from a deficit perspective. As a result, the programmatic transition caused significant disruption of students' learning experiences that eventually undermined DLBE program goals. Similarly, a study included two-way immersion high school students who had attended a two-way immersion program since Kindergarten but were placed in a traditional world language Advanced Placement class. In reflecting on their experiences, the students described differences between their language abilities and experiences and those of their foreign language peers in terms of grammatical knowledge versus the ability to actually use the language for communicative purposes. One of the students observed that, while the non-TWBE (two-way bilingual education) students might have a better grasp of grammar, their ability to comprehend text was quite different. He notes, "they read a passage and it takes us an hour and a half to figure out what's going on" (de Jong & Bearse, 2011, p. 116). This quote also illustrates the challenge for teachers when both world language and DLBE students enroll in the same class.

Horizontal Program Coordination

Since what students learn in one language is accessible to them in the other language (Cummins, 1979; MacSwan et al., 2017), an important principle of DLBE has always been to not repeat what is taught in one language but to extend and build on what was learned in one language in the partner language. To effectively coordinate instruction across languages at each grade level and provide continuity of language and literacy development, DLBE teachers (including specialized support teachers, such as special education or reading intervention teachers) need to engage in horizontal planning efforts. There is little empirical research on such explicit curricular and programmatic planning between teachers. There are, however, several examples of planning practices in support of cross-linguistic transfer, metalinguistic awareness, as well as content-related connections. This section briefly describes such efforts: the Bridge, counterbalanced instruction, the preview/view/review (P/V/R) strategy, and curriculum transformation through translanguaging. It should be kept in mind that these activities take place within a range of instructional activities in DLBE programs.

The Bridge

The first example is the Bridge, a planning tool introduced by Beeman and Urow (2013). They describe the Bridge as

> the instructional moment when teachers bring the two languages together to encourage students to explore the similarities and differences in the phonology (sound system), morphology (word formation), syntax and grammar, and pragmatics (language use) between two languages, that is, to undertake contrastive analysis and transfer what they have learned from one language to the other. (p. 4)

The following example illustrates how the Bridge works. A DLBE classroom has finished learning about the parts of a solar system during their Spanish medium science class time. The class also completed various reading and writing activities in Spanish. During the Bridge, the teacher and students created a bilingual anchor chart of solar system vocabulary words. On the left-hand side of the chart, the vocabulary words were in Spanish and students were invited to provide the English equivalent of those words. Through this activity, "students had an active role in making meaning and generating language. They took the concepts they learned in Spanish and, building on the knowledge they have in both languages, bridged them to English" (Beeman & Urow, 2013, p. 137). In short, the Bridge is a structured block of time for students to make active connections across both languages.

Counterbalanced Approach

Roy Lyster and colleagues developed an approach to systematically integrate language and content learning within and across languages of instruction (Lyster, 2007; Lyster et al., 2009; Tedick & Lyster, 2020). An example of how the counterbalanced approach can support connections between instruction is through the use of children's books in both languages. Tedick and Lyster (2020) worked with a pair of teachers who utilized Tomi Ungerer's *Crictor*. The teachers (one French and one English) made explicit connections between English and French vocabulary. The two teachers focused on suffixes in both languages. For example, the English teacher focused on the suffix -ic while the French teacher drew attention to the suffix -ique which encouraged students to discover the connections between the two suffixes. In this way, the teachers helped students draw explicit comparisons between the two languages and supported their metalinguistic awareness.

Preview/View/Review

A third tool for planning and coordinating instruction between the two languages of instruction is through bilingually constructed thematic units (Collier & Thomas, 2009). One curriculum strategy to support cross-linguistic and conceptual connections is the P/V/R approach (Lessow-Hurley, 2009; Mercuri, 2015). P/V/R sequence is a three-step structure which consists of previewing or introducing key concepts in the students' native language, teaching the content in the target language, and reviewing key learning in the native language. In Mercuri (2013), Mrs. Lee makes connections (preview) to previous lessons and the students' background knowledge in Spanish. Then, she teaches (view) in the form of minilectures, whole group discussions, or hands-on activities that are explained and engaged with in English. Finally, the lesson closes with a review of the concepts taught and an extension activity in the form of homework or a preview activity the next day in the students' home language. P/V/R can promote language transfer, make content comprehensible, and build and/or activate background knowledge (Mercuri & Musanti, 2018). Effective implementation of P/V/R avoids direct repetition of content and invites a continuous cycle of deepening and expanding content learning.

Translanguaging as Curriculum

When considered from an instructional planning lens, translanguaging "describes the process whereby teachers build bridges between [home] language practices and the language practices desired in formal school settings" (Flores & Schissel, 2014, p. 462). Sánchez et al. (2018) describe the necessity to provide space for bilingual language users to bring their languages together for critical metalinguistic analysis while affording an opportunity for creative language use by having access to their full linguistic repertoire which they refer to as "translanguaging transformation" (Sánchez et al., 2018; see also Kleyn & García, 2019). Woodley (2016) documents how one teacher incorporates translanguaging into his classroom. At the beginning of the lesson, the students are provided with the essential question in English and a Google-translated version in their native language. The students then modify or correct the sentence in the L1 which engages them in metalinguistic analysis. Students then compare the content material (slavery) to examples of oppressive structures from their home countries. Through strategic planning for translanguaging, teachers encourage students to draw on their entire linguistic repertoire in a systematic way.

Standards-Based Instruction

The second principle emphasizes that DLBE programs implement a standards-based curriculum. Since DLBE is positioned as a mainstream ("standard") program, the reliance on local, state, and national professional standards is not surprising. However, an uncritical adoption of existing national and/or state standards is problematic. This section discusses how monolingual assumptions and practices that often guide such standards interfere with DLBE program goals.

Standardization and Sameness

When state frameworks are not inclusive of DLBE students' cultural backgrounds, it can be challenging for DLBE teachers. Two-way immersion middle school teachers who taught both mainstream and two-way immersion social studies and language arts classes felt the pressure to adhere to the mainstream curriculum at the expense of being able to include culturally relevant content and pedagogies (de Jong & Bearse, 2014). Moreover, standards based curricula (i.e., Common Core State Standards) expect bilingual students to perform linguistically as monolingual anglophone students do (García & Flores, 2013). When blindly following existing standards, districts may therefore rely on a scope and sequence of literacy development in the partner language that merely mirrors the teaching of English literacy. Such a "translation" may fail to acknowledge curricular aspects that are unique to partner language and literacy development. For example, Goldenberg et al. (2014) examined the differences between literacy instruction in the United States and Mexico. Specifically, the authors investigated if there was a connection between phonemic awareness and Spanish reading skills. In the United States, students received explicit instruction targeting phonemic awareness, but the students in Mexico did not. The study found that by the end of second grade, the Mexican students still scored lowest on phonemic awareness but had caught or surpassed their American counterparts in Spanish reading skills. This finding led Goldenberg et al. (2014) to conclude, "these results call into question whether phonemic awareness instruction actually helps promote, much less is necessary for acquiring, Spanish reading skills" (p. 624) and that phonemic awareness instruction might be superfluous for students learning to read Spanish in certain contexts. Escamilla and Coady (2001) observe the need to recognize differences in writing approaches in Spanish and English. Similarly, a monolingual approach may lead to a scope and sequence that reflects literacy development for each language individually rather than one designed to support biliteracy development (Howard et al., 2018; Mercuri & Musanti, 2018). In DLBE programs, standards based curricula need to take students' bilingualism into account (García & Flores, 2014; Flores & Schissel, 2014). Escamilla et al. (2014) note that a bilingually oriented curriculum needs to reflect students' bilingual trajectories and growth holistically.

Standards and Sociocultural Competence

Another area where a mere "same standards" approach fails is related to DLBE program's sociocultural goals. Although content standards may reflect disciplinary literacy and knowledge, they rarely address the development of intercultural competencies, that is "identity development, cross-cultural competence, and multicultural appreciation" (Howard et al., 2018, p. 3). As such, it is crucial for educators to consider and plan for the development of sociocultural competence. How educators address teaching for sociocultural competence can include the content/material chosen or the pedagogies and instructional practices used to deliver the content or both. An example of incorporating content or material for sociocultural competence can be the use of bilingual children's books, bilingual poems, or selecting inquiry topics situated to students' lived experiences (e.g., using immigration for argument writing; Fránquiz et al., 2019; La Serna, 2020). Pedagogically, educators can incorporate the creation of student made bilingual texts or create brave spaces – spaces that require students to participate in risk-taking as part of learning (Navarro Martell, 2021). When the definition of the intercultural competence goal also includes critical consciousness (Palmer et al., 2019), transformative curricular practices can be embraced. Heiman and Yanes (2018) provide examples of the impact critical consciousness has on curriculum. Through the inclusion of controversial topics and figures, the teacher in their study engaged students in critical classroom dialogue by highlighting the experiences of marginalized figures, who were not highlighted by the general education curriculum.

Standards and Representation

DLBE educators must also critically examine access to and quality of materials in both languages. The lack of quality partner language materials from which teachers can choose is problematic when trying to equalize language status within the program (Freire & Valdez, 2017). Fewer materials are typically available in the partner language than in English which forces partner language teacher to develop their own materials (de Jong & Bearse, 2014). Self-made materials are often translations from materials published in English as creating one's own materials is labor-intensive and time-consuming (Amanti, 2019). Amrein and Peña's (2000) study demonstrates how inequitable the distribution of resources is between English and the partner language. They found that Spanish materials accounted for less than 20% of total shelving area. In practical terms, this means that students in their study were five times more likely to find and select a book in English than a book in Spanish. Inequity also exists in the quality of books that are available to students. As Freeman et al. (2018) conclude, "if the books in English have colorful illustrations and clear charts, but the books in Spanish have few illustrations and small print that is difficult to read, then there is no equity" (p. 65). Moreover, having the same materials (i.e., an English text translated into Spanish) does not necessarily count as having "quality" materials in both languages.

The implementation of a standards-based curriculum must be accompanied by efforts that ensure that all students, families, and communities are represented. Most mainstream materials leave out the histories, voices, and experiences of marginalized communities. However, as Howard et al. (2018) note, "most of these standards have not been designed with English learners in mind and therefore curriculum adjustments may need to be made to reflect contextualized funds of knowledge of students and their families" (p. 32). Without such adaptations, minoritized languages and cultures become seen as less than and/or devalued (Reyes & Vallone, 2007). Palmer (2018) observes:

> more than merely providing the mainstream curriculum in two (or more) languages, a DLBE program must center its curriculum upon the voices and knowledges of the members of its own community, particularly the often-marginalized members of that community whose experiences will not necessarily be reflected in the mainstream curriculum. (p. 3)

DLBE teachers thus must spend time selecting materials which match both state and local educational requirements and materials that are reflective of their students' linguistic and cultural backgrounds. Fránquiz et al. (2019) documented how two exemplar DLBE teachers incorporated different materials in their classrooms which addressed state and local requirements while representing their students' cultural backgrounds. Both teachers in the study specifically selected bilingual children's literature books which matched state content standards and were culturally relevant to the students in the classroom. With these materials, the teachers incorporated different pedagogical practices to value students' cultural backgrounds, including read alouds, interactive discussions, and bilingual identity texts (Fránquiz et al., 2019).

Conclusion

Despite the centrality of curriculum and the importance of the alignment and integration of language and literacy development and conceptual development in DLBE programs, empirical research in this area is still limited. More research is needed on programmatic articulation as students move from grade to grade and transitions between school levels. Another area of research is on how DLBE teachers coordinate instruction at their grade level and, in the case of a two-teacher model, how they collaborate to support linguistic and conceptual connections for their students. Finally, more research is needed on how DLBE administrators and teachers interpret, appropriate, and enact practices that align with yet also question and critique content standards developed for non-DLBE contexts. This issue, in turn, poses a challenge for teacher and leadership preparation (see also Chapter 20 in this handbook).

References

Amanti, C. (2019). The (invisible) work of dual language bilingual education teachers. *Bilingual Research Journal*, *42*(4), 455–470.

Amrein, A., & Peña, R. A. (2000). Asymmetry in dual language practice: Assessing imbalance in a program promoting equality. *Education Policy Analysis Archives*, *8*, 08.

Beeman, K., & Urow, C. (2013). *Teaching for biliteracy*. CASLON.
Collier, V. P., & Thomas, W. P. (2009). *Educating English learners for a transformed world*. Dual Language Education of New Mexico–Fuente Press.
Cummins, J. (1979). Linguistic interdependence and the educational development of bilingual children. *Review of Educational Research*, *49*(2), 222–251.
de Jong, E. J., & Bearse, C. (2011). The same outcomes for all? High school students reflect on their two-way immersion program experiences. In D. Christian, D. Tedick, & T. Fortune (Eds.), *Immersion education: Pathways to bilingualism and beyond* (pp. 104–122). Multilingual Matters.
de Jong, E. J., & Bearse, C. I. (2014). Dual language programs as a strand within a secondary school: Dilemmas of school organization and the TWI mission. *International Journal of Bilingual Education and Bilingualism*, *17*(1), 15–31.
Escamilla, K., & Coady, M. (2001). Assessing the writing of Spanish speaking students: Issues and suggestions. In J. Tinajero & S. Hurley (Eds.), *Handbook for literacy assessment for bilingual learners* (pp. 43–63). Allyn & Bacon.
Escamilla, K., Hopewell, S., Butvilosfky, S., Sparrow, W., Soltero-González, L., Ruiz-Figeroa, O., & Escamilla, M. (2014). *Biliteracy from the start. Literacy squared in action*. Caslon Publishing.
Flores, N., & Schissel, J. L. (2014). Dynamic bilingualism as the norm: Envisioning a heteroglossic approach to standards-based reform. *TESOL Quarterly*, *48*(3), 454–479.
Fránquiz, M. E., Leija, M. G., & Salinas, C. S. (2019). Challenging damaging ideologies: Are dual language education practices addressing learners' linguistic rights? *Theory into Practice*, *58*(2), 134–144.
Freeman, Y. S., Freeman, D. E., & Mercuri, S. (2018). *Dual language essentials for teachers and administrators*. Heinemann.
Freire, J. A., & Valdez, V. E. (2017). Dual language teachers' stated barriers to implementation of culturally relevant pedagogy. *Bilingual Research Journal*, *40*(1), 55–69.
García, O., & Flores, N. (2013). Multilingualism and common core state standards in the United States. In S. May (Ed.), *The multilingual turn: Implications for SLA, TESOL, and bilingual education* (pp. 157–176). Routledge.
Goldenberg, C., Tolar, T. D., Reese, L., Francis, D. J., Ray Bazán, A., & Mejía-Arauz, R. (2014). How important is teaching phonemic awareness to children learning to read in Spanish? *American Educational Research Journal*, *51*(3), 604–633.
Greenman, L. J., & Hansen, M. (2019). *Crossing the border: Connecting middle and high School language programs*. Paper presented at the Central States Conference on the Teaching of Foreign Languages, Columbus, Ohio.
Heiman, D., & Yanes, M. (2018). Centering the fourth pillar in times of TWBE gentrification: "Spanish, love, content, not in that order". *International Multilingual Research Journal*, *12*(3), 173–187.
Howard, E. R., Lindholm-Leary, K., Rogers, D., Medina, N., Kennedy, B., Sugarman, J., & Christian, D. (2018). *Guiding principles for dual language education* (3rd ed.). Center for Applied Linguistics.
Jong, E. d., & Howard, E. (2009). Integration in two-way immersion education: Equalising linguistic benefits for all students. *International Journal of Bilingual Education and Bilingualism*, *12*(1), 81–99. https://doi.org/10.1080/13670050802149531
Kennedy, B. (2019). *Effective practices in bilingual education program model implementation: A review of the literature*. Texas Education Agency, Division of English Learner Support, Austin, Texas.

Kleyn, T., & García, O. (2019). Translanguaging as an act of transformation. In L. de Oliveira (Ed.), *The handbook of TESOL in K–12* (pp. 69–82). Wiley Blackwell. https://doi.org/10.1002/9781119421702.ch6

La Serna, J. J. (2020). Culturally relevant pedagogy in two-way immersion classrooms. *Bilingual Research Journal*, *43*(4), 400–416.

Lessow-Hurley, J. (2009). *The foundations of dual language instruction* (6th ed.). Pearson.

Lord, G., & Isabelli-García, C. (2014). Program articulation and management. In M. Lacorte (Ed.), *The Routledge handbook of Hispanic applied linguistics* (pp. 166–183). Routledge.

Lyster, R. (2007). *Learning and teaching languages through content: A counterbalanced approach* (Vol. 18). John Benjamins Publishing.

Lyster, R., Collins, L., & Ballinger, S. (2009). Linking languages through a bilingual read-aloud project. *Language Awareness*, *18*(3–4), 366–383.

MacSwan, J., Thompson, M. S., Rolstad, K., McAlister, K., & Lobo, G. (2017). Three theories of the effects of language education programs: An empirical evaluation of bilingual and English-only policies. *Annual Review of Applied Linguistics*, *37*, 218–240. https://doi.org/10.1017/S0267190517000137

Mercuri, S. (2013). Re-conceptualizing science instruction for English language learners. *MEXTESOL Journal*, *37*(2). https://www.mextesol.net/journal/index.php?page=journal&id_article=471

Mercuri, S. (2015). Teachers' understanding of practice: Planning and implementing preview/view/review in the dual language classroom. In Y. S. Freeman & D. E. Freeman (Eds.), *Research on preparing inservice teachers to work effectively with emergent bilinguals* (pp. 81–106). Emerald Group Publishing Limited.

Mercuri, S., & Musanti, S. I. (2018). Interdisciplinary biliteracy: Leveraging biliteracy development for all bilingual learners. *Language Magazine 34–37*. (October [4th quarter/Autumn])

Merritt, S. (2011). *Conflicting ideologies about using and learning Spanish across the school years: From two-way immersion to world language pedagogy* [Unpublished dissertation, University of California].

Navarro Martell, M. A. (2021). Ciencias bilingües: How dual language teachers cultivate equity in dual language classrooms. *International Journal of Bilingual Education and Bilingualism*, 1–17. https://doi.org/10.1080/13670050.2020.1870925

Palmer, D. (2018). *Equity and dual language immersion: Curriculum*. Paper presented at the Confronting the Equity Issues in Dual Language Immersion Programs, University of California. https://civilrightsproject.ucla.edu/research/k-12-education/language-minority-students/equity-and-dual-language-immersion-curriculum/Palmer-Curriculum-EquityInDL-2018-11-for-post.pdf

Palmer, D. K., Cervantes-Soon, C., Dorner, L., & Heiman, D. (2019). Bilingualism, biliteracy, biculturalism, and critical consciousness for all: Proposing a fourth fundamental goal for two-way dual language education. *Theory Into Practice*, *58*(2), 121–133.

Reyes, S. A., & Vallone, T. L. (2007). Toward an expanded understanding of two-way bilingual immersion education: Constructing identity through a critical, additive bilingual/bicultural pedagogy. *Multicultural Perspectives*, *9*(3), 3–11.

Rubio, F. (2018). Language education in elementary schools: Meeting the needs of the nation. *Foreign Language Annals*, *51*(1), 90–103.

Sánchez, M. T., García, O., & Solorza, C. (2018). Reframing language allocation policy in dual language bilingual education. *Bilingual Research Journal*, *41*(1), 37–51.

Tedick, D. J., & Lyster, R. (2020). *Scaffolding language development in immersion and dual language classrooms*. Routledge.

Woodley, H. H. with Brown, A. (2016). Balancing windows and mirrors: Translanguaging in a multilingual classroom. In O. García & T. Kleyn (Eds.), *Making meaning of translanguaging: Learning from classroom moments*. Routledge.

28

TOWARD A BILITERATE PEDAGOGY

Susan Hopewell, Jody Slavick, Kathy Escamilla

The United States is a multi-racial multilingual country with a history of supporting and sustaining institutions and policies that uphold monolingualism and white supremacy. Among these are both public and private schools. Dual language bilingual education (DLBE) programs, which espouse and promote values and policies that elevate bilingualism, biliteracy, and cross-cultural competence, have always had to defend their existence and their efficacy. In the United States, the sociopolitical and historical debates regarding DLBE have centered largely around the appropriateness and the role of languages other than English during academic instruction. Research, however, has demonstrated consistently that DLBE results in academic achievement that is as efficacious, if not superior, to English-only instruction and that it simultaneously results in the loftier outcomes of bilingualism and biculturalism (Collier & Thomas, 2004, 2017; Genesee & Lindholm-Leary, 2021; Steele et al., 2017). Bilingually educated students have greater cognitive flexibility, executive functioning, and working memory. Additionally, they are better able to multitask (Bialystok, 2001; Bialystok et al., 2012). Those who maintain their bilingualism into high school are more likely to go to four-year colleges and less likely to drop out (Rumbaut, 2014; Santibañez & Zárate, 2014). Finally, and importantly, sound DLBE programs help children develop and express pride in their communities and their cultural heritages while also maintaining and sustaining meaningful communication channels with their families (Wong Fillmore, 2000). In other words, DLBE works, is efficacious, and contributes to the overall well-being of its participants. Its efficacy and benefits, however, should not be confused with the misguided notion that it is a one-size-fits-all solution to multilingual education. As August and Hakuta cautioned in their seminal edited review of research

DOI: 10.4324/9781003269076-40

(1997), "The key issue is not finding a program that works for all children and all localities, but rather finding a set of program components that works for the children in the community of interest, given that community's goals, demographics, and resources" (p. 138). To this end, they espoused a series of five lessons that were meant to guide the field in moving forward: (1) the field needs higher quality program evaluations, (2) local-level evaluations must be more meaningful and informative, (3) theory-based interventions need to be created and evaluated, (4) focusing on program components is more important than politically motivated labels, and (5) a developmental model is required to predict the effects of program components on children in different learning environments. Though more than two decades have passed since they offered these observations, we would argue that the field would do well to revisit them. In our discussion of the need to develop a biliterate pedagogy that is responsive to the ontology of being bilingual, we will intentionally surface and discuss two: (1) the need for the creation and evaluation of theory-based interventions and (2) the importance of examining how the individual program components contribute differentially to overall efficacy.

We begin this chapter from the assumption that the research evidence is conclusive that the use of languages other than English is beneficial, particularly for simultaneous bilingual learners as well as for those learners who come from homes where a language other than English is prevalent as is the case for newly arrived immigrants. We argue that it is imperative that we abandon the stale debate about whether languages other than English should be used in the education of students in the U.S. school system and pivot to the more fruitful and urgent need to develop and research pedagogies of bilingualism that recognize the unique ontology of being bilingual. Refining practices and attending to the quality of instruction have the potential to escalate the linguistic and learning outcomes of bilingual learners participating in DLBE. Well-designed and implemented programs that are responsive to the communities' needs should encourage the use of curricular materials and pedagogical strategies that support and sustain cross-cultural competencies and boost self-esteem and cultural pride. A goal is that these pedagogies establish a counter-hegemonic, decolonizing, culturally affirming, and sustaining alternative to the prevailing monolithic, English-only, one-size-fits-all approaches to educating bilingual learners.

The Ontology of Bilingualism

What does it mean to be bilingual? What is different about the bilingual brain and how might that affect cognition and learning? What are the implications for how bilingual people experience the world and how should educators take this information into consideration in educational contexts?

Bilingualism involves the intersection of two or more languages within the mind and life experiences of an individual. It shapes and mediates the collective experiences of those with shared repertoires. In other words, it is both an individual and a social experience. Bilingualism develops in a language ecology that ranges from individuals who are raised in fully bilingual environments from birth and are actively engaged in bilingual living throughout life to those who acquire bilingualism later in life and have limited opportunities to process and activate all their linguistic knowledge. An intricate web of variables interacts in the process of becoming bilingual resulting in a complex phenomenon that is difficult to define, describe, or measure. These variables include linguistic, cognitive, social, psychological, cultural, and political factors. Further complicating the bilingual experience is that language proficiency can fluctuate along receptive/productive abilities and oral/written capacities (Solano-Flores, 2010). One attempt to capture the intersecting and variable nature of this has been the Continua of Biliteracy (Hornberger, 2008). The Continua of Biliteracy explicates the interrelated and intersecting aspects of the totality of the fluctuating factors affecting language proficiency and emphasizes that the more a learning context attends to all the factors, the more fully an individual's bilingualism and biliteracy will develop. The Continua lays the foundation for, and champions, holistic learning opportunities that offer expansive, inclusive, and evidence-based opportunities to establish mature bilingualism.

Importantly, evidence demonstrates that the entirety of a bilingual person's linguistic repertoire is activated when they experience language, whether orally or in print (Kroll et al., 2015; Marian & Spivey, 2003). In fact, we know from brain activation research that language processing in the bilingual mind differs from that of the monolingual mind (Pierce et al., 2015). When bilingual individuals engage in phonological working memory (PWM) tasks designed to examine their executive functioning in terms of their ability to store and manipulate incoming speech sounds, their brains are not only activated in the same language-focused areas as the brains of their monolingual peers, but they also show activity in brain areas related to cognitive control, indicating that exposure to bilingualism, no matter when it occurs in life, activates unique neural pathways that influence language processing. Stated differently, bilingual individuals enlist non-language regions of the brain when processing linguistic input (Abutalebi & Green, 2008). Some researchers have interpreted this more complete engagement of the brain as contributing to a bilingual advantage (Bialystok et al., 2012).

Not only does cognition affect language and language processing, but language affects cognition. Steven Levinson (2003), a noted psycholinguist, tells us, "... language and thought closely parallel one another, and thus linguistic diversity is reflected in cognitive diversity" (p. 2). If a language, for example, requires a person to use only cardinal directions (i.e. north, south, east, west) to describe location, that person must develop the cognitive ability to stay oriented in space, even in novel locations, in order to communicate (Boroditsky, 2011). Further, we know that despite the fact that the human eye can technically perceive more than 10 million colors, individual languages have organized and coded the color spectrum differently using a limited number of terms. These terms delimit and influence how the brain understands and interprets color signals. Research has demonstrated that if you teach a person new words for colors, they learn to perceive colors differently (Winawer et al., 2007). Distinctions in perception, gender, agency, spatial orientation, numeracy, and the organization of the passage of time are only a few of the cognitive distinctions researchers have associated with individual languages. In fact, researchers have documented that teaching people new ways to talk results in changing the way they think (Boroditsky, 2011). From an educational perspective, this raises interesting possibilities for the inclusion of diverse perspectives or worldviews into the meaning-making and problem-solving inquiries that saturate the learning environment.

Theorizing Pedagogies of Bilingualism

A paradox within bilingual education is that it maintains an explicit goal of bilingualism, biliteracy, and biculturalism, yet the approach to teaching and learning is largely derived from research and pedagogies designed for monolingual speakers of a single language. Often the language policies within bilingual education settings keep languages separated and siloed. This approach is referred to as parallel monolingualism (Fitts, 2006; Heller, 2001), code-segregation (Guerra, 2012), or two solitudes (Cummins, 2005). In parallel monolingual models, parts of the day, or perhaps designated subject matters, are assigned to a single language. During the demarcated time period or subject matter, both the teacher and the students remain in the designated language. All materials used to teach and learn and all oral communications are in the authorized language. The primary justification for this model is the need for a dedicated safe time to practice a language and to counteract the hegemony of the language of greater power or prestige (Ballinger et al., 2017; Cenoz & Gorter, 2017). We know, however, that there is zero empirical evidence to demonstrate that this is the most effective way to educate bilingual learners (Cummins, 2014) and that strict language separation does not mirror or capitalize upon the lived experiences of bilingual individuals (Flores & García, 2017; Gort & Sembiante, 2015).

DLBE models that adhere to parallel monolingual frameworks are well intentioned and are adhering to a theory that minoritized languages must be preserved and protected; however, they lack attention to the ontology of being bilingual. Certainly, the worry about protecting and preserving minoritized languages is a valid and important mission within DLBE; however, as others have forwarded (see, e.g., Cook & Li, 2016; Cummins, 2007), we argue that what is missing in the theoretical frameworks and empirical research on DLBE is focused attention to the quality of instruction in two languages that attends to the specific ontology of being bilingual.

Stated differently, learning in and through two languages differs fundamentally from learning in and through only one (Jarvis & Pavlenko, 2008). Biliterate pedagogies go beyond teaching two languages. Rather, they intentionally connect language environments and provide explicit opportunities for students to make cross-language and cross-cultural connections (Escamilla et al., 2014). Biliterate pedagogies must include content teaching that is anti-racist and that addresses issues of language status and xenophobia (Alim et al., 2016). This is not to say that there are not areas of overlap with pedagogies enacted in monolingual environments, but the field needs to consider that pedagogies and methodologies designed primarily for mainstream, white, middle-class, monolingual English-speaking children may be inadequate for the vast majority of bilingual students. For example, in many DLBE classrooms, we have witnessed kindergarten students being taught alphabetic principles by focusing on letter names or by practicing onset – rime activities during Spanish literacy. While there is an empirical base for using this approach in English, it is completely inappropriate in Spanish where a focus on letter sounds, syllabication, and the morphology of word endings is more appropriate. Further, we see too little attention to how the languages operate vis-à-vis one another. We need pedagogies and materials that are developed from the onset using a bilingual lens not simply translated from one language to another and applied with the assumption that the outcomes will be the same.

When we begin from the understanding that the outcome of interest is bilingualism, biliteracy, and biculturalism, we are better positioned to select materials and pedagogies that reject parallel monolingualism, decenter whiteness, and challenge English-centric ways of knowing and teaching. This is true regardless of program type, student profile, or program languages. The charge to the field, therefore, is to determine which elements overlap from one language to the other and will, therefore, transfer; and which differ and will, therefore, require explicit and focused attention.

We often use the metaphor of a tandem bicycle to elucidate this. Imagine starting out learning to ride a bike, but with the caveat that you must do so while coordinating with another person. The process itself (mounting, balancing, coordinating, and communicating) would be substantially different than learning to ride solo. Certainly, much about riding a bike solo (pedaling, steering, etc.) overlaps with what one needs to understand about riding tandem, but the effect of two riders changes the experience in meaningful ways. Similarly, we propose that the effect of two languages changes the language acquisition and academic learning process in meaningful ways.

Those changes are what we need to attend to as we think about conceptualizing bilingual pedagogies.

Theorizing bilingual pedagogies requires that we consider the sociolinguistic environment in which learning occurs. Bilingual pedagogies will vary according to the program model (one-way versus two-way), the number of bilingual students, the status of the languages involved, the needs and desires of the community, and the sociopolitical context (Cenoz & Gorter, 2015). In other words, any theory providing the justification for a particular approach to bilingual education must take into consideration not only how instruction will be coordinated, but the precise demographics and profiles of the community of learners (Genesee, 2018). It will also recognize that despite individual contexts, a student's languages, cultures, and life experiences form an indivisible whole. If we understand that what is known and understood in one language contributes to what is known and understood in the other, then we must begin from a core premise that languages are reciprocally reinforcing in a bidirectional and supportive manner and must constitute the foundation for all learning opportunities (Dworin, 2003; Pavlenko & Jarvis, 2002).

Designing a bilingual pedagogy that considers the ontology of being bilingual means accepting that it is not unusual, or unexpected, to witness bilinguals accessing multiple linguistic codes to interpret, understand, and communicate their experiences. The result is that normal bilingual behaviors that were once viewed as deficits or evidence of confusion or language interference, such as code-switching or language mixing, must be reinterpreted as assets that enhance communication and understanding. If language shapes how we construe reality, it stands to reason that a bilingual bicultural reality would differ in significant ways from a monolingual monocultural way of understanding and interpreting the world. Knowing this, it becomes imperative that we dismantle paradigms and pedagogies that insist on fractionalizing languages and concomitantly the related ways of knowing and understanding, so that we can explore more holistic and inclusive approaches to teaching and assessing bilingual students.

In a nation in which whiteness and English are often privileged in school spaces, we have the opportunity through the design and enactment of bilingual pedagogies to center students' bilingual and multicultural experiences and to recognize that these learning environments are essential to their growth and development as human beings (Bartolomé, 1994; Fránquiz & Salazar, 2004; Salazar, 2013). Bilingual pedagogies create the conditions in which students' languages are not constrained, but rather sustained and cultivated in ways that ensure that students' humanity and dignity, as reflected in their use of their full repertoire of languages, are recognized and supported through affirming pedagogical practices. We maintain that biliteracy is a greater and more complex form of literacy (Hopewell & Escamilla, 2014).

This complexity and the corresponding differential learning and teaching experience requires an evidence-based approach.

Quality Instruction: What Do We Know?

Determining the component elements of a quality bilingual educational program begins with analyzing the institutional conditions to support evidence-based instructional components. As early as 2011, Calderón and her colleagues reviewed the available data with regard to the education of bilingual learners and came to the conclusion, "… what matters most in educating English Learners is the quality of instruction" (p. 107). In their review of research on programs and practices proven effective with bilingual learners, their primary recommendation was for comprehensive school reform. Within school reform, they outlined the necessary conditions for reform, including effective and committed leadership; constant collection and use of data to monitor implementation and outcomes; ongoing and focused hands-on professional development for all staff; explicit and structured language and literacy instruction with an emphasis on vocabulary instruction, oral language development, reading instruction, writing instruction, and strategic use of primary language; and cooperative small-group heterogeneous interactions, parent and family support teams, and one-on-one tutoring and interventions for those who need it. In short, the authors argue that while quality instruction occurs inside of the classroom, the conditions that support quality instruction occur in the larger school and district environments which include language policies, assessment practices, and professional development opportunities. Further, it is important to institutionalize support systems for families and students to ensure their overall well-being and achievement. With these in place, one can turn to the classroom-based instructional components of a well-designed DLBE pedagogy.

Two comprehensive summaries of research related to the scholarship about the education of bilingual learners were published in 2006: (1) the National Literacy Panel for Language-Minority Children (NLP) report and (2) the Center for Research on Education, Diversity, and Excellent (CREDE) report. The NLP looked at research from around the world and considered first- or second-language outcomes in the area of literacy (August & Shanahan, 2006). The CREDE report considered only research conducted in the United States with outcomes in English but included content areas beyond literacy (Genesee et al., 2006). Due to these differences, each made unique contributions to our understanding of the field but, interestingly, reached similar conclusions with regard to effective instruction (Goldenberg, 2008). While they both touted the benefits of first-language instruction and the fact that there are overlaps with monolingual instructional strategies, such as direct vocabulary instruction and cooperative learning models, they emphasized that modifications and accommodations are beneficial, as are increased opportunities for oral language development. The corpus of studies included, however, mostly considered English language outcomes in English-medium schools. In other words, while these syntheses moved the field forward in terms of English language acquisition, they did little to define the coordination of instruction across languages.

Following these syntheses, the Institute of Educational Science's (IES') What Works Clearinghouse (WWC) was created. The practice guides produced through this endeavor advocate a series of research-supported recommendations for teaching bilingual learners (Baker et al., 2014; Gersten et al., 2007). The guides are meant to build upon each other and to be used in conjunction with one another. Again, however, the authors delimited the scope of the research to that which reported outcomes related to bilingual learners' learning in and through English. Despite this limitation, in the most recent iteration (Baker et al., 2014), the authors contend that,

> ... regardless of the particular approach a school district takes toward language of instruction – whether it is dual immersion, structured immersion, or transitional bilingual education – the recommendations articulated in this guide are relevant for English language academic instruction. (p. 3)

Proficiency in English is, indeed, necessary in the attainment of bilingualism and biliteracy; however, the ability to capitalize upon the use and knowledge of other languages has not been adequately explored. If we are to better understand the component parts of efficacious holistic bilingual pedagogies, it is imperative that researchers be embedded in bilingual classrooms collecting and analyzing data about specific approaches and strategies that capitalize on bilingualism. Further, we need to develop assessment practices and interpretation procedures that center bilingualism and biliteracy recognizing that a biliterate trajectory may vary in important and significant ways from monolingual trajectories in either language. It is only through deeply theoretical and classroom-based research that we will be able to identify, highlight, measure, and understand the art and science of bilingual instruction. In particular, we need studies that examine how to coordinate instruction across languages while exploring how best to capitalize on the bilingualism and biculturalism of the students and staff.

Despite the dearth of such studies, there are promising frameworks that are attempting to build bilingual models that are grounded in the available research, holistic in their conception of bilingualism, innovative in their instructional strategies, coordinated across languages, and that collect classroom- and school-level data to analyze and evaluate the effects. One such model is Dr. José Medina's C6 Biliteracy Instructional Framework which highlights the need to create, connect, collaborate, communicate, consider, and commit. Stated differently, this additive dual language framework asks schools and districts to establish a bilingual learning ecology that centers the bilingual student, elevates oral and written language development that is grounded in students' lived cultural and linguistic realities, and builds in reflection and self-assessment that brings together content, language, and culture. The model is currently being evaluated in a six-year longitudinal research design (Medina & Izquierdo, 2021). Another is the Gómez and Gómez 50-50 Content Model that is employed extensively throughout Texas and Washington. This model focuses on program design and fidelity of implementation. The language of instruction is designated by content area, students are flexibly grouped heterogeneously linguistically, content development is privileged over language development, and content-based bilingual learning centers support first- and second-language development (Gómez et al., 2005). Each model is an attempt to synthesize and enact a bilingual learning ecology that centers bilingualism and biculturalism, elevating research findings that value bilingual outcomes in contrast to English-only outcomes. A challenge for all who strive to develop such frameworks and models, however, is the paucity of research collected in two languages that describes classroom practices and measures results bilingually. Hence, it is our plea to the field to design and report qualitative, quantitative, and mixed-methods studies that will generate knowledge to contribute to the refinement of biliteracy pedagogies.

Despite the absence of an extensive body of conclusive research, we understand the importance of summarizing the knowledge base that exists and building/extending the foundation. We will do this by sharing and summarizing some of what has been learned thus far through a model titled Literacy Squared. The model has been implemented over a period of nearly 20 years and illustrates the kinds of studies one might conduct to validate the efficacy of a bilingual pedagogy to move the field forward in terms of the development of holistic bilingual pedagogies that are responsive to individual communities.

Promising Frameworks

Literacy Squared

While there are many frameworks that are viable for developing biliterate pedagogies, we present one, Literacy Squared, a biliteracy model that is implemented in bilingual education settings in 9 states and 15 school districts. Literacy Squared is a holistic paired literacy model that requires coordinated lessons across language environments with attention to cross-language and cross-cultural connections (Escamilla et al., 2014). We include and discuss its research base in depth because it is familiar to us, and because we have developed a robust empirical research base in the framework that is inclusive of what previous researchers have cited as needs in the field. We have conducted research on the totality of the Literacy Squared framework, including (1) research on student outcomes in Spanish and English reading and writing in Literacy Squared schools; (2) research related to classroom strategies that comprise components of the Literacy Squared instructional framework; (3) research that establishes the limits of English-only assessments for understanding the literacy development of emerging bilingual learners as well as research documenting the benefits of documenting developing biliteracy; and (4) research on professional development. Rather than summarize all the research that has been conducted in Literacy Squared schools, we limit our synthesis of research findings in this chapter to research on student outcomes and research on classroom strategies. Importantly, our findings examine biliteracy outcomes rather than monolingual English language outcomes or parallel monolingual outcomes and add to the research base in terms of effective bilingual pedagogy.

Language Acquisition and Academic Learning

We begin our synthesis of research with a summary of four studies related to student outcomes. These longitudinal studies examine student outcomes in Spanish and English in reading and writing in selected schools and districts. Soltero-González et al. (2016) conducted a longitudinal study that examined whether the implementation of a Spanish-English paired literacy approach provided an academic advantage to emerging bilingual students over a sequential literacy approach. Paired literacy requires that students learn to read and write in Spanish and English simultaneously with content, themes, standards, and texts being coordinated across languages. Employing a quasi-experimental design, the study compared the biliteracy outcomes of third-grade emerging bilingual learners participating in a paired literacy instruction from grades K-3 (n = 167) to those of students from the same schools who received sequential literacy instruction in K-2 and started to participate in the paired literacy model in third grade (n = 191). Students' writing and reading were assessed in both languages using informal measures. Third-grade reading scores on a high-stakes state assessment were also examined. Independent-sample t-tests were conducted to compare means on the four measures (Spanish and English writing and reading), and Cohen's d was calculated to generate effect sizes for each assessment in each language. Frequencies were run to determine the percentage of students who met or exceeded the state test performance standards. Findings indicated that the paired literacy group scored considerably higher than students in the comparison group on all measures. Furthermore, differences between groups were statistically significant for each outcome measure in each language with moderate to large effect sizes (.42–.90). Also, a larger percentage of students in the paired literacy group met or exceeded the state test performance standards. These findings suggest that paired literacy instruction leads to stronger literacy outcomes in both languages as compared to sequential literacy. This is significant in that a tenet of Literacy Squared's pedagogy has been the introduction of paired literacy (simultaneous literacy instruction) in Spanish and English beginning in kindergarten rather than the more traditional approach to begin literacy instruction in one language in kindergarten and refraining from adding on a second language until second or third grade.

A second study (Sparrow et al., 2021) was a six-year longitudinal single subject study to examine the effects of paired literacy (simultaneous literacy instruction in Spanish and English). The study utilized descriptive statistics and correlational analyses to analyze Spanish and English reading and English language proficiency data on a cohort of 58 Spanish-speaking emerging bilingual learners from grades kindergarten to fifth in four Literacy Squared schools. Data showed that students could develop literacy in two languages simultaneously without impeding development in either language. Especially impressive was student progress in oral English proficiency. When students started in kindergarten, 82% were at beginning and early intermediate levels in English, and by fifth grade, 97% of students reached early advanced and advanced proficiency levels. Growth in reading in two languages was equally impressive. Data showed that over five school years, from the end of kindergarten through the end of fifth grade, students grew just under five years in Spanish reading (4.97 years), and over four years of school, from the end of first grade through the end of fifth grade, they grew over four years in English reading (4.15 years). To determine the relationship between Spanish and English reading from kindergarten through fifth grade, Pearson's correlation coefficients (r) were calculated for Spanish (EDL2) and English (DRA2) reading scores each year. At each grade level, correlations were all significant at the .01 level, and they were high and positive, ranging from .61 to .72. These data further corroborate the value of introducing paired literacy beginning in kindergarten and maintaining it throughout elementary school in order to develop sustained literacy in both Spanish and English.

Butvilofsky et al. (2017a) conducted a single subject longitudinal study that documented the biliterate development (reading and writing) of emerging bilingual students. The purpose of the study was to examine the effect of paired literacy. From 2009 to 2012, data were collected from a total of 182 Spanish-English emerging bilingual children from kindergarten through grade 5. Four separate grade-level cohorts of students were followed across three grades: Cohort I included students from kindergarten through second grade (n = 45), Cohort II students from first through third grade (n = 39), Cohort III students from second through fourth grade (n = 53), and Cohort

IV students from third through fifth grade ($n = 45$). Growth occurred in all grade levels, but the greatest growth in English occurred between the fourth and fifth grades. Building on the results of other studies in the program, this study added the element of cumulative effects in the pedagogy in that while positive results are demonstrated at each grade level, accelerated growth is seen at the upper elementary grades. Further and equally as important to building a biliterate pedagogy was the finding that children in the cohort that started in Literacy Squared in kindergarten made greater gains than children starting at second grade. One implication is that starting paired literacy sooner and sustaining it longer seems to have greater long-term effects on biliteracy development.

Finally, a fourth longitudinal study (Escamilla et al., 2019) examined the biliterate writing growth of students participating in a one-way Spanish/English dual language program under two different conditions: biliteracy program treatment ($n = 38$) and biliteracy program control ($n = 72$) over two school years. The study utilized a longitudinal study design that examined growth in students' writing in Spanish and English in grades 1–3 from a quantitative perspective. Results indicated a statistically significant difference between the Spanish/English writing abilities of students in the Literacy Squared program as compared to those of control group students.

All outcome-based studies conducted thus far have established that a pedagogy that employs paired literacy and begins literacy instruction in Spanish and English in kindergarten is beneficial to students in that it does not impede literacy development in either reading or writing in either Spanish or English and may be more effective for the growing numbers of simultaneous bilingual children. Further, evidence seems to indicate that while growth is consistent in two languages at each grade level, it is not until upper elementary that accelerated growth begins, signaling that biliterate trajectories likely develop and should be evaluated at a different pace than monolingual trajectories.

Sociolinguistic Environments and Classroom Ecologies

As outlined above, centering bilingual students' entire linguistic repertoires and ways of knowing and interacting in the world is an assets-based approach to conceiving of biliteracy frameworks and pedagogies that reject and decenter English-centric curricula, pedagogy, and materials. Creating a sociolinguistic ecology that explicitly values and capitalizes on multilingualism encourages productive and receptive language development and provides concrete experiences for students to connect their languages and examine how they interact with one another as a starting place.

We continue with a summary of Literacy Squared research that examines specific pedagogical strategies we recommend teachers use within the paired literacy model. Again, if DLBE programs are going to adhere to a bilingual pedagogy that assures attention to quality of instruction, they must be grounded in classroom-based research that teases out the effects of particular strategies within a holistic model. The importance of the classroom strategy studies in building biliterate pedagogies is to ascertain if a particular strategy is stronger or more beneficial than another strategy in paired literacy programs. Four of these strategies are reviewed below.

LOTTA LARA

Lotta Lara is a repeated reading strategy that has been paired with oracy and writing strategies in Literacy Squared classrooms in both Spanish and English with Spanish Lotta Lara designed for grades K-2 and English for grades K-5 (Butvilofsky, et al., 2017b). This quasi-experimental study tested the efficacy of Lotta Lara. Its purpose was to investigate whether the biliterate reading strategy, which focuses on reading fluency, comprehension, and oracy through whole-group instruction, impacted first-grade emerging bilingual learners' biliterate reading development. The study utilized an Ordinary Least Squares regression model to compare students' biliterate reading outcomes in the treatment group ($n = 23$) to those of the control group ($n = 21$). Despite the small sample size, positive and statistically significant effects were found on students' Spanish reading outcomes. While students made growth in their English reading, significant effects were not detected on English reading outcomes. Our findings support the need to provide emerging bilingual learners with explicit and interactive biliterate reading instruction to promote biliterate reading development that includes opportunities for oracy and writing connections.

ASÍ SE DICE

Así se dice (that's how you say it) is a strategy that is designed to help students develop bilingualism/biliteracy through translation exercises. These translation exercises encourage the development of translanguaging skills, critical thinking, side-by-side language analyses, and attention to the development of metalinguistic awareness. *Así se dice* asks Spanish-English bilingual students to translate and discuss text-based passages. This particular pedagogical strategy is specific to bilingual contexts. Hopewell and Escamilla (2018) reported the results of a qualitative case study that included 3.5 hours of classroom observation data and 4.5 hours of teacher interview data. Findings were important in that teachers contributed to the creation of recommended guidelines for the implementation of *Así se dice*. For example, the teachers emphasized that selection of passages for *Así se dice* lessons be under 25 words. Further, teachers identified phrases or passages in texts that were seemingly simple but proved difficult to translate. Additionally, teachers emphasized the need for students to be familiar with the genre of the text they were translating and indicated that the strategy is more effective if it is connected to a unit teachers are teaching. It is important for teachers to know students' language proficiency levels. Finally, teachers need to translate the texts before having students do them.

This study provides evidence through teacher testimonials of the benefits of the *Así se dice* strategy in the development of cross-language metalinguistic skills which are an important aspect of the biliteracy instructional. However, the study is also an important example of how Literacy Squared strategies have been, and can be, refined and modified over time through collaboration with teachers and schools in our partnership.

DIARIO DUO

Diario Duo is a strategy implemented and researched in Literacy Squared classrooms in Texas (Alvarez & Butvilofsky, 2021). This study examined the biliterate writing abilities and development of 25 Spanish-English Latinx children over the course of their first-grade year. As part of their regular classroom instruction, each student created 16 writing compositions over the year, once a month, 8 entries each in Spanish and English. Using embedded mixed methods and a holistic view of bilingualism, nearly 400 writing samples were analyzed for various aspects of writing development: ideas expressed, spelling, punctuation use, and grammar, as well as cross-language transfers. Through their analyses, the authors documented the children's biliterate writing growth across time, although growth was not always linear across languages or in all writing abilities. At the beginning of the year, children demonstrated greater abilities in Spanish than English in all writing abilities, but as the year progressed, abilities across languages were comparable. This work is significant to understand biliterate writing development.

ENGAGEMENT OF STUDENTS' HOLISTIC LINGUISTIC REPERTOIRES

Finally, in an observational descriptive study, Hopewell (2017) documented and examined how a second-grade bilingual teacher and her students explicitly and intentionally practiced and enacted translanguaging as a form of humanizing and resistant bilingual pedagogy. We offer this as an example of the importance of ecologically valid studies that document complex language ecologies and the pedagogies enacted within. Data were collected three days per week over a period of four months and findings documented the employment of two powerful biliterate strategies. The first was the development and use of thematic biliteracy boards that were co-created with students to capture and capitalize on students' full bilingual repertoires. The second were pre-planned home-school connected lessons that involved reading texts in English during school, discussing the content at home with families in Spanish, and then returning to school to write in Spanish about their parent's opinions. In this way, classroom practices reflected the teacher's understanding of the theory that a student's learning burden is lessened when comprehension and learning is facilitated by access to all previous knowledge regardless of the language of acquisition (Nation, 2001). Findings include the understanding that the opportunity to teach and learn is stifled when educators insist on strict separation of languages. This study was important to the development of a biliterate pedagogy with regard to the inclusion of translanguaging practices and deemphasizing previous policies of strict language separation.

Anti-racist Curricula and Materials

Anti-racist teaching strives to include the perspectives, histories, and experiences of people who have been marginalized and excluded from U.S. curricula. It actively aims to dismantle and challenge monolingual, monocultural, and monolithic worldviews that perpetuate white supremacy. The paired literacy practices and sociolinguistic ecologies and practices outlined above are shored up in Literacy Squared through intentionally selected materials that challenge white normativity and racial/linguistic injustice. Rather than be limited by content and language standards, we expand our work through the inclusion of Social Justice Standards (https://www.learningforjustice.org/frameworks/social-justice-standards). Our students and teachers openly explore ancestry, immigration, and racism. While we lack space to provide an extensive list of children's texts that serve to support our paired literacy units, here are just a few titles related to immigration and racism that we appreciate: *Diarou's Not So Different* (Bayo et al., 2020, *What is a Refugee*? (Gravel, 2019), *Race Cars: A children's book about white privilege* (Devenny, 2021), *Something Happened in our Town: A child's story about racial injustice* (Celano et al., 2018), and *Stamped: el racismo, el antirracismo y tú* (Reynolds & Kendi, 2020). When possible, we include multilingual versions. When not, we find similarly themed texts to pair across languages. Children need to see themselves and their histories in the texts and curricula we provide. They also need to have the language and ability to confront biases and stereotypes based on age, language, race, gender, ability, etc. These lessons begin early.

This brief synthesis provides a snapshot of how one promising biliteracy framework, Literacy Squared, has incorporated research into the development of a bilingual pedagogy. It serves as an illustrative example of research that centers bilingualism/biliteracy into its frameworks and instructional practices and examines program efficacy from a developing bilingual/biliterate lens. Many more such research-informed perspectives are needed.

Conclusion

In this chapter, we argued that there is a critical need for the development of a bilingual pedagogy that responds to and embraces the ontology of being bilingual such that the quality of instruction in DLBE programs is elevated and maximized. Research to date has largely focused on outcomes that reify English as the pinnacle as opposed to the more complex outcome of bilingualism, biliteracy, and biculturalism. It is imperative that bilingual pedagogies begin from a position of anti-racist, counter-hegemonic, and decolonizing lenses. The goal of education should not be that students leave with less than they began, but that we build upon and strengthen the linguistic and cultural capital they embody. To this end, we offered one example of a promising framework that embraces a multilingual multicultural holistic approach to developing biliteracy. To be sure, this is not the only model, and we recognize that it is limited in that it focuses solely on the area of biliteracy. Pedagogies of bilingualism and biliteracy must look at not only the whole child, but the whole curriculum. More comprehensive models are needed that are responsive to the myriad of communities that desire bilingualism and biculturalism for their children. This, however, will require that we attend to a number of challenges.

Firstly, the scholarly community needs to establish research agendas that include classroom-based inquiry into innovative instructional strategies that are unique to DLBE contexts. A recent search in the ERIC (Proquest) database with the terms "classroom-based research" and "dual language," for example, yielded a single study (de Jong & Bearse, 2014). A broader search for peer-reviewed research produced in the past decade attending to "bilingual instructional strategies" only increased this number to 41. Granted, this was not a systematic or methodical search, but the paucity of initial literature is alarming and should raise concern in the field.

Secondly, bilingual pedagogies will not elevate the quality of instruction if we lack bilingual teachers with the knowledge to enact them. In the past three years, more than 61% of states have reported shortages in the number of available ESL/Bilingual teachers (U.S. Department of Education, n.d.). This has resulted in the current need for many schools and districts to recruit teachers from abroad who speak Spanish but may not know the U.S. context and are even further removed from the pedagogies of bilingualism we are advocating. We call upon U.S. teacher preparation programs to institute coursework grounded in bilingual pedagogies and to strive to promote and champion consistency in-state credentialing that requires said coursework of teachers (Alfaro, 2019; Johnson & Thorne Wallington, 2021; Leider et al., 2021).

Finally, sound pedagogies of bilingualism and biliteracy are undermined by English language assessment systems that do not value the bilingual and bicultural knowledge and skills that are being fostered in DLBE programs. The time and attention they are afforded takes away from the ability to instruct in ways that advance holistic bilingualism. Time, in fact, is at a premium in DLBE contexts. Teachers and students are being asked to accomplish more in the same amount of time. We call upon districts and administrators to reevaluate what is being required of bilingual teachers using a framework of bilingualism and abandoning the colonial and white supremacist orientation that students educated bilingually should emerge only as valued for the skills they can demonstrate in English.

If we aspire to dismantle systems and institutions that perpetuate white supremacy and monolingualism, we must begin by reframing our DLBE pedagogies in such a way that they begin from the premise that we are all better off in a world that is diverse and multilingual. Our bilingual students, families, and teachers deserve nothing less.

References

Abutalebi, J., & Green, D. W. (2008). Control mechanisms in bilingual language production: Neural evidence from language switching studies. *Language and Cognitive Processes*, *23*(4), 557–582.

Alfaro, C. (2019). Preparing critically conscious dual language teachers: Recognizing and interrupting dominant ideologies. Reimaging dual language education in the US. *Theory Into Practice Journal*, *58*(2), 194–203.

Alim, S. H., Rickford, J. R., & Ball, A. F. (Eds.) (2016). *Raciolinguistics: How language shapes our ideas about race*. Oxford University Press.

Alvarez, A., & Butvilofsky, S. A. (2021). The biliterate writing development of bilingual first graders. *Bilingual Research Journal*, *44*(2), 189–212.

August, D., & Hakuta, K. (Eds.). (1997). *Improving schooling for language-minority children: A research agenda*. National Academy Press.

August, D., & Shanahan, T. (Eds.). (2006). *Developing literacy in second-language learners: Report of the national literacy panel on language-minority children and youth*. Lawrence Erlbaum.

Baker, S., Lesaux, N., Jayanthi, M., Dimino, J., Proctor, C. P., Morris, J., Gersten, R., Haymond, K., Kieffer, M. J., Linan-Thompson, S., & Newman-Gonchar, R. (2014). *Teaching academic content and literacy to English learners in elementary and middle school* (NCEE 2014-4012). Washington, DC: National Center for Education Evaluation and Regional Assistance (NCEE), Institute of Education Sciences, U.S. Department of Education. Retrieved from the NCEE website http://ies.ed.gov/ncee/wwc/publications_reviews.aspx

Ballinger, S., Lyster, R., Sterzuk, A., & Genesee, F. (2017). Context-appropriate crosslinguistic pedagogy considering the role of language status in immersion education. *Journal of Immersion and Content-Based Language Education*, *51*(2017), 30–57.

Bartolomé, L. (1994). Beyond the methods fetish: Toward a humanizing pedagogy. *Harvard Educational Review*, *64*, 173–195.

Bayo, D., Campbell, R., & Cooke, A. (2020). *Diarou's not so different*. Shout Mouse Press.

Bialystok, E. (2001). *Bilingualism in development: Language literacy, and cognition.* Cambridge University Press.
Bialystok, E., Craik, F. I. M., & Luk, G. (2012). Bilingualism: Consequences for mind and brain. *Trends in Cognitive Sciences, 16*(4), 240–250.
Boroditsky, L. (2011). How language shapes thought: The languages we speak affect our perceptions of the world. *Scientific American, 304*(2), 63–65.
Butvilofsky, S. A., Hopewell, S., Escamilla, K., & Sparrow, W. (2017a). Shifting deficit paradigms of Latino emerging bilingual students' literacy achievement: Documenting biliterate trajectories. *Journal of Latinos and Education, 16*(2), 85–97.
Butvilofsky, S., Sparrow, W., Roberson, N. D., & Hopewell, S. (2017b). Lotta Lara: A promising biliterate reading strategy. *Literacy Research and Instruction, 56*(4), 269–289.
Celano, M., Collins, M., & Hazzard, A. (2018). *Something happened in our town: A child's story about racial injustice*. Magination Press.
Cenoz, J., & Gorter, D. (Eds). (2015). *Multilingual education: Between language learning and translanguaging*. Cambridge University Press.
Cenoz, J., & Gorter, D. (2017). Minority languages and sustainable translanguaging: Threat or opportunity? *Journal of Multilingual and Multicultural Development, 38*(10), 901–912.
Collier, V., & Thomas, W. (2004). The astounding effectiveness of dual language education for all. *NABE Journal of Research and Practice*, 2(1), 1–20.
Collier, V., & Thomas, W. (2017). Validating the power of bilingual schooling: Thirty-two years of large-scale, longitudinal research. *ARAL*, 1–16. https://static1.squarespace.com/static/5d854ac170e64a71d1de71d3/t/5d9cb55f26d64b44562c6069/1570551181085/ARAL±2017±%28typed%29.PDF
Cook, V., & Li, W. (Eds.). (2016). *The Cambridge handbook of linguistic multi-competence*. Cambridge University Press.
Cummins, J. (2005, September). Teaching for cross-language transfer in dual language education: Possibilities and pitfalls. In *TESOL symposium of dual language education: Teaching and learning two languages in the EFL setting*. Istanbul, Turkey. September 23.
Cummins, J. (2007). Rethinking monolingual instructional strategies in multilingual classrooms. *Canadian Journal of Applied Linguistics, 10*(2), 221–240.
Cummins, J. (2014). Rethinking pedagogical assumptions in Canadian French immersion programs. *Journal of Immersion and Content-Based Language Education*, 2(1), 3–22.
de Jong, E. J., & Bearse, C. I. (2014). Dual language programs as a strand within a secondary school: Dilemmas of school organization and the TWI mission. *International Journal of Bilingual Education and Bilingualism, 17*(1), 15–31.
Devenny, J. (2021). *Race cars: A children's book about white privilege*. Quarto Publishing.
Dworin, J. E. (2003). Insights into biliteracy development: Toward a bidirectional theory of bilingual pedagogy. *Journal of Hispanic Higher Education*, 2(2), 171–186.
Escamilla, K., Fine, C., & Hopewell, S. (2019). Enhancing writing outcomes in Spanish/English biliteracy programs. *The Bilingual Review-La Revista Bilingüe*, 34(1), 77–96. http://bilingualreview.utsa.edu/index.php/br/article/view/253
Escamilla, K., Hopewell, S., Butvilofsky, S., Sparrow, W., Soltero-Gonzalez, L., Ruiz Figueroa, O., & Escamilla, M. (2014). *Biliteracy from the start: Literacy squared in action*. Caslon Publishing.
Fitts, S. (2006). Reconstructing the status quo: Linguistic interaction in a dual-language school. *Bilingual Research Journal, 30*, 337–366.

Flores, N., & García, O. (2017). A critical review of bilingual education in the United States: From basements and pride to boutiques and profit. *Annual Review of Applied Linguistics*, *37*, 14–29.

Fránquiz, M., & Salazar, M. (2004). The transformative potential of humanizing pedagogy: Addressing the diverse needs of Chicano/Mexicano students. *High School Journal*, *87*(4), 36–53.

Genesee, F. (2018). Taking stock: Lessons on dual language education. In M. B. Arias & M. Fee (Eds.), *Profiles of dual language education in the 21st century*. Multilingual Matters.

Genesee, F., & Lindholm-Leary, K. (2021). The suitability of dual language education for diverse students. *Journal of Immersion and Content-Based Language Education*, *9*(2), 164–192.

Genesee, F., Lindholm-Leary, K., Saunders, W., & Christian, D. (2006). *Educating English language learners*. Cambridge University Press.

Gersten, R., Baker, S. K., Shanahan, T., Linan-Thompson, S., Collins, P., & Scarcella, R. (2007). *Effective literacy and English language instruction for English learners in the elementary grades: A practice guide* (NCEE 2007-4011). Washington, DC: National Center for Education Evaluation and Regional Assistance, Institute of Education Sciences, U.S. Department of Education. http://ies.ed.gov/ncee/wwc/publications/practiceguides

Goldenberg, C. (2008). Teaching English language learners: What the research does and does not say. *American Educator*, 8–44. https://digitalcommons.georgiasouthern.edu/esed5234-master/27

Gómez, L., Freeman, D., & Freeman, Y. (2005). Dual language education: A promising 50:50 model. *Bilingual Research Journal*, *29*(1), 145–164.

Gort, M., & Sembiante, S. F. (2015). Navigating hybridized language learning spaces through translanguaging pedagogy: Dual language preschool teachers' languaging practices in support of emergent bilingual children's performance of academic discourse. *International Multilingual Research Journal*, *9*(1), 7–25.

Gravel, E. (2019). *What is a refugee?* Schwartz & Wade.

Guerra, J. C. (2012). From code-segregation to code-switching to code-meshing: Finding deliverance from deficit thinking through language awareness and performance. In P. J. Dunston, S. K. Fullerton, C. C. Bates, K. N. Headley, & Stecker (Eds.), *61st Literacy research association yearbook* (pp. 29–39). Literacy Research Association.

Heller, M. (2001). Undoing the macro/micro dichotomy: Ideology and categorization in a linguistic minority school. In N. Coupland (Ed.), *Sociolinguistics and social theory* (pp. 261–296). Pearson.

Hopewell, S. (2017). Pedagogies to challenge monolingual orientations to bilingual education in the United States. In B. Paulsrud, J. Rosén, B. Strazer, & A. Wedín (Eds.), *New perspectives on translanguaging and education* (pp. 72–89). Multilingual Matters.

Hopewell, S., & Escamilla, K. (2014). Biliteracy development in immersion contexts. *Journal of Immersion and Content-Based Language*, 2(2), 181–195.

Hopewell, S., & Escamilla, K. (2018). Exploring cross language connections in Spanish and English through *Así se dice*. Paper presented at LRA, Indian Wells, CA.

Hornberger, N. H. (Ed.). (2008). Continua of biliteracy. *Encyclopedia of language and education* (pp. 3152–3169). Springer. https://doi.org/10.1007/978-0-387-30424-3_237

Jarvis, S., & Pavlenko, A. (2008). *Crosslinguistic influence in language and cognition*. Routledge.

Johnson, A. M., & Thorne Wallington, E. (2021). From theory to implementation: Examining EL certification requirements through the lens of local context. *Education Policy Analysis Archives*, *29*(105), 1–32. https://doi.org/10.14507/epaa.29.5253

Kroll, J., Dussias, P., Bice, K., & Perrotti, L. (2015). Bilingualism, mind, and brain. *Annual Review of Linguistics*, 1(1), 377–394. https://www.annualreviews.org/doi/abs/10.1146/annurev-linguist-030514-124937

Leider, C. M., Colombo, M. W., & Nerlino, E. (2021). Decentralization, teacher quality, and the education of English learners: Do state education agencies effectively prepare teachers of els? *Education Policy Analysis Archives*, *29*(100), 1–44. https://doi.org/10.14507/epaa.29.5279

Levinson, S. (2003). *Space in language and cognition: Explorations in cognitive diversity*. Cambridge University Press.

Marian, V., & Spivey, M. (2003). Bilingual and monolingual processing of competing lexical items. *Applied Psycholinguistics*, *24*(2), 173–193.

Medina, J., & Izquierdo, E. (2021). Equity commitment in large-scale dual language bilingual education. *Multilingual Educator*, pp. 6–10. https://www.gocabe.org/wp-content/uploads/2021/03/ME_2021-FINAL.pdfNation

Nation, I. S. P. (2001). *Learning vocabulary in another language*. Cambridge University Press.

Pavlenko, A., & Jarvis, S. (2002). Bidirectional transfer. *Applied Linguistics*, *23*(2), 191–214.

Pierce, L. J., Chen, J., Delcenserie, A., Genesee, F., & Klein, D. (2015). Past experience shapes ongoing neural pathways for language. *Nature Communications*, *6*, 1–11.

Reynolds, J., & Kendi, I. X. (2020). *Stamped: el racismo, el antirracismo y tú*. Penguin Random House.

Rumbaut, R. G. (2014). English plus: Exploring the socioeconomic benefits of bilingualism in Southern California. In R. M. Callahan & P. C. Gándara (Eds.), *The bilingual advantage: Language, literacy, and the labor market* (pp. 182–205). Multilingual Matters.

Salazar, M. D. C. (2013). A humanizing pedagogy: Reinventing the principles of education as a journey toward liberation. *Review of Research in Education*, *37*, 121–148.

Santibañez, L., & Zárate, M. E. (2014). Bilinguals in the U.S. and college enrollment. In R. M. Callahan & P. C. Gándara (Eds.), *The bilingual advantage: Language, literacy, and the labor market* (pp. 211– 233). Multilingual Matters.

Solano-Flores, G. (2010). Function and form in research on language and mathematics education. In J. N. Moschkovich (Ed.), *Language and mathematics education: Multiple perspectives and directions for research* (pp. 113–150). Information Age.

Soltero-González, L., Sparrow, W., Butvilofsky, S., Escamilla, K., & Hopewell, S. (2016). Effects of a paired literacy program on emerging bilingual children's biliteracy outcomes in third grade. *Journal of Literacy Research*, *48*(2), 1–25.

Sparrow, W., Schepers, O. C., & Escamilla, K. (2021). A six year trajectory toward better biliteracy: Results of a paired literacy program for emerging bilingual students. *NABE Journal of Research and Practice*. https://doi.org/10.1080/26390043.2021.1977593

Steele, J. L., Slater, R. O., Zamarro, G., Miller, T., Li, J., Burkhouser, S., & Bacon, M. (2017). Effects of dual-language immersion programs on student achievement: Evidence from lottery data. *American Educational Research Journal*, *54*(1S), 282s–306s.

U.S. Department of Education. (n.d.) *Teacher shortage areas*. https://tsa.ed.gov/#/reports

Winawer, J., Witthoft, N., Frank, M. C., Wu, L., Wade, A. R., & Boroditsky, L. (2007). Russian blues reveal effects of language on color discrimination. *Proceedings of the National Acadamies of Science*, *10*(19), 7780–7785.

Wong Fillmore, L. (2000). Loss of family languages: Should educators be concerned? *Theory Into Practice*, *39*(4), 203–210.

Discourses, Power, and School Research

29

THE HEGEMONIC POWER OF ENGLISH (AND SPANISH OF ELSEWHERE) AND ITS IMPACT IN DUAL LANGUAGE EDUCATION

Christian Faltis

Within the field of bilingual education, vibrant bilingualism and full biliteracy have not ever been the primary goal of programs that are labeled bilingual education in the United States (Flores & García, 2017). By *vibrant bilingualism*, I mean an understanding of bilingualism, following Pennycook (2017) and Canagarajah (2013), that decenters humans in the construction of meaning so that communication necessarily transcends language users toward an understanding of bilingualism as "embodied, embedded, and distributed across people, places, and time" (Pennycook, 2017, p. 276). Accordingly, bilingualism is vibrant and dynamic to the extent it grows in unpredictable ways and lives among both humans and non-human objects and things. Vibrant bilingualism is complex and its users include multilayered histories, identities, and experiences in the world that surrounds them.

In bilingual education, a vibrant understanding of language is visibly absent. Languages are named, taught, and used as if they belong only to the learners/users and communication occurs only when humans share the same narrowly constructed meaning systems that exclude non-human factors and experiences. The primary goal of most bilingual programs has been the replacement of students' vibrant home language and literacy practices with a predefined, standard spoken, and written English, "our language" as some state policy makers describe it (Freire et al., 2022). For bilingual education programs that express an "additive" goal, the students' vibrant home language and literacies may be considered a pedagogical resource for learning English, the ways English users speak it, based on the research finding

DOI: 10.4324/9781003269076-42

among certain mainstream and mainly cognitive researchers that, when the minoritized language students have engaged with home language practices in educational contexts for meaningful communication, what they learn can be applied to other educational contexts (in English) (Cummins, 2017; de Jong, 2016; Lambert, 1974; Landry et al., 1991). This "additive" argument for bilingual education originates from a separate, non-vibrant, linear, monoglossic approach of bilingualism: Learners who "do well" on language and content presented and assessed in standard language are likely to excel in learning the new language, owing to the "transfer" of standard language and literacy practices learned in academic contexts where the home language is used to the new language (August & Shanahan, 2017).

Similarly, in other iterations of bilingual education, that is, **dual** language education and **dual** language immersion, parents, teachers, and students are placed in classrooms where the teacher likely insists on language separation for teaching children. A particular feature of dual language education is that minority language and English speakers who are learning the non-English language are placed together in classrooms, creating "a learning context where fluent and less fluent speakers of the target language could interact and learner together" (de Jong & Howard, 2009). In the United States, the most common type of dual language program includes the named languages of Spanish and English taught preferably separately by different teachers or by one teacher who uses the two languages separated for content or time blocks (though the one-teacher model does occur in many programs). Some dual language programs follow a 50:50 model (Gómez et al., 2005), where half of the largely whitestream curriculum[1] (Urrieta, 2009) is taught by one teacher and half by another, using each of the languages monolingually and separately, to better fit monoglossic language (García, 2009) and "true or real" bilingualism spoken by native speakers of each language (Valdés, 2015, p. 39). Other dual language programs use a 90:10 model where immersion into the non-English language through literacy and content areas is steadily reduced by the fourth grade to 50:50 allocation of both languages for instruction. According to Sánchez et al. (2018), dual language education is but one approach to dual language bilingual education, which is a broader term that includes various ways of teaching students bilingually.

For the English-speaking students of various ethnic and racial backgrounds, dual language immersion programs provide a way to enrich their academic preparation, and to add the target language, Spanish, to their communicative repertoire, with the understanding that they are also building on their home language and literacy proficiency, standard English, which is also the preferred language of the nation, of business, and of higher education that schools force on children (Freire et al., 2022). For children who come from Spanish-speaking homes and are able to enroll in dual language programs, there are different reasons that come into play. One reason is that parents want their children to maintain their home language and identities as Spanish speakers. Dual language education provides an avenue for these children to develop spoken and written Spanish and English for multiple academic years. In many cases, for Spanish-speaking students to qualify for enrollment, however, they must already be bilingual; i.e., they also must have developed advanced English language proficiency to be eligible for admission. This is because many dual language programs have developed in recent years for white English-speaking families wishing to add a second language, a phenomenon found especially widespread in Utah, which Valdez et al. (2016) refer to more broadly as the gentrification of dual language education (also see Dorner et al. (2021) who discuss gentrification as coloniality in dual language programs). Another reason Spanish-speaking parents enroll their children in dual language programs is for developing their oral and written standard Spanish through monolingual instruction, because of the widespread belief spread by both monolingual Spanish and English speakers that their bilingualism is inferior because they alternate between Spanish and English haphazardly (Freire et al., 2017; Palmer, 2010; Valdés, 1997).

Hegemony of Language and How It Impacts Beliefs and Actions

Let us begin with two crucial questions: Why are dual language programs oriented toward standard language and monolingual bilingualism rather than for the development of fully vibrant bilingualism and biliteracy for Spanish-speaking children? Where do these orientations come from? The answers, I believe, partially reside in the concept of *hegemony*, first introduced by Gramsci (Bates, 1974) as taken-for-granted national, cultural, and social ways of being and doing that benefit the dominant group. As Gramsci understood, people are not ruled by people alone, but by the ideas these people hold about certain people. In the case of language, hegemony works to create messages about what kind of language counts, who counts as representatives of that language, and how language within a nation thrives. Language hegemony works in part because nations are imagined communities (Anderson, 1983). Most members of communities within a nation-state will never come to encounter each other, but the communities, most well connected with the dominant group, the colonizers, and their subsequent generations of settler colonizers, will continue to act in ways that reflect the demands of the dominant group. Moreover, immigrants who are granted citizenship or legal status, as well as undocumented immigrants, will be expected to be, act, and communicate in ways implied or insisted by the dominant group. The dominant group, with the power of their written text, dictionaries, media outlets, schools, banks, and businesses to define and use language in ways they determine as the best for their continued domination

(Lippi-Green, 2012) This means that the dominant group has the power to name the language and type of language used in these and other contexts as being the most intelligent and elaborate, and that the type of language of the named language must be modeled after speakers and writers who "sound intelligent" and use standard language in speaking and writing as it is taught in schools, colleges, and universities.

The common denominator of these proclamations is an imagined homogeneity of language and language users, when, in fact, all nation-states are heterogenous and vibrantly multilingual. Despite this fact, hegemons seek to maintain their language dominance even when alternative ways of being, doing, languaging, and teaching in languages other than English are proposed, implemented, and valued in schools and communities (Macedo et al., 2003).

Lest we forget, the United States is a colonial country, which began with the original 13 colonies, and over the next 200 years, the entire country was overtaken by colonizers moving westward to the Pacific Ocean and beyond. It is important to understand how language hegemony came to be as colonizers slowly began taking land from indigenous populations, and acquiring Louisiana and the present-day Southwest states of Arizona, California, western Colorado, Nevada, New Mexico, Texas, and Utah (Del Castillo, 1992). The next section offers a brief historical account of the development and consequences of language hegemony in the United States. The account begins with the indoctrination of indigenous children in the late 1800s, as public schools began developing across the expanding colonization of the country.

A Brief History of Language Hegemony in the United States

During the 19th and 20th centuries, tens of thousands indigenous children in the southwestern United States (and Canada) were taken from their parents and placed into residential boarding schools where they were treated as "savages" in need of being civilized, and where their languages were extirpated and replaced with English (Romero-Little et al., 2007; Voicu, 2020). These horrific mandates were partially driven by beliefs in language ideologies that positioned English as the language of the nation, standard English as the language of schooling, and languages used by indigenous families as non-literate and incapable of expressing abstract ideas. Note that the hegemons in power who produced and believed in these language ideologies were the ones committing the savagery because they mandated the obliteration of the indigenous ways of knowing, being, and languaging. Davilla (1978) provides an explanation of the ideological principles that promote these beliefs and actions as follows:

> Culturally, colonialization has a adopted a negation to the [indigenous culture's] symbolic systems [including their language practices], forgetting or undervaluing them even when they manifest themselves in

> action. This way, the eradication of the past and the idealization and the desire to relive the cultural heritage of the colonial societies constitute a situation and a system of ideas which along with other elements, situates the colonial society as a class.
>
> *(cited in Macedo et al., 2003 p. 66)*

Among the "other elements" were justifications, such as language ideologies that position English as the language of civilized peoples, for placing indigenous children in residential boarding schools to rid them of their symbolic systems. As was recently revealed, owners of residential boarding schools in the United States and Canada throughout the 19th and 20th centuries murdered and physically harmed for life thousands of indigenous children, all of whom were expected to learn and use English in schools designed to stop them from speaking their home languages (Estes, 2019; Mosby & Millions, 2021). While it is not clear that language ideologies that favored standard English and despised the languages of indigenous children were entirely to blame for these murders, it is clear that the schools believed that these children's languages were unworthy of any support. Likewise, up until the end of the Civil War (1865), white slave owners often beat their slaves who were taken from various African countries and prohibited them from using their home languages (Baugh, 1999) by insisting that they use English only. However, few were allowed to learn to read and write in English, owing to a belief that they were incapable of developing standard English.

Since the 1920s, a primary goal of public education has been the Americanization of "new immigrants"(especially Southern and Eastern European darker skinned immigrants) into whitestream life through assimilationist and melting pot practices that aim to have immigrants rid themselves of ethnic and language markers (Ovando, 2003). One of the ways the dominant groups did this was by making English the designated language for all instruction in public schooling up until the late 1960s, when bilingual education is finally approved for use in schools with a certain number of students for whom English was a new language (Faltis & Hudelson, 1998). English-only instruction favored English-speaking families and made learning in schools very difficult for non-English-speaking children. For example, in the late 1940s in Driscoll, Texas, the school district there, run by white English-speaking administrators, held Mexican American young children who entered school speaking Spanish back, keeping them in the first grade for three years, until they deemed them English-ready for second grade. The school claimed that the emergent bilingual Mexican descent children deprived white students of white teachers' attention and instruction in English and that the Mexican children were not learning proper English (San Miguel, 1983). Parents of the Mexican children sued the Driscoll school district in 1954 claiming language and racial discrimination. U.S. District Judge James

V. Allred ruled in 1957 that it was unreasonable to place students in separate classrooms based on their race or origin.[2] In this case, race and origin were proxies for language abilities of these Mexican children.

The Bilingual Education Act of 1968 allowed for school districts with certain numbers of non-English-speaking children to have reading and certain content areas taught in their home language, for up to two years, in most cases (Faltis & Hudelson, 1998). It was believed that learning English in a bilingual program was a way for immigrants and children of immigrants to show that they fit into American society and to demonstrate a commitment to becoming English speakers. Yet, their rejection continued due to their accents, their racialization, their non-English names, and their type of bilingualism, mixed and impure (Mena, 2020).

During the 1980s and 1990s, white hegemons (such as white monolingual English speaker Ron Unz in California) began what is known as the modern English-only movement. This movement targeted immigrant speakers of languages other than English, primarily Mexican descent children and youth, as well as the bilingual programs that served them in Arizona, California, Colorado, and Massachusetts. Other states, such as Texas and New Mexico, where transitional bilingual education programs existed relied heavily on the dismissive message of the English-only movement to get children to stop using their non-English home languages and use only English in schools as quickly as possible, with as little cost to the school district as possible.

Relying on the political stance of U.S. English (1983) and English hegemony in general, the English-only movement gained momentum throughout the 1990s and early 2000s after Ronald Reagan and during the George Bush Sr. and George W. Bush eras, when immigration from Mexico was at its height, and the U.S. empire sought to expand its economic and military power. Since the late 1990s, 32 out of 50 states have declared English as their state's official language (Nieto, 2021). At the national level, no language has been declared as official. Nonetheless, the English-only movement has been devastating for emergent bilingual children and youth. Not only have these children fallen behind academically in states where bilingual education has been banned or restricted to transitional bilingual education programs, many lose some oral proficiency in the home languages within a generation (Fillmore, 1991; García & Wei, 2014) and few develop strong biliteracy (Herrera, 2022).

Hegemonic Language Ideologies

Language ideologies, beliefs about language, and the people who use language are often not about language itself but rather are belief systems informed by and tied to questions of identity and power (Blackledge, 2000); hence, they are hegemonic. Accordingly, language ideologies created by hegemons promote certain beliefs about different groups of people, their intelligence, and their ability to communicate ideas. Hegemonic language ideologies are intimately tied to ideas about the connection among race, intelligence, and language. These connections date back to the late 1700s and 1800s when white males invented and pushed the language ideology that a "native speaker" of English had to speak Standard American English, the registers of English used by educated white males in the mid-west territories and states, but never the English varieties used by African Americans in the South, Mexicans in the Southwest, Eastern Europeans, and Jews in the Northeast (Bonfiglio, 2002). Standard American English was considered to be inherently more intelligent, more rational, and more elaborate than the Englishes of African Americans, eastern European immigrants, bilingual Mexicans, Chinese, and indigenous peoples. These beliefs have been taken up by language hegemons and have made their way in education, especially dual language and dual language bilingual education. For example, language hegemony supports current beliefs found in dual language education programs: (1) that the languages should be presented, taught, and used separately, and (2) that dual language teachers should promote and use standard, academic varieties of the language of instruction (Valdez et al., 2016). Both of these hegemonic language requirements are attached to language ideologies about imagined language users, with reference to differences between how certain people use language poorly, while others use language well as we saw in the examples of written language contrasted above. These differences are in part a result of the eugenic movements with support from research that intends to show difference in language abilities between racial groups and social classes.

The idea that certain races are better equipped for intellectual and leadership positions stems primarily from eugenics, the study of difference of intellectual abilities between whites and other racialized groups. The next section introduces how the eugenics movement contributed to a language ideology that places certain languages and language practices above those believed to be used by racialized minorities and people of color.

Eugenics-based Language Ideology

A eugenics-based language ideology is fueled by work carried out by eugenicists between 1890 and 1930. Eugenicists believed that controlled breeding would increase the likelihood of more desirable offspring and the elimination of people viewed as intellectually inferior and less capable of logical and rational ways of speaking (Faltis, 2022).

Early eugenicists in the United States based their work on differences in IQ test results between monolingual white English speakers and African Americans, multilingual eastern European immigrants, bilingual Mexicans, and bilingual Native Americans. In 1916, Stanford University psychologist Lewis Terman set out to prove that white monolingual English speakers were genetically superior to people of color and recent eastern European immigrants (Valencia, 1997), building on the idea of a connection between genetics and intelligence, first introduced in England and then promoted heavily in the United States by Henry Goddard, a eugenicist whose subsequent IQ test, *The Binet and Simon Test of Intellectual Capacity,* was picked up by public schools as a way to show that white monolingual English-speaking children were intellectually superior based on their scores IQ tests compared to other children who were "non-native speakers" of English. The original goal of eugenics was to sterilize people deemed to be "feeble-minded" as determined by IQ test scores. By 1927, more than 64,000 people, mainly economically poor people of color and recently arrived immigrants, were no longer able to reproduce offspring. Within 30 years, eugenics moved away from physical sterilization and toward questions about the educability of people who were determined to have low IQ test scores, mainly African American, Mexican American, and Native American peoples. The new eugenics focused on language sterilization or eugenics-based language erasure (Faltis, 2022). By the 1960s, UC Berkeley eugenicist, Arthur Jensen, argued that people of color, particularly non-standard English-speaking African Americans, were at least 15 points below whites in the United States, and that it was largely a waste of time and effort to spend additional money to educate them (Jensen, 1968).

In the meantime, white anthropologist, Oscar Lewis (1966) developed his theory of the "culture of poverty," to depict poor people as "lazy, fatalistic, hedonistic, violent distrustful people living in common law unions, as well as in dysfunctional, female-centered authoritarian families who are chronically unemployed and rarely participate in local civic activities, vote or trust the police and political leaders" (Foley, 1997, p. 115). In 1974, Nobel Prize winner and eugenicist, William Shockley (1910–1989), famously stated: "My research leads me inescapably to the opinion that the major cause of the American Negro's intellectual and social deficits is hereditary and racially genetic in origin and, thus, not remediable to a major degree by practical improvements in the environment" (Episode S0145, Firing Line). Herrnstein and Murray (1994), relying on work by Arthur Jensen on genetics and intelligence, continued to make these eugenicist arguments in the book, *The Bell Curve*, in which they claim that Latino and black immigrants who perform poorly on IQ tests were contributing to a widespread lower intelligence across the United States (Giroux & Searls, 1996). Never mind that people who took the tests needed to follow test instructions and to read test questions in standard English gave a mighty and gratuitous advantage to non-immigrants and those with years of schooling in English (Fish, 2013). It is important to understand that those bilingual users were not necessarily slow readers. They make meaning and analyze multiple world systems, a practice that monolingual test takers could not even imagine. However, according to Giroux and Searls (1996), "when The *Bell Curve* appeared in 1994, few reviewers in the mainstream media denounced the text as a racist tract or, for that matter, even questioned its basic propositions regarding the measurability of intelligence, the causal relationship between intellectual ability and race, or the hereditarian justification of inequality" (p. 10). English-speaking hegemons surely felt a boost in power from what Bell Curve claimed about the role of learning standard English and showing intelligence on an IQ test conceived and written by monolinguals in standard English.

Pure and Perfect Language Ideologies

Pronouncements by eugenicists throughout the 20th century about the supposed inferiority of people of color and immigrants compared to white monolingual English speakers also served to inform language ideologies about purity and perfection. Racial and language purity go hand in hand. The purer the race, and the closer the race to some idealized form of Nordic, Germanic invention of race, the more intelligent. Ideologies of racial purity abound, as do ideologies about mixed, impure races (Bruinius, 2007). Purity and perfection in language are ideologies that show up in language education programs and the way certain people express their beliefs about language. "You speak perfect English." "You shouldn't mix languages." As Mexican poet and essayist Octavio Paz once famously responded to the question: What do you think about Spanglish? (Spanish words and expressions used along with English) "No es ni bueno, ni malo, sino abominable" [it isn't bad or good, it's abominable] (Stavans, 2003, p. 4). What Paz was supporting was the eugenics-based sterilization of mixed languaging practices.

Pure and perfect language ideologies have been around for centuries, but they gained steam in the mid- and late 20th century as increasing numbers of immigrants from Mexico moved north and began working in the fields and canneries in the Southwest. Hegemons began to build on the idea that there was a fundamental difference between whitestream standard English (pure and perfect) and all other ways of communicating in English (impure and imperfect), ways that were hegemonically positioned as incapable of expressing higher level thinking and, thus, to be successful in U. S. schools and society.

Language Hierarchies

Schatzman and Strauss (1955), indirecting drawing on eugenics-based language ideologies, were among the first white sociologists to assert that there was a distinct difference in the way members of the lower class and the middle class exchanged meaningful information. As they point out in their abstract of the article on social class and modes of communication,

> Differences in modes of communication, as revealed in interviews with lower- and middle-class respondents, are more than differences in intelligibility, grammar, and vocabulary. Differences are found in number and kinds of perspective, ability to take the listener's role, use of classifying or generalizing terms, and devices of style to order and implement communication. These differences in speech can be accounted for by differences in thinking and perceiving and in the respondent's relationship to the interviewer. (p. 329)

This sort of message played well into the hegemonic establishment's portrayal of whitestream members of Western culture in general as capable of languaging practices that rely on abstract, rational, and logical ways of organizing ideas and thoughts (Leacock, 1972), while people of color, immigrants, and indigenous people are concrete language users, incapable of higher level thinking and languaging. Their conclusions clearly align well with eugenics-based language ideologies.

The power of English used by educated whitestream speakers in the United States also received support from across the ocean, where British sociologist Basil Bernstein developed his verbal deficit hypothesis about the distinction between public and formal language use, which eventually termed "restricted" and "elaborated" codes, where codes mean ways of expressing, describing, and explaining ideas. Bernstein (1964), like Schatzman and Strauss (1955) before him, argued that

> ... restricted codes have their basis in condensed symbols, whereas elaborated codes have their basis in articulated symbols; ... restricted codes draw on metaphor, whereas elaborated codes draw on rationality; ... these codes constrain the contextual use of language in critical socialising contexts and in this way, they regulated the orders of relevance and relation which the socialized take over. (p. 200)

Bernstein contended that restricted code was used primarily among unskilled working-class families; middle-class educated families used both restricted and elaborated codes, leaning toward elaborated codes for schooling and business. According to Bernstein, the main function of restricted code was to express emotions and group solidarity; exchanging ideas and expressing more cognitive functions was secondary and difficult to obtain because, he maintained, restricted code does not rely on logical connectors. In restricted code, meanings are limited to the immediate context, and syntactic structures are highly predictable because they are likely to be "simple."

Likewise, speech in restricted code is marked by frequent use of pronouns, where it is assumed that interlocutors share knowledge of who is being discussed. Bernstein argues that elaborated code users, wishing to give direction to the rational organization of thinking, generate "accurate grammatical order and syntax" to regulate their thoughts; rely heavily on "logical modification" and "grammatically complex sentence construction, especially through the use of a range of conjunctions and subordinate clauses"; incorporate prepositions to "indicate logical relationships as well as to indicate temporal and spatial contiguity"; and select from a wide range of descriptive adjectives and modifying adverbs.

Bernstein (1964) argued that the primary difference between the speech of working-class and middle-class children was the scope of their language structure available to and used by the two groups. Because working-class children drew from a restricted code base, according to Bernstein, they were in a sense imprisoned by simple language structure and limited vocabulary, which ultimately meant that they would do poorly in school unless they reject their restricted code and become open to being taught how to use a more elaborated code in English. Middle-class children, capable of drawing on both restricted and elaborated codes, and especially able to access elaborated code in school settings, were deemed more likely to succeed in school and even excel in foreign language learning.

Nearly two decades after Bernstein's restricted and elaborated code entered the sociological discourse, Canadian educational psychologist Jim Cummins came on to the educational scene touting a "new" way of understanding language dimensions as these relate to successful schooling for bilingual children. Cummins (1980) was initially concerned with refuting the idea that children with special learning needs were failing on standardized tests because the tests were biased toward a certain kind of language style. He concluded that the tests used a language ability that was not accessible to special education children, who were relying on what he called *Basic Interpersonal Communication Skills* (BICS) Their BICS enabled them to participate in many school contexts, but it failed them when more cognitively demanding language was required for advancement in school settings. For language used in these more academic contexts, he argued that all students needed to have *Cognitive Academic Language Proficiency* (CALP). According to Cummins (1979), all children acquire BICS for face-to-face, here and now personal, interactions relatively quickly with little need for instruction. To gain CALP, however, children require a longer period of time and need to be supported by teachers or instructional-like interactions where children are socialized to use language that is highly decontextualized and cognitively more demanding. For both Bernstein (1964) and Cummins (1979), elaborated, decontextualized, rational, and cognitively demanding language is positioned as desirable and necessary for successfully schooling and higher level positions in society; basic communicative and highly contextualized language used in the here and now, for face-to-face interactions, restricts the opportunities for children to be successful in school and society.

Accordingly and increasingly, for many educators, CALP begins to stand for academic language (although Cummins [2021] argues that AL is different from CALP), and BICS as languaging sans higher order thinking. Pure and perfect language ideologies have embraced CALP as representative of what students need to develop: Cognitive uses of standard language. For them, the only way to achieve CALP is monolingually in a named academic language that has economic and political power for those who learn it well. Likewise, to be considered fully bilingual from this hegemonic perspective, children and youth who become bilingual would need to fully develop CALP in two separate named, academic languages, meaning they would also need to become fully biliterate in standard written academic languages (García & Solorza, 2021). There are scholars who have pushed back on the idea of academic language. For example, Bunch (2014) introduced the concept of the language of ideas and the language of display of ideas as a way to move teachers and educators away from conceptions of what counts as academic language (also see Bunch & Martin, 2021). But, as we learn in the next section, moving away from the idea of academic language will be difficult, because it is now associated with hegemonic ideas about language in academic contexts.

Silverstein (1996) claims that all schools in the United States operate within a "culture of the standard language," where the monolingual standard variety of language used in academic contexts resides at the highest level of purity and perfection because of its clarity and precision, and the multiple distinctions within ideas that speakers/writer can convey through its use. In this manner, speakers of local varieties of language, including dynamic bilingual languaging, are seen as having impoverished lexicons, grammars, and sound systems that can be confusing to audiences who are expecting and are accustomed to monolingual standard language varieties (Mena, 2022). Language users who fail to obey the monolingual, academic language rules of language are considered by hegemons and teachers alike to be incapable of communicating nuances of meaning and engaging in intelligible discourse with those who do use language with precision and clarity (Peregoy & Boyle, 2017).

Conjuring up the BICS and CALP distinction, Peregoy and Boyle (2017) write that "academic language differs from day-to-day conversation in terms of qualities, functions, and linguistic features at the word, phrase, and discourse levels" (p. 53). In this socially constructed contrast, there is an unstated assumption that academic language is related to social positioning, such that users of academic language belong to a higher social position and use words, phrases, and discourse styles that are appropriate for higher social levels of interaction, while the local varieties used by hoi polloi are deviant, impure, illegitimate, uncouth, and less complex and intelligible than academic language spoken in one language (also see Kramer-Dahl, 2003).

Who benefits from positioning academic language as the way to be successful in school and society? Who benefits from positioning academic language as being the only way to contrast pure and impure, cognitively superior, and socially imperfect languaging? As Gee (2004) points out, language is always involved and used for "civic, economic, and political purposes" (p. 63). As such, the power to portray language and how it is portrayed enables hegemons to socially stratify children and youth on the basis of the languaging practices they bring to school. Teachers across the United States are taught in teacher education programs that English learners and emergent bilingual language users arrive at school lacking academic language experiences in their homes. For example, Solomon and Rhodes proclaim:

> There is general agreement among educators and researchers that the distinct type of English used in classrooms, referred to as *academic language, is* a variable that often hinders the academic achievement of some language minority students, even though such students might be proficient in varieties of English used in non-academic contexts. (p. 1)

The hegemony of academic language that Solomon and Rhodes, among many others (Freeman & Freeman, 2009; Hyland, 2009; Peregoy & Boyle, 2017; Zwiers, 2009), rely on places the blame squarely on minoritized language users and purposefully ignores larger social contexts where language ideologies about language purity, language perfection, and language in academic contexts not only reify monolingual standard language use but also openly reject the languaging practices of non-English speakers and emergent, dynamic bilingual children and youth as being improper at best, and deviant and reflective of low intelligence at worst (Gándara & Contreras, 2020). Moreover, as García and Solorza (2021, p. 506) point out, "the construct of 'academic language' actively excludes the languaging practices of Latinx students, including those who are bilingual and English-speaking." In other words, academic language serves as an instrument of eugenics-based language ideologies to effectively sterilize their languaging practices, as unacceptable for learning and use in academic contexts, including dual language programs.

Bilingual Teacher Education and Language Hegemony

Last, but not least, it is important to understand the role of bilingual and dual language teacher education in the promotion and use of hegemonic language ideologies and hierarchies for preparing bilingual and dual language teachers.

Teachers and teacher educators have been socialized in an educational system that imagines language as a system that must be logical and rational, correct, and, most importantly, un-mixed (Silverstein, 1996). Following this imagined view of language, the ways languages are taught to teacher candidates in bilingual and dual language programs typically adhere to "appropriate" ways of talking and being in academic contexts (Flores & Rosa, 2015). For English, this means standard language that looks and sounds white, as described above. For Spanish, this most often means the language of "something else and something other than the language spoken in the everyday lives" of bilingual families and children (Mena, 2022, p. 80). Accordingly, Spanish, too, like English, needs to be standard, monolingual, and pure, the kind spoken in countries other than the United States to be considered legitimate. Bilingual speakers of Spanish and English must strive to have perfect language practices. Bilingual Spanish used in the local communities throughout the United States is downplayed as deficient, full of errors, imperfect, and impure (Achugar & Pessoa, 2009; de los Ríos & Seltzer, 2017). Teacher educators and teachers who promote this friendlier form of "linguistic terrorism" (Mena, 2022), however, are right in line with hegemonic language ideologies that insist upon pure and logical academic language, and especially that teacher candidates must learn and use standard English and Spanish.

Final Thoughts

What can be done to counter these narratives that terrorize bilingual children and families, and promote separate, monolingual language practices that benefit non-bilingual children and families? As we have learned, school children who come from homes believed to use and promote academic language are considered to be intelligent and teachable, and capable of learning pure and perfect language. Children who begin school with non-academic varieties who have acquired either their home language or who enter school with their home language and some English, in contrast, are often termed at-risk and in need of language sterilization. In my view, it matters little that these students are in dual language programs; the risks are the same. From a language hegemonic perspective and without ideological clarity (Alfaro & Bartolomé, 2017; Cervantes-Soon et al., 2017), dual language teachers who are forced to teach only in a standard variety of the classroom language may also be expected to be constantly vigilant for any language deviations, any Anglicized use of words and expressions, and non-standard terms that could corrupt the standard Spanish development of the youth white children who are becoming bilingual through a separate monolingual approach to "true bilingualism."

When dual language programs insist upon separate monolingual language use, they are not only obeying the hegemonic language ideologies about language purity, language perfection, and academic language, they are enhancing the hegemonic power of English and the Spanish of elsewhere and attempting to erase the languaging practices of vibrant bilingual users. While this may be a friendlier practice of language erasure than earlier forms of linguistic terrorism, it harms bilingual children, their self-esteem, and identities as Spanish and English speakers.

If dual language programs are ever to be supportive of emergent bilingualism and translanguaging as it is used in bilingual communities (García, 2019; García & Solorza, 2021), they cannot and should not ever appeal to language hegemonies of pure, perfect, and eugenics-based ideologies of language. These are highly detrimental to bilingual children and communities; they serve to keep English as the dominant language of the United States, while more than one-third of the U.S. population is bilingual and more than two-thirds of the world's communities are bi/multilingual and biliterate. In short, dual language education programs that mirror hegemonic language practices are unfit for emergent bilingual communities. Dual language bilingual biliterate programs need to be built on the languaging practices of bilingual communities that enable children and youth to sustain these languaging practices and build new literacies in the increasingly bi/multilingual world. We in the fields of bilingual and dual language education must push back on the monoglossic, separate language ideologies, and work to change dual language programs so that (1) bilingual children are enrolled, and (2) that their languaging practices of vibrant bilingualism are held up as examples of what bilingualism and biliteracy can and should become.

One approach to achieving this change in focus toward bilingual children and communities is taking a critical bilingual literacies stance (España & Herrera, 2020) to "recenter bilingual Latinx students' knowledge and ways of being" (p. 17) around the Three Ts: topics – culturally and linguistically sustaining topics and themes (Paris, 2012); texts – reading and writing materials that affirm children's identities and languaging practices; and translanguaging – creating spaces for students to use all of their languaging repertoires for learning (Herrera, 2022, p. 179). According to Herrera (2022), teacher candidates working in a dual language program began to reflect on their own invisibility when they were students. The teacher candidates also worked to unpack their own experiences and thoughts about language in order to eventually begin to embrace vibrant bilingualism and develop a strong translanguaging stance and to celebrate their students' bilingualism and the bilingualism of the community (Herrera & España, 2022).

There are myriad ways of countering the hegemony of English and (of Spanish-elsewhere), and it is up to us as scholars, social justice advocates, and bilingual and dual language educators to bring change to our schools and our teacher education programs so that our commitments in practice honor our students' cultural and languaging practices. It is up to us as educational leaders to move toward educational dignity (Valdés, 2022).

Notes

1 According to Luis Urrieta (2009), a whitestream curriculum refers to the practice in the United States that positions students of color as having to endure systematic discrimination and trauma in an educational system that was not built to serve them, to recognize their value to society, and to nurture their identities. He uses whitestream rather than mainstream to specifically point out that school practices, school curricula, and the majority of teachers are from and support white, monolingual English-speaking backgrounds. Also see Freire et al. (2022).

2 Currently, under the direction of Texas Governor Greg Abbott (R), it is prohibited to discuss this case of racial and language discrimination in Texas public schools. Abbot is presently trying to overturn Plyler v. Doe (1982) to prohibit children of undocumented immigrant parents from attending public schools.

References

Achugar, M., & Pessoa, S. (2009). Power and place: Language attitudes towards Spanish in a bilingual academic community in Southwest Texas. *Spanish in Context*, *6*(2), 199–223.

Alfaro, C., & Bartolomé, L. (2017). Preparing ideologically clear bilingual teachers: Honoring working-class non-standard language use in the bilingual education classroom. *Issues in Teacher Education*, 26(2), 11–34.

Anderson, B. (1983). *Imagined communities: Reflections on the origins and spread of nationalism*. New Left Books.

August, D., & Shanahan, T. (2017). *Developing literacy in second-language learners: Report of the national literacy panel on language-minority children and youth*. Routledge.

Bates, T. R. (1974). Antonio Gramsci and the Soviet experiment in Italy. *Societas*, *4*(1), 37–54.

Baugh, J. (1999). *Out of the mouths of slaves: African American language and educational malpractice*. University of Texas Press.

Bernstein, B. (1964). Elaborated and restricted codes: Their social origins and some consequences. *American Anthropologist*, *66*(6), 55–69.

Blackledge, A. (2000). Monolingual ideologies in multilingual states: Language, hegemony and social justice in Western liberal democracies. *Estudios de sociolingüística*, *1*(2), 25–45.

Bonfiglio, T. (2002). *Race and the rise of standard American*. Mouton de Gruyter.

Bruinius, H. (2007). *Better for all the world: The secret history of forced sterilization and America's quest for racial purity*. Vintage.

Bunch, G. C. (2014). The language of ideas and the language of display: Reconceptualizing "academic language" in linguistically diverse classrooms. *International Multilingual Research Journal*, *8*(1), 70–86.

Bunch, G. C., & Martin, D. (2021). From "academic language" to the "language of ideas": A disciplinary perspective on using language in K-12 settings. *Language and Education*, *35*(6), 539–556.

Canagarajah, S. (2013). Theorizing a competence for translingual practice at the contact zone. In S. May (Ed.), *The multilingual turn* (pp. 88–112). Routledge.

Cervantes-Soon, C. G., Dorner, L., Palmer, D., Heiman, D., Schwerdtfeger, R., & Choi, J. (2017). Combating inequalities in two-way language immersion programs: Toward critical consciousness in bilingual education spaces. *Review of Research in Education*, *41*(1), 403–427.

Cummins, J. (1979). Cognitive/academic language proficiency, linguistic interdependence, the optimum age question and some other matters. *Working papers on Bilingualism, no. 19.*

Cummins, J. (1980). The entry and exit fallacy in bilingual education. *NABE Journal*, *4*, 25–60.

Cummins, J. (2021). *Rethinking the education of multilingual learners: A critical analysis of theoretical concepts*. Multilingual Matters.

de Jong, E. (2016). Two-way immersion for the next generation: Models, policies, and principles. *International Multilingual Research Journal*, *10*(1), 6–16.

de Jong, E., & Howard, E. (2009). Integration in two-way immersion education: Equalising linguistic benefits for all students. *International Journal of Bilingual Education and Bilingualism*, *12*(1), 81–99.

de los Ríos, C. V., & Seltzer, K. (2017). Translanguaging, coloniality, and English classrooms: An exploration of two bicoastal urban classrooms. *Research in the Teaching of English*, *52*(1) 55–76.

Del Castillo, R. G. (1992). *The Treaty of Guadalupe Hidalgo: A legacy of conflict*. University of Oklahoma Press.

Dorner, L. M., Cervantes-Soon, C. G., Heiman, D., & Palmer, D. (2021). "Now it's all upper-class parents who are checking out schools": Gentrification as coloniality in the enactment of two-way bilingual education policies. *Language Policy*, *20*(3), 1–27.

España, C., & Herrera, L. Y. (2020). *En comunidad: Lessons for centering the voices and experiences of bilingual Latinx students*. Heinemann.

Estes, N. (2019). The U.S. stole generations of indigenous children to open the west. *High Country News*. October 14, 2019.

Faltis, C. (2022). Understanding and resisting perfect language and eugenics-based language ideologies in bilingual teacher education. In J. MacSwan (Ed.), *Multilingual perspectives on translanguaging* (pp. 321–342). Multilingual Matters, Ltd.

Faltis, C., & Hudelson, S. (1998). *Bilingual education in elementary and secondary school communities: Toward understanding and caring*. Pearson College Division.

Fillmore, L. W. (1991). When learning a second language means losing the first. *Early Childhood Research Quarterly*, *6*(3), 323–346.

Fish, J. M. (2013). *Race and intelligence: Separating science from myth*. Routledge.

Flores, N., & García, O. (2017). A critical review of bilingual education in the United States: From basements and pride to boutiques and profit. *Annual Review of Applied Linguistics*, *37*, 14–29.

Flores, N., & Rosa, J. (2015). Undoing appropriateness: Raciolinguistic ideologies and language diversity in education. *Harvard Educational Review*, *85*(2), 149–171.

Foley, D. E. (1997). Deficit thinking models based on culture: The anthropological protest. In R. Valencia (Ed.), *The evolution of deficit thinking: Educational thought and practice* (pp. 113–131). Routledge.

Freeman, Y. S., & Freeman, D. E. (2009). *Academic language for English language learners and struggling readers: How to help students succeed across content areas*. Heinemann.

Freire, J. A., & Delavan, M. G. (2021). The fiftyfication of dual language education: One-size-fits-all language allocation's "equality" and "practicality" eclipsing a history of equity. *Language Policy*, *20*(3), 1–31.

Freire, J. A., Gambrell, J., Kasun, G. S., Dorner, L. M., & Cervantes-Soon, C. (2022). The expropriation of dual language bilingual education: Deconstructing neoliberalism, whitestreaming, and English-hegemony. *International Multilingual Research Journal*, *16*(1), 1–20.

Freire, J. A., Valdez, V. E., & Delavan, M. G. (2017). The (dis) inclusion of Latina/o interests from Utah's dual language education boom. *Journal of Latinos and Education, 16*(4), 276–289.

Gándara, P., & Contreras, F. (2020). *The Latino education crisis*. Harvard University Press.

García, O. (2019). Translanguaging: A coda to the code? *Classroom Discourse, 10*(3–4), 369–373.

García, O., & Solorza, C. (2021). Academic language and the minoritization of U.S. bilingual Latinx students. *Language and Education, 35*(6), 1–17.

García, O., & Wei, L. (2014). *Translanguaging: Language, bilingualism, and education*. Palgrave Pivot.

Gee, J. P. (2004). *An introduction to discourse analysis: Theory and method*. Routledge.

Giroux, H. A., & Searls, S. (1996). Race talk and "The Bell Curve" debate: The crisis of democratic vision. *Cultural Critique, Autumn*(34), 5–26.

Gómez, L., Freeman, D., & Freeman, Y. (2005). Dual language education: A promising 50–50 model. *Bilingual Research Journal, 29*(1), 145–164.

Herrera, L. Y. (2022). Growing critical bilingual literacies in a bilingual teacher residency program. *Journal of Language, Identity & Education, 21*(3), 174–190.

Herrera, L. Y., & España, C. (2022). Se hace camino al andar: Translanguaging pedagogy for justice. *English Journal, 111*(5), 27–34.

Herrnstein, R. J., & Murray, C. (1994). The bell curve. *Library Quarterly, 66*(1), 89–91.

Hyland, K. (2009). *Academic discourse: English in a global context*. Continuum.

Jensen, A. (1968). Social class, race, and genetics: Implications for education. *American Educational Research Journal, 5*(1), 1–42.

Kramer-Dahl, A. (2003). Reading the "Singlish Debate": Construction of a crisis of language standards and language teaching in Singapore. *Journal of Language, Identity & Education, 2*(3), 159–190.

Lambert, W. E. (1974). Culture and language as factors in learning and education. In F. E. Abour, & R. D. Meade (Eds.), *Cultural factors in learning and education* (pp. 91–122). Bellington, Washington; 5th Western Washington Symposium on Learning.

Landry, R., Allard, R., & Théberge, R. (1991). School and family French ambiance and the bilingual development of Francophone Western Canadians. *Canadian Modern Language Review, 47*(5), 878–915.

Leacock, E. (1972). Abstract versus concrete speech: A false dichotomy. In C. Cazden, V. John, & D. Hymes (Eds.), *Functions of language in the classroom* (pp. 111–134). Teachers College Press.

Lewis, O. (1966). The culture of poverty. *Scientific American, 215*(4), 19–25.

Lippi-Green, R. (2012). *English with an accent: Language, ideology, and discrimination in the United States*. Routledge.

Macedo, D., Dendrinos, B., & Gounari, P. (2015). *The hegemony of English*. Paradigm Publishers.

Mena, M. (2022). The language-elsewhere: A friendlier linguistic terrorism. In J. Cobas, B. Urciuoli, J. Feafin, & D. Delgado (Eds.), *The Spanish language in the United States: Rootedness, racialization, and resistance* (pp. 80–95). Routledge.

Mosby, I., & Millions, E. (August 1, 2021). Canada's residential schools were a horror. *Scientific American*. https://www.scientificamerican.com/article/canadas-residential-schools-were-a-horror/

Nieto, D. G. (2021). Making it official: The institutionalization of the hegemony of English in the US. *Education Policy Analysis Archives*, *29*(96), 96–103.

Ovando, C. J. (2003). Bilingual education in the United States: Historical development and current issues. *Bilingual Research Journal*, *27*(1), 1–24.

Palmer, D. (2010). Race, power, and equity in a multiethnic urban elementary school with a dual-language "strand" program. *Anthropology & Education Quarterly*, *41*, 94–114.

Paris, D. (2012). Culturally sustaining pedagogy: A needed change in stance, terminology, and practice. *Educational Researcher*, *41*(3), 93–97.

Pennycook, A. (2017). Translanguaging and semiotic assemblages. *International Journal of Multilingualism*, *14*(3), 269–282.

Peregoy, S., & Boyle, O. (2017). *Reading, writing, and learning in ESL* (7th ed.). Pearson.

Romero-Little, M. E., McCarty, T. L., Warhol, L., & Zepeda, O. (2007). Language policies in practice: Preliminary findings from a large-scale national study of Native American language shift. *TESOL Quarterly*, *41*(3), 607–618.

San Miguel, G. (1983). The struggle against separate and unequal schools: Middle class Mexican Americans and the desegregation campaign in Texas, 1929–1957. *History of Education Quarterly*, *23*(3), 343–359.

Sánchez, M. T., García, O., & Solorza, C. (2018). Reframing language allocation policy in dual language bilingual education. *Bilingual Research Journal*, *41*(1), 37–51.

Schatzman, L., & Strauss, A. (1955). Social class and modes of communication. *American Journal of Sociology*, *60*(4), 329–338.

Silverstein, M. (1996). Monoglot "standard" in America. In D. Brenneis, & R. Macaulay (Eds.), *The matrix of language: Contemporary linguistic anthropology* (pp. 284–306). Westview.

Stavans, I. (2003). *Spanglish: The making of a new American language*. HarperCollins.

Urrieta, L. Jr. (2009). *Working from within: Chicana and Chicano activist educators in whitestream schools*. University of Arizona Press.

Valdés, G. (1997). Dual-language immersion programs: A cautionary note concerning the education of language-minority students. *Harvard Educational Review*, *67*(3), 391–430.

Valdés, G. (2015). What is bilingualism/multilingualism? In G. Valdés, K. Menken, & M. Castro (Eds.), *Common core bilingual and English language learners: A resource book for educators* (pp. 38–39). Caslon Publishing.

Valdés, G. (2022). Towards educational dignity: Translanguaging y la preparación de maestros. *Journal of Language, Identity & Education*, *21*(3), 212–216.

Valdez, V. E., Freire, J. A., & Delavan, M. G. (2016). The gentrification of dual language education. *The Urban Review*, *48*(4), 601–627.

Valencia, R. (1997). Genetic pathology model of deficit thinking. In R. Valencia (Ed.), *The evolution of deficit thinking* (pp. 41–112). Routledge Farmer.

Voicu, A. (2020). Killing the culture in the child: The contradictory intentions and effects of Native residential schools. *Essays in Development Studies*, *25*, 25–33.

Zwiers, J. (2009). *Building academic language: Essential practices for content classrooms*. Jossey-Bass.

30
DISCOURSES IN DUAL LANGUAGE BILINGUAL EDUCATION

Noah Katznelson, Katie A. Bernstein, Kathryn I. Henderson

Introduction

Gentrification, commodification, instrumentalization. Enrichment, appropriateness, languagelessness. Equity, identity, justice. In this chapter, we aim to help readers make sense of the many discourses described by language scholars to talk, write, and think about dual language bilingual education (DLBE) in the United States. We argue that these discourses are not infinite but instead cluster into discourse families: groups of discourses that draw on similar underlying logic regarding bilingualism, multilingualism, and diverse languaging practices. In Part 1 of the chapter, we develop a historically situated model of DLBE discourses. We use this model (Figure 30.1) to explain how discourses relate to each other in patterned ways and how they emerge from the larger social, political, and historical context in which they are situated. In Part 2, we use our model to map the current U.S. landscape of DLBE discourses (Figure 30.2). We conclude by suggesting what we see as a way forward—toward a humanizing DLBE that centers multilingual students and values diverse languaging practices.

Part 1: Situating Discourses of DLBE Historically

Why Do Discourses Matter?

We define discourses as culturally held, socially constructed ways of understanding the world. Discourses shape what is thinkable, knowable, and sayable, providing what Foucault (1970) called a "grid of intelligibility," or a way to organize and analyze what we see as reality. Foucault used the term *episteme*, from the Greek word for "knowledge," to name a time period in

 DOI: 10.4324/9781003269076-43

RESOURCE
English
Nationalist Episteme
Languages other than English
Linguistic Right to Civic Participation
PROBLEM
RIGHT
RESOURCE
Whitewashed Multilingualism
Neoliberal Episteme
Racialized Language Varieties/Practices
Linguistic Right to Equity & Identity
PROBLEM
RIGHT

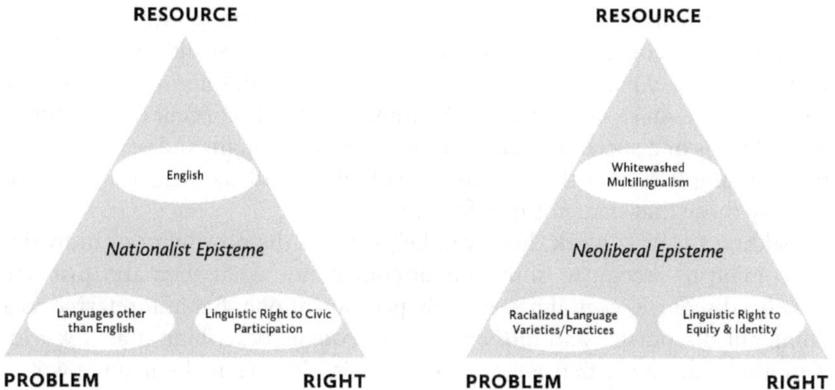

Figure 30.1 Language Orientations Across Epistemes

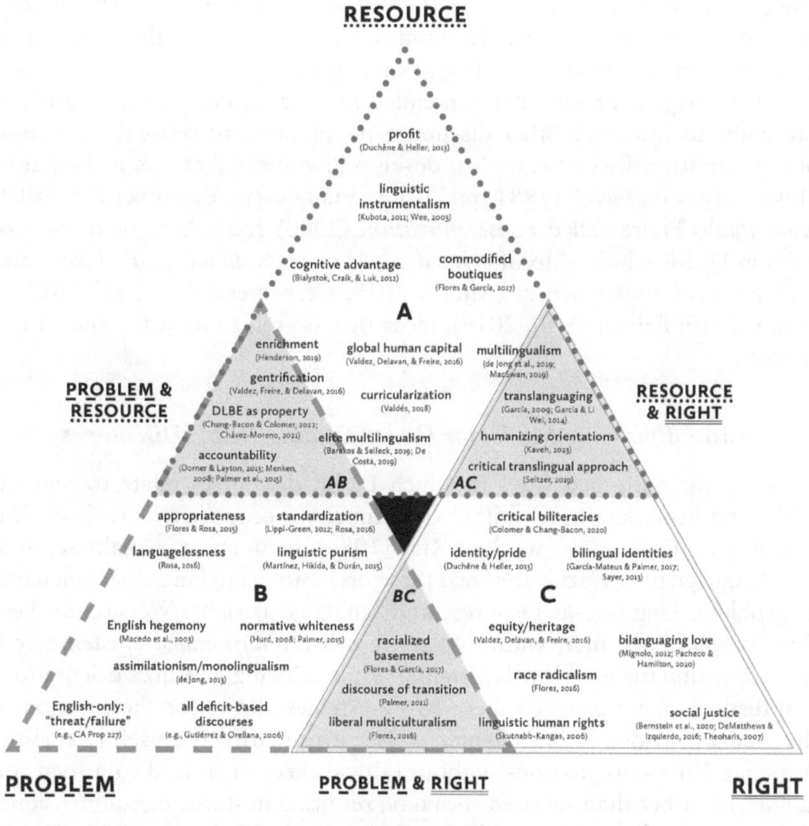

RESOURCE
profit
(Duchêne & Heller, 2013)
linguistic instrumentalism
(Kubota, 2011; Wee, 2003)
cognitive advantage
(Bialystok, Craik, & Luk, 2012)
commodified boutiques
(Flores & García, 2017)
A
enrichment
(Henderson, 2019)
global human capital
(Valdez, Delavan, & Freire, 2016)
multilingualism
(de Jong et al., 2019; MacSwan, 2019)
gentrification
(Valdez, Freire, & Delavan, 2016)
curricularization
(Valdés, 2018)
translanguaging
(García, 2009; García & Li Wei, 2014)
PROBLEM & RESOURCE
DLBE as property
(Chang-Bacon & Colomer, 2022; Chávez-Moreno, 2021)
elite multilingualism
(Barakos & Selleck, 2019; De Costa, 2019)
humanizing orientations
(Kaveh, 2023)
RESOURCE & RIGHT
accountability
(Dorner & Layton, 2013; Menken, 2008; Palmer et al., 2015)
critical translingual approach
(Seltzer, 2019)
AB
AC
appropriateness
(Flores & Rosa, 2015)
standardization
(Lippi-Green, 2012; Rosa, 2016)
critical biliteracies
(Colomer & Chang-Bacon, 2020)
languagelessness
(Rosa, 2016)
linguistic purism
(Martínez, Hikida, & Durán, 2015)
identity/pride
(Duchêne & Heller, 2013)
bilingual identities
(García-Mateus & Palmer, 2017; Sayer, 2013)
B
BC
C
English hegemony
(Macedo et al., 2003)
normative whiteness
(Hurd, 2008; Palmer, 2015)
racialized basements
(Flores & García, 2017)
equity/heritage
(Valdez, Delavan, & Freire, 2016)
bilanguaging love
(Mignolo, 2012; Pacheco & Hamilton, 2020)
assimilationism/monolingualism
(de Jong, 2013)
discourse of transition
(Palmer, 2011)
race radicalism
(Flores, 2016)
English-only: "threat/failure"
(e.g., CA Prop 227)
all deficit-based discourses
(e.g., Gutiérrez & Orellana, 2006)
liberal multiculturalism
(Flores, 2016)
linguistic human rights
(Skutnabb-Kangas, 2006)
social justice
(Bernstein et al., 2020; DeMatthews & Izquierdo, 2016; Theoharis, 2007)
PROBLEM
PROBLEM & RIGHT
RIGHT

Figure 30.2 Landscape of Current DLBE Discourses

which a particular order of discourse functions to organize meaning. Epistemes and the discourses that characterize them can be difficult for those living within them to think outside of. In this sense, Foucault's notions of episteme and discourse share similarities with Gramsci's (1971) concept of hegemony: a set of ideas or a social organization that are so dominant and pervasive that they are simply seen as the natural state of affairs and, as such, are sustained even by those that may not benefit from them.

Bakhtin's (1981) work, however, helps us see the possibility of individuals coming to recognize dominant discourses for what they are: just one *possible* discourse, even if a seemingly permanent one. Bakhtin referred to a dominant discourse as an *authoritative discourse*, describing it as a worldview that "demands that we acknowledge it, that we make it our own … we encounter it with its authority already fused to it" (p. 342). As such, authoritative discourses function in service of existing (i.e., unequal) power relations. For example, colonial discourses construct notions like *Whiteness* (Harris, 1995) which then function as a form of property, serving those in power by denying access to others (Leonardo & Broderick, 2011). Authoritative discourses are so pervasive (and seductive) that even those they marginalize often perpetuate them (e.g., skin lightening).

Yet, through a process Bakhtin called *ideological becoming*, individuals can come to recognize other discursive possibilities, to resist the demands of authoritative discourse, and to develop discourses that are, as he put it, "internally persuasive" (1981, p. 354). In many ways, this process parallels what Paolo Freire called *conscientization* (2000) and relates to recent notions in DLBE scholarship of *critical consciousness, ideological clarity*, and *sociopolitical consciousness* (Alfaro, 2019; Cervantes-Soon et al., 2017; J. Freire, 2020; Palmer et al., 2019), ideas that we return to at the end of this chapter.

Cross-Epistemic Model for Understanding DLBE Discourses

To show the patterned ways in which DLBE discourses relate to one another and how they have shifted over time, we propose a cross-historical model that draws on the work of Ruiz (1984). In an effort to make sense of U.S. language policy, Ruiz outlined three orientations to language: language-as-problem, language-as-resource, and language-as-right. We situate these three orientations, first, within what we call the *nationalist episteme* and, second, within the *neoliberal episteme*. While drawing on Ruiz's orientations and distinguishing between these two epistemes allows for the creation of the model provided in this chapter, we see it primarily as a useful heuristic. Applying Ruiz's orientations without critical theory can lead to a focus on languages rather than situated speakers, resulting in static, one-dimensional (mis)understandings of complex and intersectional languaging practices

(Kaveh, 2023). Furthermore, some have argued—and we agree—that the nationalist and neoliberal eras are, in fact, two manifestations of the larger colonial project of accumulation through dispossession predicated upon a constructed racial hierarchy (e.g., Mignolo, 2012). As we demonstrate throughout this chapter, the colonial logic of dispossession and racialization underlies both epistemes.

The Nationalist Episteme

Ruiz (1984) wrote his foundational article on language orientations in the early 1980s at the end of two centuries of U.S. nation-building that relied on the creation of several national myths: the melting pot (Heike, 2014); the American Dream (and meritocracy); the social construction of race (to justify slavery) and citizenship based on evolving constructs of Whiteness (King, 2000; Skiba, 2012); and manifest destiny (to justify Westward expansion and colonization of Native inhabitants; e.g., Horsman, 1981). Schools played a central role in the national project (Mondale & Patton, 2001) through assimilationist approaches ranging from the Americanization movement (Galindo, 2011; King, 2000) to English language education in its various forms, all serving the maintenance of White Anglo dominance. A defining feature of what we call the *nationalist episteme* is the hegemonic ideology known as "one state, one nation, one language" (May, 2012) which, in the United States, manifested in the construction of English as *the* national language (albeit unofficially). It was within this nationalist episteme that Ruiz identified and named his three orientations. He saw the first orientation, language-as-problem, as the dominant one. In this orientation, languages other than English were framed as problematic barriers to success, both for individuals (e.g., leading to poverty and low educational achievement) and for the nation (e.g., interfering with national security and social cohesion). The dominant societal solution to these problems—the way to build a strong, unified (i.e., monolingual) nation—was linguistic and cultural assimilation.

Ruiz called his second orientation *language-as-right*, describing it as emerging in direct response to the language-as-problem orientation. In a language-as-right orientation, language was framed as a civil right, guaranteeing: (1) language access (e.g., to voting materials, legal proceedings, and education) and (2) protection from language discrimination, through the U.S. legal system's notion of "protected classes." It was this orientation that helped to secure rights to bilingual education (e.g., the Bilingual Education Act, 1968; Lau v. Nichols, 1974).

Ruiz, a strong advocate of bilingual education, not only rejected language-as-problem discourses as inherently problematic but also saw language-as-right discourses as too contentious/litigious. Instead, he proposed a third orientation, *language-as-resource*, that shifted from viewing English as the resource to viewing multilingualism (English plus other languages) as a resource, benefiting the economy and national security, and leading to greater understanding across ethnic groups.

The Neoliberal Episteme

In the early 1980s, however, Ruiz could not have foreseen the epistemic shift that was beginning: a shift toward understanding everything, including language, through the lens of the market. Reagan was beginning the first years of his presidency, ushering in policies of privatization and free market economics that were already underway in other parts of the world (e.g., the UK and Chile). In subsequent decades, these economic shifts became social and even epistemic shifts, as domains formerly understood to be separate from business (e.g., medicine, education, and religion) came to be understood in market terms, and increasingly, not in any others (Harvey, 2005; Martín Rojo & Del Percio, 2019). Although the nationalist era in the United States always had economic (i.e., capitalist) foundations, what has changed in the current episteme is that neoliberal logic has become not just the form of capitalism that governs our economic system, but the lens through which we understand the whole of our social world. In education, for example, school choice policies—policies that permit parents to choose between their child's assigned public school, charter schools, other public schools, and, in some states, private schools through vouchers or education accounts—are purported to improve education overall by introducing competition into the school landscape (Ball, 2017) and to give parents the right to find the best educational product for their child. Yet simultaneously, this logic places the responsibility for a child's success on individual parents' choices, rather than on systems (Apple, 2006). In neoliberal logic, a person's success or failure cannot be attributed to structures, but to individuals, who must make good choices and acquire skills to be competitive (Martín Rojo & Del Percio, 2019).

We argue that, with this epistemic shift, what gets categorized as "problem," "right," and "resource" in language policy and language education has shifted as well (compare triangles in Figure 30.1). First, as noted by Ricento (2005) and Petrovic (2005), multilingualism—made up of discrete, school taught, and standardized languages—has become a resource to help individuals, corporations, or even nations compete. This new language-as-resource discourse relies on seeing language as a decontextualized instrument: "as commodity, displaced from its historical situatedness, a tool to be developed for particular national interests" (Ricento, 2005, p. 357). These discourses thus necessitate a de-coupling of languages from ethnic or cultural groups, thereby ignoring language as an identity marker. In DLBE, this de-coupling and unmarking is a double-edged sword. On one hand, it has promoted the expansion of DLBE programs by making learning languages like Spanish attractive to White, middle-class families looking for distinction in a globalized economy. Yet, it also serves to erase the cultural, historical, and political connections that are most salient and meaningful for language-minoritized students. For these reasons, we refer to the neoliberal version of multilingualism as *whitewashed* multilingualism. Whitewashing, or the erasure of racialized identities from multilingualism, creates an a-historical, sociolinguistically inaccurate representation of language and the people who use it. Like other forms of whitewashing, it serves dominant interests.

With this shift in the language-as-resource orientation, what constitutes language-as-problem has shifted as well. Because whitewashed multilingualism has become a resource that benefits those in power, "whole" languages themselves can no longer be problems. Instead, certain varieties—that is, "non-standard" or racialized varieties—have become problems to be remediated or fixed. Here, we see the way whitewashed multilingualism functions as a form of property (Chávez-Moreno, 2021). In order to reserve the benefits of multilingualism for dominant groups, another discourse is invoked to make certain (i.e., racialized) language varieties or practices problematic. Once again, the problem discourse acts as a powerful gatekeeper.

Finally, in response to the whitewashing of multilingualism and the problematizing of racialized language practices, the third orientation—language-as-right—has also shifted. Instead of arguing for the legal right to use/learn their home languages, speakers with familial and cultural ties to language argue for the right to equity and identity through the legitimization of their language practices.

Part 2: Mapping the Landscape of DLBE Discourses

We now use this model of language orientations within the neoliberal episteme (right triangle in Figure 30.1) to map the discursive landscape of current DLBE scholarship in the United States. We do this through a literature review of major ideas in DLBE research, situating them within—and at the intersections of—the three orientations, or as we see them, discourse families. In doing so, we illustrate how, within each discursive family, the authors draw on (or critique) similar underlying logic.

To give an example of how the three discourse families—and the intersections between them—can be used to make sense of DLBE discourses, take the "discourse of transition" (as in transitional bilingual education [TBE]; Palmer, 2011). The discourse of transition is rooted in the nationalist episteme and continues today, drawing on the idea that other languages are problems and that bilingual children should transition to English-only education as soon as they can. But the discourse of transition also draws on language-as-right discourses, as TBE exists because legal decisions such as

Lau v. Nichols (1974) have said that U.S. children have the right to access education, even before they speak English. This is not to say that all schools and teachers that implement TBE draw on Problem and Right discourses (see Palmer, 2011). Yet, if schools and teachers adopt TBE uncritically, they might understand TBE and their students' languages through the lenses of TBE policy: at the intersection of nationalist-era language-as-right but also language-as-problem discourses.

In Figure 30.2 and in the sections that follow, we use the analytic approach illustrated above to review current DLBE discourses. We note that just because these discourses co-exist within the neoliberal episteme, not all of them are neoliberal. Some, like the example we just provided (discourse of transition), are vestiges of the nationalist era still in circulation today (e.g., English hegemony, linguistic purism, and standardization); others are a reaction to and a move away from neoliberal discourse (e.g., equity/heritage and identity/pride). But as Bakhtin (1981) explained, the power of an authoritative (i.e., dominant) discourse is that all other discourses—even those that reject the authoritative discourse—are still forced to respond to it. We therefore begin our review with the current discourse that all other discourses must answer to: language-as-economic-resource.

Language as (Economic) Resource Discourses

In the neoliberal episteme, the underlying logic of the language-as-resource discourse family is that languages (other than English, but always in addition to English) are economic resources that can give a person, business, or nation a competitive edge. In this logic, languages are not associated with any particular group of speakers and are detached from any cultural, historical, familial, or political connections—what we have termed *whitewashed* multilingualism. Languages can therefore be acquired by anyone as a value-added skill. These ideas are central to what Wee (2003) and Kubota (2011) name the discourse of *linguistic instrumentalism*, in which language is viewed as a tool whose value comes primarily (or even exclusively) from the "specific utilitarian goals" it permits a speaker to achieve.[1] The logic of language as an economic tool also undergirds what Valdez et al. (2016) name *global human capital* discourse, in which language serves to help produce better and more competitive workers in the global economy. Importantly, Valdez et al. point to how global human capital discourse serves to make programs like DLBE not just palatable, but marketable to the White speaking subject (Flores & Rosa, 2015). Similarly, Duchêne and Heller's (2013) *language-as-profit* discourse (which they contrast with a *language-as-pride* discourse) draws on this logic, describing a shift toward seeing language as one of many sources of economic opportunity that a person might pursue (rather than a unique and important marker of identity).

Mena and García's (2021) concept of *converse racialization* helps to explain that shift, drawing on the language-as-resource logic of de-coupling language from a community of speakers. Converse racialization theorizes a process by which associations of particular languages with particular races, established over the last two centuries in the United States, are broken, and languages become un-marked, or unassociated with any one set of societal indexes. Through converse racialization, a language like Spanish—formerly discursively linked in language-as-problem discourses to immigration, poverty, and deficiency—can become a form of capital to be accumulated (particularly by White speaking subjects). This process can also lead to discourses of *curricularization* (Valdés, 2018), a term coined to explain how instrumentalization and de-coupling play out in educational settings. Through curricularization, languages are understood and taught as academic skills and school subjects, rather than as meaning-making systems acquired in communities.

Writing about DLBE specifically, Valdez et al. (2016) bring together the logic of instrumentalization, curricularization, and the de-coupling of languages from speakers through their idea of the *gentrification of dual language education*. This discourse aptly evokes the tensions that accompany gentrification of a neighborhood and helps to explain changes seen across the United States to the purpose of DLBE—reflecting instrumental aims—along with the population served—from Latinx, Spanish speakers to White, English speakers. Gentrification discourses often have echos of discourses of *elitism* or *elite multilingualism* (Barakos & Selleck, 2019; De Costa, 2019; Freire & Alemán, 2021)—rooted in the nationalist episteme, but still relevant today—which place value on the multilingualism of an English speaker acquiring (optional) "world" languages through school, while not placing the same value on the multilingualism of a Spanish speaker acquiring (required) English.

Relatedly, in what Henderson (2019) has called *the enrichment narrative*, DLBE stakeholders uncritically position DLBE as gifted and talented programs. In this framing, DLBE can be seen as "too challenging" for certain students (i.e., students with disabilities or English learners who do not speak one of the program languages), who may therefore be discouraged from participating. Palmer and Henderson (2016) show this explicitly in their study of program placement decisions for emergent bilingual learners in Texas: students seen as academically advanced were selected for two-way DLBE programs, while students seen as "low" were placed in one-way programs. Research demonstrating the cognitive benefits of bilingualism (Bialystok et al., 2012) and the connected discourse of *cognitive advantage* in DLBE can similarly be adopted in problematic and exclusionary ways. These last discourses point to the ways in which language-as-resource discourses intersect with—and in some cases depend on—the next family of discourses: language-as-problem.

Language (Varieties/Practices) as Problem Discourses

The underlying logic of the language-as-problem discourse family—many members of which originated in the nationalist episteme—is that "non-standard" or racialized language varieties and practices are problems to be eradicated. As languages such as Spanish and Mandarin have undergone whitewashing and converse racialization (Mena & García, 2021) to become resources in an idealized "balanced" bilingualism in two standardized varieties, language-as-problem discourses mark other multilingual practices as problematic.

This logic is evident in discourses of *standardization* (Rosa, 2016) and *standard language ideologies* (Lippi-Green, 2012), in which practices such as translanguaging and varieties like Tex-Mex, Chicano English, Spanglish, and African American English are seen as illegitimate and their speakers are marked as deficient. Similar to earlier forms of racialized languages, like Spanish, Mandarin, or Japanese, and their indexical linking to poverty, laziness, or lack of intelligence, discourses of standardization draw on raciolinguistic ideologies to "conflate certain racialized bodies with linguistic deficiency unrelated to any objective linguistic practices" (Flores & Rosa, 2015, p. 150). Thus, if a White Spanish learner in a DLBE program blends languages in a similar way to a Latinx English learner, those practices will not be evaluated in the same way: the former student may be lauded for "making a real effort with Spanish"; the latter may be labeled as "struggling" with English. In DLBE, language-as-problem logic also manifests as what Martínez et al. (2015) call the discourse of *linguistic purism*, in which language separation is privileged over translanguaging practices, and teachers work to "protect" languages such as Spanish, by keeping English out of Spanish time (e.g., Hamman-Ortiz, 2019).

The language-as-problem logic of delegitimizing certain racialized varieties and practices also undergirds discourses of *languagelessness* (Rosa, 2016), *semilingualism* (Cummins, 1994), *alingualism* (Zentella, 2007), and "*non/non*"-ness (MacSwan, 2005), in which racialized bilingual or emergent bilingual students are viewed as being non-proficient in English and in (the standard variety of) their home language. In these discourses, the bilingualism (or double monolingualism [Flores, 2013; Heller, 1999] of English plus a school-variety of Spanish) of the White speaking subject is upheld as the most valuable bilingualism, while the practices indigenous to bilingual communities in the United States are marginalized, along with their speakers. As Cervantes-Soon (2014) notes:

> Speaking Spanish is only a valuable asset when using the standard variation *and* when English is one's dominant language. If [Latinx children] cannot demonstrate their full proficiency in the language legitimized

by school—whether it is English or standard Spanish—they might as well not speak at all. In this way, students' home languages, and consequently their voices and identities, remain relegated to the margins. (p. 74)

One way in which teachers relegate home language practices to the margins is through what Flores and Rosa (2015) call the discourse of *appropriateness* (see also Leeman, 2005). To avoid explicitly labeling certain varieties as problems, appropriateness discourse frames all language varieties as legitimate "for some contexts" (i.e., home; out of school) but frames the standardized variety (sometimes euphemized as "academic language") as the most "appropriate" for professional or academic contexts. This discourse depends on the myth that by acquiring legitimate language practices, speakers will gain legitimacy. Yet as Flores and Rosa (2015) argue, "the linguistic practices of language-minoritized populations [are viewed] as deviant based on their racial positioning in society as opposed to any objective characteristics of their language use" (p. 151).

This final point captures the slipperiness and deviousness of language-as-problem discourses: as language-as-resource discourses shift, turning formerly marginalized and racialized languages into whitewashed assets for those in power, language-as-problem discourses shift too, continuing to frame racialized speakers' language practices as deficient, no matter what those practices are. In this way, language-as-problem discourses are the other side of the language-as-resource coin: in order to frame certain practices as resources, it is necessary to frame other practices as *non*-resources. Thus, language-as-resource discourses, such as elite multilingualism and DLBE as enrichment, depend on language-as-problem discourses, such as standardization, for their logic to make sense. Indeed, it is the intersection of language-as-problem and language-as-resource discourses (see triangle *AB* in Figure 30.2) that have led scholars to posit *dual language as White property* (Chávez-Moreno, 2021) and *biliteracy as property* (Chang-Bacon & Colomer, 2022), with the voices, interests, and bilingualism of White students and families being valued over those of racialized students, including the Latinx students bilingual education was created to serve.

The intersection of language-as-problem and language-as-resource discourses has also served to systematically exclude speakers of Black English language varieties (Wall et al., 2022) and emergent bilingual students labeled as disabled from DLBE programs. Cioè-Peña (2017, 2020) outlined how separate policies and classes for language acquisition and special education frequently leave students with intersectional identities out of DLBE conversations and how parents of emergent bilingual students labeled as disabled are counseled out of DLBE programs. This tendency is amplified by the decades-long trend of overrepresentation of racialized students—particularly,

African American, Native American, and Latinx students—in special education (Kramarczuk Voulgarides et al., 2017) and underrepresentation in gifted and talented programs. This pattern introduces another possible intersection of language-as-resource and language-as-problem discourses: when DLBE programs are seen as a kind of gifted and talented program, existing biases for inclusion of racialized students in those programs are applied to DLBE. This process, which Morita-Mullaney and Chesnut (2022) aptly name *deselection*, is illustrated in a quote from a DLBE principal in Bernstein et al.'s (2020) study:

> We do consider [DLBE] an advanced learning opportunity. So it's kind of marketed that way. It's not for everybody. Not everybody can handle it. And we do have some kids unfortunately that start off in dual language, and we find out maybe they have language deficits or special learning disabilities that really make it challenging for them to do both. And so we do have to move them back to monolingual. (p. 672)

When school principals see DLBE as giving students an edge precisely because of its added challenge, it is easy to argue that not all students are up for that challenge and to exclude those whose language varieties or practices or abilities are seen as a problem.

Accountability discourses (abling/disabling discourses) (Cioè-Peña, 2017, 2020; Dorner & Layton, 2013) can also serve to exclude, by positioning students as "high" or "low" based on standardized assessment of monolingual competence in prestige varieties of English or Spanish (Palmer & Henderson, 2016). Accountability discourses—rooted in processes of standardization—can serve to oppress English learners (Menken, 2008) and derail DLBE program implementation (Palmer et al., 2016) based on incompatibility with pluralist discourses that promote bilingualism and biculturalism. In sum, while discourses at the intersection of language-as-resource and language-as-problem can have consequences for all students, they are particularly dangerous for students who are already marginalized within U.S. schools, like students of color, students with disabilities, and emergent bilingual students.

When language-as-problem discourses instead intersect with language-as-right discourses (see triangle *BC* in Figure 30.2), the results are more ambiguous. For instance, as discussed, the discourse of transition affords access and a right to bilingual education, while still framing language as a problem to be fixed (i.e., transitioned out of). In Flores and García (2017), García names her early days of bilingual teaching the era of *bilingual basements*, recalling how she and her Latinx students were remanded to dingy basement-level bilingual classrooms because of their "deficient" English (language-as-problem) but found warm affinity spaces where their identities, cultures, and languages were celebrated. The authors contrast these bilingual basements with today's DLBE programs, which are marketed as *commodified boutiques*, with their attractiveness and high visibility, but which no longer "belong" to Latinx teachers and students.

Language-as-problem and language-as-right meet in a slightly different way in Flores' (2016) discourse of *liberal multiculturalism*. Flores argues that liberal multiculturalism frames "bilingual education as a tool to provide Latinos access to the idealized language practices of a reconfigured bilingual vision of hegemonic Whiteness" (p. 23). In other words, liberal multiculturalism provides a vision for DLBE that does nothing to disrupt current societal power structures, instead seeking to repair bilingual students' language practices to better fit a White norm. Similarly, in Dorner et al.'s (2020) work, a school founded on ideas of equity for Black students in DLBE failed to live up to its aims when it understood students' language and literacy through discourses of languagelessness and standardization, seeing "ending word poverty" and "increasing social capital" for Black students as paths to equity (p. 100). These discourses eventually undermined goals of equal access to DLBE for all students, when the school decided that students should not learn literacy in Spanish, Mandarin, or French until they had demonstrated proficiency in English literacy.

Language as Right (to Equity and Identity) Discourses

In contrast to discourses that problematize marginalized students' language practices, the logic of the language-as-right discourse family (see triangle C in Figure 30.2) is that speakers have a right to all of their language practices, because language maintenance is tied to both identity and equity. In the nationalist episteme, language-as-right discourses focused on legal rights for emergent bilingual students; in the neoliberal episteme, this family of discourses instead focuses on re-coupling languages to identity, history, and culture. This discourse family is thus a rebuke to the dominant, language-as-resource discourse and its whitewashing of languages.

Two prominent discourses in this family are discourses of *linguistic rights* (Fránquiz et al., 2019) and *linguistic human rights* (Skutnabb-Kangas, 2006). Both frame the right to maintain and use one's language as equal to other human rights and essential to one's personhood (Zúñiga, 2016). Through this lens, access to home language education, through programs like DLBE, is never just about language learning, but about creating conditions in which students "are not forced to assimilate, can feel their linguistic identities as respected, and learn that their linguistic human rights matter" (Fránquiz et al., 2019, p. 141). Yet, linguistic human rights discourse can become problematic when it focuses more on language preservation than on speakers and listeners in communities (Kaveh, 2023). Scholars have therefore encouraged alternative approaches and discourses that center speakers. Valdez et al.

(2016) apply the idea of linguistic rights in their equity/heritage discourse—framing DLBE as a way to support students' right to their linguistic heritage and cultural identification—but they add the element of "equity," framing DLBE as a way to counter the inherent inequality in schools and larger society. Discourses of *race radicalism* in bilingual education (Flores, 2016), which arose during the civil rights movement, also framed bilingual education as much more than language learning. Instead, for the Puerto Rican activists that Flores writes about, bilingual education was part of the larger revolutionary project of transforming society by educating students to stand in solidarity with other marginalized peoples, resist the oppression of White supremacy, and fight for decolonization. These aims read as revolutionary but are echoed in the more recently described *equity and social justice* discourses (Bernstein et al., 2020; DeMatthews et al., 2017; Izquierdo et al., 2019). In these discourses, language learning within DLBE is framed not as the end goal but as just one means—embedded in larger critical education—to address past wrongs, support emergent bilinguals in developing strong identities and connections to their past, and teach all children to recognize inequalities and work toward social transformation (Bernstein et al., 2020; DeMatthews et al., 2017). *Critical biliteracies* (Chang-Bacon & Colomer, 2022) also explicitly addresses language and literacy alongside power, race, and culture. This approach combines criticality with biliteracy, acknowledging the history and richness of both traditions within the fields of literacy and bilingual education, respectively, but pushing for an integration of the two.

Finally, several discourses in the language-as-right family emphasize the formation of positive *bilingual identities*, in addition to language practices, as key to DLBE (García-Mateus & Palmer, 2017; see also Chapter 24). Pacheco and Hamilton (2020) advocate for the enactable discourse of *bilanguaging love* (Mignolo, 2012) in which Latina/o/x students adopt and contest identity positions, including Spanish speaker, bilingual, Latina and Mexicana/o in ways that reflect agency and display borderland knowledges and sensibilities, resisting clear boundaries between languages and identities.

Finally, the intersection of language-as-right with language-as-resource discourses (depicted in triangle *AC* in Figure 30.2) represents another space of possibility, in which diverse linguistic practices and identities are validated AND in which they are viewed and utilized as resources for emerging bilinguals. An important contribution of scholarship in this area provides ways to name and identify the dynamic and fluid languaging practices of bi/multilinguals from a pluralist perspective, including bilanguaging (Mignolo, 2012), codemeshing (Canagarajah, 2011), hybrid language practices (Gutiérrez et al., 1999), and others. Within the field of DLBE in the United States, *multilingualism* and *translanguaging* are two such frameworks.

Multilingualism from a pluralist perspective—rather than an assimilationist one (de Jong, 2013; see also Piller, 2016)—offers one lens for understanding diverse language practices and promoting discourses at the intersection of language as a right and resource (Durán & Palmer, 2014; MacSwan, 2019). Adopting this view allows educators to see DLBE as a space to serve an increasingly diverse community of speakers (de Jong et al., 2019), such as students who speak Spanish and an indigenous language or students who speak neither target language. Pluralist multilingual discourses afford opportunities to promote inclusive DLBE. At the same time, multilingualism discourse brings potential challenges and its usefulness for promoting social justice has been contested (Blackledge & Creese, 2014), which is why we place it along the border of language-as-resource. The vulnerability of multilingualism to contestation in the neoliberal era is also a result of its terminological sloganization (Schmenk et al., 2019)—that is, the way it has been emptied of its meaning and decontextualized into near-mythic form, resulting in detachment from speakers and communities. An important argument that aims to prevent this problematic de-coupling is to move away from Ruiz's (1984) orientations to languages entirely and to instead center speakers and their complex, intersectional languaging practices, through *humanizing orientations* (Kaveh, 2023). Consistent with the perspective that the national and neoliberal epistemes are manifestations of the broader colonial project, shifting to humanizing orientations necessitates a paradigm shift toward decolonial and indigenous perspectives. Adopting a translanguaging stance represents a pathway toward paradigmatic re-orientation. *Translanguaging* can be understood as the language practices and meaning-making processes of bilinguals and is a concept that explicitly disrupts deficit perspectives of emerging bilinguals by understanding their dynamic bilingualism (García, 2009; García & Wei, 2014). Translanguaging pedagogy involves educators adopting a stance and design that embraces translanguaging as a classroom resource and that responds to translanguaging shifts in classroom interaction (García et al., 2017; see also Chapter 28). A *critical translingual approach* (Seltzer, 2019) builds on the tenets of translanguaging and pushes boundaries for inclusive transformative education with an explicitly critical lens. Similarly, translanguaging in combination with universal design for learning (TrUDL) has been proposed as a framework to further ensure and guide DLBE into an inclusive and transformational space for bilingual students with disabilities (Cioè-Peña, 2021). Substantial research depicts the way translanguaging pedagogy creates classroom spaces that counter dominant language-as-problem discourses to serve emerging bilingual learners (Sánchez & García, 2021), including within DLBE contexts (García-Mateus et al., 2022; Henderson & Ingram, 2018; Palmer et al., 2014; Tian, 2022). In sum, DLBE programs and policies should strive to adopt and promote discourses that begin at the intersection of right and resource which, as argued in the following section, can only be achieved through a critical interrogation of historical and current dominant discourses.

From Right+Resource to Humanizing Spaces: Ideological Becoming as a Pathway Forward

In this chapter, we have used Ruiz's (1984) orientations to language as a heuristic to make sense of a vast and complex set of ideas within DLBE. We believe that metadiscursive awareness—or the ability to identify and name discourses—can equip DLBE educators with tools to disrupt language-as-problem discourses and promote discourses, practices, and pedagogies at the intersection of language-as-right and resource. We see this as a critical part of *ideological becoming* (Bakhtin, 1981) and the development of related concepts of *critical consciousness* (Cervantes-Soon et al., 2017; Palmer et al., 2019; see also Chapter 3), *sociopolitical consciousness* (J. Freire, 2020; see also Chapter 11), and *ideological clarity* (Alfaro, 2019; see also Chapter 34). We situate these ideas, not in any of the sections of the triangle discussed so far, but in the space at the center of the triangle, as shown in Figure 30.3. From this position, scholars and educators can observe all of the discourses circulating around them and come to decide which discourses are internally persuasive. We see it as a space of potential, a not-as-yet defined space for developing humanizing and liberatory discourses.

Conclusion

Multiple discourses shape DLBE policy, programs, and classrooms. Language-as-problem and language-as-resource discourses—often the authoritative discourses in DLBE—can serve to marginalize racialized speakers by framing their language varieties and practices as problems and by stripping them of special claims to languages through the whitewashing of multilingualism. As DLBE educators, we are forced to recognize and reckon with these dominant discourses and the institutional and political authority fused to them (Bakhtin, 1981). Yet, these discourses need not be internally persuasive to us. Identification and critical awareness of authoritative discourses and their history are necessary to disrupt them. Instead, we can engage with non-dominant discourses at the intersection of language-as-right and language-as-resource. These discourses offer a vision of linguistic rights that re-contextualizes languages, re-animating language as a living expression of identity, culture, and history. Promoting a process of ideological becoming for students, educators, administrators, and researchers alike would provide the opportunity for critical engagement with and reflection on our discursive landscape. While we cannot—and should not—control which discourses become internally persuasive to others, we hope that providing an unencumbered view of the complex histories and power relations (in)forming this landscape will allow more non-dominant and counter-hegemonic discourses to emerge. There is a history and legacy of bilingual education advocates

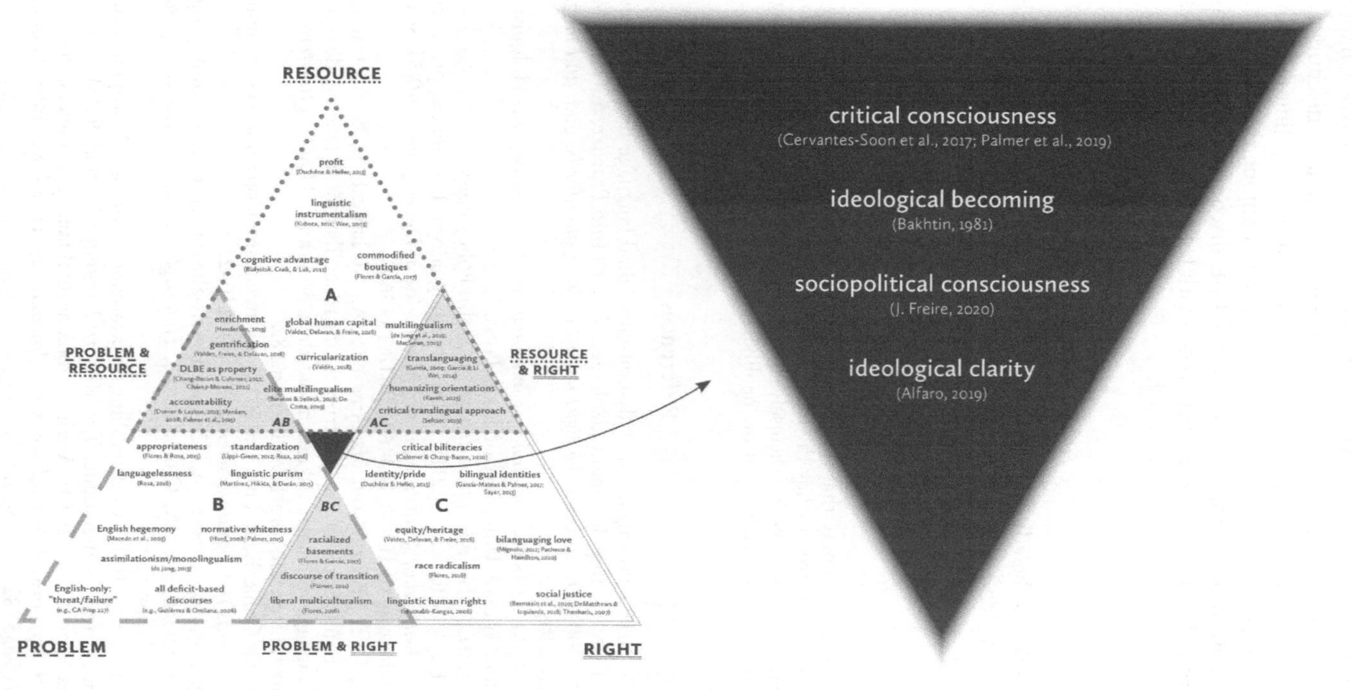

Figure 30.3 A Pathway Forward

driven by internally persuasive non-dominant discourses (see Chapter 4). These advocates recognize the ways in which dominant discourses have been oppressive through the erasure and/or vilification of linguistically and racially minoritized speakers. We count ourselves among these advocates in calling for more liberatory and healing DLBE discourses in which historically marginalized students are centered—with fully contextualized lives that are valued and voices that are heard.

Acknowledgments

Many thanks to the editors and to Deb Palmer, Nelson Flores, Chris Chang-Bacon, and Yalda Kaveh for pushing our thinking with your feedback on this chapter. We are grateful to be able to learn from you.

Note

1 It is important to note that the ideas reviewed in this section are meant to name and critique the trends they theorize. Thus, it is the discourses these scholars describe (and not the scholars themselves) that draw on and perpetuate the language-as-economic-resource logic of the neoliberal episteme.

References

Alfaro, C. (2019). Preparing critically conscious dual-language teachers: Recognizing and interrupting dominant ideologies. *Theory Into Practice*, *58*(2), 194–203.

Apple, M. (2006). *Educating the right way: Markets, standards, god, and inequality* (2nd ed.). Routledge.

Bakhtin, M. M. (1981). *The dialogic imagination: Four essays* (M. Holquist & C. Emerson, Trans.). University of Texas Press.

Ball, S. J. (2017). *The education debate* (3rd ed.). Policy Press.

Barakos, E., & Selleck, C. (2019). Elite multilingualism: Discourses, practices, and debates. *Journal of Multilingual and Multicultural Development*, *40*(5), 361–374. https://doi.org/10.1080/01434632.2018.1543691

Bernstein, K. A., Katznelson, N., Amezcua, A., Mohamed, S., & Alvarado, S. L. (2020). Equity/social justice, instrumentalism/neoliberalism: Dueling discourses of dual language in principals' talk about their programs. *TESOL Quarterly*, *54*(3), 652–684. https://doi.org/10.1002/tesq.582

Bialystok, E., Craik, F., & Luk, G. (2012). Bilingualism: Consequences for mind and brain. *Trends in Cognitive Sciences*, *16*(4), 240–250.

Blackledge, A., & Creese, A. (2014). Heteroglossia as practice and pedagogy. In A. Blackledge, & A. Creese (Eds.), *Heteroglossia as practice and pedagogy* (pp. 1–20). Springer.

Canagarajah, S. (2011). Codemeshing in academic writing: Identifying teachable strategies of translanguaging. *The Modern Language Journal*, *95*(3), 401–417.

Cervantes-Soon, C. G. (2014). A critical look at dual language immersion in the new Latin@ diaspora. *Bilingual Research Journal*, *37*(1), 64–82. https://doi.org/10.1080/15235882.2014.893267

Cervantes-Soon, C. G., Dorner, L., Palmer, D., Heiman, D., Schwerdtfeger, R., & Choi, J. (2017). Combating inequalities in two-way language immersion programs: Toward critical consciousness in bilingual education spaces. *Review of Research in Education*, *41*(1), 403–427.

Chang-Bacon, C. K., & Colomer, S. E. (2022). Biliteracy as property: Promises and perils of the seal of biliteracy. *Journal of Literacy Research*, *54*(2), 182–207. https://doi.org/10.1177/1086296X221096676

Chávez-Moreno, L. C. (2021). Dual language as White property: Examining a secondary bilingual-education program and Latinx equity. *American Education Research Journal*, *58*(6), 1107–1141. https://doi.org/10.3102/00028312211052508

Cioè-Peña, M. (2017). The intersectional gap: How bilingual students in the United States are excluded from inclusion. *International Journal of Inclusive Education*, *21*(9), 906–919. https://doi.org/10.1080/13603116.2017.1296032

Cioè-Peña, M. (2020). Dual language and the erasure of emergent bilinguals labeled as disabled (EBLADs). In N. Flores, A. Tseng, & N. Subtirelu (Eds.), *Bilingualism for all?: Raciolinguistic perspectives on dual language education in the United States* (pp. 63–87). Multilingual Matters.

Cioè-Peña, M. (2021). TrUDL, a path to full inclusion: The intersectional possibilities of translanguaging and universal design for learning. *TESOL Quarterly*. https://doi.org/10.1002/tesq.3074

Cummins, J. (1994). Semilingualism. In R. R. Asher (Ed.), *International encyclopedia of language and linguistics* (2nd ed., pp. 3812–3814). Elsevier Science Ltd.

De Costa, P. (2019). Elite multilingualism, affect and neoliberalism. *Journal of Multilingual and Multicultural Development*, *40*(5), 453–460. https://doi.org/10.1080/01434632.2018.1543698

de Jong, E. J. (2013). Policy discourses and U.S. language in education policies. *Peabody Journal of Education*, *88*, 98–111.

de Jong, E. J., Yilmaz, T., & Marichal, N. (2019). A multilingualism-as-a-resource orientation in dual language education. *Theory Into Practice*, *58*(2), 107–120.

DeMatthews, D., Izquierdo, E., & Knight, D. S. (2017). Righting past wrongs: A superintendent's social justice leadership for dual language education along the U.S.-Mexico border. *Education Policy Analysis Archives*, *25*, 1. https://doi.org/10.14507/epaa.25.2436

Dorner, L. M., & Layton, A. (2013). What makes a good school? Data and competing discourses in a multilingual charter network. In D. Anagnostopoulos, S. Rutledge, & R. Jacobsen (Eds.), *The infrastructure of accountability: Mapping data use and its consequences across the American education system* (pp. 145–162). Harvard Educational Press.

Dorner, L. M., Moon, J. M., Bonney, E. N., & Otis, A. (2020). Dueling discourses in dual language schools: Multilingual 'success for all' versus the academic 'decline' of Black students. In N. Flores, A. Tseng, & N. Subtirelu (Eds.), *Bilingualism for all?: Raciolinguistic perspectives on dual language education in the United States* (pp. 88–110). Multilingual Matters.

Duchêne, A., & Heller, M. (Eds.). (2013). *Language in late capitalism: Pride and profit*. Routledge.

Durán, L., & Palmer, D. (2014). Pluralist discourses of bilingualism and translanguaging talk in classrooms. *Journal of Early Childhood Literacy*, *14*(3), 367–388. https://doi.org/10.1177/1468798413497386

Flores, N. (2013). Silencing the subaltern: Nation-state/colonial governmentality and bilingual education in the United States. *Critical Inquiry in Language Studies*, *10*(4), 263–287.

Flores, N. (2016). A tale of two visions: Hegemonic whiteness and bilingual education. *Educational Policy*, *30*(1), 13–38.
Flores, N., & García, O. (2017). A critical review of bilingual education in the United States: From basements and pride to boutiques and profit. *Annual Review of Applied Linguistics*, *37*, 14–29. https://doi.org/10.1017/S0267190517000162
Flores, N., & Rosa, J. (2015). Undoing appropriateness: Raciolinguistic ideologies and language diversity in education. *Harvard Educational Review*, *85*(2), 149–171. https://doi.org/10.17763/0017-8055.85.2.149
Foucault, M. (1970). *The order of things: An archaeology of the human sciences*. Pantheon Books.
Fránquiz, M. E., Leija, M. G., & Salinas, C. S. (2019). Challenging damaging ideologies: Are dual language education practices addressing learners' linguistic rights? *Theory Into Practice*, *58*(2), 134–144.
Freire, P. (2000). *Pedagogy of the oppressed* (M. B. Ramos, Trans.; 30th Anniversary ed.). Bloomsbury Academic.
Freire, J. A. (2020). Promoting sociopolitical consciousness and bicultural goals of dual language education: The transformational dual language educational framework. *Journal of Language, Identity & Education*, *19*(1), 56–71.
Freire, J. A., & Alemán, E. Jr. (2021). "Two schools within a school": Elitism, divisiveness, and intra-racial gentrification in a dual language strand. *Bilingual Research Journal*, *44*(2), 249–269. https://doi.org/10.1080/15235882.2021.1942325
Galindo, R. (2011). The nativistic legacy of the Americanization era in the education of Mexican immigrant students. *Educational Studies*, *47*(4), 323–346. https://doi.org/10.1080/00131946.2011.589308
García, O. (2009). Education, multilingualism and translanguaging in the 21st century. In *Social justice through multilingual education* (pp. 140–158). Multilingual Matters.
García, O., & Wei, L. (2014). *Translanguaging: Language, bilingualism and education*. Palgrave Macmillan. https://doi.org/10.1057/9781137385765
García, O., Johnson, S., & Seltzer, K. (2017). *The translanguaging classroom. Leveraging student bilingualism for learning*. Caslon.
García-Mateus, S., & Palmer, D. (2017). Translanguaging pedagogies for positive identities in two-way dual language bilingual education. *Journal of Language, Identity, and Education*, *16*(4), 245–255.
García-Mateus, S., Henderson, K. I., Palmer, D. K., & Tellez-Arste, M. (2022). Pre–K Latinx students in the borderlands: A counter-hegemonic transformative experience of biliteracy and bilingual identity development. In M. T. Sánchez & O. García (Eds.), *Transformative translanguaging espacios in bilingual education-US Latinx bilingual children rompiendo fronteras* (pp. 156–179). Multilingual Matters.
Gramsci, A. (1971). *Selections from the prison notebooks*. International Publishers.
Gutiérrez, K. D., Baquedano-López, P., & Tejeda, C. (1999). Rethinking diversity: Hybridity and hybrid language practices in the third space. *Mind, Culture, and Activity*, *6*(4), 286–303.
Hamman-Ortiz, L. (2019). Troubling the "two" in two-way bilingual education. *Bilingual Research Journal*, *42*(4), 387–407. http://dx.doi.org/10.1080/15235882.2019.1686441
Harris, C. I. (1995). Whiteness as property. In K. Crenshaw, N. Gotanda, G. Peller, & K. Thomas (Eds.), *Critical race theory: The key writings that formed the movement* (pp. 276–291). New Press.

Harvey, D. (2005). *A brief history of neoliberalism*. Oxford University Press.
Heike, P. (2014). *The myths that made America: An introduction to American studies*. Transcript Verlag.
Heller, M. (1999). *Linguistic minorities and modernity: A sociolinguistic ethnography*. Longman.
Henderson, K. I. (2019). The danger of the dual-language enrichment narrative: Educator discourses constructing exclusionary participation structures in bilingual education. *Critical Inquiry in Language Studies*, *16*(3), 55–77. https://doi.org/10.1080/15427587.2018.1492343
Henderson, K. I., & Ingram, M. (2018). "Mister, you're writing in Spanglish": Fostering spaces for meaning making and metalinguistic connections through teacher translanguaging shifts in the bilingual classroom. *Bilingual Research Journal*, *41*(3), 253–271.
Horsman, R. (1981). *Race and manifest destiny*. Harvard University Press.
Izquierdo, E., DeMatthews, D. E., Balderas, E., & Gregory, B. (2019). Leading dual language: Twenty years of innovation in a borderland elementary school. In D. E. DeMatthews & E. Izquierdo (Eds.), *Dual language education: Teaching and leading in two languages* (pp. 163–180). Springer.
Kaveh, Y. (2023). Re-orienting to language users: Humanizing orientations in language planning as praxis. Language Policy, 22(1), 1–23.
King, D. (2000). *Making Americans: Immigration, race and the origins of democracy*. Harvard University Press.
Kramarczuk Voulgarides, C., Fergus, E., & King Thorius, K. A. (2017). Pursuing equity: Disproportionality in special education and the reframing of technical solutions to address systemic inequities. *Review of Research in Education*, *41*(1), 61–87. https://doi.org/10.3102/0091732x16686947
Kubota, R. (2011). Questioning linguistic instrumentalism: English, neoliberalism, and language tests in Japan. *Linguistics and Education*, *22*(3), 248–260. https://doi.org/10.1016/j.linged.2011.02.002
Leeman, J. (2005). Engaging critical pedagogy: Spanish for native speakers. *Foreign Language Annals*, *38*(1), 35–45.
Leonardo, Z., & Broderick, A. (2011). Smartness as property: A critical exploration of intersections between Whiteness and disability studies. *Teachers College Record*, *113*, 2206–2232.
Lippi-Green, R. (2012). *English with an accent: Language, ideology and discrimination in the United States* (2nd ed.). Routledge.
MacSwan, J. (2005). The "non-non" crisis and academic bias in native language assessment of linguistic minorities. In J. Cohen, K. McAlister, K. Rolstad, & J. MacSwan (Eds.), ISB4: *proceedings of the 4th international symposium on bilingualism* (pp. 340–375). Cascadilla Press.
MacSwan, J. (2019). A multilingual perspective on translanguaging. In D. Macedo (Ed.), *Decolonizing foreign language education* (pp. 186–219). Routledge.
Martín Rojo, L., & Del Percio, A. (2019). Neoliberalism, language, and governmentality. In L. Martín Rojo & A. Del Percio (Eds.), *Language and neoliberal governmentality* (pp. 1–25). Routledge.
Martínez, R. A., Hikida, M., & Durán, L. (2015). Unpacking ideologies of linguistic purism: How dual language teachers make sense of everyday translanguaging. *International Multilingual Research Journal*, *9(*1), 26–42. https://doi.org/10.1080/19313152.2014.977712
May, S. (2012). *Language and minority rights: Ethnicity, nationalism and the politics of language*. Routledge.

Mena, M., & García, O. (2021). 'Converse racialization' and 'un/marking' language: The making of a bilingual university in a neoliberal world. *Language in Society*, *50*(3), 343–364. https://doi.org/10.1017/S0047404520000330

Menken, K. (2008). *English language learners left behind: Standardized testing as language policy*. Multilingual Matters.

Mignolo, W. D. (2012). *Local histories/global designs: Coloniality, subaltern knowledges, and border thinking*. Princeton University Press.

Mondale, S., & Patton, S. (Eds.). (2001). *School: The story of American public education*. Beacon Press.

Morita-Mullaney, T., & Chesnut, C. (2022). Equity traps in the deselection of English learners in dual language education: A collective case study of school principals. *NABE Journal of Research and Practice*, *12*(2), 49–68. https://doi.org/10.1080/26390043.2022.2079390

Pacheco, M., & Hamilton, C. (2020). Bilanguaging love: Latina/o/x bilingual students' subjectivities and sensitivities in dual language immersion contexts. *TESOL Quarterly*, *54*(3), 548–571.

Palmer, D. K. (2011). The discourse of transition: Teachers' language ideologies within transitional bilingual education programs. *International Multilingual Research Journal*, *5*(2), 103–122. https://doi.org/10.1080/19313152.2011.594019

Palmer, D. K., & Henderson, K. I. (2016). Dual language bilingual education placement practices: Educator discourses about emergent bilingual students in two program types. *International Multilingual Research Journal*, *10*(1), 17–30.

Palmer, D. K., Cervantes-Soon, C., Dorner, L., & Heiman, D. (2019). Bilingualism, biliteracy, biculturalism, and critical consciousness for all: Proposing a fourth fundamental goal for two-way dual language education. *Theory Into Practice*, *58*(2), 121–133. https://doi.org/10.1080/00405841.2019.1569376

Palmer, D. K., Martínez, R. A., Mateus, S. G., & Henderson, K. I. (2014). Reframing the debate on language separation: Toward a vision for translanguaging pedagogies in the dual language classroom. *The Modern Language Journal*, *98*(3), 757–772. https://doi.org/10.1111/modl.12121

Palmer, D. K., Henderson, K. I., Wall, D., Zúñiga, C. E., & Berthelsen, S. (2016). Team teaching among mixed messages: Implementing two-way dual language bilingual education at third grade in Texas. *Language Policy*, *15*(4), 393–413.

Petrovic, J. E. (2005). The conservative restoration and neoliberal defenses of bilingual education. *Language Policy*, *4*(4), 395. https://doi.org/10.1007/s10993-005-2888-y

Piller, I. (2016). Monolingual ways of seeing multilingualism. *Journal of Multicultural Discourses*, *11*(1), 25–33.

Ricento, T. (2005). Problems with the "language as resource" discourse in the promotion of heritage languages in the U.S.A. *Journal of Sociolinguistics*, *9*, 348–368. https://doi.org/10.1111/j.1360-6441.2005.00296.x

Rosa, J. (2016). Standardization, racialization, languagelessness: Raciolinguistic ideologies across communicative contexts. *Journal of Linguistic Anthropology*, *26*(2), 162–183. https://doi.org/10.1111/jola.12116

Ruiz, R. (1984). Orientations in language planning. *NABE Journal of Research and Practice*, *8*(2), 15–34. https://doi.org/10.1080/08855072.1984.10668464

Sánchez, M. T., & García, O. (Eds.). (2021). *Transformative translanguaging espacios: Latinx students and their teachers rompiendo fronteras sin miedo*. Multilingual Matters.

Schmenk, B., Breidbach, S., & Kuster, L. (2019). Sloganization in language education discourse: Introduction. In B. Schmenk, S. Breidbach, & L. Kuster (Eds.),

Sloganization in language education discourse: Conceptual thinking in the age of academic marketization (pp. 1–18). Multilingual Matters.

Seltzer, K. (2019). Reconceptualizing "home" and "school" language: Taking a critical translingual approach in the English classroom. *TESOL Quarterly*, *53*(4), 986–1007.

Skiba, R. (2012). "As nature has formed them": The history and current status of racial difference research. *Teachers College Record*, *111*, 1–49.

Skutnabb-Kangas, T. (2006). Language policy and linguistic human rights. In T. Ricento (Ed.), *An introduction to language policy: Theory and method* (pp. 273–291). Blackwell.

Tian, Z. (2022). Translanguaging design in a third-grade language arts class. *Applied Linguistics Review*, *13*(3), 327–343.

Valdés, G. (2018). Analyzing the curricularization of language in two-way immersion education: Restating two cautionary notes. *Bilingual Research Journal*, *41*(4), 388–412. https://doi.org/10.1080/15235882.2018.1539886

Valdez, V. E., Delavan, G., & Freire, J. A. (2016). The marketing of dual language education policy in Utah print media. *Educational Policy*, *30*(6), 849–883. https://doi.org/10.1177/0895904814556750

Valdez, V. E., Freire, J. A., & Delavan, M. G. (2016). The gentrification of dual language education. *The Urban Review*, *48*(4), 601–627. https://doi.org/10.1007/s11256-016-0370-0

Wall, D. J., Greer, E., & Palmer, D. K. (2022). Exploring processes in a district-wide dual language program: Who is it for? Who is left out? *Journal of Latinos and Education*, *21*(1), 87–102. https://doi.org/10.1080/15348431.2019.1613996

Wee, L. (2003). Linguistic instrumentalism in Singapore. *Journal of Multilingual and Multicultural Development*, *24*(3), 211–224. https://doi.org/10.1080/01434630308666499

Zentella, A. C. (2007). "Dime con quién hablas, y te diré quién eres": Linguistic (in)security and Latina/o unity. In J. Flores & R. Rosaldo (Eds.), *A Companion to Latina/o Studies* (pp. 25–38). John Wiley & Sons, Ltd. https://doi.org/10.1002/9781405177603.ch3

Zúñiga, C. E. (2016). Between language as problem and resource: Examining teachers' language orientations in dual-language programs. *Bilingual Research Journal*, *39*(3–4), 339–353.

31

RESEARCH ON THE USE OF LANGUAGE(S) AND DISCOURSES IN DUAL LANGUAGE AND MULTILINGUAL MATHEMATICS AND SCIENCE CLASSROOMS

Melissa A. Navarro Martell, William Zahner

This chapter summarizes the state of research on mathematics and science education in dual language (DL) and multilingual classrooms. Attending to language(s) in mathematics and science classrooms is important because current research and policy documents focus on promoting student participation in discourse and mathematical and scientific practices (Lee et al., 2013; Moschkovich, 2015). Recently, mathematics and science education researchers who focus on the interaction of using languages and engaging in disciplinary learning have produced research summarizing asset-based teaching practices to promote bilingual students' participation in disciplinary discourses and practices. This chapter aims to provide an overview of trends and tensions in mathematics and science education research within DL bilingual education (DLBE) programs. We intentionally elevate ideological clarity and the critical consciousness (Alfaro, 2019) necessary to honor the assets of language-minoritized and other racialized students by focusing on research that highlights students' assets rather than their erroneously perceived deficits.

As we consider mathematics and science teaching and learning in DL environments, limited research explicitly focuses on DLBE classrooms. Instead, most research that addresses languages and mathematics and science teaching and learning focuses on meeting the needs of "language minority"

 DOI: 10.4324/9781003269076-44

students to develop their perceived missing academic language and, in most cases, specifically in English. Historically, most of the research in this body of work centers on deficit perspectives of multilingual learners. Additionally, when considering the three goals of DL and bilingual education programs – bilingualism and biliteracy, academic achievement, and sociocultural and global competencies (Howard et al., 2018) – even less is known about how to fulfill these goals in the content areas of mathematics and science. Another aspect to acknowledge is the analysis and critiques of experts in the field of DL, noting that the previously mentioned three goals lack the aspect of critical consciousness, which is foundational and has the potential to better serve the needs of racialized students (Palmer et al., 2019).

We begin by providing an orientation to current scholarship in science, technology, engineering, and mathematics (STEM) education, focusing on research examining the interplay of language(s), discourse, and disciplinary practices. We then summarize research on science and mathematics teaching and learning in multilingual settings, highlighting key issues that cut across science and mathematics education research. We follow by presenting a brief example to illustrate the critical issues in current research. Finally, we conclude by discussing the implications and future directions for math and science research in DLBE programs.

Shifts in STEM Education Research and Needed Focus on Dual Language and Bilingual Education

Over the past 20 years, there has been an increase in attention to the role of language(s) and discourse practices in shaping students' reasoning in mathematics and science education. The increased attention to language and culture in STEM learning can be seen in the content of the traditionally published handbooks in mathematics and science education research. For example, in the 2007 *Handbook of Research in Mathematics Education* (Lester, 2007), no chapter focused exclusively on language, though two chapters focused on culture, equity, and diversity (Bishop & Forgasz, 2007; Diversity in Mathematics Education (DiME) Center for Learning and Teaching, 2007). These two chapters highlighted such topics as the interaction of culture(s), power, and the institutional policies and practices of school mathematics in realizing more or less equitable outcomes in mathematics education for historically excluded students. In contrast, the 2017 *Compendium of Research in Mathematics Education* (Cai, 2017) included one chapter summarizing research on classroom discourse (Herbel-Eisenmann et al., 2017), as well as a chapter on mathematics teaching and learning in multilingual settings (Barwell et al., 2017). Barwell et al. (2017) organized the chapter by three dominant traditions in research on mathematics and language: cognitive, sociocultural, and sociopolitical perspectives. Another comprehensive review of research on

English learners in mathematics education was organized by the categories of student learning, teaching, and teacher education (de Araujo et al., 2018). However, neither de Araujo et al. (2018) nor Barwell et al. (2017) explicitly disaggregated their reviews based on the type of language program in use (e.g., DL, bilingual, immersion, or sheltered instruction).

When considering handbooks in science education, the trend is similar. For example, both the 2007 *Handbook of Research in Science Education* (Abell & Lederman, 2007) and the 2014 edition of the *Handbook* (Lederman & Abell, 2014) include chapters on language and cultures in science education (Buxton & Lee, 2014; Lee & Luykx, 2007). Yet, notably, no chapters specifically focus on science learning in DLBE settings. Nevertheless, while there is evidence of growing interest in language in mathematics and science education research, there continues to be an absence of research on STEM education in DL settings.

Alongside an increased focus on language(s) and discourse patterns shaping research on students' mathematical or scientific thinking, there have been changes in the intellectual traditions prevalent in the field and the context of schools and schooling. Three specific and critical shifts over the past 20 years have been: (a) a conceptual re-orientation of research related to language(s) and discourse in school science and mathematics; (b) a contextual shift in student demographics in K-12 schools; and (c) a change in the focus of school curriculum guidelines, standards, and policy documents to include some discussion of multilingual learners.

Shift 1: Conceptual Re-orientation of Research Related to Language(s) and Discourse

The first shift has been from deficit-focused theories about multilingual learners' science and mathematics education to asset-focused theories. This conceptual shift occurred alongside a shift from conceptualizing mathematical or scientific language as words to considering "language" more broadly in terms of developing disciplinary discourse practices and literacies (Moschkovich, 2002, 2015; Warren et al., 2001). For instance, early research on "language issues" in mathematics focused on bilingual and multilingual students' struggles to translate specific words or phrases from natural language into mathematical equations (Mestre & Gerace, 1986). However, more recent work has taken a broader view of language(s) and mathematics and science education, which have expanded to focus on registers and discourse practices (Moschkovich, 2002, 2015; Setati & Adler, 2001; Warren et al., 2001). This focus on discourse practices and disciplinary literacies decreases the focus on using "correct" terminology in mathematics and science. Instead, it engages students in disciplinary practices such as argumentation from evidence, proof, and explanation of processes (Buxton & Lee, 2014).

An early example of such re-framing is the study of the assets of Haitian Creole-speaking students for learning science (Warren et al., 2001). As minoritized students are becoming the numerical majority in many schools and school systems (National Center for Educational Statistics, 2021), such students' languages and social and cultural community assets are no longer peripheral to the focus on education. In recent work, math and science education researchers (Cuauhtin, 2019; Pelaez et al., 2023) have used frameworks such as community cultural wealth (Yosso, 2005) to explicitly highlight the assets of multilingual learners and their communities, including in math and science classrooms.

Simultaneous with this first conceptual shift, science and mathematics education researchers who work in multilingual settings have started to adopt a more critical approach to describing the "language of instruction" and the language-related goals of mathematics and science education in multilingual settings (Civil & Planas, 2011). For example, in some foundational research on the mathematics and science education of multilingual students that adopted a focus on disciplinary literacies and practices (e.g., Fradd et al., 2001), the unstated assumption was that the purpose of education is to acquire fluency in the dominant language – e.g., English in the North American context. However, more recent research in mathematics and science education has explored a more open stance toward linguistic heterogeneity, not seeing fluency in the dominant language(s) as a prerequisite for learning science or mathematics (e.g., LópezLeiva et al., 2013; Navarro Martell, 2021). Similarly, the sociopolitical turn in STEM education (Gutiérrez, 2013) has added a critical focus on *whose* language is privileged in the classroom, *how* that language privileging is done, and why.

Shift 2: Contextual Shift in Student Demographics in K-12 Schools

Second, school contexts and student demographics have shifted. For example, the proportion of multilingual students in the United States has increased dramatically over the past 20 years (National Center for Educational Statistics, 2021). A similar trend of increasing linguistic heterogeneity in schools is occurring across the globe as more people move – either willingly or due to social and economic disruption (OECD, 2019). Simultaneously, the teaching force does not reflect the diversity of students. For example, in the United States, most teachers are white and female and do not reflect the diversity of the K-12 student population (National Center for Educational Statistics, 2021). The shift in student demographics and the slow pace of change in teacher demographics and language background have led to both tensions and opportunities. In the research literature, these demographic realities have added urgency to shifting the discourse about language(s) and discourse practices in mathematics and science education to recognize students' assets from nondominant communities.

Shift 3: Change in the Focus of School Curriculum Guidelines, Standards, and Policy Documents

Finally, with the rise of new standards such as the Common Core State Standards in Mathematics (CCSSM, National Governors Association Center for Best Practices & Council of Chief State School Officers, 2010) and the Next Generation Science Standards (NGSS, Next Generation Science Standards, 2013), there has been an increased focus in STEM education research on "practices" in addition to "content." For example, in the CCSSM, the eight standards for mathematical practice describe ways of reasoning mathematically that are expected to be valued across grades K-12. Some practices, such as "attend to precision," highlight how language is integral to doing and learning mathematics. Correspondingly, mathematics education researchers such as Moschkovich (2013) have argued that educators may focus on the mathematical practices to better meet the educational needs of multilingual learners without focusing on what students *lack*. A similar argument applies to the science practices and crosscutting concepts that are core to the NGSS.

While the shifting focus on language in mathematics and science education standards indicates a positive step in acknowledging the assets that multilingual students bring to classrooms, these new standards do not intentionally or specifically address the learning needs of multilingual students. For example, regarding the NGSS (Next Generation Science Standards, 2013), there was an intentional conversation as the standards were planned to ensure all students had opportunities to engage in scientific inquiry around a phenomenon (Lee et al., 2013). In addition, when considering non-traditional students, NGSS authors added appendices to supplement the standards and serve as educators' resources. However, when exploring Appendix D, "All Standards, All Students: Making the Next Generation Science Standards Accessible to All Students," it is evident that multilingual learners were not central to the conceptualization of this document. Regrettably, the NGSS uses labels from No Child Left Behind (NCLB), such as "students with limited English proficiency," an antiquated deficit term that has been criticized for years (Hernández et al., 2022).

Scholarship at the Intersection of Science, Mathematics, and Language(s)

This section highlights research related to science and mathematics teaching and learning with multilingual learners. Specifically, we present research related to three themes: designing mathematics and science instruction in multilingual settings, translanguaging in mathematics and science classrooms, and teacher preparation for working with multilingual learners.

Designing Instruction

First, in science education, Beltran et al. (2013) focus on how multilingual learners can develop their academic language through inquiry-based instruction. The book centers on multilingual learners, and the authors discuss the English Language Development (ELD) standards, inquiry-based projects, the 5E method of instruction, and assessment. Next, Beltran et al. (2013) provide an overview of language development to understand what they refer to as academic language proficiency for English language learners (ELs). Then, they present a framework for decision-making in developing academic language in which they describe five essential principles for academic language development instruction for teachers of ELs. The first principle consists of teachers scaffolding language learning to make learning comprehensible and relevant. The second focuses on the teacher supporting explicit academic language instruction "for authentic social and academic language purposes" (p. 76). The third principle discusses differentiation of instruction to meet the diverse needs of ELs. The fourth principle suggests that the teacher optimizes language use "through the cognitive engagement and social interaction of ELs" (p. 65). Lastly, the fifth principle addresses the teacher bridging the "diverse social, cultural, and linguistic resources" multilingual learners bring to the classroom to identify student assets (p. 76). In addition to Beltran et al.'s valuable work, newer frameworks for considering teaching science in DLBE settings have emerged – such as translanguaging, critical science education, and postcolonial science education. Below we summarize some of this new research.

Research is relatively limited in designing instruction for DL science programs with multilingual learners compared to the extensive work focused on developing a target language in science. At the preschool level, Rumper and colleagues (2021) discuss how science assessment results in English and Spanish compare with children in DL preschool programs. They base their comparison on three areas: the role of the language used in the assessment, what they refer to as "language dominance," and the teachers' language used during instructional play. Rumper et al. (2021) found that only teachers' use of academic science language in Spanish impacted the children's performance in their science assessments.

At the primary level, Aguirre-Muñoz and Gregory (2019) name the benefits of developing science literacy in English to improve achievement by embedding language authentically as something that must be intentionally planned for multilingual learners. Relatedly, Navarro Martell (2018) discusses teachers' ideological clarity as they create equitable learning spaces for multilingual learners during science instruction time, including using translanguaging to access content. Additionally, Esquinca et al. (2018) conducted an ethnographic study in a transborder context in a fourth-grade DL school with a majority immigrant and transnational student population. During the first year of the study, they reported that the STEM curriculum utilized was not taught following DL goals, reproducing hegemonic practices in DL programs that further marginalized Latinx multilingual learners. However, Esquinca et al. (2021) further reported that DL teachers at the site continued to develop their DL pedagogies to integrate science and engineering learning experiences in meaningful ways for immigrant and transnational students at their schools.

At the middle school level, Infante and Licona (2021) mention translanguaging as a pedagogical approach that provides multilingual learners access to content and scientific practices. In another middle school study, Lachance (2018) considers teachers' perspectives on biliteracy development in science and sociocultural perspectives to inform teacher education programs that focus on preparing middle school teachers in DL. Finally, other papers that addressed science in DL aspects primarily described how language usage impacted test scores for children in DL programs (e.g., Garza-Reyna, 2019).

In mathematics, education research efforts have focused on developing frameworks for integrating mathematics and language learning that go "beyond good teaching" (Celedon-Pattichis & Ramirez, 2012). Erath et al. (2021) summarize a body of research that has spanned multiple national contexts, describing six design principles and six teaching moves aligned with these principles. In the review by Erath et al., it is evident that the national-political-linguistic context of various studies shapes the linguistic milieu and the relevant language ideologies that shape learning contexts and policies. In the U.S. context, specifically, two frameworks for teaching mathematics to multilingual learners have come from the work of Driscoll and colleagues (2016) and Chval and colleagues (2014, 2021). Both works highlight, for example, the importance of incorporating language support structures in mathematics instruction, particularly when considering teaching and learning in multilingual settings. For example, Driscoll et al. (2016) emphasize how visual representations of mathematics problems can be a valuable resource for multilingual learners to express their thinking using multiple modes of communication. In addition, many school mathematics problems are posed in "real life" contexts. Chval et al. (2014) explicated the importance of developing contextual knowledge (and addressing associated language demands) when teaching mathematics in multilingual classrooms. Finally, Chval et al. (2021) also discuss how classroom interactions can be used to position multilingual learners in either productive or unproductive ways. Precisely, teachers can position multilingual students as capable mathematical thinkers or as students who "need help" and are a problem. This focus on how students' language(s) are positioned invokes Ruíz's (1984) discussion of language and how it can be framed as a problem versus language as a resource.

In designing instruction for multilingual secondary mathematics classrooms, Zahner et al. (2021) and Zahner and Wynn (3) challenged conventional ideas about mathematical learning trajectories and developed design principles for mathematics instruction to foster robust discussions in multilingual secondary mathematics classrooms. In their work, Zahner et al. (2021) illustrate how applying these design principles led to transformed discourse patterns in a linguistically diverse ninth-grade classroom. However, they also cautioned that the sociopolitical context of the urban school within which they worked (including an assumed goal of English acquisition) also appeared to limit the effectiveness of the intervention developed and tested in this study.

While there is research on developing mathematics education in multilingual settings, there is relatively less research on developing mathematics instruction specifically for bilingual and DL classrooms. Some of the foundational work in this area is from out-of-school and after-school settings. For example, LópezLeiva and colleagues described the power of a bilingual after-school mathematics program in which bilingual students could use their entire repertoire of linguistic assets to do mathematics (LópezLeiva et al., 2013). Yet, LópezLeiva and Khisty (2014) also noted the tensions and interpersonal conflicts that arose in designing and implementing the program. Such tensions often revolved around students and teachers taking up the dominant ideology that prioritized English in school interactions. In their discussions of the interactions observed in the setting, LópezLeiva and collaborators noted that students and teachers needed additional support to develop biliteracy in bilingual mathematics classrooms.

Finally, Martínez Hinestroza (2020) offers a perspective that illustrates the complexity of studying language use in DLBE mathematics classrooms. Specifically, Martínez Hinestroza argues that a focus on verbal language in bilingual settings can slide into an approach to research where words and specifically verbalizations receive more attention than other resources that may support student thinking. Martínez Hinestroza's work highlights the importance of focusing on nonverbal communication and silence as resources for student learning in DL and bilingual classrooms.

Translanguaging in Science and Mathematics Classrooms

Second, another aspect addressed in research considers the role of translanguaging in the bilingual science classroom (Mazak & Herbas-Donoso, 2014; Navarro Martell, 2021; Poza, 2018; Stevenson, 2013). In recent years, mathematics and science education researchers have used translanguaging (García, 2019; García & Wei, 2015) to describe bilingual students and their teachers' use of multiple languages to do mathematics and science. For example, language can be used as a resource (Ruíz, 1984) when considering the goal of a science lesson, such as comprehending and applying science content and skills to accomplish this lesson goal. Poza (2018) asserted that providing multilingual learners with spaces to use their entire bilingualism assists in the process of making meaning. On the other hand, Stevenson (2013) warned that for multilingual learners to develop and advance a rich vocabulary creatively, teachers must be purposeful in creating the spaces, opportunities, and scaffolds to use language(s). In a study with fifth graders in Hong Kong, Williams (2022) researched content language integrated learning and translanguaging during a biology and physics unit. In this study, Williams (2022) illustrated that multilingual learners utilize four distinct non-linguistic modes (e.g., gestures and tactile meanings) to support their science discourse while translanguaging. Moreover, other scholars have invited us to problematize and question what is considered "science" and the role that language, English specifically, plays in labeling science as a content area for the privileged (Mazak & Herbas-Donoso, 2014; Mensah & Jackson, 2018; Sammel, 2009).

Mathematics education researchers have also examined multilingual students' use of multiple languages when doing mathematics (Moschkovich, 2007; Setati & Adler, 2001; Zahner & Moschkovich, 2011). Early research in this area built on non-deficit framings of code-switching examined the conversational and disciplinary functions of switching languages during a mathematical discussion. In one finding, Zahner and Moschkovich (2011) demonstrated that when Spanish-English bilingual students in a DL school switched languages during a mathematical discussion, they used their entire linguistic repertoire to manage the interactional demands of the conversation. For example, students switched from Spanish to English or vice versa to emphasize a point and/or to gain the conversational floor.

Work that focuses on translanguaging builds on and responds to the prior work that used code-switching as a framework for examining students' and teachers' use of languages in multilingual mathematics classrooms. For example, Garza (2018) examined the uses of language in one seventh-grade classroom in a DL school and noted that the teacher used translanguaging to integrate Spanish and English and their associated ways of saying and doing things (e.g., linguistic markers) into a single communication system. In subsequent work, Garza Ayala (2020) highlighted how, in the context of DL schools, the use of translanguaging by students and teachers can be a powerful resource for the development of biliteracy. Garza Ayala's use of the translanguaging framing challenges the language planning focus of many DL schools where languages are intentionally separated and taught in different classes at different times. A recent special issue of *Teaching for Excellence and Equity in Mathematics* presented several articles that examined translanguaging practices in K-12 mathematics. For example, Maldonado

Rodríguez et al. (2020) used the image of the "translanguaging corriente" (García & Wei, 2015) to describe how, in the flow of language use in a classroom, including multilingual learners and teachers, teachers can support students' development in multiple ways, including developing bilingual identities, mathematical proficiencies, and supporting students' socioemotional wellbeing. A study group of mathematics educators who came together to read, discuss, and consider the implications of research on translanguaging for mathematics education recently published a research summary. The group concluded their article by posing a series of questions for the field: "(1) What instructional practices support bilingual students in the mathematics classroom when we take a translanguaging perspective? (2) How might we prepare preservice teachers to understand and enact practices consistent with this perspective? (3) How might mathematics education research be transformed with and through a translanguaging perspective?" (Translanguaging Study Group, 2020, p. 13)

Math and Science Teacher Preparation

How do teachers in DL and bilingual classrooms address modern mathematics and science standards, namely the NGSS and CCSSM, in which teachers must teach using an inquiry approach? Such teaching may require all students to conduct purposeful investigations (Aguilar-Valdez et al., 2013; Bybee, 2013; Quinn et al., 2012), and this can be supported by using practical pedagogical approaches such as the biological sciences curriculum study's (BSCS) 5E instructional model (Bybee, 2014). Yet, the level of rigor is contingent upon teachers' comfort with teaching science.

A study by Lyon et al. (2018) examined the uptake of a framework for preparing science teachers that incorporated four dimensions: scientific sense-making, scientific discourse, language, and disciplinary literacy development, and contextualized science activity. They found that science teacher educators were most successful in increasing student interaction and facilitating talk. However, another level added to teaching to the NGSS entails teaching science for social justice. Thus, in-service and pre-service teachers need to be prepared to teach the new math and science standards. Following the NGSS, multilingual learners must be able to explain procedures and sequential actions and must be able to defend their findings in scientific investigations. Additionally, they must also develop the skills needed to conduct the investigations. However, what is not as visible in the research is how teachers of multilingual learners in DL settings can teach language and content while considering and valuing the assets multilingual learners bring to their learning environments.

In work focused on the transition from mathematics teacher education to practice, Yeh (2017) described the complexities of teaching a reform vision of mathematics in a bilingual elementary mathematics classroom. Yeh's comparative case study of two bilingual elementary mathematics teachers highlighted the time, support, and preparation required for bilingual teachers to develop as bilingual mathematics educators. In describing the teachers' experiences in their preparation programs, Yeh noted that "there was little emphasis on preparing teachers to support students' development of language skills to engage meaningfully in disciplinary discourse" (p. 28). As a result, the bilingual teachers implemented the discourse-centered mathematics program unevenly.

While paradigm and conceptual shifts in mathematics and science education have taken place, the legacy of educational debt (Ladson-Billings, 2006) continues to pose challenges in contemporary DL and bilingual education, especially in science and mathematics. In our review for this chapter, we found relatively little research focused on teacher preparation and professional learning for DL or bilingual mathematics and science. Additionally, we know from current research that there are ongoing shortages of DLBE teachers, and most DLBE teachers lack adequate curriculum materials for teaching multilingual learners (Hernández et al., 2022). These challenges in the field relate to systemic design and the hegemony of English (Macedo et al., 2015), as well as restrictive language policies such as Proposition 227 in California, which has limited bilingual education (Hernández et al., 2022).

In the next section, we present one illustration of forward-looking research that examined science teaching and learning from the perspective of one DL teacher.

Example from Current Research: "Todavía No Están en Español, Verdad?"

To illustrate current issues in DL math and science research, we share an example from a case study of Maestra Barrett, a fourth-grade Spanish/English DL teacher. Maestra Barrett considers herself a multilingual learner and teaches in a school near the U.S.-Mexico border that follows a 90-10 DL program model. The school has a large representation of military families and serves primarily Latinx (45%) and Filipinx (20%) students. Interviews were conducted as part of a phenomenological study of critically conscious DL science teachers (CCDLSTs, Navarro Martell, 2018, 2021, 2022). CCDLSTs are DL teachers who center racial, social, linguistic, and environmental justice in their science pedagogy to create equitable learning spaces.

The Issues with Teaching for Social Justice

Maestra Barrett had seven years of experience as a DL teacher when she was interviewed for the study. When asked to discuss whether she felt prepared to teach science in Spanish, with a social justice perspective while using the newly released NGSS, Maestra Barrett shared the following:

> ... pero así de que dices al principio me sentí preparada, claro que no porque no tenía material, tenía que hacer esas investigaciones, tenía que leer. Entonces uno tiene que ser autodidacta y buscar una forma de entender lo que les estaba pidiendo entonces, y más porque los estándares están en inglés y no en español así que buscar vocabulario, traducirlo, descomponer el estándar y todavía no están en español, ¿verdad?
>
> [... but if you ask if at the beginning I felt prepared, of course not because I did not have material, I had to do that research, I had to read. So more if one has to be self-taught and look for a way to understand what they (NGSS) were asking, and more because the standards are in English and not in Spanish, so looking for vocabulary, translating it, deconstructing the standard and they are not in Spanish yet, right?

In this dialogue, Maestra Barrett describes how unprepared she felt when she first began implementing a vision of standards-aligned science teaching in Spanish. Being enrolled as a graduate student, however, provided Maestra Barrett with the tools needed to conduct her research on how to teach and implement the new standards, especially since the standards were, and still are, only available in English. In addition, advancing her education was important to her because she completed her bilingual teaching credential program before the NGSS were released. However, not all K-12 teachers have the privilege of being enrolled in professional degree programs past their teaching credentials, so what worked for Maestra Barret may not work for others. As Yeh (2017) discusses, Maestra Barret's experiences exemplify the complexities of teaching science to multilingual learners. However, the need for teacher preparation programs to better address teaching for social justice, as demonstrated in the following quote.

In her interviews, Maestra Barrett repeatedly mentioned how she wished for more professional development opportunities to teach NGSS from a social justice perspective. "I was researching more about this because, like I said previously, we don't have professional development really on social justice." She then added,

> I think I need more professional development. I need to read more and tap into the history behind science ... because this is not [only] from the past but there are problems that are happening around the world that we're not teaching students .... And as a teacher, I have to maintain current on the issues that are happening and see how students can petition and maybe help out...and tapping into the standards they need to learn.

As a critically conscious teacher, it was important for Maestra Barrett to learn and understand global issues to help her students develop into globally conscious and agentic leaders. Notably, she first mentioned and prioritized being informed about global issues before discussing the standards (to learn more, please read Navarro Martell et al., 2022).

While the NGSS have appendices intended to support the teaching of science (Next Generation Science Standards, 2013), teachers in schools with DLBE programs where science is taught in a language other than English continue to struggle to find culturally relevant material that aligns with social-political and environmental justice, and the NGSS. This example provides more evidence of a gap in the third shift in mathematics and science education research in DL contexts, which is the shift in the focus of school curriculum guidelines, standards, and policy documents to address multilingual learners.

The Issues with Curriculum and Instructional Materials

Maestra Barrett mentioned that she used a Spanish language curriculum during her Spanish language arts time that connected to the science unit she was teaching. As a fourth-grade teacher in a 90-10 model, 70% of instruction was in Spanish and 30% in English. However, she noted that the language in her Spanish language curriculum was, at times, too advanced for her and her students; "using [our textbook], it's really difficult information ... in Spanish because even for teachers .... [we] haven't been exposed to [it]." In addition, when instructional materials are used without being supplemented or critically analyzed, this can perpetuate inequities through the hidden curriculum (Darder, 2015). Nonetheless, Maestra Barrett mentioned using teacher-created chants, charts, and songs highlighting content facts as a Project Guided, Language, Acquisition, Design (GLAD; OCDE Project GLAD®, 2020) strategy to process and review the information within the dense science curriculum materials, see Figure 31.1.

Sources of energy

Maestra Barret is an exemplary example of what we describe in the first conceptual shift in mathematics and science education in DL education. We know teachers are interested in doing liberatory work and teaching for social justice; however, many tensions remain. For a wider group of teachers to reach this point of ideological clarity and critical consciousness, teachers can benefit from continuous professional learning and spaces for reflection. Teachers can also benefit from continuous learning to stay current with state-adopted standards as well as equitable ways of teaching linguistically, culturally relevant, and sustaining pedagogies in multilingual and diverse classroom settings.

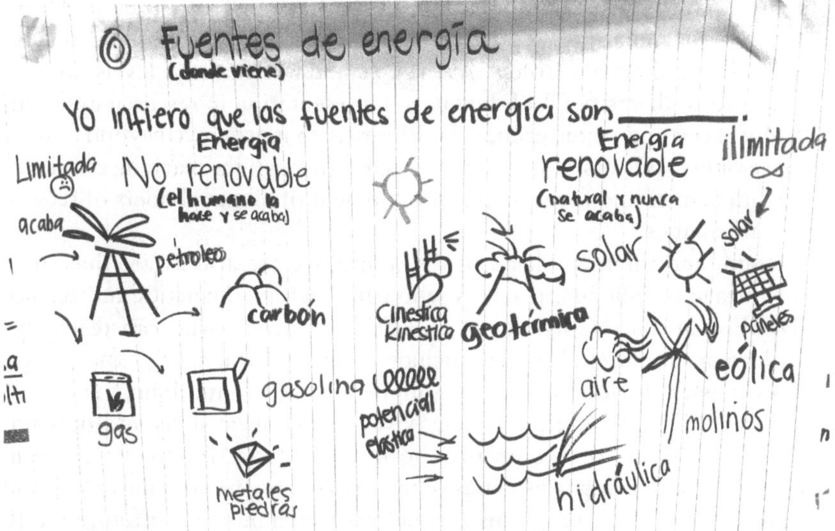

Figure 31.1 Fuentes de energía

Discussion and Conclusion

In this chapter, we have described shifts in mathematics and science education research that has considered language(s), summarized scholarship at the intersection of mathematics and science education and language, and presented an example from current research illustrating issues faced by critically conscious mathematics and science educators in DL and bilingual programs. Finally, we conclude this chapter with three specific calls for more research. First, more research is needed around DLBE and mathematics and science education in general, including research that addresses mathematics and science curricula and quality instructional materials for use in DLBE programs. Second, more research is needed explicitly on DLBE mathematics and science teacher education, both pre-service and ongoing.

Regarding the first call, we acknowledge that limited research in DLBE mathematics and science education is partly a result of policies that banned bilingual education (such as Proposition 227 in California and similar measures in other states, Hernández et al., 2022). Restrictive language policies have hindered and limited research on teaching, curriculum, and teacher preparation in this area (Alfaro, 2018). Thus, new research is in demand, especially research that centers on questions that approach multilingual learners and their families and communities from an asset-based perspective (e.g., Chval et al., 2021). We also highlight that as researchers and practitioners, we must continue unpacking the transformations in DLBE language education and who is qualified to be a mathematics and science teacher of multilingual learners. At the U.S. and international levels, there is also a need to diversify DLBE language representation in research and with different racial and ethnic groups. DLBE research must move beyond a focus on developing students as speakers of English through the teaching of science and mathematics and focus on the development of bilingual doers of science and mathematics.

Second, and thinking ahead to the future, we are also aware that there is a shortage of bilingual teachers who can teach mathematics and science in DLBE contexts (Hernández et al., 2022). Teachers who can teach this must have a specific skill set that includes content and language knowledge. However, with the long history of suppression of DL and bilingual education in U.S. K-12 schools, very few have the linguistic skills and domain-specific knowledge to take on this work in K-12 classrooms, let alone in teacher education programs. Thus, one area ripe for future innovation and research is developing programs that cultivate communities of future DLBE mathematics and science teachers and studying the effects of those programs. Building on the rich traditions of asset-based, liberatory pedagogies and incorporating insights from current research in the disciplines and in language, mathematics, and science education can become a new edge in the growth of DL and bilingual education.

References

Abell, S. K., & Lederman, N. G. (2007). *Handbook of research on science education.* Lawrence Erlbaum Associates.

Aguilar-Valdez, J. R., LópezLeiva, C. A., Roberts-Harris, D., Torres-Velásquez, D., Lobo, G., & Westby, C. (2013). Ciencia en Nepantla: The journey of Nepantler@s in science learning and teaching. *Cultural Studies of Science Education*, *8*(4), 821–858. https://doi.org/10.1007/s11422-013-9512-9

Aguirre-Muñoz, Z., & Gregory, M. O. (2019). Concept-based teaching in dual language science classrooms: Using oral language routines to develop scientific descriptions and arguments. In P. Spycher & E. F. Haynes (Eds.), *Culturally and linguistically diverse learners and STEAM: Teachers and researchers working in partnership to build a better tomorrow* (pp. 45–75). Information Age Publishing.

Alfaro, C. (2018). The sociopolitical struggle and promise of bilingual teacher education: Past, present, and future. *Bilingual Research Journal*, *41*(4), 413–427.

Alfaro, C. (2019). Preparing critically conscious dual language teachers: Recognizing and interrupting dominant ideologies. *Reimaging Dual Language Education in the U.S. Theory Into Practice Journal*, *58*(2), 194–203.

Barwell, R., Moschkovich, J. N., & Setati-Phakeng, M. (2017). Language diversity and mathematics: Second language, bilingual, and multilingual learners. In J. Cai (Ed.), *Compendium for research in mathematics education* (pp. 583–606). National Council of Teachers of Mathematics.

Beltran, D., Sarmiento, L. E., & Mora-Flores, E. (2013). *Science for English language learners: Developing academic language through inquiry-based instruction*. Shell Educational Publishing.

Bishop, A. J., & Forgasz, H. (2007). *Issues in access and equity in mathematics education* (Vol. 2). Information Age Publishing.

Buxton, C. A., & Lee, O. (2014). English learners in science education. In N. G. Lederman & S. K. Abell (Eds.), *Handbook of research on science education* (Vol. II, pp. 204–222). Routledge, Taylor & Francis.

Bybee, R. W. (2013). *Translating the NGSS for classroom instruction*. National Science Teaching Association Press.

Bybee, R. W. (2014). The BSCS 5E instructional model: Personal reflections and contemporary implications. *Science and Children*, *51*(8), 10–13.

Cai, J. (Ed.). (2017). *Compendium for research in mathematics education*. National Council of Teachers of Mathematics.

Celedon-Pattichis, S., & Ramirez, N. G. (2012). *Beyond good teaching: Advancing mathematics education for ELLs*. National Council of Teachers of Mathematics; WorldCat.

Chval, K. B., Pinnow, R. J., & Thomas, A. (2014). Learning how to focus on language while teaching mathematics to English language learners: A case study of Courtney. *Mathematics Education Research Journal*, 27(1), 103–127. https://doi.org/10.1007/s13394-013-0101-8

Chval, K. B., Smith, E., Trigos-Carrillo, L., & Pinnow, R. (2021). *Teaching math to multilingual students grades K-8: Positioning English learners for success*. Corwin.

Civil, M., & Planas, N. (2011). Language policy and the teaching and learning of mathematics. In M. Setati, T. Nkambule, & L. Goosen (Eds.), *Proceedings of the ICMI study 21 conference: Mathematics education and language diversity* (pp. 36–45). ICMI.

Cuauhtin, T. (2019). We have community cultural wealth!: Scaffolding Tara Yosso's theory for classroom praxis. In T. Cuauhtin, M. Zavala, C. Sleeter, & W. Au (Eds.), *Rethinking Ethnic Studies*, (pp. 244–256). Rethinking Schools.

Darder, A. (2015). *Culture and power in the classroom: Educational foundations for the schooling of bicultural students*. Routledge.

de Araujo, Z., Roberts, S. A., Willey, C., & Zahner, W. (2018). English learners in K–12 mathematics education: A review of the literature. *Review of Educational Research*, *88*(6), 879–919. https://doi.org/10.3102/0034654318798093

Diversity in Mathematics Education (DiME) Center for Learning and Teaching. (2007). Culture, race, power, and mathematics education. In F. K. Lester (Ed.), *Second handbook of research on mathematics teaching and learning* (pp. 405–433). Information Age.

Driscoll, M., Nikula, J., & Neumayer DePiper, J. (2016). *Mathematical thinking and communication: Access for English learners*. Heinemann.

Erath, K., Ingram, J., Moschkovich, J., & Prediger, S. (2021). Designing and enacting instruction that enhances language for mathematics learning: A review of the state of development and research. *ZDM – Mathematics Education*, *53*(2), 245–262. https://doi.org/10.1007/s11858-020-01213-2

Esquinca, A., de la Piedra, M. T., & Herrera-Rocha, L. (2018). Hegemonic language practices in engineering design and dual language education. *Association of Mexican American Educators Journal*, *12*(2), 44–68.

Esquinca, A., de la Piedra, M. T., & Herrera-Rocha, L. (2021). Engineering design in dual language: How teachers leveraged biliteracy practices to add engineering disciplinary literacy practices. *Bilingual Research Journal*, *44*(3) 298–317.

Fradd, S. H., Lee, O., Sutman, F. X., & Saxton, M. K. (2001). Promoting science literacy with English language learners through instructional materials development: A case study. *Bilingual Research Journal; Philadelphia*, *25*(4), 479–501.

García, O. (2019). Decolonizing foreign, second, heritage and first languages: Implications for education. In D. Macedo (Ed.), *Decolonizing foreign language education* (pp. 152–168). Routledge.

García, O., & Wei, L. (2015). Translanguaging, bilingualism, and bilingual education. In W. E. Wright, S. Boun, & O. García (Eds.), *The handbook of bilingual and multilingual education*. Wiley Blackwell.

Garza, A. (2018). A translanguaging mathematical space: Latina/o teenagers using their linguistic repertoire. In P. C. Ramírez, C. J. Faltis, & E. J. de Jong (Eds.), *Learning from emergent bilingual Latinx learners in K-12: Critical teacher education* (pp. 139–157). Routledge.

Garza Ayala, A. (2020). At the intersection of culture, bilingualism, and mathematics: Breaking language norms in a seventh-grade dual-language classroom for biliteracy development. *International Journal of Bilingual Education and Bilingualism*, 1–15. https://doi.org/10.1080/13670050.2020.1859984

Garza-Reyna, G. L. (2019). The academic preparedness of Latino students in dual language and transitional bilingual education programs. *Journal of Latinos and Education*, *18*(4), 340–348.

Gutiérrez, R. (2013). The sociopolitical turn in mathematics education. *Journal for Research in Mathematics Education*, *44*(1), 37–68.

Herbel-Eisenmann, B., Meaney, T., Bishop, P., & Heyd-Metzuyanim, J. (2017). Highlighting heritages and building tasks: A critical analysis of mathematics classroom discourse literature. In J. Cai (Ed.), *Compendium for research in mathematics education* (pp. 583–606). National Council of Teachers of Mathematics.

Hernández, S. J., Alfaro, C., & Navarro Martell, M. A. (2022). Bilingual teacher educators as language policy agents: A critical language policy perspective of the Castañeda v. Pickard case and the bilingual teacher shortage. *Language Policy*

Howard, E. R., Lindholm-Leary, K. J., Rogers, D., Olague, N., Medina, J., Kennedy, B., Sugarman, J., & Christian, D. (2018). *Guiding principles for dual language education* (3rd ed.) Center for Applied Linguistics.

Infante, P., & Licona, P. R. (2021). Translanguaging as pedagogy: Developing learner scientific discursive practices in a bilingual middle school science classroom. *International Journal of Bilingual Education and Bilingualism*, *24*(7), 913–926. https://doi-org.libproxy.sdsu.edu/10.1080/13670050.2018.1526885

Lachance, J. (2018). A case study of dual language teaching in science class: Implications for middle level teachers. *Research in Middle Level Education Online*, *41*(5), 1–14.

Ladson-Billings, G. (2006). From the achievement gap to the education debt: Understanding achievement in U.S. Schools. *Educational Researcher*, *35*(7), 3–12. https://doi.org/10.3102/0013189X035007003

Lederman, N. G., & Abell, S. K. (2014). *Handbook of research on science education*. Lawrence Erlbaum Associates.

Lee, O., & Luykx, A. (2007). Science education and student diversity: Race/ethnicity, language, culture, and socioeconomic status. In S. K. Abell & N. G. Lederman (Eds.), *Handbook of research on science education* (pp. 171–197). Lawrence Erlbaum Associates.

Lee, O., Quinn, H., & Valdés, G. (2013). Science and language for English language learners in relation to next generation science standards and with implications for common core state standards for English language arts and mathematics. *Educational Researcher*, *42*(4), 223–233. https://doi.org/10.3102/0013189X13480524

Lester, F. K. (Ed.). (2007). *Second handbook of research on mathematics teaching and learning*. Information Age Publishing.

LópezLeiva, C. A., & Khisty, L. L. (2014). "Juntos pero no revueltos": Microaggressions and language in the mathematics education of non-dominant Latinas/os. *Mathematics Education Research Journal*, *26*(2), 421–438. https://doi.org/10.1007/s13394-013-0105

LópezLeiva, C. A., Torres, Z., & Khisty, L. L. (2013). Acknowledging Spanish and English resources during mathematical reasoning. *Cultural Studies of Science Education*, *8*(4), 919–934. https://doi.org/10.1007/s11422-013-9518-3

Lyon, E. G., Stoddart, T., Bunch, G. C., Tolbert, S., Salinas, I., & Solis, J. (2018). Improving the preparation of novice secondary science teachers for English learners: A proof of concept study. *Science Education*, *102*(6), 1288–1318. https://doi.org/10.1002/sce.21473

Macedo, D., Dendrinos, B., & Gounari, P. (2015). *Hegemony of English* (1 ed.). Routledge. https://doi.org/10.4324/9781315634159

Maldonado Rodríguez, L. A., Krause, G. H., & Adams-Corral, M. (2020). Flowing with the translanguaging corriente: Juntos engaging with and making sense of mathematics. *Teaching for Excellence and Equity in Mathematics*, *11*(2), 17–24.

Martínez Hinestroza, J. (2020). "Hush it up!": Silence as a pedagogical resource in a language immersion mathematics classroom. *Teaching for Excellence and Equity in Mathematics*, *11*(3), 8–14.

Mazak, C. M., & Herbas-Donoso, C. (2014). Translanguaging practices and language ideologies in Puerto Rican university science education. *Critical Inquiry in Language Studies*, *11*(1), 27–49. https://doi.org/10.1080/15427587.2014.871622.

Mensah, F. M., & Jackson, I. (2018). Whiteness as property in science teacher education. *Teachers College Record*, *120*(1), 1–38.

Mestre, J. P., & Gerace, W. J. (1986). A study of the algebra acquisition of Hispanic and Anglo ninth graders: Research findings relevant to teacher training and classroom practice. *The Journal for the National Association for Bilingual Education*, *10*, 137–167.

Moschkovich, J. N. (2002). A situated and sociocultural perspective on bilingual mathematics learners. *Mathematical Thinking and Learning*, *4*(2–3), 189–212. https://doi.org/10.1207/S15327833MTL04023_5

Moschkovich, J. N. (2007). Using two languages when learning mathematics. *Educational Studies in Mathematics*, *64*, 121–144.

Moschkovich, J. (2013). Principles and guidelines for equitable mathematics teaching practices and materials for English language learners. *Journal of Urban Mathematics Education*, *6*(1), 45–57.

Moschkovich, J. N. (2015). Academic literacy in mathematics for English learners. *The Journal of Mathematical Behavior*, *40*, 43–62. https://doi.org/10.1016/j.jmathb.2015.01.005

National Center for Educational Statistics. (2021). *English language learners in public schools*. https://nces.ed.gov/programs/coe/indicator/cgf

National Governors Association Center for Best Practices & Council of Chief State School Officers. (2010). *Common core state standards for mathematics*. Authors.

Navarro Martell, M. A. (2018). *A critical examination of dual-language science educators: Ideology, pedagogy, access and equity*.

Navarro Martell, M. A. (2021). Ciencias bilingües: How dual language teachers cultivate equity in dual language classrooms. *International Journal of Bilingual*

Education and Bilingualism, 1–17. https://doi.org/10.1080/13670050.2020.1870925

Navarro Martell, M. A., Yanga-Peña, J., & Barret, G. (2022). Growing globally conscious citizens: Documenting two dual language maestras' pedagogical approaches to teaching science. In M. Y. Medina & M. Machado-Casas (Eds.), *Encyclopedia of critical understandings of Latinx and global education* (pp. 199–225). Brill.

NGSS Lead States. Next Generation Science Standards: For States, By States. *Read the Standards*. (2013). https://www.nextgenscience.org/

OCDE Project GLAD®. (2020). *Project GLAD*. Orange County Department of Education. https://ntcprojectglad.com/

OECD. (2019). *PISA 2018 results* (Vol. II). https://www.oecd-ilibrary.org/content/publication/b5fd1b8f-en

Palmer, D. K., Cervantes-Soon, C., Dorner, L., & Heiman, D. (2019). Bilingualism, biliteracy, biculturalism, and critical consciousness for all: Proposing a fourth fundamental goal for two-way dual language education. *Theory Into Practice*, *58*(2), 121–133. https://doi.org/10.1080/00405841.2019.1569376

Pelaez, K., Calleros, E. D., Parra, J., & Zahner, W. (2023). Examining community cultural wealth of a transfronteriza multilingual student in mathematics classrooms. *Journal of Qualitative Studies in Education.* https://doi.org/10.1080/09518398.2023.2178036

Poza, L. E. (2018). The language of *ciencia*: Translanguaging and learning in a bilingual science classroom. *International Journal of Bilingual Education and Bilingualism*, *21*(1), 1–19. https://doi.org/10.1080/13670050.2015.1125849

Quinn, H., Lee, O., & Valdés, G. (2012). *Language demands and opportunities in relation to next generation science standards for English language learners: What teachers need to know.* Paper presented at the Understanding Language Conference, Stanford, CA. https://ul.stanford.edu/resource/foundational-papers

Ruíz, R. (1984). Orientations in language planning. *NABE Journal*, *8*(2), 15–34. https://doi.org/10.1080/08855072.1984.10668464

Rumper, B. M., Frechette, E., Greenfield, D., & Hirsh-Pasek, K. (2021). Impacts on head start dual language learning children's early science outcomes. *Education Sciences*, *11*(6), 283. https://doi.org/10.3390/educsci11060283

Sammel, A. (2009). Turning the focus from 'other' to science education: Exploring the invisibility of whiteness. *Cultural Studies of Science Education*, *4*(3), 649–656.

Setati, M., & Adler, J. (2001). Between languages and discourses: Language practices in primary multilingual mathematics classrooms in South Africa. *Educational Studies in Mathematics*, *43*, 243–269. https://doi.org/10.1023/A:1011996002062

Stevenson, A. R. (2013). How fifth grade Latino/a bilingual students use their linguistic resources in the classroom and laboratory during science instruction. *Cultural Studies of Science Education*, *8*(4), 973–989.

Translanguaging Study Group. (2020). Translanguaging and the mathematics classroom. *Teaching for Excellence and Equity in Mathematics*, *11*(2), 8–14.

Warren, B., Ballenger, C., Ogonowski, M., Rosebery, A., & Hudicourt-Barnes, J. (2001). Rethinking diversity in learning science: The logic of everyday sense-making. *Journal of Research in Science Teaching*, *38*, 529–552.

Williams, M. (2022). Fifth graders' use of gesture and models when translanguaging during a content and language integrated science class in Hong Kong. *International Journal of Bilingual Education and Bilingualism*, *25*(4), 1304–1323.

Yeh, C. (2017). Math is more than numbers: Beginning bilingual teachers' mathematics teaching practices and their opportunities to learn. *Journal of Urban Mathematics Education*, *10*(2), 106–139.

Yosso, T. J. (2005). Whose culture has capital? A critical race theory discussion of community cultural wealth. *Race Ethnicity and Education*, *8*(1), 69–91. https://doi.org/10.1080/1361332052000341006

Zahner, W., Calleros, E. D., & Pelaez, K. (2021). Designing learning environments to promote academic literacy in mathematics in multilingual secondary mathematics classrooms. *ZDM – Mathematics Education*, *53*(2), 359–373. https://doi.org/10.1007/s11858-021-01239-0

Zahner, W., & Moschkovich, J. N. (2011). Bilingual students using two languages during peer mathematics discussions: ¿Qué significa? Estudiantes bilingües usando dos idomas en sus discusiones matemáticas: What does it mean? In K. Tellez, J. N. Moschkovich, & M. Civil (Eds.), *Latinos and mathematics education: Research on learning and teaching in classrooms and communities* (pp. 37–62). Information Age Publishing.

Zahner, W. & Wynn, L. (2023). Rethinking learning trajectories in light of student linguistic diversity. *Mathematical Thinking and Learning*, *25*(1), 100–114. https://doi.org/10.1080/10986065.2021.1931650

32
WHAT HAVE WE DONE?
A Brief Synthesis of STEM and Social Studies Research in Dual Language Bilingual Education

Armando Garza Ayala

English learners, or better yet, emergent bilingual students[1] (EBs) are the fastest growing student population in public schools in the United States (Ardasheva et al., 2018; National Center for Education Statistics, 2020). According to the U.S. Department of Education (n.d.), EBs represent about 12% of the total student population in the U.S. K-12 education system, and 77% of this student body is reported to be identified as Hispanic or Latina/o/x having Spanish as their home language. While school districts across the nation have placed English language arts (ELA) and mathematics as the most important content-areas in schools, educational interdisciplinarity has become more relevant trying to dissipate [opportunity] gaps between student populations (Jeynes, 2015). For instance, during the last decade, school districts have given a crucial importance to STEM (science, technology, engineering, and mathematics) education; yet, [opportunity] gaps between EBs and their English-speaking counterparts—especially in science, mathematics, and ELA—are not reducing at a desirable pace (Olson et al., 2020). Furthermore, a report by the National Academy of Sciences, Engineering and Medicine (2018) describes a persistent and growing marginalization of EBs in STEM education as they enroll into secondary school. Given these statistics, several departments of education across the nation have implemented bilingual education programs to better serve the EB students. Although across the United States, bilingual education may have a number of different programs, dual language bilingual education (DLBE) has been effective to better provide academic results for marginalized bilingual learners (BLs) (Cervantes-Soon et al., 2020; DeMatthews & Izquierdo, 2018; Garza-Reyna, 2019; Henderson & Palmer, 2020; Tran et al., 2015).

 DOI: 10.4324/9781003269076-45

DLBE programs are most commonly found at the elementary level. However, during the last decade, these types of bilingual programs are emerging in middle- and high-school levels due to the evident academic student success (Lindholm-Leary, 2012), and readiness to college (Garza-Reyna, 2019; Tran et al., 2015). Most of these types of programs foster an additive, enrichment academic model for the development of the bilingualism and biliteracy of their students, which is directly associated with high academic achievement (Lindholm-Leary, 2005; Steele et al., 2017; Watzinger-Tharp et al., 2018). Having these ideas into consideration, this chapter focuses on what researchers and practitioners, within the field of DLBE, have investigated on content area subjects, particularly in STEM and social studies (STEM&SS) and best learning and teaching practices for dual language bilingual learners (DLBLs).[2] In doing so, this manuscript provides a brief research review on what is happening in such subjects within DLBE programs across the United States. To explore these activities currently present in DLBE classrooms, the following overarching line of inquiry guided this review: what kind of research has been conducted by STEM&SS researchers focusing on learning and teaching practices in DLBE classrooms or programs?

Methods: The Review, the Reviewer, and Reviewing

This brief research synthesis of literature is guided by Lather's (1999) conceptualization of a review. She points out that a "review is gatekeeping, policing, and productive ... [it] is not exhaustive; it is situated, partial, perspectival ... [which can be] a critical interpretation and unpacking of a problematic [issue] that situates the work historically and methodologically" (p. 3). This review focuses on outcomes in STEM&SS in DLBE programs where DLBLs are situated as capable bilingual students regardless grade level or linguistic proficiency. In doing so, Lather's conceptualizations are important due to the scarcity of research in DLBE settings regarding teaching and learning practices in STEM&SS, without paying attention to language acquisition and development; bilingualism; students' identities; reading and writing literacies; and issues of power, race, and policy-making—themes and constructs that are typically explored in DLBE research.

According to Lather (1999), all scholarly manuscripts in a review are shaped by the author's background, experiences, positionality, and expertise; this review is not an exception. Thus, I had to reflect on my own work as a Latino bilingual teacher educator and scholar whose research studies mostly lie on language-use and STEM; and language and literacy justice for culturally and linguistically marginalized student populations. Thus, it is difficult to detach my work from politics and race; "language is always ... racialized" (Flores et al., 2021, p. 6), and whether "we choose to discuss it or not, there is no language without politics" (Zentella, 1997, p. 14). Although politics and race were always on my mind while I conducted the search for manuscripts, I had the purpose abovementioned constantly present so the search was not influenced by my own research orientations.

In order to locate the literature, I conducted a focused search on leading educational online databases: Educational Resources Information Center (ERIC), APA PsychInfo®, EBSCO, and ProQuest. I searched for peer-reviewed scholarly articles that combined three major areas: bilingual education, STEM, and SS. Although the search was restricted to these three areas, I had to resort to other terminology such as dual language/immersion education, bilingual students, science, mathematics, technology, engineering, SS, emergent bilingual, and dual language learners/students. I excluded terms such as K-12 education, specific grade level, private schooling, specific cultural groups, as well as works that explored EBs in mainstream classrooms or transitional bilingual education, and international programs—there are some exemptions explained in the specific sections where these works appear throughout the chapter. I set these limitations to focus on DLBE in the United States; specificity regarding grade level would not have been necessarily applicable, and foreign bilingual education programs would have been too broad—there are substantive differences between bilingual education programs that exist outside of the United States (see Baker & Lewis, 2015). Additionally, I did not set specific dates to make the search broader; nevertheless, most of the articles included are not older than 20 years. Other materials such as book chapters that I have collected over the years that fit the criteria were also included. In addition, the search was complemented by citation chaining.

Organization of the Chapter

This literature review is not exhaustive by any means. Nonetheless, it sheds light on research gaps in DLBE that scholars in the field need to consider for further research, elaboration, and discussion. The organization of the chapter was based on the guided question, having four main sections: (a) an examination of STEM research in DLBE; (b) a section that is dedicated to SS in DLBE classrooms; (c) a small compilation of works related to DLBLs and STEM&SS after-school programs; and (d) implications for DLBE STEM&SS researchers. Given the scarcity of manuscripts on DLBE and STEM&SS, the articles included in this section are not clustered according to their foci; instead, the organization alludes mainly to teaching and learning practices in the DLBE classrooms and pedagogical approaches at the district level, and some assessment practices.

Examination of STEM Research in Dual Language Bilingual Education

This section of the manuscript is designated to research in DLBE classrooms/programs or studies that is exploring the disciplines that specifically compose STEM teaching and learning—science, technology, engineering, and mathematics. Mostly all of the pieces included here include a linguistic component brought up by authors from different lenses; after all, language is the tools of tools for teaching and learning (Vygotsky, 1978, 1986). Nevertheless, the linguistic components observed in these works are not always the main focus areas of these manuscripts. In fact, it is worth noting that all articles included throughout this review do not observe issues of language and power, language and politics/policies, linguistic ideologies, race, gender, and the like; instead, they look at STEM meaning making in DLBE classrooms. As Domínguez (2021a) argues, "in a world where economic, political, racial, religious, sexual, and research forces have, for decades, reinforced ontological divides, one consequential place for innovation is ... precisely the ontologies we use in our research" (p. 403). Therefore, I remind the audience that this section of the review, STEM research, is guided by the following question line of inquiry, what kind of research has been conducted by STEM researchers focusing on learning and teaching practices in DLBE classrooms or programs? In order to answer this line of inquiry, the search for STEM literature brought up 19 articles relating either DLBE or DLBLs and any, or a combination, component of STEM—some exceptions are explained. This section was divided into three main subsections, mathematics, science, and technology; in this way, the organization of the literature is clearer and more focused. Unfortunately, articles where engineering is added to the K-12 DLBE curriculum were not found; however, there are some pieces in the afterschool programs section presented later.

Mathematics

This section of mathematics teaching and learning research in DLBE comprises 11 articles (Celedón-Pattichis & Turner, 2012; Domínguez, 2021a, 2021b; Domínguez & Adams, 2013; Goodrich et al., 2021; Musanti & Celedón-Pattichis, 2013; Reeder, 2020; Turner & Celedón-Pattichis, 2011) two of which overlap with science (Brenneman et al., 2019; Li et al., 2016), and one (LópezLeiva & Sung, 2016) which does not exactly focus on DLBE or DLBLs; however, I believe that it was pertinent due to the multidisciplinary approach it presents while fostering mathematics learning with specific linguistic minoritized student populations—approach that is not commonly found in mainstream or bilingual classrooms. Most of the works presented in this subsection are empirical studies, having one practitioner-based (Reeder, 2020), and one conceptual piece (LópezLeiva & Sung, 2016).

Mathematical thinking and doing was a salient theme for some articles in particular. For instance, Celedón-Pattichis and Turner (2012), using a sociocultural framework, examined DLBE preschoolers' ways of problem-solving while observing the tools that students utilized through language and actions. They observed a DLBE classroom for an entire year paying attention to the progressions that students enacted while orally describing their mathematical thinking and procedures. They concluded that Latina/o/x DLBE kindergarteners used a variety of resources such as visual representations, actions on quantities, gestures, and symbols to mediate and support their mathematical thinking through discursive moments. In a similar way, detaching from a language-focused interactionist model, Domínguez (2021a), using concepts from Indigenous ways of knowing and Western materialist feminist perspectives, explored the multiple relationalities between students and materials by observing how they made sense of equivalent fractions. The author describes how DLBLs utilized their linguistic resources in their own terms; however, Domínguez explains that by detaching mathematics research from a language-interactionist lens, we can observe DLBLs' vibrant and expressive material worlds in which they are able to show their mathematical lives. That is, the materialist approach that the author uses allowed him to see how students were intra-acting with material bodies—such as cameras, figures, cardboard—and mathematical concepts. In addition, Domínguez (2021b) brings up ideas about the role of *noticing* in the DLBE mathematics classroom challenging readers to think differently about such construct—considering its materiality and reciprocity along with movement while doing mathematics. Domínguez discusses his findings as noticing and decentering the human, noticing and mobilizing mathematical concepts, and noticing and sensing and making sense; as he put it, "this perspective on reciprocal noticing as located not in the minds of individual teachers or students, but in the space and time that these vibrant bodies cocreate with other vibrant nonhuman bodies" (p. 53). Domínguez (2021a, 2021b) and Domínguez and Adams (2013) are challenging mathematics DLBE researchers to detach themselves from a language-interactionist perspective and to conceptualize mathematical learning and teaching from different theoretical frames to see how students think in and do mathematics.

Solving problem and cognitively guided instruction (Carpenter et al., 2015) is not widely studied in DLBE classrooms. Looking at such pedagogical approach for teaching and learning mathematics, Turner and Celedón-Pattichis (2011) explored the construct of *opportunities-to-learn* in which they looked at time, quality, and how teachers provided appropriate tasks so students have plenty of practice manipulating mathematical concepts. The authors observed three fourth-grade classrooms, two DLBE, and one English as a second language (ESL) classroom. Something the authors found when comparing the classrooms was that DLBL students outperformed the

ESL students, due to the ample opportunities that their bilingual teacher (BT) provided. In addition, DLBLs were able to use their full range of linguistic resources while manipulating word problems with a variety of math operations. This mixed-methods study suggests that the more opportunities students have to do mathematics—including variety of tasks, linguistic tools, and teachers' dispositions—the better they perform. The authors emphasize the role of the mathematics teacher when giving students a variety of opportunities to learn and do mathematics.

The role of BTs while using specific STEM curriculum and pedagogies is underexplored; practice- and classroom-based ethnographic research in such field is needed. Reeder (2020) provides a practitioner-based work where she describes a 21-day approach to nurture mathematics and language in a first-grade DLBE classroom. As the teacher-researcher herself, she was able to see the growth in both mathematics and language. She suggests that these types of teaching practices with DLBLs are crucial and require constant routines and formal instruction; especially during the first two years of DLBE instruction. According to Reeder, BTs' training and dispositions toward specific approaches have vital importance where promoting units that promote both mathematics content and language growth. Similarly, Musanti and Celedón-Pattichis (2013) focused their study on the practices of a BT of a predominantly Mexican-American classroom. The authors discuss teaching practices such as authentic mathematics stories, the use of multimodality when presenting problem-solving tasks, opportunities for students to collectively do math, and how teachers can promote participation so they create a mathematical discursive community. The researchers argue that these practices encompass pedagogical features of confidence, care, and understanding. These features, according to them, may create a learning environment that supports DLBLs by promoting engagement in tasks that develop mathematical thinking through mathematical linguistic tools.

As is well known, in the United States, assessment is always an issue for many DLBE schools and districts; equity has to be considered (Navarro Martell, 2022). Mainstream and DLBE pre- and in-service teachers' common inquiry asks whether or not DLBL students need translations of specific concepts to nurture academic growth, and to have more equitable tools to assess learning. Goodrich et al. (2021) conducted a study looking at equitable mathematics assessments for DLBLs. Their results suggest that using a translation of an assessment instrument of mathematics is an equitable and unbiased accommodation for young DLBLs. This statement pushes the DLBE field to create practical implications for designing standardized equitable assessments for DLBLs; especially in mathematics.

Professional development for BTs is very much in need (Varghese, 2004). Although innovative programs for DLBLs exist, they usually belong to their company creators and research is scarce (Figueras-Daniel & Li, 2021).

In this regard, Brenneman et al. (2019) proposed a STEM professional development program for early childhood BTs. Although the authors specify that they focus on science and mathematics, they, as other scholars, use the term STEM to broaden their content and leaving some space for technology and engineering. According to the authors, this program, titled SciMath-DLL, is research-based, and it has been implemented in several school districts with a high number of DLBLs. The program aims to improve STEM teaching in preschool classrooms by providing a three-part professional development training consisting of manipulating math and science content, addressing teachers' ideologies toward such content, and highlighting research-based evidence on best STEM teaching practices for DLBLs.

As mentioned earlier, research on STEM teaching and learning practices in DLBE is not abundant; however, as this short section has shown, there are scholars focusing on DLBLs and STEM performance. Another example is a large-scale study conducted by Li et al. (2016) exploring the strategies used in DLBE classrooms and mainstream classrooms in order to compare and contrast how instruction in core classes such as mathematics, science, and language arts was conducted. Although this study does not focus on a particular subject-area, it is worth to point out their findings so policy makers and other stakeholders are aware of the potential of DLBE programs for historically linguistically marginalized students. This is important because as researchers have pointed out, though bilingualism is currently seen as positive in the United States (Flores et al., 2021), there is criticism that DLBE programs may not work as expected (Olivos & Lucero, 2020).

This section ends with LópezLeiva and Sung's (2016) conceptual piece on *exploring Latino stories through mathematics*. Although this work does not focus on DLBE programs per se, it provides a structure to design and implement mathematics units that involve the culture and histories of minoritized students in a DLBE program. As is well known, ELA and mathematics are the so-called most important subjects in school (Schleppegrell, 2010). Thus, LópezLeiva and Sung propose a framework to create multidisciplinary units that include multiple literacies—such as reading, writing, and storytelling—to foster mathematical knowledge. Using a Mestizo lens for storytelling and time, the authors present seven moments in their pedagogical approach which integrates cultural children's stories and elapsed time to teach about cultural identities and the mathematical concept of time. These researchers suggest that reading and writing [and perhaps talking] about culture and identity should be included in mathematics tasks.

Science

This part of the chapter includes four articles which investigate science learning in DLBE classrooms; specifically, the chosen articles explore culturally responsive teaching practices through proverbs, riddles, and DLBLs' metaphorical creations (Arreguín-Anderson & Ruiz-Escalante, 2016; Martínez-Álvarez et al., 2018); teachers' adaptations to planned and unplanned scientific classroom interactions as a teaching process (Solís, 2017); and inclusive approaches to assess the scientific knowledge that DLBLs manipulate in their classroom (Fine & Furtak, 2020). While these four works are focusing exclusively on science in DLBE settings, other works already mentioned above explore the intersections of either science and mathematics (Brenneman et al., 2019); or science, mathematics, and language arts (Li et al., 2016).

Using culturally responsive teaching practices is crucial in diverse classrooms (Ladson-Billings, 2021). Responding to this need, Arreguín-Anderson and Ruiz-Escalante (2016) argue that not using these types of pedagogies is a disservice to DLBLs; especially those who are linguistically and culturally marginalized. The authors suggest the use of *dichos y adivinanzas* to promote science and literacy instruction that is relevant to Latina/o/x DLBLs. They argue that BTs working with marginalized DLBLs should "design interdisciplinary science lessons that are culturally congruent with [Latina/o/x DLBLs so] inquiry lessons such as those based on the 5E model [are infused with ample] opportunities to connect with proverbs and riddles" (p. 179). Similarly, Martínez-Álvarez et al. (2018) examine DLBLs' metaphorical initiations and how bilingual teacher candidates (BTCs) use such tools to create culturally responsive science lessons. The authors describe how the use of metaphors in the DLBE K-6 science classrooms foster the creation of hybrid spaces where rich cultural knowledge is utilized as a teaching and learning tool so students acquire and develop scientific content. Both pieces emphasize DLBLs' culture as an important component to make science learning relevant and meaningful.

Teaching in bilingual settings should be understood as flexible and fluid (García et al., 2017). Solís (2017) responds to this statement by examining how *adaptation,* as a theoretical framework, is a pedagogically productive approach that provides a lens for understanding both planned and unplanned scientific classroom interactions as collaborative processes. Solís reminds us that adaptations "as a theory and method for understanding classroom life of bilingual settings ... while institutional spaces and timelines [promote] normative plans for learning, [such spaces] are also porous and ever shifting" (pp. 210–211). The author argues that bilingual science teachers can benefit from being aware of how adaptations in their lesson plans promote productive spaces, especially when students bring up their cultural knowledge and language styles while manipulating scientific content. This flexibility also provides teachers with inclusive opportunities to assess students' scientific knowledge. Furthering this idea, Fine and Furtak (2020) place emphasis on more inclusive approaches to assess scientific understandings of linguistically marginalized student populations. These researchers, while suggesting the use of clear scientific objectives aligned with the Next Generation Science Standards and academic rigor, state that DLBE schools should use appropriate and equitable assessments for DLBLs. Fine and Furtak urge BTs to acquire a holistic bilingualism perspective when assessing DLBLs' scientific knowledge; a perspective that includes the use of students' full range of cultural and linguistic resources, such as translanguaging (García, 2009a).

Technology

The use of technology is widely used in U.S. K-12 classrooms due to the flexibility to promote multimodal literacy enhancement in which students can display their personal meanings and cultural experiences with academic content (Dagenais et al., 2017; Sakr et al., 2016). Nevertheless, more research is needed on how technology is used in DLBE settings (LópezLeiva et al., 2019; Rowe & Miller, 2016). This section includes four articles that represent some of the work that teachers and researchers have done while incorporating technology-based practices in their work. The first two pieces are Brown and Allmond (2021) and Rowe and Miller (2016); although they do not explore DLBE settings, their multilingual participants' experiences with technology and academic literacies are important for BTs. In addition, it is believed that the findings and arguments of these two works may potentially influence the work in DLBE classrooms. Both studies look at how multilingual students use multimodalities for creative writing. Brown and Allmond (2021) describe a case study of a second-grade Tagalog-speaking student and his interaction with technology to express their cultural experiences while learning the English language. In a similar way, Rowe and Miller (2016) explore multilingual classrooms and how multilingual students create eBooks showing their creative writing. Both works suggest that the use of multimodal strategies, which encompass the free use of linguistic and cultural resources and technology, enhances the writing abilities of BLs in both their home language and English. This is an implication for all types of educators working with multilingual students in mainstream classrooms, regardless their multilingual skills.

In the same way that technology-use promotes writing abilities, research suggests that it also enhances the reading comprehension of any kinds of texts (e.g., Lange, 2019; Walker et al., 2017). In this regard, Walker et al. (2017) report a technological intervention that they call Enhanced Moved by Reading to Accelerate Comprehension in English (EMBRACE) which is designed to enhance the reading comprehension of Latina/o/x DLBLs. Having the premise that *simulation* is based on theories of embodied cognition which posits that language comprehension is a cognitive simulation process, the authors investigated the use of technology-enhanced books and its benefits for DLBLs to understand written scientific texts (circulatory system). The authors found that when DLBLs were reading in English at a grade level, there was a clear benefit of simulation. In addition, using Spanish support, these second graders further the meaning of specific scientific words. The authors stated that having both languages scaffolding understandings, students were able to excel. Walker et al. strongly argue that when DLBLs are reading grade-appropriate texts, interaction in the form of simulation (technology-based software) helps students to comprehend scientific text.

This small section ends with a quantitative piece in which Foster et al. (2018) utilized computer-assisted instruction (CAI) as a viable tool to deliver supplemental mathematics instruction, and assessed the mathematical skills of DLBE kindergarteners in both Spanish and English. The authors made use of the software Building Blocks, which includes resources guides, assessments, and manipulatives with the purpose of promoting fluency in numeracy (number sense) and geometry. These researchers separated languages to assess mathematical knowledge growth; while they found increased growth in mathematics knowledge in Spanish, their results were not significant in English. Although this study has potential to prepare DLBE teachers in the early grades to alternatively teach and assess mathematics effectively, it lacks theories of bilingualism and biliteracy in regard to mathematical knowledge transferability. Foster et al. suggest that DLBLs should be assessed in both languages separately, which most sociocultural scholars in language, bilingualism, and biliteracy would oppose.

Through all the above-described studies, STEM researchers are strongly suggesting scholars in the field to take different frames to see DLBE learning and teaching practices. In doing so, they also urge sociocultural academics to take an advocacy stance for minoritized DLBLs and teach their pre- and in-service teachers to be sociopolitical and culturally conscious. This perspective will equip teachers with a new mindset which will allow them to take risks—risks that will be translated into teaching with culturally and responsive practices; flexibility and fluid assessments; paying attention to what DLBLs bring into their classrooms; teaching with a multimodality perspective; among many others.

Social Studies in the Dual Language Bilingual Education Classroom

SS education is often overlooked and obscured by the importance that is given to state-mandated assessments that are usually perceived as reliable measures of students' knowledge, their critical thinking, and (social) problem-solving skills (Valenzuela, 2005). As a consequence, teachers are left with the task of either adapting the SS curriculum to their school districts' mandates or simply not giving the importance to such crucial element of the

K-12 curriculum, a conflict that many researchers across the United States are trying to eradicate (Valdez, 2020).

The NCSS, National Council for the Social Studies, (1994) adopted the following definition of SS in 1992:

> Social studies is the integrated study of the social sciences and humanities to promote civic competence. Within the school program, social studies provides coordinated, systematic study drawing upon such disciplines as anthropology, archaeology, economics, geography, history, law, philosophy, political science, psychology, religion, and sociology, as well as appropriate content from the humanities, mathematics, and natural sciences. The primary purpose of social studies is to help young people make informed and reasoned decisions for the public good as citizens of a culturally [and linguistically] diverse, democratic society in an interdependent world.

Despite this definition, many educators use the SS curriculum only to provide a small glimpse of historical events of the past and the present. Although the NCSS and research-based studies continue to advocate for a reorganization of such content, curriculum scripts and the lack of use of culturally relevant pedagogies persist with a tremendous strength (Valdez, 2020).

In the same way that research on STEM pedagogies and practices and DLBE is scarce, the picture for SS in such programs does reflect an even more obscure panorama. Thus, this section includes seven studies that directly explore SS teaching and learning in DLBE classrooms (Ciechanowski, 2012; Di Stefano & Camicia, 2018; Di Stefano & Uribe, 2020; Martínez-Álvarez & Ghiso, 2017; Peterson & Chamberlain, 2015; Salinas et al., 2016; Soto Huerta, 2017). Although it can be stated that some sociocultural and/or sociolinguistic researchers might not agree, all these works try to pursue social justice in the DLBE classroom, which is expected as majority of DLBLs are marginalized students.

Having a functional linguistic and discourse analyses perspective, Ciechanowski (2012) explored competing discourses about a historical American Indian text and how DLBLs manipulated ideas of social justice through their languaging. The author emphasizes how DLBLs are exposed to language that belongs to the dominant culture without an explicit instruction/discussion of their positioning as minoritized students. Ciechanowski urges teachers and teacher educators to acquire and develop knowledge and skills on how to instruct DLBLs with explicit instruction on language and social justice; specifically, how these marginalized student populations navigate the dominant culture and its discourses. Because language and politics are inseparable, bilingual identities are always threatened by dominant discourses. Di Stefano and Camicia (2018) explore how DLBLs shaped their bilingual identities through the use of culturally responsive teachings in DLBE programs. The authors strongly suggest that the DLBE classroom should be a third-space where DLBLs are able to understand their identities as bilingual citizens in a dominant culture that fosters monolingualism.

Drawing from cultural and historical activity theory, Martínez-Álvarez and Ghiso (2017) describe how first-grade DLBLs engage in critical inquiry and conversations through the use of photographs in transnational spaces. The authors document how the students manipulated their full range of linguistic resources to describe the communities they photographed. They argue that using translanguaging, as a cultural and historical tool, is necessary in DLBE settings to mediate DLBLs' social justice meanings. While Martínez-Álvarez and Ghiso focused on a more sociolinguistic approach for instructing DLBLs, Di Stefano and Uribe (2020), arguing that English speakers in DLBE take advantage from DLBLs with a Latin American heritage, focused their study on the development of academic Spanish—construct that brings much debate among sociocultural bilingual scholars. According to the authors, by bringing academic Latin American literature to the DLBE classroom, teachers promote linguistic equity and justice for minoritized Latina/o/x DLBLs. Similarly, but using Freire's (1970) frame on conscientização, Soto Huerta (2017) examines how BLs manipulated informative texts in Texas. Specifically, the author observed how students developed critical perspectives on social justice and equity about slavery in Texas. Although this work was conducted in a transitional bilingual education classroom, Soto Huerta's findings are important for DLBE schools because her work demonstrates that teachers can easily integrate critical frameworks to the bilingual SS curriculum to elevate the instructional quality for marginalized DLBLs.

Guiding student inquiry through the use of critical readings is a teaching practice supported by the National Association for Multicultural Education in their position statement (National Association for Multicultural Education [NAME], 2015). Therefore, reading these types of texts is highly encouraged in the DLBE classroom. In this regard, Peterson and Chamberlain (2015) describe how a DLBE teacher promotes read-aloud discussions with fourth-grade DLBLs. The authors emphasize that these kinds of teaching practices allow students to manipulate texts with specific social justice issues that deepen students' understandings of what is happening around them; critical in the DLBE SS curriculum. Furthermore, Salinas et al. (2016) state that the experiences of BTCs in the SS methods courses, in their teaching preparation programs, are critical so they reproduce those events in their future classrooms. The authors explain how bilingual Latina teacher candidates build historical narratives of marginalized communities of Color in their teacher preparation courses. They suggest that teacher educators should integrate critical frameworks, such as LatCrit, in their courses and assignments so critical epistemologies influence how prospective Latina teachers are prepared to counteract the exclusion of minoritized narratives in the SS curriculum.

What these short reviews of SS manuscripts show is that we, as social justice scholars in the field of DLBE, need to pay more attention to how injustices and social justice issues are being taught in the K-12 DLBE classroom. We can no longer afford for teachers to use scripted curriculum as Valdez (2020) strongly criticizes. Teacher educators need to equip their pre- and in-service teachers to give justice to minoritized DLBLs in broken educational systems.

Dual Language Learners and STEM&SS After-School Programs

After-school programs is a common educational practice in U.S.-educational system. Often, these programs target underserved student populations and focus on critical subject areas such as mathematics and language. Through the use of these educational models and regardless the rationale of such programs, educators, researchers, and members of society in general come together to make an impact on their communities. This section of the chapter describes some impactful after-school programs that are either carried out in DLBE schools, bilingual settings, or just serving DLBLs and their communities.

Many of these spaces are non-formal learning settings where participants collaborate with each other modeling variations of what Cole (1996, 2006) conceptualized as fifth-dimension after-school projects. These rich educational settings are developed and designed as hybrid spaces (see e.g., Gutiérrez et al., 1999) where multiple academic literacies, cultural, and linguistic tools come together. These hybrid spaces, also conceived as third-spaces (e.g., Gutiérrez et al., 1999; Moje et al., 2004; Vomvoridi-Ivanović, 2012), create authentic formal and informal interactions where participants utilize a variety of academic tools to negotiate, mediate, create, and develop new STEM&SS meanings; they provide culturally and linguistically marginalized students with ample opportunities to acquire and develop academic literacies in content areas. After-school programs usually involve K-12 marginalized children, undergraduate students, community members, and university researchers who constantly negotiate their roles as they participate in a variety of academic and social activities.

Particularly to DLBE, and based on a network of fifth-dimension after-school models in California, *La Clase Mágica* (LCM) (Vásquez, 2003) emerged as a bicultural, bilingual, biliterate, and intergenerational approach computer-based project in which participants interact in non-formal environments working on problem-solving activities and creating zones of proximal (academic and linguistic) development. Informed by multiple sociocultural and historical theories of learning and development, LCM has inspired multiple ecological learning environments in the United States and internationally. Researchers and educators in these settings have urged academics in the field of bilingual education to create these kinds of rich learning spaces for marginalized DLBLs. In response to this call, scholars have designed and carried out projects that have impacted a great number of DLBL minoritized students and their communities. The following represent just an example of these fifth-dimension programs for bilingual/multilingual marginalized communities: *Las Redes* (Gutiérrez et al., 1999; Gutiérrez et al., 1999); *Los Rayos* (Razfar, 2013; Vomvoridi-Ivanović, 2012; Willey et al., 2014); *LCM at UTSA* (Bustos Flores et al., 2014); *El Pueblo Mágico* (Schwartz et al., 2015); *Academia Cuauhtli* (Valenzuela, 2017; Valenzuela et al., 2015); Robotics at LCMs (Yuen et al., 2013); and engineering, mathematics, technology, and bilingual Latina/o/x middle-school students, through the *Advancing Out-of-School Learning in Mathematics and Engineering* (AOLME) project (Celedón-Pattichis et al., 2013; LópezLeiva et al., 2019). All these projects take into consideration the cultural, literacy, and linguistic tools that participants possess to challenge the traditional ways of seeing what constitutes as *formal* STEM&SS *academic knowledge.*

After-school programs for minoritized DLBLs should be a priority in every school district across the nation. The outcomes that these programs offer cross multidisciplinary boundaries along with multiple affordances that every sociocultural context is able to provide. According to researchers abovementioned, these programs allow students and their families with safe spaces where they can not only learn but also create familial relationships with other members of the community. Researchers urge STEM academics to look for grant opportunities from the National Science Foundation (NSF), which is able to support formal and informal programs in K-12 educational settings.

Implications for Researchers of Dual Language Bilingual Education in STEM&SS

As mentioned earlier and implied by the articles included in this review, it is clear that more research that explores STEM and SS teaching and learning practices in DLBE classrooms is needed. Although there is a growing body of research in DLBE settings, most of this research is focused on program structure, language acquisition, language policies, language allocation, language ideologies, power relations, and similar constructs. To provide an illustration of this necessity, we can look at three compilation of works on bilingual/multilingual (Wright et al., 2015) and dual language education (Ramírez & Faltis, 2019, 2020). While Wright et al.'s (2015) work provides global-international and critical perspectives on bilingual/multilingual education, there is no specific research on STEM or SS pedagogical approaches. Similarly, in the works edited by Ramírez and Faltis (2019, 2020), while focusing on DLBE, none of the articles included explore teaching and learning approaches in STEM&SS classrooms or programs—some discuss issues of social justice in teaching and learning; however, they do not explicitly discuss pedagogical practices. Thus, this brief review of literature provides a critical call for DLBE researchers and practitioners already involved in research in bilingual settings to develop empirical contributions to the field, adding crucial components on how DLBLs are performing in STEM&SS content-area classes. It is time to give the importance that our minoritized DLBLs deserve in such crucial subject-area-classes. It is the hope that this brief synthesis of research plants the seed on many DLBE scholars so they extend their research agendas and integrate issues of STEM&SS teaching and learning in the DLBE classroom along with other constructs mentioned above.

Notes

1 García (2009b) introduced the term emergent bilingual (EB) which "refers to the children's potential in developing their bilingualism; it does not suggest a limitation or a problem ... bilingualism is recognized as a potential resource ... [these students] are seen as having an advantage over those who speak English only and for whom becoming bilingual will be more difficult" (p. 322). Although the use of EB is not at the center of this chapter, it is used to counteract the negative connotations attached to the label English learner.

2 Researchers and authors of bilingual education use different labels such as bilingual learners, multilingual learners, English learners, EBs, bilingual students, dual language students, etc. For this manuscript, the term "dual language bilingual learner" (DLBL) was chosen, for consistency purposes, and due to the nature of this handbook on DLBE, first of its kind. It is believed that these students, while they may be multilingual, they are learning content-area in two-nation-named languages in U.S. public schools beyond kindergarten—in some states, school districts have K-12 [two-way immersion] dual language bilingual education. Thus, DLBL seems appropriate.

References

Ardasheva, Y., Wang, Z., Roo, A. K., Adesope, O. O., & Morrison, J. A. (2018). Representation visuals' impacts on science interest and reading comprehension of adolescent English learners. *Journal of Educational Research*, *111*(5), 631–643.

Arreguín-Anderson, M. G., & Ruiz-Escalante, J. (2016). Dichos y adivinanzas: Literary resources that enhance science learning and teaching in the bilingual classroom. In E. Riojas Clark, B. Bustos Flores, H. L. Smith, & D. A. González (Eds.), *Multicultural literature for Latino bilingual children: Their words, their worlds* (pp. 167–182). Rowman & Littlefield.

Baker, C., & Lewis, G. (2015). A synthesis of research on bilingual and multilingual education. In W. E. Wright, S. Boun, & O. García (Eds.), *The handbook of bilingual and multilingual education* (pp. 109–126). John Wiley & Sons, Inc.

Brenneman, K., Lange, A., & Nayfeld, I. (2019). Integrating STEM into preschool education; designing a professional development model in diverse settings. *Early Childhood Education Journal*, *47*(1), 15–28. https://doi:10.1007/s10643-018-0912-z

Brown, S., & Allmond, A. (2021). Constructing my world: A case study examining emergent bilingual multimodal composing practices. *Early Childhood Education Journal*, *49*(2), 209–221. https://doi:10.1007/s10643-020-01062-4

Bustos Flores, B., Vásquez, O. A., & Riojas Clark, E. (Eds.). (2014). *Generating transworld pedagogy: Reimagining la clase mágica*. Lexington Books.

Carpenter, T. P., Fennema, E., Franke, M. L., Levi, L., & Empson, S. B. (2015). *Children's mathematics: Cognitively guided instruction*. Heinemann.

Celedón-Pattichis, S., LópezLeiva, C., Pattichis, M., & Llamocca, D. (2013). An interdisciplinary collaboration between computer engineering and mathematics/bilingual education to develop a curriculum for underrepresented middle school students. *Cultural Studies of Science Education*, *8*(4), 873–887. https://doi:10.1007/s11422-013-9516-5

Celedón-Pattichis, S., & Turner, E. E. (2012). "Explícame tu respuesta": Supporting the development of mathematical discourse in emergent bilingual kindergarten students. *Bilingual Research Journal*, *35*(2), 197–216. https://doi:10.1080/15235882.2012.703635

Cervantes-Soon, C., Gambrell, J., Kasun, G. S., Sun, W., Freire, J. A., & Dorner, L. M. (2020). "Everybody wants a choice" in dual language education of El Nuevo Sur: Whiteness as the gloss for everybody in media discourses of multilingual education. *Journal of Language, Identity & Education*, 1–17. https://doi:10.1080/15348458.2020.1753201

Ciechanowski, K. (2012). Conflicting discourses: Functional linguistic and discourse analyses of Pocahontas texts in bilingual third-grade social studies. *Journal of Literacy Research*, *44*(3), 300–338. https://doi:10.1177/1086296X12450699

Cole, M. (1996). *Cultural psychology: A once and future discipline*. Belknap Press of Harvard University Press.

Cole, M. (2006). *The fifth dimension: An after-school program built on diversity*. Russell Sage.

Dagenais, D., Toohey, K., Bennett Fox, A., & Singh, A. (2017). Multilingual and multimodal composition at school: "ScribJab" in action. *Language and Education*, *31*(3), 263–282.

DeMatthews, D., & Izquierdo, E. (2018). The importance of principals supporting dual language education: A social justice leadership framework. *Journal of Latinos and Education*, *17*(1), 53–70. https://doi:10.1080/15348431.2017.1282365

Di Stefano, M., & Camicia, S. P. (2018). Transnational civic education and emergent bilinguals in a dual language setting. *Education Sciences*, *8*, 1–22.

Di Stefano, M., & Uribe, N. E. (2020). Sor Juana Inés de la Cruz en la clase de doble inmersión. *Dialnet*, (45). https://dialnet.unirioja.es/servlet/articulo?codigo=7524016

Domínguez, H. (2021a). Fraction detectives: Bilingual students investigate the hidden identities of equivalent fractions. *ZDM*, *53*(2), 393–404. https://doi:10.1007/s11858-020-01218-x

Domínguez, H. (2021b). Students and teachers mobilizing mathematical concepts through reciprocal noticing. *ZDM-Mathematics Education*, *53*(1), 43–55. https://doi:10.1007/s11858-020-01209-y

Domínguez, H., & Adams, M. (2013). Más o menos: Exploring estimation in a bilingual classroom. *Teaching Children Mathematics*, *20*(1), 36–41. https://doi:10.5951/teacchilmath.20.1.0036

Figueras-Daniel, A., & Li, Z. (2021). Evidence of support for dual language learners in a study of bilingual staffing patterns using the classroom assessment of supports for emergent bilingual acquisition (CASEBA). *Early Childhood Research Quarterly*, *54*, 271–285. https://doi:10.1016/j.ecresq.2020.09.011

Fine, C. G. M., & Furtak, E. M. (2020). A framework for science classroom assessment task design for emergent bilingual learners. *Science Education*, *104*(3), 393–420. https://doi:10.1002/sce.21565

Flores, N., Tseng, A., & Subtirelu, N. (2021). Bilingualism for all or just for the rich and white? Introducing a raciolinguistic perspective to dual language education. In N. Flores, A. Tseng, & N. Subtirelu (Eds.), *Bilingualism for all?: Raciolinguistic perspectives on dual language education in the United States* (pp. 1–18). Multilingual Matters.

Foster, M. E., Anthony, J. L., Clements, D. H., Sarama, J., & Williams, J. J. (2018). Hispanic dual language learning kindergarten students' response to a numeracy intervention: A randomized control trial. *Early Childhood Research Quarterly*, *43*, 83–95. https://doi.org/10.1016/j.ecresq.2018.01.009

Freire, P. (1970). *Pedagogy of the oppressed*. Herder and Herder.

García, O. (2009a). *Bilingual education in the 21st century: A global perspective*. Wiley-Blackwell Pub.

García, O. (2009b). Emergent bilinguals and TESOL: What's in a name? *TESOL Quarterly*, *43*(2), 322–326. https://doi:10.1002/j.1545-7249.2009.tb00172.x

García, O., Ibarra Johnson, S., & Seltzer, K. (2017). *The translanguaging classroom: Leveraging student bilingualism for learning*. Caslon.

Garza-Reyna, G. L. (2019). The academic preparedness of Latino students in dual language and transitional bilingual education programs. *Journal of Latinos and Education*, *18*(4), 340–348. https://doi:10.1080/15348431.2017.1394858

Goodrich, J. M., Koziol, N. A., & Yoon, H. (2021). Are translated mathematics items a valid accommodation for dual language learners? Evidence from ECLS-K. *Early Childhood Research Quarterly*, *57*, 89–101. https://doi:10.1016/j.ecresq.2021.06.001

Gutiérrez, K. D., Baquedano-López, P., Alvarez, H. H., & Chiu, M. M. (1999). Building a culture of collaboration through hybrid language practices. *Theory Into Practice*, *38*(2), 87–93. https://doi:10.2307/1477228

Gutiérrez, K. D., Baquedano-López, P., & Tejeda, C. (1999). Rethinking diversity: Hybridity and hybrid language practices in the third space. *Mind, Culture & Activity*, *6*(4), 286–303.

Henderson, K. I., & Palmer, D. K. (2020). *Dual language bilingual education: Teacher cases and perspectives on large-scale implementation*. Multilingual Matters.

Jeynes, W. H. (2015). A meta-analysis on the factors that best reduce the achievement gap. *Education and Urban Society*, *47*(5), 523–554. https://doi:10.1177/0013124514529155

Ladson-Billings, G. (2021). *Culturally relevant pedagogy: Asking a different question*. Teachers College Press.

Lange, A. A. (2019). Technology, instructional methods, and the systemic messiness of innovation: Improving reading fluency for low socio-economic elementary school students. *Educational Technology Research and Development*, *67*(5), 1333–1350. https://doi:10.1007/s11423-019-09675-2

Lather, P. (1999). To be of use: The work of reviewing. *Review of Educational Research*, *69*(1), 2–7.

Li, J., Steele, J., Slater, R., Bacon, M., & Miller, T. (2016). Teaching practices and language use in two-way dual language immersion programs in a large public school district. *International Multilingual Research Journal*, *10*(1), 31–43.

Lindholm-Leary, K. J. (2005). Review of research and best practices on effective features of dual language education programs. *Center for Applied Linguistics*.

Lindholm-Leary, K. J. (2012). Success and challenges in dual language education. *Theory Into Practice*, *51*(4), 256–262. https://doi:10.1080/00405841.2012.726053

LópezLeiva, C. A., Pattichis, M. S., & Celedón-Pattichis, S. (2019). Modelling and programming of digital video: A source for the integration of mathematics, engineering, and technology. In B. Doig, J. Williams, D. Swanson, R. Borromeo Ferri, & P. Drake (Eds.), *Interdisciplinary mathematics education: The state of the art and beyond* (pp. 135–153). Springer International Publishing.

LópezLeiva, C. A., & Sung, Y. K. (2016). Tiempo y cultura: Exploring Latino stories through mathematics. In E. Riojas Clark, B. Bustos Flores, H. L. Smith, & D. A. González (Eds.), *Multicultural literature for Latino bilingual children: Their words, their worlds* (pp. 183–204). Rowman & Littlefield.

Martínez-Álvarez, P., & Ghiso, M. P. (2017). On languaging and communities: Latino/a emergent bilinguals' expansive learning and critical inquiries into global childhoods. *International Journal of Bilingual Education and Bilingualism*, *20*(6), 667–687. https://doi:10.1080/13670050.2015.1068270

Martínez-Álvarez, P., Sáez, N., & Ghiso, M. P. (2018). Mediating hybrid spaces in the bilingual science class by learning to cultivate children's metaphors. *Linguistics and Education*, *47*, 68–83. https://doi:10.1016/j.linged.2018.08.003

Moje, E. B., Ciechanowski, K. M., Kramer, K., Carrillo, E., & Collazo, R. (2004). Working toward third space in content area literacy: An examination of everyday funds of knowledge and discourse. *Reading Research Quarterly*, *39*(1), 38–70.

Musanti, S. I., & Celedón-Pattichis, S. (2013). Promising pedagogical practices for emergent bilinguals in kindergarten: Towards a mathematics discourse community. *Journal of Multilingual Education Research*, *4*, 41–62.

National Council for the Social Studies. (1994). *Expectations of excellence: Curriculum standards for social studies* (vol. 3). NCSS.

National Academies of Sciences, Engineering and Medicine (2018). *Promoting the educational success of children and youth learning English: Promising futures*. The National Academies Press.

National Association for Multicultural Education (NAME). (2015, May 30). *Definition updated 2013*. https://www.nameorg.org/2003_name_position_statements.php

National Center for Education Statistics. (2020). *English language learners in public schools*. https://nces.ed.gov/programs/coe/indicator_cgf.asp

Navarro Martell, M. A. (2022). Ciencias bilingües: How dual language teachers cultivate equity in dual language classrooms. *International Journal of Bilingual Education and Bilingualism*, *25*(6), 2142–2158. https://doi:10.1080/13670050.2020.1870925

Olivos, E. M., & Lucero, A. (2020). Latino parents in dual language immersion programs: Why are they so satisfied? *International Journal of Bilingual Education and Bilingualism*, *23*(10), 1211–1224. https://doi:10.1080/13670050.2018.1436520

Olson, C. B., Woodworth, K., Arshan, N., Black, R., Chung, H. Q., D'Aoust, C., Dewar, T., Friedrich, L., Godfrey, L., Land, R., Matuchniak, T., Scarcella, R., & Stowell, L. (2020). The pathway to academic success: Scaling up a text-based analytical writing intervention for Latinos and English learners in secondary school. *Journal of Educational Psychology*, *112*(4), 701–717. https://doi:10.1037/edu0000387

Peterson, K. E., & Chamberlain, K. (2015). 'Everybody treated him like he was from another world': Bilingual fourth graders develop social awareness through interactive read-alouds focused on critical literacies. *Literacy Research and Instruction*, *54*(3), 231–255. https://doi:10.1080/19388071.2015.1027020

Ramírez, P. C., & Faltis, C. (2019). This issue. *Theory Into Practice*, *58*(2), 101–106. https://doi:10.1080/00405841.2019.1569401

Ramírez, P. C., & Faltis, C. (Eds.). (2020). *Dual language education in the US: Rethinking pedagogy, curricula, and teacher education to support dual language learning for all* (1st ed.). Routledge.

Razfar, A. (2013). Multilingual mathematics: Learning through contested spaces of meaning making. *International Multilingual Research Journal*, *7*(3), 175–196.

Reeder, R. (2020). Twenty-one days of first grade Spanish dual immersion: A nurturing mathematics and linguistic incubation. *Teaching for Excellence and Equity in Mathematics*, *11*(1), 14–21.

Rowe, D. W., & Miller, M. E. (2016). Designing for diverse classrooms: Using iPads and digital cameras to compose eBooks with emergent bilingual/biliterate four-year-olds. *Journal of Early Childhood Literacy*, *16*(4), 425–472. https://doi:10.1177/1468798415593622

Sakr, M., Connelly, V., & Wild, M. (2016). 'Evil cats' and 'jelly floods': Young children's collective constructions of digital art making in the early years classroom. *Journal of Research in Childhood Education*, *30*(1), 128–141.

Salinas, C. S., Fránquiz, M. E., & Rodríguez, N. N. (2016). Writing Latina/o historical narratives: Narratives at the intersection of critical historical inquiry and LatCrit. *The Urban Review*, *48*(3), 419–439. https://doi:10.1007/s11256-016-0361-1

Schleppegrell, M. J. (2010). Language in mathematics teaching and learning: A research review. In J. N. Moschkovich (Ed.), *Language and mathematics education: Multiple perspectives and directions for research* (pp. 73–112). Information Age Publishing, Inc.

Schwartz, L. H., DiGiacomo, D., & Gutiérrez, K. D. (2015). Designing "contexts for tinkerability" with undergraduates and children within the el pueblo mágico social design experiment. *International Journal for Research on Extended Education*, *3*(1), 94–113.

Solís, J. L. (2017). Adaptation and the language of learning science in a bilingual classroom. In J. Langman, & H. Hansen-Thomas (Eds.), *Discourse analytic perspectives on STEM education* (pp. 195–215). Springer.

Soto Huerta, M. E. (2017). Transformative pedagogy: Emergent bilinguals and perspective taking. *Journal of Latinos and Education*, *16*(3), 192–202. https://doi:10.1080/15348431.2016.1229613

Steele, J. L., Slater, R. O., Zamarro, G., Miller, T., Li, J., Burkhauser, S., & Bacon, M. (2017). Effects of dual-language immersion programs on student achievement: Evidence from lottery data. *American Educational Research Journal*, *54*, 282S–306S.

Tran, N. A., Behseta, S., Ellis, M., Martinez-Cruz, A., & Contreras, J. (2015). The effects of Spanish English dual language immersion on student achievement in science and mathematics. *eJEP: eJournal of Education Policy*, 57–77. https://in.nau.edu/ejournal/summer-2015-special-issue/#

Turner, E. E., & Celedón-Pattichis, S. (2011). Mathematical problem solving among Latina/o kindergartners: An analysis of opportunities to learn. *Journal of Latinos and Education*, *10*(2), 146–169.

U.S. Department of Education. (n.d.). *Our nation's English learners: What are their characteristics?* https://www2.ed.gov/datastory/el-characteristics/index.html#one

Valdez, C. (2020). Flippin' the scripted curriculum: Ethnic studies inquiry in elementary education. *Race Ethnicity and Education*, *23*(4), 581–597. https://doi:10.1080/13613324.2018.1497959

Valenzuela, A. (2005). Introduction: The accountability debate in Texas: Continuing the conversation. In A. Valenzuela (Ed.), *Leaving children behind: How "Texas style" accountability fails Latino youth* (pp. 1–32). University of New York Press.

Valenzuela, A. (2017). Academia Cuauhtli: (Re)locating the spiritual, if crooked, path to social justice. *International Journal of Qualitative Studies in Education*, *30*(10), 906–911.

Valenzuela, A., Zamora, E., & Rubio, B. (2015). Academia Cuauhtli and the eagle: "Danza Mexica" and the epistemology of the circle. *Voices in Urban Education*, (41), 46–56.

Varghese, M. (2004). Professional development for bilingual teachers in the United States: A site for articulating and contesting professional roles. *International Journal of Bilingual Education and Bilingualism*, *7*(2–3), 222–237. https://doi:10.1080/13670050408667810

Vásquez, O. A. (2003). *La clase mágica: Imagining optimal possibilities in a bilingual community of learners*. Lawrence Erlbaum Associates, Publishers.

Vomvoridi-Ivanović, E. (2012). Using culture as a resource in mathematics: The case of four Mexican-American prospective teachers in a bilingual after-school program. *Journal of Mathematics Teacher Education*, *15*(1), 53–66. https://doi:10.1007/s10857-011-9201-0

Vygotsky, L. S. (1978). *Mind in society: The development of higher psychological processes*. Harvard University Press.

Vygotsky, L. S. (1986). *Thought and language* (Translation newly revised and edited by A. Kozulin, ed.). MIT Press.

Walker, E., Adams, A., Restrepo, M. A., Fialko, S., & Glenberg, A. M. (2017). When (and how) interacting with technology-enhanced storybooks helps dual language learners. *Translational Issues in Psychological Science*, *3*(1), 66–79. https://doi:10.1037/tps0000100

Watzinger-Tharp, J., Swenson, K., & Mayne, Z. (2018). Academic achievement of students in dual language immersion. *International Journal of Bilingual Education and Bilingualism*, *21*(8), 913–928. https://doi:10.1080/13670050.2016.1214675

Willey, C., LópezLeiva, C. A., Torres, Z., & Licón Khisty, L. (2014). Chanzas: The probability of changing the ecology of mathematical activity. In B. B. Flores, O. A. Vásquez, & E. R. Clark (Eds.), *Generating transworld pedagogy: Reimagining la clase mágica* (pp. 159–176). Lexington Books.

Wright, W. E., Boun, S., & García, O. (Eds.). (2015). *The handbook of bilingual and multilingual education*. John Wiley & Sons, Inc.

Yuen, T. T., Ek, L. D., & Scheutze, A. (2013, August 26–29). *Increasing participation from underrepresented minorities in STEM through robotics clubs*. [Paper presentation]. Proceedings of 2013 IEEE International Conference on Teaching, Assessment and Learning for Engineering (TALE), Kuta, Indonesia.

Zentella, A. C. (1997). *Growing up bilingual: Puerto Rican children in New York*. Blackwell Publishers.

Family and Community

33

FAMILIES, COMMUNITIES, AND ACTIVISM IN DUAL LANGUAGE BILINGUAL EDUCATION

Paradigms of Parental Engagement

Edward M. Olivos, Alberto M. Ochoa

Parent involvement is a popular concept in educational research and practice (Boethel, 2003; Henderson & Mapp, 2002; Jordan et al., 2001). Involving parents in their children's education is a high priority among many in professional education. Researchers for their part overwhelmingly support the notion that when caregivers (parents, families, etc.) are involved in schools, children excel in a multitude of ways. Parent involvement has been linked to better student behaviors in schools, literacy gains, math gains, high school graduation, and college preparedness (Pomerantz et al., 2005). Few openly question that there appears to be some form of positive return for students when their parents are involved in educational matters and when school personnel make explicit efforts to reach out to them (Epstein, 2001; Henderson & Mapp, 2002). Policymakers also consider parent involvement an essential component of effective educational programs and education reform and have included "more" parental "voice" in decisions that affect children (like special education) and schools (like school committees around school budgets and the use of categorical funds).

Parental Involvement in Schools

Parent involvement is a broad term used to describe both home- and school-based parental participation (Pomerantz et al., 2007; Theodorou, 2007). Home-based participation is school-related support such as helping children with their homework or daily reading in the home. It may also include more

DOI: 10.4324/9781003269076-47

general parental responsibilities believed to make children more attentive and productive in schools such as making sure children get enough sleep, are well-fed, and receive positive emotional support and encouragement. School-based participation differs from home-based participation in that it requires parental presence at the school. This category of participation includes a wide range of activities from volunteering in classrooms and on fieldtrips to participation on decision-making committees. It is often assumed that this latter form of school involvement has greater influence not only on student achievement but also on parent and community agency and self-perception (Barton et al., 2004; Shirley, 1997).

It is not uncommon to find in the research literature a "hierarchy" of parent involvement activities with home-based participation "put to the very bottom of the involvement scale [often] regarded as minimal and insufficient in comparison to 'higher' or 'more desirable' ways of involvement, more likely to be encountered among middle- or upper middle-class families" (Theodorou, 2007, p. 90). It has also been argued that each level (or layer) of involvement produces different outcomes, ranging from individual, child-specific academic gains to broader changes in school practices or policies (Marschall & Shah, 2016). Therefore, some researchers have been inclined to distinguish between "parent involvement" and "parent engagement" (Olivos et al., 2011; Shirley, 1997).

Parent involvement is often conceptualized as participation on school terms, focusing on individual child-specific achievement and on identifiable school-valued outcomes (such as test scores, reading scores, and behavior). Barton and colleagues (2004) argue that "parents' roles and involvement in schools have been understood largely in terms of 'what they do' and how that fits or does not fit with the needs of the child or the goals of the school" (p. 4). Parent engagement on the other hand has come to be understood as being more advocacy- and parent-centered. Outcomes are not only child-specific but also more population- and community-centered such as advocating for better learning conditions and outcomes for historically underachieving communities to empowering immigrant and working-class parents to navigate school bureaucracies and broader sociopolitical policies and practices (Pomerantz et al., 2007; Shirley, 1997; Terriquez & Rogers, 2011).

Though often included in the latter "category," community (grassroots) organizing as a more "empowering" process or form of parent engagement may not completely capture the uniqueness of advocacy that originates in the community and not in the school. There are a growing number of researchers who have been examining grassroots organizing and community organizing as a promising model for involving bicultural parents in schools (Freire et al., 2021; Hong, 2011; Mediratta et al., 2009; Oakes & Rogers, 2006; Shirley, 1997; Warren, 2021; Warren & Mapp, 2011). This form of engagement strays a bit from the more "traditional" forms of involvement mentioned in the research literature as it has as one of its goals "school reform" and not just individual student academic improvement. An additional goal is developing "civically engaged" parents who then "transfer" these skills to address concerns and issues at the community, state, and national levels (Mediratta et al., 2009; Warren, 2021; Warren & Mapp, 2011). Terriquez and Rogers (2011), for example, document how a Los Angeles organization, comprised mostly of immigrant parents, helps parents develop skills such as analyzing data, surveying neighbors, and communicating concerns with school officials. Through their engagement with the organization, some of the parents simultaneously develop a civic engagement "consciousness" which prompts them to want to be more involved in other issues that concern their communities such as safety or housing.

Community organizing and grassroots organizing are the most used terms to describe the process in which community members harness local resources and power in order "to create institutional and policy change on their own behalf" (Warren & Mapp, 2011, p. 7) (see also Hong, 2011 and Mediratta et al., 2009). There are many reasons that would prompt individuals to organize, or to join, a community group. This can range from meeting immediate personal objectives or goals to working toward meeting longer term strategic initiatives that will benefit a larger community (Freire et al., 2021; Warren, 2021). Often though, community organizing, or the mobilization of people, particularly people of color (i.e., ethnically, and linguistically diverse), comes out of frustration—frustration with confronting power structures that are often inaccessible to low-income and working-class bicultural individuals (Freire et al., 2021; Warren, 2005, 2021). In the school context, community and grassroots organizing goals are equally diverse as are the forms they take for developing navigational capital, social capital, and power to strengthen individual parents' involvement in their children's schools and, at times, collective participation in larger issues of social, civic, and community life (Mediratta et al., 2009; Shirley, 1997; Terriquez & Rogers, 2011; Warren, 2005, 2021; Warren & Mapp, 2011).

Critiques and Challenges to Parental Involvement

There have been challenges to the idea that parent involvement is a uniform, value-free, and identifiable set of school-like behaviors or attitudes that can be "measured" and to the argument that parent involvement is even effective in, and directly linked to, promoting academic achievement, considering larger sociopolitical and economic forces (Barton et al., 2004; de Carvalho, 2001; Robinson & Harris, 2014; Theodorou, 2007). Drummond and Stipek (2004) contend, for example, that "despite broad support for parent involvement among policymakers and educators, empirical evidence on its effects on student achievement is inconsistent" (p. 200). While many studies have linked parent involvement to increased student achievement, Drummond and Stipek question if increased parent participation causes "higher student achievement, or perhaps it is easier and more pleasant [for parents] to become involved in [their] children's learning when they are performing well" or more urgent "when their children are not doing well" (p. 200).

Meanwhile, others question the possibility of even replicating parent involvement "promising practices" given the uniqueness of each context and situation. de Carvhalo (2001) writes that "from a practical and dynamical point of view, experimental programs tend to create unique situations and, if successful, ideal models. Thus, there is no guarantee that the conditions and incentives fostered by a particular program, in a particular context, will be successfully reproduced elsewhere, let alone everywhere" (p. 14). Therefore educators "continue to struggle with designing and implementing strong family involvement programs that link to student success and research identifying what does and does not work remains insufficient" (Marschall & Shah, 2016, p. 3).

Another critique found in the parent involvement literature is around access for non-white, working-class parents and the barriers and challenges they encounter as they attempt to participate and engage with schools (Baquedano-López et al., 2013; Barton et al., 2004). These barriers may be due to the parents' life circumstances which make it difficult for them to participate in manners that require consistent presence at school: due to work schedules, not speaking the language of the school, childcare, etc. This body of research generally does not question the concept of parental involvement as important for student achievement and parental agency but rather views as problematic the lack of access certain parent groups have to the school's resources and power structure.

A similar body of literature examines how the barriers and challenges bicultural parents encounter in schools are explicitly and implicitly shaped by school authorities. These barriers could be in the form of school policies and/or school practices that minimize or neutralize the impact and agency of non-white, working-class parents and/or in general deficit-oriented mindsets and beliefs educators may hold about minoritized families and communities (Baquedano-López et al., 2013; Olivos, 2006). For example, class and/or racial biases against working-class or non-white communities may instill in educators the belief that academic deficiencies originate in the home, the home culture, or in parental motivation. As a result, less is expected of these children and of their parents and since less is expected, then less opportunities for participation are provided. Opportunities that do arise for minoritized parents focus on "fixing" them and not on reimagining or restructuring schools to make them more inclusive.

Parents in Two-Way Immersion (TWI)

One program model that is found under the general dual language bilingual education umbrella term is the two-way immersion (TWI) program (sometimes also referred to as Dual Language Immersion). By design, TWI programs must bring together two populations with different linguistic characteristics and sociocultural attributes (Howard et al., 2018). These programs are offered in numerous languages, yet the majority are in English and Spanish. TWI programs are unique educational settings for language-minoritized parent involvement. While many of the participation "barriers" found in English-only settings may still hold true, there are certain features within these programs that would suggest greater access for language-minoritized communities. For example, in Spanish-English TWI programs, there are bilingual teachers and often bilingual office staff and administrators who can speak to Spanish-speaking parents without translators and thus communicate with them in a more personal manner. Second, TWI programs claim to promote cultural pluralism so school officials may tend to hold more favorable views of minoritized cultures and may even have a greater level of understanding of their histories and value systems (Casas et al., 2005). Third, language-minoritized families are needed. TWI programs simply cannot exist without target-language-speaking children and families. And finally, parent involvement is a fundamental principle of a "good" TWI program (Casas et al., 2005; Howard et al., 2018). Howard and colleagues (2018) identify "equity and a positive school environment" as an important component of successful TWI programs.

TWI programs are often based on a set of principles (or strands), the most widely recognized are those laid out in the *Guiding Principles for Dual Language Education* from the Center for Applied Linguistics (CAL) (Howard et al., 2018). Family and community engagement is one of the seven strands deemed vital for an effective and welcoming TWI program. Some of the recommended practices for engaging families (it is assumed that the authors are referring exclusively to the target-language (minoritized) families in this strand based on the nature of the recommendations) include viewing families from an asset-based perspective, providing linguistically and culturally appropriate outreach and services to parents, creating a welcoming and multicultural school climate with the appropriate bilingual staff and teachers, and addressing barriers that may preclude target-language parents from participating equally in school matters.

Key Findings in Parents in TWI

Given the nature of TWI programs, the student and parent populations they serve, their professed biliteracy and bicultural outcomes for all students, their underlying principles around cultural and linguistic equity, and their political nature as a bilingual education program model in a country that has long devalued and problematized linguistic diversity, it is not surprising that many researchers have documented the inequitable participation and academic outcomes these programs produce. A large body of research starting in 2000 has focused on parental opinions about, and satisfaction with, TWI programs, including the reasons parents may choose these programs for their children. Many researchers have also delved into issues around fairness and what some believe is the disparate treatment of parent groups by educators and/or between parent groups. A smaller number of publications examined the role of parents in influencing the academic achievement of their children (a popular area of research in the general parent involvement literature) or their participation in their children's schools. Most of the research on parents and TWI programs is on the Latinx population with a few notable exceptions (see Ee, 2017, 2018; Lee & Jeong, 2013; Michael-Luna, 2013; Palmer, 2010).

Ee (2107, 2018) and Lee and Jeong (2013), for example, examined Korean parent involvement in English-Korean TWI programs. Ee (2017) used social capital theory to investigate how Korean parents interacted with other parents in seven English-Korean TWI schools in the Los Angeles area, as well as how they participated in their children's schools and the obstacles they faced. As could be expected, lack of English proficiency was a noticeable obstacle for some parents, as were work schedules and childcare. What is unique about Ee's study, however, is that the parent populations in her study consisted of three parent groups: Koreans, Latinx, and white parents who all had children in the English-Korean TWI programs. Lee and Jeong, for their part, examined the experiences of Korean-American students and parents in a newly instituted English-Korean TWI school. Their findings were similar to those that focus on Latinx parents in that the parents understood the value and benefits of having their children enrolled in a bilingual program but nonetheless held concerns about the organization and instruction. They had particular concerns about their children's language development in both English and Korean and the quality of instruction at the school. For example, the parents were "uneasy about the teachers' proficiency levels in both English and Korean … [and] many parents believed that their own Korean was better than the teachers" (p. 99).

Parental Opinions, Satisfaction, and Choosing Programs

Much of the research literature on parents and TWI programs published between 2000 and 2021 examined parental opinions about, and their satisfaction with, their children's programs. Studies included factors that influenced parents' decisions in choosing TWI programs for their children (Call et al., 2018; Dorner, 2012; Ee, 2018; Gerena, 2011; Giacchino-Baker &

Piller, 2006; Lee & Jeong, 2013; López, 2013; Parkes, 2008; Shannon & Milian, 2002; Whiting & Feinauer, 2011), the bilingual outcomes parents desired for their children from these programs (Dorner, 2010; Lindholm-Leary, 2001; López, 2013; Michael-Luna, 2013; Olivos & Lucero, 2018; Ramos, 2007), parental satisfaction with and commitment to these programs (Giacchino-Baker & Piller, 2006; Parkes, 2008; Parkes & Ruth, 2011; Ramos, 2007; Saucedo, 1997), and differences in opinion, motivation, and involvement that may exist between parent groups and/or parents and educators (Craig, 1996; Giacchino-Baker & Piller, 2006; Oliveira et al., 2020; Olivos & Lucero, 2018; Ryan et al., 2010; Whiting & Feinauer, 2011).

Craig (1996) surveyed both white and Latinx parents who had children enrolled in a Spanish-English TWI program. She studied their opinions about their children's school and their "attitudes toward bilingualism in general" (p. 390). Both parent groups held favorable views toward "all aspects of bilingualism" and showed "substantial agreement ... that minority language maintenance is important" (pp. 392–393). Where white and Latinx parents differed however was in their reasons for enrolling their children in the program in the first place. White parents generally viewed TWI as an enrichment opportunity for their children as well as an opportunity to increase their children's future career opportunities. Spanish-speaking parents, on the other hand, "cited Spanish language and cultural maintenance as the major reasons for enrolling their children" (p. 399). Craig's study made an important contribution to future research in that she connected her findings to the work of Gardner and Lambert (1972) who originally identified "instrumental" and "integrative" motivations for learning a second language. She applied these concepts not to the actual learners themselves but to the parents to explain their motivations for seeking bilingual outcomes for their children and thus influence their decisions in choosing a bilingual educational program for them.

Subsequent studies also argued that white and non-white parents tend to choose TWI programs for their children for different reasons (see Giacchino-Baker & Piller, 2006; Parkes, 2008). The conceptualizations of "integrative" v "instrumental" reasons for learning a second language learning continued to be used to distinguish the differences between white and non-white parents' choices (see also Olivos & Lucero, 2018; Olivos, 2021; Parkes, 2008; Shannon & Milian, 2002). Findings continued to suggest that English-speaking parents choose TWI programs to secure future financial and career benefits associated with knowing a second language. Language-minoritized parents, on the other hand, had reasons that included wanting their children to maintain their heritage language so that they could speak to extended family members (grandma, for example), to wanting their children to maintain a connection (or a bond) with the heritage community and culture (Gerena, 2011; Giacchino-Baker & Piller, 2006; Lindholm-Leary, 2001;

López, 2013; Ramos, 2007; Shannon & Milian, 2002; Whiting & Feinauer, 2011).

Another finding that has appeared in the TWI/parent involvement literature is the high levels of satisfaction and the favorable views that both language-majoritized and language-minoritized parents express about their children's programs and bilingualism in general (Craig, 1996; Lindholm-Leary, 2001; Olivos & Lucero, 2018; Parkes & Ruth, 2011; Saucedo, 1997). Some researchers noted subtle differences between parents' reasons for their satisfaction (Gerena, 2011; Lindholm-Leary, 2001; Parkes & Ruth), while others cautioned reading too much into these high levels of satisfaction (Olivos, 2021; Olivos & Lucero, 2018). Gerena (2011), for example, noted integrative v instrumental reasons influencing parental satisfaction patterns. In her study, "both sets of parents" (English-speaking and Spanish-speaking) "expressed a high level of satisfaction with the program." The Spanish-speaking parents however focused more "on the fact that they felt that their children [enjoyed] school more, whereas English-speaking parents were pleased that their children were not falling behind ... and were becoming culturally aware and sensitive" (p. 354). In terms of which program features were most important to them, "English-speaking parents focused on the employment opportunities and benefits ... whereas Spanish-speaking parents focused on the maintenance of cultural and heritage ties and ... strong family bonds and relationships" (p. 355).

Disparate Treatment and Outcomes

Despite the seductive nature of TWI programs and the general consensus among researchers and educators that these programs provide the "strongest" and most "authentic" form of bilingual education, caution has been raised as to the pitfalls that may exist in an educational program designed to create identical outcomes (biliteracy and biculturalism) for different student populations (Cervantes-Soon, 2014; Scanlan & Palmer, 2009; Shannon, 2011; Valdés, 1997; Valdez et al., 2016; Varghese & Park, 2010). This caution is often raised in the context of Spanish-English TWI programs (Valdés, 1997; Valdez et al., 2016) and what some researchers believe is the unrealistic likelihood that educators can reconcile different (and at times) competing parent and community interests within one educational program (Burns, 2017; Cervantes-Soon, 2014; Chaparro, 2019; Shannon, 2011).

Since TWI programs laud bilingualism and biculturalism as their outcomes and tend to center equity as one of their educational principles, promoting language and cultural status equalization in the classroom is one means of achieving these outcomes for language-minoritized children as well as for English-speaking children. However, these highly popular programs do not only present hopeful educational possibilities for bicultural students, but they also present unique challenges for their parents (Burns, 2017; Cervantes-Soon, 2014; Chaparro, 2019; Muro, 2016; Olivos, 2021; Olivos & Lucero, 2018). TWI programs can become settings where the competing interests of two distinct groups of parents can become crystalized (Shannon, 2011; Valdez et al., 2016). Researchers suggest that regardless of the stated mission of equity and inclusion that TWI programs profess, language-minoritized parents tend to experience differential treatment and attention (Cervantes-Soon, 2014; Chaparro, 2019; Palmer, 2010; Shannon, 2011).

Interest convergence theory is often used to explain the complex relationship between parent groups (white and non-white) and why white parents may choose TWI programs for their children in the first place (Burns, 2017; Morales & Maravilla, 2019; Olivos, 2021; Palmer, 2010; Shannon, 2011). This theory "broadly applied holds that minority interests are upheld by courts and supported in other arenas when minority interests converge with the interests of the majority" (Kelly, 2018, p. 1). In other words, in return for their support of a minoritized community's agenda, the majoritized community expects to get something in return. Shannon (2011) contends that there is an "interest convergence dilemma" inherent in all TWI programs. Middle- (and upper-) class white parents' support for Spanish-English TWI programs is primarily driven by their desire to secure bilingualism for their children rather than by noble intentions toward their Latinx counterparts (Burns, 2017). Indeed, it's been suggested that "while English-speaking Americans might value bilingual proficiency for their own children, they are not as convinced of the importance of non-English home language maintenance for minority language children" (Craig, 1996, p. 386).

To summarize, the research on parent involvement and TWI has raised the following issues: (1) despite being designed to be bicultural and bilingual, TWI programs often get molded to reflect white parents' interests and expectations (Burns, 2017; Kelly, 2018); (2) dual language educators are often pulled between working to satisfy white, English-speaking parents' desires and expectations and fostering the meaningful engagement of language-minoritized families (Burns, 2017); (3) school officials come to depend on white parental satisfaction for "political coverage" (Palmer, 2010); and (4) white parental satisfaction must constantly be attended to so that they do not pull their children out of the program (Chaparro, 2020).

Paradigms of Parent Involvement in DLBE

What exactly is meant by parent involvement in a DLBE school or program? What does it look like? Are all forms of parental involvement the same? If not, what are the differences? Do all parents have equal access and opportunity to participate in DLBE schools? If not, where are the challenges? In addition, can the involvement of bicultural parents in schools lead to broader social changes, political consciousness, civic engagement, or involvement in policy development and decision-making? These are some of the issues that remain to be examined in the existing empirical research on parents in DLBE. Our own research suggests that these types of questions can best be understood by examining the underlying philosophies and principles that frame the involvement of bicultural parents in institutions that have long worked to serve the majoritized population (Olivos et al., 2011).

In past research, we broadly identified four parent involvement models (which we will call here: paradigms) as follows: the *Family Influence Paradigm*, the *Alternative School Reform Paradigm*, the *Cooperative School Paradigm*, and the *Transformative Education Context Paradigm* (Olivos et al., 2011). In the examination of these parent involvement paradigms, we acknowledge that it is possible for practices and mindsets from one paradigm to carry over to the others. Likewise, it is possible that these philosophies be implemented in various ways according to the school administrator or the particular schools' culture. Nonetheless, using these four paradigms, we apply them to the DLBE context with the goal of assisting DLBE educators toward recognizing the underlying principles and/or philosophies of each. Each of the four paradigms has assumptions that perceive parents as either having a passive or active voice or role in schools.

The *Family Influence Paradigm*, also referred to as the *Schools Transmission Model* by McCaleb (1997), frames parent involvement as school authorities deploying techniques and strategies that work to change the family and their home practices. As Delgado-Gaitán (1990) notes "academic deficiencies are presumed to be corrected by school designed interventions and make home socialization congruent with the school culture" (p. 50). Thus, school personnel believe that deficiency in learning is centered in homelife rather than in school policies or practices. Their belief is that if somehow the students' home situation (culture, lifestyle, epistemology, etc.) can be changed and/or corrected, then their academic future can be improved.

This paradigm is driven by deficit thinking, which frames bicultural communities as lacking or deficient in their intelligence, culture, and/or social adjustment (Baquedano-López et al., 2013; Valencia, 2010). The underlying assumption of viewing bicultural parents as lacking instead of an asset can be seen in the parent education classes that are often offered by schools in which minoritized parents are given guidelines, materials, and/or trainings to carry out school-like activities in the home (McCaleb, 1997). Equally popular are the efforts of teaching parents about effective parenting and the legitimacy of the school culture. For bicultural parents, this model is an effort to assimilate them into the majoritized school culture.

The overall goal of the paradigm is for the school to provide opportunities for parents to improve their home condition in order to mirror that of the school culture, while no attention is paid to other factors (both outside and inside) of the school that contribute to limiting the bicultural community's ability to effectively participate in the schooling process of their children. Furthermore, school personnel are accepted as the owners and purveyors of legitimate knowledge and culture, thus putting forth a notion that bicultural communities have nothing of value to offer. Ironically, despite the obvious shortcoming and disrespect this paradigm has for all communities, particularly bicultural, it continues to be the most accepted among U.S. public schools.

The *Alternative School Reform Paradigm* is another framework we have identified in past work and provides a shift to the *Family Influence Paradigm* in that the parents and the community work to change the schools to make them more responsive to them and their children (Delgado-Gaitán, 1990). This is done by parents exercising their power at the school, challenging school personnel to be more accountable to their children's needs. It is important to note that this paradigm is more prevalent and more effective among community members from the majoritized culture. That is, middle-class and upper-class white parents have more success in demanding their children's educational rights than do bicultural parents of lower resources (Olivos, 2006). This is, of course, because there is a closer symmetrical power and status relationship between the school and the majoritized community. Furthermore, school personnel are generally more inclined to respond to the needs of parents whom they view as their equals and/or to high-status parents with social networks and resources to hold school personnel accountable. In the DLBE setting, this paradigm is operationalized when school authorities come to consider the white, English-speaking parents as their main audience and become most attentive to their needs.

The *Cooperative Systems Paradigm* is the third framework. It is all-encompassing and general in that this approach integrates the parents into various roles within the school, even as employees (such as lunch duty helpers, instructional assistants, and school security). The philosophy behind this third model argues that "factors in the home, school and community are interrelated" (Delgado-Gaitán, 1990, p. 54). It sees the parent as a volunteer, paid employee, teacher at home, school participant, decision-maker, and adult learner. The *Cooperative Systems Paradigm* attempts to integrate the economic, social, and educational interests of the parents under the general umbrella term of parent involvement. These multiple roles, particularly that of a paid employee, make direct parent advocacy less likely since parents who are working in the school have developed an economic interest in the continuation of the status quo in the educational system since it is a source of their livelihood. Furthermore, parents who challenge the school system and are active players in school activities are often co-opted by becoming employees of the school or members of school-sanctioned committees. In the DLBE context, this is involving minoritized parents in "important" school committees to demonstrate a representation but having little impact or say in educational decisions.

The *Transformative Education Context Paradigm* is the fourth framework and is based on the notion that knowledge and power are socially constructed between participants and as such, all are equally responsible and capable of contributing to transforming the educational process. A philosophy within this paradigm is that "through analysis and critique all people are capable of engaging in actions that may transform their present realities" (McCaleb, 1997, p. 26). Parent involvement is a process of transformation in which critical consciousness is achieved by all the participants for the benefit of student literacy, academic achievement, and school and community transformation.

This process of transformation can be possible, for example, via the Freirian principles of dialogue and problem-posing education that seeks to name the problem, understand the conditions creating the problem, and offer alternatives and solutions to the problem (Freire, 2007). In addition, dialogue promotes a language not only of resistance but also of possibilities for positive change. This form of change is rooted in the belief that collaboration within the entire school population will build a community of learners in which learning is not isolated, but collective, historical, social, authentic, and transformational. Bicultural parents under this paradigm act to promote their interests, those of their children, those of other people's children, and those of their community while at the same time participating in the sociocultural and agency process of changing their lives from objects to subjects, that is from passive (conforming) to active involvement (biliteracy as a right). In the DLBE context, this process could involve language-minoritized parents participating in grassroots "language activism" and developing "navigational" and "resistance" capital to promote programs and policies that benefit their children's language goals and their communities' interests (Freire et al., 2021; Olivos, 2006).

Reexamining Parent Involvement in DLBE

Using the *Transformative Education Context Paradigm*, we examine what this approach may offer bicultural parents who have children in DLBE programs. In other words, will a "paradigm shift" in how educators view parent involvement in general allow language-minoritized parents the opportunity to be more deeply engaged in their school community and to reimagine education through dual language bilingual settings? Traditionally, parents from marginalized communities have been invited into schools using mindsets and approaches which have been contradictory to authentic involvement (Mapp et al., 2014). Dual language education programs can and have the equal responsibility and power to transform a school community so they can meet the educational and social needs of all children while protecting the interests of the minoritized. DLBE schools and the communities they serve have the status to generate the necessary conditions to create an equitable and democratic schooling experience for a culturally and linguistically diverse society.

The importance of a "transformative" approach to parent involvement in DLBE is in its ability to consider the social, cultural, and economic factors impacting the school community's quality of life. The model sociologically addresses the issue of how knowledge and power are constructed and normalized based on an individual's or group's position in society. Additionally, it does not ignore or conceal the strong political interest found in schooling; therefore, parent engagement is a political and empowering act, particularly for community members who are marginalized in other sectors of social and civic life (minoritized parents, undocumented parents, working-class parents, etc.). Parent involvement from this approach is a political project in which parents from diverse backgrounds work to transform a system that has long produced inequitable outcomes. Furthermore, it presents a counter perspective which views the home knowledge and culture of the participants as equally valid and powerful for social change. It is this paradigm that forms the basis of a shift that seeks to transform parent involvement into a meaningful act of empowerment with the goal of making education a democratic and reflective action.

In our present and previous work with low-income ethnically and linguistically diverse school communities, we called for an alternative paradigm to reconceptualize and actualize bicultural parent engagement (Olivos et al., 2011). For decades, researchers have reached similar conclusions and have made multiple pleas for educators to reach out and engage bicultural parents within their schools to develop meaningful and authentic relationships which value, honor, and capitalize on their assets and contributions (Delgado-Gaitán, 1990; Mapp et al., 2014; McCaleb, 1997; Valdés, 1997). There has been a call for educators to engage bicultural parents and communities who have often been driven by the need to counteract longstanding and deeply ingrained negative beliefs about their biculturalism and bilingualism and even overlook the positive contributions they make to their school communities, their children, and schools.

Recognizing and interpreting "resistance" is also important for understanding "transformative" parent engagement. Transformative resistance encompasses the motivation for "social justice" (Solórzano & Delgado Bernal, 2001). Through the development of social consciousness, parents begin to overcome self-defeating behaviors of assimilating to the status quo of school practices and developing voice and agency to change the conditions of existing practices that work against one's right to bilingualism and bicognition. An example is the microaggression act of reclassification that often celebrates a student once classified as an English learner (EL) as meeting English proficiency and marks the practice of eliminating support of their home language (Spanish,

Hmong, Vietnamese, Mixteco, Somali, Mandarin, Tagalog, etc.). Participants under this paradigm of parent engagement can develop a deep understanding of social and educational inequity and an orientation in seeking to act on injustices. Freire et al. (2021) use the terms "grassroots language activism" and "bottom-up resistance" to document how language-minoritized communities in Utah challenge one-size-fits-all language policies which ignore community wishes and empirical research on language usage and allotment in DLBE programs. This is an example of a "paradigm shift" in which the language-minoritized parents used "navigational capital" and "resistance capital" to create space for their interests and equity for their children.

Implications for DLBE

DLBE is considered the "gold standard" of bilingual education and these programs are highly sought after by both language majoritized and language-minoritized communities. Yet DLBE is a setting where minoritized parents' interests are in daily contact and struggle with those of majoritized parents. In this rush to satisfy high-status parents' wishes, DLBE educators may tend to overlook or ignore the desires and interests of the minoritized parents. As a program that promotes linguistic diversity and cultural pluralism, educators must be aware of the educational desires of the minoritized parents and that, at times, these parents may have to use all the means at their disposal to be heard. Being aware of the "interest convergence" may also help DLBE educators work to support or "elevate" the voices of minoritized parents who may have concerns or ideas for the school that may not resonate with the more "powerful" parent group.

Several major issues arise from this overview of parent engagement and DLBE. One major issue that consistently emerges in the research is that of equity, and the tension that arises between the ideal of TWI program and the reality of its implementation in the United States, a monolingual English society. Another issue is that, for the most part, bicultural parent involvement is practiced as a mode of participation (things to do) and not of transformation (things that need to change). A final issue is that dual language programs operate in a variety of policy contexts in schools around the country, which implement the model in diverse ways. Given the professed benefits and growing use of dual language education programs, it is important to understand the status of DLBE and the gaps that exist to be a model for schooling that can engage all parent groups regardless of status. An examination of the paradigms that inform parental involvement practices at school may be an important first step for DLBE educators interested in supporting the power of language-minoritized parents and in developing "grassroots resistance and activism [that] can clearly work to create change that can benefit language-minoritized communities" (Freire et al., 2021, p. 14).

References

Baquedano-López, P., Alexander, R. A., & Hernández, S. T. (2013). Equity issues in parental and community involvement in schools: What teacher educators need to know. *Review of Research in Education*, *37*, 149–182.

Barton, A. C., Drake, C., Perez, J. G., St. Louis, K., & George, M. (2004). Ecologies of parental engagement in urban education. *Educational Researcher*, *33*(4), 3–12.

Boethel, M. (2003). *Diversity: School, family, & community connections.* National Center for Family & Community: Connections with Schools.

Burns, M. (2017). "Compromises we make": Whiteness in the dual language context. *Bilingual Research Journal*, *40*(4), 339–352.

Call, A., Domenech Rodríguez, M. M., Vázquez, A. L., & Corralejo, S. M. (2018). Predicting participation in dual language immersion using theory of planned behavior. *Bilingual Research Journal*, *41*(1), 23–36. https://doi.org/10.1080/15235882.2018.1425935

Casas, J. F., Ryan, C. S., Kelly-Vance, L., Ryalls, B. O., Ferguson, A., & Nero, C. L. (2005). *Examining the impact of parental involvement in a dual language program. Implications for children and schools.* Report prepared for the Office of Latino/Latin American Studies. University of Nebraska.

Cervantes-Soon, C. G. (2014). A critical look at dual language immersion in the new Latin@ diaspora. *Bilingual Research Journal*, *37*(1), 64–82.

Chaparro, S. (2019). Schools, parents, and communities: Leading parallel lives in a two-way immersion program. *International Multilingual Research Journal.* https://doi.org/10.1080/19313152.2019.1634957

Chaparro, S. (2020). Pero aquí se hablan inglés: Latina immigrant mothers' experiences of discrimination, resistance, and pride through autopoesía. *TESOL Quarterly*, *54*(3), 599–628. https://doi.org/10.1002/tesq.593.

Craig, B. A. (1996). Parental attitudes toward bilingualism in a local two-way immersion program. *The Bilingual Research Journal*, *20*(3&4), 383–410.

de Carvalho, M. E. P. (2001). *Rethinking family-school relations: A critique of parental involvement in schools.* Lawrence Erlbaum Associates Publishers.

Delgado-Gaitán, C. (1990). *Literacy for empowerment: The role of parents in children's education.* The Falmer Press.

Dorner, L. (2010). English and Spanish 'para un futuro'-or just English? Immigrant family perspectives on two-way immersion. *International Journal of Bilingual Education and Bilingualism*, *13*(3), 303–323. https://doi.org/10.1080/13670050903229851

Dorner, L. (2012). The life course and sense-making: Immigrant families' journeys toward understanding educational policies and choosing bilingual programs. *American Educational Research Journal*, *49*(3), 461–486. https://doi.org/10.3102/0002831211415089

Drummond, K. V., & Stipek, D. (2004). Low-income Parents' beliefs about their role in Children's academic learning. *The Elementary School Journal*, *104*(3), 197–213. https://doi.org/10.1086/499749

Ee, J. (2017). Two dimensions of parental involvement: What affects parental involvement in dual language immersion? *Bilingual Research Journal*, *40*(2), 131–153. https://doi.org/10.1080/15235882.2017.1306598

Ee, J. (2018). Exploring Korean dual language immersion programs in the United States: Parents' reasons for enrolling their children. *International Journal of Bilingual Education and Bilingualism*, *21*(6), 690–709. https://doi.org/10.1080/13670050.2016.1208144

Epstein, J. L. (2001). *School, family, and community partnerships: Preparing educators and improving schools*. Westview Press.

Freire, P. (1974, 2007). *Education for critical consciousness*. Continuum Books.

Freire, J. A., Delavan, G., & Valdez, M. (2021). Grassroots resistance and activism to one-size-fits-all and separate-but-equal policies by 90:10 dual language schools en comunidades latinas. *International Journal of Bilingual Education and Bilingualism*. https://doi.org/10.1080/13670050.2021.1874868

Gardner, R. C., & Lambert, W. E. (1972). *Attitudes and motivation in second language learning*. Newbury House.

Gerena, L. (2011). Parental voice and involvement in cultural context: Understanding rationales, values, and motivational constructs in a dual immersion setting. *Urban Education*, *46*(3), 342–370. https://doi.org/10.1177/0042085910377512

Giacchino-Baker, R., & Piller, B. (2006). Parental motivation, attitudes, support, and commitment in a Southern Californian two-way immersion program. *Journal of Latinos and Education*, *5*(1), 5–28.

Henderson, A. T., & Mapp, K. L. (2002). *A new wave of evidence: The impact of school, family and community connections on student achievement*. Southwest Educational Development Laboratory.

Hong, S. (2011). *A cord of three strands: A new approach to parent engagement in schools*. Harvard Education Press.

Howard, E. R., Lindholm-Leary, K. J., Rogers, D., Olague, N., Medina, J., Kennedy, B., Sugarman, J., & Christian, D. (2018). *Guiding principles for dual language education* (3rd ed.). Center for Applied Linguistics.

Jordan, C., Orozco, E., & Averett, A. (2001). *Emerging issues in school, family, & community connections*. Southwest Educational Development Laboratory.

Kelly, L. B. (2018). Interest convergence and hegemony in dual language: Bilingual education, but for whom and why. *Language Policy*, *17*, 1–21.

Lee, J. S., & Jeong, E. (2013). Korean-English dual language immersion: Perspectives of students, parents, and teachers. *Language, Culture, and Curriculum*, *26*(1), 89–107. https://doi.org/10.1080/07908318.2013.765890

Lindholm-Leary, K. (2001). *Dual language education*. Multilingual Matters LTD.

López, M. M. (2013). Mothers choose: Reasons for enrolling their children in a two-way immersion program. *Bilingual Research Journal*, *36*(2), 208–227. https://doi.org/10.1080/15235882.2013.818595

Marschall, M. J., & Shah, P. R. (2016). Linking the process and outcomes of parent involvement policy to the parent involvement gap. *Urban Education*, *55*(5). https://doi.org/10.1177/0042085916661386

McCaleb, S. P. (1997). *Building communities of learners: A collaboration among teachers, students, families, and community*. Routledge.

Mediratta, K., Shah, S., & McAlister, S. (2009). *Community organizing for stronger schools: Strategies and successes*. Harvard Education Press.

Michael-Luna, S. (2013). What linguistically diverse parents know and how it can help early childhood educators: A case study of a dual language preschool community. *Early Childhood Education Journal*, *41*, 447–455. https://doi.org/10.1007/s10643-013-0574-9

Morales, P. Z., & Maravilla, J. V. (2019). The problems and possibilities of interest convergence in a dual language school. *Theory into Practice*, *58*(2), 145–153. https://doi.org/10.1080/00405841.2019.1569377

Muro, J. (2016). "Oil and water"? Latino-white relations and symbolic integration in a changing California. *Sociology of Race and Ethnicity*, 2(4), 516–530.

Oakes, J., & Rogers, J. (2006). *Learning power: Organizing for education and justice*. Teachers College Press.

Oliveira, G., Chang-Bacon, C. K., Cho, E., & Baez-Cruz, M. (2020). Parent and teacher perceptions of a Brazilian Portuguese two-way immersion program. *Bilingual Research Journal*, *43*(2), 212–231. https://doi.org/10.1080/15235882.2020.1773961

Olivos, E. M., Jiménez-Castellanos, O., & Ochoa, A. M. (Eds.) (2011). *Bicultural parent engagement: Operationalizing advocacy and empowerment*. Teachers College Press.

Olivos, E. M. (2021). Silencing bicultural parental voices through educational satisfaction: What do we need to know? *Theory into Practice*. https://doi.org/10.1080/00405841.2020.1829378

Olivos, E. M. (2006). *The power of parents: A critical perspective of bicultural parent involvement in public schools*. Peter Lang.

Olivos, E. M., & Lucero, A. (2018). Latino parents in dual language immersion programs: Why are they so satisfied? *International Journal of Bilingual Education and Bilingualism*, *23*(10), 1211–1224. https://doi.org/10.1080/13670050.2018.1436520

Palmer, D. (2010). Race, power, and equity in a multiethnic urban elementary school with a dual language "strand" program. *Anthropology & Education Quarterly*, *41*(1), 94–114.

Parkes, J. (2008). Who chooses dual language education for their children and why? *International Journal of Bilingual Education and Bilingualism*, *11*(6), 635–660.

Parkes, J., & Ruth, T. (2011). How satisfied are parents of students in dual language education programs?: 'Me parece maravillosa la gran oportunidad que le están dando a estos niños'. *International Journal of Bilingual Education and Bilingualism*, *14*(6), 701–718.

Pomerantz, E. M., Grolnick, W. S., & Price, C. E. (2005). The role of parents in how children approach achievement: A dynamic process perspective. In A. J. Elliot, & C. S. Dweck (Eds.), *Handbook of competence and motivation* (pp. 229–278). Guilford Publications.

Pomerantz, E. M., Moorman, E. A., & Litwack, S. D. (2007). The how, whom, and why of parents' involvement in children's academic lives: More is not always better. *Review of Educational Research*, *77*(3), 373–410.

Ramos, F. (2007). What do parents think of two-way bilingual education? An analysis of responses. *Journal of Latinos and Education*, *6*(2), 139–150. https://doi.org/10.1080/15348430701304807

Robinson, K., & Harris, A. L. (2014). *The broken compass: Parental involvement with children's education*. Harvard University Press.

Ryan, C. S., Casa, J. F., Kelly-Vance, L., Ryalls, B. O., & Nero, C. (2010). Parent involvement and views of school success: The role of parents' Latino and white American cultural orientations. *Psychology in the Schools*, *47*(4), 391–405.

Saucedo, L. (1997). *Parents' attitudes toward dual language immersion*. ERIC Document. ED 405 730.

Scanlan, M., & Palmer, D. (2009). Race, power, and (in)equity within two-way immersion settings. *Urban Review*, *41*(5), 391–415.

Shannon, S. (2011). Parent engagement and equity in a dual language program. In E. M. Olivos, O. Jiménez-Castellanos, & A. M. Ochoa (Eds.), *Bicultural parent engagement: Advocacy and empowerment* (pp. 83–102). Teachers College Press.

Shannon, S., & Milian, M. (2002). Parents choose a dual language program in Colorado: A survey. *Bilingual Research Journal*, *26*(3), 681–696. https://doi.org/10.1080/15235882.2002.10162584

Shirley, D. (1997). *Community organizing for urban school reform*. University of Texas Press.

Solórzano, D. G., & Delgado Bernal, D. (2001). Examining transformational resistance through a critical race and LatCrit theory framework: Chicana and Chicano students in an urban context. *Urban Education*, *36*(3), 308–342. https://doi.org/10.1177/0042085901363002

Terriquez, V., & Rogers, J. (2011). Becoming civic: The active engagement of Latino immigrant parents in public schools. In E. M. Olivos, O. Jiménez-Castellanos, & A. M. Ochoa (Eds.), *Bicultural parent engagement: Advocacy and empowerment* (pp. 186–205). Teachers College Press.

Theodorou, E. (2007). Reading between the lines: Exploring the assumptions and implications of parental involvement. *International Journal about Parents in Education*, *1*(0), 90–96.

Valdés, G. (1997). Dual-language immersion programs: A cautionary note concerning the education of language-minority students. *Harvard Educational Review*, *67*(3), 391–429.

Valdez, V. E., Delavan, G., & Freire, J. A. (2016). The marketing of dual language education policy in Utah print media. *Educational Policy*, *30*(6), 849–883. https://doi.org/10.1177/0895904814556750

Valencia, R. (2010). *Dismantling contemporary deficit thinking: Educational thought and practice*. Routledge.

Varghese, M. M., & Park, C. (2010). Going global: Can dual-language programs save bilingual education? *Journal of Latinos and Education*, *9*(1), 72–80. https://doi.org/10.1080/15348430903253092

Warren, M. (2005). Communities and schools: A new view of urban education reform. *Harvard Educational Review*, *75*(2), 133–173.

Warren, M. (2021). *Willful defiance: The movement to dismantle the school to prison pipeline*. Oxford University Press.

Warren, M. R., & Mapp, K. L. (2011). *Match on dry grass: Community organizing as a catalyst for school reform*. Oxford University Press.

Whiting, E. F., & Feinauer, E. (2011). Reasons for enrollment at a Spanish–English two-way immersion charter school among highly motivated parents from a diverse community. International *Journal of Bilingual Education and Bilingualism*, *14*(6), 631–651. https://doi.org/10.1080/13670050.2011.560931

SECTION IV

Teacher and Administrator Preparation

Teacher Education and Professional Development

34

DUAL LANGUAGE BILINGUAL TEACHER PREPARATION

The Braided Relationship of Ideology, Identity, Language, and Culture

Cristina Alfaro, Ana M. Hernández

Due to ideological and political language education debates across the nation, bilingual teacher preparation programs have fought to survive due to their vulnerability and the ever-present risk of being eliminated during politically contentious times (Alfaro, 2018; Gándara & Hopkins, 2010). In the United States, anti-bilingual and anti-im/migrant movements, such as California's Proposition 227 (1998), ban bilingual education after 20 years of implementation under the Bilingual Education Act (1968). Promptly, other similar state initiatives subsequently passed in Arizona's Prop 203 and Massachusetts' Sheltered English Immersion mandate had a definitive impact on public schools by severely limiting students' access to bilingual programs. Even after California and Massachusetts overturned state rulings, irreparable harm of language loss, shame for culture, and fractured identities plagued vulnerable and diverse communities. To date Arizona remains the only state still upholding an anti-bilingual education law. This national anti-bilingual movement had a direct impact on bilingual teacher preparation; established credential programs that mainly focused on early or late transitional bilingual education (Cummins, 1994; Thomas & Collier, 2002) faced discontinuation or less state/federal assistance for preparing bilingual teachers, even though an unmet demand for bilingual teachers meant that bilingual aides provided instruction without any prior preparation – the only requirement was to speak a language other than English (Crawford, 1997). Furthermore, existing bilingual teacher preparation programs had insufficient support, limited bilingual faculty, and difficulty in

DOI: 10.4324/9781003269076-50

sustaining a high-quality bilingual teacher preparation program. In many cases, only one or two bilingual faculty were responsible for creating, maintaining, and administering their university programs (Alfaro, 2018). Given this, today teacher educators' conversations orbit around the challenges to identify and name issues regarding the comprehensive preparation of dual language bilingual education (DLBE) teacher candidates (hereafter teacher candidates).

After an overview of programmatic and organizational issues related to DLBE teacher education, this chapter centers on braiding three fundamental research themes engaged in the development of bilingual teacher candidates: (1) critical ideological consciousness that recognize and interrupt dominant ideologies and hegemonic practices, (2) identity and self-authorship to provide opportunities to reflect on how owning individual histories informs and impacts their practice, and (3) critical awareness of their diverse languages and cultural assets for powerful content teaching and learning. Finally, the chapter concludes with recommendations for DLBE teacher preparation.

Dual Language Bilingual Education Teacher Preparation

The Civil Rights Act of 1964, the Bilingual Education Act of 1968, the 1974 Lau v. Nichols decision, and other federal legal mandates in support of bilingual education (e.g., Castañeda v. Pickard, 1981) created the impetus for the creation of bilingual teacher preparation programs in Institutions of Higher Education. Nonetheless, this did not mean that the hegemonic ideologies in teacher preparation were eradicated but rather the beginning of the struggle to create and implement bilingual teacher preparation programs nationwide (Alfaro, 2018). Moreover, the 1974 reauthorization of the Bilingual Education Act provided a stronger definition of bilingual education and required schools receiving Title VII grants to teach a curriculum in students' home language to enable bi/multilingual students to progress successfully through the educational system (Wiese & Garcia, 2001). Critical to the success of DLBE are those who teach bi/multilingual students. Given the cultural and linguistic diversity of our nation's schools, it is imperative that we take a close and critical look at the effectiveness of DLBE teacher education programs.

According to the National Center for Education Statistics, there is an urgent demand for subject-area teacher preparation, and the turnover rate for bilingual educators is considerably higher (National Center for Education Statistics [NCES], 2022) due to the demand for content knowledge and the rigor of the partner language(s) (Tedick & Lyster, 2020). Much of the existing literature on bilingual teacher preparation has concentrated on program characteristics, organizational issues (e.g., recruitment, retention),

Spanish language proficiency, and assessment that is shifting toward teacher identity, beliefs, and critical consciousness (Caldas, 2017; Cervantes-Soon, 2018; Freire, 2016; Sarmiento-Arribalzaga & Murillo, 2010; Wall & Hurie, 2017). Research in DLBE repeatedly states the importance of a teacher candidate's well-articulated critical ideological stance with an elevated critical consciousness that establishes a foundation where teacher candidates can powerfully traverse the cyclical ideological-political eruptions surrounding DLBE (Alfaro & Bartolomé, 2018; Bartolomé, 2002; Dorner et al., 2023; Freire, 2016). Moreover, this stance must include a set of cultural and linguistic beliefs, fundamental commitments, and values that lie beneath the diverse socio-political realities of bi/multilingual students, families, and communities. Unless DLBE teacher candidates engage in the process of questioning the status quo and how their beliefs impact their classroom practices, they will, at best, become technicians that continue to perpetuate the existing dominant ideologies and social order (Giroux, 2010; Téllez & Varghese, 2013).

As amply depicted in the above research, the need for bilingual teacher candidates who are well prepared to work with bi/multilingual learners has been converted into a call to action (Alfaro, 2018, 2019; Carver-Thomas & Darling-Hammond, 2017; Hernández et al., 2022; Kennedy, 2018), see Chapter 20 in this volume. Feuer et al. (2013) highlight how the general evaluation of teacher preparation programs conducted by state and national agencies typically center on input measures such as admission criteria, faculty qualifications, course requirements, quality of student teaching experiences, and fieldwork requirements. Output measures include teacher candidates' licensure exams, program graduate surveys, employer surveys, and ultimately the impact on student learning. In DLBE teacher preparation, these measures are important but insufficient for informing program development, innovation, and improvements to prepare DLBE teacher candidates. Much of the research accentuates attitudinal surveys and outcomes of exams rather than critical feedback and development of curriculum to define pedagogical strategies teacher candidates need in the field, including candidates' feedback for continuous program improvement and evaluation of practices (Alvarado & Proctor, 2022; Flores et al., 2011).

Some scholars have identified additional dimensions essential for DLBE teacher preparation. In an effort to fill some of the existing gaps, Guerrero and Lachance (2018) proposed the National Dual Language Education Teacher Preparation Standards which include objectives designed for the implementation and evaluation of teacher candidates. To bridge the distance between teacher education and school contexts, Aquino-Sterling et al. (2022) discussed critical aspects of innovative curricular and pedagogical designs in bilingual teacher candidate preparation where language(s), content, social justice, and culturally sustaining pedagogical practices are integrated. Clark and Flores (2010) contended that teacher candidates must be provided opportunities for identity development through critical reflection and action to transform their pedagogy. They further argue that such programs must foster teachers' identity reconstruction to deepen their knowledge of ideological forces in teaching and learning. Additional research highlights the importance of developing teacher candidates' knowledge around language policy issues and how they are enacted throughout the educational system but also ways to become advocates for their students' linguistic rights (Hernández et al., 2022; Parkes et al., 2009).

In teacher preparation, there is a strong connection between pedagogical efficacy and program satisfaction (Lindholm-Leary & Genesee, 2014), including how mentor teachers provide positive experiences during clinical practice. Learning from research that applies to DLBE teacher preparation are the positive correlations between teacher candidates' perceptions about the quality of their clinical experience with their preparedness, teaching efficacy, and interest in working with traditionally underserved students, particularly Black and Latinx students (Ronfeldt & Reininger, 2012). Another critical element that applies to DLBE clinical practice is the quality of the mentor teachers as they exhibit great influence on the teacher candidates' ideology and pedagogy, since mentors monitor theory into practice dependent on their own dispositions and knowledge, rather than on the program's conceptual or structural elements (Bullough et al., 2003). In the case of DLBE clinical practice, mentor teachers need culturally and linguistically relevant professional development congruent to the program's standards and coursework. Hernández and Daoud (2022) analyzed mentor teachers' surveys indicating deficit-oriented uses of assessments with bi/multilingual students. By using a "learning about my students" framework (Pang, 2018), mentor teachers focused on the counter constructs, strengths, linguistic resources, and cultural background of students in using asset-based assessments to inform their pedagogy. The framework derived from valuing diversity and equity in the classroom, allowing teachers to develop strong trusting and reciprocal relationships with students. Opportunities for teacher preparation programs to work with mentor teachers reduce expressed concerns about racism, anti-immigrant sentiment, and unique needs overlooked in instruction (Ram, 2022).

This body of research foregrounds the importance of addressing DLBE teacher candidate preparation in more critical, comprehensive, strategic, relevant, meaningful, and sustainable ways. For DLBE teacher candidate preparation to be liberating and humanizing, it must go beyond subject matter in two languages and must have an ideological and pedagogical stance aligned to equitable student learning (Alfaro et al., 2017; Bartolomé, 2004; Freire, 1993). The following section synthesizes three critical areas from the literature on the efficacious preparation of DLBE teacher candidates.

Dual Language Bilingual Teacher Critical Ideological Consciousness

Given the socio-political and ideological nature of DLBE, it is imperative that teacher candidates learn to embrace discomfort to identify harmful dominant ideologies and their manifestation, so that they can be prepared to intervene and develop humanistic bilingual pedagogical practices for all students (Alfaro & Bartolomé, 2017; Darling-Hammond, 2012; Joseph & Evans, 2018; Lopez & Kleyn, 2022). Alfaro and Bartolomé (2018) responded by specifying that teacher candidate preparation must adopt "developing ideological clarity" in their programs. In many bilingual teacher preparation programs, the state/national standards are the basis for building teachers' content knowledge in all their languages, by ways to "increase bilingual teachers' ideological clarity and discover ways to honor and build on the language varieties that bi/multilinguals bring to the classroom" (Alfaro & Bartolomé, 2017, p. 25). How is this implemented in DLBE teacher preparation? Alfaro et al. (2017) discuss and document how a progressive teacher education program, in Southern California, developed five guiding principles to support the knowledge, dispositions, and skills critical to DLBE teacher preparation. This framework and guiding principles are rooted in bilingual education empirical research (Faltis & Valdés, 2016; Flores et al., 2011; Freire, 1993; Hollins & Torres-Guzman, 2005; Hollins & Warner, 2021; Palmer & Martínez, 2013) as well as from extensive dialogical forums with public school teachers, program graduates, administrators, faculty, community, and state standards (Alfaro, 2018). The first guiding principle in this framework explicitly addresses teacher candidates' critical ideological clarity development. This primary principle is included in all courses, but explicitly in the biliteracy and English language development methods courses where students are guided in developing and writing about how their ideology braids their pedagogy. Through this framework, teacher candidates are driven into a space of discomfort with the support of their professors and likeminded mentor teachers. This process creates a safe pathway to embrace discomfort, critical listening, and dialogue that allows teacher candidates to identify how their ideological stance braids their pedagogy (Alfaro et al., 2017; Dorner et al., 2023). For teacher candidates to engage in new understandings, this place of tension is where the ideological self develops (Bakhtin, 1981).

Paulo Freire's teachings (1993) extend to teacher education – given that the curriculum and goals are typically based on dominant ideologies – education never is, has been, or will be a neutral enterprise (Freire, 1993, p. 127). A teacher candidate's neutrality becomes a major impediment to a well-articulated and implemented DLBE program; as it perpetuates a dysfunctional and biased-based school culture, it negates the political act to transform (Bartolomé, 2008; Freire, 1993, 1998). Hence, DLBE teacher candidates need to engage in a critical self-reflection and personal interrogation to confront their implicit biases as a focus on building on students' assets and their own development of critical ideological consciousness (Alfaro & Hernández, 2016; Dorner et al., 2023; Freire, 2016). To propel the development of critical ideological consciousness, teacher preparation programs need to engage teachers in the examination of self-knowledge, defined as a personal understanding about one's lived experiences and ongoing conversations about selfhood as they braid their language(s) and cultural identities.

Identity, Self-Authorship, and Owning Our Histories

Jackson et al. (2010) discuss how most bilingual candidates enter the teaching profession with a limited understanding of their own cultural self, selfhood, and identity. They explain that "Telling *nuestros cuentos* (our narratives) as well as critical analysis of assumptions and beliefs about bilingualism and biliteracy can contribute to constructing and reconstructing identity and agency of bilingual educators" (p. 36). A study by Sheets et al. (2011) explored bilingual teacher candidates' lived experiences where they examined and reconstructed their self-identities through the meaning of critical pedagogy and entered the field of bilingual education with multiple figured worlds which influenced how they perceived their role as DLBE teachers. Parkes and colleagues (2009) argue for integrating cross-cultural competence in bilingual teacher preparation curriculum; "cross-cultural competence needs to be explicated in terms of the practices, behaviors, knowledge, and attitudes that comprise it" (p. 21). Evidently, this becomes essential in the preparation of DLBE teacher candidates as they navigate the culture and socio-political aspects in their field experiences and careers (Alfaro et al., 2014; Parkes et al., 2009).

DLBE teacher preparation programs must provide opportunities for teacher candidates to think about their practice, receive input, and make changes to their instruction through self-reflection – who we are and who we teach. It is important for teacher candidates to write and dialogue about their historical narratives, explore their own cross-cultural and linguistic identities, and use their voices to establish who they are as teachers, learners, and human beings (Alfaro et al., 2017; Clark & Flores, 2010; Jackson et al., 2010; Parkes et al., 2009; Yosso, 2006). This kind of examination connects a teacher's self-authorship to their cultural, racial, and linguistic identities and experiences as raced, classed, and gendered children and teachers of the world.

Because language and culture are tightly braided, if students lose a sense of who they are, they are also likely to lack connections and communication with teachers, family, and community members (Catalano & Hamann, 2016;

Mordechay & Alfaro, 2019). It is not uncommon for teacher candidates to have multiple identities as transnationals, and im/migrants with a unique set of linguistically and culturally diverse individualities that are rooted in strong historical ties to their homeland and national languages (Hernández & Alfaro, 2020). According to teacher candidates' *testimonios*, they recount stories of displacement from K- to 12-grade bilingual programs into monolingual settings or having no access to bilingual programs in their own communities. Others recount stories of border crossings, fragmented schooling, language loss, and origins in im/migrant communities that are closely linked with their ethnic, cultural, and linguistic pride (Alfaro & Gándara, 2021).

Cochran-Smith (1993) reminds us about the tacit assumptions we make regarding children and the practices we deem most appropriate for learners who look and sound like us or those who do not.

> To learn to teach in a society that is increasingly culturally and linguistically diverse, prospective teachers, as well as experienced teachers, need opportunities to examine much of what is usually unexamined in the tightly braided relationships of language, culture, and power in schools and schooling. (p. 500)

Teacher candidates need to feel proud of their histories, languages, and personal narratives that uphold their values to avoid the perils of assimilation because of living life as teachers with a fractured identity (Hernández & Alfaro, 2020). What's more, teaching academic discourses in both English and the partner language cannot be accomplished without first taking a detour through teachers' and their students' sociolinguistic and sociocultural contextual realities.

Critical Awareness of Diverse Languages and Cultural Assets

A fundamental challenge is to teach dominant culture "school language" varieties in intellectually honest and bias-free ways (Alfaro & Bartolomé, 2018; Faltis & Valdés, 2016; Palmer & Martínez, 2016). Given this challenge, the complex and diverse language proficiency profiles of teacher candidates make it difficult to fully develop the linguistic abilities needed to teach in a DLBE program when we consider the limited span of time spent in their credential programs, approximately one academic year (Hernández & Alfaro, 2020). Authors identified 25 distinct linguistic typologies of bilingual teacher candidates due to varied experiences in PreK- to 12-grade schooling, spoken languages at home, and their personal investments in the development of their linguistic abilities (Hernández & Alfaro, 2020). Due to this complex reality, DLBE teacher preparation must inspire teacher candidates' personal agency for growth and development in all their languages, abilities, and ideology to fully understand how it will impact their students' education (Ferreyra & Venegas-Weber, 2022; Palmer, 2011; Palmer & Martínez, 2016). Professional growth in the partner language is necessary to achieve higher levels of proficiency for effective bilingual teacher preparation (Guerrero & Lachance, 2018; Howard et al., 2018; Rodríguez-Valls & Aquino-Sterling, 2016).

Hernández and Alfaro (2020) found that teacher candidates value family interactions and cultural spaces to enhance the development of their native languages by acknowledging parents as teachers and models of languages, engaging in family conversations, attending cultural events, participating in religious events, viewing Spanish television/movies, reading books/novelas, and cultural activities that nurtured their heritage language (Hernández, 2017, 2018; Hernández & Alfaro, 2020). It is critical to develop DLBE teacher candidates' home languages through their preparation programs and professional development, since heritage languages in contact with the dominant language (e.g., English) diminish their form over time through the reduction and simplification of semantics, functions, and structures of the language (Silva-Corvalán & Enrique-Arias, 2017).

Briceño et al. (2018) argue the criticality of having DLBE teacher candidates examine the raciolinguistic beliefs that influence heritage Spanish speakers. This is critical given the current political situation related to anti-im/migrant sentiments in the United States and how these policies are internalized by teacher candidates as rejections of their culture and language (Hernández & Alfaro, 2020). Ferreyra and Venegas-Weber (2022) examined how DLBE teacher candidates' own language ideologies either aligned or conflicted with those in their school placements. Their study concluded that language ideologies emerged as both an asset and a commodity that granted access to social and professional opportunities.

In addition, it is important to braid teachers' cultural and linguistic assets, while also addressing the multiple layers of ideological variance and complexity in creating inclusive and student-valued spaces. Recent research goes beyond linguistic and cultural strategies for effective DLBE teacher preparation to address the linguistic and cultural resources that bi/multilingual learners bring to the classroom (Briceño et al., 2018; Lavadenz & Baca, 2017). DLBE teacher preparation should include culturally relevant and anti-racist curriculum and pedagogy in their methods courses (Faltis & Valdés, 2016; Garza et al., 2020; Martínez-Álvarez, 2020). Linguistic and cultural knowledge for powerful content teaching and learning allows teachers to make learning relevant and linguistically flexible. Alvarado and Proctor (2022) argue that DLBE teacher candidates must be exposed to varied perspectives, roles, and functions of language, including psycholinguistics, linguistic anthropology, sociolinguistics, and raciolinguistics to deepen their knowledge of how language functions develop – see Chapter 14 in this volume.

Another critical area of research that affirms linguistic and cultural practices is translanguaging coined in the early 2000s as a dynamic communicative practice which has always been a common and natural practice among bi/multilinguals. Translanguaging can be understood as a theory as well as pedagogy; it offers a view of all linguistic resources as legitimate for teaching and learning. Translanguaging consists of the ways bi/multilinguals move between languages for communicative meaning-making through their worlds (García, 2009). Translanguaging is complex and dynamic and has critical implications for teacher preparation. Orcasitas-Vicandi and Perales-Fernández-de-Gamboa (2022) conducted a study with teacher candidates on translanguaging and materials' design, the outcomes revealed common traces among the materials they developed for translanguaging to affirm their students' cultural and linguistic realities. Additionally, Musanti and Rodríguez (2017) conducted a qualitative case study where they found that Latina teacher candidates created translanguaging spaces through writing in multiple ways, to defy the monolingual tradition prevailing in bilingual teacher preparation. More information on translanguaging is available in Chapter 26 in this volume.

A plethora of research now exists that clearly supports the need for continued development of teacher candidates' cultural and linguistic assets, while also addressing the multiple layers of ideological variance and complexity of their identities, including their raciolinguistic beliefs. Bilingual teacher candidates have varied experiences and linguistic typologies that allow them to translanguage through their worlds. Considering teacher candidates' multiple and complex identities, the final section outlines recommendations for DLBE teacher preparation.

Conclusion

DLBE teacher candidates must be prepared to unapologetically contest inequalities in DLBE programs to drive the field of education toward a more humane, accessible, and equitable teaching and learning space for diverse groups of learners, their families, and communities (Alfaro, 2017; Freire, 2016). Past and present research and cautionary notes by critical scholars regarding the issue of equity in DLBE have equipped teacher educators with a heightened awareness of the essentiality for DLBE teacher candidates to braid critical ideological clarity, identity and self-authorship, and language and culture at the onset of their preparation. Hence, critical teacher educators clearly see the importance of intentionally elevating teacher candidates' consciousness and engaging them in a process of self-interrogation, "asking the tough questions" (Alfaro & Hernández, 2016), to enable them to recognize and interrupt dominant ideologies and engage in counterhegemonic practices within their DLBE school/community (Alfaro, 2019; Palmer & Martínez, 2016, 2013; Valenzuela, 2016).

To fulfill the promise and intent of DLBE, it is imperative that we prepare critically ideologically conscious teacher candidates with the knowledge, disposition, and skills to build on their students' cultural and linguistic foundations (García, 2009; Yosso, 2006). In fact, more research is needed to help teacher educators better prepare teachers to develop greater global sociocultural and sociolinguistic awareness in order to counter hegemonic practices via a cultural wealth orientation that assists students to reach their full potential as *linguistic geniuses* (Alfaro & Bartolomé, 2018).

The braided relationship of ideology, identity, language, and culture is critical to the development of DLBE teacher candidates; this begins by understanding competing ideologies, their varied self-identities/authorships, and languages and cultural histories. We end with an essential challenge for DLBE teacher educators regarding the enormous responsibility we have for the generations of teacher candidates we prepare. It is incumbent on teacher educators to demonstrate, through their teachings and by explicit example, the process of braiding their identities as teachers through their languages and cultural ties to students, families, and communities.

References

Alfaro, C. (2017). Growing ideologically clear and linguistically efficacious dual language teachers. *Multilingual Educator*, 36–40.

Alfaro, C. (2018). The sociopolitical struggle and promise of bilingual teacher education: Past, present, and future. *Bilingual Research Journal*, *41*(4), 413–427.

Alfaro, C. (2019). Preparing critically conscious dual-language teachers: Recognizing and interrupting dominant ideologies. *Theory into Practice*, *58*(2), 194–203.

Alfaro, C., & Bartolomé, L. (2017). Preparing ideologically clear bilingual teachers: Honoring working-class non-standard language use in the bilingual education classroom. *Issues in Teacher Education*, *26*(2), 11–34.

Alfaro, C., & Bartolomé, L. I. (2018). Preparing ideologically clear bilingual teachers to recognize linguistic geniuses. In B. Berriz, V. Poey, & A. Wager (Eds.), *Arts as a way of talking for emergent bilingual youth: A foundation for literacy in K-12 schools* (pp. 44–59). Routledge.

Alfaro, C., & Gándara, P. (2021). Binational teacher preparation: Constructing pedagogical bridges for the students we share. In *The students we share: Preparing US and Mexican teachers for our transnational future* (pp. 45–69). SUNY Press.

Alfaro, C., & Hernández, A. M. (2016). Ideology, pedagogy, access and equity (IPAE): A critical examination for dual language educators. *Multilingual Educator*, 8–11.

Alfaro, C., Cadiero, K., & Ochoa, A. (2017). Teacher education and Latino emergent bilinguals: Knowledge, dispositions, and skills for critically conscious pedagogy. In P. Ramirez, C. Faltis, & E. de Jong (Eds.), *Critical teacher education: Learning from Latino English language learners in K-12*. Routledge.

Alfaro, C., Durán, R., Hunt, A., & Aragón, M. J. (2014). Steps toward unifying dual language programs, common core state standards, and critical pedagogy: Oportunidades, Estrategias y Retos. *Association of Mexican American Educators Journal*, *8*(2), 17–30.

Alvarado, J., & Proctor, P. (2022). Cultivating bilingual education in Massachusetts: From survival to restoration. In C. R. Aquino-Sterling, M. Gort, & B. Flores (Eds.), *Innovative curricular and pedagogical designs in bilingual teacher education* (pp. 51–63). Information Age Publishing.

Aquino-Sterling, C. R., Gort, M., & Flores, B. (Eds.). (2022). *Innovative curricular and pedagogical designs in bilingual teacher education*. Information Age Publishing.

Bakhtin, M. M. (1981). *The dialogic imagination: Four essays*. University of Texas Press.

Bartolomé, L. I. (2002). Creating an equal playing field: Teachers as advocates, border crossers, and cultural brokers. In Z. F. Beykont (Ed.), *The power of culture: Teaching across language difference* (pp. 167–191). Harvard Education Publishing Group.

Bartolomé, L. I. (2004). Critical pedagogy and teacher education: Radicalizing prospective teachers. *Teacher Education Quarterly*, *31*(1), 97–122.

Bartolomé, L. I. (Ed.). (2008). *Ideologies in education: Unmasking the trap of teacher neutrality*. Peter Lang.

Briceño, A., Rodriguez-Mojica, C., & Muñoz-Muñoz, E. (2018). From English learner to Spanish learner: Raciolinguistic beliefs that influence heritage Spanish speaking teacher candidates. *Language and Education*, *32*(3), 212–226.

Bullough, R. V., Young, J., Birrell, J. R., Clark, D. C., Egan, M. W., Erickson, L., Frankovich, M., Brunetti, J., & Welling, M. (2003). Teaching with a peer: A comparison of two models of student teaching. *Teaching and Teacher Education*, *19*, 57–73.

Caldas, B. (2017). Shifting discourses in teacher education: Performing the advocate bilingual teacher. *Arts Education Policy Review*, *118*(4), 190–201.

Carver-Thomas, D., & Darling-Hammond, L. (2017). *Addressing California's growing teacher shortage: 2017 update*. Learning Policy Institute.

Catalano, T., & Hamann, E. T. (2016). Multilingual pedagogies and pre-service teachers: Implementing "language as a resource" orientations in teacher education programs. *Bilingual Research Journal*, *39*(3–4), 263–278.

Cervantes-Soon, C. G. (2018). Using a Xicana feminist framework in bilingual teacher preparation: Toward an anticolonial path. *The Urban Review*, *50*(5), 857–888.

Clark, E. R., & Flores, B. B. (2010). The metamorphosis of teacher identity: An intersection of ethnic consciousness, self-conceptualization, and belief systems. In P. Jenlink (Ed.), *Teacher identity and the struggle for recognition*. Routledge.

Cochran-Smith, M. (1993). Color blindness and basket making are not the answers: Confronting the dilemmas of race, culture, and language diversity in teacher education. *American Educational Research Journal*, *32*(3), 493–522.

Crawford, J. (1997). *Best evidence: Research foundations of the bilingual education act* (National Clearinghouse for Bilingual Education Report). Office of Bilingual Education and Minority Languages Affairs.

Cummins, J. (1994). Primary language instruction and the education of language minority students. In California State Department of Education. *Schooling and language minority students: A theoretical framework* (2nd ed.). California State University, Los Angeles.

Darling-Hammond, L. (2012). The right start: Creating a strong foundation for the teaching career. *Phi Delta Kappan*, *94*, 8–13.

Dorner, L. M., Palmer, D., Cervantes-Soon, C. G., Heiman, D., & Crawford, E. R. (Eds.). (2023). *Critical consciousness in dual language bilingual education: Case studies on policy and practice*. Taylor & Francis.

Faltis, C. J., & Valdés, G. (2016). Preparing teachers for teaching in and advocating for linguistically diverse classrooms: A vade mecum for teacher educators. In D. H. Gitomer & C. A. Bell (Eds.), *Handbook of Research on Teaching* (pp. 549–592). American Educational Research Association.

Ferreyra, P., & Venegas-Weber, P. (2022). 'What language does grandma speak?' An understanding of dual language teacher candidates' language ideologies in elementary placements. *International Journal of Bilingual Education and Bilingualism*, 1–14.

Feuer, M. J., Floden, R. E., Chudowsku, N., & Ahn, J. (2013). *Evaluation of teacher preparation programs: Purposes, methods, and policy options*. National Academy of Education.

Flores, B. B., Hernández, A., García, C. T., & Claeys, L. (2011). Teacher academy induction learning community: Guiding teachers through their zone of proximal development. *Mentoring & Tutoring: Partnership in Learning*, *19*(3), 365–389.

Freire, J. A. (2016). Nepantleras/os and their teachers in dual language education: Developing sociopolitical consciousness to contest language education policies. *Association of Mexican American Educators Journal*, *10*(1), 36–52.

Freire, P. (1993). *Pedagogy of the city*. Continuum.

Freire, P. (1998) *Teachers as cultural workers: Letters to those who dare teach*. Westview Press.

Gándara, P., & Hopkins, M. (2010). *Forbidden language: English learners and restrictive language policies*. Teachers College Press.

García, O. (2009). *Bilingual education in the 21st century: A global perspective*. Wiley Blackwell.

Garza, E., Espinoza, K., Machado-Casas, M., Schouten, B., & Guerra, M. J. (2020). Highly effective practices of three bilingual teacher preparation programs in us Hispanic-serving institutions (HSIs). *EHQUIDAD. Revista Internacional de Políticas de Bienestar y Trabajo Social*, *14*, 95–128.

Giroux, H. A. (2010). Rethinking education as the practice of freedom: Paulo Freire and the promise of critical pedagogy. *Policy Futures in Education*, *8*, 715–721.

Guerrero, M. D., & Lachance, J. R. (2018). The national dual language education teacher preparation standards. *Dual Language Education of New Mexico*, 1–84.

Hernández, A. M. (2017). Reflective and transformative practice in bilingual teacher preparation: Examining cross-cultural and linguistic equity. In M. Lavadenz & R. Baca (Eds.), *Issues in Teacher Education: Preparing Bilingual Teachers*, *26*(2), 63–82.

Hernández, A. M. (2018). Bilingual teacher candidates speak of peace, language and identity: Reflecting on an era of restrictive language policies in California. In E. Mikulec, S. Bhatawadekar, C. McGivern, & P. C. Iida-Miller (Eds.), *Readings in language studies (vol. 7): Intersections of peace and language studies* (pp. 151–171). International Society for Language Studies.

Hernández, A. M., & Alfaro, C. (2020). Naming and confronting the challenges of bilingual teacher preparation: A dilemma for dual language education in California–lessons learned. *NABE Journal of Research and Practice*, *10*(2), 31–46.

Hernández, A. M., & Daoud, A. (2022). Learning about my students: Examination of cultural asset-based assessments in dual language education. In M. Machado-Casas, S. I. Maldonado, & B. B. Flores (Eds.), *Assessment and evaluation in bilingual education* (Vol. 28, pp. 245–266). Peter Lang International Academic Publishers.

Hernández, S. J., Alfaro, C., & Martell, M. A. N. (2022). Bilingual teacher educators as language policy agents: A critical language policy perspective of the Castañeda v. Pickard case and the bilingual teacher shortage. *Language Policy*, *21*, 1–23.

Hollins, E., & Torres-Guzman, M. E. (2005). The preparation of candidates for teaching diverse student populations. In M. Cochran-Smith, & K. M. Zeichner (Eds.), *Studying Teacher Education: The Report of the AERA Panel on Research and Teacher Education* (pp. 201–225). Lawrence Erlbaum associates, Inc.

Hollins, E. R., & Warner, C. K. (2021). *Rethinking teacher preparation program design*. Routledge.

Howard, E. R., Lindholm-Leary, K., Rogers, D., Medina, N., Kennedy, B., Sugarman, J., & Christian, D. (2018). *Guiding principles for dual language education* (3rd ed.). Center for Applied Linguistics.

Jackson, L. G., Guzman, S. B., & Ramos, G. (2010). Learning a borderland professional identity. In L. D. Soto & H. Kharem (Eds.), *Counterpoints, Teaching Bilingual/Bicultural Children: Teachers Talk about Language and Learning* (Vol. 371, pp. 29–37). Peter Lang.

Joseph, T., & Evans, L. M. (2018). Preparing preservice teachers for bilingual and bicultural classrooms in an era of political change. *Bilingual Research Journal*, *41*(1), 52–68.

Kennedy, B. (2018). Teacher preparation for dual language classrooms. In *Profiles of dual language education in the 21st century* (pp. 103–114). Multilingual Matters.

Lavadenz, M., & Baca, R. (2017). Introduction: Preparing bilingual teachers. *Issues in Teacher Education*, *26*(2), 3–9.

Lindholm-Leary, K., & Genesee, F. (2014). Student outcomes in one-way, two-way, and indigenous language immersion education. *Journal of Immersion and Content-Based Language Education*, 2(2), 165–180.

Lopez, D., & Kleyn, T. (2022). Centering immigrant voices and experiences in a dual language bilingual school: Teachers as critical pedagogues and policymakers. In L. M. Dorner, D. Palmer, C. G. Cervantes-Soon, D. Heiman, & E. R. Crawford (Eds.), *Critical consciousness in dual language bilingual education: Case studies on policy and practice*. Taylor & Francis.

Martínez-Álvarez, P. (2020). Essential constructs in the preparation of inclusive bilingual education teachers: Mediation, agency, and collectivity. *Bilingual Research Journal*, *43*(3), 304–322.

Mordechay, K., & Alfaro, C. (2019). The binational context of the students we share: What do educators on both sides of the border need to know? *Kappa Delta Pi Record*, *55*(1), 30–35. https://doi.org/10.1080/00228958.2019.1549438

Musanti, S. I., & Rodríguez, A. D. (2017). Translanguaging in bilingual teacher preparation: Exploring pre-service bilingual teachers' academic writing. *Bilingual Research Journal*, *40*(1), 38–54.

National Center for Education Statistics (NCES). (2022). English learners in public schools. *Condition of Education*. U.S. Department of Education, Institute of Education Sciences.

Orcasitas-Vicandi, M., & Perales-Fernández-de-Gamboa, A. (2022). Promoting pedagogical translanguaging in pre-service teachers' training: Material design for a multilingual context with a regional minority language. *International Journal of Multilingualism*, 1–21.

Palmer, D. (2011). The discourse of transition: Teachers' language ideologies within transitional bilingual education programs. *International Multilingual Research Journal*, *5*(2), 103–122.

Palmer, D., & Martínez, R. A. (2013). Teacher agency in bilingual spaces: A fresh look at preparing teachers to educate Latina/o bilingual children. *Review of Research in Education*, *37*(1), 269–297.

Palmer, D. K., & Martínez, R. A. (2016). Developing biliteracy: What do teachers really need to know about language? *Language Arts*, *93*(5), 379.

Pang, V. O. (2018). *Diversity and equity in the classroom*. Cengage Learning.

Parkes, J., Ruth, T., Angerg-Espinoza, A., & de Jong, E. (2009). *Urgent research questions and issues in dual language education*. Dual Language Education of New Mexico.

Ram, S. (2022). Understanding educators' experiences teaching multilingual learners: A qualitative research study about educator preparation, classroom experiences, institutional barriers, and requests for state support. *Public Advocates*. Retrieved from Understanding Educators' Experiences Teaching Multilingual Learners.

Rodríguez-Valls, F., & Aquino-Sterling, C. (2016). Maestros de secundaria y preparatoria, maestros de lenguaje: la importancia de propiciar el aprendizaje de la lengua a través de contenidos curriculares. *Journal of Bilingual Education Research and Instruction*, *18*(1), 106–120.

Ronfeldt, M., & Reininger, M. (2012). More or better student teaching? *Teaching and Teacher Education*, *28*, 1091–1106.

Sarmiento-Arribalzaga, M. A., & Murillo, L. A. (2010). Pre-service bilingual teachers and their invisible scars: Implications for preparation programs. *SRATE Journal*, *19*(1), 61–69.

Sheets, R. H., Flores, B. B., & Clark, E. R. (2011). Educar para transformar: A bilingual education teacher preparation program model. In B. B. Flores, R. H. Sheets, & E. R. Clark (Eds.), *Teacher preparation for bilingual student populations: Educar para transformar* (pp. 9–24). Routledge.

Silva-Corvalán, C., & Enrique-Arias, A. (2017). *Sociolingüística y pragmática en español* (2nd ed.). Georgetown University Press.

Tedick, D. J., & Lyster, R. (2020). *Scaffolding language development in immersion and dual language classrooms*. Routledge.

Téllez, K., & Varghese, M. (2013). Teachers as intellectuals and advocates: Professional development for bilingual education teachers. *Theory Into Practice*, *52*(2), 128–135.

Thomas, W. P., & Collier, V. P. (2002). *A national study of school effectiveness for language minority students' long-term academic achievement* (Final report). Center for Research on Education, Diversity & Excellence.

Valenzuela, A. (Ed.). (2016). *Growing critically conscious teachers: A social justice curriculum for educators of Latino/a youth*. Teachers College Press.

Wall, D. J., & Hurie, A. H. (2017). Post-observation conferences with bilingual pre-service teachers: Revoicing and rehearsing. *Language and Education*, *31*(6), 543–560.

Wiese, A.-M., & Garcia, E. E. (2001). The bilingual education act: Language minority and US federal educational policy. *International Journal of Bilingual Education and Bilingualism*, *4*(4), 229–248.

Yosso, T. J. (2006). *Critical race counterstories along the Chicano/Chicana educational pipeline*. Routledge.

35

RECONSIDERING LANGUAGE ASSETS

A Critical and Integrative Examination of Language Proficiency and Biliteracy in Dual Language Teacher Education

Eduardo R. Muñoz-Muñoz, Allison Briceño

Interrogating Language Proficiency and Literacy Knowledge in DLBE

White, monolingual, standardized norms often dominate dual language (DL) programs, thereby omitting – and attempting to replace – students' rich cultures and languaging practices (Cervantes-Soon et al., 2017; Palmer et al., 2019; Valdés, 2018). Bilingual teacher candidates (BTCs) have often internalized such hegemonic messages of linguistic inferiority (Arce, 2004; Briceño et al., 2018; Brito et al., 2004). In order to break this cycle, bilingual teacher preparation programs must actively counteract existing norms and practices. This work includes the creation of counterhegemonic spaces where language ideologies and literacy pedagogies enable transformative practices that build on students' linguistic assets and provide equitable instruction to the diverse learners in DL programs (Alfaro, 2019; Alfaro & Bartolomé, 2017). While much of the literature has focused on Spanish DL programs, there is a need for critical bilingual teacher candidates irrespective of their language focus to be aware of the sociolinguistic status and power relations inside their speaker communities in the U.S. context (Guerrero & Lachance, 2018).

The complex praxis of bilingual teacher preparation for DL programs is empirically understudied. BTCs require significant knowledge of and in two languages, as well as deep understanding of the interdependence among language development, biliteracy, and bilingual pedagogy, which are a precondition for the leveraging of marginalized students' language and literacy

DOI: 10.4324/9781003269076-51

assets (Alfaro & Bartolomé, 2017). In this chapter, we address some of these complexities, including the need to deconstruct and unlearn the harmful stereotypes candidates have been taught about their languaging and literacy practices. We synthesize the literature on language proficiency and holistic biliteracy, and argue for an integrative critical approach to these topics in communities of practice (Lave & Wenger, 2001) that support BTCs and bilingual faculty.

What Counts as Bilingual Teacher Language Proficiency?

As Anzaldúa (1987) reminds us, "So, if you want to hurt me, talk badly about my language" (p. 39). Public education labels, catalogs, compares, contrasts, and denigrates the linguistic repertoires of multilingual students who, over time, may (or may not) become sorely needed bilingual teachers. Language proficiency and the political, sociological, economical, and linguistic regime under which it is constructed need to be critically examined if DLBE is to live up to its promise of social justice (Howard et al., 2018). Therefore, as states enact legal mandates for proficiency (Boyle et al., 2015) and individual preparation programs establish their local selection processes, all agents involved in the implementation of measurements ought to pause (as we authors do) to scrutinize our backgrounds, projections, and biases that may continue to perpetuate linguistic violence against bilingual educators (Ek et al., 2013). A holistic approach to bilingual teacher language proficiency exceeds the confines of instruments of professional control: It defines the core of the profession at the intersection of identity, pedagogy, and social justice. The issue of proficiency is twofold for BTCs. It has traditionally concerned proficiency assessment but it requires, most importantly, that we examine how programs are nourishing the BTCs' linguistic repertoires during their formative period. If BTCs are intended to serve as "bilingual role models" as the profession has often been conceptualized (Guerrero et al., 2017), the field needs to inquire critically into the standard of "linguistic appropriateness" as a purportedly self-evident concept (Flores & Rosa, 2015).

Any discussion about fitness cutoffs is conditioned by the context of the "shortage" of bilingual teachers and the policies and instruments influencing the pipeline and labor market. For example, Arroyo-Romano (2016) describes how the development of comprehensive language tests with an increased focus on formal properties of language and the written mode led to a reduction in the number of certified BTCs. Ultimately, the author points out that the test "should not be blamed for low passing rates; these data show the reality of the current development of bilingual education throughout the state" (p. 285). In the California context, Muñoz-Muñoz and colleagues (2022) discuss the implications of the bilingual legislation such as proposition 227 in California as feeding the vicious cycle of the bilingual teacher shortage.

Breaking Monolingual Inertia

Guerrero and colleagues have consistently reminded the field of the situation of Spanish in K-20 education in a context of English-centric organizations (Guerrero, 1997, 2003; Guerrero & Guerrero, 2008, 2013, 2020) and how these revitalization struggles are not recent (see Gaarder, 1977). In his 2003 "We have correct English teachers. Why can't we have correct Spanish teachers? It is not acceptable," Guerrero aims at identifying the causes that prevent the development of academic Spanish for many BTCs. The nefarious interaction between limited access to academic Spanish in formal education and an internalized sense of inappropriate linguistic skills undermines the potential of bilingual teachers.

Guerrero and Guerrero (2008) focus on structural causes and how political, economic, and social psychological factors undermine academic Spanish in the same institutions charged with safeguarding it. The article makes a plea for academics to publish in Spanish and create Spanish academic language communities that undo ideologies and create a new academic Spanish habitus. Such impetus is behind "Abriendo Brecha," (2017) an anthology of articles in Spanish edited by Guerrero and colleagues intended to "hacer más leve el peso que por décadas hemos llevado injustamente a nuestras espaldas los usuarios del español académico en este país" (p. v).

Breaking Monoglossic Pressure

A demographic imperative requires that monolingual education in the United States be reconstructed to embrace a diverse and democratic society. It also demands that the field revisits the ontology of language as lived and experienced by those people driving such change in the United States, including among teacher educators (Rodriguez-Mojica et al., 2019). Thus, DLBE ought to problematize notions such as academic language, standardization, and native speakers. Such monoglossic ideologies favor the hierarchization of language varieties and the stigmatization of language practices through covert paralinguistic judgments, as has been argued by raciolinguistics (Flores & McAuliffe, 2020; Flores & Rosa, 2015). Ideologies privileging the "white gaze" of "listener perspectives" have a direct impact on the sense of appropriateness that BTCs experience from enrollment in teacher preparation programs to their lives as teachers of record. As the internalization of oppressive ideologies has often occurred alongside the BTC's own early educational experiences (Briceño et al., 2018; Rodriguez-Mojica et al., 2019), it stands to reason that a counterhegemonic decolonization and reconstruction of the speaker self encompasses a parallel empowerment of the BTC's critical awareness (Alfaro, 2019; Caldas, 2019; Caldas & Heiman, 2021; Ostorga & Farruggio, 2014; Ostorga et al., 2020; Lindahl et al., 2021) in the BTC credentialing program.

Ek and colleagues (2013) described linguistic violence Latinx bilingual teacher candidates experienced in South Texas, explaining that the varieties of Spanish spoken by Latinx candidates in the United States are marked and intersect with anti-immigrant, racist sentiments. The relevance of this work is still felt in the work of Fallas Escobar and Treviño (2021) who incorporate the raciolinguistic notions of "listening others" and "speaker others" (Rosa & Flores, 2017) to understand the account of two transnational BTCs as their speaker identity and sense of proficiency unfold against the hegemonic U.S. ideologies.

To counteract linguistic oppression, Freire and Feinauer (2022) call for the use of vernacular Spanish and translanguaging in DL classrooms to combat deficit language ideologies and practices and build children's critical consciousness, the fourth goal of DL programs (Cervantes-Soon et al., 2017; Freire, 2020; Palmer et al., 2019). Such practices might include observation and critique of linguistic practices in schools, the engagement of fluid repertories in the classroom, using children's books that include local varieties of Spanish, and incorporation of dialogical approach to address the relationship between language and power and its impact on local communities (Freire & Feinauer, 2022).

Other studies on BTC preparation that evidence development of critical consciousness and translanguaging pedagogy include the use of both Spanish and English across the curriculum, incorporating critical reflection of candidates' language ideologies, raciolinguistics, and discussions of specific readings (Alfaro, 2018; Collins et al., 2023; Rodriguez-Mojica & Briceño, 2019; Rodriguez-Mojica et al., 2020). Alfaro (2018) recounts how one university's bilingual teacher preparation program develops critically conscious bilingual teachers by emphasizing biliteracy across the content areas, family and community engagement, critical literacy, and inclusive learning environments. These studies provide examples of bilingual programs intentionally enacting counterhegemonic, translingual practices to develop critically conscious bilingual teachers.

The creation of bilingual professional communities in K-20 institutions does not shield programs from a culture of monoglot standardization (Silverstein, 1996). Just as there is an inertia to keep pure English at the center of teaching in the United States, there can be an ideological pressure to keep any language other than English "pure," with similarly deleterious effects for BTCs. Accordingly, Flores and Rosa (2015) have argued for the debunking of concepts such as bilingual proficiency and linguistic dexterity as linguistically objective constructs, evidencing the inextricable coconstruction of race and language in a racialized field like bilingual education. In his development of "languagelessness," Rosa (2016) emphasizes the impossibility of making a proficiency judgment without considering the embodied racialized histories of bilingual educators. Thus, linguistic performances by bilingual educators are commonly stigmatized as illegitimate as they fail to satisfy ideologies of standard and pure language embodied in Eurocentric listeners.

Teacher educators need to think urgently about our stance toward the inherent linguistic potential of BTCs who may identify as heritage speakers (Valdés, 2005). Embracing decolonial, antiracist epistemologies necessarily changes the landscape of bilingual teacher preparation not only in approaches to content instruction or cultural relevance, but also in the nature of language as a primordial learning vehicle. When Cervantes-Soon (2018) argues for the use of a Xicana Feminista Framework in bilingual teacher preparation, she is taking issue with the violence inherent in the transmission of ideologies that enshrine standardized hegemonic languages over the language practices of the subaltern. In this perspective, colonial blindness (Calderon, 2014) creates the illusion of being able to teach a hegemonic language while leaving at the margins its body of ideologies, histories, and oppressions.

Envisioning and Enacting New Perspectives on Proficiency Development for BTCs

Bilingual education, by virtue of societal and epistemic progress, has been challenged to think about alternative models of language and their operationalization. What it means to be a DLBE teacher necessarily changes over time.

Elaborating on a Language for Specific Purposes framework, Aquino-Sterling (2016) posited a model of bilingual teacher proficiency in the concept of pedagogical Spanish and supports it with some empirical work in his own illustrative practice. The author articulates the idea of a teaching-specific proficiency tailored to the contextualized demands of the bilingual education context articulated in academic pedagogical (subject area linguistic performance) and professional (the performance of professional duties and socialization in a community) discourse demands. Setting this model aside from generalist language tests to date, Aquino-Sterling argues that teachers do not need just superior language proficiency, but also the professional practices at the intersection of disciplinary language and communication in their communities.

Heteroglossic stances pour in as Aquino-Sterling and Rodríguez-Valls (2016) push this model beyond what is merely linguistically appropriate to focus on cultural, linguistic, and professional relevance to the profession. The authors build their framework on the notion of pedagogical language knowledge or PLK, which Galguera (2011) and Bunch (2013) develop with an emphasis on critical language awareness (Alim, 2005), literacy, and functional linguistics for English learner instruction. Pedagogical Spanish is extended to include hybrid practices such as translanguaging in a conceptualization that works to harmonize the high expectations placed on the linguistic proficiency of BTCs with the irreducible creativity of their linguistic repertoires. These conceptualizations pave the way for transformative teacher preparation courses that aspire to decenter monolingual and monoglossic perspectives.

Much remains to be researched about specific models of DLBE preparation, and the role and articulation that proficiency has in them, but some promising examples begin to emerge. In "Speaking educación," Caldas et al. (2019) describe the experiences of developing linguistic proficiency in a bilingual teacher preparation program in the U.S.-Mexico border, with an emphasis on the influence of the context, the negotiation of language demands, the harnessing of translingual repertoires, and the development of critical language awareness. These processes are developed simultaneously and in an integrated manner. A second detailed approach to this experience, described in Caldas' "To switch or not to switch" (2019), advances heteroglossic stances in BTC preparation and higher education by creating a translanguaging space as a pivotal pedagogical foundation for the BTCs' experience.

More recently, the experiences at City University of New York (CUNY) have been captured by Collins et al. (2023) who have described the transformation of a bilingual preparation program starting in 2016 with an increase of instruction in Spanish, raciolinguistic lenses, and the explicit inclusion of heteroglossic components as part of culturally sustaining pedagogies (Paris & Alim, 2017) which have resulted in the validation of BTC identities. In particular, the authors argue, the openness to translanguaging practices in instruction and assignments led to an increased desire to develop Spanish proficiency and language-specific performances.

The breaking of new ground in states and regions that are embracing DLBE brings the imperative need to reconceptualize the what and the how of language proficiency. Amanti and colleagues (2022) describe how they reconsidered linguistic assets for BTCs in Georgia, part of the New Latinx South. While their program was initially poised to keep high proficiency expectations based on testing evidence to secure the success of nascent programs in new regions, the authors reconceptualized their criteria and how to capture language development over time (as opposed to on admission) in the belief that "language 'proficiency' is not a settled concept" (p. 8).

Interrogating Biliteracy Instruction in DBLE

Like language proficiency, biliteracy is deeply intertwined with issues of culture, identity, and power (Ceballos, 2012; Flores, 2016; Flores & Rosa, 2015; Musanti, 2014). To combat inequities in DL spaces, bilingual teacher educators must prepare BTCs to recognize and interrogate the power structures and ideologies of schools' biliteracy programs. In contrast to monoglossic ideologies that focus on students' discrete literacy abilities one language at a time, a *holistic biliteracy* approach (Dworin, 2003, Escamilla et al., 2014) maintains that a bilingual's language and literacy practices are mutually reinforcing, as bilinguals use all of their linguistic resources when languaging and processing text. A holistic biliteracy perspective challenges the literacy learning Spanish/English binary, instead offering a frame for understanding the dynamic literacy and languaging practices of multilinguals (Escamilla et al., 2014, 2019). As such, we question what counts as biliteracy instruction and provide suggestions for building on students' linguistic and literacy capital (Compton-Lilly & Nayan, 2016; Yosso, 2005) for more equitable biliteracy practices.

What Counts as Biliteracy Instruction?

White, monoglossic cultural and linguistic norms pervade DL literacy instruction. Too often multilingual students and students of color are not represented in the curriculum (Dahlen, 2020). There is a dearth of books that reflect multilingual students' authentic lived experiences to serve as mirrors (Bishop, 1990), with only 5% of children's books published in 2018 containing Latinx characters, while 77% contain White characters or animal/non-human characters (50% and 27%, respectively; Park Dahlen & Huyck, 2019). Considering that most DL programs enroll one-third to one-half of students who speak Spanish in the home and other Latinx students attend as English speakers, it is clear that DL students are not well represented in the books used to teach literacy.

As such, BTCs must learn to center the diversity of their bilingual students in various ways, including the use of translanguaging. Teachers can diversify their classroom libraries to include books that incorporate translanguaging and multilingualism and have students create texts in which their families' authentic, lived experiences are told in their own words in books, personal narratives, and various forms of multimodal, multilingual creations (España & Herrera, 2020). For example, a study that explored the creation of DL books about family treasures provided students with opportunities for identity formation, development and exhibition of cultural pride, and the acquisition of basic technology skills while developing their early literacy knowledge and abilities (Roessingh, 2012).

A holistic approach to biliteracy instruction intentionally pairs literacy instruction in Spanish and English so that biliteracy instruction is integrated and builds across languages (Escamilla et al., 2014). To counteract monoglossic norms, BTCs need to teach biliteracy in ways that support students' metalinguistic knowledge and development of translingual, cross-linguistic skills as well as their identity and criticality (Rodriguez-Mojica & Briceño, 2018). While DL programs traditionally separate literacy instruction by language (Howard et al., 2018), students learn and do literacy using their full linguistic repertoire (García & Wei, 2014; García & Kleifgen, 2020). For example, Velasco and García (2014) analyzed five written texts produced by young multilingual writers and demonstrated that students used their entire linguistic repertoire in the planning, drafting, and production stages of writing, even when the final product was monolingual.

Since students learn and use language dynamically, bilingual programs should make space for translanguaging opportunities (García & Kleifgen, 2020) and explicitly help students make cross-linguistic connections during literacy instruction (Escamilla et al., 2014). Instructional strategies might include cognate instruction (García et al., 2020), use of both languages in discussions about texts, bilingual annotations, use of bilingual texts, contrastive analysis, generating multilingual texts, intentionally developing multilingual students' *confianza* in performing literacies, fostering metalinguistic awareness (García & Kleifgen, 2020), the Dictado, and Así se Dice (Escamilla et al., 2014). Briceño and Zoeller (2022) developed a Transliteracy Framework to incorporate translanguaging in literacy instruction. The framework asks teachers to use holistic observation to identify a specific literacy strength in one language and leverage that strength to support students' literacy development in the other language. In summary, BTCs must learn to counter sequential monolingual perspectives of biliteracy instruction and aim for biliteracy instruction and assessment that enables Latinx BTCs and their students to genuinely self-express (Cervantes-Soon, 2018), including translingually, rather than self-censor as a result of internalized monoglossic expectations.

Implications and Future Directions: Integration, Coordination, Transformation

A consistent thread in the literature about both bilingual teacher proficiency and biliteracy has been the intimate connection among language, identity, personal and professional trajectories, and the development of critical consciousness (Cervantes-Soon et al., 2017; Palmer et al., 2019). The language and literacy ideologies of BTCs, inherited, developed through experience, and reinforced by structural circumstances, influence their judgment of what appropriate proficiency is. Accordingly, we posit that the preparation of resilient, committed BTCs requires the conceptual integration of both areas into the curricular pathway and formative experiences of BTCs. Similarly, the foundations of any professional experience for inservice bilingual teachers must consider critically the ongoing interaction between what teachers think that "knowing" a language is and how it manifests recurrently in literacy approaches. Such an approach is exemplified by The National Dual Language Education Teacher Preparation Standards (Guerrero & Lachance, 2018) which integrates Bilingualism and Biliteracy in its standard 1 with a substantial emphasis on the scrutiny of the self and institutions with regard to language skills, affordances, and ideologies.

The criticality and urgency of bilingual teacher development for the growth of heteroglossic DLBE requires that more case study research be conducted on model bilingual teacher education programs (e.g., Alfaro, 2018). As we have seen in the extant literature in this chapter, the coordination of courses and language pedagogies together with the concerted effort to sustain bilingual teacher educators is essential to ensure an increased, intentional exposure to dynamic language and literacy models.

Last, but certainly not least, an integrated critical language proficiency and holistic biliteracy is a cornerstone aspect of the emancipatory aspirations of equity-based DLBE. Future research must deepen its analysis into the heteroglossic implications of debunking models of native-speakerhood and decentering canonical references in literacy development. For example, as the ideology of standard monoglot is brought into question as it applies to Spanish and a nascent body of literature explores African-American linguistic and literacy identities in bilingual education (Bauer et al., 2020; Frieson, 2019; Zoeller & Briceño, 2023), how will the field of DLBE embrace African-American Vernacular English into PreK-20 DLBE contexts? As it concerns BTC certification, how will tests and other mechanisms required as evidence to document linguistic fitness and literacy pedagogical readiness resist or adapt to the influence of the decolonial and emancipatory pedagogies that are currently energizing bilingual teacher preparation programs across the nation?

We want to end this chapter with a call to action that echoes what the field has voiced as the most pressing and necessary cause in the field of DLBE and bilingual education in general: An integrated, coordinated, and transformative move to engage with the linguistic and literacy energy in our communities as a way to curb the bilingual teacher shortage. While the country may have a numerical shortage of certified bilingual teachers, there is an overwhelming qualitative potential that can turn a vicious cycle into a virtuous one. An area of further development and emphasis pointed out by most authors in this research area is the role played by colleges of education and BTC preparation programs in the creation of institutionalized spaces for sequences of culturally and linguistically sustaining courses where Spanish is elevated and where faculty are also sustained in their linguistic development. In our quest to undo oppressive, linguistic structural conditions, this is one of several perfect points to start.

References

Alfaro, C. (2018). The sociopolitical struggle and promise of bilingual teacher education: Past, present, and future. *Bilingual Research Journal*, *41*(4), 413–427.

Alfaro, C. (2019). Preparing critically conscious dual-language teachers: Recognizing and interrupting dominant ideologies. *Theory into Practice*, *58*(2), 194–203.

Alfaro, C., & Bartolomé, L. (2017). Preparing ideologically clear bilingual teachers: Honoring working-class non-standard language use in the bilingual education classroom. *Issues in Teacher Education*, *26*(2), 11–34.

Alim, H. S. (2005). Critical language awareness in the United States: Revisiting issues and revising pedagogies in a resegregated society. *Educational Researcher*, *34*(7), 24–31.

Amanti, C., Domke, L. M., & Larraga Jauregui, L. (2022). "I didn't even know that was a thing": Preparing dual language bilingual education teachers in the New Latinx South. *Journal of Latinos and Education*, 1–16.

Anzaldúa, G. (1987). *Borderlands/La frontera: The new mestiza*. Aunt Lute Books.

Aquino-Sterling, C. R. (2016). Responding to the call: Developing and assessing pedagogical Spanish competencies in bilingual teacher education. *Bilingual Research Journal*, *39*(1), 50–68.

Aquino-Sterling, C. R., & Rodríguez-Valls, F. (2016). Developing teaching-specific Spanish competencies in bilingual teacher education: Toward a culturally, linguistically, and professionally relevant approach. *Multicultural Perspectives*, *18*(2), 73–81.

Arce, J. (2004). Latino bilingual teachers: The struggle to sustain an emancipatory pedagogy in public schools. *International Journal of Qualitative Studies in Education*, *17*(2), 227–246. https://doi.org/09518390310001653880

Arroyo-Romano, J. E. (2016). Bilingual education candidates' challenges meeting the Spanish language/bilingual certification exam and the impact on teacher shortages in the state of Texas, USA. *Journal of Latinos and Education*, *15*(4), 275–286.

Bauer, E. B., Colomer, S. E., & Wiemelt, J. (2020). Biliteracy of African American and Latinx kindergarten students in a dual-language program: Understanding students' translanguaging practices across informal assessments. *Urban Education*, *55*(3), 331–361.

Bishop, R. S. (1990). Mirrors, windows, and sliding glass doors. *Perspectives*, *6*(3), ix–xi.

Boyle, A., August, D., Tabaku, L., Cole, S., & Simpson-Baird, A. (2015). *Dual language education programs: Current state policies and practices*. Office of English Language Acquisition, US Department of Education.

Briceño, A., Rodriguez-Mojica, C., & Muñoz-Muñoz, E. (2018). From English learner to Spanish learner: Raciolinguistic beliefs that influence heritage Spanish speaking teacher candidates. *Language and Education*, *32*(3), 212–226.

Briceño, A., & Zoeller, E. C. (2022). "Subestimamos las habilidades de los estudiantes:" Bilingual teacher candidates building on multilingual assets. *Bilingual Research Journal*, *45*(1), 8–25.

Brito, I., Lima, A., & Auerbach, E. (2004). The logic of non-standard teaching: A course in Cape Verdean language, culture and history. In B. Norton & K. Toohey (Eds.), *Critical pedagogies and language learning* (pp. 181–199). Cambridge University Press.

Bunch, G. C. (2013). Pedagogical language knowledge: Preparing mainstream teachers for English learners in the new standards era. *Review of Research in Education*, *37*(1), 298–341.

Caldas, B. (2019). To switch or not to switch: Bilingual preservice teachers and translanguaging in teaching and learning. *TESOL Journal*, *10*(4), e485.

Caldas, B., & Heiman, D. (2021). Más allá de la lengua: Embracing the Messiness as Bilingual Teacher Educators. *Journal of Language, Identity & Education*, *20*(1), 58–70.

Caldas, B., Palmer, D., & Schwedhelm, M. (2019). Speaking educación in Spanish: Linguistic and professional development in a bilingual teacher education program in the US-Mexico borderlands. *International Journal of Bilingual Education and Bilingualism*, *22*(1), 49–63.

Calderon, D. (2014). Uncovering settler grammars in curriculum. *Educational Studies*, *50*(4), 313–338.

Ceballos, C. B. (2012). Literacies at the border: Transnationalism and the biliteracy practices of teachers across the US-Mexico border. *International Journal of Bilingual Education and Bilingualism*, *15*(6), 687–703.

Cervantes-Soon, C. G. (2018). Using a Xicana feminist framework in bilingual teacher preparation: Toward an anticolonial path. *The Urban Review*, *50*(5), 857–888.

Cervantes-Soon, C. G., Dorner, L., Palmer, D., Heiman, D., Schwerdtfeger, R., & Choi, J. (2017). Combating inequalities in two-way language immersion programs: Toward critical consciousness in bilingual education spaces. *Review of Research in Education*, *41*(1), 403–427. https://doi.org/10.3102/0091732X17690120

Collins, B. A., Sanchez, M., & España, C. (2023). Sustaining and developing teachers' dynamic bilingualism in a re-designed bilingual teacher preparation program. *International Journal of Bilingual Education and Bilingualism*, *26*(2), 97–113. https://doi.org/10.1080/13670050.2019.1610354

Compton-Lilly, K., & Nayan, R. (2016). Literacy capital in two immigrant families: Longitudinal case studies. In P. Ruggiano Schmidt & A. M. Lazar (Eds.), *Reconceptualizing literacy in the new age of multiculturalism and pluralism* (2nd ed., pp. 191–214). Information Age Publishing.

Dahlen, S. P. (2020). "We need diverse books": Diversity, activism, and children's literature. In N. op de Beeck (Ed.), *Literary cultures and twenty-first-century childhoods* (pp. 83–108). Palgrave Macmillan.

Dworin, J. E. (2003). Insights into biliteracy development: Toward a bidirectional theory of bilingual pedagogy. *Journal of Hispanic Higher Education*, *2*(2), 171–186.

Ek, L. D., Sánchez, P., & Quijada Cerecer, P. D. (2013). Linguistic violence, insecurity, and work: Language ideologies of Latina/o bilingual teacher candidates in Texas. *International Multilingual Research Journal*, *7*(3), 197–219.

Escamilla, K., Fine, C., & Hopewell, S. (2019). Enhancing writing outcomes in Spanish/English biliteracy programs. *Bilingual Review/Revista Bilingüe*, *34*(1), 77–96.

Escamilla, K., Hopewell, S., Butvilofsky, S., Sparrow, W., Soltero-González, L., Ruiz-Figueroa, O., & Escamilla, M. (2014). *Biliteracy from the start: Literacy squared in action*. Caslon Publishing.

España, C., & Herrera, L. Y. (2020). *En comunidad: Lessons for centering the voices and experiences of bilingual Latinx students*. Heinemann.

Fallas Escobar, C., & Treviño, A. (2021). Two Latina bilingual teacher candidates' perceptions of language proficiency and language choice options: Ideological encounters with listening and speaking others. *Bilingual Research Journal*, *44*(1), 124–143.

Flores, N. (2016). A tale of two visions: Hegemonic whiteness and bilingual education. *Educational Policy*, *30*(1), 13–38.

Flores, N., & McAuliffe, L. (2022). 'In other schools you can plan it that way': a raciolinguistic perspective on dual language education. *International Journal of Bilingual Education and Bilingualism, 25*(4), 1349–1362.

Flores, N., & Rosa, J. (2015). Undoing appropriateness: Raciolinguistic ideologies and language diversity in education. *Harvard Educational Review*, *85*(2), 149–171.

Freire, J. A. (2020). Promoting sociopolitical consciousness and bicultural goals of dual language education: The transformational dual language educational framework. *Journal of Language, Identity & Education*, *19*(1), 56–71.

Freire, J. A., & Feinauer, E. (2022). Vernacular Spanish as a promoter of critical consciousness in dual language bilingual education classrooms. *International Journal of Bilingual Education and Bilingualism*, *25*(4), 1516–1529.

Frieson, B. L. (2019). *(Re) mixin'& flowin': Examining the literacy practices of African American language speakers in an elementary two-way immersion bilingual program* [Doctoral dissertation, University of Illinois at Urbana-Champaign].

Gaarder, A. B. (1977). *Bilingual schooling and the survival of Spanish in the United States*. Newbury House Publishers, Inc.

Galguera, T. (2011). Participant structures as professional learning tasks and the development of pedagogical language knowledge among preservice teachers. *Teacher Education Quarterly*, *38*(1), 85–107.

García, O., & Kleifgen, J. (2020). Translanguaging and literacies. *Reading Research Quarterly*, *55*(4), 553–571.

García, G. E., Sacco, L. J., & Guerrero-Arias, B. E. (2020). Cognate instruction and students' improved literacy performance. *The Reading Teacher*, *73*(5), 617–625.

García, O., & Wei, L. (2014). *Translanguaging: Language, bilingualism and education*. Palgrave Pivot.

Guerrero, M. D. (1997). Spanish academic language proficiency: The case of bilingual education teachers in the US. *Bilingual Research Journal*, *21*(1), 65–84.

Guerrero, M. D. (2003). Acquiring and participating in the use of academic Spanish: Four novice Latina bilingual education teachers' stories. *Journal of Latinos and Education*, 2(3), 159–181.

Guerrero, M. C., & Guerrero, M. D. (2020). La creación de un nuevo espacio: se buscan profesores de español y educación bilingüe comprometidos. *Journal of Latinos and Education*, *22*(1) 144–156.

Guerrero, M. D., & Guerrero, M. C. (2008). El (sub)desarrollo del español académico entre los maestros bilingües: ¿Una cuestión de poder? *Journal of Latinos and Education*, *8*(1), 55–66.

Guerrero, M. D., & Guerrero, M. C. (2013). El discurso del español académico en una zona fronteriza: Un caso de colonización benevolente. *Journal of Latinos and Education*, *12(*4), 239–253.

Guerrero, M. D., & Lachance, J. R. (2018). *The national dual language education teacher preparation standards*. Dual Language Education of New Mexico.

Guerrero, M. D., Guerrero, M. C., Soltero-González, L., & Escamilla, K. (2017). *Abriendo brecha: Antología crítica sobre la educación bilingüe de doble inmersión*. Dual Language Education of New Mexico/Fuente Press.

Howard, E. R., Lindholm-Leary, K. J., Rogers, D., Olague, N., Medina, J., Kennedy, B., & Christian, D. (2018). *Guiding principles for dual language education* (3rd ed.). Center for Applied Linguistics.

Lave, J., & Wenger, E. (2001). Legitimate peripheral participation in communities of practice. In *Supporting lifelong learning* (pp. 121–136). Routledge.

Lindahl, K., Fallas Escobar, C., & Henderson, K. I. (2021). Linguistically responsive instruction for Latinx teacher candidates: Surfacing language ideological dilemmas. *TESOL Quarterly*, *55*(4), 1190–1220.

Muñoz-Muñoz, E. R., Poza, L. E., & Briceno, A.(2022). Critical translingual perspectives on California multilingual education policy. *Educational Policy*.

Musanti, S. I. (2014). "Porque sé los dos idiomas." Biliteracy beliefs and bilingual preservice teacher identity. In Y.S. Freeman & D. E. Freeman (Eds.), *Research on preparing preservice teachers to work effectively with emergent bilinguals* (pp. 59–87). Emerald Group Publishing Limited.

Ostorga, A. N., & Farruggio, P. (2014). Discovering best practices for bilingual teacher preparation: A pedagogy for the border. In Y.S. Freeman & D. E. Freeman (Eds.), *Research on preparing preservice teachers to work effectively with emergent bilinguals*. Emerald Group Publishing Limited.

Ostorga, A. N., & Farruggio, P. (2020). Preparing bilingual teachers on the US/Mexico border: Including the voices of emergent bilinguals. *International Journal of Bilingual Education and Bilingualism*, *23*(10), 1225–1237.

Ostorga, A. N., Zúñiga, C. E., & Hinton, K. A. (2020). Bilingual teacher educators at an HSI: A border pedagogy for Latinx teacher development. In J. M. Schall, P. A. McHatton, & E. L. Sáenz (Eds.), *Teacher education at Hispanic-Serving Institutions* (pp. 137–155). Routledge.

Palmer, D. K., Cervantes-Soon, C., Dorner, L., & Heiman, D. (2019). Bilingualism, biliteracy, biculturalism, and critical consciousness for all: Proposing a fourth fundamental goal for two-way dual language education. *Theory Into Practice*, *58*(2), 121–133.

Paris, D., & Alim, H. S. (2017). *Culturally sustaining pedagogies: Teaching and learning for social justice in a changing world*. Teachers College Press.

Park Dahlen, S., & Huyck, D. (2019). *Diversity in children's books 2018*.

Rodriguez-Mojica, C., & Briceño, A. (2018). Sentence stems that support reading comprehension. *The Reading Teacher*, *72*(3), 398–402.

Rodriguez-Mojica, C., & Briceño, A. (2019). Critical consciousness in bilingual teacher preparation for emancipatory biliteracy. *Bilingual Review/Revista Bilingüe*, *34*(1), 1–21.

Rodríguez-Mojica, C., Briceño, A., & Muñoz-Muñoz, E. R. (2019). Combating linguistic hegemony. *Teacher Education Quarterly*, *46*(3), 57–78.

Rodriguez-Mojica, C., Muñoz-Muñoz, E., & Briceño, A. (2020). Preparing bilingual teachers to enact culturally sustaining pedagogy. In S. Keengwe (Ed.), *Handbook of research on diversity and social justice in higher education*. IGI Global.

Roessingh, H. (2012). Family treasures: A dual-language book project for negotiating language, literacy, culture, and identity (enhanced). *Canadian Modern Language Review*, *66*(Supplement 1), S123–S148.

Rosa, J. D. (2016). Standardization, racialization, languagelessness: Raciolinguistic ideologies across communicative contexts. *Journal of Linguistic Anthropology*, *26*(2), 162–183. https://doi.org/10.1111/jola.12116

Rosa, J., & Flores, N. (2017). Unsettling race and language: Toward a raciolinguistic perspective. *Language in Society*, *46*(5), 621–647.

Silverstein, M. (1996). *Monoglot 'standard' in America: Standardization and metaphors of linguistic hegemony*. The Matrix of Language: Contemporary Linguistic Anthropology.

Valdés, G. (2005). Bilingualism, heritage language learners, and SLA research: Opportunities lost or seized? *Modern Language Journal*, *89*(3), 410–426.

Valdés, G. (2018). Analyzing the curricularization of language in two-way immersion education: Restating two cautionary notes. *Bilingual Research Journal*, *41*(4), 388–412.

Velasco, P., & García, O. (2014). Translanguaging and the writing of bilingual learners. *Bilingual Research Journal*, *37*(1), 6–23.

Yosso, T. J. (2005). Whose culture has capital? A critical race theory discussion of community cultural wealth. *Race, Ethnicity, and Education*, *8*(1), 69–91.

Zoeller, E. C., & Briceño, A. (2023). Linguistic justice: Lessons learned from teaching black multilinguals. *Language Arts*.

36

PROFESSIONAL DEVELOPMENT FOR IN-SERVICE DUAL LANGUAGE TEACHERS

The Dominguez Hills Colectivo Plurilingüe

The process by which in-service dual language (DL) teachers develop professionally has mirrored the tensions, contradictions, and ways in which DL education as a project of linguistic justice has been circumscribed by power. Broad debates about multilingual education and its guiding language ideologies are intertwined with historically and culturally situated processes of power and politics (Castagno & McCarty, 2017). The resulting programs are never only about language: they inherently connect to broader discourse about national identity, sovereignty, race, immigration, and civil rights (Anderson, 2009). For some, DL education represents threats of cultural pollution and the "death of the nation" (Handler & Saxton, 1988, p. 169), "linguistic welfare", and a drain to the national coffers because it does "not really teach English" and undermines "white identity" (Morganthau, 1997, p. 58). For others, DL programs directly challenge schools' role in settler-colonial projects, deeply connected to issues of racism, and attached to struggles for sovereignty and epistemic justice (Goodyear-Ka'opua, 2013). The current embrace of DL education by dominant, white stakeholders adds a problematic layer of interest convergence (Morales & Maravilla, 2019) to the conversation. Dominant, neoliberal framing of DL education recognizes multilingualism as the development of transactional skills instead of as sustenance of identities, cultures, and futures.

Positioned at the heart of these matters are practicing DL teachers who confront tense sociopolitical contexts that simultaneously demand and criminalize critical pedagogy. How, then, are DL teachers developing professionally within this reality? DL teachers are called to enact anticolonial practices founded upon contemporary language theories that are culturally

 DOI: 10.4324/9781003269076-52

and linguistically sustaining and support rich content learning. Supporting teachers and advancing these goals require situating dual language professional development (DLPD) within complex, ideological, sociopolitical frameworks, while making this messy reality a central component in DLPD to foster critical consciousness and activism.

In this chapter, we review the literature about professional development experiences of in-service DL teachers. We begin by situating DLPD within today's sociopolitical context followed by a review of the professional learning opportunities specifically designed for DL teachers, exposing promises and challenges. Next, we illuminate DL teachers' realities and contemplate how/if DLPD meets their professional needs. We conclude with a call for an ideological shift to align DLPD in solidarity with the movement for linguistic justice and to fully embrace the liberatory potential of DL education. We suggest a critical approach to DLPD that is dialogical, centers teachers' community cultural wealth, supports activist networks, and supports teachers on their path toward ideological clarity.

Sociopolitical Context of Dual Language Professional Development

Complex constellations of struggle in which different groups with varied political, economic, and cultural visions seek to define and control the purpose, values, and practices of DL education have shaped in-service teachers' development. While the 1968 Elementary and Secondary Education Act: Bilingual Education Act served as a cornerstone in the movement to address inequities for multilingual learners in U.S. schools, neoliberal forces effectively coopted this progress by promulgating assimilatory English-only policies and practices. The infamous passage of Proposition 227 and the dismantling of the Bilingual Education Act under No Child Left Behind have lasting impact on DLPD, despite Proposition 227's repeal and Every Student Succeeds Act's (ESSA) slight acknowledgment of multilingualism. Administrators are anguished by lack of funding for DLPD (Stavely & Marquez Rosales, 2021) and caught in a bind: while Title III of the ESSA provides PD monies, these must be used to center the development of English language proficiency. State funding, like the California Bilingual Professional Development Grant, also centers on English learning. These policies have structurally functioned to limit DLPD even while DL education experiences a rejuvenation.

DL programs have recently multiplied in part due to interest convergence, the notion that interests of students of color are accommodated only when they align with interests of "powerful whites" (Morales & Maravilla, 2019). As such, many DL programs are often formed for the advantage of white mainstream English (WME)-speaking students. Critics contest that one driving force behind DL is the "hegemonic interest in preparing students from the dominant culture for a complex and global economy, rather a desire to support students from linguistic minorities" (Kelly, 2018, p. 4). Others note that many DL programs marginalize language customs (e.g., regionalisms, codeswitching, and non-standard varieties) of multilingual students (Kelly, 2018), causing these students' language to be muffled and fractured. Commodification of minoritized languages further complicates the neoliberal landscape that practicing DL teachers navigate and affects available PD, experiences within PD, and research about DLPD.

Not surprisingly, DLPD opportunities for teachers are mostly available as monolingual training about teaching English learners and supporting English development. Frankly, "teachers are not receiving adequate PD to support the language programs in which they teach" (Franco-Fuenmayor et al., 2015, p. 346). Research lumps DL teachers' development experience with that designed for teaching English to multilingual learners in monolingual settings, making it difficult to decipher research specific to teaching in two languages. For example, Craft-Coleman (2013) asserted that, in her research, "the terms classroom teachers, mainstream teachers, and dual language teachers are used interchangeably to suggest that mainstream and classroom teachers need the same knowledge and skills as a dual language teacher" (p. 22). At best, this has resulted in DL teachers' specific professional learning being lost in the literature. At worst, it advances gentrifying rhetoric in the literature. These oversights devalue minoritized languages, dismiss DL teachers' specialized pedagogical skills, and reject calls for educational equity and linguistic justice.

How Are Dual Language Teachers Developing Professionally?

A broad theme throughout the literature illuminates DL teachers' dissatisfaction with monolingual training and points to the need for more PD congruent to the demands of teaching in and about two languages (Bhattacharya, 2016; Capdevila-Gutiérrez et al., 2020; Franco-Fuenmayor et al., 2015; Jaar, 2017). *The Guiding Principles for Dual Language Education* (Howard et al., 2018) reinforce that DLPD should be aligned with schools' instructional programs and include specialized training in philosophies of DL education, (bi)language education pedagogy, curriculum, materials, and assessment. It articulates topics that high-quality DLPD should address partner-language development, educational equity, biliteracy instruction integrated with content teaching/learning, critical thinking, and reflective practice. While teachers may participate in DLPD addressing some of these during the onset of a program's implementation, training is limited and not sustained over time (Henderson & Palmer, 2020). This leaves teachers wanting more PD to understand and uphold the promises of DL education.

Holistic, Aligned, and Sustained: Promising DLPD Frameworks

Successful DL programs need district-wide support since a lack of buy-in can be detrimental (Freire & Valdez, 2017; Murillo, 2018) For this to happen, the complexity of the context of professional development design must be taken into consideration, including its micro and macro influences and how teachers interact with support structures (Bhattacharya, 2016). Teachers point to incongruencies between schools' hopes for DL programs and their day-to-day expectations, calling for PD to align with a consistent DL curricular framework and supplemental resources (Franco-Fuenmayor et al., 2015). In Henderson and Palmer's (2020) study of a Texas district, DL teachers from two and one-way Spanish-English DL programs expressed frustration that DL program implementation conflicted with the district's emphasis on high-stakes, standardized testing. Scholars also advocate that PD must be offered in a program's partner language to support partner-language equivalent pedagogy and teachers' language use and development (Bhattacharya, 2016; Stacy et al., 2020).

PD that focuses on the specific needs of DL teachers, dialogic, localized, programmatic, and sustained over time, has positive outcomes. Torres-Guzmán and Swinney (2009) detailed a holistic approach to DLPD for teachers in a Spanish-English program, which included development of teacher portfolios, study/inquiry groups about language variations, mutual collaboration with universities, and opportunities for teachers to network. Centering intellect and agency allowed DL teachers to "explore their individual freedom while retaining a sense of being part of a concerted effort that shared principles or shared conceptions of what is good and right for bilingual children" (p. 98). In their study of the peer-learning model in two Chilean intercultural bilingual education (IBE) preschools where students learn Mapuche and Spanish, Becerra-Lubies and Varghese (2019) found that Mapuche preschool teachers in Chile were positioned as knowledge experts about the indigenous community and its aims for preservation of language and culture, leading to more equitable collegial partnerships.

DL teachers cultivate support systems through confianza (mutual respect and trust) that can be intentionally systematic. Cohorts and interdisciplinary teaching teams enhance DL teachers' motivation to learn collaboratively and build relationships (Rosal et al., 2018) while problem-solving to implement DL programs and create curricula (Cruz, 2000). Professional learning communities help DL educators engage in agency, advocacy, and identity formation (Jaar, 2017) while emphasizing a pedagogy of listening, valuing vulnerability and growth, and strengthening self-efficacy (Gillespie, 2011). Furthermore, steady partnerships with universities can sustain iterative praxis, support programmatic restructuring, and transform stakeholders

(Clark et al., 2002). Coyle et al. (2017) studied a diverse group of European content and language integrated learning (CLIL) teachers and found that a cyclical approach to examining praxis supported them in arriving at sophisticated context-specific understanding of CLIL. Similarly, centering DL teachers' agency in a 14-week PD allowed third-grade teachers in a Spanish-English DL, integrated co-teaching classroom to experience physical, social, and knowledge structures involved in science teaching, and they eventually drew upon physical, social, and knowledge structures beyond the curriculum to guide praxis (Rivera Maulucci et al., 2015).

Professional Development for Transformation

Contemporary research highlights promising shifts in DLPD that center teachers' agency, support development of ideological clarity, and foster critical pedagogies. Téllez and Varghese (2013) clarify DL teachers' political position and assert that DLPD must "prepare bilingual teachers for intellectual and advocacy roles" (p. 132). Topics like learning local political landscapes, building alliances across teacher unions and organizations, and becoming teacher researchers can become part of DLPD (Téllez & Varghese, 2013). Freire (2020b) engaged DL teachers in a two-way immersion, 50:50 Spanish-English program in long-term, collaborative PD that included group pláticas focused on self-reflection and critique of beliefs and practices. Teachers needed an intentional space to begin grappling through this learning process and this approach supported developing sociopolitical consciousness. Stacy et al. (2020) documented a two-week summer institute for DL teachers from all types of bilingual programs that used a critical professional development model (Kohli et al., 2015). Conducted entirely in Spanish, El Instituto drew upon LatCrit theory and Freirean pedagogies to integrate sociopolitical realities (e.g., Black Lives Matter, COVID-19), intersecting identities, and community cultural wealth with a sociocultural understanding of language-learning. Participation in critical pedagogy rejuvenated teachers' praxis, empowered them to try humanizing pedagogies, and facilitated network building.

Spaces Where DL Professional Learning Happens

While professional conferences for DL teachers are well-attended, it is difficult to know the degree of access that DL teachers have to these events and the amount of support (financial or otherwise) from their schools. National organizations that sponsor annual conferences include the National Association for Bilingual Education (NABE), La Cosecha, and the Association of Two-Way Dual Language Education (ATDLE). Some organizations, like the American Council on the Teaching of Foreign Languages and the Center for Applied Linguistics, focus generally on language-learning but include topics on DL education. National and state grant funding has facilitated innovative DLPD by organizations like the BUENO Center for Multicultural Education, the Center for Transnational and Multilingual Education, CUNY-New York State Initiative on Emergent Bilinguals, the Center for Advanced Research of Language Acquisition, and the International Coalition for Multilingual Education and Equity. Likewise, state-level organizations like the California Association for Bilingual Education (CABE) offer conferences and similar Associations for Bilingual Education can be found in Michigan (MABE); Texas (TABE); Colorado (CO-CABE); Washington (WABE); and Idaho (IABE). In some instances, multiple states have partnered to offer training opportunities, including The Central States Conference on the Teaching of Foreign Languages in the Midwest and the Southern Conference on Language Training in the South. Many districts are developing their own DLPD and/or partnering with universities.

Still, it is not surprising that many institutionalized DLPD opportunities do not meet the needs of critical DL educators. In search of knowledge that will result in transformative education, DL teachers use social media as a source of instant pedagogical inspiration. Instagram, Twitter, TikTok, and Facebook allow educators to continuously engage with networks of critical educators and tap into their self-organizing abilities. For example, *The Heritage Team Extraordinaire* is an international coalition of culturally responsive bilingual teachers. Besides serving as fugitive spaces for critical educators, these resources also provide authentic examples of epistemic pluralism (Saavedra & Pérez, 2018).

These formal, informal, and digital spaces cultivate important relationships, professionalism, and confianza (Bonilla, 2017). However, more research is needed to understand how they are experienced by in-service DL teachers and the degree to which they advance critical DL education.

What Is Needed in DLPD?

Certainly, DL teachers' knowledge about instructional programs, materials, assessments, and bilingual language education (Howard et al., 2018) and knowledge about/proficiency in multiple languages are important. But programs, materials, pedagogies, and languages are embedded in broader sociopolitical contexts. To advance justice, DLPD must be approached as a messy process which includes teachers' development of critical consciousness, knowledge about linguistic trauma, and critical content-language integration.

Expanding Critical Consciousness

Critical consciousness, defined as "learning to perceive social, political, and economic contradictions, and to take action against the oppressive elements of reality" (Freire, 2005, p. 35), must be continuously fostered throughout teachers' careers to be responsive to shifting macro and micro realities. Freire (2014, 2020a) named sociopolitical consciousness as a goal of the transformational DL education framework. To achieve this, teachers must "identify and interpret social inequities, such as racism, classism or other dominant ideologies and macrostructures that affect their lives and their communities, resist them, and be able to fight against them" (Freire, 2014, pp. 36–37). Alfaro and Hernández (2016) advise that DLPD should purposefully support teachers in gaining ideological and pedagogical clarity to effectively advance equitable praxis, naming that "a teacher's critical consciousness is the anchor needed to connect the ideological with the pedagogical, programmatic, curricular, and evaluative dimensions for establishing cultural and linguistic democracy in dual-language learning spaces" (Alfaro, 2019, p. 195). DLPD can create space for teachers to engage in critical self-reflection, interrogate beliefs and the broader systems that inform those values, and consider the implications of these on their treatment of students, families, and communities. This process supports DL teachers in gaining agency, becoming advocates, and leveraging students' linguistic and cultural capital in teaching and learning (Alfaro, 2019).

Because DL teachers are "arbiters of their own classroom language policies" (Palmer & Martínez, 2013, p. 270), their ideologies guide if/how they construct critical DL classrooms. Freire (2020b) captured how DL teachers integrated the bicultural and sociopolitical goals of DL education on different levels: (1) contributions, (2) additive, (3) transformative, and (4) social action. He observed that most teachers' pedagogy hovered at the first two levels and called for greater effort to incorporate sociopolitical consciousness into DLPD. Murillo (2018) found that DL Latinx teachers' past personal and professional experiences with, and resistance against, oppressive education affects their teaching. Varghese and Snyder (2018) recommend that DLPD include discussion about teachers' identities and their relation to the broader arc of DL history, policy, and practice. Freire (2020a) suggests that PD can help teachers of color and white teachers identify and unpack conscientization calls, defined as "lessons individuals learn related to injustice and inequity affecting minoritized populations" (p. 3), and leverage these for transformative praxis. Teachers appreciate when space is made for their identities and lived experiences in DLPD, noting that they are more engaged and empowered (Stacy et al., 2020; Torres, 2017).

Unpacking Traumatic Linguistic Landscapes

A robust understanding of bilingualism and interactional dynamics of bilingual contexts can influence DL teachers' ideological shifts and beget critical consciousness (Palmer & Martínez, 2013). Teachers, students, and community stakeholders come to DL classrooms embodying centuries of hegemonic linguistic trauma residual from years of assimilatory language ideologies. Essential to this is utilizing DLPD to engage teachers in critical conversations that upend traditional thinking about language-learning. For example, the charge to teach "standard" varieties of languages is guised in the false dichotomy of "academic/non-academic" language and views racialized students from a deficit lens (Flores, 2020). The word "standard" asserts a correct form, but this term is rooted in politics, not language (Lessow-Hurley, 2012). Standard language varieties are imposed by the socially dominant majority (Milroy & Milroy, 2012), codify broader ideologies about who and what is valuable, and extend to teaching (Varghese & Snyder, 2018). Heritage learners in particular experience trauma as they confront these forces at the intersections of their racial, ethnic, and linguistic identities (Palmer, 2018) and DL teachers (many who are heritage learners) must have deep understanding of these linguistic characteristics and experiences so that they can implement culturally sustaining practices. Furthermore, taken-for-granted practices like using the terms "target" or "minority" language, strict separation of languages, and "balanced" recruitment of WME students reinforce power structures and inequities. Thus, DLPD must focus on topics such as language ideologies and power, language varieties and vernacular language, translanguaging, and raciolinguistics (Freire & Feinauer, 2022).

DLPD should also engage in critical pedagogies and develop practices that actively undo linguistic trauma (Stacy et al., 2020). Culturally sustaining pedagogies (CSP) can intentionally be used to sustain students' language and culture, yet teachers express that they do not feel prepared to do so and that schools do not provide training or time to create such content (Freire & Valdez, 2017; Franco-Fuenmayor, 2015). Barriers to implementing CSP in DL classrooms included lack of time, materials and knowledge, and a belief that social justice topics were "inappropriate" for young children (Freire & Valdez, 2017). DLPD should be the place where these issues are explored and integrated with conversations about troubleshooting and transforming praxis.

Intersections of Content and Language

DL teaching becomes even more complex when the same criticality is applied to language content instruction. Most research advocates that effective programs align professional development to the goals and strategies of the instructional program, with a high emphasis on biliteracy skills across the content areas (Howard et al., 2018). Researchers and educators have discussed the importance of specialized training in language education pedagogy and curriculum, materials and resources, and assessment (Genesee & Hamayan, 2016) in the face of stringent academic language requirements in educational policy (Valdés et al., 2015). However, DLPD about academic multilingual content teaching must integrate the aforementioned linguistic characteristics and be configured to embrace heritage learners and localized language varieties (Eckerson, 2015) while also teaching content from a critical lens.

There is contention regarding the intersection of language and content and best pedagogical practices. Aquino-Sterling (2016) identifies the need for teachers to use pedagogical language while teaching content. Some DLPD initiatives have used a content and language integrative learning (CLIL) approach (Lyster & de Zarobe, 2017. CLIL asserts that DL teachers must develop "language knowledge for content teaching" and become fluent in common and specialized language of the focal discipline(s) (Morton, 2018). Others promote specialized pedagogies that support "subject-specific language", like language skills required to participate in arguments regarding economics and politics in Austria (Hüttner & Smit, 2018). However, much of this literature reinforces the hegemonic notion that there is an objective divide between "academic" and "social" language: a perspective that "frames racialized students as deficient and in need of remediation" (Flores, 2020, p. 22).

Alternatively, many understand language-content learning as multifaceted and integrative of teachers' and students' identities and lived experiences, paying attention to form-focused functions of language in different disciplines while centering an asset-based framework and intentional balance between content and language teaching (Tedick & Young, 2018). Capdevila-Gutiérrez et al. (2020) advocate for middle and high school DL teachers' development to incorporate strategic language planning across disciplines (e.g., shared rubrics, cross-references to linguistic assets, transversal use of textual types, and complementary linguistic opportunities) and integrate sociocultural competence. Comparatively, language arts and social studies teachers collaborated to support students in deconstructing primary and secondary sources in the partner language, amplifying knowledge about content and function of language (Rodríguez-Valls et al., 2017). Certainly, sustained, long-term PD support teachers in developing well-integrated instructional models focused on language, biliteracy, and discipline knowledge (Cammarata & Haley, 2018). Still, resources in the partner language are limited and often an afterthought, creating invisible, unpaid, and unvalued working conditions for DL teachers (Amanti, 2019). DLPD, then, must include issues of power and analysis of content, language, and relationships among colleagues.

Toward Critical Dual Language Professional Development

To move toward the liberatory aims of DL education, DLPD must move beyond a neoliberal "methods fetish" (Bartolomé, 1994) that upholds banking methods and deliverables (Kohli et al., 2015) and support teachers in rethinking notions of bilingualism through the process of conscientization that develops understandings of topics like language as practice, hybridity in language, asymmetries of power in DL classrooms, nexus of language and identity, and multilingual teacher and student agency. We call for critical professional development (C-DLPD) to frame DL educators as intellectually and politically engaged actors who actively participate in shaping society (Kohli et al., 2015). C-DLPD supports professional learning within the advancement of social and political struggle of multilingual communities. C-DLPD is dialogical and prepares teachers to actively undo oppressive practices by becoming advocates who leverage their own and their students' linguistic and cultural capital in teaching and learning (Alfaro, 2019). However, such a shift will not happen on a large scale without concerted efforts from policy makers, researchers, school leaders, teachers, and community members who understand C-DLPD as a pivotal player in transforming DL education.

We urge scholars, leaders, and practitioners to advance C-DLPD by cultivating and studying spaces that center teachers' process of conscientization and eradicating approaches that aim to transactionally replicate skills. To achieve this, we suggest:

1 developing brave spaces for learning about and reflecting on linguistic trauma;
2 modeling critical praxis through immersive experiences and cultivating teachers' implementation through sustained support;
3 conducting C-DLPD in the partner language while learning about sociolinguistic complexities;
4 following generative frameworks that reflect teachers' localized realities and facilitate network building;
5 including C-DLPD for administrators;
6 moving toward anticolonial understandings of language, pedagogy, and content that center indigenous knowledges.

References

Alfaro, C. (2019). Preparing critically conscious dual-language teachers: Recognizing and interrupting dominant ideologies. *Theory Into Practice*, *58*(2), 194–203. https://doi.org/10.1080/00405841.2019.1569400

Alfaro, C., & Hernández, A. (2016). Ideology, pedagogy, access, and equity (IPAE): A critical examination for dual language educators. *The Multilingual Educator*, 8–11.

Amanti, C. (2019). The (invisible) work of dual language bilingual education teachers. *Bilingual Research Journal*, 42(4), 455–470. https://doi.org/10.1080/15235882.2019.1687111

Anderson, K. (Ed.). (2009). *War or common cause?: A critical ethnography of language education policy, race, and cultural citizenship*. Information Age Publishing.

Aquino-Sterling, C. R. (2016). Responding to the call: Developing and assessing pedagogical Spanish competencies in bilingual teacher education. *Bilingual Research Journal*, *39*(1), 50–68. https://doi.org/10.1080/15235882.2016.1139519

Bartolomé, L. (1994). Beyond the methods fetish: Toward a humanizing pedagogy. *Harvard Educational Review*, *64*(2), 173–194. https://doi.org/10.17763/haer.64.2.58q5m5744t325730

Becerra-Lubies, R., & Varghese, M. (2019). Expansive learning in teachers' professional development: A case study of intercultural and bilingual preschools in Chile. *International Journal of Bilingual Education & Bilingualism*, 22(8), 940–957. https://doi.org/10.1080/13670050.2017.1325832

Bhattacharya, B. (2016). *Professional development experiences and practices: The case of a dual language bilingual program* (Publication No. 3721449) [Doctoral dissertation, Michigan State University]. ProQuest Dissertation Publishing.

Bonilla, C. M. (2017). Relational professionalism in a bilingual teacher association: Promoting occupational identities and pedagogic agency. *Bilingual Research Journal*, *40*(3), 304–317. https://doi.org/10.1080/15235882.2017.1351009

Cammarata, L., & Haley, C. (2018). Integrated content, language, and literacy instruction in a Canadian French immersion context: A professional development journey. *International Journal of Bilingual Education and Bilingualism*, *21*(3), 332–348.

Capdevila-Gutiérrez, M., Muñoz-Muñoz, E., Rodríguez-Valls, F., & Solsona-Puig, J. (2020). The time is now! Preparing middle and high school teachers for dual immersion programs (Spanish-English) in California: A readying examination of current practices, needs, and potentialities. *International Journal of Bilingual Education & Bilingualism*, 1–12. https://doi.org/10.1080/13670050.2020.1844635

Castagno, A. E., & McCarty, T. (Eds.). (2017). *The anthropology of education policy: Ethnographic inquiries into policy as sociocultural process*. Taylor & Francis.

Clark, E. R., Flores, B. B., Riojas-Cortez, M., & Smith, H. L. (2002). You can't have a rainbow without a tormenta: A description of an IHE's response to a community need for a dual-language school. *Bilingual Research Journal*, *26*(1), 123–147.

Coyle, D., Halbach, A., Meyer, O., & Schuck, K. (2017). Knowledge ecology for conceptual growth: Teachers as active agents in developing a pluriliteracies approach to teaching for learning (PTL). *International Journal of Bilingual Education and Bilingualism*, *21*(3), 349–365. https://doi.org/10.1080/13670050.2017.1387516

Craft-Coleman, S. L. (2013). *Preparing dual language teachers to educate English language learners* (Publication No. 3578042) [Doctoral dissertation, University of Phoenix]. ProQuest Dissertation Publishing.

Cruz, G. I. (2000). *Collegial networks: A team of sixth-grade teachers in a two-way bilingual program.* University of Albany, School of Education, B–9. https://files.eric.ed.gov/fulltext/ED447701.pdf

Eckerson, J. M. (2015). *Teacher perspectives on professional development needs for better serving Nebraska's Spanish heritage language learners.* (Publication No. 3738830) [Doctoral dissertation, University of Nebraska-Lincoln].

Flores, N. (2020). From academic language to language architecture: Challenging raciolinguistic ideologies in research and practice. *Theory Into Practice*, *59*(1), 22–31. https://doi-org.libproxy.csudh.edu/10.1080/00405841.2019.1665411

Franco-Fuenmayor, S. E., Padrón, Y. N., & Waxman, H. C. (2015). Investigating bilingual/ESL teachers' knowledge and professional development opportunities in a large suburban school district in Texas. *Bilingual Research Journal*, *38*(3), 336–352. https://doi.org/10.1080/13670050.2020.1775778

Freire, P. (2005). *Education for critical consciousness.* Continuum.

Freire, J. A. (2014). *Spanish-English dual language teacher beliefs and practices on culturally relevant pedagogy in a collaborative action research process* (Publication No. AAI3672850) [Doctoral dissertation, University of Utah]. ProQuest Dissertations Publishing.

Freire, J. A. (2020a). Conscientization calls: A white dual language educator's development of sociopolitical consciousness and commitment to social justice. *Education and Urban Society*, *53*(2), 231–248. https://doi.org/10.1177/0013124520928608

Freire, J. A. (2020b). Promoting sociopolitical consciousness and bicultural goals of dual language education: The transformational dual language educational framework. *Journal of Language, Identity & Education*, *19*(1), 56–71. https://doi.org/10.1080/15348458.2019.1672174

Freire, J. A., & Feinauer, E. (2022). Vernacular Spanish as a promoter of critical consciousness in dual language bilingual education classrooms. *International Journal of Bilingual Education and Bilingualism*, *25*(4), 1516–1529. https://doi.org/10.1080/13670050.2020.1775778

Freire, J. A., & Valdez, V. E. (2017). Dual language teachers' stated barriers to implementation of culturally relevant pedagogy. *Bilingual Research Journal*, *40*(1), 55–69. https://doi.org/10.1080/15235882.2016.1272504

Genesee, F., & Hamayan, E. (2016). *CLIL in context: Practical guidance for educators*. Cambridge University Press.

Gillespie, M. (2011). *The impact of a Reggio-inspired professional learning community on two-way immersion teachers' self-efficacy* (Publication No. 3483138) [Doctoral dissertation, Texas A&M University Commerce].

Goodyear-Ka'opua, N. (2013). *The seeds we planted: Portraits of a native Hawaiian charter school*. University of Minnesota Press.

Handler, R., & Saxton, W. (1988). Dyssimulation: Reflexivity, narrative, and the quest for authenticity in "living history." *Cultural Anthropology*, *3*(3), 242–260. https://doi.org/10.1525/can.1988.3.3.02a00020

Henderson, K. I., & Palmer, D. K. (2020). *Dual language bilingual education: Teacher cases and perspectives on large-scale implementation*. Multilingual Matters.

Howard, E. R., Lindholm-Leary, K. J., Rogers, D., Olague, N., Medina, J., Kennedy, B., Sugarman, J., & Christian, D. (2018). *Guiding principles for dual language education* (3rd ed.). Center for Applied Linguistics.

Hüttner, J., & Smit, U. (2018). Negotiating political positions: Subject-specific oral language use in CLIL classrooms. *International Journal of Bilingual Education and Bilingualism*, *21*(3), 287–302. https://doi.org/10.1080/13670050.2017.1386616

Jaar, A. (2017). *Professional development of dual-language teachers: Learning communities as potential sites of teacher identity, agency, and advocacy* (Publication No. 10275096) [Doctoral dissertation, Teachers College, Columbia University].

Kelly, L. B. (2018). Interest convergence and hegemony in dual language: Bilingual education, but for whom and why? *Language Policy*, *17*(1), 1–21. https://doi.org/10.1007/s10993-016-9418-y

Kohli, R., Picower, B., Martinez, A. N., & Ortiz, N. (2015). Critical professional development: Centering the social justice needs of teachers. *The International Journal of Critical Pedagogy*, *6*(2), 7–24.

Lessow-Hurley, J. (2012). *Foundations of dual language education* (6th ed.). Pearson.

Lyster, R., & de Zarobe, Y. R. (2017). Introduction: Instructional practices and teacher development in CLIL and immersion school settings. *International Journal of Bilingual Education & Bilingualism*, *21*(3), 273–274. https://doi-org.libproxy.csudh.edu/10.1080/13670050.2017.1383353

Milroy, J., & Milroy, L. (2012). *Authority in language: Investigating standard English*. Routledge.
Morales, Z. P., & Maravilla, J. V. (2019). The problems and possibilities of interest convergence in a dual language school. *Theory Into Practice, 58*(2), 145–153. https://doi.org/10.1080/00405841.2019.1569377
Morganthau, T. (1997). The face of the future. *Newsweek*.
Morton, T. (2018). Reconceptualizing and describing teachers' knowledge of language for content and language integrated learning (CLIL). *International Journal of Bilingual Education and Bilingualism, 21*(3), 275–286. https://doi.org/10.1080/13670050.2017.1383352
Murillo, R. (2018). *Dual language teachers: Personal and professional testimonios* (Publication No. 10978425) [Doctoral dissertation, California State University].
Palmer, D. (2018). Equity and dual language immersion: Curriculum. *For the Forum on Equity and Dual Language Education:* UCLA Civil Rights Project/Proyecto Derechos Civiles. https://civilrightsproject.ucla.edu/research/k-12-education/language-minority-students/equity-and-dual-language-immersion-curriculum
Palmer, D., & Martínez, R. A. (2013). Teacher agency in bilingual spaces: A fresh look at preparing teachers to educate Latina/o bilingual children. *Review of Research in Education, 37*(1), 269–297.
Rivera Maulucci, M. S., Brotman, J. S., & Fain, S. S. (2015). Fostering structurally transformative teacher agency through science professional development. *Journal of Research in Science Teaching, 52*(4), 545–559. https://doi.org/10.1002/tea.21222
Rodríguez-Valls, F., Solsona-Puig, J., & Capdevila-Gutiérrez, M. (2017). Teaching social studies in Spanish in dual immersion middle schools: A biliterate approach to history. *Cogent Education, 4*(1), 1326202. https://doi.org/10.1080/2331186X.2017.1326202
Rosal, K., Roman, D., & Basaraba, D. (2018). Debemos escuchar a los maestros: Perspectives of bilingual teacher candidates in teacher education partnerships. *Bilingual Research Journal, 41*(2), 187–205. https://doi.org/10.1080/15235882.2018.1456986
Saavedra, C. M., & Pérez, M. S. (2018). Global South approaches to bilingual and early childhood teacher education: Disrupting global North neoliberalism. *Policy Futures in Education, 16*(6), 749–763. https://doi.org/10.1177/1478210317751271
Stacy, J., Fernández, Y., & Reyes McGovern, E. (2020). Centering language, culture, and power in dual language teacher preparation. *Journal of Culture and Values in Education, 3*(2), 120–137. https://doi.org/10.46303/jcve.2020.16
Stavely, Z., & Marquez Rosales, B. (2021, June). Why training California bilingual teachers just got harder. *EdSource*. https://edsource.org/2021/why-training-california-bilingual-teachers-just-got-harder/656558
Tedick, D. J., & Young, A. I. (2018). Two-way immersion students' home languages, proficiency levels, and responses to form-focused instruction. *International Journal of Bilingual Education and Bilingualism, 21*(3), 303–318. https://doi.org/10.1080/13670050.2017.1383354
Téllez, K., & Varghese, M. (2013). Teachers as intellectuals and advocates: Professional development for bilingual education teachers. *Theory Into Practice, 52*(2), 128–135. https://doi.org/10.1080/00405841.2013.770330
Torres, K. N. (2017). *50/50 two way immersion program implementation perspectives* (Publication No. 10759873) [Doctoral dissertation, University of Houston Clear-Lake].

Torres-Guzmán, M. E., & Swinney, R. (2009). *Freedom at work: Language, professional, and intellectual development in schools*. Paradigm Publishers.

Valdés, G., Poza, L., & Brooks, M. D. (2015). Language acquisition in bilingual education. In, W.E. Wright, S. Boun, & O. García (Eds.) *The Handbook of Bilingual and Multilingual Education* (1st ed., pp. 56–74). Wiley-Blackwell.

Varghese, M. M., & Snyder, R. (2018). Critically examining the agency and professional identity development of novice dual language teachers through figured worlds. *International Multilingual Research Journal*, *12*(3), 145–159. https://doi.org/10.1080/19313152.2018.1474060

Leadership and Partnership

37

LEADING EQUITY-DRIVEN DUAL LANGUAGE BILINGUAL EDUCATION

Elena Izquierdo, Sarah De La Garza, David DeMatthews

Background

Researchers, practitioners, and advocates in the bilingual education community have noted the rapid expansion of dual language bilingual education (DLBE)[1] across the country. The promise of DLBE rests on its three pillars: (1) bilingualism/biliteracy; (2) high academic achievement; and (3) social-cultural competence (Howard et al., 2018). Research has also emerged that proposes critical consciousness as a fourth goal for DLBE in providing equal access to educational opportunities for emergent bilingual[2] students and families (Cervantes-Soon et al., 2017; Palmer et al., 2019).

Across the nation, K-12 schools continue to increase their emergent bilingual enrollment (OELA, 2020). Districts and schools are rapidly shifting from a few DLBE programs into large-scale implementation to provide more emergent bilingual students with an effective and culturally responsive education. The increase in DLBE may play a role in decreasing academic achievement gaps, especially if these programs are appropriately implemented and replace less effective transitional and English-only instructional programs (López et al., 2013).

Dual language is a bilingual education program initially developed to support the schooling of emergent bilingual students. High-quality DLBE aims to support emergent bilingual children to continue language and academic development in their primary language while learning through both languages across the curriculum throughout their schooling (Collier & Thomas, 2012). Research consistently documented dual language as the most effective model of bilingual education for emergent bilingual students (Collier & Thomas, 2004; Lindholm-Leary & Block, 2010; Steele et al., 2017; Thomas & Collier, 2012). DLBE is a paradigm shift which extends beyond simply learning Spanish (or another

DOI: 10.4324/9781003269076-54

partner language) and English, to developing bilingualism, biliteracy, critical thinking skills in two languages across the curriculum, and advancing sociocultural competence (Izquierdo, 2021). District-wide DLBE implementation advocates equitable access to academic success for all emergent bilingual students. DLBE has evolved into one-way and two-way models depending on the student composition. One-way models serve linguistically homogeneous groups such as all emergent bilinguals or speakers of the same language (Collier & Thomas, 2012). Student composition in two-way models consists of both English and Spanish (or another partner language) (Collier & Thomas, 2012). All students serve as first language models and second language learners in two-way programs. As interest grows and many English-speaking parents increasingly enroll their children in DLBE, one-way models quickly convert to two-way models in response to changing demographics (Henderson & Palmer, 2020). However, growing research reveals how, in this process of large-scale DLBE and rapid expansion of two-way models, the focus on equity and equality is being compromised (Cervantes-Soon et al., 2017; Palmer et al., 2019).

The unique needs of emergent bilingual students in DLBE should shape principals' equity-driven leadership. For example, four equity issues specific to this population include educational programming that addresses linguistic and academic needs, quality DLBE curriculum, appropriate assessments, resources, and parent and community engagement (García et al., 2008). To address these equity issues, principals must know and understand bilingual education as foundational to DLBE. Principals need to harness their instructional expertise, build capacity in their teaching and building staff, implement necessary programs and services, and build a positive school culture (Callahan et al., 2019; DeMatthews & Izquierdo, 2019). Aspiring, current, and veteran principals need opportunities to develop critical consciousness and deconstruct their experiences and ideologies to lead and implement DLBE effectively and equitably (Izquierdo, 2021). Critical consciousness is necessary for principals to lead with equity.

This chapter is organized into three strands: (1) a framework for equity-driven leadership in DLBE, (2) review of preparation standards, and (3) recommendations for principal preparation programs to address each component within the framework. The chapter concludes with recommendations for future research.

A Framework for Equity-Driven Leadership in DLBE

Equity-driven leadership requires principals to be wholeheartedly committed to DLBE and their own professional development and growth. Radd et al. (2021) state,

> Equity leadership requires that kind of commitment, courage, and self-reflection from all of us. It requires us to imagine equitable spaces and

> ideas that we have not seen in practice. To do this, leaders need a bold vision, significant knowledge and skills, and collaboration with many people. (p. xii)

Equally important is the principals' understanding of the specialized nature and historic struggle for DLBE. As critically conscious leaders, DLBE principals need to recognize and address any deficit preconceived notions that they might hold about students or families' linguistic or cultural backgrounds. Developing a critical consciousness requires the interrogation of power structures, learning the historical context of the school, and listening to silenced voices (Palmer et al., 2019). Essentials of equity-driven leadership in DLBE require principals to develop a historical awareness of emergent bilinguals' marginalization and examine existing practices, policies, and structures, build professional capacity, revisit instructional practices, build a positive school culture, and evaluate program effectiveness.

Historical Awareness of Emergent Bilinguals' Marginalization

School leaders must understand how emergent bilinguals have been marginalized to fully appreciate how DLBE implementation can combat historical inequities in academic performance and family engagement. According to Akerman and Tazi (2015), close to 26% of preschool-age Latinx children are U.S.-born and have at least one immigrant parent. Many children enter kindergarten with reading and mathematics gaps (Han et al., 2012) and these gaps persist, as evident in national and state accountability measures (López et al., 2013). Correlations between lower performance on state assessments and increased dropout rates have been noted (Gándara & Contreras, 2009; McNeil et al., 2008). In addition, schools have historically neglected to meet the needs of their Latinx immigrant community by not validating their culture and language and failing to promote positive self-identity or create welcoming school environments (Arias & Morillo-Campbell, 2008). The home-school connection may be overlooked, and the important "funds of knowledge" students and parents bring from home may be unnoticed or deemphasized (De Gaetano, 2007; Moll et al., 1992). Latinx immigrant families (transnational students) often feel positioned as "outsiders," forced to cope with the physical and social-emotional stress of establishing a new life away from their home country while also struggling to determine how they will access education, housing, and healthcare for their families (Alfaro & Gándara, 2021; Good et al., 2010). Families experiencing poverty and families with undocumented status deal with additional stress. These conditions create unequal power dynamics that do not allow families to effectively advocate for their children. Parents perceive that they are not respected by schools which contributes to their lack of participation in school activities (Carreón et al., 2005). Paradoxically, Olivos (2020) found Latinx parents were highly satisfied with their children's bilingual education program. Parental satisfaction, however, accounted for parents' knowledge about the language program model, engagement in school events, and "access to the school's power structure to affect change if they are dissatisfied" (Olivos, 2020, p. 79). Principals must understand how emergent bilingual students and their parents have been historically marginalized.

Other potential challenges in leading DLBE include state and local policies, unequal power dynamics between parents from different racial and economic backgrounds, bureaucratic demands, teacher preparation, in-service professional development, the hegemony of English in schools, and the deficit-framing of Spanish (Cervantes-Soon et al., 2017; Zúñiga et al., 2018). Subsequently principals need not only understand the foundations and sociocultural goals of DLBE, but they also need to be able to negotiate issues of status, English-only mandates, and/or ideologies within their school community. The principal is critical to leading the development, implementation, and sustainability of DLBE on their campus. A growing body of research has already begun to document the principal's critical role (Menken, 2017). Effective DLBE principals promote bilingualism and biliteracy through the reallocation of resources, strengthening of family and community relationships, monitoring DLBE implementation, providing teachers with coaching, support, planning opportunities to adapt pedagogy and quality DLBE curriculum, and attending to power dynamics within the broader community (Alanís & Rodríguez, 2008; Black, 2006; DeMatthews & Izquierdo, 2019; Menken, 2017; Rosa, 2011; Scanlan & López, 2012; Wiemelt & Welton, 2015).

Practices, Policies, and Structures

Principals must be ready to address educational injustices entrenched within district policies and practices. They are the primary catalyst for change by addressing their schools' shortcomings via community engagement and leveraging the technical and administrative skills endemic to their positions (DeMatthews, 2015). For DLBE principals, these skills include understanding how to reallocate and adapt budgets, policies, master schedules, teacher caseloads, and other administrative structures necessary to create more equitable classrooms and schools for the success of emergent bilingual children (Knight et al., 2016). Leadership for equity attends to dismantling and eliminating inequities via structures, policies and processes, staff capacity, and capital resources.

Building Leadership Capacity

DLBE principals must be able to engage in their own leadership development in the theory and practice of dual language, content development, quality DLBE curriculum, and biliteracy in order to support, build capacity, and monitor their teachers, staff, and students' growth. Rosa (2011) found effective principals constantly seek ways to push staff toward innovative instructional methods to meet the needs of emergent bilinguals. Less effective principals could not be critically reflective of their practices, lacked prerequisite instructional knowledge, and were less willing to engage in professional development with teachers (Rosa, 2011). Black (2006) found that principals were unprepared to support emergent bilingual students, partly because they struggled to understand critical aspects of language acquisition models. Principals reported struggling with tensions of English-first ideologies and the beliefs that language and culture were foundational and important assets to be preserved (Black, 2006). Warhol and Mayer (2012) and Black (2006) also found some well-intended principals maximized English instruction at the expense of students' home language or underestimated the program's effectiveness due to their state-standardized assessment data. The principalship is critical to creating a supportive teaching and learning culture for teachers, staff, and students.

Instructional Practices

Theoharis and O'Toole (2011) stress that principals must know about language development, effective instructional practices, assessment, classroom management, and collaborative inquiry. DLBE principals need to continuously receive and provide training on specific DLBE pedagogies such as language acquisition, biliteracy, translanguaging, bridging content across both languages, cross-linguistic connections, cognates, and appropriate assessments in both languages. Principals must encourage, support, mentor, and monitor the implementation of these culturally and linguistically responsive DLBE pedagogies. Successful implementation requires DLBE principals to actively engage all stakeholders in collaborative planning to promote inclusive DLBE classrooms, identify and access quality curricular resources, progress monitor, and adjust programs and supports as needed (Scanlan & López, 2012; Theoharis & O'Toole, 2011).

School Culture

One of the DLBE goals is the development of social-cultural competence. DLBE principals recognize the cultural and linguistic assets that students bring to school. Menken (2017) notes, "school leaders – particularly principals – are extremely influential in shaping a school's language policy and the overall quality of schooling that emergent bilinguals receive" (p. 2). When cultural and linguistic diversity are viewed as assets, principals and teachers have the power to cultivate positive life-long attitudes for all languages and cultures within their students, and this impacts the school and community in powerful ways. DLBE principals support the schooling of emergent bilingual children and foster welcoming and inclusive schools for their families by promoting culturally responsive practices and actions. In creating inclusive schools, principals challenge dominant beliefs, co-construct new and empowering narratives, advocate for comprehensive change, and publicly engage in ongoing candid discussions about race, ethnicity, social class, disability, gender, sexual orientation, and other marginalization conditions (Furman, 2012; Jean-Marie, 2008; Jean-Marie et al., 2009; Theoharis, 2007).

Program Evaluation

Ongoing program evaluation informs the school community on program strengths and areas of need in order to make adjustments. This process of ongoing evaluation supports the sustainability of the school's DLBE program. Equity-driven DLBE promotes a collaborative and comprehensive evaluative process that authentically engages all stakeholders in a number of areas. For instance, leaders could assess their campus climate by identifying levels of support for bilingualism and biculturalism, productivity, collaboration, inquiry, and the contributions of teacher-leaders and parents (DeMatthews & Izquierdo, 2016). Evaluations should also focus on teachers and parents' knowledge of DLBE curriculum and assessment, and community engagement in decision-making (DeMatthews & Izquierdo, 2016; Howard et al., 2018).

Principal Preparation

Extant research on principal preparation, specifically for DLBE, is limited but growing. Anderson et al. (2022) found 608 universities nationally offer over 1,100 different pathways to the principalship, including traditional face-to-face, fully online, and hybrid pathways. However, no study to date has provided a systematic or descriptive portrait of how DLBE is addressed in principal preparation programs nationally. The available literature focuses on current principals' leadership in DLBE settings such as case studies of a single principal (Alanís & Rodríguez, 2008; DeMatthews & Izquierdo, 2016, 2017, 2020a, 2020b; Menken, 2017; Menken & Solorza, 2015; Wiemelt & Welton, 2015) or groups of principals (Morita-Mullaney & Chesnut, 2022). Frameworks such as Howard et al. (2018) provide invaluable tools to guide schools in DLBE implementation, but practicing principals are still left to navigate challenges such as parent perceptions, dismantling structural challenges, and limited bus transportation for emergent bilinguals to attend DLBE schools (Morita-Mullaney & Chesnut, 2022). Nevertheless, the question remains *how* preparation programs can prepare future principals to confront inequities and lead equity-driven DLBE schools.

There is a dearth of literature that documents how leadership preparation programs engage in reform efforts to address the needs of emergent bilingual students. Baecher et al.'s (2013) study explored the extent to which a preparation program focused on emergent bilingual students and bilingual education. They reviewed syllabi and explored student perspectives on readiness to serve as leaders for emergent bilingual students. Most responses indicated that few issues were discussed in-depth (Baecher et al., 2013). Some faculty stated the need for a required course on the historical foundation of bilingual education and instructional methods of teaching ELLs (Baecher et al., 2013). Another faculty said, "The topic seems to be ghettoized or ignored" (Baecher et al., 2013, p. 290). Hess and Kelly's (2007) study suggested that less than 3% of curricula were devoted toward issues of diversity and multiculturalism. Nevertheless, some programs have engaged in efforts to specifically address the needs of emergent bilinguals. For example, Project Preparing Academic Leaders (PAL), a five-year multi-million national professional development grant, has trained 120 aspiring principals specifically for bilingual and dual language settings (Irby et al., 2020). This unique program includes a summer residency at a DLBE campus, bimonthly mentoring, and targeted professional development on the state's bilingual standards (Irby et al., 2020). All leadership programs should review their program activities, structures, and curriculum to evaluate the extent emergent bilingual students and DLBE are addressed.

Leadership Standards for Equity-Driven Dual Language Education

The Professional Standards for Educational Leaders (PSEL) (2015) set the expectations for effective leaders to facilitate student success. However, the PSEL are broad and lack a critical focus on bilingual education, its history, language policy, and program models as important dimensions of the knowledge base for equity-driven DLBE leadership. Terms such as emergent, bilingual, English learner, or language acquisition are absent in the standards. Two standards that make reference to "language" are Standard 3, Equity and Cultural Responsiveness, and Standard 5, Community of Care and Support for Students. For example, Standard 3.E calls for leaders to "confront and alter institutional biases of student marginalization, deficit-based schooling, and low expectations associated with race, class, culture and language, gender and sexual orientation, and disability or special status" (National Policy Board for Educational Administration, 2015, p. 11).

A second example is Standard 5.F that states effective school leaders should "infuse the school's learning community with the cultures and languages of the school's community" (National Policy Board for Educational Administration, 2015, p. 13). The inclusion of culture, language, and equity in the standards is important, but given the demographics of schools across the nation, the standards should include the specialized knowledge required for equity-driven DLBE leadership. However, the ambiguity leaves it to the interpretation of principal preparation programs. The next iteration of the PSEL standards should include the history, policies, programs models, theories of bilingual education, and language acquisition across the ten standards.

Recommendations for Principal Preparation Programs

Institutions of higher education (IHE) can support equity-driven DLBE through their vocal program commitment and program structures. IHE program commitment can materialize leadership program redesigns to include DLBE district-university partnerships, proactive recruitment efforts of faculty experts in DLBE, and interdepartmental collaboration between teacher education and principal preparation. Programs should provide all instructors and faculty affiliated with the principal preparation program to participate in targeted leadership development grounded in critical consciousness and focused on the history, policies, programs models, theories of bilingual education, quality DLBE curriculum, and acquisition of languages. In addition, programs should seek additional federal and state grants to facilitate internships at DLBE campuses. The following are specific recommendations for principal preparation curriculum:

- Redesign existing courses to review and interrogate past legislation, policy, and court cases like the Bilingual Education Act of 1968, the Lau Remedies, and *Castañeda v. Pickard* (1981), along with state language policies.
- Incorporate principals' reflective practices on ideologies and the understanding and development of critical consciousness.
- Incorporate culturally responsive projects that promote engagement with families of all linguistic and cultural backgrounds.
- Incorporate campus visits and learning walks on DLBE campuses and classrooms and model how to create communities of practice for teachers and their peer administrators working with emergent bilingual students and families.
- Ensure quality DLBE curriculum which are culturally relevant texts, other texts written by local authors, and materials specifically developed for DLBE and not merely a translation from the general curriculum.
- Develop a mentoring or internship model at campuses with effective DLBE principals.

- Prepare principals to observe a teacher's pedagogical repertoire that promotes biliteracy, bilingualism, translanguaging, and sociocultural awareness.
- Include program evaluation topics in coursework such as program monitoring, data collection, and data analysis specific to the progress of emergent bilingual students in DLBE.
- Work with alumni via group reflection activities or focus groups targeting DLBE implementation in their respective districts.
- Connect with consultants or program evaluators specializing in DLBE.

Future Directions

Equity-driven DLBE requires knowledgeable and skilled leadership to take purposeful action. Principal preparation programs have the responsibility to build the capacity of future principals in the development, implementation, and sustainability of equity-driven DLBE. Given the demographics in our schools there is an urgency to redesign principal preparation programs to address DLBE, policies and structures, school culture, instructional practices, engagement of families, and program evaluation through a critical consciousness framework. Furthermore, programs should go beyond the PSEL and prepare aspiring principals of DLBE to advocate, support, and protect cultural and linguistic diversity.

Further research is needed to focus on redesign efforts of principal preparation programs in addressing DLBE and the needs of emergent bilingual students. In addition, research can be conducted with recent graduates of principal preparation programs in documenting their challenges and successes in implementing DLBE at their campuses. Furthermore, a national evaluation of states' principal standards and the extent of their inclusion of DLBE, bilingual education, and/or working with emergent bilingual students would be useful for principal preparation programs. As student demographics continue to change, we call upon educational leadership and principal preparation programs to ensure that future principals have bilingual education knowledge, critical consciousness, commitment, and bold actions to lead schools with equity and specifically for DLBE. Our collective work should continue to raise community agency and critical consciousness at all levels, particularly with those of us that teach, lead, and prepare educators.

Notes

1 Dual language is grounded in the history, policies, program models, and struggles in bilingual education.

2 We use the term emergent bilinguals rather than English Language Learners (ELLs) or Limited English Proficient (LEP). ELLs or LEP students are those students who speak a language other than English and are acquiring English in school.

We prefer to use the term emergent bilinguals because we believe that when policymakers, educators, and researchers ignore bilingualism and its role in schooling, they perpetuate numerous inequities and discount the needs of children from linguistically diverse backgrounds.

References

Akerman, D. J., & Tazi, Z. (2015). Enhancing young Hispanic dual language learners' achievement.: Exploring strategies and addressing challenges. *ETS Research Report Series*, 2015, 1–39. http://dx.doi.org/10.1002/ets2.12045

Alanís, I., & Rodríguez, M. A. (2008). Sustaining a dual language immersion program: Features of success. *Journal of Latinos and Education*, 7(4), 305–319. https://www.tandfonline.com/doi/full/10.1080/15348430802143378

Alfaro, C., & Gándara, P. (2021). Binational teacher preparation: Constructing pedagogical bridges for the students we share. In P. Gandara, & B. Jensen (Eds.), *The students we share: Preparing US and Mexican educators for our transnational future* (pp. 45–69). SUNY Press.

Anderson, E., Budhwani, S., & Perrone, F. (2022). State of States: Landscape of university-based pathways to the principalship. *Journal of School Leadership*, *32*(2), 103–125. https://doi.org/10.1177/1052684620980360.

Arias, M. B., & Morillo-Campbell, M. (2008). *Promoting ELL parental involvement: Challenges in contested times.* Arizona State University Education Policy Research Unit.

Baecher, L., Knoll, M., & Patti, J. (2013). Addressing English language learners in the school leadership curriculum: Mapping the terrain. *Journal of Research on Leadership Education*, *8*(3), 280–303 https://journals.sagepub.com/doi/abs/10.1177/1942775113498377

Black, W. R. (2006). Constructing accountability performance for English language learner students: An unfinished journey toward language minority rights. *Educational Policy*, *20*(1), 197–224. https://doi.org/10.1177/0895904805285948

Callahan, R., DeMatthews, D. E., & Reyes, P. (2019). The impact of *Brown* on E.L. students: Addressing linguistic and educational rights through school leadership practice and preparation. *Journal of Research on Leadership Education*, *14*(4), 281–307.

Carreón, G. P., Drake, C., & Barton, A. C. (2005). The importance of presence: Immigrant parents' school engagement experiences. *American Educational Research Journal*, *42*(3), 465–498. https://doi.org/10.3102/00028312042003465

Castañeda v. Pickard, 648 F. 2nd 989 5th Cir. (1981). https://casetext.com/case/castaneda-v-pickard

Cervantes-Soon, C., Dorner, L., Palmer, D., Heiman, D., Schwerdtfeger, R., & Choi, J. (2017). Combating inequalities in two-way language immersion programs: Toward critical consciousness in bilingual education spaces. *Review of Research in Education*, *41*(1), 403–427.

Collier, V. P., & Thomas, W. P. (2004). The astounding effectiveness of dual language education for all. *NABE Journal of Research and Practice*, *2*(1), 1–20. https://www.berkeleyschools.net/wp-content/uploads/2011/10/TWIAstounding_Effectiveness_Dual_Language_Ed.pdf?864d7e

Collier, V. P., & Thomas, W. P. (2012). What really works for English language learners: Research-based practices for principals. In G. Theoharis, & J. S. Brooks (Eds.), *What every principal needs to know to create equitable and excellent schools* (pp. 155–173). Teacher College Press.

De Gaetano, Y. (2007). The role of culture in engaging Latino parents' involvement in school. *Urban Education*, *42*(2), 145–162. https://doi.org/10.1177/0042085906296536

DeMatthews, D., & Izquierdo, E. (2020a). Supporting Mexican American immigrant students on the border: A case study of culturally responsive leadership in a dual language elementary school. *Urban Education*, *55*(3), 362–393. https://doi.org/10.1177/2F0042085918756715

DeMatthews, D., & Izquierdo, E. (2020b). Leadership for social justice and sustainability: A historical case study of a high-performing dual language school along the U.S.-Mexico Border. *Journal of Education for Students Placed at Risk (JESPAR)*, *25*(2), 164–182. https://doi.org/10.1080/10824669.2019.1704629

DeMatthews, D. E., & Izquierdo, E. (Eds.) (2019). *Dual language education: Teaching and leading through two languages*. Springer International Publishing.

DeMatthews, D. E., & Izquierdo, E. (2017). Authentic and social justice leadership: A case study of an exemplary principal. *Journal of School Leadership*, *27*(3), 333–360.

DeMatthews, D. E. (2015). Making sense of social justice leadership: A case study of a principal's experiences to create a more inclusive school. *Leadership and Policy in Schools*, *14*(2), 139–166.

DeMatthews, D. E., & Izquierdo, E. (2016). School leadership for dual language education: A social justice approach. *Educational Forum*, *80*(3), 278–293.

Furman, G. (2012). Social justice leadership a praxis: Developing capacities through preparation programs. *Educational Administration Quarterly*, *48*, 191–229.

Gándara, P. C., & Contreras, F. (2009). *The Latino education crisis: The consequences of failed social policies*. Harvard University Press.

García, O., Kleifgen, J. A., & Falchi, L. (2008). *From English Language Learners to Emergent Bilinguals*. A Research Initiative of the Campaign for Educational Equity, Teachers College Columbia University. https://files.eric.ed.gov/fulltext/ED524002.pdf

Good, M. E., Masewicz, S., & Vogel, L. (2010). Latino English language learners: Bridging achievement and cultural gaps between schools and families. *Journal of Latinos and Education*, *9*(4), 321–339. https://doi.org/10.1080/15348431.2010.491048

Han, W. J., Lee, R., & Waldfogel, J. (2012). School readiness among children of immigrants in the U.S.: Evidence from a large national birth cohort study. *Children and Youth Services Review*, *34*(4), 771–782. https://doi.org/10.1016/j.childyouth.2012.01.001

Henderson, K. I., & Palmer, D. K. (2020). *Dual language bilingual education*. Multilingual Matters. https://doi.org/10.21832/9781788928106

Hess, F., & Kelly, A. (2007). Learning to lead: What gets taught in principal preparation programs. *The Teachers College Record*, *109*(1), 244–274.

Howard, E. R., Lindholm-Leary, K. J., Rogers, D., Olague, N., Medina, J., Kennedy, B., Sugarman, J., & Christian, D. (2018). *Guiding principles for dual language education* (3rd ed.). Center for Applied Linguistics.

Irby, B. J., Lara-Alecio, R., Tong, F., Abdelrahman, N., & Torres, M. (2020). A model for preparing academic leaders (Project PAL) for teachers of English learners building instructional capacity within a socially-responsible principal preparation program. *International Journal of Educational Leadership Preparation*, *15*(1), 29–47. https://files-eric-ed-gov.ezproxy.lib.utexas.edu/fulltext/EJ1254580.pdf

Izquierdo, E. (2021). *The shift to equity review of the book dual language bilingual education: Teacher cases and perspectives on large-scale implementation*. International Journal of Bilingual Education and Bilingualism.

Jean-Marie, G. (2008). Leadership for social justice: An agenda for 21st century schools. *Educational Forum*, *72*(4), 24–354.

Jean-Marie, G., Normore, A. H., & Brooks, J. S. (2009). Leadership for social justice: Preparing 21st century school leaders for a new social order. *Journal of Research on Leadership Education*, *4*(1), 1–31.

Knight, D., Izquierdo, E., & DeMatthews, D. E. (2016). A balancing act: School budgeting and resource allocation on a new dual language campus. *Journal of Cases of Educational Leadership*, *19*(4), 32–46.

Lindholm-Leary, K., & Block, N. (2010). Achievement in predominantly low SES/Hispanic dual language schools. *International Journal of Bilingual Education and Bilingualism*, *13*(1), 43–60.

López, F., Scanlan, M., & Gundrum, B. (2013). Preparing teachers of English language learners: Empirical evidence and policy implications. *Education Policy Analysis Archives*, *21*(20), 20. https://doi.org/10.14507/epaa.v21n20.2013

McNeil, L. M., Coppola, E., Radigan, J., & Vasquez Heilig, J. (2008). Avoidable losses: High-stakes accountability and the dropout crisis. *Education Policy Analysis Archives*, *16*(3), 3. https://doi.org/10.14507/epaa.v16n3.2008

Menken, K., & Solorza, C. (2015). Principals as linchpins in bilingual education: The need for prepared school leaders. *International Journal of Bilingual Education and Bilingualism*, *18*(6), 676–697. https://doi.org/10.1080/13670050.2014.937390

Menken, K. (2017). *Leadership in dual language bilingual education*. Center for Applied Linguistics.

Moll, L. C., Amanti, C., Neff, D., & Gonzalez, N. (1992). Funds of knowledge for teaching: Using a qualitative approach to connect homes and classrooms. *Theory Into Practice*, *31*(2), 132–141. https://doi.org/10.1080/00405849209543534

Morita-Mullaney, T., & Chesnut, C. (2022). Equity traps in the deselection of English learners in dual language education: A collective case study of school principals. *NABE Journal of Research and Practice*, 1–20. https://doi.org/10.1080/26390043.2022.2079390

National Policy Board for Educational Administration. (2015). *Professional standards for educational leaders 2015*. Author. https://www.npbea.org/wp-content/uploads/2017/06/Professional-Standards-for-Educational-Leaders_2015.pdf

OELA. (2020, February). *English learners: Demographic trends*. Office of English Language Acquisition (OELA), United States of America Department of Education. https://ncela.ed.gov/files/fast_facts/19-0193_Del4.4_ELDemographicTrends_021220_508.pdf

Olivos, E. M. (2020). Silencing bicultural parental voices through educational satisfaction: What do we need to know? *Theory Into Practice*, *60*(1), 72–82. https://doi.org/10.1080/00405841.2020.1829378

Palmer, D. K., Cervantes-Soon, C., Dorner, L., & Heiman, D. (2019). Bilingualism, biliteracy, biculturalism, and critical consciousness for all: Proposing a fourth fundamental goal for two-way dual language education. *Theory Into Practice*, *58*(2), 121–133. https://doi.org/10.1080/00405841.2019.1569376

Radd, S. I., Givens Generett, G., Gooden, M. A., & Theoharis, G. (2021, February). *Five practices for equity-focused school leadership*. ASCD.

Rosa, M. (2011). A mixed-methods study to understand the perceptions of high school leaders about English language learners: The case of mathematics. *Jornal Internacional de Estudos em Educação Matemática*, *4*(2), 71–116.

Scanlan, M., & López, F. (2012). ¡Vamos! How school leaders promote equity and excellence for bilingual students. *Educational Administration Quarterly*, *48*(4), 583–625. https://doi.org/10.1177/0013161X11436270

Steele, J. L., Slater, R., Zamarro, G., Miller, T., Li, J., Burkhauser, S., & Bacon, M. (2017). Effects of dual-language immersion programs on student achievement. *American Educational Research Journal*, *54*(1), 282S–306S. https://doi.org/10.3102/0002831216634463

Theoharis, G. (2007). Social justice educational leaders and resistance: Toward a theory of social justice leadership. *Educational Administration Quarterly*, *43*(2), 221–258. https://doi.org/10.1177/0013161X06293717

Theoharis, G., & O'Toole, J. (2011). Leading inclusive ELL social justice leadership for English language learners. *Educational Administration Quarterly*, *47*(4), 646–688. https://doi.org/10.1177/0013161X11401616

Thomas, W. P., & Collier, V. P. (2012). *Dual language education for a transformed world*. Fuente Press.

Warhol, L., & Mayer, A. (2012). Misinterpreting school reform: The dissolution of a dual-immersion bilingual program in an urban New England elementary school. *Bilingual Research Journal*, *35*(2), 145–163. https://doi.org/10.1080/15235882.2012.703636

Wiemelt, J., & Welton, A. (2015). Challenging the dominant narrative: Critical bilingual leadership (liderazgo) for emergent bilingual Latin@ students. *International Journal of Multicultural Education*, *17*(1), 82. https://doi.org/10.18251/ijme.v17i1.877

Zúñiga, C. E., Henderson, K. I., & Palmer, D. K. (2018). Language policy toward equity: How bilingual teachers use policy mandates to their own ends. *Language and Education*, *32*(1), 60–76.

38

CRITICAL MULTILINGUAL POLICY ECOLOGY

University-District Partnerships in Dual Language/Bilingual Teacher Education

Magaly Lavadenz, Elvira G. Armas, Jongyeon Ee, Hoan Thi Thu Do

The rapid growth and expansion of dual language (DL) programs across the nation has intensified the demands on university educator preparation programs to increase the numbers of certified/licensed bilingual/DL teachers (American Councils for International Education, 2021; Garcia, 2017; Garcia et al., 2019). The emerging literature on district-university partnerships in DL/bilingual teacher education (DLBTE) is situated in local contexts in response to this rapid growth and expansion. However, DLBTE partnerships are affected by and susceptible to historical, social, political, and economic factors that have limited access, equity, and representation of linguistically and culturally diverse and minoritized populations in education, thus exacerbating bilingual teacher shortages. This necessitates transformative approaches that counter K-12 cultural and linguistic hegemonic practices.

This chapter provides a brief history of university-district partnerships (Table 38.1), followed by our conceptualization of DLBTE partnerships through a critical multilingual policy ecology (CMPE) framework. We use this framework and Onwuegbuzie and Frels' (2016) comprehensive literature review (CLR) methodology to analyze the existing multimodal literature on DLBTE partnerships. Informed by the work of critical scholars (Garcia et al., in this volume) and this multimodal CLR review, we suggest a CMPE as a set of strategic and transformative directions for university-district DLBTE partnerships to increase access, engagement, and equity in the educator preparation pipeline. We conclude with implications for bilingual teacher education programs, local policy planning, and research.

 DOI: 10.4324/9781003269076-55

Table 38.1 Types of university-district partnerships

Type	*Timeline*	*Description*
Laboratory/ demonstration schools	1894—Founded by John Dewey at the University of Chicago	• Formal agreement • Focus on teacher preparation, innovation, educational research, and professional development (PD)
Collaborative/ consortia	± 1983	• Formal or informal • Multiple districts and multiple universities • Common pedagogic, content, or context-specific agreement • Focus on field work, student teaching, and clinical experiences • Advisory boards • Informed by the 1983 "Nation at Risk Report" and the 1986 Carnegie Foundation's Report "A Nation Prepared: Teachers for the 21st Century"
Professional development schools	Holmes Group (1995)	• Provide ongoing PD for current educators • Encourage joint school-university faculty investigation of education-related issues • Promote P-12 student learning of P-12 students (National Association of Professional Development Schools, 2008, p. 1)
Teacher residency programs	Primarily as a result of Higher Education Opportunity Act of 2008	• Modeled on medical residencies • Combine coursework in education with extensive on-the-job training • Develop teachers for specific school districts or charter networks • Pair a district with an institution of higher learning and/or a nonprofit partner
Research-practice partnerships	~2010	• Long-term collaborations between practitioners and researchers • Investigate problems of practice and solutions for improving schools and districts (Coburn et al., 2013)

University-District Partnerships in Teacher Education

> Years of working in university partnerships have convinced several colleagues and me that the symbiotic joining of the two cultures, however difficult, is essential in the renewal of both schools and the education of educators, and that the two processes are best undertaken simultaneously.
>
> *(Goodlad, 1994, p. 280)*

Goodlad alludes to schools and universities as inherently distinct institutions. Despite a similar focus on the educational endeavor, each has unique cultures and incentive structures (Alemán et al., 2017; Boyer, 1996). Higher education faculties are obligated to the three principles of "teaching, research, and service", and K-12 partnerships have largely been relegated to the "service" principle. Boyer's call for the "scholarship of integration" prioritizes collaboration between schools/districts with teacher preparation faculties. Table 38.1 highlights several types of partnerships and locates these in larger education reform movements.

National school-district-university movements reside within larger historical, political, social, and cultural systems and can serve to inform partnerships for DLBTEs; our conceptual framework describes DLBTE ecosystems.

Conceptual Framework: Critical Multilingual Policy Ecology

We draw on the conceptual framework of CMPE to achieve two objectives: (1) to synthesize the extant literature based on the critical understanding of the current policy landscape shaping language education and teacher education programs and (2) to suggest strategic and transformative directions for DLBTE university-district partnerships by identifying the vacuum of the conscious endeavor to promote equity in DLBTE in prior studies. Specifically, we conceptualize CMPE as a framework (Figure 38.1)—a multi-faceted approach to form, critique, strengthen, and actualize university-district partnerships in DLBE with equity as a centralizing principle. This approach facilitates the analysis of "the many contexts and influences swirling around a policy process" (del Rosal et al., 2018; Weaver-Hightower, 2008, p. 162). Thus, it considers how policy processes are mediated by various actors, relationships, structures, and power over time and space regarding DL access, participation, and outcomes. Mitigated by sociopolitical factors such as race, class, and language ideologies, CMPE foregrounds historical and political consciousness around language and education policies (Heiman et al., this volume) that problematize the nature of university-district partnerships as institutional and individual actors in DLBE teacher preparation and program implementation. Inspired by Einar Haugen's essays on the Ecology of Language (1972), Hornberger (2003) extended this framework to analyze more complex, interdependent relationships and to galvanize diverse actors. We apply CMPE as a lens to examine access, equity, and justice issues for immigrant and emergent bilingual populations whose participation has been limited by "white privileging" and the gentrification of DLBE. We also extend this lens to disrupt the "colonization" of DLBE (Delavan, this volume; Chávez-Moreno, 2021).

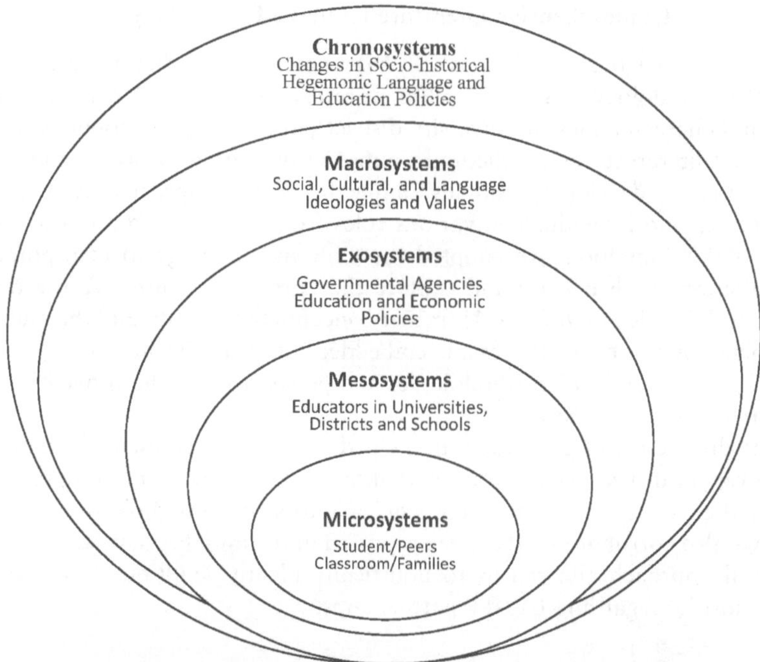

Note. Critical Multilingual Policy Ecology. Adapted from Bronfenbrenner's Ecological Systems Theory, In *The Psychology Notes Headquarters*, n.d. *https://www.psychologynoteshq.com/bronfenbrenner-ecological-theory/. Copyright 2021 by The Psychology Notes Headquarters. Adapted with permission.*

Figure 38.1 Critical Multilingual Policy Ecology

Building on the corpora of language and education policies over time, we situate university-district partnerships in the multiple intersectional systems—ecology—where bilingual schooling occurs and partners converge. This ecology is influenced by sociopolitical and ideological forces and micro- and macro processes that shape language use and policies (De Leon & Lavadenz, 2020; Freire & Alemán, 2021; Hornberger, 2003; Ricento, 2000). As policy actors, leaders in higher education and schools/districts serve as program and policy planners who address their communities' larger, often competing and conflicting interests (Cervantes-Soon et al., 2017; Corson, 1999). They have agency with which to shape and influence systems. University-district partnerships serve multiple K-12 schools that employ various DLBE target languages and program types. Galvanized by several states and local policy decisions—policy changes at the exo- and-meso-system levels—numerous districts continue to expand DLBE programs in terms of grade levels and languages offered.

Comprehensive Literature Review Methodology

We use Onwuegbuzie and Frels' (2016) comprehensive literature review (CLR) methodology to guide our literature review. Given the complex nature and characteristics of university-district partnerships, we found a conventional literature review method limited in delivering priorities and the importance of developing and sustaining the partnerships, mainly involving entities and individuals in various roles from academia to the field. To address this limitation, we adopted the CLR methodology to incorporate consultations with experts and explore the "grey" literature. We use this multimodal CLR as a *tool* to (1) further conceptualize CMPE and the multiple spheres in this ecosystem as an "embedded" study of the literature (p. 65) and (2) to "decolonize" methodologies and perspectives in the conventional research literature reviews.

The diverse list of grey literature helped our review represent the nature of university-district partnerships and allowed the review to be comprehensive and current. The iterative content validation process through experts' reviews also corroborated the areas captured in the initial review stage. This bilateral approach allowed us to holistically identify multiple dimensions and priorities regarding DLBTE partnerships.

Procedures

Varied combinations of the following keywords were employed: DL, bilingual education, university-district partnership(s), university-district collaboration, school-university, network, bilingual teacher preparation, and pre-service teacher preparation. We conducted our search using traditional academic search tools and broader venues[1] to ensure proper coverage of non-peer-reviewed sources or unpublished studies. We found limited empirical literature on university-research partnerships for DLBTE preparation. We then selected a multi-modal approach that broadens the sources to the grey literature and scholars and practitioners. Next, using the purposeful sampling technique (Patton, 2015), we identified 14 experts from prolific authors/often-cited researchers to veteran DLBTE practitioners with diverse professional roles to reflect the applied nature of partnerships. We administered a survey asking experts to review our sources and identify additional sources for insights and views regarding DLBTE. Eight content experts, including two from our research team, responded to the survey, yielding a response rate of 57%. The expert respondents had an average of 14.7 years of experience in university-district partnerships, and an average of 11.6 years of experience in DLBTE. Respondents reported their engagement in a variety of university-district partnerships, including (1) clinical, field-based/student teaching partnership; (2) residency program; (3) research-practice partnership; and (4) internships. Clinical, field-based/student teaching partnership was the most popular in our sample, with six out of eight respondents reporting their participation in this type of university-district partnership. Respondents also assumed diverse roles in the DLBTE program, including program director, clinical supervisor of pre-service teachers, bilingual teacher and mentor trainer, and statewide coordinator for clinical practice. The expert panel's feedback was affirmative; five rated the initial sources as extremely helpful in assisting us to identify key categories in DLBTE university-district partnerships, and two experts found them very helpful. Additionally, we asked experts to evaluate the relative importance of the identified categories. On a scale from 1 (not important) to 5 (very important), expert respondents rated these very positively (mean ratings ranged from 4.57 to 5.00 for all the identified themes).

From the initial categories generated and confirmed by the experts in this review, we engaged in a dialectical analytic process in iterative rounds to further synthesize and interpret selected sources. We next propose a coherent set of tenets for equity-informed DLBTE university-district partnerships.

Toward a Critical Multilingual Policy Ecology Movement in Dual Language/Bilingual Teacher Education University-District Partnerships

> Central to the language ecology movement, as for other ecology movements, is that it is about not only studying and describing those potential losses, but also counteracting them.
>
> *(Hornberger, 2003, p. 3)*

Informed by several bodies of work of critical scholars (see Garcia et al., this volume), and this multimodal CLR review of DLBTE partnerships, we suggest CMPE as a set of strategic and transformative directions for university-district partnerships in DLBTE to increase access, engagement, and equity in the educator preparation pipeline. District-wide K-12 DLBE growth and expansion require that districts prioritize target language(s) and program models that are responsive to their context and have implications for recruiting, retaining, and developing multilingual teaching staff. Therefore, we identify and report on the limited literature on partnerships supporting elementary-level Spanish DLBE, corresponding to national trends (American Councils for International Education, 2021). Nevertheless, our framework can inform a variety of program types and target languages because of the framework's holistic nature, allowing contextualized interpretations of other DLBE languages and programs. Accordingly, we assert the following four tenets.

Tenet 1: The Centrality of Equity, Rigor, and Support in University-District Partnership Contexts

Portland State University stated on its bilingual teacher pathway program website that "Our education system progresses only if it offers equitable learning experiences" (n.d.). Without a deep understanding of the chronosystems' hegemonic historical, social, cultural, political, and economic forces that shape local and contemporary contexts and how those forces influence DLBTE, partners as actors in multiple policy spaces are susceptible to reifying and perpetuating the larger inequities facing DL education, including, but not limited to:

- the commodification of languages as marketable/economic resources
- the access and equitable participation of non-Latino language minoritized and other marginalized groups, including African American students from a variety of income levels
- subtractive and deficit orientations contributing to low expectations for minoritized populations
- the need to address knowledge and practice regarding the non-academic impacts of participation, including the micro-social interactions occurring between actors in two-way immersion classrooms

Within the exosystem of CMPE, we localize DLBE certification policies to include preparation standards, which vary across the United States. As indicated in a US Department of Education report (Boyle et al., 2015), 25 states and the District of Columbia currently offer some types of bilingual teacher certification. Federal scholarship/tuition support for bilingual teacher preparation virtually disappeared during the No Child Left Behind era, resulting in shortages of bilingual or English as a second language teachers (Garcia et al., 2019). Professional organizations developed DLBE teacher standards that are largely devoid of equity considerations (Alfaro, this volume). As policy actor implementers, university and district partners develop agreements to (1) ensure that minimum standards are met; (2) high expectations are held; and (3) provide adequate support to maximize candidate and program success and to mentor and retain teachers (Leong et al., 2018).

As a result of Texas Senate Bill 1882, in the University of Texas at San Antonio, DL Community Lab Schools Partnerships was created in June 2021 to build a school network and provide competent teachers, principals, counselors, school psychologists, and others dedicated to educating bilingual students. The partnership also aims to ensure that the district's educators receive support in implementing research-based, rigorous DL practices.

In another type of partnership between a community college and university, Flores et al. (2007) describe how the simultaneous goals of excellence, equity, and support are operationalized in a "learning ecology" model in Academy for Teacher Excellence. In reimagining equity language and learning ecology spaces for DLBTE (Foy et al., 2018), partners co-create local school/classroom level policies in which teacher-peers continue their pre-service pedagogic development and hone their expertise to mentor students in envisioning their futures. Accompanied by guidance, mentorship, and coaching, teachers also receive support through various bilingual professional development experiences (Guilamo, 2020). Applying Beck's concept of the "third space" (2018) to DLBTE partnerships, iterative cycles of practice and research have the potential to respond to the mutually negotiated counter-narrating and questioning about who is served and whose interests are being served.

Tenet 2: Ensuring Critical Consciousness, Agency, and Clarity in Relationships and Roles

> Power relations cannot be established, maintained, extended, resisted or mobilised into action, or given material form, without the mediation of discourse.
>
> *(Doherty, 2007, p. 195)*

University-district partnerships have the potential to address the uniqueness of DLBE candidates by building a common understanding of partnership relationships and roles to guide decision-making and interactions between university faculty/staff, DLBE candidates, and school-site-level personnel (Brown et al., 2008; Garcia, 2017; Garcia et al., 2019). However, there is often a lack of attention to how critical consciousness—the fourth pillar and driving force in DLBE (Heiman et al., this volume)—can be galvanized as partners seek to balance institutional power dynamics while simultaneously centering equity for minoritized students. The opportunity to identify, question, and reject historical inequalities that affect DLBE contexts leads to the development of critical agency among all partners. Thus, we can move beyond a traditional relationship and affirm the linguistic and cultural strengths of bilingual candidates to address the socioeconomic and linguistic diversity of the students, families, and communities they serve.

Our review of DLBTE university-district partnership multimedia and web resources yielded a few promising cases wherein a more prominent approach to critical conscientiousness leading to critical agency can be fostered, systematized, and researched. For example, Rodríguez (2003) describes Project Alianza's "Circle of Influence" which creates, adapts, and expands bilingual curricula to include courses of study that affirm and uplift existing knowledge. They incorporate practical experiences and research-based family-engagement practices to enhance the capabilities of teachers, parents, administrators, school board members, and community leaders to co-create partnerships (Webb et al., n.d.). This encourages relationship-building and results in creating "lasting bridges" for effective partnerships. California State University San Marcos' Project GLOBAL (Global Learning Opportunities in Bilingual and Leading, n.d.) is a university-district partnership focused on doubling the number of bilingual teachers, tripling the number of graduating high school seniors with a Seal of Biliteracy, and quadrupling the number of DL programs. Drawing on foundations from the US PREP Framework[2] and California's Global 2030 initiative,[3], the project specifies four Global Competence domains: (1) investigate the world beyond their immediate environment; (2) recognize different perspectives; (3) communicate in multiple languages, and (4) take action to improve conditions. Their commitment to strengthening partnerships with school districts can facilitate engaging and supporting all university and district policy actors in creating contexts that allow bilingual teachers to develop critical conscientiousness and uncover their confidence to challenge inequalities at the micro- and macro level of the multilingual policy ecology.

Defining roles and specialized criteria for DLBTE personnel at the university and district levels is critical for success. Key personnel must be qualified to mentor, coach, and support DLBE candidates. Qualifications include target language fluency, DLBE pedagogy, content knowledge, and experience with biliteracy assessment (del Rosal et al., 2018; Garcia, 2017; Heineke et al., 2020; Lavadenz et al., 2019). Experts who maintain a site-level liaison are critical to ensuring candidates feel connected and supported in the partner-school context. In a policy highlight, Garcia et al. (2019) described lessons learned from Western Washington University's Woodring College of Education partnership with Highline Public Schools (n.d.) in the implementation of the Grow Your Own (GYO) program to address the bilingual teacher shortage. One of the key lessons included developing a unique job description for the P-12 bi/multilingual fellows in their program who simultaneously served as paraprofessionals. The distinction of roles allowed the district to increase and sustain the program's visibility and justified a higher pay rate.

Tenet 3: Privileging Community Social, Linguistic, and Cultural Wealth in DLBE Teacher Recruitment and Retention

Hernández (this volume) proposes key considerations and contextual factors to move from short-term solutions to sustainable teacher education practices that address the bilingual teacher shortage, including the expansion of bilingual teacher pathways such as GYO programs (Gist et al., 2018), career ladders (Valenciana et al, 2005), Bilingual Teacher Residencies (Lavadenz et al., 2019), and U.S. Department of Education grants, programs, and initiatives (e.g., U.S. Department of Education, 2016, 2017). Through conceptualization of CMPE, we contend that intersectionality across these policy ecosystems allows university-district partners the opportunity to employ the community cultural wealth (CCW) perspective to validate DLBE candidates' assets: aspirational, navigational, social, linguistics, familiar, and resistant capital. The degree to which the sources explicitly expressed their intent to address these assets varied. However, the analysis of the Portland State University consortium program elucidated how candidates benefitted from this practice, "The candidates described language as a powerful aspect of identity in their own lives, defining who they were. They found that their ability to be 'border crossers' made them in demand in their school districts, not only to translate materials and carry out similar linguistic tasks but also because of their ability to reach across cultures" (Brown et al., 2008, p. 60).

The sources we reviewed primarily provided descriptions of strategies that support entry into programs (recruitment) and approaches to professional development or mechanisms that support retention in the program and profession. Garcia (2017) and Garcia et al. (2019) detailed how GYO and other alternative certification routes address the bilingual teacher shortage through targeted recruitment and support of school staff such as paraprofessionals, translators, and high school students, including hiring a full-time program coordinator to support candidates in the application and district hiring procedures. Another example is the Project 29 Pathways program (Sakash & Chou, 2007). This program provided academic advising (e.g., individualized course plans to meet general education requirements) and social-emotional support (e.g., organization of small groups to discuss life-work issues, English/Spanish communication) and adapted its curriculum to leverage participants' personal and cultural attributes through targeted professional English Learner development. In rural contexts, Klitzing (2020) identified three common barriers: distance to public universities, cost of private online programs, and lack of reliable internet connectivity. These areas are concerning given they signal systemic inequities coupled with a call to action to apply lessons learned, namely (1) develop a systemic approach that engages multiple stakeholders, (2) align with state/local initiatives, and (3) identify and address bureaucratic hurdles (e.g., prerequisite coursework, required exams).

To develop an integrated system, Leong et al. (2018) offer a Recruiting, Training, and Retaining Framework focusing on (1) Partnership and Recruitment, (2) Teacher Preparation, and (3) Induction and Mentoring, Professional Learning, and Supportive Leadership. These areas include nine strategies with discussion questions to guide reflection and implementation. Experts agree that the greatest impact can occur when a shared vision across the partnership includes a comprehensive implementation and evaluation plan, clearly defined roles (see Tenet 2), ongoing communication, procedures, and structures to support candidates.

Tenet 4: Transforming Biliteracy/Bicultural "Zones of Development"

Most multimodal sources on partnerships apply frameworks, research, or practices based on traditional notions of university-district partnerships (see Table 38.1) to adapt to their DLBTE context. These spaces or "archaeologies" of multilingual knowledge and practices offer apprenticeship into the profession that occurs through multiple teacher preparation pathways as described in Tenet 3. To address the socioeconomic and linguistic diversity of targeted neighborhoods, Loyola University Chicago and the Chicago Public Schools leveraged "horizontal" partnerships with other universities and "vertical" partnerships with P-12 schools to apprentice bilingual teachers across "multiple planes of practice" that address individual, interpersonal, and institutional factors (Heineke et al., 2020). These "zones" of biliteracy/bicultural knowledge and pedagogy facilitate the allocation of space(s) and time(s), challenge hegemonic notions, policies, and practices, and decolonize bilingual teacher education partnerships to extend and include the broader ecology (Bhabha, 1994; Gutiérrez, 2008).

Yet, such emphasis on the transformation of ideologies around DLBTE at the university level is not fully shared with school/district leaders. In a recent survey where 223 district and school site leaders participated, the results show that leaders prioritize beginning teachers' language skills and abilities and bilingual pedagogic competencies. However, they identified lower priority and less capacity to allocate resources or plan for ongoing professional learning for new bilingual teachers (Lavadenz et al., 2021). Bilingual mentors play a significant role in the early development and retention of bilingual educators and contribute to sustainability and longevity (Mead et al., 2015; Rodríguez, 2003). University and site-level leaders are mutually interested in the short- and long-term success of DL programs (ibid). For partnerships to privilege community social, linguistic, and cultural wealth (Tenet 2), partners need to integrate international and binational collaboration as zones for potential development (Archy, this volume). Yet, the policy ecology landscape for developing as educators remains fairly parochial and is limited to the most immediate geographic boundaries although emergent bilingual families and communities are transnational, bicultural, and dynamic. Only a few partnerships emphasize "the students that we share" (Center for U.S.-Mexican Studies, 2017).

Conclusion and Implications for Equity in University-District Partnerships in DLBTE

This multimodal CLR via an applied use of the CMPE framework allowed us to examine and identify transformative directions in DLBTE university-district partnerships to increase access, engagement, and equity in the educator preparation pipeline. This section draws from our findings as well as the four equity-informed tenets to discuss implications and address the complex and dynamic nature of DLBTE university-district partnerships.

Mapping the Multilingual Policy Ecology Landscape in DLBTE Partnerships

Challenging and decolonizing the discourse around extant partnerships require a new movement that coalesces "actors" as change agents within the ecosystem (Olsen, 2021). Actors engaged in multiple policy spaces are less susceptible to reifying and perpetuating larger inequities. It is imperative to develop a deep understanding of the chronologies of hegemonic historical, social, cultural, political, and economic forces that shape specific local and contemporary contexts. Only then can we effectively "map the course" to transform DLBTE university-district partnerships to promote equity-based mindsets and practices at the various levels of the CMPE framework. Acknowledging the complexity of the intersections across the systems, we focus on the immediate ecology spaces in which we primarily situate DLBE partnerships to discuss implications for multilingual policy actors in and across the system.

Implications for Bilingual Teacher Education Programs and District Partnerships

It is clear from our review that there must be a critical understanding of the local context for the university and district teams at the micro level. Uplifting community and cultural wealth among students, families, and communities allows university-district partnerships to develop an ideologically clear and shared vision. Establishing a comprehensive implementation and evaluation policy to support ongoing communication, procedures, and structures for DLBE candidates is also vital. It is noteworthy that explicit attention to and mutual accountability for equity-focused DLBE program implementation includes equity-driven and sustainable teacher education practices, especially when existing partnerships have previously been established and expanded to include DLBTE (Education First, 2016). Addressing the bilingual teacher shortage to expand bilingual teacher pathways can also increase racial, ethnic, linguistic, and socioeconomic status diversity among students to enrich the quality of DLBE programs (Osterling & Buchanan, 2003).

At the meso-system level, we illuminate critically conscious and co-constructed relationships to inform university and district/school partnerships. Several key components include (1) clarifying roles and support areas based on research in bilingual pedagogy and practice, (2) establishing horizontal and organic liaisons among agencies to respond to DLBE program design and implementation, and (3) building the research-practice system between universities and districts to identify lessons that oppose hegemonic notions and decolonize bilingual teacher education partnerships (Umansky et al., 2015).

Policy coherence and articulation are essential characteristics of equity-driven DLBTE university-district partnerships. These intersect, interact, and are informed by local, state, and national policies as they are supported and co-led by university and district leaders to ensure systemic development for DLBE support and advocacy (Umansky et al., 2015). Mapping the multilingual policy ecology landscape in DLBTE partnerships and research requires intentionality and action to build a comprehensive support system and benefit minoritized students and educators in schools, districts, and universities.

Notes

1 Various search platforms include the university library search engine, Google Scholar, Google, ERIC, AERA Open, AERA Online Paper Repository, government/organizations' websites, and multimedia.
2 US PREP (n.d.)
3 California Department of Education (2018).

References

Alemán, E. Jr., Freire, J. A., McKinney, A., & Delgado Bernal, D. (2017). School–university–community pathways to higher education: Teacher perceptions, school culture and partnership building. *The Urban Review*, *49*(5), 852–873.

American Councils for International Education. (2021). *2021 Canvass of dual language and immersion (DLI) programs in US public schools*. https://www.americancouncils.org/sites/default/files/documents/pages/2021-10/Canvass%20DLI%20-%20October%202021-2_ac.pdf

Beck, J. S. (2018). Investigating the third space: A new agenda for teacher education research. *Journal of Teacher Education*, *71*(4), 379–391. https://doi.org/10.1177/0022487118787497

Bhabha, H. (1994). *The location of culture*. Routledge.

Boyer, E. (1996). The scholarship of engagement. *Journal of Public Service and Outreach*, *1*(1), 11–20.

Boyle, A., August, D., Tabaku, L., Cole, S., & Simpson-Baird, A. (2015). *Dual language education programs: Current state policies and practices*. U.S. Department of Education, Office of English Language Acquisition. https://ncela.ed.gov/files/rcd/TO20_DualLanguageRpt_508.pdf

Brown, J. E., Smallman, S., & Hitz, R. (2008). Partnerships to recruit and prepare bilingual teachers. *Metropolitan Universities*, *19*(3), 54–67. http://archives.pdx.edu/ds/psu/11085

California Department of Education. (2018). *Global California 2030: Speak. Learn. Lead.* California Department of Education. https://www.cde.ca.gov/eo/in/documents/globalca2030report.pdf

California State University San Marcos School of Education. (n.d.). *Project GLOBAL competence*. https://www.csusm.edu/soe/collaborationandoutreach/global/index.html

Carnegie Forum on Education and the Economy. (1986). *A nation prepared: Teachers for the 21st century: The report of the Task Force on Teaching as a Profession*. The Forum.

Center for U.S.-Mexican Studies. (2017). *The students we share: At the border – San Diego & Tijuana* (Policy Brief). University of California San Diego's School of Global Policy and Strategy. https://usmex.ucsd.edu/_files/mmfrp_policy%20brief_2017.pdf

Cervantes-Soon, C. G., Dorner, L., Palmer, D., Heiman, D., Schwerdtfeger, R., & Choi, J. (2017). Combating inequalities in two-way language immersion programs: Toward critical consciousness in bilingual education spaces. *Review of Research in Education*, *41*(1), 403–427. https://doi.org/10.3102/0091732X17690120

Chávez-Moreno, L. C. (2021). Dual language as White property: Examining a secondary bilingual-education program and Latinx equity. *American Educational Research Journal*, *58*(6), 1107–1141. https://doi.org/10.3102/00028312211052508

Coburn, C. E., Penuel, W. R., & Geil, K. E. (2013). *Research-practice partnerships: A strategy for leveraging research for educational improvement in school districts*. William T. Grant Foundation. https://eric.ed.gov/?id=ED568396

Corson, D. (1999). *Language policy in schools*. Lawrence Erlbaum.

De Leon, T., & Lavadenz, M. (2020). A new ecology of biliteracy in California: A study of the early implementation of the seal of biliteracy. In A. Heineke & K. Davin (Eds.), *The seal of biliteracy: Case studies and considerations for policy implementation* (pp. 49–66). Information Age Publishers.

del Rosal, K., Roman, D., & Basaraba, D. (2018). Debemos escuchar a los maestros: Perspectives of bilingual teacher candidates in teacher education partnerships. *Bilingual Research Journal*, *41*(2), 187–205. https://doi.org/10.1080/15235882.2018.1456986

Doherty, R. (2007). Critically framing education policy: Foucault, discourse and governmentality. In M. A. Peters & T. Besley (Eds.), *Why Foucault? New directions in educational research* (pp. 193–204). Peter Lang.

Education First. (2016). *Ensuring high-quality teacher talent: How strong, bold partnerships between school districts and teacher preparation programs are transforming the teacher pipeline*. https://education-first.com/wp-content/uploads/2016/01/Ensuring-High-Quality-Teacher-Talent.pdf

Flores, B. B., Clark, E. R., Claeys, L., & Villarreal, A. (2007). Academy for teacher excellence: Recruiting, preparing, and retaining Latino teachers through learning communities. *Teacher Education Quarterly*, *34*(4), 53–69. http://eric.ed.gov/?id=EJ795187

Foy, K., del Prado, P., Patti, A., & Davis, J. (2018). Esperanza e imaginación: PDS partners working together to help bilingual middle school students build hope and imagination for their futures. *School-University Partnerships*, *11*(1), 60–63. https://eric.ed.gov/?id=EJ1179968

Freire, J. A., & Alemán, E. Jr. (2021). "Two schools within a school": Elitism, divisiveness, and intra-racial gentrification in a dual language strand. *Bilingual Research Journal*, *44*(2), 249–269.

Garcia, A. (2017). *Building a bilingual teacher pipeline: The Portland Public Schools and Portland State University dual language teacher partnership*. New America. https://na-production.s3.amazonaws.com/documents/FINAL_SupportingVisionELEquity.pdf

Garcia, A., Manuel, A., & Buly, M. R. (2019). Washington policy spotlight: A multifaceted approach to grow your own pathways. *Teachers Education Quarterly*, *46*(1), 69–78. https://www.jstor.org/stable/26558183

Gist, C. D., Bianco, M., & Lynn, M. (2018). Examining grow your own programs across the teacher development continuum: Mining research on teachers of color and nontraditional educator pipelines. *Journal of Teacher Education*, *70*(1), 13–25. https://doi.org/10.1177/0022487118787504

Goodlad, J. I. (1994). *Educational renewal: Better teachers, better schools*. Jossey Bass.

Guilamo, A. (2020). *Coaching teachers in bilingual and dual-language classrooms: A responsive cycle for observation and feedback*. Solution Tree Press.

Gutiérrez, K. D. (2008). Developing a sociocritical literacy in the third space. *Reading Research Quarterly*, *43*(2), 148–164. https://doi.org/10.1598/RRQ.43.2.3

Haugen, E. I. (1972). *The ecology of language*. Stanford University Press.

Heineke, A. J., Roudebush, A., Papola-Ellis, A., Davin, K. J., Cohen, S., & Wright-Costello, B. (2020). Apprenticing educators of emergent bilingual learners: Partnerships to promote linguistically responsive practice in classrooms, schools, and communities. *The Professional Educator*, *43*(1), 70–80. https://eric.ed.gov/?id=EJ1276090

Higher Education Opportunity Act of 2008, Pub. L. §§110–315, USC (2008).

Holmes Group. (1995). *Tomorrow's schools of education*. Holmes Group, Inc. https://files.eric.ed.gov/fulltext/ED399220.pdf

Hornberger, N. H. (2003). Afterword: Ecology and ideology in multilingual classrooms. *International Journal of Bilingual Education and Bilingualism*, *6*(3–4), 296–302. https://doi.org/10.1080/13670050308667787

Klitzing, M. (2020, November 15). *New partnership addresses California's rural bilingual educator shortage*. San Diego State University NewsCenter. https://newscenter.sdsu.edu/sdsu_newscenter/news_story.aspx?sid=78233

Lavadenz, M., Armas, E. G., & Robles, N. (2019). *Bilingual teacher residency programs in California: Considerations for development and expansion* (Education and Policy Briefs No. 7). Loyola Marymount University Center for Equity for English Learners. https://doi.org/10.15365/ceel.policy.7

Lavadenz, M., Ee, J., Armas, E. G., & López, G. V. (2021). *Leaders' perspective on the preparation of bilingual/dual language teachers* (Education and Policy Briefs No. 9). Loyola Marymount University Center for Equity for English Learners. https://doi.org/10.15365/ceel.policy.10

Leong, M., Motamedi, J., & Yoon, S. (2018). *Common practices for recruiting, training, and retaining bilingual and diverse teachers*. https://ies.ed.gov/ncee/edlabs/regions/northwest/pdf/common-bractices-bilingual.pdf

Mead, S., Aldeman, C., Chuong, C., & Obbard, J. (2015). *Rethinking teacher preparation: Empowering local schools to solve California's teacher shortage and better develop teachers*. Bellwether Education Partners. https://bellwethereducation.org/sites/default/files/Bellwether_TFA-CA.pdf

National Association of Professional Development schools. (2008). *What it means to be a professional development school*. https://www.gcsu.edu/sites/files/page-assets/node-1573/attachments/nine-essentials.pdf

National Commission on Excellence in Education. (1983). *A nation at risk: The imperative for educational reform*. https://edreform.com/wp-content/uploads/2013/02/A_Nation_At_Risk_1983.pdf

Olsen, L. (2021). *A legacy of courage and activism: Stories from the movement for educational access and equity for English learners in California*. Californians Together.

Onwuegbuzie, A. J., & Frels, R. (2016). *Seven steps to a comprehensive literature review: A multimodal and cultural approach*. Sage.

Osterling, J. P., & Buchanan, K. (2003). Tapping a valuable source for prospective ESOL teachers: Northern Virginia's bilingual paraeducator career-ladder school–university partnership. *Bilingual Research Journal*, 27(3), 503–521. https://doi.org/10.1080/15235882.2003.10162605

Patton, Q. (2015). *Qualitative research and evaluation methods: Integrating theory and practice* (4th ed.). Sage.

Portland State University. (n.d.). *Bilingual teacher pathway (BTP)*. https://www.pdx.edu/education/btp

Ricento, T. (2000). Historical and theoretical perspectives in language policy and planning. *Journal of Sociolinguistics*, *4*(2), 196–213.

Rodríguez, R. G. (2003, May). The power of partnerships – How Alianza is reshaping bilingual teacher preparation. *Intercultural Research Development Association Newsletter*. https://www.idra.org/resource-center/the-power-of-partnerships/

Sakash, K., & Chou, V. (2007). Increasing the supply of Latino bilingual teachers for the Chicago Public Schools. *Teacher Education Quarterly*, 34(4), 41–52. http://eric.ed.gov/?id=EJ795186

U.S. Department of Education. (2016). *National Professional Development Grant Program 84.365Z cohort 2016 – Project abstracts-summaries*. https://www2.ed.gov/programs/nfdp/npd2016abstracts.pdf

U.S. Department of Education. (2017). *National Professional Development Grant Program 84.365Z cohort 2017 – Project abstracts-summaries*. https://www2.ed.gov/programs/nfdp/npd2017abstracts.pdf

US PREP. (n.d.). Preparing the foundation: What should you do before you begin? https://toolkit.usprepnationalcenter.com/step-zero

Umansky, I. M., Reardon, S. F., Hakuta, K., Thompson, K. D., Estrada, P., Hayes, K., Maldonado, H., Tandberg, S., & Goldenberg, C. (2015). *Improving the opportunities and outcomes of California's students learning English: Findings from school district–university collaborative partnerships* (Policy brief 15-1). Policy Analysis for California Education. https://files.eric.ed.gov/fulltext/ED562543.pdf

University of Texas at San Antonio. (2021, June 14). *UTSA partners with SAISD to establish Dual Language Community Lab Schools*. UTSA Today. https://www.utsa.edu/today/2021/06/story/utsa-saisd-establish-dual-language-community-lab-schools.html

Valenciana, C., Morin, A. J., & Morales, S. R. (2005). Meeting the challenge: Building university-school district partnerships for a successful career ladder program for teachers of English learners. *Action in Teacher Education*, 27(1), 82–91. https://doi.org/10.1080/01626620.2005.10463376

Weaver-Hightower, M. B. (2008). An ecology metaphor for educational policy analysis: A call to complexity. *Educational Researcher*, *37*(3), 153–167. https://doi.org/10.3102%2F0013189X08318050

Webb, J., Abdelrahim, S., Mahmoud-Tabana, S., & Banes, L. (n.d.). *REEd framework for bilingual family-school partnerships: Executive summary*. Resourcing Excellence in Education. https://education.ucdavis.edu/sites/main/files/file-attachments/reed_framework_for_bilingual_family-school_partnerships_executive_summary.pdf?1618948040

Western Washington University. (n.d.). *Woodring multilingual teaching fellows*. https://wce.wwu.edu/wmtf

NAME INDEX

Note: Page references in **bold** denote table.

SUBJECT INDEX

Note: Page references in *italics* denote figures, in **bold** tables and with "n" endnotes.